ARCHAEOLOGICAL RESOURCE MANAGEMENT IN THE UK

AN INTRODUCTION

SECOND EDITION
COMPLETELY REVISED AND UPDATED

EDITED BY JOHN HUNTER AND IAN RALSTON

SUTTON PUBLISHING

First published in the United Kingdom in 1993 by
Sutton Publishing Ltd
Phoenix Mill · Thrupp · Stroud · Gloucestershire · GL5 2BU

This revised edition first published in 2006

British Library Cataloguing in Publication Data
A catalogue record for this book is available from the British Library

ISBN 0-7509-2789-5

Typeset in Times 10/11 pt.
Typesetting and origination by
Sutton Publishing Limited
Printed and bound in England by
J.H. Haynes & Co. Ltd, Sparkford.

CONTENTS

PREFACE TO THE SECOND EDITION

The following volume replaces the first edition of *Archaeological Resource Management in the UK: An Introduction*, on which we collaborated as editors in the early 1990s. Some of the following chapters have been entirely rewritten, some by new authors; all have been substantially updated. The contents thus encapsulate 'the state of the art' with regard to applied archaeological practice in the United Kingdom in 2004/5. It will readily be apparent to the reader that, given the amount of change that has affected this field over the previous decade, practices can be expected to continue to evolve, and thus trying to compile an up-to-date guide in this field is like trying to design an up-to-date warship or aircraft.

In the Preface to the previous edition, which is reproduced below since it outlines our perceptions of the archaeological world at the time this book was initially produced and explains why we coined the neologism 'Archaeological Resource Management' to describe its scope, we highlighted many of the factors contributing to rapid change in applied archaeological practice. None of these has abated in the meantime. Reviews of policy and procedures are becoming increasingly numerous, and often seem to represent good reasons to hold off embarking on a publication of this kind, since major change may always be about to occur. Some of these proposed changes are, in any case, stillborn. Potentially, at least, too, matters will become more complicated, since applied archaeology is effectively a devolved issue within the UK, giving scope for more internal diversity in practices in future than is already the case. The main regional variation within the UK in terms of legislation concerns Northern Ireland, and we are grateful to Claire Foley of ENS/DoE (NI) for her contributions, revising and updating those of the late Ann Hamlin in the first edition. We have not been able systematically to include reference to practices in the Channel Islands, or the Isle of Man, although some variations in practice there are indeed highlighted below.

New elements in this edition include a list of acronyms pertinent to the domain under consideration, and citation of some of the key websites, which are of increasing significance. In the first edition, we made reference to the ephemerality of, or difficulty of access to, numbers of the printed sources relevant to the subject area. While this has continued to be the case – and was to be matched by increasing quantities of 'grey literature' – a welcome development has been the compilation of a substantial quantity of key sources and resources accessibly on the Internet. If web-based resources (not really an issue at all when the first edition came out) are here to stay, so too are acronyms. There are those who lament their burgeoning number, and those who welcome them as useful shorthand. Bearing in mind a student readership and the requirements of those who come into contact with field archaeologists as part of their professional activities, reason and realism dictate that a guide to the subject area needs to unlock the secrets hidden in these little bits of code.

We are grateful to all our contributors, both new and old. Many of the 'old hands' – and in this we would include ourselves – were surprised how much revision and updating were required since they first composed their contributions; this is a reflection of the extent of the rapid evolution, and occasional revolutionary changes, that have affected professional practice over the intervening years. The new contributors are thanked for producing pieces that can be readily grafted into the overall work. Some of our colleagues, fitting this commitment into hectic schedules, produced their contributions more speedily than others: we are obliged to the speedy for their forbearance as we assembled all the contributions; and to the less quick for responding to our cajoling. Archaeological resource management is not the simplest of topics to illustrate, and we are therefore grateful to the photographers whose photographs are included.

As ever, Margaret and Sandra, and at least some of our children and now one granddaughter at least some of the time, had to live with this book too.

John Hunter and Ian Ralston
Kinross, December 2005

PREFACE TO THE FIRST EDITION

In the twenty-two chapters of this book, we have asked our colleagues to try to draw together diverse aspects of the structure, outlook and operation of archaeology in the UK at the present time, and in some instances to consider its relevance to modern society. We felt, on the basis of archaeology's transformation during the last two decades, that there was need for stock to be taken and an overview given. The contexts of British archaeological practice have altered radically since the late 1970s: changes in planning controls, heritage legislation, land-use practices and social awareness have drawn the archaeologist into important new professional arenas affecting the whole of archaeology's broad spectrum, from legislation to tourism, from churches to underwater sites, as well as in the processes by which archaeological sites and landscapes are selected for examination, academic study, preservation and public interpretation. Nowhere, it seemed, had these changes been monitored, listed and commented upon in any detail in a single volume.

Both of us have also been directly concerned with the teaching of cultural resource management at our respective universities. One of the problems has always been in trying to assemble not only the strands of the subject itself, but also the published sources. There are a few glossy books that deal with the broader generalities, but little that charts the development of the individual components that make up the whole. Such information survives in our files as short papers from journals, pamphlets, leaflets, government circulars and advice notes, unreadable statutes and newspaper cuttings, now mostly inaccessible or obscure and almost invariably out of print. This book will, in part, serve as a permanent replacement for such collections.

To some extent this is also a history of public archaeology. Our present students entered this life in the mid-1970s when archaeology was shrill with the voices of rescue archaeology and implications surveys; and when hundreds of people were prepared to work at a moment's notice for next to nothing. But today the students' first encounter with the subject belongs to an age of contractors, curators, tendering, mitigation strategies and PPG 16. This book also recounts why practices have changed.

The chapters and extensive bibliography do not constitute a textbook per se of archaeological resource management. Rather, we hope to have provided a handbook that will be of use to students and colleagues both in the archaeological and heritage worlds. We trust, too, that the book will serve as a vade mecum to the increasing range of professionals in neighbouring subjects – for example, planning, development, environmental assessment, engineering and recreation – for whom contact with field archaeology in one of its new guises has become a more or less regular occurrence.

The title includes, as far as we are aware, a new coining in the phrase 'archaeological resource management', an amalgam of two phrases currently used as definitions: cultural resource management, and archaeological heritage management. The former is a linguistic immigrant from North America already used to describe the content of courses at a number of UK universities and to identify one of the 'Areas of Competence' for Membership of the Institute of Field Archaeologists (IFA). It is thus reasonably embedded in English as a challenger to archaeological heritage management, again used in the title of university courses (IFA 1992) and in publications (Cleere 1989). In trying to find a form of words that fairly reflected the contents of this book, we were keen to avoid misrepresentation, whether by commission or omission. Thus 'archaeological' seemed preferable to 'cultural' as a description of the material covered. Furthermore, at a time of increasing recognition of the erosion of the archaeological record, we considered it more appropriate to focus attention on the significance of archaeological remains as 'resources' rather than as 'heritage'.

This book is the first to carry the joint imprint of the IFA, an organisation now a decade old that links archaeologists working in different sectors of British archaeology (central and local government, education, the private sector and charitable trusts, as well as the self-employed). The IFA now serves as the most important forum in the UK for the development of archaeological practice and professionalism. External pressures, especially politically inspired changes, have ensured that concern with the practice of archaeology has been central to the IFA's deliberations, although not its sole function, during its first ten years. We are grateful to the IFA's councillors in session 1991–2 for allowing us to persuade them to devote some of the IFA's modest financial resources to underwriting the production of this collection of essays, which seek to take stock of the transitions and to provide a guide to the new terrain.

Although most of our authors are IFA members, the contents of this book represent the authors' personal opinions and must not be taken either as an official IFA perspective (except in the case of direct citation of its documentation) or as that of their employers. It will rapidly become clear to the reader that the management of archaeological resources is a subject undergoing rapid evolution in which professional attitudes, ethical positions, and consideration of the relationships between theory and practice are all actively debated. We have attempted to exercise editorial control as lightly as possible in the matter of allowing place for different opinions, so that we hope that something of the competing flavours of, and tensions within, contemporary archaeological resource management are apparent.

We are grateful to our contributors, all of whom produced copy to a very tight timetable – many of them exactly on schedule. Our thanks also go to Ann Hamlin, DoE (Northern Ireland), for her assistance with our contribution; David Breeze, Historic Scotland, for advice on terminology; Bill Finlayson, Manager, CFA, University of Edinburgh, for making seemingly countless incompatible disks readable; and to Mark Pollard, University of Bradford, for access to facilities that much simplified final editing. Rupert Harding of Alan Sutton Publishing Ltd guided our relations with the publisher expertly.

Finally Ellie, Natalie, Edward, Tom, Tom and Ben deserve the apologies of two fathers who were just a little preoccupied over Christmas 1992.

John Hunter and Ian Ralston
Bradford, January 1993

THE CONTRIBUTORS

David Baker is joint Director of Historic Environment Conservation, Bedford.

Robert H. Bewley is English Heritage's Planning and Development Regional Director for the South-West, based in Bristol.

Carl Bianco was formerly at the Cathedrals Fabric Commission for England, London, and is now working in visual effects for films.

David Breeze now leads the bid for World Heritage status for the Antonine Wall as part of the *Frontiers of the Roman Empire* initiative, having been Chief Inspector of Ancient Monuments in Historic Scotland.

Henry Cleere has been a consultant to the International Council on Monuments and Sites in Paris since 1992 and is also Visiting Professor in Archaeological Heritage Management at the Institute of Archaeology, University College, London.

Simon Collcutt is Managing Director of Oxford Archaeological Associates Ltd.

Timothy Darvill is Professor of Archaeology in the School of Conservation Sciences, Bournemouth University.

Graham Fairclough is the London-based Head of English Heritage's Characterisation Team.

Antony Firth is Head of Coastal and Marine Projects for Wessex Archaeology, based in Salisbury.

Claire Foley is Senior Inspector, Built Heritage, Environment and Heritage Service, Department of the Environment, Northern Ireland.

Peter Fowler is now a heritage consultant, having been Secretary of the RCHME and then Professor of Archaeology at Newcastle University.

David Fraser was until recently English Heritage's Planning and Development Regional Director for Yorkshire, based in York, and is now DEFRA's Rural Director for Yorkshire.

Chris Gaffney is a Director of GSB Prospection, Bradford.

John Gater is a Director of GSB Prospection, Bradford.

Jane Grenville is a Senior Lecturer in Archaeology at the University of York.

The late Ann Hamlin was Principal Inspector of Historic Monuments, Environmental Services, Department of the Environment (Northern Ireland), Belfast.

Catherine Hills is University Senior Lecturer in Archaeology, University of Cambridge.

John Hunter is Professor of Ancient History and Archaeology at the University of Birmingham.

Andrew J. Lawson recently stepped down as Head of Wessex Archaeology to concentrate on consultancy and writing.

Gavin Lucas is Assistant Director of *Fornleifastofnun Íslands*, the independent charity which provides an archaeological service for Iceland.

Lesley Macinnes is a Principal Inspector in Historic Scotland, Edinburgh.

Linda Monckton was formerly Assistant Secretary of the Cathedrals Fabric Commission for England and is now a Senior Architectural Investigator at English Heritage.

Martin Newman is Datasets Development Manager in the Data Services Unit, National Monuments Record, English Heritage, Swindon.

Susan Pearce is Professor Emerita of Museum Studies, University of Leicester.

Michael Parker Pearson is Professor of Archaeology at the University of Sheffield.

Francis Pryor is Director of Archaeology for the Fenland Archaeological Trust and has recently served as President of the Council for British Archaeology.

Ian Ralston is Professor of Archaeology at the University of Edinburgh.

Julian D. Richards is Professor of Archaeology at the University of York, where he is also Director of the Archaeology Data Service.

Alan Saville is a Curator in the Archaeology Department, National Museums of Scotland, Edinburgh and Head of the Treasure Trove Unit for Scotland.

Ian Shepherd is Principal Archaeologist for Aberdeenshire Council, Aberdeen.

Ken Smith is Manager of the Peak District National Park Authority's Cultural Heritage Team, Buxton, Derbyshire.

Roger M. Thomas is Head of Urban Archaeology for English Heritage, London.

Jason Wood is Director of Heritage Consultancy Services, Carnforth, Lancashire.

ACRONYMS USED IN THE TEXT

AAHRG	Avebury Archaeological and Heritage Research Group
AAI	Area of Archaeological Importance
AARG	Aerial Archaeology Research Group
ABRC	Advisory Board for Redundant Churches
ACAO	Association of County Archaeological Officers
ACHWS	Advisory Committee of Historic Wreck Sites
ACOP	Approved Codes of Practice
ADS	Archaeology Data Service
ADU	Archaeological Diving Unit
AHRB/C	Arts and Humanities Research Board/Council
AIFA	Associate of the Institute of Field Archaeologists
AIP	Archaeological Investigations Project
ALGAO	Association of Local Government Archaeology Officers
ALSF	Aggregates Levy Sustainability Fund
AMAA Act	Ancient Monuments and Archaeological Areas Act (1979)
AMB	Ancient Monuments Board (England)
AMBS	Ancient Monuments Board for Scotland
ANO	Air Navigation Order
AOC	Air Operator's Certificate
AOC	Area of Competence (Institute of Field Archaeologists)
APPAG	All-Party Parliamentary Archaeology Group
APU	Air Photographic Unit (English Heritage)
ARC	Archaeological Research Centre (York)
ARCHNET	Website: the World Wide Web Virtual Library for Archaeology
ARGE	Website: Archaeological Resource Guide for Europe
ARIA	Association of Regional and Islands Archaeologists
ARM	Archaeological Resource Management
BADLG	British Archaeologists and Developers Liaison Group
BAG	Buildings Archaeology Group (Institute of Field Archaeologists)
BAN	*British Archaeological News*
BIAB	*British and Irish Archaeological Bibliography*
BMAPA	British Maritime Aggregates Producers Association
BSI	British Standards Institute
CAA	Civil Aviation Authority
CAD	Computer Aided Design
CADW	*Cadw* is Welsh for 'to keep', and this title is used for the historic environment agency within the Welsh Assembly Government.
CANMAP	Is the map-based interface of CANMORE
CANMORE	Canmore is RCAHMS's principal searchable database, accessible via the Internet.
CASE	Cooperative Awards in Science and Engineering
CASG	Contract Archaeology Study Group
CAWP	Contract Archaeology Working Party

CBA	Council for British Archaeology
CBI	Confederation of British Industry
CCC	Council for the Care of Churches
CCM	Care of Cathedrals Measure
CCT	Churches Conservation Trust
CEU	Central Excavation Unit
CFCE	Cathedrals Fabric Commission for England
CMW	Council of Museums in Wales
CoE	Council of Europe
CPD	Continuing Professional Development
CPL	Commercial Pilot's Licence
CRAAGS	Committee for Rescue Archaeology in Avon, Gloucestershire and Somerset
CRM	Cultural Resource Management
CSA	Council for Scottish Archaeology
CSS	Countryside Stewardship scheme
CT	Competitive Tendering
CUCAP	Cambridge University Committee for Aerial Photography (now Unit for Landscape Modelling)
DAC	Diocesan Advisory Committee
DAMHB	Directorate of Ancient Monuments and Historic Buildings
DCA	Department for Constitutional Affairs
DCMS	Department for Media, Culture and Sport
DoE	Department of the Environment
DoE (NI)	Department of the Environment (Northern Ireland)
DEFRA	Department for Environment, Food and Rural Affairs
DETR	Department of Environment, Transport and the Regions
DFBO	Design, Fund, Build and Operate
DMRB	*Design Manual for Roads and Bridges*
DNH	Department for National Heritage
DTLGR	Department for Transport, Local Government and the Regions
EA	Environmental Assessment (synonym of EIA)
EAA	European Association of Archaeologists
EIA	Environmental Impact Assessment (synonym of EA)
EH	English Heritage
EHS	Environment and Heritage Service (Northern Ireland)
END	Extended National Database
EOP	*Exploring our Past* (English Heritage)
ESA	Environmentally Sensitive Area
EU	European Union
EUS	Extensive Urban Surveys (EH's urban programme)
FAC	Fabric Advisory Committee
FCO	Foreign and Commonwealth Office
FISH	Forum on Information Standards in Heritage
FJC	Faculty Jurisdiction Commission
FJR	Faculty Jurisdiction Rules
FLO	Finds Liaison Officer
GIS	Geographic Information System
GNVQ	General National Vocational Qualification
GPR	Ground Penetrating Radar
HBMC	Historic Buildings and Monuments Commission

HEEP	Historic Environment Enabling Programme
HEIRPORT	Website: Historic Environment Information Resources Portal
HELPS	Historic Environment List for Projects and Societies
HER	Historic Environment Record/Review
HLA	Historic Landuse Assessment
HLC	Historic Landscape Characterisation
HLF	Heritage Lottery Fund
HLS	Higher Level Stewardship
HS	Historic Scotland
HSIS	Heritage Spatial Information System
HUMBUL	Website: part of the Resource Discovery Network, this Oxford University-based service includes a guide to many online archaeological resources
IAM	Inspector(ate) of Ancient Monuments
IAPA	Irish Association of Professional Archaeologists
ICAHM	International Committee on Archaeological Heritage Management
ICE	Institute of Civil Engineers
ICOMOS	International Council on Monuments and Sites
IFA	Institute of Field Archaeologists
IHBC	Institute for Historic Building Conservation
IPN	Interim Preservation Notice
JNAPC	Joint Nautical Archaeology Policy Committee
LAARC	London Archaeological Archive and Research Centre
LARA	Lincoln Archaeological Research Assessment
LBC	Listed Building Consent
LBS	Listed Buildings System
MAFF	Ministry of Agriculture, Fisheries and Food
MAGIC	Multi-Agency Geographic Information for the Countryside
MAP2	*Management of Archaeological Projects* (2nd edition) (EH)
MARS	Monuments at Risk Survey (EH)
MCA	Maritime and Coastguard Agency
MCD	Monument Class Designation
MDA	Museums Documentation Association
MGC	Museums and Galleries Commission
MID	Mean Intervention Distance
MIDAS	Monument Inventories Data Standard
MIFA	Member of the Institute of Field Archaeologists
MLA	Museums, Libraries and Archives Council
MoD	Ministry of Defence
MOLAS	Museum of London Archaeological Service
MPP	Monuments Protection Programme (English Heritage)
MS Act	Merchant Shipping Act
NAPLIB	National Association of Aerial Photographic Libraries
NDVI	Normalised Difference Vegetation Index
NERC	Natural Environment Research Council
NH Act	National Heritage Act
NMP	National Mapping Programme (EH)
NMR	National Monuments Record
NMRS	National Monuments Record of Scotland
NMRW	National Monuments Record of Wales
NPPG	*National Planning Policy Guideline* (followed by number) (Scotland)

OIA	Organisation of Irish Archaeologists
OASIS	Website: this signifies 'Online access to the index of archaeological investigations' (for England) and can be accessed via http://ads.ahds.ac.uk/project/oasis/
ODPM	Office of the Deputy Prime Minister
OS	Ordnance Survey
PAN	*Planning Advice Note* (followed by number) (Scotland)
PAS	Portable Antiquities Scheme
PIFA	Practitioner of the Institute of Field Archaeologists
PMR Act	Protection of Military Remains Act
PO	Preservation Order
POW	Prisoner of War
PPG	*Planning Policy Guidance* (followed by number)
PPL	Private Pilot's Licence
PPS	Planning Policy Statement
PW Act	Protection of Wrecks Act
QAA	Quality Assurance Agency
QA	Quality Assurance
QLTR	Queen's and Lord Treasurer's Remembrancer
R&D	Research and Development
RAE	Research Assessment Exercise
RAO	Registered Archaeological Organisation (Institute of Field Archaeologists)
RCAHMS	Royal Commission on the Ancient and Historical Monuments of Scotland
RCAHMW	Royal Commission on the Ancient and Historical Monuments of Wales
RCHME	Royal Commission on the Historical Monuments of England
RSM	Record of Scheduled Monuments
SAM	Scheduled Ancient Monument
SAPPP	Scottish Architects Papers Preservation Project
SBAC	Science-Based Archaeology Committee
SCAUM	Standing Committee of Archaeological Unit Managers
SCFA	Subject Committee for Archaeology
SCRAN	Scottish Cultural Resources Access Network
SDD	Scottish Development Department
SEA	Strategic Environmental Assessment
SHARP	Sedgeford Archaeological and Historical Research Project
SHER	*State of the Historic Environment Report*
SMA	Society of Museum Archaeologists
SMC	Scheduled Monument Consent
SMR	Sites and Monuments Record
SOEnD	Scottish Office Environment Department
TQM	Total Quality Management
UAD	Urban Archaeological Databases (EH)
UGC	University Grants Committee
UKIC	United Kingdom Institute for Conservation
UNCLOS	United Nations Convention on the Law of the Sea
UNESCO	United Nations Educational Scientific and Cultural Organisation
URL	Unique Reference
VAT	Value Added Tax
VCH	*Victoria History of the Counties of England*
WAG	Welsh Assembly Government

CHAPTER 1

ARCHAEOLOGY IN A MATRIX

Peter Fowler

INTRODUCTION

Archaeology is about the past, in part at least: Archaeological Resource Management (ARM), by definition, is in the present (Cleere 1989; Berry and Brown 1995). Furthermore, ARM is based on an assumption that there will be a future, indeed that the future will require a past. 'Past' with the indefinite article, or better still 'pasts', rather than 'the' past in the sense of something finite and definite that has happened, was a conceptual shift picked up in the first paragraph of the first edition of this chapter. The subsequent decade justified both the thought and its placement. Particularly is that so in the light of one interesting discussion of the topic which, among other points, remarked that 'most archaeologists consider themselves . . . as students of the past, who may operate in the present but are not students of present society' (Carman *et al.* 2000 in general: p. 303 for the quotation). The basic contention of this opening essay is that that statement is not good enough, indeed that it is now simply unrealistic.

Where there was once a past, not only are there now many of them but they are ubiquitous (Fig. 1.1; Fowler 1992, with many references up to 1990 inclusive; Hodder *et al.* 1997; Graham *et al.* 2000). In the First World's age of multiple everything, not least of eclectic personal consumption, a concept of a single past is now anachronistic and was already so by 1990; post-modernity rules and pasts proliferate (Harvey 1989; Kolb 1990; Boyne and Rattansi 1990). The 1990s then underwrote that view (Samuel 1994; Lowenthal 1996; Ucko 2000). Such a vision is a long way from the traditions of historicity, the corridors of absolutism, in which archaeology developed (Daniel 1975; Daniel and Chippindale n.d.; cf. *Archaeological Dialogues* 1994). The accretional, linear model of scientific, academic based progress in our acquisition of what was delusorily thought to be knowledge (Bowler 1989) fragmented from the 1960s onwards. This fragmentation is seen in almost every facet of the subject: its rationale, scope, objectives, organisation and personnel (Shanks and Tilley 1987b; Hodder *et al.* 1997) but, curiously perhaps, not its methodologies, which have homogenised as they have expanded (cf. Renfrew and Bahn 1991).

Archaeological resource management as a concept developed in the USA following the publication of McGimsey's (1972) seminal book *Public Archaeology*. The very title was a shock to many, for it implied that not only should a lot of archaeology be carried out in public (as Wheeler had been advocating from the 1930s), but that a major objective of archaeology was to act in the public interest. This was a far cry from the traditional exclusivity of much archaeology, from the almost private nature of much that archaeologists did; but there is absolutely no point in or to ARM unless, while accepting the precepts of the subject as academic discipline, it posits its existence on the public good. That said, 'good' is of course a relative concept, ethically, culturally and sociologically adjustable, shifting with intangibles like mood, taste, and the very sands of time that are the matter of archaeology (Green 1984); but the focus here is not so much on concepts of 'goodness' as on the word 'public', in contrast to the privacy, even introspection, that archaeology can so easily project about itself. We have nevertheless reached the point when, without being controversial, a well-known practitioner of ARM

1

Figure 1.1. Where there was once a past, now there are many, even for the best-known of monuments: Silbury Hill, Wiltshire, technically an artificial Neolithic mound of uncertain purpose but now recognised as possessing numerous 'meanings' for many different people alongside rational, scientific-based, strictly archaeological interpretations. Repairing the mound's structural weakness in public is demanding much of management.

can write: 'The key question . . . is not whether our cultural heritage matters – that argument is well behind us – but how it may be integrated into and made to contribute to the socio-economic fabric of our society' (Wainwright 2003).

A MATRIX: THEORY, PRACTICE AND SOCIETY

Interest in the past is prominent in contemporary life. Why? Does it touch a raw nerve in the public psyche, sensitised at a time of considerable political, economic and religious uncertainty and great sociological change? Ancient monuments, archaeological sites, historic buildings, it can be argued, are seen by many people as some of the few fixed points in personal landscapes, things that are old, revered, visitable and touchable. Such are things too that not only 'belong' to the people in a general sense but that also give people a sense of belonging to a place, a community. In a time of post-modernist mood, when so much bespeaks attitudes of 'take anything and anything goes', a deeply conservative reaction of clinging to some elements of the known is to be both expected and respected.

The interest ranges widely. It is as much concerned with 'Why?' as with 'What?' and 'When?' Historic buildings and archaeological sites clearly have a role to play here, possibly as psycho-sociological placebos, but personally and probably communally significant nevertheless. This line of thought has been identified as a basis for action by several organisations which are not primarily archaeological, for instance the European Union, the Council for Europe, the Countryside Agency and the Heritage Lottery Fund. All provide encouragement in the form of grants for communal action in places and with materials that have hitherto been regarded by archaeological bodies as solely their own concern. Conversely, this field has hitherto been regarded by officialdom as of no interest to other than a very minor fringe special interest group. Many non-specialist groups outside – and often seemingly ignorant of – archaeological organisations are consequently now being publicly funded to pursue what is basically archaeological work such as parish recording and preparing tourist trails. Traditional, often long-established, local archaeological groups, and indeed the scale of non-specialist activity in the archaeological field, are in places being superseded in terms of local involvement and public participation by new, populist leisure pursuits involving an engagement with the past.

Recent examples would include the encouragement for direct involvement offered by *Time Team's Big Dig* (on UK Channel 4 TV, summer 2003) and the British Museum/ BBC's promotion of archaeological treasure hunting with metal detectors (*pace* the titular euphemism of 'detectorist'; BBC 2, *Hidden Treasure*, autumn 2003; BM exhibition 2003–05) as an academically and socially acceptable mode of behaviour. In parallel, under the aegis of the Portable Antiquities Scheme, publicly funded officers all over England are now briefed to offer free academic advice to metal-detector enthusiasts. The latter 'find' archaeological material – that is, by definition remove it from its context, characteristically, it appears, using methods well short of professionally acceptable norms. Society's increasing engagement with its pasts is further exemplified by something rather different: in *The Observer* of 25 January 2004, an article entitled 'Living with Britain's population time bomb' contained a box feature that highlighted five topics directly affected by 'the age revolution'. The one on 'Culture' remarked that 'archaeology . . . and many other reflective activities have all received major boosts as more and more older people seek stimulation in retirement'. Nowadays and in future, perhaps more of these third agers will take up metal-detecting and fewer go on Swan cruises? Whatever the details and the ambiguities of such developments, this populist trend in matters archaeological is likely to continue, presenting a challenge to archaeological resource managers who will have to think long and hard about their own, and their organisation's, stance in such matters.

A former English Heritage (EH) chairman famously opined that part of the resource in his care consisted of 'only bumps in fields' (Wainwright 1992). That he thereby dismissed a major part of the patrimony – the earthwork evidence of former land use that constitutes such a vital element in the UK's glorious historic landscapes (e.g. Roberts and Wrathmell 2000, 2002) – unconsciously exemplified the fact that 'the heritage' is a fairly tightly circumscribed notion even in well-educated circles. Over twenty years ago this was all too well illustrated in the debates on the National Heritage Bill in 1982–3 and in the First Report of the House of Commons Environment Committee (HMSO 1987; cf. Fowler 1987). Now, a serious attempt is being made to improve the quality of both understanding and debate in parliament with the formation, led by two archaeologists, Lords Renfrew and Redesdale, of the All Party Parliamentary Archaeology Group (APPAG). It initiated a fact-finding enquiry, published in 2002, into the state, and particularly the funding, of archaeology in a Britain where not a single political party at the time had thought to produce a policy on archaeology. Another contemporary attempt to pull together the disparate organisational elements and voices in the heritage field, including archaeology, is represented by Heritage Link. This brings together non-governmental bodies in the field such as the Ancient Monuments Society and the Council for British Archaeology (CBA) with others such as the Youth Hostels Association (www.heritagelink.org.uk). It 'brings people together who care about our heritage to formulate policy, influence opinion and achieve change on issues of common concern . . . through undertaking research, gathering data, marshalling arguments and deploying all of these through intelligent lobbying [and acting] as a hub through which information is shared between our members'. This seems on the face of it to duplicate the purposes of the 'old' CBA, formed in 1944, and maybe expresses a frustration with the CBA's efficacy just as did the creation of RESCUE, a trust for British archaeology, in 1971. Such structural fission at the national level seems to occur in archaeology roughly generationally, and perhaps that is a sign of its vibrancy as both the subject and the context in which it has to operate change shape and expand.

The archaeological manager's view of the scope of his or her responsibility, extending to 'bumps in fields' and their equivalents, could well run up against limits of understanding and preconceptions across a range from international to very local in space and from politicians to specialists in other fields to local householders across society. Most archaeological resource managers should expect most of their professional time to be spent, not working from a shared agenda with fellow archaeologists, but in trying to understand and persuade others coming with different assumptions and knowledge (Fig. 1.2). This can lead to agonising appraisal of whether precedence lies with professional or lay perception of the nature and significance of the resource. Professionally there can be only one answer: the professional archaeological judgement based on academic criteria. But the distinction clearly to be drawn in such clashes is that between the archaeological view on the one hand and the political/financial/legal on the other. Colleagues, probably superiors, in the latter fields may well have to take a final decision, perhaps against the professional advice of the archaeologist; or the senior archaeological manager, with responsibilities wider than his or her purely archaeological ones, may have to do so accordingly. In the latter case, then obviously the senior manager, albeit an archaeologist at heart, will have to make the correct decision in the light of the other aspects of the situation, for example, in managing a National Trust estate or a National Park. Nevertheless, that cannot involve knowingly destroying 'bumps in fields' merely because they are such. Such action is only acceptable if it has been established, for example, that the 'bumps' are only a fragment of, say, common, late and insignificant ridge-and-furrow and not a fragment of rare, early and highly significant ridge-and-furrow.

Significance is all and a resource without academic value is ultimately difficult to defend. Rather more difficult in a way, however, is the challenge confronting a manager

Figure 1.2. Specialists from several different disciplines, including only one archaeologist, debate the nomination of the Loire Valley as a World Heritage site.

who is, or perhaps was initially, also an archaeologist. He or she will know the need for long-term policies to be based on good data and intellectual fibre, but at the same time he or she will also know that success depends empirically on persuading others. In practice, it is not sufficient merely to know that one's view is archaeologically correct. Powers of persuasion, in committee, with local councillors, with bureaucrats, with non-archaeological peers, are additionally required, adding to the requisites of a good archaeological manager.

PRESENT ISSUES: LATE 1992 AND 2002–5

Two cases studies

The end of 1992, when the first version of this chapter was written, happened to illustrate numerous facets of archaeology in public. My two original case-studies-as-metaphors concerned Windsor Castle and an incident involving EH. They were used not because they were particularly significant in themselves but because they raised a range of issues relevant to ARM in the late twentieth century. They may seem rather dated now, but they nevertheless illustrate well the bones of my matter here; so, in reduced form and with new material from 2002–5, they are retained. Readers can easily supply their own later equivalents.

The Windsor Castle fire (November 1992)

A fire at Windsor Castle was immediately shocking; news of it by live television was visually dramatic. Almost before the embers had cooled, the story as news changed into seriously debated public controversy about three issues: safety precautions and conservation in historic buildings; the power of heritage to trigger strong reactions, in this case of a basic constitutional issue; and the old chestnut, re-emerging in a public debate that William Morris would have recognised, about whether to restore the old or build anew – that is, pastiche or creativity, replication or innovation, exact replacement for the sake of visual continuity or historical continuity by replacing the old with the new? All three issues are central to archaeological management.

Behind them, however, the archaeological resource manager will nowadays have in place, on paper and in practice, his risk assessment procedure designed to minimise the chances of such issues having to be raised after disaster (Stovel 1998). The relevance of the Windsor Castle fire even after a decade and more is that since ARM often involves both site works and artefact conservation, those who would manage archaeology have clear general, and specific statutory, responsibilities over such potential hazards as fire, health and safety, exactly as does any other manager in the 'real world'. Just because such work begins from academic assumptions or is pursued for research or aesthetic reasons is totally beside the point; intellectual elitism or scholarly 'ivory towerism' are no excuse for managerial ignorance or carelessness in such matters. The point is certainly well known to, and accepted by, professional archaeological managers. It is stressed here both for its own importance and to counteract any starry-eyed romanticism about the practice of twenty-first-century public archaeology.

An aspect of the Windsor Castle fire which seemed to make it different was that it concerned royalty and a place central to the concept of Englishness. The same could well have been said of the slightly later fire at Hampton Court. It is highly likely, however, that many other structures and sites under the responsibility of an archaeological resource manager will have iconographic values, perhaps neither regal nor national but nevertheless of sufficient power to trigger all sorts of consequences, predictable and otherwise. And this does happen: fire is a constant threat in 'heritage houses'. In the National Trust's Uppark,

West Sussex, it triggered all sorts of responses. Managers quickly realised that the place 'meant' many things to many people, and not just volunteers. Later, it acquired another overlay of 'value' as remedying the disaster was seen as providing the opportunity for a generation of craftspeople to develop their skills. Part of Edinburgh Old Town burnt in 2002; extensive tracts of Kakadu World Heritage site in Australia's Northern Territory went up in flames in 2003. In both and elsewhere where fire, or any other disaster like flooding, occurs, or where major, archaeologically destructive change is proposed, similar philosophical and practical issues as at Windsor and Uppark have to be confronted:

- build anew or restore?
- who pays?
- what are the future uses?
- who benefits?
- how to avoid repetition?

Such examples have a double relevance here. They are particularly apposite if, as other chapters in this book claim, archaeology would embrace, in addition to its abandoned sites and empty ruins, standing buildings, such as people's homes (Chapter 8) and cathedrals (Chapter 9) (which can also burn, for example, York Minster). Managers of that archaeology should never underestimate its power to possess, and therefore release, strong emotions. Particularly is that so when the resource in question, perhaps through its history but more probably through associations acquired irrespective of its scientific value, has crossed a magic line, transmuting itself from being merely archaeological to emerge as 'heritage' (Hewison 1987; Fowler 1992; Lowenthal 1996). People may or may not be indifferently content to leave archaeology to archaeologists, but heritage belongs to them. One of the most difficult judgements for an archaeological manager to make is whether his or her charge has enjoyed that transformation; and often the manager will not know until, for any one of a whole host of reasons, a particular site suddenly comes into the public gaze. Practically any locality can provide a recent example of a furore about a local site (e.g. Hayes and Patton 2001: 45–9, with excellent references in this field). They describe heated passions at the megalith, La Houge Bie, Jersey, and analyse issues there and at two other comparable situations in terms of crisis management; and, just down the road from where I write, a continuing saga about the future of the closed, Victorian public lavatories in the middle of that most iconic of historical English open spaces, Clerkenwell Green, where the local council proposed to build on what it saw as an empty and wasted asset and predictably, but to its apparent surprise, reaped the whirlwind of public objection.

While, of course, management of an archaeological resource has to be archaeologically correct, the decision itself and its implementation have to occur within some sort of public parameter: pastness, at least in the UK, performs now in the present, not just for its own sake or that of its practitioners. In a sense, ARM is not only now political but is on a par with other issues, such as education and health, that are sensitive to and debated by the public interest (Gathercole and Lowenthal 1990). The point is emphasised by the media coverage of the proposed treatment of Stonehenge and its environs as finally revealed in the government's roads programme, the subject of two public enquiries early in 2004. But for every Stonehenge there will be a dozen equivalents going on at regional, county and local level.

The Windsor fire stressed by implication another unromantic aspect of ARM: record that for which you are responsible. Record all changes on site whether planned or by chance. The former Royal Commission on the Historical Monuments of England (RCHME) had prepared a photographic archive of Windsor Castle some years earlier; after the fire, this proved of immense value. The cost to the public purse since the 1980s of fully recording every aspect of the heritage landscape around Stonehenge runs into millions of pounds (but what a record!). The full-time, professional archaeological staff of the National Trust has risen from none to about fifty since the 1970s largely because of the organisation's acceptance of the need to record before and during every change in its heritage resource, whether it be routine maintenance or new development.

Every archaeological manager is likely to face such issues. Even without a fire or other disaster, the management of buildings, ruins and earthworks requires at least their maintenance, probably their enhancement, and sometimes, not least for public presentation, their rebuilding in one form or another (e.g. Clark 2001). The official, traditional British response has always been 'consolidate as found' (Apted *et al.* 1977; Thompson 1981). To consolidate – the minimalist approach – or to rebuild, restore, replicate, renovate, reinstate, replace, recreate? All these options, and more, are nuances of response involving management decisions. The outcome is often as much not to take a particular step as actively to do something that will change the site or building in question. The fact, little-appreciated, is that 'heritage' is not unchanging; the very fact that any item has been identified as heritage means that it is paradoxically bound to change as a direct result of its selection and the consequential need to keep it. A consequence is that the appearance of a heritage item, and sometimes its actual nature, is not fixed but the product of successive decisions involving factors of the kinds just listed. ARM is therefore to some extent creative and, even when consciously neutral, almost bound to be so. Often the issue is not just whether to restore or not, but what to restore to? The birthplace and home of George Stephenson at Wylam, Northumberland, for example, was subtly changed by the National Trust early in the 1990s from a vaguely nineteenth-century ambience to a specifically late eighteenth-century interior. On a rather different scale, restoration after the genuinely disastrous fire at Hampton Court seized the opportunity to replace a former stylistic mishmash in the state apartments, not as it was before the fire, but to their condition when built by King William III (Mellor 1992).

Such decisions are not, however, confined to the seeming *recherché* dimensions of architectural authenticity and interior decoration; they are as much present out of doors too. They lie behind such creations as the Butser Ancient Farm (Reynolds 1979), the building of a 'genuine', new gateway into the Roman fort at South Shields, the less obvious restoration-cum-reconstruction of the 5,000-year-old west end of the Stonehenge cursus by the National Trust, and an 'Anglo-Saxon landscape' overlooking the River Tyne near the monastic church of the Venerable Bede at Jarrow (Fowler and Mills 2004; see generally Stone and Planel 1999). These issues are about theory and ethics but they are also about practical site management, conservation of fabric and objects, the emotive power of heritage, especially as a trigger for the expression of public concern, and the propriety and practice of various restorative strategies. Of course such issues must be publicly discussed, but someone has to take a decision about them for actions to proceed. Whatever that decision, it and its outcome will probably be both controversial and very publicly debated.

Here is the nub for contemporary ARM. The issues are not new, for cultural conservationists have been struggling with them since conscious preservation began to be thought about in the seventeenth century. Nowadays, however, controversy and public debate simply have to be accepted and preferably welcomed. This applies whether the resource (a landscape, building, site or object) is at the top of the heritage hierarchy – national, royal, big, old and a major tourist attraction (and it might even be scientifically significant too) – or whether it is an anonymous bump in, or a mundane object from, a local field. It will mean something to someone; someone will 'own' it. It is bound to possess a public interest, or a potential for one; if it does not, then its mishandling through failure to recognise that interest will ensure that it quickly acquires one. This encapsulates the single biggest difference in terms of ARM between the 1960s and the early twenty-first century: the public interest. Woe betide the archaeological manager who ignores, is ignorant of or, worse, despises, that interest; for with it go what individual members of our society, and those speaking for that society collectively, now regard as their 'rights'. Real or imagined, it matters not; such rights, and the means to express concern about them, exist.

English Heritage and England's heritage

An EH press conference on 26 October 1992 was primarily to announce the plan for EH, acting as the heritage executive of the state, to dispose of part of the patrimony (EH 1992a). The 'part' was a long list of monuments and archaeological sites constituting a significant portion of the portfolio of Guardianship Monuments, or Properties in Care looked after directly by EH, a portfolio built up over more than a century since the first Ancient Monuments Act in 1882. That the impression was initially given of privatisation, of even selling some of the monuments, did not help the course of rational discussion. Whatever the merits of the plan (aspects of which have since been implemented), its publication immediately illustrated a wide schism between what the managers (EH) thought was reasonable and what its constituency thought. Part of the reason for this was that no justification, other than pragmatism deeply tinged with market-place economics, was provided to buttress a plan that actually involved fine matters of theory and professional knowledge. Far more significant was the misjudgement evident in the failure to anticipate public and professional concern. The problem was aggravated by Sir Jocelyn Stevens's, the then EH chairman, widely quoted dismissal of the latter as arrogant while admitting his surprise at the scale and force of the former. The good archaeological resource manager should not be caught out on either score, but he/she should note that big errors of this sort can be made in fields other than ARM. Monsanto, for example, made such a misjudgement in the late 1990s, compounded in its case by ignorance and arrogance, in the matter of growing genetically modified crops in Britain.

The significant feature in the EH instance was that the adverse publicity was entirely media led; it was not archaeologically inspired or stimulated, nor did it have to be. The first point is, therefore, that archaeological managers nowadays have to be adept at handling the media as well as performing for it; rather more discriminatingly, they must also be able to judge when to push and when merely to follow a public bandwagon that is careering along under its own momentum. More fundamentally, they must so position themselves that they are actually in touch with their constituency; they must have some awareness of what their publics think, are likely to think, and how they will probably react. In this case EH, like many other organisations, clearly had no idea at all of how its proposals would be seen by those regarding themselves as having a stake in the same field. Worse, it conveyed an impression that it cared even less (the Blair government made a similar mistake in early 2003 as it prepared for its war in Iraq). The message projected was 'We know; you don't', and alienation was assured.

PRESENT TO FUTURE

Dictatorship is predictably a recipe for disaster in heritage matters and in the sort of society that inhabits Britain in the early twenty-first century. The days of an unquestioning respect for authority are over (*vide* the reception of the report of the Hutton Inquiry, January 2004). Archaeological managers must, therefore, whatever their private feelings on this score, professionally invest their effort and time in consultation (a process which can, of course, take several forms). You have to carry people with you, and especially when they pay the manager and already 'own' that which their manager manages. In my example, EH seemingly confused the needs of EH with those of England's heritage. That lessons have been learnt is illustrated by considerable subsequent consultation initiated by EH on various matters, for example locally, as over Stonehenge, and nationally on England's heritage itself (EH 2000a) and (in 2003–04) on the future of the National Monuments Record, the record of that heritage. Pastness is now public property; interest in and concern for it are now matters of public debate. Archaeological and heritage managers must now, therefore, discharge their responsibilities not only with an eye to the public interest but very much in the public domain. They are being watched, and are publicly accountable not just for what they do but for why and how they do it. A BBC TV series in 2004 about The National Trust's stewardship brought that out very well as it showed local people interacting with Trust management and Trust staff trying to hold the line on basic principles while trying to accommodate sensible public wishes (in exposing the self-interest and indeed sheer nastiness of particular individuals it also silently emphasised the difficulty of the resource manager's role). Reasons for this shift lie in different strands of activity and thought: a string of individual incidents, certainly, but perhaps more the result of trends rather than events. Such would include the long-term effects of realistic television and radio programmes, of countless lectures by the small army of adult education missionaries, and of the increasingly concerted effort by organisations to take archaeology to people locally through a diversity of mechanisms such as open days on excavations, special evenings at museums and the designation of heritage trails. It is called education in the best sense of that word (Binks *et al*. 1988; cf. Stone and Mackenzie 1990; Chapter 20).

Such education is not entirely altruistic, perhaps, for its strong motivation comes from conviction, but the result is beneficial to the tutor, the participator and the subject. Of course, other, non-archaeological, trends in British society have also contributed to the shift, perhaps even created the conditions in which it has been able to happen. For the archaeological manager, however, the important point is that it has happened: for example, with the arrival of a politically driven emphasis on 'access', including access to the past, has come a recognition that heritage can be a factor in, even a trigger of, economic and/or social regeneration. Powerful and emotional ideas such as 'Black history' have emerged. There is, for example, much to be done in increasing the appreciation and availability of the British countryside among minority groups. The archaeological manager is therefore in a very different situation now compared to that in which this writer started, an enviable but somewhat irresponsible one largely devoid of such concerns. In it, the only due was to the highest academic standards of the subject and my employing organisation, with virtually the only expression of public interest along the lines of 'Fancy anyone paying you to do that'. As many have found before and since then, it was the hard graft of teaching adults in the extramural departments, which were then a key part of many universities, that taught me about another, legitimate and more pressing public interest. It seems to me that such person-to-person contact is an essential of archaeological management, for nowadays it has to consist not just of what the manager thinks but of what his or her constituency thinks.

Clearly many pasts other than the archaeological one exist. A lot of people, in all sorts of ways, now want to have access to some of them (Chippindale *et al*. 1990; Devereux 1991; Bender 1993; Schama 1995; and, for a European example, Pickard 2002; and globally, Bianchi and Boniface 2002). Whatever their wishes, and whatever their own interpretations – and obviously many of them will be far from the core of archaeological 'correctness' – that which is desired is often closely related to actual sites, the resource at the heart of the archaeological manager's role. Paradoxically, nevertheless, much that the latter would regard as within his or her remit would not be seen by others as archaeological. This applies, for example, to buildings, townscapes including urban parks, countryside, landscapes and historic gardens. The countryside in particular is generally not seen as artefactual; rather others see it as natural, a divide meantime represented in England by the tripartite bureaucracy of the Countryside Agency, English Nature and EH (though the first two have been subsumed in single agencies in Scotland and Wales). The biggest landowner of them all is the Forestry Commission, which for some years now, in accepting recreational and conservation as well as timber-producing objectives, has also embraced archaeology as a factor in its land management. With all such bodies, it would be nice to think that the case for the archaeological, cultural or historic resource had been successfully made. In principle, such is indeed the case. In practice, however, the archaeological manager must still expect in the early twenty-first century to spend much time in denying limitations of his or her remit to Scheduled Ancient Monuments, single sites and material underground, and of his or her activities to excavating. Simultaneously and more positively, opportunities to advise others of the archaeological implications of their proposals and activities must be seized. It is still relatively rare for the archaeological factor to be taken into account in normal land management unless some development is in mind. Exceptions would include the admirably holistic management approach of the National Trust and, increasingly, of the National Parks.

The Parks, however, have responsibilities to allow, indeed encourage, access by the public, and not far down that road lies the whole question of tourism, interpretation, the 'visitor experience', the ambivalences of community involvement (e.g. Hodges and Watson 2000), what has been termed 'heritat' and what might be termed the 'heritage economy' (Tabata *et al.* 1992; Boniface and Fowler 1993; Hall and Page 1999; Boniface 2001). Many themes and particular aspects can be identified within that generalisation, especially in relation to interpretation, for example, post-colonial heritage (Long 2000), religious sites (Shackley 2001), montane pastoral tradition (Olwig 2001) and ethnography (Karpodini-Dimitriadi 1995). Willingly or otherwise, the archaeological resource manager is almost inevitably an active participant in this sort of issue within wider contexts such as access, sustainability, economic regeneration, revenue-enhancement and political correctness (e.g. Urban Practitioners 2002). His or her decisions might, for example, not create the best revenue-producing honeypot site required by the financial targets of the relevant organisation; decisions about opening and closing times, or about the route of a tourist trail, could well not serve the commercial needs of coach-tour operators. In such a situation, now common, the manager of the past is very much bound up with the needs of the present, yet constrained by the long-term needs of the resource. The question is clearly: what, in the last resort, is ARM about? The local matrix in which it occurs and operates should indicate at least part of the answer.

The matrix being outlined here is certainly in part local; but it is also regional, national and international. Witness a selection from the topics and issues of direct relevance to ARM that have been publicly aired on or in any one or more of television, radio, web pages and newspapers either side of New Year's day, 2005. Locally – just look in your local newspaper and there is bound to be something about a local site or archaeological find, the local museum, or some conservation issue: Allerton Hall, North Yorkshire, a Grade 1 listed building, was gutted by fire, for example, while in my case plans are on display in the local library for the conversion of the Old Town Hall into a dancing school with commercial attachments. Under current government proposals, could these by any chance possibly hide a future casino? Regionally, the remarkable archive recording prehistoric rock art in northern England, compiled through a lifetime's endeavour by an outstanding amateur archaeologist, was recently deposited in the appropriate university and has now become available on the web.

Nationally, many of the events and announcements characteristically share the common theme of money: starry-eyed youth, weaned on the romantic trivia of so much televisual archaeology and considering a career in ARM, should realistically recognise that finance will increasingly demand their time the more successful they are. At the moment, cuts in national budgets dominate: for example, of EH, with serious implications for the practice of field archaeology and ARM, and of its grants to only twenty of sixty-one cathedrals (down from £4 million to £1 million). In Scotland, concern is about the implications, including financial ones, of its Parliament's proposals which would deprive major national cultural institutions of their charitable status. But money also has its plus side – for the winners: grants from the Heritage Lottery Fund will allow three projects to proceed, namely on a new museum and education centre focused on the UK's recently discovered earliest cave art at Creswell Crags (£4.26 million, over four times the EH annual cathedral maintenance grant); on finding the site of the Battle of Bosworth (£1.4 million, see previous parenthesis); and on maintaining the biodiversity of Britain's biggest extent of ancient woodland east of Lincoln, characterised by small-leaved lime and a remnant of 'wildwood' surviving from prehistoric clearance (£700,000). Whatever the merits of those projects, their flavour seems somehow more wholesome than the news on the national/international interface of a not very original and somewhat gratuitous exhibition of Tutankhamunia including '50 items from the tomb which have not previously been shown in Britain' according to the *Sunday Times*. And where will this necrological feast be displayed? – in the Millennium Dome in 2007, 'the first year of the dome's new existence as a commercially run arena and leisure centre' according to the same source. This just about sums up the thirty-three years since the legendary 'Treasures of Tutankhamun' exhibition at the British Museum in 1972, a not entirely implausible date for the invention of ARM (McGimsey 1972). The target is clear: the 1.7 million visitors. So is the motive: to raise funds to protect sites in the Valley of the Kings, Egypt.

Internationally, three stories characterise the sort of reportage which, sadly in some respects, is continually current and which, at base, is almost invariably also about money. Academics and fundraisers are promoting the desirability of excavating the rest of the Villa of Papyri at Herculaneum, believing that it still contains 'lost' works of Classical authors such as Sophocles which, even if carbonised, will be readable using multi-spectral imaging (www.herculaneum.ox.ac.uk). The imperative is to find 'copies of known masterpieces and to recover works lost to humanity for two millennia, A treasure of greater cultural importance can scarcely be imagined', according to proponents in a letter to *The Times*. And, playing the 'rescue' card, they aim to do so before the next eruption of Vesuvius buries the site forever. Professor Fowler – not this one, I hasten to add – argues that 'we owe it to the world to dig' (as quoted in the *Sunday Times*, 23 January 2005). £10.6 million is needed, but a counter-argument posits that resources are much more urgently needed to conserve the site as a whole, a viewpoint that most visitors are likely to share. A public appeal would raise little to alleviate that however, whereas the allure of 'buried treasure', albeit well disguised as literary heritage for propriety, is likely to bring the dollars in. The place itself is meanwhile a scandal.

Such a strong word in that context can all too easily be applied to both my other examples. Recent detective work by the Israeli Antiquities Authority has exposed a long-term forgery scam that appears to have landed many a museum as well as private collectors with expensive fakes or, at the least, the possibility that their biblical objects might be fakes. Reports claim that thousands of artefacts have been forged over some twenty years. True or false, a very big question mark now hangs over not just many a Bible-related object but also, and not for the first time, the aspirations, collecting methods and academic competence of many supposedly professional curators, collectors and their advisers.

Even worse in its way is the tragedy of archaeology in Iraq since 2003 – worse because none of the archaeological waste, loss, damage and destruction need have happened. The dramatic and increasingly confused story of its national and other museums emerged in the immediate aftermath of invasion, and continues; stories of looting of and damage to sites came through too, and continue; to both was added in January 2005 the sober, awful and all-too believable report by the Keeper of the Ancient Near East Department, British Museum, about Babylon, one of the world's more numinous places, a major scientific resource and a cultural icon too. Suffice it to say that the Americans established a military camp actually on the site, one which expanded to 150 hectares housing 2,000 soldiers and which was handed over to the Polish military. The report speaks of areas flattened, trenches dug, structures damaged, stratigraphy impaired, artefacts littering the place. The whole is a near-total disaster, the exact opposite of what archaeological resource management is about and aspires to. The CBA pointed out that 'Archaeological organisations on both sides of the Atlantic were warning British and American governments about these issues months in advance of the conflict, and we have repeated our concerns many times since . . . we must press ahead rapidly with the ratification of the 1954 Hague Convention for the Protection of Cultural Property in the Event of Armed Conflict'. The simple fact that that convention has not been signed by the UK fifty years after its approval, and that in 2005 the UK government is apparently unconcernedly party to the world archaeological tragedy that is Iraq, presents ARMUK with something of a challenge for the twenty-first century.

CONCLUSION

To prolong the life of the resource has for long been a principal objective of archaeological management. It is now embedded in a matrix of significant changes which have occurred since the mid-twentieth century. One is the remarkable increase in the range of other objectives, or at least functions, of archaeology. Another is also quantitative, namely the increase in the scope of the resource to be managed and the vastly increased size of its audience. The constituency for the past, and its expectations, are now simply of a different order.

In one sense, then, ARM is necessary to counter and meet the needs of large numbers of people with increased leisure, expendable cash, fantastically improved mobility, better education and higher expectations of their personal quality of life. People also have and expect better access, both physically and also, notably through the web, intellectually. The world of information now available is revolutionary to the extent that it is affecting not just the quantity of data we can store about the past but also the very nature of learning and of our understanding of our pasts. This development may help explain why many people voluntarily choose to spend a proportion of their hard-earned improved standard of living in visiting, really and/or virtually, manifestations of what was often the dullest of subjects at school; though perhaps Alan Bennett is nearer the mark in his play *The History Boys* (2004) when he remarks that 'Archaeology is the nearest that history gets to shopping'. Nostalgia has been examined as another major motor (Shaw and Chase 1989), but nowadays that can hardly apply in terms of direct personal memory to anything earlier than about 1910 (though the vaguer late nineteenth-century world of grandparental memories is even more attractive).

Presumably, 'heritage time' will move forward in calendrical time. A good example is provided by the International Council on Monuments and Sites. ICOMOS exists, *inter alia*, 'to provide a forum for all those involved in the conservation of cultural heritage' and 'to facilitate professional dialogue and exchange on both specialist and general conservation issues' (web page). Its UK section published in 2004 a first list of the twentieth century's best buildings in Britain; some are already listed (for listing, see Chapter 8). This follows EH's *Preserving Post-War Heritage: The Care and*

Figure 1.3. The past is closing on the present and the range of 'archaeology' widens: twentieth-century military defences, Fortress of Suomenlinna, near Helsinki, Finland.

Conservation of Mid-twentieth-century Architecture. The interwar years are also in focus as suitably 'old' (cf. Frayling 1992, and the Art Deco exhibition at the Victoria and Albert Museum, 2003). The National Trust acquired in summer 2002, largely with public money, a big country house near Bristol, justifying the purchase not so much because the building was about a century old but because it had been untouched since the 1920s. The Trust also now owns two very ordinary-looking houses in Liverpool where individual Beatles spent their formative years. Similarly, in also being about material of the not-so-very long-ago (which would not have been considered 'archaeology' by many at the time of the first edition of this book: Fig. 1.3), EH, Historic Scotland and the CBA, in a rare UK-wide initiative, have undertaken a national survey of Second World War archaeology. To set beside the more conventional image of archaeology in a military context exemplified in *The Field Archaeology of Salisbury Plain Training Area*, we can now read such as *Fields of Deception: Britain's Bombing Decoys of World War II* and consult a large archive of records of anti-invasion defences under the project title 'Defence of Britain'.

The past is very close behind, and closing. Just how close was pointedly and poignantly illustrated before the author's eyes at noon on Monday, 29 November 2004 (Fig. 1.4). I was unexpectedly able to join an official UN party paying a diplomatically respectful visit to the grave of the recently deceased Yasser Arafat in his battered and bombed compound at Ramallah, West Bank. As we watched, workmen were erecting the superstructure over the heads of the soldiers standing guard at the grave's four corners, making a shrine over and around a grave piled high with funereal offerings. It was already a site of homage. We were watching the conversion of a contemporary burial place into a future heritage site starting today, into an embryonic place of pilgrimage.

That oddest of human attributes, curiosity, is a strong motivator too. With it can go a sense of personal quest, perhaps a sense of pilgrimage, not necessarily religious in any formal

Figure 1.4. Future heritage: the grave of Yasser Arafat, Ramallah, West Bank, with the structure enclosing it nearing completion, 29 November 2004.

sense, but nevertheless a journey, often physical but sometimes intellectual or emotional. Behind the holiday or weekend desire for a good day out, with opportunities to eat well and shop needlessly, may lie a perhaps unconscious wish simply to find out, not just to discover what the past or a place was like but equally how these archaeologists and historians know what they say they know (cf. Layton 1989b; Shennan 1989). If something like this be so, then performance as much as product is a key to successful presentation by those charged with responsibilities for the past in contemporary society. Especially is this so now that tourism is a major prop of the world's economy. Just note what has happened in this respect during the economic down-turn in tourism in the opening years of the twenty-first century, not only in particular tourism-dependent localities, but to major players like global airlines. While it is clear that ARM in the UK will in future be operating in an increasingly complex local society, it will also be performing for a whole series of overlapping cross-sections of the world's diverse societies as tourists (Featherstone 1990; Boniface and Fowler 1993). The concept and practice of World Heritage and its associated tourism exemplifies this trend (Fowler 2004), especially as the UK has led the way with the development of management plans for all its World Heritage sites. So here too is another field for ARM – and for the creation of another raft of posts for archaeologists and similar specialists.

In 2003 a World Heritage Project Coordinator was needed for the World Heritage Jurassic Coast of Dorset and East Devon. The requirement of the post as stated in the job specification fairly accurately summed up my matrix here: to oversee 'a portfolio of projects covering conservation, tourism, interpretation, education, access and regeneration'. Archaeological resource managers, in other words, have to operate in the present. They can surely do that more effectively if, in addition to refreshing their knowledge of the past, they are also students of present society.

CHAPTER 2

CHANGING CONFIGURATIONS: THE RELATIONSHIPS BETWEEN THEORY AND PRACTICE

Gavin Lucas

INTRODUCTION

As in any discipline, the language of archaeology is a fusion of words and phrases that stretch along a continuum from specialist jargon to the vernacular or everyday usage. It is perhaps ironic that the words 'theory' and 'practice' are often understood in a very vague, everyday sense, yet discourses of theoretical or practical archaeology commonly employ the most complex and specialist languages in the discipline. Perhaps this only adds to the oft-felt distance between the two: how can post-processualism have anything to do with a Harris Matrix or a Development Control Brief? But it is not simply that these two fields of archaeology have their own languages, there is also a more general, often unstated perspective that places theory and practice at either end of another continuum, between the abstract and the concrete. Theory is often perceived as purely conceptual, speculative, something done in an armchair, while practice is down-to-earth, empirical, and conducted in the 'real world'. Sometimes this is expressed in a stereotypical fashion such as 'fieldworkers don't read' and 'theoretical archaeologists can't dig'. Sometimes it is even expressed in the way archaeology is done in Britain, namely by two distinct types of archaeologists – respectively those teaching and researching in universities and those working in cultural resource management, whether in contract units or county archaeology offices. But these distinctions are neither as parallel, nor as distinct, as these categorisations would suggest. There are tensions within these different fields, but there are also cross-overs and blurrings of differences that demand a much more considered review of the relationship between theory and practice. In short, this relationship is much more complex than the following 'Parody Table' might suggest:

Theory	*Practice*
Abstract	Concrete
Speculative	Empirical
Academic Research	Resource Management

What do archaeologists mean by theory? Theory can imply any number of different senses: it can imply something speculative, as in the juxtapositions above, but the way it is usually understood in the context of theoretical archaeology is the (study of the) body of concepts and ideas that articulate practice. One of the most important realisations to come out of the development of theoretical archaeology since the 1960s is the understanding that whatever archaeologists do is *always* informed by theory, whether this is made explicit or not – and better by far to make it as explicit as possible. For example, one of the major consequences of this realisation was the development of research strategies and project designs, now a standard part of the archaeological process (Binford 1964; EH 1991a). More importantly, though, it implies that a 'common-sense' archaeologist is just as theoretical as a post-processualist, even if he or she does not know it – and perhaps a more dangerous one for just that reason. Observations or facts are never absolute or uncontestable, but always occur or are produced within a certain framework or way of perceiving the world. For many, the best framework is a scientific one. But science itself – and we might even contest the unity of this framework – is just as determined by its theoretical context as any other discipline, a feature now long recognised (Kuhn 1962). Theoretical archaeology is simply an examination of the varied theoretical contexts in which archaeology is practised, scientific or otherwise. It provides both a critique and alternative ways of thinking about practice and the different -isms, or broader schools such as processual and post-processual archaeology, which simply reflect the diversity of such critiques and alternatives. Archaeology has always been theoretical and an archaeology that engages with theory is ultimately one which is self-aware and reflexive, and from which it can only profit.

But archaeology has also always been practical. What made archaeology a distinct discipline in the late nineteenth century was that its practitioners went into the field and engaged with the remains of past cultures, that at its heart was an engagement with material culture. This engagement can take place in many ways, from digging holes in the ground, to running museums, from studying artefacts to development control. But any one of these engagements takes place within a conceptual framework, which largely influences the way in which archaeological practice is carried out. This framework changes over time, and between regions or countries and it is a mistake to think that archaeologists practise the discipline in the same way everywhere. There are many different ways to excavate a site, display artefacts or mitigate development, and these ways all depend on what questions one has, and what theoretical perspectives are informing those questions.

FIELDWORK AND THE DEVELOPMENT OF ARCHAEOLOGY

The very existence of archaeology as a practice depends on a certain view of the past that developed in Europe from the sixteenth century (Schnapp 1996). Being aware of the remains of the past, engaging with them, is not synonymous with archaeology – even the prehistoric societies we study did this (Bradley 2002a). Rather, the development of archaeology is linked to specific cultural and historical contexts, and if it has spread into a global practice today, this is largely because of the imperial expansion of the countries, such as Britain, where it first emerged. A general theoretical framework was already in place before archaeology, as we know it today, developed. Many of our practices, particularly those associated with museums and the display of artefacts, are linked into this longer history. Nonetheless, much of the work archaeologists undertake today has a shorter history and these activities are more directly the offspring of the emergence of archaeology as a distinct discipline and profession in the late nineteenth century. In Britain, the first academic posts, archaeological societies and journals all emerged at this time, as did the first government inspector of ancient monuments and, in 1882, corresponding legislation (Levine 1986). What perhaps unites all these emerging features and defined archaeology as a new discipline, is a totally new outlook on the recovery of the remains of the past: the development of fieldwork. It is no coincidence, as Grahame Clark noted long ago, that the first Inspector of Ancient Monuments was also the paragon of this new approach to the remains of the past and subsequently remembered as the 'father of fieldwork' – General Pitt Rivers (Clark 1934).

Archaeology has, since its inception, been largely defined by the fact that it requires fieldwork. As with many other sciences that developed at the same time, such as geology, botany or zoology, fieldwork became one of the cornerstones of the discipline, guaranteeing its scientific and academic status (Kuklick 1997). The field *was* the archaeologist's laboratory – at least until it adopted the more conventional, 'white-coated' type as well from the 1950s. But this field laboratory did not come ready made with a manual on how to use it; it was something that had to be constructed, to be built and rebuilt on every site investigated. How did the first archaeologists create such a 'mobile laboratory'; how were the rules of excavation and survey established? It is far too easy, and naïve, to answer with vague allusions to common sense or progress. As in any laboratory, one chooses the equipment according to the questions one has, and in archaeology these have developed and changed over time. There are many obvious ways in which such questions have affected fieldwork – perhaps the most commonly cited is the retrieval of non-artefactual data such as animal bones or seeds, which clearly relate to developing interests in economic and environmental aspects of the past. But there is a much more fundamental way in which theory influences field practice and this is in the understanding of context. It has often been remarked that the chief difference between archaeology and antiquarianism is this concern for context. Knowing where an object came from or understanding the nature of a site pulls archaeology away from art history or treasure hunting. But what exactly do we mean by context? This understanding has changed according to larger theoretical orientations.

For example, Pitt Rivers's fieldwork texts tend to be very find-oriented and up until the 1930s, most archaeological site reports give much more space to the finds than to the site itself. This focus on the finds can be seen as part of the major theoretical concern of the time, specifically evolutionary typology, which formed the main bulk of Pitt Rivers's other writings (e.g. Pitt Rivers 1906; Bradley 1983). Pitt Rivers's excavation methods, in particular their carefulness, were directed primarily at establishing an accurate context for finds, so these could be reliably employed within evolutionary typologies, a goal also shared by many of his contemporaries, such as Petrie (1899). The complexity of the deposits themselves or the characteristics of the composition of the site, especially in terms of stratigraphy, is often noticeably lacking. Full awareness of such issues only emerged with Wheeler and others in the 1920s and 1930s. This new recognition of the complexity of sites (both stratigraphically and horizontally) and the emphasis on excavating new types of sites (especially settlements), show a very different theoretical perspective in fieldwork, one much more concerned for the site as the context of a past community or society and the specific way in which it expressed itself through its material culture. The field methods that developed in the 1920s and 1930s were directly linked to broader shifts in theoretical perspectives, particularly the notion of the culture group and culture historical archaeology as most famously articulated by Gordon Childe (e.g. Childe 1929). Yet despite the concern for stratigraphy, fieldwork texts of the 1930s to 1950s largely present the site as a static entity – a frozen manifestation of a society, even if one culture replaces another in the stratigraphic sequence it contained. It was not until the 1960s that archaeologists started to challenge this normative view of society and seek more dynamic interpretations of past communities. This New Archaeology also radically changed the way fieldwork was practised – in particular, greater attention was paid to spatial patterning of deposits and finds, and this necessitated new methods of excavation and survey, such as sampling techniques (from trench location to sieving) or excavation in plan rather than through sections (from open area excavation to single context recording).

This bare summary of the detailed histories of fieldwork in Britain is only intended to demonstrate that archaeological practice has always been influenced by theoretical perspectives (see Lucas 2001a for a fuller discussion). The attention given here to fieldwork is a reflection of its importance in the definition of the discipline, an importance that is perhaps even more central in archaeological resource management. Perhaps the most significant development in the postwar decades was the gradual rise in developer-led archaeology and correspondingly, cultural or archaeological resource management (Butcher and Garwood 1994; Jones 1984; Rahtz 1974). Theoretical frameworks emerging at the same time deeply affected the way this archaeology has been, and continues to be, practised. One of the key terms in this theory, as much of the language makes explicit, is the notion of archaeology as a *resource* and all the attendant discourse that this term brings such as sustainability (Fowler 1976). This term is now so deeply embedded in current archaeological language that we are perhaps unaware of a host of conceptual problems it brings with it. In particular, the notion that archaeological remains are a resource in the manner of, say, minerals or other raw materials views them as something with a value independent of our intervention with them. The consequence of this way of thinking has been to orient the whole discourse of development in terms of the preservation of these remains (whether *in situ* or by record), with the actual meaning of these remains taking a second, much poorer place (Lucas 2001b). That this has been deleterious from the start is obvious from the various initiatives to have emerged from English Heritage since the 1980s, from the backlog programme to the development of period and regional research agendas (Butcher and Garwood 1994; Wainwright 2000). These attempts to patch up the flaws in developer-led archaeology, though important, do not see that perhaps the very reason they are needed is a result of the very language and theoretical perspective that informs this practice.

A greater theoretical awareness can offer much in this direction and yet, ironically, since the development of the specialist sub-field of theoretical archaeology, theory appears to have become more and more esoteric to many practitioners and far removed from everyday practice. As both archaeological theory and archaeological resource management have developed, particularly since the 1980s, they have diverged further and further and now would seem at times almost to inhabit different disciplines and speak different languages. While many might accept that theory is important and articulates practice, as described earlier, many also feel, perhaps justifiably in some cases, that archaeological theory does not live up to this role; sometimes it is hard to see how theory has any relationship to practice at all. The question that is increasingly pressing today is how can this burgeoning discourse in abstract theory be relevant to concrete practice? Specifically, how can such theory make a difference to the way we practise archaeology?

FUTURE CONFIGURATIONS

Some of the earliest fruits of theoretical archaeology came from studies directed at the heritage industry – radical critiques of museums, exhibitions and, more generally, the presentation of the past to the public all had immediate relevance for the way archaeology was practised in this sphere (e.g. Shanks and Tilley 1987a; Merriman 1991; Hooper-Greenhill 1992; Pearce 1992). However, the impact of theory on fieldwork was, until just recently, minimal. Since some of the central issues surrounding the development of archaeological practice are articulated through fieldwork, it is useful to continue using this area as a means of exploring future directions. There have in fact been several recent attempts to explore alternative or supplementary ways of conducting fieldwork (e.g. Bender *et al.* 1997; Woodward and Hughes 1998; Cooper and Garrow 2000). Many of these examples share the insertion of an 'embodiment' into the site, marked by the archaeologists concerned thinking about and recording the site in terms of human scales of perception and experience. After all, if presence in the field provides anything, it provides one obvious ready-made tool for analysis – the human body. Yet in so much excavation, we routinely ignore this in favour of abstract scales of measurement, in the name of objectivity. Yet this very objectivity can obscure and prevent the recording of much useful information about a site, in terms that encapsulate how it may have been experienced in the past. There are an increasing number of similar experiments in archaeological fieldwork, and many are done not in research but contract situations. However, these are often small-scale experiments running alongside more conventional fieldwork; major attempts to rethink the nature of fieldwork – and with greater implications for archaeological practice as a whole – are inevitably rarer but they also perhaps demonstrate the potential in such an approach. The two most significant projects of this nature have been Çatalhöyük and Framework Archaeology, one a foreign research project run from the University of Cambridge, the other a contract company set up in the developer-funded world (Hodder 1997; 1999; Andrews *et al.* 2000).

The general approach of the Çatalhöyük project incorporates four themes: reflexivity, relationality, interactivity and multivocality (Hodder 1999: 193–5; see also Chapter 19). By reflexivity is meant critical self-awareness of the theoretical component of fieldwork; by relationality, recognition of the dependent and situated nature of knowledge production; by interactivity, the facilitation of communication between different groups, such as specialists and diggers; and by multivocality, the acceptance and incorporation of diverse and potentially competing interests concerning the past. These four themes influence the practice of archaeology and an enormous amount of thought has gone into producing a style of fieldwork that promotes these goals, from on-site methods of recording to the ambitious use of web-based media in the presentation of the project. Çatalhöyük is of course a multinational and interdisciplinary project, and many of the issues it faces are peculiar to a project working abroad and with a team drawn from several different countries. This is not to downplay the relevance or significance of any of these issues, but because of its particular characteristics, there are other issues relating to practice, such as might be found in a domestic context in Britain, that it does not encounter. These are issues that, for example, Framework Archaeology sets out to engage with (see also Chapter 14).

Framework Archaeology was set up to produce a style of field archaeology in a developer-led context that promoted more on site interpretation through an engaged and reflexive team of excavators and specialists. Based within the redevelopment of Heathrow Airport, this style of fieldwork is termed 'historical research', in order to assert its interpretive rather than merely technical nature, and that this is a fundamental rather than an add-on aspect of such fieldwork. At its heart is a critique of archaeological practice that separates fieldwork from post-excavation interpretation or analysis; this is particularly problematic in the context of developer-led archaeology that sees excavation as preservation by record. Deferral of interpretation in such situations only impoverishes the quality of work done and is regarded as a seriously inadequate approach to cultural resource management. At a basic level, the authors of the Framework project argue for similar points to those advocated in the Çatalhöyük project – despite some criticism of the latter. Critical and theoretical awareness of the interpretive nature of fieldwork and the need to encourage much more thoughtful and integrated practices are common to both, even though they articulate these in different ways and on quite different sites. Moreover, both situate their projects within a broader social context, either in terms of multivocality and competing interests, as with Çatalhöyük, or in terms of cultural resource management and developer-led archaeology, as with Framework.

These two examples provide current and exciting examples of new approaches to fieldwork, but they are only a start and, inevitably, their practice can sometimes fall short of their ideals (e.g. Chadwick 1998, 2003). Nevertheless, they contain many valuable insights and offer many useful directions. Drawing from these approaches and extending the discussion to a wider field of archaeological practice, I would like to suggest five key areas in which archaeology can, and often does, benefit from a more theoretically aware and informed stance. These areas encompass the diversity of archaeological practice and show how theory is relevant at all levels, not just the most abstract – from the coal-face of contract digging to government legislation, from local projects to national frameworks. Theory is implicated at both extremes and in everything that lies in between.

Fieldwork and the archaeological process

The problem of deferred interpretation is part of a larger issue about the fragmentation of the archaeological process. It has even been argued that the principles behind MAP2 and its very structure enshrine this fragmentation (Adams and Brooke 1995; Hodder 1999: 172). On many archaeological projects, for example, not only might interpretation of a feature or site be deferred, but many kinds of analysis, particularly of finds, are usually held over until a post-excavation stage. But the more an archaeologist can know about the feature or site being excavated while it is happening, the better that excavation can be, and rapid feedback of specialist information would facilitate this. The current structure has little practical basis. Furthermore, the more archaeologists know about what they want to say in the field, the more they can critically assess the nature of the archive they want to produce and preserve, and the story they want to disseminate. This therefore also has implications for archiving and publication. This is not to deny that there will always be a post-excavation stage, but perhaps the distinction should be less clear-cut; and more careful consideration needs to go into what might be better done when.

Management of the archaeological heritage

Directly leading on from the first point is the question of how to think about archaeological heritage. Should we continue to view it as a resource, recognising that new conceptions of fieldwork increasingly regard it in very different ways? Perceiving the archaeological heritage as a resource asserts an intrinsic valuation, which does not recognise the creative aspect of archaeology. It leads to views of fieldwork as data extraction rather than interpretation, to views that promote preservation as always the first and best choice. Under the initial threat of development, this was a positive strategy, but it is one we should perhaps now be rethinking, for ironically this philosophy only makes archaeology redundant at best or contradictory at worst (cf. Biddle 1994). *How* we value remains is more important that the simple fact that we do value them, and in this respect, theory is a crucial part of the process. Preservation or excavation should be a decision made on the basis of the unique features of each site in relation to larger theoretical issues, both archaeological and socio-political, not a blanket law applied to all remains regardless of wider considerations.

Interpreting the past

The recent development of research agendas is a sure sign that theory is having an impact on archaeological practice, for it is no longer sufficient to justify developer-led excavation in terms of the percentage of the remains rescued or the deployment of adequate standards of recording. We want to know what and how this site will add to our understanding of the past and how the excavation methodology will affect this. What we regard as archaeologically important or valuable is directly dependent on current theoretical paradigms and academic agendas. Archaeologists working in heritage or resource management need to know what the issues are and to be as informed as possible in order to make the best assessments of the work required under development conditions. This means everything from what the current approaches are in Bronze Age studies to what actually constitutes archaeological remains. The period of post-medieval or modern archaeology for example, especially of the nineteenth and twentieth centuries, is extremely variable in its valuation as part of our heritage – from being seen as modern disturbance at one extreme to being regarded as crucial to our understanding of the contemporary world at the other (Tarlow and West 1999; Buchli and Lucas 2001).

Archaeology and the public

The recognition that archaeology has a responsibility to the wider public has long been appreciated. At one level, this interrelationship touches on issues of how archaeology is disseminated and presented outside the disciplinary discourse through media such as museums, popular publications or television. But at another level it concerns the nature of *who* this public is – particularly the recognition of the diversity of people and interests contained within the phrase 'the public' and also the active relationship archaeology should have with these groups. Questions about *whose past* and *on whose behalf* archaeologists are speaking, are both central concerns and have been major topics in theoretical debate. Archaeologists working in regions such as North America or Australia have to negotiate their objectives with those of indigenous peoples when it comes to disturbing sites or ancient remains, but even in Britain, archaeologists still need to engage with local communities and interest groups, as the recent example of 'Seahenge' demonstrates (Skeates 2000).

Archaeology as a profession

If archaeology needs theory to evaluate how it conducts fieldwork, manage our heritage, interpret the past and engage with the public, then it just as equally needs theory to evaluate the state of its own profession. How we perceive the structure of archaeology and its varied practitioners is informed by our theoretical perspective. For example, the low valuation of 'diggers' – both intellectually and financially – is directly related to their usually tacit, ascribed status as technicians; yet the new approaches to fieldwork would seem to contradict this ascription. Similarly, the division that has emerged between archaeology practised in commercial units and government institutions on the one hand, and that within universities on the other, has effectively produced two, almost mutually exclusive career paths in archaeology. Despite many units working through university departments and some individuals crossing over between these career paths, this division is fairly well set. That it is a potential problem is clear to see from the recent establishment of research agendas within archaeological resource management with the implication that contract archaeology has lost touch with broader interpretive themes as developed in universities. But equally, university academics may be working in blissful ignorance of new sites and new evidence excavated in contract situations, which could overturn conventional interpretations of the past.

CONCLUSION

Looking back at the previous version of this chapter written by Ian Hodder for the 1993 edition, it is encouraging to see how much this topic has developed over the past decade. It seems that for a long time there has been tacit or explicit recognition of the interpretive and theoretical nature of fieldwork and the need to see the relationship between theory and practice as mutually beneficial (e.g. Carver 1989; Hodder 1992; Richards 1995; Tilley 1989). But it is only in the past five years or so that this has progressed into critically new ways of *doing* archaeology, especially fieldwork. Debates about the theoretical nature of other practices within archaeology, especially the more science-based, laboratory work are more recent but are clearly heading in the same direction (see Jones 2001), while those in heritage and museum studies are perhaps the most advanced (e.g. Merriman 1999). There is a feeling, however, that archaeology is entering a new period in the relationship between practice and theory, one in which there is much more integration and mutual interaction which go beyond the mere statement of their connection. In concluding, however, it is perhaps worth raising a major omission in the presentation so far. I have discussed at length how practice is and should be theoretically informed, and how it is only improved the more aware we are of this relationship. But what of theory? Is this just a one-way process – is practice always to defer to theory, or should theory not equally defer to practice?

I would argue that theory in archaeology, to be both useful and relevant, needs to be practical, to be grounded. All this really means is that archaeological theory must, first and foremost, be *archaeological*. The alienation of many archaeologists from theory comes precisely because theory is sometimes written and presented in a disengaged manner. In many ways of course, theory is, by definition, abstract and generalising; but, even then, it does not necessitate a separation from practical application. Its very success as a convincing idea is in fact largely dependent on specific examples. Nevertheless, theory is sometimes difficult and there is no getting around that fact; sometimes abstract arguments and concepts are essential to articulate complex ideas. And this really brings me back to the issue with which I opened this chapter: the languages of archaeology. For many archaeologists, the irrelevance of theory is fostered by the fact that theoretical archaeology seems to speak another language, almost unintelligible to the uninitiated. Yet how many archaeologists understand the language of micromorphological thin-section descriptions or lipid analysis through gas chromatography? We accept that specialist fields within archaeology require their own language, and just the same is true of theory.

Ultimately, just as we expect the results of micromorphology or lipid analysis to be communicated intelligibly in terms every archaeologist can understand, so the same applies to theoretical discourse. If those carrying out fieldwork and other practical aspects of archaeological work should try harder to be theoretical, those refining theory should equally try harder to be practical. Post-processualism has everything to do with a Harris matrix, and it should equally be able to change the way we excavate and understand a site. The challenge facing theoretical archaeology is, as always, to make theory work. Theory needs to be practical, as much as practice needs to be theoretical. Indeed, perhaps archaeological theory at its best is theory performed when digging out a ditch or writing a development control brief. Equally, archaeological practice, at its best, is archaeology done in a reflexive and informed manner, with a critical awareness of why it is done and why in a particular way. In many ways, if we reach this point, there will no longer be any distinction between the two terms.

CHAPTER 3

THE BRITISH ARCHAEOLOGICAL DATABASE

David Fraser and Martin Newman

TOWARDS A DEFINITION

Any attempt to describe the British archaeological database must begin by recognising that there has not been a single successful attempt to compile a set of archaeological information that is complete and consistent. There is no such entity as the British archaeological database: rather, archaeologists have to manage with a complex set of overlapping collections of information gathered by different individuals and organisations at different times for different purposes. There have been some attempts to achieve complete coverage to some consistent standard for some geographical areas, and there have been some attempts to draw together information from various sources to improve accessibility; but there is no single British source of archaeological information. Enquiries of the sort 'How many thirteenth-century pele towers are there in Britain?' and 'Provide a list of all Bronze Age barrows in modern urban areas' can only be answered by consulting a large number of individual records in disparate locations, and there is no guarantee of uniform information quality. The single major source of discontinuity is the division of Britain into England, Wales and Scotland: although the Scottish and Welsh Royal Commissions and English Heritage (EH) have made largely successful attempts to ensure that their records are consistently compiled, there is no single organisation that has a duty or objective to compile and maintain the British archaeological database.

But this rather pessimistic statement ignores the pragmatic fact that there is a wealth of excellent archaeological data in Britain used daily by several thousand professional archaeologists and many more interested, and no less competent, unpaid archaeologists. Indeed, once it is recognised that archaeological data is messy, ill defined and constantly being refined, then the nature of the existing systems becomes easier to understand, and the power of those systems to inform is better placed in context.

INCLUSIONS AND EXCLUSIONS

A definition of the existing British archaeological database is best attempted by referring to inclusions and exclusions. Every component record in the database includes locationally referenced descriptions of sites and monuments. These descriptions cover human activity from the earliest Palaeolithic period to the present day. Inclusion in an archaeological record generally implies that the human activity has ceased or has survived beyond its normal time span. 'Sites' and 'monuments' are interpreted very widely, and there is a tendency to include rather than exclude information if there is an easily available source.

Nevertheless, some types of information are generally excluded. Descriptions of natural history and non-human biology are usually seen as the remit of other record systems, and it is only recently that historic buildings have been more accepted as part of the archaeological database. There is a commonly held view that information concerning archaeology, architectural history, natural history and biology is all part of the same fuzzily defined resource management database, but beyond a few locally based attempts, there has been no serious effort to define or construct such a record.

One class of data with an uneasy relationship with the archaeological database is that concerning collections of artefacts, commonly held in museums. There is a vast and productive enterprise devoted to cataloguing and describing the contents of museums, and many collections contain objects and information of central importance to field archaeologists. A county planning department might hold a record of the place where a gold torc was found, while the county museum might maintain a catalogue entry giving much detail of the same torc, displayed in its galleries. Even if each record contains a cross-reference to the other, the basic divide between field archaeology and museum archaeology is maintained, and there is little formal uniformity between the records.

A second class of data sitting uneasily on the margins of the archaeological database can be broadly defined as countryside heritage: ancient woodlands, flora-rich grasslands, medieval land divisions, and landscape features of all sorts that owe their origins to human management at some period in the past. Few archaeologists would deny that such information is properly part of the archaeological database, and in the last decade the Historic Landscape Characterisation (HLC) project in England (Fairclough 1999b; Chapter 17) has started to incorporate such material (extending also into urban areas) in archaeological databases using geographical information systems (GIS).

THE CONSTRUCTION OF THE DATABASE

The archaeological database has been constructed in two basic ways. The first method is by systematic field observation, where trained field archaeologists have walked selected areas of the land of Britain and have compiled consistent records of all archaeological entities they have observed. The outstanding example of this endeavour was the work of the field surveyors of the now-defunct Archaeology Division of the Ordnance Survey (OS), whose remit was to provide data concerning visible archaeological sites for display and publication on topographic maps. The second method is by documentary trawl of published information of all kinds, including academic reports, journals of learned societies and many kinds of ephemeral literature. The principal and enduring example of this work is that carried out by the recorders of the OS and the Royal Commissions.

The fundamental unit of recording in the archaeological database is not uniform. In essence, there are three different methods: by land parcel, by event and by archaeological entity (IAM 1984). The land-parcel method creates a new record for each piece of defined land, such as an agricultural field, or an urban block, or the land owned by a single person, or simply the land enclosed within a line drawn on a map or plan. Everything of archaeological interest within that land parcel is attributed to the record. The prime example of a land-parcel record is the Record of Scheduled Monuments (RSM), where each entry is defined by a verbal description and a plan showing an area of land within a drawn line.

Another method of defining a record in an archaeological database is by event. These may include major excavations, minor field investigations, the finding of an artefact, the observation of structures during building work, or simply the taking of an aerial photograph. Examples of such event-based records include the *NMR Excavation Index for England* (initiated by the Royal Commission on the Historical Monuments of England (RCHME) and now curated by EH) and the catalogues of aerial photographs compiled by many organisations. Characteristically, event-based records include little interpretation of the information they contain.

The third method of defining a record is by archaeological entity. In such records, the unit of recording is a distinct feature or structure that is well understood and has a comprehensive definition (even if that definition is the subject of intense academic debate). Examples are 'henge', 'hillfort', 'moated site', 'castle' and 'smelt-mill'. The spatial extent of such records may not be clearly defined, and may overlap with other entities, but the record refers to a concept that is part of the common archaeological vocabulary. One attempt to provide a dictionary for this is the *Thesaurus of Monument Types* (RCHME with EH 1998).

In reality, most components of the archaeological database contain records that are defined by all three methods – by land parcel, event and entity. This is a result of pragmatism: few records have the resources to interpret fully the information they receive (especially if this requires a field visit) and so it is accessed in the format in which it arrives. The common thread in all three methods is locational referencing: every record is tied to a specific place. Sometimes the place is very accurately defined down to a unique exact point or area, and sometimes the place is more vaguely described, as within a field, or within a certain distance of a known point, or even within a parish. But the vast majority of records in the British archaeological database is referred to in some way by location. The application of GIS in archaeological databases is an obvious development which has started in some limited applications: for example, point locations for Scheduled Ancient Monuments are displayed on Multi-Agency Geographic Information for the Countryside (www.magic.gov.uk). Clearly the use of GIS has great potential to develop still further.

THE COMPONENTS OF THE ARCHAEOLOGICAL DATABASE

The record of Scheduled Monuments

The Ancient Monuments Protection Act of 1882 was the first public and legal recognition of the need for what would now be called an archaeological database. The legislation incorporated a schedule of monuments throughout Great Britain and Ireland (Chapter 5), which forms the basis for the current schedule of ancient monuments. After successive revisions, the statutory authority for the schedule now resides in Section 1 of the Ancient Monuments and Archaeological Areas Act 1979 (AMAA Act).

In addition, Section 2 of this legislation requires the publication of the schedule, a duty fulfilled by the responsible organisations in the form of county or region-based lists showing the location and name of each monument in the schedule (e.g. for Scotland www.pastmap.org.uk; www.historic-scotland.gov.uk/index/ancientmonuments/searchmonuments.htm; EH 1999a). For new schedulings in England a notification is sent out including a description assessment of importance and a map extract.

The published lists of Scheduled Monuments are only an extract from a comprehensive archaeological database – the Record of Scheduled Monuments (RSM) – curated by Historic Scotland (HS), EH, and CADW and the DoE in Northern Ireland. The number of entries is relatively small, with about 7,500 for Scotland, 3,400 for Wales, 19,400 for England and 1,500 in Northern Ireland. The number of protected monuments and hence entries will continue to rise in the next decade. In England this is thanks to the Monuments Protection Programme (MPP), which made an average of 1,250 scheduling recommendations per year (EH 2000b). On the other hand, the amount of information contained in each entry is extensive and constantly updated by means of regular visits by field monument wardens, reflecting the national importance of this select, protected group of monuments. The RSM does not generally hold original archive material, but will contain references to the records held by the Royal Commissions, Historic Environment Records (HERs)/Sites and Monuments Records (SMRs) and other records.

Taking the English RSM as an example, each Scheduled Monument entry includes sub-records for different archaeological entities, or 'items', and contains data in four categories:

1. Location and identification
    *   Scheduled Monument title
    *   archaeological item title(s)
    *   Scheduled Monument grid reference
    *   archaeological item grid reference(s)
    *   county
    *   district
    *   parish
    *   height above Ordnance Datum

2. Descriptive
    *   Scheduled Monument description
    *   confirmation of boundary of protected area
    *   Scheduled Monument assessment of importance
    *   archaeological item description
    *   archaeological item assessment of importance
    *   monument class
    *   period
    *   components
    *   history of events
    *   sources

3. Management
    *   Scheduled Monument management statement
    *   area of protected site
    *   other designations on site
    *   other designations around site
    *   current land use
    *   form
    *   condition
    *   stability
    *   vulnerability

4. Administration
    *   file reference
    *   administrative history
    *   owner(s)
    *   occupier(s)
    *   other interested parties
    *   record compilation date.

In addition, the three component parts of the RSM include a map record capable of defining the exact extent of each Scheduled Monument, and subsidiary records of legal, administrative and conservation action, including records of visits by field monument wardens.

Other statutory and quasi-statutory data

Computerised records of other heritage-based designations are also maintained by EH. These include the Listed Buildings System (LBS), over 373,000 records (including delistings, building preservation notices and certificates of immunity), the Parks and Gardens Registration System (1,550 records) and the Buildings at Risk Register (1,400 records) (EH 2001). Spatial records of designations are held in EH's corporate GIS, formerly the Heritage Spatial Information Service (HSIS). Records of Conservation Areas are held by local authorities. EH is also managing the Images of England Project, which will make a photograph of every listed building available via the Internet (www.imagesofengland.org.uk).

The Royal Commissions

Britain has three organisations with the duty of compiling a national archaeological record. All three were originally granted Royal Warrants by Edward VII in 1908. In order of seniority, and using the shortened versions of their titles, they are:

The Royal Commission on the Ancient and Historical Monuments of Scotland (RCAHMS)

The Royal Commission on the Ancient and Historical Monuments of Wales (RCAHMW)

EH which was amalgamated with the Royal Commission on the Historical Monuments of England (RCHME) in 1999, with the RCHME ceasing to exist legally in 2002.

Each (until the revision of their Royal Warrants in 1992) had a similar remit: 'to make an inventory of the ancient and historical monuments and constructions connected with or illustrative of the contemporary culture, civilisation and conditions of life of the people from the earliest times, and to specify those which seem most worthy of preservation'.

Since 1908 this remit has been interpreted in several ways. For the greater part of the century, the Royal Commissions concentrated on the publication of volumes, known as *Inventories*, based on detailed field survey carried out by their own investigators. *Inventories* are normally county-based, each volume containing descriptions of several hundred monuments, and are well illustrated with drawings and photographs of the highest quality. Perhaps a third of the land area of Britain has been covered by *Inventories*, beginning with the old counties of Berwickshire in 1909, Hertfordshire in 1910, and Montgomery in 1911. Where an *Inventory* entry exists for a particular site or monument, it will reflect the highest standards of scholarship prevailing at the time of publication. For example, the Scottish Royal Commission in 1992 published the seventh and last volume in the *Inventory* of the former county of Argyll (RCAHMS 1992): the seven volumes are a remarkable distillation of knowledge completely fulfilling the objectives of the original warrant.

The Royal Commissions came to recognise that publication to *Inventory* standard was too slow, given currently available resources, to meet modern archaeological needs. Each attempted a contemporary restatement of its objectives, with the English Royal Commission's reading: 'to compile, and assess, curate and make available the national record of England's ancient monuments and historic buildings for the use of individuals and bodies concerned with understanding, interpreting and managing the historic environment' (RCHME 1992a). These restatements were formalised in the issue of new Royal Warrants in all three countries and the later integration of the work of the English Royal Commission with that of EH. The three organisations have adopted a variety of strategies to reflect the changed context of their work. The Scottish Royal Commission embarked in the 1980s on a series of rapid identification surveys, carrying out more selective and less intensive fieldwork, and publishing lists of sites and monuments in outline detail (e.g. Lamb 1982). It has also published more synthetic accounts with detailed information held in a central archive (e.g. RCAHMS 1990). The English Royal Commission and now EH have given much attention to studies of selected topics limited in scope and area, such as the textile mills of Yorkshire (RCHME 1992b), the earthworks of Bokerley Dyke (RCHME 1991a) and the physical remains of the jewellery industry in Birmingham (Cattell *et al.* 2002).

All three government organisations have also recognised that the modern archaeological database is not the sum total of published volumes but rather a continually evolving, constantly updated, mechanically accessible collection of information from a variety of disparate sources, not all of which can be equally validated. A constituent part of each National Monuments Record (NMR) is an archaeological database containing more than the material published in *Inventories*. Indeed, 'the Archaeological Database, and the Architectural Register together with the Collections of photographs, drawings and manuscripts now provide the Inventory . . . first envisaged' (Murray 1992: 210).

The (English) National Monuments Record, based in Swindon (www.english-heritage.org.uk/nmr) holds records of about 400,000 sites and more than 2,500,000 photographs of archaeological, architectural and historic interest dating from the 1860s onwards. The English NMR also includes archives of the former OS Archaeology Division and reports, drawings, and photographs compiled by RCHME/EH and other fieldworkers. The (English) National Library of Air Photographs, also based at the NMR in Swindon, contains 600,000 oblique and 2,000,000 vertical air photographs providing a complete record of the landscape since the beginning of the Second World War. The (English) National Monuments Record also holds the NMR Excavation Index which contains details of over 70,000 events pertaining to archaeological investigations including desk-based assessments, surveys, building recording, watching briefs and evaluations as well as excavations. These data sets are recorded in the National Monuments Records database system AMIE and the HSIS GIS system. EH supplies heritage information to the Multi-Agency Geographic Information for the Countryside (MAGIC) (www.magic.gov.uk).

The National Monuments Record of Scotland (NMRS), based in Edinburgh (www.rcahms.gov.uk) contains records of 225,000 sites, of which about 60 per cent represent archaeological sites, held on a database and GIS. The archive contains some 250,000 drawings, of which 150,000 are drawings in the Scottish Architects Papers Preservation Project (SAPPP) and 35,000 in the Dick, Peddie and McKay Collection. The NMRS also holds about 1,500,000 air photographs, of which about 75,000 are RCAHMS's own oblique air photographs, and 500,000 other photographs on open access in the NMRS public area. The NMRS also maintains CANMORE, an online database launched in 1998, and CANMAP, an online GIS launched in 2002. There were over 180,000 remote searches of NMRS data through in 2002, and this figure is increasing every year.

The RCAHMW's National Monuments Record of Wales, based in Aberystwyth (www.rcahmw.org.uk) has around 60,000 records in the core sites database, although this includes historic buildings and monuments of all periods excluded from the totals mentioned above for England and Scotland. All three NMRs are recognised places of deposit for public records, and the NMRW archive includes 1,250,000 terrestrial and air photographs, 30,000 drawings and plans, and 30,000 large-scale maps in the national collection. These include RCAHMW records, excavation archives, other public and private archives relating to archaeology as well as the Welsh sections of the former OS Archaeology Division records.

The curators of each of the three national monuments records have been forced to tackle the difficult question of whether their record is the record or simply an index to the record housed in many different places. In England a cooperation statement between RCHME, EH and the Association of Local Government Archaeological Officers (ALGAO) was published in 1998 (prior to the merger of RCHME and EH). This stated that, as part of its lead role for SMRs, RCHME would 'develop the NMR inventory as a high level index to all records of sites and monuments wherever held, including EH, SMRs and voluntary bodies' (RCHME *et al.* 1998: 7). The nature of overlap and divergence between the National Monuments Record and local SMRs is currently under investigation by EH. In Scotland the National Monuments Record of Scotland is seen as 'the most comprehensive record available for archaeological monuments in Scotland' (Murray 1992: 210). In many ways this question is only relevant in the context of local and central government politics: the national archaeological records are both the best single accessible source of national data, and an index to many other local databases, including county-based sites and monuments records.

Sites and Monuments Records (SMRs) and Historic Environment Records (HERs)

Another component of the British archaeological database is the network of locally based SMRs or HERs. The early history of this network has been summarised by Burrow (1984; see also Chapter 10): in response to a growing need for accurate archaeological information to be fed into the planning system, from the 1970s onwards local authorities invested in the staff and resources required to compile and maintain a database for their own administrative area. In England the movement received considerable political and financial support from the Inspectorate of Ancient Monuments. In early years there was scant recognition of SMRs, but their authority and usefulness is now enshrined in the English and Welsh General Development Order (Statutory Instrument No. 1813, 1988) – an adjunct to the formal planning system and the Town and Country Planning Acts – and in formal planning advice published in England (DoE 1990a) and Scotland (SOEnD 1994a, 1994b). SMRs are also specifically mentioned in the Hedgerow Regulations (DoE and MAFF 1997).

Since 1989 EH (initially RCHME) and the Scottish and Welsh Royal Commissions have been given the lead role for the oversight of SMRs. Each (starting with Wales) commissioned an assessment of the SMRs in their area (Baker 1996, 1999a, 1999b). These reports form a valuble point-in-time benchmark of the state of SMRs. The picture in England has since been in part updated by the SMR Content and Computing Survey 2002 (Newman 2002).

As part of its lead role, RCHME instigated a programme of wide-ranging audits of SMRs including their data, resourcing and services. This programme was continued after the merger with EH, and has been the subject of a review which showed the audits to have been of considerable benefit to those SMRs who had undertaken them (Newman 2001).

Another initiative in England has been the creation of a network of Urban Archaeological Databases (UADs). These new SMRs have a more specific remit and were designed to address identified weakness in SMRs for deeply stratified urban deposits. Some of these are new databases, held mainly by city or district councils, while others are the enhancement of part of an existing SMR. Another part of this programme is the extensive urban survey which enhances SMR records for smaller towns (EH 1992b).

There have also been improvements in data standards in SMRs. These include the widespread acceptance of MIDAS (the Monuments and Inventories Data Standard) (Lee 1998) and the controlled terminologies recommended by the Forum on Information

Standards in Heritage (FISH), via Inscription (www.mda.org.uk/fish/inscript.htm). To promote standards in SMRs RCHME (now EH) and ALGAO entered into a partnership with a commercial software company exeGesIS SDM Ltd to produce a database and GIS package for SMRs. This system, now in its third release, is entitled Historic Buildings Sites and Monuments Records (HBSMR) and is in use by over half the SMRs in England. EH has also published (in association with ALGAO and the Archaeology Data Service (ADS)) an SMR manual called *Informing the Future of the Past: Guidelines for SMRs* (Fernie and Gilman 2000).

More recently, there have been calls for SMRs to be made a statutory requirement of local authorities in England and Wales. An amendment was introduced into the Culture and Recreation Bill by Lord Renfrew to do just this, stating that 'the Secretary of State may by order prescribe . . . standards to which Sites and Monuments Records shall conform' (Renfrew 2001). The amendment and bill were lost because of the 2001 general election. However, calls for statutory status have continued, and this has proved the impetus for the setting of minimum standards for SMRs. EH and ALGAO have agreed the draft Historic Environment Records Benchmarks for Good Practice (Chitty 2002). The new name of Historic Environment Records (HERs) for SMRs which appears here denotes the wider remit they now fulfil, including, for example, historic buildings. This originated in EH's review of the historic environment in England *Power of Place*. This recommended the government to 'ensure that local authorities have access to properly curated Historic Environment Record Centres' (EH 2000a: 39). The government's response, *A Force for our Future*, welcomed the recommendations on HERs and committed itself to producing a consultation paper covering a range of options for their future (DCMS and DTLR 2001: 15). Another initiative to emerge from *Power of Place* and *A Force for our Future* was the annual *State of the Historic Environment Report, Heritage Counts*. The first of these included a short section on SMRs, which may be expanded in future editions to include indicators (EH 2002a: 8).

A structural weakness of SMRs is that they are dependent upon the continued existence of their parent authorities, and local government is in a continual state of review. However, experience to date (notably the abolition of the English metropolitan counties and the creation of unitary authorities) suggests that the SMRs are sufficiently robust, with sufficient political support, to survive the reorganisation of local government. This may in part be a result of the publication by RCHME of guidance to new authorities on the role of SMRs (RCHME 1995a). Also, ALGAO seeks to ensure that the SMRs operate together for their mutual benefit and improvement and has published its own strategy for SMRs (ALGAO 2001). In Scotland the equivalent of ALGAO, the Association of Regional and Island Archaeologists (ARIA), is in the process of becoming ALGAO Scotland.

In England there are a total of 101 SMRs. The majority cover counties or former county areas and nearly all have local authorities as their parent organisation. The former metropolitan counties (e.g. South Yorkshire) have SMRs that cover part of their area, monitored by formal or informal joint committees of district or borough councils: these are based in a variety of institutions. The SMR for Greater London is curated by the London Region of EH. Of the SMRs housed in county councils, the most common location is the department responsible for planning or economic development, but a significant proportion are housed in other departments, notably museum or leisure services. There are other anomalies: for example Greater Manchester SMR is curated by the University of Manchester, which receives funding from the local authorities in the former county. There are also SMRs that have been outsourced to commercial companies, as happened with five of the authorities which make up most of the former county of Berkshire, where the SMRs were run by Babtie, the engineering and environmental company. There are also two SMRs held by large land owners, the National Trust and the Ministry of Defence. ALGAO estimate that English SMRs contain over one million records (ALGAO 2001: 11). Among the largest SMRs in terms of numbers of records are Devon (65,000) and Cornwall (52,000).

The Welsh SMRs are grant-aided by RCAHMW and contain around 100,000 site-based database records in total. RCAHMW coordinates the Extended National Database partnership of archaeological organisations in Wales, which exchanges information between the NMRW, the SMRs, CADW and the Archaeology and Numismatics Department of the National Museums and Galleries of Wales and makes available an online index, CARN, at www.rcahmw.org.uk/data.

All councils in Scotland (except for two) now have access to archaeological provision, including SMRs. The most recent estimate of the number of records in Scottish SMRs is 122,450 (Baker 1999b: 77).

In Northern Ireland the functions of NMR and SMRs are combined by the Environment and Heritage Service, which is part of the DoE. This maintains the Northern Ireland SMR, which contains approximately 15,000 sites covering the six counties that make up the province. It also maintains the Northern Ireland buildings database which contains details of over 9,000 historic buildings (www.ehsni.gov.uk).

In the Isle of Man, a self-governing dependency of the British Crown, Manx National Heritage is the Statutory Government Agency providing an integrated cultural and natural heritage service within one organisation. The Manx National Monuments Record holds 5,269 individual records. Of these, sixty sites have received statutory protection as listed monuments under the Manx Museum and National Trust Act (the closest Isle of Man equivalent to Scheduled Monuments). In addition, all the 204 medieval decorated stones and cross slabs on the island (whether *in situ* or removed to local or central protection) are listed monuments.

Although primarily established for development control purposes, SMRs have become more widely used and are increasingly seen as a public record. This has been recognised by the Heritage Lottery Fund (HLF), which is making funding available for SMRs to create outreach programmes including making SMR data available over the Internet (HLF 1999). There is an e-mail discusion list for SMRs and two formal meetings a year of SMRs, users and other interested parties, the results of which are publicised in *Historic Environment Record News* (formerly *SMR News*).

The single overwhelming strength of the network of SMRs is, paradoxically, the same as the weakness alluded to earlier: they are locally based. Most SMRs are accessible to all working archaeologists in the county or region, and the SMR staff are well placed to take note of new discoveries, newly found sources of material and threats of all kinds to archaeological resources. Perhaps most significant of all, SMR staff are the best source of information on the gaps and shortcomings of their own records, since a number of years of constant use of a relatively small database encourages familiarity with the archaeological resource in a way that is no longer possible for a single individual to acquire (because of the sheer quantity of data) with a national record.

Other components of the database

There are many other organisations that have claim to be important parts of the British archaeological database. These include the *Victoria History of the Counties of England* (VCH), which has published many valuable volumes on the early history and archaeology of selected counties, mostly broken down into parish surveys. They also include the many museums that maintain and curate locational records as part of their duty to maintain contextual information relating to their physical holdings. There are also books, pamphlets, articles, unpublished archives, research documents with limited circulation, and the unspoken thoughts and theories of thousands of archaeological workers – all are indisputably part of the database. But none constitutes a primary record in the way the RSM, the NMR and the SMRs have become such: ideally, the three major components of the database will contain references or indexes to every other source of archaeological information.

The most diverse and interesting of these components are the holdings of special interest groups, societies and projects which undertake recording, thus giving them a claim to be primary records. Many of these are computerised records and some have been made available through the Internet. These range from the work of local history and archaeological societies to national groups such as the Tiles and Architectural Ceramics Society. There are also large national projects, such as the National Inventory of War Memorials and the Survey of the Jewish Built Heritage. Many of these make their data available to the three National Monuments Records and the SMRs on completion of the project, as has happened with the Defence of Britain Project. Data sources such as these, known as HEIRS (Historic Environment Information Resources) are included on a register called HEIRNET (www.britarch.ac.uk/HEIRNET). Some of these can also be searched on the Archaeology Data Service's (ADS) online catalogue ARCHSearch (ads.ahds.ac.uk/catalogue/collections.cfm). A discussion forum called HELPS (Historic Environment List for Projects and Societies) has been set up to assist such groups in sharing information and advertising their work.

USERS OF THE ARCHAEOLOGICAL DATABASE

In one sense, most users of the British archaeological database never consult the database themselves: the public dissemination of information on archaeology is carried out by means of television and radio programmes, newspaper and magazine articles, classroom teaching, talks, lectures and exhibitions (Chapter 19). All these media rely heavily on the distillation of information that has been processed and accessed into the various components of the archaeological database, and subsequently retrieved, interpreted, and synthesised into comprehensible and interesting packages. Even the most populist pamphlet for the visitor to Hadrian's Wall relies on a mosaic of facts and ideas about the Roman occupation of Britain, the Roman army and the native population that has been built up over the last century as a result of archaeological and historical research based on information contained in the common archaeological database.

In 2002 the Cultural Heritage Consortium conducted secondary research on the more immediate users of historic environment databases (Cultural Heritage Consortium 2002). The conclusions were inconclusive: although there is a large and increasing demand for such information, there is little known about the actual user profiles, or the use to which such information is put. Nevertheless, it is possible to informally describe the three main categories of users: conservationists, researchers and educators. These categories are not distinct, and all three may be represented in the same individual at a single time. Nevertheless, they do articulate three distinct reasons for using the database. 'Conservationists', in the broadest sense and including planning archaeologists, are concerned with the positive management of change in the landscape, with protecting the archaeological resource from being depleted or destroyed, and in steering land managers towards constructive and positive exploitation of the archaeological past. 'Researchers', including excavators, are more concerned with constructing images of the past and interpreting the remains of past human activity in a way that is understandable and attractive or interesting to modern people. 'Educators' are responsible for translating and transmitting these constructed images to a wide audience. All three categories of user have a common desire to see the archaeological database maintained and expanded, and they speak with a common voice in seeking to protect the database from being reduced or dismembered.

Conservationists

The conservationist users of the archaeological database include Inspectors of Ancient Monuments employed by government heritage bodies, local government archaeologists employed by local authority development and planning departments, archaeological officers employed by major land-hungry organisations supplying goods, power, entertainment and transport, and archaeological consultants employed by a wide variety of clients assessing the heritage implications of their operations. The objective of all these users is to collect and interpret the available archaeological information to assist several government ministers, local planning committees, other statutory and non-statutory bodies, and organisations concerned with the investment of money. All these decision-makers need to make informed and rational choices about the future of the land for which they are responsible, and will frequently be required to balance archaeological considerations against a host of other social and economic factors.

Conservationists have become, without any question, the heaviest users of the archaeological database in the last decade or so, with many specific enquiries of short duration and many complex enquiries requiring deep interrogation of the database. This pattern is substantiated by the fact that local planning authorities have become heavy investors in the database, with local authority SMRs being the rapidly expanding component of the database. SMRs are the most frequently consulted, by a wide margin, of all of the publicly accessible records. A survey by Lang in 1989 (Lang 1992: 175) suggested that strict planning-related enquiries accounted for more than 70 per cent of all enquiries to SMRs. On the whole, the Royal Commission databases have failed to capture this large growth of conservation-related endeavour: many archaeologists would like to see the power and accessibility of the NMRs being harnessed to assist in the achievement of conservation objectives.

Example 1: a conservation plan of an historic property

EH is the manager of some 410 historic properties. Setting standards for the profession, it has compiled conservation plans (or their more compact counterparts, conservation statements) for each of these properties with a view to planning their future management to the highest standards of archaeological heritage management. The completed report for Richmond Castle in North Yorkshire (Grenville *et al.* 2001) consists of three volumes. The first, *Understanding the Site*, contains a historical description of events at the castle over ten periods from earliest times to the twentieth century, and describes the physical fabric of the castle in ten zones. It also lists all the relevant primary sources for archaeological, historical and environmental material, including SMR references to more than ten archaeological interventions. The second volume sets out in detail a statement of significance for Richmond Castle, and outlines conservation policies designed to preserve that significance. The third volume is a detailed gazeteer of each element of the castle.

Example 2: an archaeological assessment of a large urban development site

In accordance with the planning regulations governing large-scale development proposals, a consortium of developers headed by Crosby Homes, Evans of Leeds and Land Securities prepared an Environmental Statement in support of their application for the comprehensive mixed-use development of a 5-hectare area of land known as Hungate within the medieval city walls of the historic city of York. Technical Appendix D in the very lengthy statement was an archaeological assessment commissioned from Mike Griffiths & Associates (2003). This document collated all the known information from previous archaeological interventions in the area, reported the results of field work, and drew conclusions about the quantity and quality of archaeological deposits in the area: 'the Hungate site contains extensive archaeological deposits ranging from the Roman to Modern Periods . . . of significance on a regional to European scale' (Griffiths Associates 2003: vol. 1: 102).

Example 3: a local development plan

Every local authority in Britain is required to produce one or more development plan to provide guidance in the reaching of decisions under the planning legislation. Since the archaeological consequences of proposed development are a material consideration, many plans (and a great variety of formal and informal planning guidance produced by local authorities) contain policies that depend on an appreciation of the archaeological database. As one example, the Local Plan for Newbury, Berkshire (NDC 1990) refers to the SMR maintained by Berkshire County Council. It identifies four broad areas where it is most likely that development will have archaeological implications: the Saxon and medieval centres of six historic towns; the alluvium-covered bottoms of four river valleys; the Berkshire Downs; and two civil war battle sites. The plan then sets out three policies designed to mitigate the effects of any development proposals on the archaeological heritage of the district.

Researchers

Archaeological researchers are those users of the database who most closely correspond to the popular view of the field archaeologist. Typical researchers might include university and college lecturers, undergraduate and postgraduate students, excavators and surveyors exploring the context of their field projects, and post-excavation assistants searching for comparable sites.

Example 4: the palaeoenvironment and archaeology of a wetland area

As the fifth part of of a wider research project into the wetland archaeology and palaeoenvironments of the Humber estuary, the Centre for Wetland Archaeology at the University of Hull published *Wetland Heritage of the Hull Valley* (Van der Noort and Ellis 2000). Much of the data comes from artefactual and scientific evidence gathered through field survey, but there are two important record sources: the database of the SMR for the East Riding and Hull curated by the Humber Archaeology Partnership, and the documentary collections of the Hull and East Riding Museum.

Example 5: a regional study of a specific class of monument

The physical structure and the contents of the Neolithic chambered cairns of Scotland have long been the subject of detailed research by Miss Audrey Henshall. In recent years this has taken the form of updated regional surveys accompanied by analytical discussion. Four publications have successively covered Orkney (Davidson and Henshall 1989), Caithness (Davidson and Henshall 1991), Sutherland (Henshall and Ritchie 1995) and Ross and Cromarty and Inverness-shire (Henshall and Ritchie 2001). Each volume describes the present appearance of each known chambered cairn, all modern archaeological activity and all the recovered artefacts. In their acknowledgements, the primary locational archive quoted by Davidson and Henshall and Ritchie is the National Monuments Record of Scotland (NMRS). Throughout the inventory there are frequent references to the NMRS and to the surveys carried out by other field archaeologists.

For many researchers the archaeological database is only the starting point of their work, and they frequently contribute more, in the long term, than they extract from it. In terms of magnitude of use, researchers are probably the least significant users, but their enquiries are rarely short or simple and usually require complex interrogation of the database. For this reason, researchers are among the most skilful and experienced of users.

Educators

Educational users of the archaeological database cover the full spectrum of formal education from the nursery school to higher and further education, and also takes in the expanding field of life-long education, which shades into leisure and recreation. Typical users might be the primary school teacher preparing for a visit of his class to a local guardianship monument, the extramural lecturer delivering a course on the Roman antiquities of her local region, and the tourist guide responsible for showing coachloads of visitors around heritage attractions.

An important tool for all educators (and, indeed, for conservationists and researchers) are the OS maps that portray archaeological sites: EH and the Royal Commissions provide information to the OS to update continually all OS maps. In most cases, educators' use of the archaeological database results in a verbal presentation to a limited audience, so the examples below of published or widely distributed material are perhaps more typical of generic educational uses.

Example 6: a popular guide to the heritage of a region

In the 1980s and 1990s two new authoritative series of regional guides to archaeological monuments and buildings have emerged, *Exploring Scotland's Heritage*, published by the Scottish Royal Commission in eight volumes; and *Exploring England's Heritage*, published in eleven volumes in association with EH. Each volume, covering a small number of counties or regions, contains general essays on selected topics, and a short description of a hundred or more of the best archaeological sites. The intent of both series is well expressed by Professor Barry Cunliffe in his introduction to the English series. England, he writes, is 'a beautiful, gentle country full of fascinating corners, breathtaking sights – an eclectic mix of insurpassable [*sic*] quality. All you need is someone with vision to show you how to start looking' (Weaver 1992: vii). Each volume relies on the personal knowledge of the distinguished archaeologist author, as well as formal access to the archaeological database. For example, the volume for the former Grampian region (Shepherd 1986; update reissued as Shepherd 1996) was written by the regional archaeologist, who acknowledges the assistance of the staff of RCAHMS, his own department and several smaller archives.

Example 7: a teachers' guide to a medieval castle

Pickering Castle, in North Yorkshire, is a property in the care of EH. To assist the enjoyment and education value of visits by schools and colleges, the Education Service has published several leaflets (Goddard 1998) including one specifically to provide information for tutors and students of GNVQ Leisure and Tourism. They describe the castle and its historical background, point out the architectural features and visible archaeological features, outline several educational approaches to the castle, and pose, with suitable material to help in the framing of answers, several questions relating to the heritage management of the site. Although there are direct references to the primary archaeological database, the list of resources for teachers include publications specific to Pickering Castle, and publications on medieval archaeology and castle archaeology, each of which rely for their fundamental information on the archaeological database.

Educators are the broadest and most disparate set of users, and include many individuals who may only ever make a small number of enquiries of the database. Despite this, among their number are the most influential of users and several SMRs have deliberately set out to court this sector, anticipating an increase in its importance in the future.

CONCLUSIONS

Baker's assessments of British SMRs (1996: 23–5, 1999a: 3–5, 1999b: 3–5) make a large number of recommendations for the future of SMRs. The English and Scottish reviews start with a definition of an SMR as 'a definitive permanent, general record of the Local Historic Environment in its national context, publicly maintained, whose data is accessible and retrievable for a wide range of purposes'. The specific recommendations then cover how an SMR should be managed in order to fulfil this role, including areas such as policy, resourcing, content, use and standards. Considerable progress has since been made with these recommendations with the SMR audit programme assisting greatly in individual SMRs. With the arrival (in England) of *Benchmarks for Good Practice* (Chitty 2002) this definition has been widened and new aspirational targets for SMRs set. The future of SMRs as Historic Environment Records now seems assured. These combined with the national records of the Royal Commissions, EH, HS and CADW create a comprehensive record of the heritage of the Britain.

This brief description of the British archaeological database allows two general conclusions to be drawn. The first is that the components of the database contain a vast amount of archaeological information collected over the last century by many archaeologists for different purposes. That information is now used for many other purposes and there is no necessary correlation between the source of information and the use to which it is now being put. Unevenness in the quality of data collection is recognised to be a problem, but information is constantly being updated and validated as needs are perceived and as resources are made available to fulfil those needs.

The second inescapable conclusion is that the dynamic nature of all archaeological records requires every record to be professionally curated. A record needs staff trained professionally in field survey and documentary research, experienced in the technical aspects of maintaining a computerised database, and competent in the art of structuring and answering partly formed enquiries. Without such staff, the record becomes a weighty megalith, impressive in its unrealised potential for enhancing knowledge, but dumb and very capable of being completely misinterpreted.

ACKNOWLEDGEMENTS

We are grateful to those with whom we have discussed the contents of this chapter and those who have provided information: Mark Barrett, Philip Ellis, Mike Evans, Andrew Foxon, Rebecca Jones, Jason Lowe, Donnie Mackay, Diana Murray, Henry Owen-John, Ian Ralston, Ian Shepherd, Bill Startin and David Thomas. The archaeological profession is indebted to all curators, past and present, of the various components of the archaeological database.

CHAPTER 4

THE STRUCTURE OF BRITISH ARCHAEOLOGY

John Hunter and Ian Ralston
with contributions by Ann Hamlin and Claire Foley

INTRODUCTION

Even a cursory investigation of the development of field archaeology in the UK over the last half century immediately highlights its underdeveloped structure in any formal sense. Structure implies an organised framework of functions administered within an overall authority. Archaeology exhibits none of this, except in Northern Ireland (below); instead, it shows piecemeal, if quantum, evolution between 1970 and 1990 in which central government, local government, learned societies, universities, amenity groups and individuals responded, in large measure autonomously, to an unprecedented set of changes threatening the archaeological environment. Since 1990, and largely as a result of the effects of PPG 16 and NPPG 5, which brought a degree of financial stability to field archaeology, these individual components became consolidated and their separation more emphatic.

In the beginning (if such a phrase can be used to mark a point in the 1960s that might epitomise the old order of field archaeology's public function), professional, applied field archaeology was essentially practised by the small archaeological staffs of state or quasi-state bodies backed by long-established statute or Royal Warrant and was supported by enthusiastic amateur involvement. Elsewhere, the keyword was research – essentially museological, seasonal and performed by those who were either interested enough or could afford to participate. Thereafter, and with increasing impetus through the 1970s and 1980s, this arrangement was progressively changed in response to a set of unprecedented demands posed by the recognition of the quickening pace of the impacts of modern development on the archaeological resource, and the increasing recognition that the latter was finite. The emergence of archaeological units, trusts, county archaeologists and indeed many university departments, although some of the last-mentioned remained aloof from such changes, stems from this period. These new organisations belong to the era of so-called rescue archaeology (Rahtz 1974; Jones 1984; Owen-John 1986; Barker 1987), which witnessed changes in the dynamics of archaeology, in funding and in legislation, and which widened the professionialisation of archaeological practice. This reorientation brought into focus, for many more archaeologists than had previously deemed this a central concern, the need for basic philosophies of heritage management (see also Chapter 1).

Rescue archaeology spawned responses at all levels: it created an ad hoc, ungainly, evolving structure that largely compounded earlier geographical inequalities in archaeological attention and resources within the UK, despite contrary advice (CBA 1974). The rapid expansion of rescue work, although widely welcomed, also resulted in disparate and inconsistent policy control. The acquisition of resources to carry through interventions was heavily dependent on the public purse, and was thus modified by governmental initiatives, notably those that saw many young unemployed engaged on archaeological work-experience schemes. These developments were acceptable to the archaeological community not because they were especially effective, but in considerable measure because they made available an exponential leap in the financial support available for field archaeology, although much less so in the concomitant activities fieldwork necessitates. Further, the number of separate agencies underwriting this work multiplied: retrospectively, the unwieldy system must have appeared to many impossible to alter – a fait accompli, for better or for worse, of historical accident ('Gildas' 1988).

The rescue boom was not, however, a unitary phenomenon. It underwent progressive modifications resulting from external influences and internal re-evaluation. It has, nevertheless, bequeathed an important legacy to archaeology today (Mytum and Waugh 1987; Spoerry 1992a). Efforts to formalise the disparate structures inherited from the rescue phase produced a proliferation of committees and liaison bodies, some longer lived than others, and even one laudable attempt to audit the relevant resources (Hart 1987). The need for rationalisation, including that of the disbursement of the restricted research funding available to British field archaeology, eventually bore fruit in the establishment of the Forum for Co-ordination in the Funding of Archaeology. But this, like many other aspects of the 'old order', became obsolete when, from the late 1980s, the demands of environmental impact assessment and subsequently PPG 16 and its equivalents made fashionable a new framework of curators, clients and contractors in a dominantly commercial environment. The same actors remained on stage, but the relative importance of their roles had changed and it was the financial and other considerations of the developer rather than the public purse that now took the lead and dictated the course of the drama.

A new, if rather clinical, kind of applied archaeology resulted. It provided greater employment opportunities (Aitchison 1999) but in clearly focused areas: in central government in the form of English Heritage (EH), Historic Scotland (HS), CADW and the DoE (Northern Ireland) as ostensible monitors and policy makers, or at least advisors; in local authority planning departments, which carried the brunt of curatorial activity; and in the field units, which undertook increased contractual work staged ahead of development. A new group of varying influence appeared in the form of specialist consultants, whereas at least some of the universities effectively withdrew into their own private research environment, at least as far as involvement in British archaeology was concerned. The amateur archaeologists – the *prima movens* for archaeology in Britain – were forced to find a different role, not least in the safety of the new Council for Independent Archaeologists and in community involvement for which considerable financial support was found in the form of the Heritage Lottery Fund.

For good or bad, this period from 1990 marked the rise of a new era of professionalism in archaeology. Working within the development and construction industries, archaeologists became more conscious of health, safety and employment issues. Ethics moved higher up the agenda in the wake of the competitive pressures many archaeologists felt to be impinging on their practices and eddying from external developments such as the Vermillion Accord (1989) (http://www.wac.uct.ac.za/archive/content/vermillion.accord.html), dealing with reburial of human remains. British archaeology became for the first time the subject of a parliamentary all-party group (APPAG 2003) and its higher public profile was reflected in popular television series, many drawing on new evidence that was coming to light through applied work, such as *Time Team*, *Meet the Ancestors* and *Down to Earth*. As a result, the public perception of the archaeologist shifted significantly away from Indiana Jones towards a more acceptable caricature. Career routes within British archaeology became less weakly established and, while there still remained no formal organisation capable of speaking with authority for the whole of British archaeology, the individual components that made archaeology tick in Britain had firmly dug themselves in.

Figure 4.1. Since 1990 excavation in advance of development has become relatively commonplace. Here excavations take place at Giles Street, Leith, Scotland. *Photo: Headland Archaeology*

CENTRAL GOVERNMENT

State involvement with field antiquities can be traced back to Henry VIII, whose dissolution of monastic holdings led to the Office of the King's Works taking on responsibility for the care of redundant monastic and ecclesiastical buildings as well as outmoded royal strongholds. A fundamental change in emphasis in state involvement with historic and archaeological remains had to wait until late Victorian times. The passing of the first Ancient Monuments legislation during Gladstone's administration in 1882 was accompanied by the creation of the position of Inspector of Ancient Monuments, held by General Pitt Rivers, the first of a distinguished series of early antiquarians holding that and equivalent official posts in other parts of the UK.

The appropriate government office, originally housed within the Ministry of Public Building and Works, was eventually subsumed, in England, within the Department of the Environment in 1969. Much of its present function developed there as a response to the rapid changes in the political and economic climates from the 1970s. Policy and funding were implemented via a body of inspectors answerable to the Ancient Monuments Board; the inspectorate was charged with regional responsibilities for both rescue archaeology and relevant areas of statutory preservation. In England, it was assisted by area advisory committees composed of local academics, fieldworkers, senior archaeological personalities and participating local authorities, although this devolved advisory structure was not paralleled elsewhere. These and other 'quango' committees were progressively abolished as a result of changes in outlook and procedure emanating from government since 1979.

Statutory powers were increased, albeit relatively marginally, by the passing of the Ancient Monuments and Archaeological Areas Act 1979 (AMAA Act 1979, see Chapter 5). Additional funding enabled the establishment in England of a mobile Central

Excavation Unit (Anon 1986), the functions of which have been modified in recent years, and the development of a strong central laboratory facility then in London to cover conservation, analytical, palaeoenvironmental and geophysical demands. Despite the addition of regional contract laboratories, post-excavation resources of these types remained wholly overloaded (DoE 1978). A smaller equivalent service was developed in Scotland, although Wales followed a different route, founded on a network of regional archaeological trusts.

In England, almost the whole facility was nominally removed from civil service status in 1983 by the creation of the Historic Buildings and Monuments Commission (HBMC, popularly known as English Heritage). HBMC combined the functions of the Ancient Monuments Board and the Historic Buildings Council in a 'super-quango' deliberately established at arm's length from government: the intention was to optimise the potential benefits of a degree of funding flexibility and operational versatility that had been unavailable to the preceding civil service department. A parallel although slightly later change saw the creation of CADW in Wales. In Scotland the appropriate government department remained until late in the decade largely uninfluenced by the quasi-governmental English model; the name was changed, however, to HS, but it remained closer to the executive as a government agency.

The activities and the funding policy of EH are best reflected in its Annual Reports from which can be gleaned issues of central concern, notably policy and funding distribution according to region, period and priority (see Chapter 13). Included within the typical budget were allowances for education (in accord with EH's role of public dissemination), for basic survey cover (as a portion of the overall state funding of this key activity), as well as for excavation. A substantial part of the budget continued to be earmarked for publication, of both backlog and current fieldwork funded by central government. Publication problems resulting from rescue archaeology, characterised by an upswing in field endeavour wholly unmatched by support for all subsequent processing, were identified and partly resolved in an Ancient Monuments Board report popularly known as the Frere Report (DoE 1975a). Sequels also addressed this issue, notably the Cunliffe Report (Cunliffe 1983), and thereafter the combined voices of a consortium of organisations led by the Society of Antiquaries (1992), this last being an attempt to answer the publication problems posed by increased developer funding, including the issue of 'grey literature' (see Chapter 19).

The introduction of new planning directives and guidance from 1990 (see Chapter 10) was part of a wider recognition of archaeology's importance within Britain's urban and rural fabric. Archaeology and heritage issues concurrently became firmly embedded as a consideration across a range of land use schemes and designations, including increasingly MAAF (now DEFRA) matters. These new directives also altered the status of EH from major national funding agency and policy coordinator to that of a lesser funding agent as a consequence of the 'polluter pays' philosophy being extended into field archaeology. Instead, the agency had the potential to offer proactive support in the field and could release limited funding for defined research areas by competition or tender. Among key aspects sponsored or instigated in England were the *Monuments at Risk Survey* (Darvill and Fulton 1998), a review of research frameworks (EH 1996), and experimentation in sampling strategies (Hey and Lacey 2001). HS followed a similar path and continues to draw up championed research themes for which application for financial support can be made. The national agencies also began to provide a greater advisory capability, for example with respect to project management (EH 1991a), policy guidelines (EH 1991b), or to issues of practicality such as the treatment of human remains (HS 1997) or the acquisition and disposal of artefacts (HS 2001). The same environment of developer funding also led to greater autonomy in field units, as they increasingly moved to arm's-length relationships with the organisations that had formerly housed them. Increasingly, commercial practices dictated that competition among them became more widespread (below): territoriality – the safeguarding of particular regional expertises by individuals or groups – disintegrated and degrees of privatisation occurred (see Chapter 14), which even spread to components of central facilities. Thus HS's former Central Excavation Unit – now Archaeological Operations and Conservation Ltd (AOC) – is now part of the private sector and its staff work from southern England northwards and indeed abroad.

The national agencies of England, Wales and Scotland, whether loosely or rigidly attached to central government, share particular responsibilities, both for the day-to-day curation of archaeological resources (EH 1991c; HS 1991) as well as for 'the Estate' (that is, those monuments and their surroundings held in state care). Processes of internal devolution within Britain since the late 1990s have generated some divergence of cultural attitude and policy here, but the binding legislative framework for their activities is that still furnished by the AMAA Act 1979; for Northern Ireland, see below. However the new planning directives have, *inter alia*, served to emphasise not only the rigidity and mothballing effects of the scheduling process but also the feasibility of devising preservation processes that can absorb change and still maintain a sustainable historic environment. The concurrent shift in terminology from SMR (sites and monuments record) to HER (historic environment record) is a response to changing attitudes and is a reflection of government policy to make heritage part of a living and more accessible environment at both local and national level (DCMS and DTLGR 2001; WAG 2003).

In terms of the oversight of legislation affecting ancient monuments and field archaeological resources, the government departments holding the principal responsibilities were the Department of the Environment, the Welsh and Scottish Offices, and the Department of the Environment (Northern Ireland). In England, from 1997, control has been vested in the Department for Culture Media and Sport (DCMS) which took over statutory responsibilities for listing and scheduling, including the potential impact of the convention on archaeological protection (CoE 1992) signed in Malta in early 1992 and finally ratified by the UK government in 2001. In England and Wales, despite the creation of EH and CADW respectively, the statutory responsibility for the safeguarding of monuments remains vested with the respective Secretaries of State. The system continues to function through the staff of the Inspectorate of Ancient Monuments. The processes of scheduling Ancient Monuments, including the former enhancement scheme in England known as the Monuments Protection Programme (Darvill *et al.* 1987), and the maintenance of Guardianship sites remain statutory functions of government irrespective of the vehicle through which government operates (Davies 1985). Moreover, field remains have been given some further protection in the form of the new Treasure Act, which has radically altered factors of ownership of and reward for any artefacts or other buried remains discovered in England and Wales since 1996. Associated schemes for metal detecting and the appointment of portable antiquities staff operate in tandem, and in this instance central government funding has stepped in to replace necessarily short-term funding from Heritage Lottery sources (Chapter 6).

SURVEY AND RECORD AT NATIONAL LEVEL

In the first decade of the twentieth century, and partly as a result of sustained extra-parliamentary pressure, the Royal Commissions on Ancient and Historical Monuments were created by Royal Warrant with the unenviable remit of preparing an inventory of the sites and monuments illustrating the 'culture, civilisation and conditions of the life of the people . . . from earliest times and to specify those which seem most worthy of preservation'. The warrants have since been redefined and were reissued in 1992, taking into account gradual changes in practice and scope (Chapter 3). The commissions were, and remain, funded by central government, including its devolved components such as the Scottish Executive, but are not part of the civil service. Policy and decisions are ratified by commissioners appointed by relevant ministers on behalf of the Crown and are implemented by skilled investigators.

In all cases (including in Northern Ireland, below) the warrant was for long implemented primarily by county-based surveys of both upstanding as well as buried remains at a level of detail and a rate which, while permitting the display of very considerable scholarship, became incompatible with the changing requirements of field survey during the 1970s. The production of these lavish and expensive *Inventory* volumes, necessarily at a slow pace, was increasingly acknowledged as difficult to justify in the rescue environment. Instead, a need to implement a more basic level of survey cover was acknowledged, but one more extensive in both area and thematic terms, and offering wider appeal and usefulness than the traditional narrow academic remit required. A variety of new styles of publication has ensued. The commissions were able to take an advisory role in this reorientation: for example, the Royal Commission on the Ancient and Historical Monuments of Scotland (RCAHMS) now archives and publishes the work of notable architects, offers an important outreach and education provision, and has pioneered online services such as the CANMORE and CANMAP websites.

The significance of non-intensive National Monuments Records (NMRs), held by the respective commissions, developed from the 1980s, as did diversification into thematic publications and more popular works, drawing on the commissions' survey activities. It is, however, the development of NMR facilities, including aerial photographic resources that, despite constraining changes in aerial operating licences (Chapters 3 and 18), most reflect the changing needs of modern field archaeology. These include the provision of a database for SMRs (now HERs) to underpin evaluation needs, and the provision of central archive repositories for the outcomes of increasing amounts of fieldwork. Consistency of terminology and compatibility of systems have become increasingly essential. More proactive work by the commissions now includes the use and refinement of increasing digitisation of data using geographical information systems (GIS) in the analysis of survey data, and in the development of both terrestrial and aerial/satellite data capture, for example in *Lidar* and *Cyrax* systems. The growth of electronic mapping (e.g. *Digimap*) continues to revolutionise field recording, planning and presentation.

During the early part of the period under review, the Royal Commissions were also obliged to absorb the work of the Archaeological Division of the Ordnance Survey (below). Initially, the commissions were largely unaffected by the changes that altered, for example, EH's relationships with central government in the early 1980s. Since 1992, however, the commissions have additionally taken over responsibility for making inventories of sites within UK territorial waters (Chapter 7), reflecting further rationalisation in governmental procedures, and by 1999 the English Commission had effectively lost its independence and became merged with EH. The Scottish and Welsh Commissions continue to retain their autonomy, albeit within new structures responsible to their devolved paymasters.

Another strand of considerable importance in the quantification and depiction of Britain's field archaeological resources developed early in this country through the recording of field antiquities by the Ordnance Survey (OS), the state's official cartographic agency. Much archaeological data was collected during the mid-Victorian detailed survey of the UK; that which did not appear on the published version of the maps

Figure 4.2. Field survey remains the single most important technique for the systematic recording of sites and monuments.

was incorporated in the OS *Name Books*, those for England unfortunately having been a casualty of the bombing of Southampton during the Second World War (Davidson 1986); the Scottish examples are now held in the National Library in Edinburgh.

In 1920 the OS appointed O.G.S. Crawford as its first archaeological officer, a post which was subsequently expanded to become a branch and latterly a division of the OS, prior to its demise, when the Serpell Committee thought fit to pass central responsibility for archaeological survey entirely to the Royal Commissions. Pride of place must, however, still be accorded here to the OS's former band of field archaeological surveyors: the OS remains the sole body to have attempted field survey on the ground of Britain's entire field archaeological resources on a nationwide basis. The records, in card form, assembled by the OS field surveyors, now underpin both the NMRs, constituent parts of the Royal Commissions (see above), and intensive SMRs (HERs) assembled at local authority level (see below and Chapter 10).

LOCAL GOVERNMENT

During the 1970s and 1980s local authorities, encouraged by central government, did much to improve the curation of the archaeological resource. Beyond their museum services, the employment of archaeologists by local authorities was rare until the early 1970s; thereafter, with Department of the Environment encouragement, many county and metropolitan councils in England established SMRs (HERs) for their areas, appointing the additional specialist staff necessary to achieve this. The exercise was primarily intended to enable the creation of a database of archaeological remains to serve decision-making within the context of local planning; it additionally provided a strong curatorial facet as forward-planning strategies developed (see Chapter 10). The compilation of the database often took the form of implications surveys, an early overview of which (Heighway 1972) pointed to the particular severity of the threat within ancient towns. It is ironic that the existing museum services, although locally funded and often with a resident core of archaeologically trained personnel, and supporting analytical, conservation and other facilities, played little formal part in the development of these locally based archaeological structures. Latterly, however, outreach and education, storage and archiving requirements, among other factors, have caused the relationships between field- and museum-based archaeologists to be reassessed (Museums Association 1989; Lewis 1989; Chapter 21).

In many instances, archaeologists (often located on the staffs of local authority planning departments) were complemented by the establishment of field teams, with the capacity to undertake rescue excavations, to conduct programmes of survey and fieldwalking, and also, in some cases, to undertake educational work. By the end of the 1970s this regional network, although weighted heavily towards the south and south-east of England, was consolidated by the presence of county archaeologists in nearly all county planning departments in England, and in the new regional areas of Wales (where the creation of multi-function archaeological trusts was the norm: see below). Equivalent posts were established, albeit altogether less densely, in Scotland (Beresford Dew 1977; Spoerry 1992a; Chapter 10). Variability in the speed of compilation and the level of detail incorporated in the new regional and county SMRs reflected the uneven distribution of financial and manpower resources – factors that the Royal Commission's *Survey of Surveys* (RCHME 1978) and subsequent work by EH (IAM 1984) did much to highlight.

The impetus of this development in archaeological provision at the local level was considerable. Sustained and effective pressure orchestrated by the pressure group RESCUE (below), underpinned by the results of intensive fieldwork ahead of motorway and building construction, demonstrated that the threats to finite and irreplaceable archaeological resources were many and severe. The work of influential small groups like the Rescue Archaeology Group in Wales (Owen-John 1986) demonstrated that high-quality fieldwork, including excavation, was achievable over prolonged field seasons employing small teams of professional archaeologists – a radical departure from previous practices. The pace of redevelopment in the cores of historic towns, and the scale, wealth and complexity of archaeological deposits (most especially perhaps in York and London, but demonstrated most effectively to a surprised public in Deansgate, Manchester (Jones 1984)), equally demanded an archaeological response not deliverable within the rhythms of previous archaeological fieldwork. This had been, in most cases, limited to relatively short field seasons when staff of other archaeological organisations, notably universities, were either available or at liberty to take on such responsibilities in addition to their other duties.

The Department of the Environment's strategy at that time in England was thus to build up a system of territorially based multi-county units, loosely reflecting the Council for British Archaeology's regional structure. This operated with an admixture of funding drawn from central and local government sources, although a small level of developer funding had begun to appear in the input figures by 1974. In some instances it became increasingly possible to obtain voluntary financial support from developers (Hobley 1987; Anon 1989); in London in particular a substantial, integrated archaeological service was created, drawing on the particular circumstances of economic development and ability on the part of developers to fund additional responsibilities that characterised the capital. Latterly, the obligation for pre-development assessments nationwide to consider the treatment of cultural heritage as a necessary component of timescales for development and working costs (below) led to further reorientation. However, before this became government policy, government spending on rescue archaeology rose spectacularly in England at least and to a lesser extent elsewhere in line with increasing fieldwork needs and rising standards of practice (Beresford

Dew 1977; Chapter 14). Additional funding also became available locally from various Manpower Services Commission programmes – training schemes that artificially boosted the available fieldwork resource from the public purse. Many excavations, especially those in urban environments, of which Perth is a notable example, became possible as a result. Such projects lasted until the second half of the 1980s, when changes in the ground rules for such schemes radically diminished the scope for using them in the furtherance of archaeological work (Drake and Fahy 1987; Mellor 1986, 1988).

The pattern that developed in Wales and Scotland was somewhat different. In Wales (CBA Wales 1988; Owen-John 1986), a number of multi-function regional trusts was established, not directly integrated with the local authorities, but often consulted by them on planning-related matters. Contrastingly, the employment of archaeologists within local authority planning departments (Manley 1987) was relatively rare, such that these trusts generally fulfilled both curatorial and contracting roles. In Scotland, decentralisation of the control of archaeological resources developed much more slowly (Chapter 10). State support for rapid survey was initially made available through the Society of Antiquaries of Scotland, but was thereafter reallocated directly to RCAHMS, which subsequently received further financial inputs from the Scottish Office specifically for strategic survey in relation to afforestable lands, which were rapidly being cloaked in conifers as a by-product of tax incentive schemes. Certain regional and island authorities employed archaeologists (in no case more than two), from the mid-1970s, essentially in the first instance to compile SMRs (now HERs) and to advise on planning matters. On the urban front, the City of Aberdeen, exceptionally, developed a small integrated archaeological service. By contrast, the Perth-based but territorially wide-ranging Scottish Trust for Urban Archaeology was again set up initially under the aegis of the Society of Antiquaries of Scotland, but with a heavy reliance on Scottish Office funding at the outset, initially to deal with the need to provide a rescue service for threatened archaeology in towns.

The start of a new decade in 1990 brought the beginnings of major changes as a result of the implementation of new planning guidelines. Not only did this directly affect the level of developer funding available but it also provided a significant new workload for archaeologists based in local authority planning departments (increasingly termed 'curators') in the preparation of briefs and specifications. Archaeological remains and/or the possibility of significant archaeological deposits at the relevant location became a pertinent factor for consideration in planning applications, and local authority archaeologists took on a heavy responsibility in implementing the new system to deal with a range of issues that were coming into being. This radical realignment of roles and responsibilities ensuing from the changeover to the 'polluter pays' system was not without problems, notably in Wales, but subsequent reviews of the impact of PPG 16 indicated general, if qualified, satisfaction (e.g. Darvill and Russell 2002). The absence of a research dynamic in the 'polluter pays' process that engulfed applied archaeology in Britain was soon flagged up by Biddle (1994), and renewed calls for a more academic basis for specifications for development-led archaeological work and local authority policies on the archaeological heritage were formalised in an EH document *Frameworks for our Past* (EH 1996). EH funding was released thereafter in order to facilitate the establishment of regional research frameworks to this end, again in an innovative move not directly paralleled elsewhere in the UK.

ARCHAEOLOGICAL UNITS AND TRUSTS

Archaeological organisations, usually initially designed as field units, emerged throughout the 1970s and became consolidated in England and to some extent fossilised during the cutbacks in public spending in the 1980s. By the end of that decade, many such organisations responded to the new scope of planning procedures (notably initially the *Environmental Assessment Regulations* from 1988). Subsequently, the role of the development control function of the planning system in curating archaeological resources was formalised in policy guidance to local authorities (DoE 1990a; Welsh Office 1991; SOEnD 1994a, 1994b). Resources for archaeological work were increasingly obtained from a wider range of private clients (Chapter 14), the majority being commercial developers, for whom the need to commission archaeological fieldwork was a new experience. In acting thus as contractors to the corporate sector, a number of units, particularly those still based within local government, saw potential conflicts arising with their existing area-based curatorial roles (Chapter 16). The greater diversity of funding sources, and ongoing relations with client organisations, also enabled certain units to develop a remit geographically distinctly wider than their home 'territory' as originally defined by local or central government spending patterns. Underpinning this change was the need to carry out archaeological surveys, and to develop mitigation strategies, on major infrastructure projects such as pipelines that traversed several local authority boundaries. New units, unrelated to the local authority system, and thus not bound by the older territorial conventions, also came into being. One key impact of this change, the demise of terrritoriality, was to introduce new stresses within the archaeological community with the rise of competitive tendering (CT) for fieldwork projects, previously allocated effectively to a monopoly supplier on a territorial basis (Chapters 15 and 16).

Although the subsequent evolution of units has been remarkably rapid, and a few now offer national coverage for their services, the pattern to this day reflects in part the piecemeal fashion in which organisations emerged in a variety of different administrative guises, in local authority departments, as independent charitable trusts or, latterly, in some universities and as private companies. Most large ancient towns, and especially those in the south of England, have long had their own resident units – for example, those at Oxford, York and London – although most of these now work well beyond their original geographical areas of operation. A small number of these centres at one stage received greater legal protection with the full implementation of provisions in the 1979 AMAA Act (Chapter 5), but the archaeological protection of, and intervention in, the cores of selected historic towns, made possible by Section 2 of the 1979 Act, was never employed outside England. At Winchester, however, the archaeological group was uniquely proactive, consisting of a research unit undertaking urban excavations at an unprecedented and unrepeated scale. This pioneering group was later supplemented and eventually replaced by a more reactive archaeological agency.

The location of units and trusts was to a large extent initially dependent on the activities of individuals and pressure groups within the relevant areas. Success depended on a number of factors, not least of which was local authority sympathy (expressed in part financially) and public cooperation. Sociologically, the most responsive areas were predominantly the wealthier middle-class regions of the south of England; less successful were parts of northern England, south-west England and most of Scotland. Restrictions in public funding in the early 1980s effectively brought to a close the creation of units of this type at that point in the evolution of regional archaeological presence (Beresford Dew 1977: 5). The present picture to a decreasing extent still reflects that position, although there is a fundamental difference. In their origins, most units were heavily funded from local authority resources; and as a result their operational remits were strictly contained within local authority boundaries (Chapter 14).

The original concept of the multi-county unit, as promoted in England, would have permitted a more even distribution of archaeological services, each unit being provided with back-up facilities, a career structure for its staff and a means through which policy could have been directed centrally (Chapter 13). Instead, an inequitable system emerged: policy-making in relation to applied archaeology was largely vested at the local level, and considerable inconsistencies in practices and approaches arose from one area to the next. Some units were specific to ancient towns (for example, York), some to metropolitan authorities (for example, Greater Manchester), some to whole counties (for example, West Yorkshire) and a small number to multi-county areas (for example, Wessex). The nature of their funding lay substantially within the confines of rescue work, and was related especially to excavation. Research objectives generally played a lesser role, although these could be combined, albeit crudely, with threat-oriented work. Only in places like Wessex could a more rigorous academic approach be implemented, for example, on a thematic basis (Ellison 1981), because the larger geographical canvas allowed research objectives such as the development of urban infrastructure, the scope of trade or the impact of religion to be pursued within the rescue opportunities that arose at the regional level.

By 1990 the employment structure of individual units varied relatively little, but each usually embraced in-house both excavation and post-excavation staff; less usual specialist requirements were sometimes outsourced. The management was headed by a director (an archaeologist), often aided by an administrator. The organisation may additionally have contained conservation, photographic and other post-excavation facilities. Larger units also undertook educational work: an early but useful organisational model, including this role, was proposed for London (Biddle and Hudson 1973: 41–6). Later, and in tandem with the move towards a measure of independence from central and local government financial support, many units had to adopt more sophisticated management systems, marketing ploys and costing strategies in keeping with the commercial environment in which they found themselves. Since 1990 this commercial environment has taken over almost completely (see Chapter 14) and is reflected in the more ubiquitous presence of project managers, project monitors and finance officers in the staffing profile of the average unit. Furthermore, this same commercial environment that encouraged the development of substantial units staffed to deal with the archaeological requirements of major developments also provided the opportunity for the emergence of small archaeological organisations. These, often consisting of no more than two or three individuals and operating within a market niche, could undertake minor activities such as development assessments, evaluations, or watching briefs, or develop specialist skills. Costs associated with increasing distance and overhead regimes in bigger organisations mean that the smaller units can often compete well for smaller jobs or ones remote from their bigger competitors. Other specialist units, concentrating for example on aerial photography or geophysical survey, generally work on subcontracts from other archaeological units, providing services it would be uneconomic to take in-house. Developments in some high-cost specialist areas, notably in the use of ground penetrating radar (GPR, Chapter 18) have to some extent been driven to satisfy the needs of evaluation in the planning process.

Much of this development has occurred concurrently with the evolution of digital technologies that enable units to create, disseminate and archive massive amounts of data. Sadly, much of this information is less than exciting and consists of data structure reports (the minimal interim report now considered acceptable) or 'grey' literature which is ostensibly unimportant, and is difficult or sometimes even impossible to access. Nevertheless, the rapid progress made in electronic data collection has also necessitated commensurate strides in archiving facilities. These are being achieved, for example, at York through an initiative known as the Archaeology Data Service (Richards 2003; see Chapter 19); the NMRs are also increasingly geared up to take in digital data rather than paper records. While many developer-funded projects lead only to relatively minor publications, it would be grossly unfair to characterise all such outputs thus. Numbers of high profile discoveries, as well as significant information in research terms, have been generated.

Based on changes in planning controls, these developments in contracting units and local authority roles occurred in tandem with the emergence of archaeological consultants, the latest group to be spawned by the demands of the commercial world (Chapter 15). Most units also acted in this role, but the new, wider system of operation gave scope for individuals and small groups to set up in private practice to provide services within this niche. Their role has tended to be as agent for a client, or as an intermediary within the curatorial/contractual process. The provision of consultancy services can be particularly attractive to larger commercial developers wishing to obtain advice, often confidentially, regarding archaeology in planning matters, without 'revealing their hand' at a preliminary stage. The practice of field archaeology thus finds itself in the front line of commercial and contractual operations (Chapter 16); and thus, to an extent previously unparalleled, exposed to direct involvement in planning enquiries and potentially litigious situations. An increasing number of the larger construction or engineering companies, for example Gifford and Partners, employ their own in-house archaeological expertise, a move now spreading to planning or environmental consultancies and to landscape architecture firms. At the time of writing, however, most such organisations seek archaeological input from archaeological units and consultancies, retaining their own staff essentially for office-based, decision-making roles.

Very few predominantly archaeological units claim to have the expertise to take on the full scope of, for example, environmental assessments, although the profession has now effectively responded to the challenges of a number of massive developments on a scale that was unthinkable in the 1980s. This has been undertaken by alliances such as the formation of *Framework Archaeology*, a consortium put together by two of the country's largest units, now known as 'Oxford Archaeology' and 'Wessex Archaeology', to work on major projects for the British Airports Authority.

ARCHAEOLOGICAL MANAGEMENT IN NORTHERN IRELAND

The organisation of archaeology in Northern Ireland is so different from that in the rest of the UK that brief separate treatment is appropriate. The differences arise from a different historical development and different legislation (see Appendix to Part Two). Responsibility for State Care of monuments goes back to the disestablishment of the Church of Ireland in 1869. The 1920s and 1930s saw the addition of powers to protect by scheduling, to control archaeological excavation by licensing and to administer the law relating to archaeological finds. To these responsibilities were added others in 1950 with the establishment of the Archaeological Survey of Northern Ireland within the Ministry of Finance. The two staff members were appointed to carry out archaeological and architectural survey on the pattern of the commissions in Great Britain, though without a Royal Warrant. During the 1960s and especially the 1970s the number of staff increased and much effort was directed to rescue excavation, as elsewhere in the UK, as well as protection, record-building and continuing survey.

The present range of work is therefore very wide (Hamlin 1989; DoE (NI) 1990). State Care monuments numbering 181 are conserved, maintained and presented. There are just over 1,700 scheduled historic monuments and in 1992 the first three field monument wardens were appointed. This was expanded to four field monument wardens in 2003. An SMR was built up during the 1970s, as elsewhere in the UK, and now, with information on about 16,000 pre-1700 sites, it provides the basis of the protection work through monitoring all planning applications and agricultural development schemes potentially affecting monuments. Only one survey volume has been published – *An Archaeological Survey of County Down* (HMSO 1966) – but one further county survey is in preparation, on Armagh. The basic identification survey of all six counties was completed in 1995, and this information is now available to the public both at the Monuments and Buildings Record and on the website www.ehsni.gov.uk. Architectural and industrial surveys are largely taken up with recording threatened buildings.

Excavation work is mainly concentrated now on developer-funded projects with a small number of research excavations from time to time. *Planning Policy Statement 6* (PPS 6) replaced *Planning Policy Guidance Note 16* (PPG 16, DoE 1990a) in 1999 and is the principal policy document used in development control decisions for archaeological sites. Since the commencement of the Northern Ireland Peace Process in 1995, commercial development in Northern Ireland, including road improvements and pipeline construction, has greatly increased, creating a growing need for archaeological mitigation. Large greenfield sites are increasingly turning up important prehistoric settlements, both Neolithic and Bronze Age. Where possible, remains, once identified, are preserved *in situ* beneath structures and roadways. The Northern Ireland Monuments and Buildings Record (MBR) has grown greatly since it was opened to the public in 1992. This is the Northern Ireland equivalent of the (non-intensive) National Monuments Records, with its constituent parts (Sites and Monuments, Industrial Heritage, Architectural and Parks and Gardens as well as the less well-developed Defence Heritage and Battlefield sites) all housed in one location. A Maritime Heritage Record, an inventory of sites in territorial waters (see Chapter 7), is being developed in partnership with the University of Ulster at Coleraine. This is combined with a curatorial role: under an agency agreement with the Department of Culture, Media and Sport, the Department of the Environment for Northern Ireland is responsible for administering the Protection of Wrecks Act (1973). Under the Northern Ireland Historic Monuments and Archaeological Objects (Northern Ireland) Order 1995 (see Appendix to Part Two) the Department of the Environment is also responsible for administering the law relating to archaeological finds and pursuing breaches of the law, for example, unlicensed searching for archaeological material with a metal detector. Finally, there is a wide range of public relations and educational work, including cooperation with district councils, schools, contributions to exhibitions, organisation of events, production of popular publications, and talks.

Northern Ireland thus has a centralised, integrated archaeological service that combines the functions of many central, regional and county bodies in Great Britain, and this service is part of an entirely centralised structure of administration. The Built Heritage work is carried out within the Environment and Heritage Service (EHS), a grouping created within the Department of the Environment for Northern Ireland in 1990 to bring together responsibility for countryside and wildlife, environmental protection (see Chapter 22), and historic monuments and buildings. Under devolved government, DoE (NI) is also responsible for planning, road safety, driver and vehicle testing and local government services. There is no county tier of local government, but EHS provides advice and consultancy to twenty-seven district and borough councils proactively as resources allow or on demand. These have very limited powers at present. Some run local museums, in which a few archaeologists are employed, but there are no local authority curatorial archaeologists and no county units or SMRs.

To a certain extent the Northern Ireland provision may seem to resemble the 1960s Great Britain position already characterised as 'applied field archaeology practised by the small archaeological staff of state . . . bodies' (above), and in scale it may seem to resemble a large English county. Yet it covers a far wider range of functions than any single body in Great Britain, combining protecting and recording, acting as both curator and contractor. In the particular circumstances of Northern Ireland, with 80 per cent of the land under agriculture, a population of 1.8 million, and no site more than about two hours' drive from Belfast, this integrated organisation makes for a very effective operation. The work is firmly based on the philosophy of stewardship and the protection and best management of the inherited resource for present and future generations.

NON-GOVERNMENTAL AND VOLUNTARY ORGANISATIONS

Since the eighteenth century (but more particularly from the reign of Queen Victoria), the creation of learned and/or amenity societies has been a major factor in the development of British field archaeology and in the dissemination of information and opinion. The senior organisation is the Society of Antiquaries of London, established in 1707, followed by the Society of Antiquaries of Scotland, founded towards the end of the same century. The nineteenth century saw these complemented by further national societies, such as the Royal Archaeological Institute, as well as by a range of county-based organisations. Of the latter, the Society of Antiquaries of Newcastle upon Tyne (1813) is the oldest (Jobey 1990). Some of these are exclusively archaeological in their interests, but many also embrace local and/or natural history. The county organisations normally have between 500 and 1,500 members, publish journals (and in some instances monograph series), and may have amassed libraries and archives of importance, as is the case notably with the Yorkshire Archaeological Society. Some also run museums. The largest of these 'broad-canvas' societies in membership terms is the Society of Antiquaries of Scotland, with some 3,400 members (in 2005).

The principal characteristic of many of the societies formed in the twentieth century has been a kind of balkanisation, either in terms of geographical scope or of period interests. In the latter category, the earliest foundation (1911) is the Society for the Promotion of Roman Studies, with some 3,700 members (2005) the biggest in the UK, although its interests are empire-wide and not exclusively British. The Prehistoric Society was formed in 1935, by a takeover of the East Anglian Society and the widening (in this instance to world-scale) of its geographical scope. Other national societies with period-based or more specific remits were established between the mid-1950s and the mid-1970s: medieval, nautical (again international in scope), post-medieval, and industrial. Many of these have developed policy statements on the need for support for research (and its prioritisation) or legislative changes required to safeguard the archaeological resource (as in the case of the Nautical Archaeology Society) within their domains (Chippindale and Gibbins 1990; CBA 1988a, 1988b). Others have developed as institutions that have attracted considerable academic respect, for example the Cambridge Committee for Aerial Photography (now the Unit for Landscape Modelling), whose archives now constitute one of the main national photographic databases (see Chapter 18).

Since the Second World War, and more especially between the mid-1950s and the early-1980s, a large number of smaller, local groups has been established. Indeed, by the 1990s, the median date for the establishment of all archaeological societies (over 150) listed in an earlier *Current Archaeology* survey is about 1960 (Selkirk 1990). With typical memberships of between 50 and 200, these groups are a product of the popularisation of archaeology in the postwar period, and in many instances of the perceptions of threats to the archaeological resource at the local scale: such groups normally lay stress on active fieldworking among their interests. This may be conducted in their own right, or in collaboration with locally based professional archaeologists. This relationship has been placed under some stress by the changing nature of the organisation and funding of much field archaeological endeavour, as noted above and elsewhere in this volume (Chapter 20).

In Northern Ireland there is widespread general good will towards monuments, but amateur archaeology is underdeveloped compared with Great Britain. There has been a huge growth in local history societies since the 1970s and there is an active Federation for Ulster Local Studies. These societies often number archaeology among their interests, but their activities rarely extend to practical archaeology.

Archaeology was for long traditionally viewed as an amateur pastime whose manpower resources were coordinated by the Council for British Archaeology (CBA), established in 1944 as the successor to the Congress of Archaeological Societies, with a regional network. The CBA's activities were based mainly on active local fieldwork (usually in England), with regular meetings of groups interested in a wide range of relevant topics. The CBA responded to the demands of modern archaeology with a committee structure representing areas such as scientific applications and policy, the countryside, urban affairs, churches and education; membership of these was drawn from the professional, academic and voluntary sectors. In 1996, however, these were replaced by a single, strategic, UK-wide Research and Conservation Committee. Not only does the CBA have a strong publication record, including the popular journal *British Archaeology*, but it also sits at the front of information technology in the discipline. Its webpage (www.britarch.ac.uk) is the gateway into various areas of archaeology as well as offering an international electronic journal. The CBA is unique in representing all elements of British archaeology; in Scotland, its sister organisation, the Council for Scottish Archaeology (CSA), takes a similar role (Proudfoot 1986). Independent and funded substantially by annual grants from the British Academy, the CBA is of established reputation and respected opinion: its policy recommendations have been widely implemented. In the case of churches and cathedrals, for example, where redevelopment has significant archaeological implications and where different legal constraints apply from those in the secular world (see Chapter 9), the CBA instigated a network of archaeological consultants within the Anglican diocesan framework, in effect creating a specialist tier of archaeological activity and/or advice within the national structure. Arrangements for archaeological input can now be found in other national or regional organisations, for example, within the National Trusts (Thackray and Hearn 1985; Smith 1986), the National Parks (White and Iles 1991; Cleere 1991), the successors to the Nature Conservancy Council and the Forestry Commission (Forestry Commission 1991; Chapter 22) as well as within former utilities in the gas and water industries.

Also active in identifying the awareness and expansion of archaeology in Britain is RESCUE, the Trust for British Archaeology set up in 1971 as a pressure group without the establishment or restrictions of public funding. Much of the initial, and inevitably reactive, response by concerned archaeologists and their public supporters to the recognition of the threat to archaeological resources can be attributed to RESCUE's voice and to the tireless efforts of those who worked within it (Rahtz 1974; Jones 1984; Barker 1987). The organisation was also highly important in the generation of increased government funds and in the creation of archaeological units. RESCUE's independent contribution, although diminished by the changing focus of archaeological practice since the 1980s, nevertheless remains relevant (Spoerry 1992a).

Inevitably, groups representing the divergent but related interests of different professional sectors have emerged. Their names, but not their functions, have changed over time. They include the Society of Museum Archaeologists (SMA), the Standing Conference of Archaeological Unit Managers (SCAUM) and the Subject Committee for Archaeology (SCFA) which represents the subject in higher education. The foregoing are all UK-wide; the local authority sector is covered by the Association of Local Government Archaeology Officers (ALGAO), and in Scotland, the Association of Regional and Islands Archaeologists (ARIA), presently in course of merging with ALGAO, in a move which on the surface at least seems to run counter to devolutionary trends within the UK. All provide the voice and opinion of specialist professional interests within the overall framework.

Figure 4.3. Standing buildings recording is now an accepted part of archaeological investigation. The division between upstanding and buried deposits is now seen as largely artificial. *Photo: Wessex Archaeology*

The most broadly based professional organisation is the Institute of Field Archaeologists (IFA), which received Board of Trade approval in the early 1980s. There are also two professional associations covering all of Ireland: the Irish Association of Professional Archaeologists (IAPA) and the Organisation of Irish Archaeologists (OIA), the latter originating with a group of archaeologists outside permanent established posts in that country. More than any other indicator, the emergence of the IFA marks the arrival of archaeology in Britain in the professional world. The functions of the IFA embrace the establishment of working standards, the development of codes of practice, the provision of training and the dissemination of information, as well as the implementation of a disciplinary framework for the profession. Membership is by proven competence and ability at a number of levels: member, associate, practitioner and affiliate. Members are validated according to their training, competence and experience. This was originally defined through one or more areas of competence (e.g. excavation, survey, aerial archaeology, finds study, recording and analysis of standing buildings, or research and development) but these designations were later abandoned as the profession became more complex and roles more varied. Membership is thus a reflection of peer judgement by other archaeologists within the IFA, and is also an indication to associated professionals such as architects, engineers and surveyors with whom the archaeologist may be working of his or her particular expertise. More recently, the IFA has expanded its remit to provide registration for archaeological units as well as individuals. Organisations wishing to become Registered Archaeological Organisations (RAOs) are required to make available to the IFA much of the detail of their annual activities and working practices, and must agree to conform to the IFA's standards. RAOs, many of whose staff will be individual members of the institute in their own right, are also open to biennial inspection. The IFA also has a number of committees attending to a range of issues such as professional standards, contractual practices, disciplinary matters, equal opportunities and career development and training (www.archaeologists.net).

THE EDUCATION SECTOR

During the postwar period, the provision of archaeological teaching in the universities expanded rapidly, especially in relation to the muted exposure of the discipline in the remainder of the higher education sector. Joint- or combined-honours archaeology courses (typically with Classics, History or English) blossomed into single-honours courses (Tindall and McDonnell 1979) and by the early 1980s, around half of the UK's (then) fifty universities had archaeologists on their teaching staff, usually within specifically designated archaeology departments; their total number was approximately 200 (Austin 1987). Now some fifty of the hundred-plus universities in Britain offer archaeology at least as a named component within one or more of their degrees. Several universities also found it opportune to create archaeological field units on campus (see Drewett 1987) and these existed with varying degrees of success until in some instances the post-PPG 16 commercialisation required rethinking of functional and operational effectiveness. Others continue to flourish. As with local authority and private sector units, much of the work of these teams consisted of short-term evaluation and other fieldwork generated by developments such as the Environmental Assessment Regulations 1988, PPG 16 (DoE 1990a; Welsh Office 1991) and the Department of Transport's Trunk Roads Programme (Friell 1991), although certain institutions have targeted more specialist markets, such as forensic applications of archaeological practice. Numbers of archaeological units remained housed within, or associated with, university academic departments, but changing regimes of cost recovery instigated by government and other pressures within universities may lead to more of these moving into the private sector.

The teaching of the subject in most departments was (and remains) avowedly directed at the liberal arts, with few departments placing emphasis, more particularly at undergraduate level, on vocational aspects of the discipline. Provision for science-based teaching at more than a basic level was initially restricted to relatively few departments, but has been spreading through the system. Although most departments include the archaeology of the British Isles within their focus, geographical and temporal coverage beyond the British Isles varies widely (Binns and Gardiner 1990 for an early summary), with many departments priding themselves on the width of their geographical and chronological coverage.

There has been periodically an indication that the number of home students wishing to take degrees in archaeology has reached a plateau, although this has as yet not proved to be a long-term trend. Some, albeit ambiguous, evidence that numbers of applicants for the discipline had peaked by the mid-1980s was put forward; attempts at University Grants Committee (UGC) *dirigisme*, coupled with other external pressures, provoked a crisis at this

Figure 4.4. Students carrying out a geophysical survey as part of their degree training in field archaeology.

time (UGC 1989). Retraction in public spending combined with a trend towards more vocational training at tertiary level during the 1980s witnessed a process of rationalisation into fewer, larger departments, although ironically some more favourably financed institutions were able to add new courses. A UGC subcommittee also expressed the view that departments should be concerned with regional reviews of the academic priorities for archaeological research. Opportunities for this role to develop were restricted at the time, partly because many university teachers were not primarily concerned with the archaeology of their institution's immediate hinterland and partly because the funding and organisational structure of field archaeology had increasingly resulted in the development of area-based strategies becoming the preserve of archaeologists in local authority employment. Ironically, and some two decades later, this position is being reversed in England with the preparation and implementation of research frameworks (above), in which some university staff are directly involved. Additionally at that time, the limited availability of funding for non-threat-oriented field research within Britain fuelled the tendency for university-based British archaeologists to work abroad, and thus to train their students overseas.

Developments during the 1980s included the establishment of an umbrella organisation, the Standing Committee of University Professors and Heads of Archaeology (SCUPHA), more recently rebranded as the Subject Committee for Archaeology (SCFA) to represent the discipline in its dealings with funding councils and other agencies. This became all the more important as the Higher Education Funding Council for England (HEFCE) and successor to the UGC increasingly demanded representation from, or more usually rapid consultation with, individual subject areas. Specific areas of relevance appeared with the emergence of the Research Assessment Exercise (RAE), the Quality Assurance Agency (QAA) and the need for subject benchmarking.

The great majority of single- and joint-honours archaeology graduates pursue careers other than in field archaeology: this is usually a deliberate choice and reflects the value of transferable skills and breadth of knowledge which study of the subject brings. The limited career opportunities in the sector identified in the 1980s (Joyce *et al.* 1987) can be set against the range and number of archaeological posts a decade later (Aitchison 1999), even if the available salaries leave much to be desired. More pertinent, perhaps, has been the government requirement to increase student numbers to a target figure of 50 per cent of the age cohort, as well as pressures to import revenue-generating overseas students for tertiary education in the UK. Without commensurate resources this has inevitably entailed a simplification (or 'dumbing down' by some definitions) of existing undergraduate programmes, which to many are now seen as an educational rite of passage rather than a process of developing an understanding of, and an ability actively to participate in, a specific field of learning. Implicitly, this now places the intermediate-level higher degree (typically the MA, M.Sc. or M.Phil.) as the vocational platform, as well as that for progression to academic research. Students wishing to enter the profession are now well advised to consider a Master's degree from one of the many programmes available from British universities. These range from scientific and computer applications through to cultural resource management, and are also available as conversion courses for those wishing to enter archaeology from a related disciplinary background.

Opportunities for research have always been restricted by the availability of financial support, and a useful early overview of funding is best addressed in the Hart Report (SERC 1985). However, research received a considerable boost in the 1980s with the vote to the Science-Based Archaeology Committee (SBAC) of the Science and Engineering Research Council (Pollard 1989, 1990), as well as funding from the British Academy (usually for archaeological research, including fieldwork) and both the Scottish and Northern Ireland Education Departments also funding doctoral research. SBAC funded both the innovative application of techniques as well as pure scientific development on a competitive basis; funded support for more routine applications of proven methods was harder to obtain, although the Co-operative Awards in Science and Engineering (CASE) award scheme offered opportunities for collaborative work between universities and external organisations, including archaeological units. Research Council funding subsequently shifted to the Natural Environment Research Council (NERC) where initially a ring-fenced amount was made available for science-based archaeology. This is now no longer available, and archaeological researchers are obliged to rub competitive shoulders with the rest of the academic world on a level playing field with the appropriate Research Council. However, in the late 1990s much of the archaeological research originally funded through the British Academy was transferred to the newly formed Arts and Humanities Research Board (AHRB), which has recently achieved Research Council status as the Arts and Humanities Research Council (AHRC). Archaeologists have also been able to compete for increased sums for collaborative research, for example through the Leverhulme Trust, which has awarded large individual grants in excess of £1 million.

Although the university system plays no formal part in any state or regional archaeological structure, the growth in professionalism and other contemporary pressures developing within the tertiary education sector itself have resulted in the staff of university departments generally playing an increasingly small role in external archaeological activities. As a result there has developed a perceived divergence between academic and field activities, which has become more pronounced as commercial developer-led archaeology continues to predominate. However, steps are being taken by EH to identify student field training programmes, allocate bursaries and support research framework programmes that will help to break down this divide. The IFA now includes university departments within its RAO scheme in a further welcome effort to maintain a balance between applied and research-led initiatives.

CONCLUSIONS

Compared even with the earlier 1990s, the number and variety of organisations employing archaeologists has grown considerably. In many ways, the range of employment positions of archaeologists is now comparable to those of architects and planners; most are vulnerable to the same economic cycles of expansion and contraction in employment.

It is sometimes easy to forget, within this new professionalism, that the justification for professional archaeology is to safeguard resources for future generations and to examine those that cannot be preserved according to the best prevailing academic standards. There must remain considerable doubt as to whether the still-disparate structure of British archaeology currently functioning is entirely appropriate to this end. The imposition of the concept of the 'polluter pays' has none the less generated many practical innovations in the field, in desk-based and laboratory research, and in improvements in managerial practices, as practising archaeologists come into more formal contacts with a wide range of professionals in other domains.

Despite a further ten years of evolution since we first penned these conclusions, there remain, however, fundamental issues affecting archaeological practice that are at risk of being left aside by these changing currents, as there were in 1992. Among these are issues relating to the scope for designing academic research strategies to broaden the understanding of the archaeological environment (as opposed simply to identifying and recovering more data). The establishment of consistent policies and practices for heritage management is also a key concern. This dilemma is not new: archaeology's past, present, and – no doubt – its future, will continue to be inhibited by the legacy of its historical structure.

CHAPTER 5

ANCIENT MONUMENTS LEGISLATION

David J. Breeze

INTRODUCTION

The Ancient Monuments Protection Act of 1882 was the first conservation measure passed by the British Parliament. It came over 200 years after the first conservation measure in Europe, which was undertaken by Sweden in 1660 (for the history of legislation see Kennet 1972; Boulting 1976; Thompson 1977: 58–74; Chippindale 1983; Saunders 1983; MacIvor and Fawcett 1983; Cleere 1989; Ross 1991). The 1882 legislation protected twenty-six ancient monuments in England, three in Wales, twenty-one in Scotland and eighteen in Ireland. These monuments were named in a Schedule or list appended to the Act, thus giving birth to the term 'scheduling'. The 1882 Act has been succeeded by a further eight relating to the protection of ancient monuments (for Northern Ireland see Appendix to Part Two): the current primary legislation is the Ancient Monuments and Archaeological Areas Act 1979 (AMAA Act 1979). Archaeological and historical sites and landscapes are also protected, in a general way, in other legislation, often termed 'balancing legislation', and also through formal agreements with a variety of bodies concerned with the management of different aspects of the countryside.

The AMAA Act 1979 refers to the Secretary of State throughout as the person empowered under the Act. This should now (2005) be taken to refer to the Secretary of State for Culture, Media and Sport (DCMS) in England, Scottish Ministers, and the First Minister in Wales. In Scotland, Scottish Ministers' duties are undertaken by Historic Scotland and in Wales by CADW: Welsh Historic Monuments. In England several activities under the AMAA Act 1979, for example, scheduling, the granting of Scheduled Monument Consent and the designation of areas of archaeological importance, are undertaken by DCMS on the advice of English Heritage (EH), while others are directly undertaken by EH. The aims, objectives and functions of the three state bodies – EH, HS and CADW – are detailed in their *Corporate Plans*, which are published annually.

THE ANCIENT MONUMENTS AND ARCHAEOLOGICAL AREAS ACT 1979

Scheduling

The AMAA Act 1979 states that the Secretary of State (hereafter referred to as the Minister) 'shall compile and maintain . . . a schedule of monuments' which 'may . . . include . . . any monument which appears to him to be of national importance', on land or in UK territorial waters, so long as it is not 'occupied as a dwelling house by any person other than a . . . caretaker' and is not 'used for ecclesiastical purposes'; monuments may be added to the list or excluded from the Schedule of Monuments or any entry in the Schedule relating to a monument may be amended (Sections 1 (1), (3), (4), (5); 53, 61 (8)).

Figure 5.1. The upland hill-fort of the White Caterthun, Angus was among the first sites to be added to the Schedule of Ancient Monuments in 1882. *Photo: Aberdeen Archaeological Surveys*

The Act defines a monument as:

(a) any building, structure or work, whether above or below the surface of the land, and any cave or excavation;

(b) any site comprising the remains of any such building, structure or work or of any cave or excavation; and

(c) any site comprising, or comprising the remains of, any vehicle, vessel, aircraft or other moveable structure or part thereof which neither constitutes nor forms part of any work which is a monument as defined within paragraph (a) above;

and any machinery attached to a monument shall be regarded as part of the monument if it could not be detached without being dismantled. (Section 61 (7))

In effect, only items that can be removed readily by hand are beyond the protection of scheduling, though this is yet to be tested in the courts. In general, items listed in paragraph (c) are rarely protected through scheduling (see Chapter 7 for the protection of wrecks; and the Protection of Military Remains Act 1986, the purpose of which is 'to secure the protection from unauthorised interference of the remains of military aircraft and vessels that have crashed, sunk or been stranded').

A distinction is also drawn in the Act between a monument, as described above, and an ancient monument that is defined as 'any Scheduled Monument; and any other monument which in the opinion of the Secretary of State is of public interest by reason of the historic, architectural, traditional, artistic or archaeological interest attaching to it' (Section 61 (12)).

The criteria for judging national importance in England and Wales are published in the relevant *Planning Policy Guidance Note 16: Archaeology and Planning* (PPG 16 (England) Annex 4 (DoE 1990a) and Annex 3 of *Welsh Office Circular 60/96*. The eight unranked criteria, which are indicative rather than definitive, are:

Survival/Condition: the survival of the monument's archaeological potential both above and below ground is a crucial consideration and needs to be assessed in relation to its present condition and surviving features.

Period: it is important to consider for preservation all types of monuments that characterise a category or period.

Rarity: some monument categories are so scarce in some periods that any still retaining any archaeological potential should be preserved. In general, however, a selection must be made that portrays the typical and commonplace as well as the rare. For this, account should be taken of all aspects of the distribution of a particular class of monument, not only in the broad national context but also in its region.

Fragility/Vulnerability: highly important archaeological evidence from some field monuments can be destroyed by a single ploughing or unsympathetic treatment; these monuments would particularly benefit from the statutory protection that scheduling confers. There are also standing structures of particular form or complexity where again their value could be severely reduced by neglect or careless treatment and which are well suited to protection by this legislation even though they may also be listed historic buildings.

Diversity: some monuments have a combination of high-quality features – others are chosen for a single important attribute.

Documentation: the significance of a monument may be given greater weight by the existence of records of previous investigation or, in the case of more recent monuments, by the support of contemporary written records.

Group Value: the value of a single monument (such as a field system) is greatly enhanced by association with a group of related contemporary monuments (such as a settlement and cemetery) or with monuments of other periods. In the case of some groups it is preferable to protect the whole, including the associated and adjacent land, rather than to protect isolated monuments within the group.

Potential: on occasion the nature of the evidence cannot be precisely specified but it is possible to document reasons for anticipating probable existence and importance and so demonstrate the justification for scheduling. This is usually confined to sites rather than upstanding monuments.

The Ancient Monuments Board for Scotland (AMBS 1983: Section 28) offered advice as a guide towards the scheduling of monuments in Scotland:

A monument is of national importance if, in the view of informed opinion, it contributes or appears likely to contribute significantly to the understanding of the past. Such significance may be assessed from individual or group qualities, and may include structural or decorative features, or value as an archaeological source.

In addition, the Board offered the following advice as a working definition:

For a monument to be regarded as being of national importance it is necessary and sufficient –
    first, that it belongs or pertains to a group or subject of study which has acknowledged importance in terms of archaeology, architectural history or history; and
    second, that it can be recognised as being part of the national consciousness or as retaining the structural, decorative or field characteristics of its kind to a marked degree, or as offering or being likely to offer a significant archaeological resource within a group or subject of study of acknowledged importance.

In England DCMS schedules monuments on advice from EH, whereas in Scotland the authority to schedule lies with HS, and in Wales with CADW. There is no appeal against a decision to schedule a monument (except through the process of judicial review), and the law offers no provision for the payment of compensation for scheduling per se. Although it is not a statutory requirement, owners of monuments are normally advised of the intention to schedule in advance of its implementation and time is thus available for discussion about the proposal and its implications. Scheduled sites are registered as a charge in the local land registry in England and Wales; and recorded at the Register of Sasines in Scotland. The National Monuments Record (NMR) and local authorities, including the Sites and Monuments Records (SMRs), are also notified. Lists of Scheduled Monuments are regularly published, on a county basis in England and Wales and on a national basis in Scotland (see Chapter 3).

In 1986 EH commenced the Monuments Protection Programme (MPP – see Chapter 17), which was designed to review and evaluate existing information about sites of archaeological and historical interest so that those of national importance could be identified and scheduled (Darvill *et al.* 1987: 393). CADW operates a programme of reviewing monuments by type or period with a view to selecting those suitable for scheduling. In Scotland, a review of scheduling has indicated those areas under-scheduled, and resources are being focused there. There are 3,500 scheduled areas in Wales, 7,800 in Scotland and 19,400 in England, but these figures include multiple sites, so the number of protected monuments is considerably higher.

In all three countries there are monuments that are both scheduled and listed (Chapter 8). In such circumstances, Listed Building Consent is not required for works (in England and Wales the relevant legislation is Section 61 of the Planning (Listed Buildings and Conservation Areas) Act 1990 and for Scotland Section 54 (1) of the Planning (Listed Buildings and Conservation Areas) (Scotland) Act 1997). One disadvantage of this situation is that, while both the ancient monument and the listed buildings legislation (AMAA Act 1979: Section 5 and the Town and Country Planning Act 1971: Section 99 (England and Wales), and the Planning (Listed Buildings and Conservation Areas) (Scotland) Act 1997) allows for the appropriate local or central government agency to undertake emergency repairs, it is difficult for local authorities to serve repair notices on listed buildings that are also scheduled, while only the listed buildings legislation allows such costs to be reclaimed from the owner. The overlap between scheduling and listing is being reduced as respective protection programmes proceed, though with certain monument types, for example castles and bridges, there may always be a degree of overlap, as the different legislations protect different parts of the monument.

In July 2003 DCMS issued a consultation paper, *Protecting the Historic Environment – Making the System Work Better*, in which it was proposed that there should be a unified designation system – in effect, a single list of scheduled and listed sites – and a unified regulatory regime for the integrated management of the historic environment. On the expiry of the period of consultation, EH announced that it would undertake a series of pilot projects to test the proposed arrangements.

Scheduling remains a strong protective measure. However, only archaeological (or architectural) features may be protected: the AMAA Act 1979 does not allow the protection of the setting of monuments. The AMAA Act 1979 abrogated that part of the Ancient Monuments Act 1931 concerned with 'preserving the amenities of any ancient monument' on the grounds that these matters are now best dealt with through the planning legislation. In fact, the only amenity area designated under the 1931 Act was for the protection of the amenity of part of Hadrian's Wall (roughly 17 miles of the 73-mile length of the Wall). 'The desirability of preserving an ancient monument and its setting . . . whether the monument is scheduled or unscheduled' receives explicit mention in PPG 16 (England), PPG 16 (Wales) and NPPG5 (Scotland).

Under the Town and Country Planning General Development Order 1988 (England) and the Town and Country Planning (General Development Procedure) (Scotland) Order 1992, protection for Scheduled Monuments was improved by the requirement for planning authorities to consult the Secretary of State before granting planning permission for development that might affect the site of a Scheduled Monument: this was subsequently amended by the Town and Country Planning (General Development Procedure) (Scotland) Amendment (No. 2) Order 1994 which extended the consultation to include the setting of the Scheduled Monument.

Under the AMAA Act 1979 a plea of ignorance of scheduling is possible under certain circumstances. It was partly to try to ensure that owners and occupiers were cognisant of the existence of Scheduled Monuments on their land that monument wardens were appointed by all three bodies to visit sites regularly. Such visits, which occur on regular cycles, are opportunities not just to inform owners or occupiers about monuments on their land but also to offer or arrange for advice about the best management for the monuments. The AMAA Act 1979 provides for access to land for the purpose of inspecting any Scheduled Monument (Section 6).

Scheduled Monument Consent (SMC)

The AMAA Act 1979 is not just a measure to protect monuments through scheduling, but also to control works affecting Scheduled Monuments. Thus the consent of Ministers has to be sought for any of the following:

a. any works resulting in the demolition or destruction of or any damage to a Scheduled Monument;

b. any works for the purpose of removing or repairing a Scheduled Monument or any part of it or of making any alterations or additions thereto; and

c. any flooding or tipping operations on land in, on or under which there is a Scheduled Monument. (Section 2 (2))

These proscriptions lead to requirement for Scheduled Monument Consent also to be sought for archaeological excavations.

It is illegal to undertake any of the above works at a Scheduled Ancient Monument (SAM) without consent, which must be sought through the provision of detailed proposals. The Minister may grant consent for the execution of such works either unconditionally or subject to conditions, or can refuse outright. The consent, if granted, expires after five years. Compensation may be paid for refusal of consent or for conditional consent in certain circumstances, in particular if planning permission had previously been granted and was still effective (Sections 7–9). Failure to obtain SMC for any works of the kind described in Section 2 (2) is an offence, the penalty for which may be a fine which, according to the circumstances of the conviction, may be unlimited. Provision is made for the inspection of work in progress in relation to SMC (Section 6 (3), (4)). Successful prosecutions of parties who undertook works without consent or broke SMC conditions have occurred.

Under the Ancient Monuments (Class Consents) Order 1994 and the Ancient Monuments (Class Consents) (Scotland) Order 1996, certain activities do not require SMC. These are certain categories of agriculture, horticulture and forestry works, provided that the activities formed the regular use of the land in the previous six years (but do not extend to major ground disturbance operations, such as drainage, subsoiling and tree planting); coal extraction carried out more than 30ft below ground; essential and certain repair works by the British Waterways Board; minor repairs to machinery; works essential for health or safety purposes; archaeological evaluation and work in relation to the maintenance, preservation or management of Scheduled Monuments; and, in England only, work carried out by EH.

Considerable efforts are made to discuss proposals that affect Scheduled Monuments before works are carried out so as to best mitigate the effect of such works on the monuments. In some cases agreement is not possible, and provision is made within the AMAA Act 1979 for a hearing. Such a public enquiry represents democracy at work in two ways: it allows the views of officials concerning a particular application to be scrutinised and tested; it also allows the general nature of the protection policy to be tested in a wider forum. In Scotland, for example, in 1991 a public enquiry on Arran accepted that it was possible to schedule areas between visible (and in this case upstanding) monuments because excavations elsewhere had demonstrated that archaeological remains do survive between such monuments.

Guardianship and acquisition

The AMAA Act 1979 allows for monuments (and land adjoining them) to be taken into State (or local authority) Care with the agreement of the owner through the signing of Deeds of Guardianship (Sections 12, 13, 15). This procedure was introduced by the 1882 Act (it is an indication of the importance of the monuments listed in the 1882 Schedule that most have now been taken into Guardianship). The officers charged with implementing the 1882 Act were placed within the existing Board of Works, the body that had long looked after royal castles and palaces in Britain (and some cathedrals and abbeys in Scotland). This body was the direct descendant of the Office of the King's Works, which had been in continuous existence in England since the Middle Ages (MacIvor and Fawcett 1983: 9). Thus state organisations came to look after monuments held in a variety of ways, including ownership, guardianship and tenancy. Monuments are usually taken into State Care because of their signal archaeological, architectural or historical importance. There are about 440 monuments in State Care in England, 330 in Scotland and 130 in Wales, ranging in date from the Neolithic period to the last century. The presentation and interpretation of these monuments feature highly in the activities of the three state bodies.

The AMAA Act 1979 lays a burden to maintain the monument on the guardian, who is given full powers of control and management (subject to any conditions in the deed), including the power to examine or excavate the monument or remove all or part of it for the purpose of excavation (Section 13). Provision is made for public access, its control and for charging for entry (Section 19).

The AMAA Act 1979 contains provisions allowing monuments to pass out of care: these have been used sparingly (Section 14). It also allows for the compulsory acquisition of 'any ancient monument for the purposes of securing its preservation' (Section 10). This was a development of the concept of Preservation Orders, originally introduced in the Ancient Monuments Consolidation and Amendment Act 1913 and further developed in the Ancient Monuments Act 1931 and the Historic Buildings and Ancient Monuments Act 1953. CADW moved to use these powers to acquire St Quentin's Castle, Llanblethian in the Vale of Glamorgan, but before the public enquiry took place the owner placed the monument in State Care.

Management agreements and grants to owners

Scheduling is an inherently passive form of legislation. Often further action is required to ensure the best protection of a monument. This was recognised by the Walsh Committee in its *Report . . . into the Arrangement for the Protection of Field Monuments 1966–68*. The resulting legislation, the Field Monuments Act 1972, introduced the concept of an acknowledgement payment to the 'occupier of land which is the site of a field monument'. This scheme was abrogated by the AMAA Act 1979, which introduced management agreements for ancient monuments, whether scheduled or unscheduled (Section 17). The AMAA Act 1979 also allows the Minister to give grants for the acquisition or removal of a monument for the purposes of preserving it, or to ensure its preservation, maintenance and management (Section 24). In general, management agreements relate to ongoing maintenance and management, including fencing, clearance of scrub and pest control, while grants to owners encompass capital grants for works such as the consolidation of masonry structures and, in certain circumstances, grants for interpretative schemes (on management generally, see Darvill 1987).

The Minister is also empowered to enter the site of a Scheduled Monument if it appears that works are urgently necessary for its preservation and to execute those works, after giving the owner or occupier seven days' notice in writing (Section 5).

EH placed the necessity to determine the state of the archaeological heritage, and thus enable prioritisation of resources, onto a firmer footing through the publication of *The Monuments at Risk Survey of England 1995* (Darvill and Fulton 1998).

Archaeological areas

The AMAA Act 1979 grants Ministers power to designate Areas of Archaeological Importance (Part 2). The purpose of this section is to ensure that time is allowed for the investigation of archaeological deposits in towns before redevelopment takes place. Potential developers are required to give six weeks' notice to the relevant planning authority of any proposals to disturb the ground, tip on it, or flood it. Thereafter, the investigating authority has up to four and a half months for archaeological investigation. In England, although areas within five historic towns (Canterbury, Chester, Exeter, Hereford and York) were designated, in Scotland and Wales, Ministers took the view that existing arrangements between archaeologists and planners were so sound that implementation of Part 2 of the AMAA Act 1979 was unnecessary. In practice, this part of the AMAA Act 1979 has been superseded by planning guidance and, in matters of working practice, by voluntary codes of practice.

Metal detecting

Under the AMAA Act 1979 it is an offence for anyone to use a metal detector in a protected place (i.e. on a Scheduled Monument, or one in the ownership or Guardianship of the state, or a local authority, or in an area of archaeological importance), or to remove any object of archaeological or historical interest found by the use of a metal detector from a protected site without the written consent of Ministers (Section 42). Successful prosecutions of people in breach of Section 42 have occurred in both England and Scotland.

Excavation

During the Second World War the then Ministry of Works financed excavations in advance of the construction of defence installations, and this role was expanded after 1945 to encompass the rescue excavation of archaeological sites, be they scheduled or not, in advance of developments. This work was encompassed by legislation in 1979. The AMAA Act 1979 allows Ministers to 'undertake, or assist in, or defray or contribute towards the cost of, an archaeological investigation of any land which he considers may contain an ancient monument or anything else of archaeological or historical interest' (Section 45 (1)). The wording does not preclude expenditure on non-rescue investigations, though generally the call on excavation funds has been so great as effectively to restrict activities to the examination of threatened sites (see also below under Planning Policy Guidance). The AMAA Act 1979 also indicates that publication is part of the excavation process (Section 45 (3)).

Local authorities

The AMAA Act 1979 gives local authorities many of the same powers as it grants to central government (this authority was first introduced in the Ancient Monuments Act 1900). These include Guardianship, the designation of Archaeological Areas, excavation, management agreements and grants, but not scheduling or compulsory purchase.

OTHER RELEVANT LEGISLATION AND REGULATIONS

One important development over the last twenty years has been the interlinking of government actions. Today, all government departments and related bodies must take into account the interests and activities of their sister departments, and such bodies as the former public utilities. Sometimes this is enshrined in legislation; more usually in regulations or in agreements or concordats. Major landowners, such as the Forestry Commission, take enormous care to protect ancient monuments and manage such sites on their own land using policy statements and directions to their own staff. The intention is not to list all such actions, but to concentrate on those governed by legislation.

The National Heritage Act 1983

The National Heritage Act 1983 established the Historic Buildings and Monuments Commission for England, popularly known as English Heritage (Sections 32–43). The duties of EH, as defined by the National Heritage Act 1983, are more wide-ranging than those formerly undertaken by the Department of the Environment. The primary duties, as set out in the Act, are:

   a. to secure the preservation of ancient monuments and historic buildings situated in England,
   b. to promote the preservation and enhancement of the character and appearance of Conservation Areas situated in England, and
   c. to promote the public's enjoyment of, and advance their knowledge of, ancient monuments and historic buildings situated in England and their preservation.

The National Heritage Act 1983 also encompasses the provision of educational facilities, information to the public, advice, the undertaking of research, and the creation and maintenance of records (Section 33 (2)).

It should also be noted that the National Heritage Act 2002 allows EH to trade in overseas countries and to become involved in underwater archaeology in English territorial waters.

Environment Impact Assessment (EIA)

The principles of EIA were first introduced by EC Directive 87/337/EEC on the assessment of the effects of certain public and private projects on the environment. This has been amended by Directive 97/11/EC. It confirms that 'the assessment procedure is a fundamental principle and on the principle that preventative action should be taken, that environmental damage should as a priority be recitified as source and that the polluter should pay'. The directive has been transposed into UK law by various sets of regulations that apply to those specific consent regimes for projects which may require EIA – for example, Town and Country Planning, pipelines, electricity and forestry.

The regulations require that a decision is taken on the need for EIA of development proposals likely to have significant effects on the environment by virtue, *inter alia*, of their nature, size or location. They set out the statutory procedures to be followed, provide criteria for determining whether projects are likely to have significant environmental effects, list the types of projects to which they apply, specify the information to be contained in the environmental statement to be prepared by the applicant, and identify the need to consult both expert bodies and the public. The information required for an environmental statement includes, for example, 'a description of the aspects of the environment likely to be significantly affected by the development, including in particular . . . material assets including the architectural and archaeological heritage, landscape and the inter-relationship between the above factors'.

A further European Directive, 2000/42/EC, on the assessment of the effects of certain plans and programmes on the environment (more commonly known as Strategic Environmental Assessment – SEA) was transposed by regulation into UK law in July 2004. The Scottish regulations are to be replaced by a bill to be introduced into the Scottish Parliament in 2005 that will extend their scope in Scotland. In general, SEA extends the principles of EIA to certain plans and programmes at the higher, strategic level in order to secure a clearer understanding of environmental impacts at the first stages in the planning process. It addresses criticism that the projected EIA process comes too late in the planning process. The three government heritage bodies, HS, CADW and EH are consultation authorities under these regulations.

The Agriculture Act 1986

Two sections of the Agriculture Act 1986 refer to the protection of the archaeological resource (Owen-John 1992: 92; Chapter 22). Section 17 makes provision for the 'conservation and enhancement of the natural beauty and amenity of the countryside (including its flora and fauna and geological and physiographical features) and of any features of archaeological interest there' and for 'the promotion of the enjoyment of the countryside by the public'. Section 18 provides for the establishment of Environmentally Sensitive Areas (ESAs) to protect, *inter alia*, 'buildings or other objects of archaeological, architectural or historical interest in an area' and to encourage 'maintenance or adoption of particular agricultural methods . . . likely to facilitate such conservation, enhancement or protection'. ESAs were duly designated in England, Wales and Scotland (Smith 1992:

131). This method of protection has now been superseded by wider agri-environmental schemes with archaeology being included as part of general environmental conditions (cf. Chapter 22).

Inheritance tax

Owners of national heritage property are able to make a claim for capital tax relief (Capital Transfer Tax Act 1984: Section 31 = Inheritance Tax Act 1984 (the Act was renamed in 1986); Finance Act 1985: Section 94 and Schedule 26, 2. cf. Inland Revenue 1986). Exemption from capital taxes (capital transfer tax, inheritance tax, estate duty and capital gains tax), and the designation of heritage assets as the objects of a maintenance fund, are conditional upon undertakings about the maintenance, preservation of, and public access to the property. Conditional exemption can be claimed for, among others, SAMs or any other significant archaeological remains, amenity land (in order, for example, to protect views from or of a building), and land of outstanding historic interest. Advice on such matters is provided to the Inland Revenue by EH, HS and CADW.

Planning policy guidance

In November 1990 the Department of the Environment issued, for England, PPG 16, entitled *Planning Policy Guidance: Archaeology and Planning* (DoE 1990a). This was followed in 1991 by a broadly similar document covering Wales (PPG 16 (Wales)), which has now been superseded by *Welsh Office Circular 60/96 – Planning and the Historic Environment: Archaeology*, the main points of which also feature in *Planning Policy Wales* (2002). In Scotland *National Planning and Policy Guidance: Archaeology and Planning and Planning Advice Note: Archaeology – the Planning Process and Scheduled Monument Procedures* (NPPG 5 and PAN 42) were issued in 1994 (DoE 1990a; SOEnD 1994a; 1994b).

The English document sets out its purpose: guidance is for planning authorities, property owners, developers, archaeologists, amenity societies and the general public. It sets out the Secretary of State's policy on archaeological remains on land, and how they should be preserved or recorded both in an urban setting and in the countryside. It gives advice on the handling of archaeological remains and discoveries under the development plan and control systems. The guidance pulls together and expands existing advice, within the existing legislative framework. It places no new duties on local authorities.

In particular, PPG 16 emphasises the fragility of the archaeological resource and the resulting necessity for sound management. The first priority, accordingly, is preservation and where this is not possible excavation must be undertaken ('preservation by record'). Much of the responsibility for the survival of archaeological sites and landscapes lies with local authorities through their development plans and development controls. Development plans should give appropriate cognisance to the protection and enhancement of archaeological sites, and appropriate controls should be imposed, including provision for the excavating and recording of archaeological remains. While developers should not be required to finance archaeological works in return for the granting of planning permission, the onus is placed upon the developer to ensure that the conditions of the planning consent are met: this effectively requires the developer to fund any excavations or arrange for funding from elsewhere. These guidelines thus mark an important step in the move of the primary funding of rescue archaeology in Britain from the state to developers, be they public or private. One important aspect is that acceptance of the principle of developer funding has allowed state resources for archaeology to be used on projects where there is no developer, such as coastal erosion.

Within this framework, the creation of registers has been seen as an alternative way to protect sites that can be difficult to define. In England, a Register of Historic Battlefields has been published, and consideration has been given to the production of such a register in Scotland (EH 1995a; MacSween 2001). Mention should be made of a similar approach to the protection of designed landscapes and gardens, while a Register of Historic Landscapes has been produced in Wales (CADW *et al.* 1998).

THE FUTURE

Legislation enacted in the 1980s and 1990s points to the way forward in some aspects. The National Heritage Act 1983, the Agriculture Act 1986, the Environmental Protection Act 1990 and the Natural Heritage (Scotland) Act 1991 all include reference to one or more of the requirements to: disseminate knowledge, provide an education service, offer advice and undertake research. It seems possible that such activities might be extended to the core legislation concerned with the protection of ancient monuments.

In the first edition of this book, I suggested that:

The division between 'ancient monuments' and 'historic buildings' is largely a historical accident: the protection of historic buildings was too sensitive to be included in the 1882 Act (Kennet 1972). However, the continuing existence of different legislation is seen as anachronistic in the present day. Thus, the creation of unified legislation is likely to be favoured, though such unified legislation needs to ensure that the existing protection is not diluted.

The review of legislation, *Protecting our Historic Environment: Making the System Work Better*, announced by DCMS in 2003, and a similar review in Wales, proposes such an integrated approach to the protection of the historic environment, possibly extending to one unified form of protection for both terrestrial and marine sites.

All ancient monuments legislation so far enacted has been site specific. The challenge for today is to find ways of protecting the historic element in the landscape (see Chapter 22). This is distinct from protecting large archaeological areas, from the concept of curtilage in relation to historic buildings, and even from the promulgation of conservation areas. The difficulty is finding a legislative framework to do this, and thus to date actions have focused on working with other countryside managers, harmonising landscape characterisation assessment, and/or developing registers, such as for battlefields or designed parks and gardens or, in Wales, specifically identified historic landscapes. The move away from the narrow focus upon unitary monuments that has governed the protection of archaeological sites since 1882 is likely to continue and develop. Within that framework, cross-compliance and the future of the Common Agricultural Policy assume a greater significance.

In 1882 there was only one item of conservation legislation. Now the protection of the built heritage appears in various Acts and agreements. This process started gradually, and more vaguely. The Telecommunications Act 1984 referred to the protection of the physical environment (Part 2, Section 9 (4) (a)) and since then balancing clauses have appeared in other legislation, including the Agriculture Act 1986, the Environmental Protection Act 1990 and the Natural Heritage (Scotland) Act 1991. Such requirements now refer much more specifically to the need to protect archaeological and historical sites and landscapes. Through such 'balancing' clauses, the protection of the built heritage is increasingly brought into wider countryside management and thus another development might be a move towards integrated designations (Miles 1992; cf. also Lambrick 1992). New ways of protecting sites for which scheduling is inappropriate are being invented, namely registers of particular types of sites such as battlefields and designed landscapes. Such registers are normally prepared within a planning framework. Indeed, the relationship between planning legislation and ancient monuments legislation grows ever closer, with calls for even more harmonisation and even integration.

Voluntary and formal agreements have developed additional methods of protecting archaeological sites. There may not only be further scope for expansion here, but also an important role for voluntary/amateur groups in taking action to manage and conserve archaeological sites.

Looking back, the variety of legislative measures, voluntary agreements, formal agreements and general cooperation now so common within the wider framework of countryside protection is remarkable to anyone who entered the archaeological profession more than a generation ago. This diversity is now balanced by the envelopment of concern for the protection of the historic environment within concern for the environment as a whole, as indicated by its inclusion within the White Paper on the UK's environmental strategy, *This Common Inheritance* (DoE 1990b): 'sustainability' is indeed an important buzz word for archaeologists these days.

Another major change of the last twenty years has been the widening of professional involvement in the protection of the historic environment. Where once all such activities were the preserve of state bodies, now local authorities and professional units are all involved and sometimes opposed to each other through the advice they offer. It is hardly surprising, therefore, that there has been a growth in publications on the protection of the historic environment (e.g. Pugh-Smith and Samuels 1996b; Cookson 2000 and the series edited by Magnus Fladmark: e.g. Fladmark 1993, 1994, 1995 and 2000). It seems likely that we can look forward to yet more such publications exploring different aspects of our work.

Finally, changes in terminology may be noted. We have long become used to changes in departmental titles; now the very names used for our sites are changing from ancient monuments through the built heritage to the historic environment. Is this going to be a continuing development?

ACKNOWLEDGEMENTS

I am grateful to colleagues both north and south of the Border for their comments on drafts of this paper: Mr J.R. Avent, Dr G.J. Barclay, Mr T. Cairns, Mr R.A.J. Dalziel, Mr R. Emerson, Dr N. Fojut, Mrs L. Linge, Mr R.A.C. MacDonald, Dr L. Macinnes and Dr G. Wainwright.

CHAPTER 6

PORTABLE ANTIQUITIES

Alan Saville

Since this chapter was written, for the first edition of this book (Longworth 1993), there have been many substantive changes in the treatment afforded to portable antiquities in the UK. Important new pieces of legislation – the Historic Monuments and Archaeological Objects (Northern Ireland) Order 1995, the Treasure Act 1996, the Treasure (Designation) Order 2002, and the Dealing in Cultural Objects (Offences) Act 2003 – have been introduced, and new initiatives implemented, most significantly the Portable Antiquities Scheme (www.finds.org.uk). Alongside these there has been a perceptible shift to a more informed attitude towards portable antiquities, both within the archaeological profession and among government agencies and the public at large – in fact little short of a sea change in attitudes over the past decade (cf. Morris 2004). There are now a national Standing Conference on Portable Antiquities (Renfrew 1997), a Ministerial Advisory Panel on the Illicit Trade in Cultural Objects (DCMS 2002a), an Archaeological Archives Forum (Swain 2004), and the Council for British Archaeology has an active Working Group on Portable Antiquities (Wise 2004).

Instrumental in the higher profile that portable antiquities as a whole now enjoy has been the enormous increase in the number of metal objects being recovered by detectorists, opening up new fields of study (Egan and Pritchard 1991) and sometimes leading to the identification of completely new categories of artefact (Williams 1997).

The focus in this chapter on administrative aspects does not allow for coverage of the major advances in scholarship involving portable antiquities over the past decade, but suffice it to say that continuing publication from among the millions of finds from the urban excavations of the 1960s onwards is of an increasingly high standard (selecting examples is invidious, but see Egan 1998; Mainman and Rogers 2000; Ottaway and Rogers 2002 for recent examples), as is the re-analysis of artefacts from existing museum collections (e.g. Jacobi 2004).

In this chapter I look first at the legal and administrative provisions concerning archaeological finds in different parts of the UK, and then consider the aspects of export, trade and illicit antiquities. Much of this is of necessity covered in summary form, but references to the copious publications on relevant topics over the past few years are cited for those wishing to find out more.

Maritime finds – another expanding area of interest since the previous edition of this book (Redknap 1997) – are not discussed in any detail here (see Chapter 7), though it is of interest to note that in this area there is UK-wide uniformity, since objects found anywhere within UK territorial waters are regulated under the Merchant Shipping Act 1995 (Redmond-Cooper and Palmer 1999). Under this Act maritime finds must be reported to the Receiver of Wreck at the Maritime and Coastguard Agency in Southampton (www.mcga.gov.uk). Historic wreck, which includes any portable antiquities found at sea, is defined as anything over 100 years old and government policy is that such items should be offered in the first instance to museums where they will remain accessible to the public. The Receiver of Wreck will endeavour to lodge maritime portable antiquities with a museum in a location relevant to where a find was made or which has an appropriate collection.

The Merchant Shipping Act 1995 does not apply in the Channel Islands, but there is alternative provision, including the Wreck and Salvage (Vessels and Aircraft) (Bailiwick of Guernsey) Law 1986 (and its 1998 Amendment). This law makes it clear that 'ownership of historic wreck in Guernsey waters is vested in the States of Guernsey and does not belong to the finder'. Historic wreck in this instance includes cargo or any other object lost or abandoned for fifty years or more, which must be reported to the Receiver of Wreck at St Peter Port.

ENGLAND AND WALES

Following unprecedented lobbying from the heritage sector (Morris 1996), the Treasure Act 1996 (Bland 1999; Carleton 1997; Cookson 2000; Redmond-Cooper and Palmer 1999) was enacted and came into force in September 1997, replacing the previous common law of Treasure Trove (Hill 1936; Palmer 1993; Sparrow 1982). The Act makes specific what is meant by treasure in the parts of the UK it covers. Treasure is any ownerless object at least 300 years old when found which:

1. is not a coin but has metallic content of which at least 10 per cent by weight is precious metal (gold or silver);
2. is one of at least two coins in the same find with precious metal content of at least 10 per cent; or
3. is one of at least ten coins in the same find where the metallic content is less than 10 per cent precious.

In addition, any object, whatever its composition, found together with an object which is treasure becomes treasure by association. Also, and very significantly, any class of object at least 200 years old may be designated treasure by order of the Secretary of State (by Statutory Instrument) if considered to be of outstanding historical, archaeological or cultural importance.

Treasure is the property of the Crown unless otherwise determined by the Secretary of State. Finders must notify treasure to the local coroner within fourteen days of its discovery or as soon as the find is subsequently realised to be treasure, failing which the finder is guilty of an offence punishable by fine and/or imprisonment. Coroners must notify the British Museum for English finds and the National Museums and Galleries of Wales for Welsh finds, notify the landowner and/or occupier of the findspot, and hold an inquest to determine the status as treasure or otherwise of the find. Treasure retained by the Crown and transferred to a museum requires the recipient museum to fund an ex gratia reward, normally related to market value (as determined by the government-appointed Treasure Valuation Committee), which is payable to the finder and in certain circumstances to landowners and/or occupiers and others involved in the find.

The Act stipulates that it must be accompanied by a Code of Practice which the Secretary of State is obliged to keep under review and revise when appropriate. The Code (DNH 1997; DoE (NI) 1997) is a detailed document which explains the operation of the Act and provides guidance, as well as listing all coroners' offices. It makes absolutely clear that the purpose of the Act is 'to provide a mechanism to allow the public acquisition of finds that come within its scope'. The essential difference between the Treasure Act and the previous situation under Treasure Trove is that treasure is precisely, and slightly more liberally, defined and is extended to include associated items; that the accompanying procedures are itemised; and that there is no longer any burden of proof requirement, as there was under the former system, to show that the object was hidden with the intention of recovery (the *animus revertendi* principle).

Under the Act the Secretary of State is charged with the duty of reporting annually to parliament on its operation. Five such reports have been published so far (DCMS 2000a, 2001a, 2002b, 2003a, 2004a) giving detailed, illustrated accounts of all treasure finds, including their monetary valuation and their 'disposition' (i.e., which museum acquired the find, or whether it was returned to the finder).

In October 2001 a report on a detailed review of the first five years of the Act was issued (Paintin 2001), making a considerable number of recommendations, mainly relating to the Code of Practice, but including the proposal that closed groups of two or more prehistoric base-metal, or partially precious metal, objects should become treasure. This widening of the treasure net was accepted by government with a new order in 2002 (EH 2002a: 34), in accordance with the varying clause in the Treasure Act. The new Statutory Instrument (2002–2666) is The Treasure (Designation) Order 2002, which came into force in January 2003 and marks a very distinct departure from the traditional linkage in England and Wales between treasure and precious metal. It will also be likely to lead to a significant increase in the number of cases to be dealt with under the Act and may further exacerbate problems of museum funding for the rewards involved in acquisition (Clayton 2002; Keys 2003), although some alleviation of this latter situation has recently been provided by the Headley Museums Treasure Acquisition Scheme (www.headleytreasures.org.uk), which provides financial assistance to museums seeking to acquire treasure. Revised Codes of Practice to accompany the new order have been issued for England and Wales (DCMS 2003b) and for Northern Ireland (DoE (NI) 2003), and further revisions will undoubtedly be required (for example, at the time of writing the role of coroners in the Treasure Act is under review and changes in this area are anticipated).

Although the Treasure Act has been successfully introduced and is generally regarded as a major improvement (Hobbs 2003a: 20), critics point to fundamental contradictions in the conceptualisation and treatment of those items defined as treasure on the one hand, and all other portable antiquities on the other, and also to the inherent dangers of commodifying all archaeological finds rather than prioritising their heritage, scholarly, and social values (Lambrick 2001; Tubb and Brodie 2001). Attempts to shift public opinion away from the equation of treasure with only precious metal finds, and in particular with their financial value, have met with mixed success. A recent 'top ten treasures' feature, involving the British Museum and national BBC television, scored a valuable point by ranking the Romano-British wooden writing tablets from Vindolanda as the 'number one' British archaeological 'treasure' in the British Museum (*The Times*, 28 December 2002). These tablets are fascinating objects of high historical value and cut right across traditional concepts of what constitutes treasure. However, the British Museum's subsequent 2003–05 exhibition 'Buried Treasure: Finding Our Past' (Hobbs 2003a, 2003b) gave out a rather more confused message and demonstrated many of the problems archaeologists and museum curators have with accommodating to 'treasure' in their professional practice (Hobbs 2003c). The exhibition celebrated recent major discoveries by metal detectorists and in so doing inevitably found it difficult to avoid implicit promotion of the aspect of financial gain associated with such finds. A 1992 front-page headline about the Hoxne hoard – 'Bootyful! Eric finds £10M booty' – from the *Sun* newspaper was shown in the exhibition (Hobbs 2003a: 79) and the very dominant image of gold and silver coins from this Hoxne hoard, used in the publicity for the exhibition, further underscored the impression.

At the same time as the Treasure Act was being developed, changes occurred in the provision for dealing with non-treasure portable antiquities. Following a consultation exercise (DNH 1996), the government, in conjunction with the British Museum, launched

71

Figure 6.1. Publicity leaflets for the Buried Treasure exhibition at the British Museum, London, and the National Museums and Galleries of Wales, Cardiff.

in 1997 a pilot Portable Antiquities Scheme (PAS) in five regions of England (Bland 1998, 1999; Hobbs 2001). The PAS has gradually become established and, having achieved major Heritage Lottery funding (and now under the auspices of MLA, the Museums, Libraries and Archives Council), it has been extended to cover the whole of England and Wales (Miles 2002). Essentially the PAS encourages all finders of antiquities to report them to a local competent person — in most cases a museum-based Finds Liaison Officer (FLO) employed by the PAS — so that the find can be assessed and recorded. The PAS is complementary to the Treasure Act, in that the FLOs provide an immediate way of identifying whether a find might qualify as treasure and, if so, assistance with the reporting process. It is generally accepted that the presence of a FLO in any area leads to a marked increase in the number of treasure cases reported (DCMS 2004a). In its first seven years of existence the PAS has been extremely successful. As the annual reports show (DCMS 1999, 2000b, 2001b, 2002c; Resource 2003; MLA 2004), an extraordinary number of finds have been reported to the PAS and a significant amount of new archaeological data amassed.

The latest annual figure available, for the sixth year of the PAS, indicates that over 47,000 objects were reported (MLA 2004). The majority of these were metal objects, including coins, since by far the most common method of discovery is by metal-detecting. Indeed, recognition of the growth in the finding of archaeological objects by metal-detector hobbyists was one of the spurs to the creation of the scheme, which has succeeded in achieving a long-overdue rapprochement between most archaeologists and most detectorists, arguably to the considerable benefit of both (Addyman and Brodie 2002). It is doubtful if the latest phase of the PAS would have achieved its funding had it not had the support of the National Council for Metal-Detecting. The timing for introducing such a reporting scheme was favourable, since it was able to capitalise on and foster a broadening interest in 'old things' stimulated by popular TV programmes on archaeology and antiques. Also, the ability to develop an innovative website (www.finds.org.uk) to accompany the PAS has been a major contribution to its effectiveness.

The full history of the introduction of the Treasure Act and the PAS, which together have produced such a remarkable turnaround in the recognition given to chance archaeological finds in England and Wales, has yet to be written, but for some 'insider' views see Bland (1999) and Hobbs (2003a: 19–28), and for outsiders' accounts see Faulkner (2003: 173–82) and Parsons (2003).

The expansion of the PAS to cover the whole of England and Wales was achieved with the aid of substantial funding from the Heritage Lottery Fund, and this funding will expire in March 2006. A very supportive review (Chitty and Edwards 2004), extensive promotion of the PAS's virtues, and a concerted lobbying campaign have been successful (as announced by DCMS in December 2004) in securing a guarantee from central government for the future continuation of the scheme, so it seems that the PAS will become an established part of the archaeological provision in England and Wales. Reporting under the PAS is of course wholly voluntary, and there is probably a significant level of non-reporting. If there are some 15,000 (Hobbs 2002), 30,000 (Dobinson and Denison 1995), or perhaps now even more active metal-detectorists in England and Wales, then the totals of reported finds would mean some of them must be remarkably unsuccessful at discovery (Addyman 2001). Reporting is also very variable geographically. Of the total finds recorded in the PAS's sixth year, 18,732 (40 per cent) were from Norfolk, whereas only 566 (1.2 per cent) came from the whole of Yorkshire (MLA 2004). The PAS does not address the illicit 'nighthawking' activity of a minority of detectorists (Dobinson and Denison 1995; Renfrew 1998: 7) nor antiquities market issues, other than by pursuing a long-term goal of changing public opinion. The organisers are also conscious that the PAS has not achieved uniformly high standards of finds recording or of data transfer to national or local Sites and Monuments Records, and that academic evaluation of the information being amassed has inevitably lagged behind. It has also been pointed out that the absence of any formal link between finds reporting and museum acquisition is a weakness, which allows important finds to disappear from public and scholarly access (Saville 2002: 801).

The other major category of portable antiquities to be considered here concerns finds from archaeological excavation. In England and Wales, if these are not treasure or wreck,

re:source

The Council for **Museums, Archives and Libraries**

Portable Antiquities Scheme:
Advice for Finders of
Archaeological Objects

The Portable Antiquities
Scheme was established
to promote recording
of archaeological objects
found by the public and to
broaden awareness of these
finds for understanding
our past.

Supported by the
Heritage Lottery Fund

Figure 6.2. Cover of an information leaflet for the Portable Antiquities Scheme, issued in 2003.

The Future for Portable Antiquities

In the summer of 2004 the government will announce its spending review for the next five years. The Portable Antiquities Scheme is currently principally funded by the Heritage Lottery Fund, and when this funding ends in March 2006, to sustain the scheme in the long term, government funding for the project is required. Estelle Morris, Minister of State for the Arts, has recently commented that the government will be looking sympathetically at the case for putting the scheme on a permanent footing in the next spending review.

Figure 6.3. Estelle Morris, former Minister of State for the Arts and an advocate for the Portable Antiquities Scheme. She is pictured holding the Abergavenny leopard-handle Roman bronze vessel, one of the spectacular finds reported through the scheme. Reproduced from *Groundbreaker* (Summer 2004), the magazine for the Portable Antiquities Scheme in Wales.

there is no legal process whereby they can be automatically retained for public benefit in museum collections (Owen 1995). In fact the process is rather ad hoc and relies on the excavator (or whoever manages the fieldwork contract) obtaining permission from the landowner to retain the finds, initially for study and publication and subsequently for museum deposit (cf. *IFA Standard and Guidance for Archaeological Excavation*). The Ancient Monuments and Archaeological Areas Act 1979 has a section (42) making it an offence to remove objects found using a metal-detector on a Scheduled Ancient Monument. It does not stipulate what will happen to any objects so removed after recovery, but one can assume that in England and Wales they would be retained for analysis by English Heritage (EH) or CADW respectively and then (if not treasure) handed over to the landowner. This assumption is based on another section (54) of the Act, which effectively gives temporary custody of finds from the investigation of Scheduled Ancient Monuments to the person or organisation that has the appropriate Scheduled Monument Consent for the purpose of 'examining, testing, treating, recording or preserving', but prevents custody beyond a reasonable period without the consent of the landowner, whose property they remain.

Assuming the landowner is amenable, museum deposit relies on the excavator being able to find an appropriate museum willing to take the finds, which does not always happen (Perrin 2002; Swain 1997). The situation appears to be one of some commercial excavation companies continuing to accumulate large numbers of finds in their own stores. A possible solution would be for EH/CADW to operate national clearing-house systems for all excavated finds, linked to deposit in regional archive or resource centres (Perrin 2002), akin to the one now established for London (Swain 2002). Following recent debate about such concepts as Archaeological Resource Centres (Swain 1998), Historic Environment Record Centres (EH 2000a), and the problems of accessing and actually using excavated finds (Bott 2003; CMW 2004), the London Archaeological Archive and Research Centre seems to offer a practical model for emulation.

SCOTLAND

Neither the Treasure Act 1996 nor the Portable Antiquities Scheme apply in Scotland, where portable antiquities of all kinds are covered by Scots common law precepts of Treasure Trove and *bona vacantia* ('ownerless goods'). The key legal principle, derived from feudal law, which underpins the treatment of Scottish finds through what is now generally known as the 'Treasure Trove system', is *quod nullius est fit domini regis* ('that which belongs to nobody belongs to the Crown') (Carey Miller 2002). Historically, the interpretation of Treasure Trove in Scotland has diverged in many respects from that which pertained elsewhere in the UK, most especially in not being restricted to items of precious metal; in there being no requirement to demonstrate whether objects were hidden with intent to recover; and in excluding landowners from any involvement, since they do not possess any rights of ownership over antiquities from the land (Anderson 1904; Hill 1936: 256–62). Many of the key aspects of Scottish Treasure Trove were demonstrated by a famous court case concerning the St Ninian's Isle silver Pictish treasure from Shetland (Carey Miller 2002; Small *et al.* 1973).

Case history and precedent are important to the Treasure Trove system, which undeniably is legally and administratively complex (Carey Miller and Sheridan 1996). Basically, however, all ownerless portable antiquities are the property of the Crown unless and until otherwise determined. Finders must report their objects to the Queen's and Lord Treasurer's Remembrancer (QLTR) at the Crown Office (part of the Scottish Executive), who is advised by an independent Treasure Trove Advisory Panel. Reporting is usually via a local museum or direct to the Panel's Secretariat, based at the National Museums of Scotland in Edinburgh. There are no coroners or coroner's courts in Scotland to be involved in the process, and it is the Advisory Panel that recommends to the QLTR which objects should be claimed as Treasure Trove, what their valuation should be for purposes of any ex gratia rewards, and to which museum they should be allocated. The system currently has an in-built preference for allocation to a museum local to the findspot, and there is a National Fund for Acquisitions, operated through the National Museums of Scotland on behalf of the Scottish Executive, which in all normal circumstances provides half the cost of Treasure Trove acquisitions by local museums.

The Treasure Trove Advisory Panel also deals with the claiming and allocation of finds from archaeological excavations and other organised fieldwork, unless the government agency, Historic Scotland, has been involved. In the latter case there is a separate Finds Disposal Panel to deal with the allocation of those excavated finds (HS 1994). Between the two panels there is a process whereby all excavated finds are assured to be preserved for posterity in public collections throughout Scotland, usually in a museum reasonably local to the excavation site.

Current operation of the Scottish Treasure Trove system, which has changed considerably over the past decade or so, has been described by Saville (2000, 2002) and is summarised in the existing official guidelines (Scottish Executive 1999a, 1999b), but very recently an official consultation on the future of Treasure Trove, following a comprehensive review (Normand 2003), has taken place and will result in further procedural and administrative changes (Scottish Executive 2004). The basic system is robust and potentially a very effective method of protecting and preserving portable antiquities, but it is arguably over-centralised and under-resourced and would benefit from the adoption of equivalents to the FLOs of the PAS in England and Wales. A website (www.treasuretrovescotland.co.uk) helps to promulgate knowledge about the system and foster compliance, as well as providing an educational and archive resource for studying Scottish portable antiquities.

NORTHERN IRELAND

The Treasure Act 1996 applies to Northern Ireland, but has its own specific Code of Practice adapted to local circumstances (DoE (NI) 1997; 2003). In essence the process is much the same as in England and Wales, with the Ulster Museum taking the same role as the British Museum and the National Museums and Galleries of Wales. The Code of Practice also has to take account of the Historic Monuments and Archaeological Objects (Northern Ireland) Order 1995, the Statutory Instrument for the protection of monuments and artefacts in Northern Ireland

This 1995 Order requires the finder of any archaeological object, on penalty of fine, to report it within fourteen days to a 'relevant authority' (the Ulster Museum, the Department of the Environment, or the police). The definition of an 'archaeological object' is similar to that employed in the Isle of Man, but is drawn less comprehensively. Here the definition reads: 'any object, being a chattel (whether in a manufactured or unmanufactured state) which is, or appears to be, of archaeological or historical interest and which has, by reason of such interest, a value substantially greater than its intrinsic value or the value of the materials of which it is composed'.

The finder must report the circumstances of finding, the nature of the object, and the name (if known) of the owner or occupier of the land on which the object was found. The object may be retained by the Ulster Museum for a maximum period of three months from the time at which all information regarding the discovery has been ascertained to the Museum's satisfaction. During this period the Ulster Museum has the object 'for the purpose of examining and recording it and carrying out any test or treatment which appears . . . desirable for the purpose of archaeological investigation or analysis or with a view to restoring or preserving the object'. The order does not specify what happens to finds thereafter, but they are normally returned to the person who submitted the find to the Ulster Museum, who may or may not be the finder or the landowner (usually the legal owner). If the museum wishes to acquire the object, by donation or purchase, it must establish all the details of ownership in order to obtain legal title.

The Ulster Museum must report to the Department of the Environment on every item submitted, and the order also provides for the possibility of financial assistance from the Department of the Environment towards the purchase of reported objects (which also applies in the case of treasure). It is of interest that the order also recognises that some archaeological objects may not be 'readily portable', in which case the finder must report where an authorised person may inspect the object. Because the local legal provision already requires mandatory reporting of all finds, the Portable Antiquities Scheme has not been extended to Northern Ireland.

Since the Treasure Act 1996 postdates the 1995 Order, it has miscellaneous provisions to accommodate it to the Northern Ireland situation and vice versa, but in essence the Northern Ireland version follows the English and Welsh pattern. Potential treasure objects are reported to the coroner and deposited with the Ulster Museum for study. Inquests are held by the local coroner (here sitting without a jury) and ex gratia rewards are paid at full market value, assessed by the Ulster Museum, for all discoveries promptly and fully declared. Uniquely, the reward is paid by the Department of the Environment (Historic Monuments Branch) but the Treasury retains title, the objects being placed on permanent loan in the Ulster Museum.

If the coroner finds the object to be treasure, it is sent to the Treasure Valuation Committee in London to establish the value. After this it is returned to the Environment and Heritage Service in Belfast, where it is held pending acquisition by a museum. If no museum wishes or is able to acquire it, the object is returned to the finder.

The framework for undertaking archaeological activity in Northern Ireland is also somewhat different (Hamlin 2000), since the Historic Monuments and Archaeological Objects (Northern Ireland) Order 1995 prohibits any archaeological excavation (and any search for archaeological objects) without a licence from the Department of the Environment. That licence requires the investigator to declare excavated finds in a similar way to chance finds, usually after full post-excavation recording, so the Ulster Museum is unlikely to require to record them as well. The order also, as with the Ancient Monuments and Archaeological Areas Act 1979, prohibits the use of metal detectors on protected monuments, but goes further in prohibiting even possession of a metal detector on such sites.

THE ISLE OF MAN

Common law Treasure Trove operates on the Isle of Man, but in a way more akin to that which applied until recently in most of the UK, rather than as it does in Scotland. 'Objects of gold or silver (whether coins, plate or bullion) which have been hidden in the soil or in buildings, and of which the original owner cannot be traced, are treasure trove, and by law the property of the Crown' (Isle of Man Government Circular 1972 No. 66). The administrative system allows Treasure Trove cases to be adjudicated by the High Bailiff, in the capacity of Coroner of Inquests, and only precious metal may be claimed. There is some uncertainty as to whether or not there is any requirement to demonstrate objects being hidden with the intent of reclaim, as was suggested by Dolley (1977).

The Manx Museum and National Trust Acts 1959–86 (www.gov.im/mnh) regulate portable antiquities other than treasure. All finds of archaeological objects must be reported to Manx National Heritage or the police within fourteen days. The same Act prohibits unlicensed excavation, unlicensed use of metal detectors on ancient monuments and areas of archaeological importance, unlicensed export of antiquities, and unlicensed injury, defacement or destruction of archaeological objects. An archaeological object is very significantly defined as: 'any chattel including ancient human and animal remains, whether in a manufactured or partly manufactured or unmanufactured state which by reason of the archaeological interest attaching thereto, or of its association with any Manx historical event or person, has a value substantially greater than its intrinsic (including artistic) value, and . . . the said expression includes all treasure trove'.

THE CHANNEL ISLANDS

The Treasure Act 1996 does not apply to the Channel Islands, nor has the Portable Antiquities Scheme been introduced there. There have been no recent finds of treasure and there is some uncertainty about the precise procedures which would ensue, though there is a general presumption that the broad tenets of pre-Treasure Act Treasure Trove as in England are applicable (Hill 1936: 265). The position in Jersey has been reviewed by Nicolle (2001), who concluded that 'gold and silver which is found buried or hidden is treasure trove [and belongs to the Crown], but gold and silver which is neither buried nor hidden . . . is *chose gaive* if it has not been appropriated to the use of man, i.e. unworked metal, but is not *chose gaive* if it has been appropriated to such use, i.e. worked as jewellery or coin etc.'. Thus in Jersey, to take a hypothetical instance, an Iron Age gold coin found on the surface of a ploughed field would appear to belong to the finder.

There are no other specific legal provisions for portable antiquities in the Bailiwick of Guernsey, other than those covering maritime finds as mentioned at the beginning of this chapter. Finds belong to landowners and museums negotiate with them over acquisition by donation or purchase. However, legislation such as The Ancient Monuments and Protected Buildings (Guernsey) Law 1967 does afford protection to 'all buildings, structures or objects registered in the Register of Ancient Monuments and Protected Buildings' (Sebire 2004). Although no objects are included on the current Register for Guernsey, the law seems to offer the possibility that archaeological finds could be included.

In Jersey there is also no legal provision for portable antiquities other than wreck (flotsam and jetsam) found on the beach washed up by the tide or in the sea so close to shore that it can 'be touched with the tip of a lance by a man on horseback', which belongs to the Crown. The Jersey Heritage Trust has recently made successful efforts to encourage the reporting and recording of finds, but as Nicolle (2001: 51) wryly comments, 'while it would be unlawful for the finder of a Bronze Age burial urn to export it, nothing would prevent him from drilling a hole in the bottom and using it as a flower pot'.

There are some restrictions on metal-detecting in Jersey. Searching on Crown property requires the consent of the Receiver General and on common land requires the consent of the Seigneur, while the use of detectors is prohibited on sites of special interest designated under the Island Planning (Jersey) Law 1964. Archaeological excavation requires consent from the Planning and Environment Committee.

EXPORT AND TRADE

Broadly speaking, no UK antiquity can be exported from the UK without a UK and/or a European Union (EU) licence (Brodie 2002; Cookson 2000; DCMS 2002d; Maurice and Turnor 1992; Palmer and Goyder 1992). Statutory regulation is provided by both UK and EU legislation. For export control the Isle of Man is treated as part of the UK, the Channel Islands as part of the EU. Objects that require an individual licence for export include 'archaeological material or any object more than fifty years old found in UK soil or its territorial waters, other than any object buried or concealed for less than fifty years' (DCMS 2002d). This applies irrespective of the value of the items, although there is a discretion under the relevant EU Regulation which means that licences are not required for objects of 'limited archaeological or scientific interest, e.g. common Roman coins' (DCMS 2002d). It is not clear how the latter applies in Jersey, where the Import and Export (Control) (Amendment No. 5) (Jersey) Order 1997 prohibits the export without a licence of any material of archaeological interest found within or relating to the Channel Islands (Nicolle 2001: 52).

Application must be made to the Export Licensing Unit at the Department for Culture, Media and Sport (DCMS) for an export licence for a British antiquity (for details see: www.culture.gov.uk/heritage). This applies wherever the item was originally discovered within the UK. The unit will refer the application to an Expert Adviser at the British Museum for scrutiny as to national importance. If there is no objection the licence is issued, but an objection may be lodged by the Expert Adviser with reference to the so-called Waverley criteria. These result from a committee (chaired by Viscount Waverley) that reported in 1952 on the export of works of art (HM Treasury 1952). The report proposed that three key questions must be asked with reference to any proposed export:

1. Is the object so closely associated with our history and national life that its departure would be a misfortune?
2. Is the object of outstanding aesthetic importance?
3. Is the object of outstanding significance for the study of some particular branch of art, learning or history?

An objection results in the application being passed to the independent, government-appointed Reviewing Committee on the Export of Works of Art. The applicant will be invited to attend a meeting of this committee, with the item to be exported, as will the Expert Adviser who has made the objection, and also three independent expert assessors. If the objection is overruled a licence is issued; if sustained then the recommendation to refuse the licence is passed to the Secretary of State for Culture, Media and Sport. The latter usually results in a deferral for up to six months, to give appropriate bodies the opportunity of raising funds to purchase the item at a fair market value in order to keep it in the UK. If no appropriate purchaser is forthcoming, the licence is issued. If there is a purchaser with the necessary funds the applicant is not obliged to accept the offer, but non-acceptance will leave the applicant in limbo without a licence.

The number of British antiquities that come before the Reviewing Committee is extremely small — only about six since 1995 (Brodie 2002; DCMS 2002e). In 2001–02 the committee dealt with only one archaeological case, a pair of Late Bronze Age gold hair rings which a dealer wished to take for sale at a cultural art fair in Switzerland. In this instance the export was halted and the objects purchased by the Ashmolean Museum, Oxford. A recent report by the Reviewing Committee commented that '[w]hile we have expressed surprise that so few archaeological artefacts . . . ever come before us, it is not clear to what extent, if at all, there are further breaches of the export licensing rules' (DCMS 2002e: 20).

One of the reasons the committee sees so few archaeological objects is that not all those referred to the Expert Adviser are judged to meet the fairly strict Waverley criteria, though the published data on this are hard to interpret, particularly since the figures include some items licensed for temporary export for exhibitions (DCMS 2002e: 82). The main (unspoken) reason, however, is that objects are probably bypassing the export control system altogether and are being illegally exported (see below). In those cases where a licence to export is granted, there is in theory the opportunity for experts to make a full examination and record of the object before it leaves the country; in reality there are insufficient checks or resources for this to happen (Brodie 2002).

In terms of the current working of the system, there is also some concern over the way that the unit at DCMS is dependent upon the British Museum as its source of Expert Advisers for all British antiquities. The unit relies on these advisers to consult in turn with appropriate institutions in other parts of the UK when relevant, rather than contacting them directly. This reliance, given that the Expert Advisers are expected to respond to DCMS within fifteen days, is not foolproof.

While legal export of British antiquities may be on a very small scale, there is a burgeoning trade in archaeological finds within the UK. It operates at many different levels, from the flint implements advertised for a few pounds in publications of *Exchange and Mart* type or on Internet sites, such as eBay, to an important Romano-British bronze statuette selling for thousands of pounds at a major auction house. Such trade has of course existed in various guises since at least Victorian times, but has inevitably grown, concomitant with the increase in metal-detecting, and a small-scale industry has developed to service this, including antiquities dealers operating through shops, stalls and websites (Brodie 2002: 200) and publications giving current valuations (e.g. Mills 1999; Murawski 2003; see also the adverts in the monthly detectorists' magazines *Treasure Hunting* and *The Searcher*). This trade is of course currently perfectly legal and is in some respects not to be entirely denigrated by archaeologists, since it does foster interest in antiquities and the development of expertise on archaeological finds, and plays a role in public education about the past.

There are equally many disadvantages to this trade. The focus is on the object per se, not on its provenance and associations (Tubb and Brodie 2001). Many finds made in England and Wales are bypassing the Portable Antiquities Reporting Scheme and going straight into the market, usually without any but the most general indications of their geographical origin, and this represents a huge loss of archaeological information. This aspect should not apply in Scotland and Northern Ireland, where all finds must be reported, but there is little to deter unscrupulous finders and dealers from transporting finds across internal UK borders and selling them in England or Wales with no, or falsified, provenances. Even the reverse of this can happen. Non-treasure objects found in England have been transported north and reported to the Scottish authorities as local finds, in the hope of receiving favourable ex gratia rewards through the more all-embracing Scottish Treasure Trove system.

The existence of an antiquities market also acts as a spur to the small criminal element among detector users to target Scheduled Ancient Monuments. In this case the provenance will obviously be falsified and the heritage value of such monuments accordingly diminished.

ILLICIT ANTIQUITIES

Any portable antiquities found in Northern Ireland and Scotland that are not reported are de facto illicit. In England and Wales this only applies to non-reported treasure, non-reported wreck, objects recovered from Scheduled Ancient Monuments without consent or objects recovered from land without the consent of the landowner, though there is ambiguity over the precise legal status of archaeological finds made without any landowner's authorisation from common land, beaches, parks and similar places (Palmer 1996).

It has always been difficult, for obvious reasons, to ascertain how much illegal recovery of, and handling and dealing in British antiquities goes on, but the extraordinary shenanigans over the Salisbury hoard of prehistoric artefacts did much to draw attention to the problem (Stead 1998). Other high-profile cases, such as the looting of the Wanborough Romano-British temple site (Hobbs 2003a: 142–4) and the export of the Icklingham bronzes and Snettisham bowl hoard (Hobbs 2003a: 137–42), are probably the tip of an iceberg, as suggested by the recent attack by nighthawks on the Iron Age hillfort of Yeavering Bell in Northumberland (*The Guardian*, 21 October 2002).

The increasing debate about illicit antiquities has mainly concentrated on international trade (Gill and Chippindale 2002), but with special relevance to the UK since it is dealers and auction houses in Britain, particularly in London, which have been pivotal to this market (Brodie *et al.* 2000; Renfrew 2000; Tubb 1995; Tubb and Brodie 2001). A turning point came with the ratification in 2002 by the UK government of the 1970 UNESCO Convention on the Means of Prohibiting and Preventing the Illicit Import, Export and Transfer of Ownership of Cultural Property (Clément 1995; DCMS 2004b; Redmond-Cooper and Palmer 1999; Renfrew 2000), which finally brings Britain into line with most other countries in this regard. A further step, accession to the 1995 UNIDROIT Convention on Stolen or Illegally Exported Cultural Objects (Gimbrère 1995; Redmond-Cooper and Palmer 1999; Renfrew 2000; Sidorsky 1996), has so far been resisted by the UK Government. In so doing it is supported by the majority opinion of its own Ministerial Advisory Panel on the Illicit Trade in Cultural Objects, established in 2000. The panel took this position partly because it promoted an alternative strategy of introducing a new criminal offence 'dishonestly to import, deal in or be in possession of any cultural object, knowing or believing that the object was stolen, or illegally excavated, or removed from any monument or wreck contrary to local law'.

There was an expectation that circumstances were favourable for inclusion of this offence in a new Criminal Justice Bill at the Westminster Parliament in 2001, but a situation arose whereby the bill was lost (DCMS 2002a). Pursuit of this objective to establish a new criminal offence remained a priority for the panel and was taken up by means of a Private Member's bill in the House of Commons. Richard Allan MP presented a Dealing in Cultural Objects (Offences) Bill (Gaimster 2003), to 'provide for an offence of acquiring, disposing of, importing or exporting tainted cultural objects, or agreeing to do so; and for connected purposes'. By an extraordinary set of circumstances, principally linked to the furore over the looting of antiquities in Iraq during the 2003 hostilities, the bill achieved strong government backing and all-party support and had a charmed passage through parliament, becoming law on 30 December 2003. However, the new Act does not apply in Scotland, and there is some concern that Scotland could thereby become a 'soft' country within the UK and Europe for illicit antiquities trading. Closing this loophole will require legislation in the Scottish Parliament.

Although the Dealing in Cultural Objects (Offences) Act 2003 is primarily aimed at curbing the illegal trading in Britain of illicit foreign antiquities by promoting due diligence in the trade, it will have implications for the existing provisions for British portable antiquities of all kinds, not least in the antiquities trade mentioned above (DCMS 2004c). It will also clarify the situation over the illegal status of any handling in England and Wales of Irish and Scottish antiquities that have not been fully processed through the prevailing regulations in those countries. Archaeologists from England or Wales (or elsewhere) undertaking fieldwork in Scotland and Ireland need to note that this will also apply to all excavated finds taken, even temporarily, out of either country.

The highly publicised conviction in the USA in 2002 of prominent antiquities dealer Frederick Schultz for conspiring to receive and possess antiquities stolen from Egypt

(*Archaeology*, May/June 2002: 7) sent a powerful message that the climate in this area was indeed changing, but there is still a very long way to go before effective policing of what is now a truly global problem can be achieved.

CONCLUSION

There was a considerable heightening of expectations that the UK Government's ratification in 2002 of the European Convention on the Protection of the Archaeological Heritage (Revised), otherwise known as the Malta or Valletta Convention, would have benefits in the area of portable antiquities. Specifically, Article 2.iii. of the convention requires 'the mandatory reporting to the competent authorities by a finder of the chance discovery of elements of the archaeological heritage and making them available for examination'. Although this would in theory require little change to the situation in Northern Ireland and Scotland, in England and Wales it would be revolutionary and would give the Portable Antiquities Reporting Scheme the teeth it currently lacks. However, buried in the commentary attached to the convention is a 'let-out' clause: '[a] State . . . may only require mandatory reporting of finds of precious materials or on already listed sites'. Thus the convention may in the UK disappointingly be used to support the status quo, whereas in some other European countries, as in Denmark and The Netherlands, the Valletta Convention has been an inspiration for new policy and legislation (Hvass 2001: 11; Lauwerier and Lotte 2002; www.archis.nl).

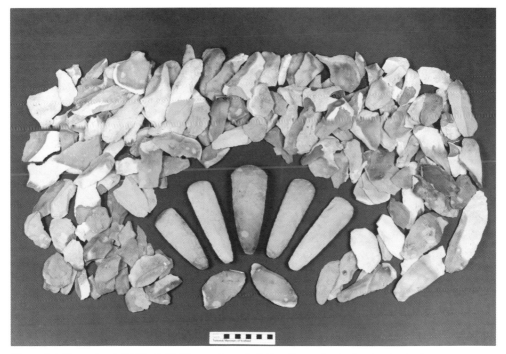

Figure 6.4. The cache of 178 Neolithic flint artefacts, including five axeheads, found at Auchenhoan, near Campbeltown in south-west Scotland in 1989. These artefacts were claimed under the Scottish Treasure Trove system. (*Photo © Trustees of the National Museums of Scotland*)

Nevertheless, so much has changed over the last decade that there must be hopes for further improvements in the next. The Dealing in Cultural Objects (Offences) Act represents an enormous step forward. Whether there will be success in persuading the public at large that the collecting and non-reporting of antiquities is as socially unacceptable as collecting birds' eggs remains to be seen (Renfrew 2000).

Meanwhile, there is a need for continuing UK-wide deliberation over many of the issues surrounding archaeological finds. Apart from anything else, there is no standard definition of what actually constitutes a portable antiquity: how large can an antiquity be and still be portable? And how old does an object have to be to be classifiable as an antiquity? It will be apparent, looked at dispassionately, that the UK arrangements are diverse, in some respects arguably to the point of perversity. To take the example of the exceptional Auchenhoan cache of Neolithic flint artefacts found in 1989 near Campbeltown in Argyll (Saville 1999), if this important prehistoric discovery had been made anywhere else in the UK there is no guarantee it would have become part of the preserved national heritage. There is a parallel lesson here from best practice in other parts of Europe, for example Finland and Sweden, where, as in Scotland, landowners do not have title to antiquities discovered on their land (Adlercreutz 1998; National Board of Antiquities n.d.). Many years ago Sir George Hill doubted that England would ever adopt the Scottish interpretation of Treasure Trove (Hill 1930), and harmonisation of the various UK systems is still unlikely and perhaps not wholly desirable, but surely an accommodation to allow for the automatic public acquisition of all important archaeological finds is a worthwhile goal?

A final thought concerns those British antiquities, whether of precious metal or otherwise, that have been in private hands for generations and are beyond any practical application of antiquities legislation. Could the MLA promote the use of the Acceptance in Lieu of Inheritance Taxation system administered by the Inland Revenue Capital Taxes Office in order to acquire these for the nation?

ACKNOWLEDGEMENTS

I am indebted to Ian Longworth for the lead provided by his original version of this chapter (Longworth 1993). Help with relevant information was kindly provided by Allison Fox and Andrew Foxon (Isle of Man), Heather Sebire (Guernsey), Olga Finch (Jersey), Declan Hurl, Sinéad McCartan, and Richard Warner (Northern Ireland), Kathy Perrin (EH), Alex Hunt (fomerly CBA), Roger Bland (British Museum) and Leena Söyrinki-Harmo (Helsinki), though the author alone is responsible for any errors.

CHAPTER 7

THE MANAGEMENT OF ARCHAEOLOGY UNDERWATER

Antony Firth

INTRODUCTION

In the decade since the first edition of this book, little may seem to have changed in the management of archaeology underwater in the UK. The control of a relatively few historic wrecks by statutory means – and the effort to reconcile protection and ownership – still take central place in management frameworks. As anticipated, procedures associated with development control and planning are generating some notable progress but, ten years on, these are still early days. For those seeking improved management in archaeology underwater, the 1990s were characterised by high expectations, repeatedly deferred.

Looking back to the 1993 version of this chapter, the amount of change that has occurred is, however, striking. One of the most important changes – the transfer of responsibility for marine archaeology in England to English Heritage (EH) – is recent, but this should not be allowed to overshadow numerous other improvements. While accepting that many of the changes have yet to take full effect – hence the lack of apparent change noted at the outset – the management of archaeology underwater today is sufficiently different from 1993 to warrant a wholesale rewrite.

As noted in 1993, archaeological material in inland waters such as rivers and lakes is subject to the same management frameworks as archaeological material on land (cf. Williams 1995). Notwithstanding this equality, archaeology under inland waters in the UK is rarely subject to any form of management. At the risk of colluding in the continued oversight of archaeology under inland waters, this chapter will concentrate on those environments where the management frameworks are different, that is, on archaeology under coastal and marine waters.

This chapter will describe the principal frameworks for protecting sites, reporting discoveries and determining ownership as they stand at present before turning to the frameworks emerging in development control (cf. Dromgoole 1999b). Reference will be made also to marine monument records, to the international context of managing archaeology underwater, and to other structures, initiatives and directions having a bearing on the management of archaeology underwater in the UK.

PROTECTING SITES

Designated wrecks

The principal means of protecting wreck sites in UK waters is – with the exception of some use of scheduling in Scotland (below) – the Protection of Wrecks Act 1973 (PW Act 1973). Protection comprises the designation of an area in which certain activities are restricted. In order to be designated, the appropriate Secretary of State or Minister must be satisfied that the site is or may prove to be that of a vessel lying wrecked on or in the seabed, and that the site ought to be protected from interference on account of the importance of the vessel or of associated objects. The scope of importance is set out as 'historical, archaeological or artistic'; there is no reference to 'national importance' (cf. Chapter 5). As protection is given effect through designating an area, the position of the wreck must be known, but the name, origin and ownership of the wreck need not.

An offence is committed in a restricted area by any person who does, causes or permits any of the following things, otherwise than under the authority of a licence: tampering with, damaging or removing any part of the vessel, or any object formerly contained in such a vessel; diving or salvage operations, or the use of diving or salvage equipment; deposition of anything that may obliterate, obstruct or damage any part of the wreck (Section 1(3)).

The history of implementing the PW Act 1973 is essential to understanding what sites have been protected using this mechanism, and how (Firth 1999, 2002). Further, as implementation of the PW Act 1973 has been a central (sometimes the only) plank in managing archaeology underwater in the UK, the history of its administration is largely synonymous with the history of official responsibility for archaeology underwater over the past thirty years. It is, therefore, worth consideration.

The power to designate sites and to license activity rests with the Secretary of State. Until 1992, the powers were exercised by the Secretary of State for Trade/Transport, advised variously by the Board of Trade/Department of Transport. Consequently, implementation of the PW Act 1973 was kept separate from the management of archaeology on land, and was carried out UK-wide. A degree of archaeological advice was provided through the Advisory Committee on Historic Wreck Sites (ACHWS), though ACHWS was intended to represent non-archaeological interests also. From 1986, the Department also had available the services of an archaeological diving contractor (the Archaeological Diving Unit (ADU)).

In 1992 implementation of the PW Act 1973 was transferred to the Secretary of State for National Heritage within the Department for National Heritage (DNH). DNH, being an offshoot of the Department of the Environment, was an England-only department, and the move was accompanied by transfers of responsibility to the Secretaries of State for Scotland, for Wales, and for the Environment (Northern Ireland). The latter, and their respective offices, were advised by the heritage services that they sponsor, namely Historic Scotland (HS), CADW, and the Environment and Heritage Service (EHS) (formerly the Historic Monuments and Buildings Branch of DoE(NI)). This had the effect in these countries of bringing the management of archaeology underwater into administrative contact with the management of archaeology on land. In England, however, the equivalent heritage service – EH – did not become involved. Consequently, the Secretary of State was advised only by the Department, supported as before by ACHWS and the ADU. In England, therefore, management of archaeology underwater remained at a considerable distance from the management of archaeology on land.

Further changes occurred following the reorganisation of government in 1997, with DNH being renamed the Department for Culture, Media and Sport (DCMS), and devolution resulting in statutory powers being exercised by the Scottish Assembly and its equivalents rather than by Secretaries of State. However, the PW Act 1973 continued to be implemented on the advice of heritage services in Scotland, Wales and Northern Ireland, and by DCMS in England.

One of the reasons that EH did not become involved in implementing the PW Act 1973 was that the statute through which EH was constituted – the National Heritage Act 1983 – was worded in such a way that EH had no powers beyond low-water mark. Although a transfer of responsibilities from DNH/DCMS to EH was accepted in principle by the mid-1990s, the necessary legal changes did not succeed until the National Heritage Act 2002.

Figure 7.1. An underwater archaeologist prepares to dive. Under the terms of the 1973 Act, archaeological work on a designated wreck is prohibited without the authority of a licence. *Photo: Wessex Archaeology*

The NHA 2002 extended EH's powers to the limit of territorial waters, paving the way for DCMS's responsibilities to be transferred. In anticipation of the transfer, EH published *Taking to the Water: English Heritage's Initial Policy for the Management of Maritime Archaeology in England* (Roberts and Trow 2002).

The situation in 2005 is, therefore, that the powers to designate areas and license activities under the PW Act 1973 are exercised on the advice of EH, HS, CADW and EHS (NI). Details of implementation vary from country to country, but the services seek to coordinate their advice through joint meetings. The four services continue to be advised by ACHWS and by an archaeological diving contractor.

It should be noted that one effect of transferring administration of the PW Act 1973 to national heritage agencies is that recourse is now available to a wider range of management tools than a single statutory mechanism. Hence in Scotland, Wales and Northern Ireland the scope of managing archaeology underwater has broadened over the past decade (e.g. HS 1999), and a similar broadening is now occurring in England.

Scheduled monuments

The Ancient Monuments and Archaeological Areas Act 1979 can be used to schedule monuments within territorial waters, largely in the same way as provided for in respect of monuments on land. The definition of 'monument' includes 'vessels'. HS has led the way in using the AMAA Act 1979 in archaeology underwater in scheduling the remains of the scuttled German High Seas Fleet in Scapa Flow, Orkney (Oxley 2002). Although scheduling has been used in England to protect sites such as the Anglo-Saxon fish weirs off the Essex coast, its current policy is to rely on the PW Act 1973 to protect wreck sites. In Wales, coastal sites have been scheduled, but no wrecks.

In Northern Ireland, monuments – including vessels and aircraft – in territorial waters can be scheduled under Section 38 of the Historic Monuments and Archaeological Objects (Northern Ireland) Order 1995 (HMAO 1995). Intertidal and marine sites have been scheduled in this way in Strangford Lough (Williams 2002). As in England and Wales, only the PW Act 1973 has been used to protect wreck sites in Northern Ireland.

Protected places and controlled sites

It is worth noting that archaeological sites under coastal and marine waters may be subject to other, principally non-archaeological, forms of protection. For example, sites within areas protected for marine conservation purposes are likely to benefit incidentally. More direct protection might arise as a result of application of the Protection of Military Remains Act 1986 (PMR Act 1986), insofar as some sites of archaeological interest might also qualify as military remains (Dromgoole 1996). The PMR Act 1986 provides for two forms of site protection applicable to shipwrecks. Vessels lost while in military service on or after 4 August 1914 can become 'protected places' by being designated; and a place that comprises the remains of a vessel lost within the last 200 years can be designated as a 'controlled site'. Importantly, a vessel can become a protected place even if its location on the seabed is not known – that is, it is possible to protect vessels by name, even if their remains have not yet been found. Also, provision is made for protected places and controlled sites to apply beyond UK territorial waters, though such application is restricted in order to comply with international law. The offences applicable to protected places include damaging, unearthing or entering the vessel. If the wreck is a controlled site, it is also an offence to carry out any excavation or diving or salvage operation; diving in a protected place is only prohibited if it is being carried out for the purpose of doing something that would constitute an offence (such as damaging, unearthing, entering, etc.). Licences to carry out activities that are otherwise prohibited can be granted by the Secretary of State. Although this was introduced in the mid-1980s, no designations were made under the PMR Act 1986 until recently. However, following public consultation in 2001, the MoD set in motion the designation of sixteen controlled sites and five protected places. The MoD also added 'historical significance' to the criteria it would use in considering designations under the PMR Act 1986, and made a commitment to a 'rolling programme of identification and assessment' of all other vessels in military service for possible designation as protected places (MoD 2001a).

The PMR Act 1986 also applies to aircraft, but in a different way. In contrast to shipwrecks, which are only protected if they have been subject to a specific designation, the PMR Act 1986 regards *any* aircraft that has crashed in military service as being a protected place. Hence, the offences outlined above in respect of designated vessels that are protected places (for example, damaging, unearthing, entering) apply automatically in respect of military aircraft. Aircraft wrecks can also be designated as controlled sites, with the effect of prohibiting unlicensed diving or excavation. The provisions of the PMR Act

1986 in respect of aircraft, including aircraft wrecked on the seabed, are administered by the RAF Personnel Management Agency (MoD 2001b). Growing recognition of the historical and archaeological importance of wrecked aircraft – including submerged sites – has prompted EH to issue guidance on the subject (EH 2002b).

CONTROLLED ACTIVITIES

Under ancient monuments legislation there are specific offences in respect of the use of metal detectors/detecting devices. Such provisions would apply in territorial waters, and are likely to encompass not only 'conventional' metal detectors deployed by divers, for example, but also surface-towed instruments such as magnetometers. However, these restrictions apply only to sites that have been specifically protected, either by being scheduled, or by being under the ownership or guardianship of national or local authorities (Ancient Monuments and Archaeological Areas Act (AMAA Act) 1979 Section 42; for Northern Ireland HMAO 1995 Section 29).

There are some instances in the UK where archaeological activities outside specifically protected sites are also controlled. For example, in Northern Ireland the activity of searching for archaeological objects is restricted (HMAO 1995 Section 41). It is an offence to excavate in or under the land for the purposes of searching generally for archaeological objects, or for exposing or examining a particular structure or thing. Such excavation can only take place under the authority of a licence granted by the Department of the Environment (NI).

Throughout the UK and UK waters it is an offence to excavate for the purpose of discovering whether any place comprises any remains of an aircraft or vessel lost in military service, except in accordance with a licence issued by the Secretary of State (PMRA 1986 Section 2 (3)(c)).

It should also be noted that archaeological activities on the seabed are also subject to non-archaeological controls applicable to all marine works. Hence a licence may be required from the owner of the seabed, and consent may be required under local and/or national regulations relating to navigation, coast protection, marine environmental protection and so on (see Marine Consents, below).

REPORTING

Wreck

Other than the PW Act 1973, the main statute relevant to managing archaeology underwater into the 1990s was the Merchant Shipping Act. The 1894 version, referred to in the first edition, was revised and consolidated as the Merchant Shipping Act 1995. The MS Act is of interest to archaeologists because it places a legal obligation on people who find wreck (including wreck of archaeological interest) to report their finds to the authorities. This obligation is not archaeological in its intent (rather, reporting is but an early stage in returning finds to their original owner, see below), but it has been seized upon as a usable proxy in the absence of a general obligation in the UK to report archaeological discoveries.

Legally, wreck comprises material that has been lost or jettisoned from a boat, ship or aircraft ((Dromgoole 1999a). Any person who finds wreck in tidal waters is obliged to notify the Receiver of Wreck (an official of the Maritime and Coastguard Agency (MCA)). The obligation to notify the Receiver also applies to people who find wreck outside the limits of the UK, but bring it within these. Reports that are of historical or archaeological interest – which form a relatively small proportion of the whole – are passed on to the relevant heritage service in each home country. Although notifying the Receiver was obligatory, it would be fair to say that until the 1990s compliance was limited. In the last decade, a great deal of effort has been put into informing the public of the obligation, and the number of reports made has increased. In an attempt to draw a line under a history of chronic under-reporting (and, consequently, a backlog of illegally held wreck), the MCA instituted a three-month wreck amnesty in January 2001. The amnesty resulted in 4,616 reports referring to approximately 30,000 individual items, mostly by recreational divers. While many of the reports related to more recent material, 840 reports were considered as 'historic' (material over 100 years old) (Maritime and Coastguard Agency n.d.).

Following its efforts in informing the public of their obligations, and the Wreck Amnesty for past infractions, the MCA has stepped up its enforcement actions. Consequently, the obligation to report wreck might be expected to continue to develop as a source of information about archaeological discoveries at sea.

It should be noted that munitions – including guns and ammunition – found at sea are subject to the Firearms Act 1968 as well as being wreck for the purposes of the MS Act 1995.

Treasure

The Treasure Act 1996 applies to objects found along tidal rivers and on the foreshore (that is, low water) if they qualify as 'treasure' (Department of National Heritage 1997: 7) and are not 'wreck' as defined by the MS Act 1995. The management of 'treasure' and other portable antiquities is discussed in Chapter 6. In Scotland, the law of treasure trove and *bona vacantia* apply to inland and some marine waters (see JNAPC *et al.* n.d.).

Non-statutory reporting

The MS Act 1995 applies only to material that is wreck, and the Treasure Act 1996 applies only to treasure found above mean low water. Other forms of material – including items that have eroded from the shore, or that were deposited on land but have since been submerged by sea-level rise – are neither wreck nor treasure. Clearly, many forms of archaeological material, such as prehistoric remains associated with former land surfaces or other submerged deposits, fall outside the established frameworks. There is no statutory mechanism to encourage or enforce the reporting of archaeological material found in or near the sea that is neither wreck nor treasure. In the absence of such provision, the Receiver of Wreck does pass on to the NMR information about non-wreck material that is inadvertently reported under the MS Act 1995, and in England and Wales Finds Liaison Officers (Chapter 6) record material from in or near the sea that is reported to them.

Some non-statutory schemes have been introduced to encourage the reporting of archaeological material, principally by facilitating understanding of and access to statutory schemes. One example is the Dorset ship timbers scheme (Dorset Coast Forum 2002). Equally, reporting protocols have been introduced in connection with a number of marine developments, supported by conditions on development consent. Such protocols require developers to report any chance discoveries in the course of dredging, for example, to a nominated archaeologist who will provide advice and liaise with archaeological curators and the Receiver of Wreck as required. This kind of approach is being promoted industry-wide in the case of marine aggregates, where the British Marine Aggregate Producers Association (BMAPA) is collaborating with EH in preparing a reporting system that will apply to all its members, as well as to individual aggregate licences through conditions on consent.

OWNERSHIP

Ownership of wreck

In UK law, ownership of material lost at sea resides in its original owners or their successors, unless it can be shown that abandonment has occurred. There is no provision to assume abandonment after any set period. In contrast to the arrangements in some countries, the Crown does not claim ownership of archaeological remains by virtue of their antiquity or public interest. The Crown does, however, claim ownership of wreck from UK territorial waters that is salvaged and reported (see above), but that remains unclaimed after one year, through the MS Act 1995. This mechanism is used to ensure good title on the disposal of wreck, rather than to benefit the Crown. Ownership is generally passed to the finder of historic wreck in lieu of a salvage award.

The MS Act 1995 only comes into play where wreck is salvaged, hence it has no bearing on the ownership of wreck while it remains on the seabed. Claims to ownership by virtue of simply discovering a site are generally unfounded.

Numerous wrecks still have current owners, because either ownership resides in the Crown (for example, wrecks of Royal Navy ships), or rights of ownership have been acquired by successive individuals or organisations such as insurance companies. Such rights are not restricted to UK citizens: foreign governments have claimed ownership of wrecks of archaeological interest. The Netherlands is a prominent example, maintaining claims of ownership to wrecks of Dutch East India Company vessels.

Rights of salvors

One area that continues to be contentious is the rights of salvors to wreck that they are in the process of removing. As noted above, the MS Act 1995 only comes into effect once wreck has been recovered, at which point salvors have a statutory entitlement to a salvage award. The rights of salvors in respect of material that is still on the seabed is governed by the common-law concept of 'salvor in possession' (Fletcher-Tomenius et al. 2000). In salvage law in general, salvors do not own wreck that they recover, but they have a link (lien) to the property that allows them to possess it until the owner provides an appropriate reward. In order to address the circumstance where two or more salvors are competing to salvage wreck, common law provides that the salvor 'in possession' has the predominant right. While this concept has its origins in salvors' efforts to save wrecks that are still afloat, it has been transferred to wrecks that have sunk, and subsequently to wrecks that are so long sunk that they are of archaeological interest. Leaving aside the question as to whether wrecks of archaeological interest are still 'in danger' and therefore capable of being salvaged, the net effect is that salvors who can establish that they are in possession can seek the support of the law in protecting their rights by excluding other would-be salvors (by, for example, injunction). Moreover, human rights law provides some support to the rights of a salvor in possession against the infringement of those rights by, for example, the application of statutory protection. Hence in the last decade legal conflicts have arisen where salvors claiming possession have challenged designation of 'their' sites under the PW Act 1973 (Fletcher-Tomenius et al. 2000).

Ownership of non-wreck material

As indicated above, wreck does not encompass all forms of archaeological material found at or near the sea. In particular, prehistoric material originating in terrestrial contexts but which is now submerged will not constitute wreck and is not subject to the MS Act 1995, to the law of wreck in general, or to salvage law. Such material is likely to be governed by the more general rules of ownership applicable in the UK, whereby objects of archaeological interest found in the soil in England and Wales belong to the owner of the land. In general terms and except where granted otherwise, the foreshore and the seabed of tidal rivers and estuaries is owned by the Crown and the Crown claims ownership of the seabed in UK territorial waters (Howarth 1992). The Crown Estate administers the Crown's ownership. Rights to the natural resources of the seabed and subsoil of the Continental Shelf are also vested in the Crown; while such rights would encompass the matrix within which archaeological objects are found, they may not include the archaeological objects themselves as they are not natural resources.

DEVELOPMENT CONTROL

Overview

Planning law, which provides a framework that is generally familiar to UK archaeologists, does not apply to most marine developments. Planning law is implemented by local development authorities, corresponding to local authorities. The boundary of the local authority usually coincides with the boundaries of the parishes of which it is formed, and these, at the coastal margin, normally correspond to mean low-water mark. Some local authorities do extend beyond low water, particularly in relatively enclosed estuaries or where other historical reasons apply. However, it is argued that, even in such cases, planning authority (as opposed to other responsibilities of the local authority generally) only extends as far as low water. The degree to which planning control – and, therefore, the policies set out in PPG 16: *Archaeology and Planning* (DoE 1990a) and its equivalents – can be exerted beyond low water is, therefore, circumscribed.

There are, however, a number of avenues through which a degree of archaeological management can be applied beyond low water through planning. For example, PPG 20: *Coastal Planning* (DoE and Welsh Office 1992) notes that 'the coastal zone also has a rich heritage both above and below low-water mark' (para. 2.8) and numerous development plans and related coastal plans include policies for coastal archaeology (Firth 1995). Planning permission may be sought for developments that have extents that straddle the low-water mark, in which case the local authority might reasonably expect archaeological requirements to address the entire scheme. Further, local authorities might be consulted by the relevant government department in the course of processing the other forms of consent for marine development (see below), in which case the local authority might expect its views to be taken into account.

Although the direct application of PPG 16 to marine archaeology is restricted to mean low water by the boundaries of planning authority, EH and RCHME have stated that 'the principles set out in *Planning Policy Guidance Note 16: Archaeology and Planning* should be applied to the treatment of sub-tidal archaeological remains in order to secure best practice' (EH/RCHME 1996).

Marine consents

Rather than being regulated by a single regime applicable to most forms of development as on land, marine development is subject to a series of specific activity-based consent schemes. The scope of marine consent schemes often overlap with each other, as well as overlapping with planning if the development footprint includes land above low-water mark. As a result, multiple consents are frequently required, to the confusion and frustration of developers and regulators alike. Consequently, the regulation of marine and coastal development is currently under review. For the time being, however, some of the principal consent schemes applicable to marine development are as follows:

Consent Scheme	Application
Food and Environment Protection Act 1985	Deposit of articles or materials in the sea
Coast Protection Act 1949	Construction, deposit and removal of materials
Local harbour acts under Harbours Act 1964	Harbour dredging and construction
Government View procedure	Marine aggregate extraction
Petroleum Act 1998	Oil and gas exploration, production and pipelines
Electricity Act 1989	Offshore renewables
Telecommunications Act 1984	Subsea cables
Transport and Works Act 1992	Major works

Some effort is being made administratively to overcome confusion and duplication, including the establishment of an integrated Marine Consents and Environment Unit. Also, most of the marine consent schemes include a requirement in common, which is for applications for major schemes to be accompanied by an Environmental Statement (see below). There are increasing signs that, whatever the system, the regulating authority will take archaeological advice from the relevant government advisor (for example, EH, CADW, HS, EHS).

Environmental assessment

The consent schemes referred to above generally require applications for major developments (that is, most marine developments) to be accompanied by an Environmental Statement (ES), which requires assessment of cultural heritage. While questions can be raised about the adequacy with which cultural heritage has been addressed in many marine Environmental Statements in the past, proper consideration is becoming more common, and marine Environmental Statements are increasingly subject to archaeological scrutiny.

A number of marine industries have also embarked on regional or strategic environmental assessments to address, in particular, the cumulative effects of anticipated development. As with scheme-specific Environmental Statements, the attention to archaeology is variable but improving.

Codes of practice

In the absence of direct archaeological control and clear curatorial advice, some constraints have been accepted voluntarily by industry. A prime example is the Joint Nautical Archaeology Policy Committee (JNAPC) Code of Practice for Seabed Developers (JNAPC 1998), to which developers are encouraged to subscribe. This approach has been further developed in the marine aggregate industry. The British Marine Aggregate Producers Association (BMAPA) has collaborated with EH to produce a guidance note on marine aggregate dredging and the historic environment, to advise developers, curators and archaeological contractors/consultants on best practice (BMAPA/EH 2003).

MARINE ARCHAEOLOGICAL RECORDS

The RCAHMS and the RCAHMW are obliged to maintain records of monuments to the limits of territorial waters by virtue of their Royal Warrants. The former RCHME was similarly obliged under its Royal Warrant, but this responsibility became incorporated within EH's statutory responsibilities following the NHA 2002, which enabled the full merger of RCHME and EH. In Northern Ireland, the EHS maintains a Monuments and Buildings Record, which includes a Maritime Record. The record of sites in territorial waters adjacent to Northern Ireland is being upgraded by the Maritime Research Unit at the University of Ulster at Coleraine.

At a local level, some local authorities have Sites and Monuments Records (SMRs) that encompass marine sites. The scope for marine SMRs is doubly limited, however, by the lack of statutory support for SMRs in general, and by the general limit of local planning powers – with which SMRs are strongly associated – to low water. Nonetheless, the role of local authorities as consultees in many marine consent and Environmental Assessment procedures is such that a reasoned case can be made for such authorities to have access to marine archaeological data through SMRs. The case for SMRs having a marine component appears to have been supported by national agencies throughout the UK, insofar as coastal SMR enhancement exercises have been widely funded. Overall, the further development of SMRs into Historic Environment Records seems likely to result in local records that transcend a terrestrial–marine divide, at least to the limit of territorial waters.

Beyond the 12-mile limit, provision for marine archaeological records is less certain. Although the UK government regulates activities, and consent procedures require applicants to consider the effects of their activities on the cultural heritage, there appears to be no provision for government – local or national – to collate or make available archaeological data. It is therefore unclear as to what information the regulators will use in determining whether an application is acceptable.

LOCAL GOVERNMENT AND ARCHAEOLOGY UNDERWATER

The difficulties facing local authorities in extending their pivotal role in archaeological resource management on land to achaeology underwater have already been raised in respect of planning and SMRs. Nonetheless, some local government archaeology services have been playing a major role in underwater archaeology for at least a decade, and such involvement seems set to increase. Direct support for archaeological projects with a coastal or marine aspect, including new surveys more or less related to SMR enhancement, have facilitated both more informed heritage management and greatly increased public awareness. Of particular note is the role of local authorities in initiating or otherwise supporting coastal archaeological fora, often linked to other coastal fora. The influence of coastal archaeological fora within these broader coastal networks can be seen in the inclusion of archaeological objectives within coastal plans, as well as in the increasing general awareness and consideration of archaeological issues among other marine users and regulators.

HEALTH AND SAFETY

Turning briefly to frameworks applicable to managing archaeological fieldwork as reported in the first edition, the *Diving Operations at Work Regulations 1981* were reviewed and replaced by the *Diving at Work Regulations 1997*, the implementation of which is subject to several Approved Codes of Practice (ACOPs). One ACOP applies to *Scientific and Archaeological Diving Projects* and is particularly suited to research- and training-led investigations, while archaeological fieldwork in development-led contexts may be more appropriately guided by the *Commercial Diving Projects Inland/Inshore* ACOP. The *Diving at Work Regulations* are administered by the Health and Safety

Executive, from which further information can be obtained. Diving Operations in Northern Ireland are subject to the *Diving Operations at Work Regulations (NI) 1994*.

Additionally, archaeologists need to be aware that any boats used in the course of archaeological fieldwork – to access intertidal areas, for example – will be subject to codes on workboats implemented by the Marine and Coastguard Agency.

Use of marine VHF radio is subject to licence under the Wireless Telegraphy Act 1949, administered by the Radiocommunications Agency.

INTERNATIONAL CONTEXT

While underwater archaeology was subject to specific rules of international law at the time of the first edition, their effect on archaeological resource management in the UK was limited and the prospects for the global community to see eye-to-eye with itself on the subject appeared – on the basis of past examples – slim. The changes that have occurred in the last decade are, therefore, remarkable, even if the implications are unclear.

The United Nations Convention on the Law of the Sea (UNCLOS)

The United Nations Convention on the Law of the Sea 1982 (commonly known as UNCLOS, and which arose – confusingly – from the Third United Nations Conference on the Law of the Sea, known as UNCLOS III) contains two provisions specifically about archaeology. Article 303 is of general application and places a duty on states to protect objects of an archaeological and historical nature found at sea, and allows them to exert a measure of control out to a distance of 24 nautical miles. Article 149 applies only to such objects found in the 'Area', which is the seabed beyond the territorial jurisdiction of states (i.e. beyond all continental shelves). Without going into detail, it would be fair to say that the provision for archaeology in UNCLOS is desperately lacking in clarity, consistency and effect. It is important, however, because notwithstanding the lack of support for UNCLOS at the time it was signed by states such as the UK, its provisions are now regarded by states such as the UK as being inviolate; i.e. any subsequent law must accord fully with UNCLOS, irrespective of its failings.

ICOMOS (International Council on Museums and Sites) Charter

In the early 1990s, a fresh initiative to improve international law in respect of archaeology at sea gathered pace, in the form of the Draft Convention on the Protection of Underwater Cultural Heritage (O'Keefe and Nafziger 1994). The draft convention put forward both a mechanism for enforcing a standard of archaeological investigation, and also the standard itself, set out in a charter to be appended to the convention. Past lack of success with international conventions prompted a two-track approach, whereby the charter was advanced as a document in its own right, becoming the ICOMOS *Charter on the Protection and Management of Underwater Cultural Heritage* (also known as the Sofia Charter), *1996* (see ICOMOS 1998). The charter includes a series of statements regarding best practice, intending 'to ensure that all investigations are explicit in their aims, methodology and anticipated results so that the intention of each project is transparent to all'.

UNESCO Convention

In the meantime, UNESCO took up the draft convention, organising a series of meetings which resulted – perhaps to some surprise – in sufficient agreement to give life to the UNESCO *Convention on the Protection of the Underwater Cultural Heritage, 2001.*

Many of the basic mechnisms of the draft convention of 1994 survived the wrangling, as did an 'Annex' based heavily on the Sofia Charter (O'Keefe 2002). The UK abstained in the vote on the final draft of the convention, but it has stated that it supports most of the articles, particularly the provisions in the annex (FCO 2001).

The Valletta Convention

In another fairly surprising move, the UK ratified the *European Convention on the Protection of the Archaeological Heritage (Revised), 1992*, known as the Valletta Convention. The implications for terrestrial archaeology in the UK are considerable. As the Valletta Convention applies to all areas within the jurisdiction of States Parties, including sea areas, then UK marine archaeology is implicated equally, but with added complications (see JNAPC 2003).

CONCLUDING REMARKS

The 1993 edition of this chapter concluded with a section entitled 'Change in the Management of Archaeology Underwater', and as this edition has demonstrated, change has indeed occurred. Looking forward, even greater changes may happen over the next decade. DCMS, in collaboration with the Welsh Assembly Government, the Scottish Executive and the Department of the Environment (Northern Ireland), has published a consultation paper on changes to marine heritage protection to accompany its equivalent consultation on terrestrial heritage protection (DCMS 2004d). Integration of marine and terrestrial protection mechanisms is being suggested, and legislation to this effect may be proposed. As noted above, the complexity and duplication of marine consent procedures are attracting attention, and the reform of the terrestrial planning system may result in changes that have implications for how archaeology is treated in major developments affecting both land and sea, such as ports. While the effects of the emerging body of international law may be slow to make themselves apparent in UK domestic management, European Directives on Strategic Environmental Assessment (2001/42/EC) and Water Frameworks (2000/60/EC), and a Recommendation on Integrated Coastal Zone Management (2002/413/EC), could have more immediate implications.

While the management of UK marine archaeology may have appeared to be in the doldrums over the last decade, even a brief look below the surface shows that strong currents have caused a fair amount of movement. We now find ourselves entering blustery latitudes. There is movement everywhere, but what progress can be made, and on what course, remains to be seen.

CHAPTER 8

HISTORIC BUILDINGS

Jason Wood

INTRODUCTION

The UK's built heritage includes historic buildings of many sizes, periods and types, ranging from the humblest barn to the grandest palace. These historic buildings are a major source of archaeological and historical information, but they also represent a finite and irreplaceable resource. Many historic buildings are therefore protected by listing because of their special architectural or historic interest. Listed Buildings are classified in grades to denote their relative importance (Grades I, II* and II in England and Wales; Grades A, B, B (Group) and C (Statutory) in Scotland; Grades A, B+, B1 and B2 in Northern Ireland). There are currently over 370,000 Listed Building entries in England covering an estimated 500,000 individual properties or items; over 27,000 in Wales; over 44,000 in Scotland; and over 8,500 in Northern Ireland. The majority of Listed Buildings are classed under the lower grades. For instance, Grade II buildings currently represent almost 92 per cent of Listed Buildings in England.

Broadly speaking, the older a building is the more likely it is to be listed. All buildings erected before 1700 that survive in anything like their original form are listed, as are most buildings erected between 1700 and 1840, although some selection is applied. After about 1840, because many more buildings have survived, greater selection is made. Buildings less than thirty years old are normally listed only if they are of outstanding quality and under threat.

In England and Wales the current principal legislation is the Planning (Listed Buildings and Conservation Areas) Act 1990; in Scotland the equivalent Act is the Planning (Listed Buildings and Conservation Areas) (Scotland) Act 1997; and in Northern Ireland the Planning (Northern Ireland) Order 1991. These Acts and Orders are supplemented by various government guidance including, in England, *Planning Policy Guidance* (PPG) *15: Planning and the Historic Environment* (DoE and DNH 1994);[1] in Wales, *Circulars 61/96* and *1/98 Planning and the Historic Environment* (Welsh Office 1996; 1998); in Scotland, the *Memorandum of Guidance on Listed Buildings and Conservation Areas* (HS 1998) and *National Planning Policy Guideline 18: Planning and the Historic Environment* (Scottish Executive 1999c); and in Northern Ireland, *Planning Policy Statement 6: Planning, Archaeology and Built Heritage* (DoE (NI) 1999). This national advice is supported by policies relating to historic buildings and development set out in various Structure Plans and Local Plans across the UK.[2]

The main purpose of listing is to ensure that buildings are not altered, extended or demolished before full consideration has been given to such proposals. Listing a building does not prohibit change. Instead, it seeks to influence the way in which change happens by requiring the owner or developer to apply to their Local Planning Authority (LPA) for Listed Building Consent (LBC) for works which would affect the building's character.[3] The majority of buildings are not listed, but many still make a significant contribution to the character of the UK's regions and the local scene. The impact of development proposals on these regionally and locally important historic buildings also warrants due consideration through the planning process. Some LPAs treat such buildings as 'locally listed' and make provision in their Local Plans for special consideration to be given to their protection. However, at present there is no power for LPAs to prevent demolition of a locally Listed Building unless it is in a Conservation Area.

In order to determine an application for LBC, or a planning application concerning an historic building, LPAs must have sufficient information to understand:

- the significance of the building
- the exact nature of the proposals and their likely effects on the special interest of the building and its setting.

Most LPAs seek to establish a sustainable approach to managing change in historic buildings. They recognise that the useful existence of buildings can be prolonged by repairing or replacing original fabric and by adaptation to alternative uses. Early consultation with the relevant archaeological and conservation staff, preferably at the planning and design stage of a conservation or development project, can aid and inform decision-making, avoid later problems and save money.

RECORDING FOR CONSERVATION AND DEVELOPMENT

The successful conservation, repair and alteration of historic buildings relies upon an adequately documented understanding of what is to be changed. Information required for planning applications can be obtained through investigations economically tailored to each case, using a progressive sequence of appraisal, assessment and evaluation. Buildings analysis and recording needed before or during works can be secured by attaching suitable conditions to planning consents. The local planning authority is able to control the process by issuing or approving briefs and specifications for such work. Its results can feed back into the conservation process through contributing to the compilation of buildings dossiers and local records systems. (ALGAO 1997)

Following the introduction of PPG 15: *Planning and the Historic Environment* (DoE and DNH 1994) an effective framework was established for the assessment and recording of historic buildings. The provisions largely paralleled those in PPG 16: *Archaeology and Planning* (DoE 1990a) in requiring assessment prior to planning decisions and conditional consents to secure fabric recording and analysis. PPG 15 recommends that:

- developers are expected '*to assess the likely impact of their proposals on the special interest of the site or structure in question, and to provide such written information or drawings as may be required to understand the significance of a site or structure before an application is determined*' (para. 2.11)
- if appropriate, applicants may be required to '*arrange suitable programmes of recording of features that would be destroyed in the course of the works*' (para. 3.23)
- '*exploratory opening up*' can be required where the LPA suspects that hidden features such as fire places, panelling, or wattle and daub partitions may be affected (para. 3.24).

Recording can inform conservation and development proposals and guide sensitive management and interpretation. It can also increase an owner's awareness of a building's value and significance. Sympathetic alteration and economic re-use of an historic building can only be achieved effectively through a good understanding of the building's history, development, functions, materials and present condition. Successful conservation and development therefore relies on adequate documentation. This is why PPG 15, and its

Figure 8.1. CgMs Consulting undertook recording prior to the redevelopment of Battersea Power Station, a landmark 1930s Grade II Listed Building in South London. Because of the volume of existing material, the record was mostly photographic, with additional historical research, phasing and a full written analysis, supplemented by annotated drawings © FH

equivalent guidance in Wales, Scotland and Northern Ireland recommend that historic buildings are recorded and analysed prior to change.

The most sensible way to develop a scheme is first to gain an understanding of the building's historic interest, relate this to the proposed changes and then examine the likely affects. For example, will the alterations obscure or remove an important feature of the building's history, or will the proposals bring a derelict building into appropriate new use? On the basis of this initial appraisal, it may be necessary to undertake more detailed recording. Clearly not all buildings need to be recorded in the same detail: different circumstances will demand different responses. The scope and level of recording will be dependent on a number of factors, such as the type and complexity of the building and the nature and scale of proposed works (Fig. 8.1). The recording may include:

- a desk-top assessment of existing information about the building
and/or
- an evaluation of the building's date and evolution, form and function, character and design, and materials and construction techniques, including photographs and measured drawings.

Figure 8.2. Stripping out of an interior during refurbishment work may provide a good opportunity to record wall and sub-floor structures. This shows an interior at 26–31 Charlotte Square, Edinburgh, as it had been left prior to purchase by the National Trust for Scotland. Targeted recording and analysis by Addyman Associates revealed important information on the fabric, form and function of the buildings. *Courtesy of The National Trust for Scotland; Photo: Ross Dallas*

The report on this work should accompany the planning and/or LBC application, and include an assessment of the historical development and significance of the building and any features of special interest, paying particular attention to those areas that are likely to be affected by the proposed works. The LPA is entitled to defer a decision until this information is available. In some cases it may also be necessary to relate the building to the built environment of which it forms a part, and to comprehend and communicate the relationship between that built environment and its cultural, social and economic contexts.

Where a proposal has been granted consent but entails alteration or loss of historic fabric, applicants may be asked to make provision for a further scheme of recording (Fig. 8.2). This may be secured by use of voluntary or legal agreement or by planning conditions. For instance, it may be necessary to arrange the recording of hidden features that might be revealed during the course of works or more detailed analysis of the parts of the building to be destroyed. In some cases records might also be required for reassembling historic fabric; for example, where it is necessary to deconstruct part of a timber roof to repair decay, or where partial demolition of masonry to remove rusting metal cramps cannot be avoided.

In all cases it is important that these records are made in advance of repair and conservation and before partial or total loss of fabric through alteration, destruction or concealment. Further records may also be required to document the works themselves and the finished result (the so-called 'as-built' record) so that it is clear which elements are original (see also Figs 8.3 and 8.4). Such recording should be an integral part of the works schedule and project budget. Following completion of the works, the records should be deposited with an appropriate archive. In most cases, recording historic buildings should be carried out by a suitably experienced contractor/consultant according to a written brief approved by the relevant LPA. Briefs and project designs are the tools against which performance, fitness for purpose and hence achievement of standards can be measured. A recording brief might contain the following elements:

- building location and status (including current use, state of repair and any physical or legal constraints)
- planning background
- description of proposed works (including health and safety provisions)
- archaeological and historical interest

Figure 8.3. The church of St George of England, Toddington, Bedfordshire, dates from the early thirteenth century and is a Grade I Listed Building. It was originally built of Totternhoe stone, but this has eroded in many places, particularly on the most exposed areas such as the tower. During the late nineteenth and early twentieth centuries, incremental repairs using tiles, bricks and flint, based on principles laid down by the Society for the Protection of Ancient Buildings, changed the character of the tower significantly. Although recent repairs sought to retain much of the interesting and attractive appearance of the tower elevations, the work did involve substantial disturbance and loss of the existing fabric. Archaeological recording and analysis provided the necessary accurate base level of information about the nature and historical development of the tower to inform the repair programme. *Courtesy of Toddington PCC; Drawing: Network Archaeology Ltd*

- aim, scope and level of recording required (documentary research, oral testimony, survey methodology and control, drawn records, photographic records, written records and, where appropriate, materials analyses and dismantling and re-erection procedures)
- archive and report contents and copyright, deposition and dissemination arrangements
- timetable
- procurement procedures
- management and monitoring procedures.

Recording requirements for larger projects involving historic buildings might include:

Plans

Basement, ground and upper level floor plans, including plans of ceilings, vaults, roof structures, showing relevant external and internal detail and features (cracks, peg and mortise holes, nail positions, etc.). The location of all sections and elevations should be identified.

Sections

Sections corresponding to the bay divisions or axes through the relevant parts of a building. These should normally consist of a line defining the principal wall plane and

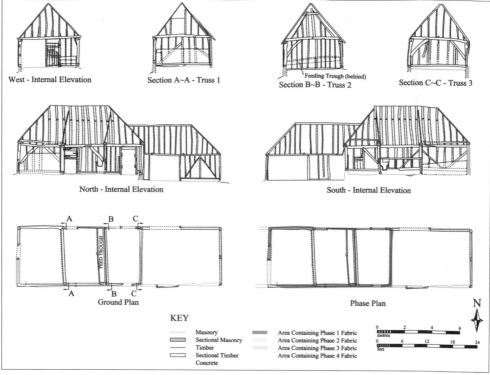

Figure 8.4. Plans, elevations and sections of a rare, timber-framed early fifteenth-century stable block at Abbey Farmstead, Faversham, Kent. The building was originally longer at its eastern end, and possibly to the west. As one of a number of listed structures on the site at risk from neglect, the building was archaeologically recorded in advance of repair and refurbishment works. *Courtesy of Oxford Archaeology and Swale Borough Council; Drawing: Lancaster University Archaeological Unit*

also include sections through adjacent openings and voids (windows, doors, passageways, put-log holes, beam sockets, etc.) which break the wall plane. Where roof and floor detail survive, such sections should include the depiction of the main timber components in elevation. The height locations of all plans should be identified.

Elevations

External and internal elevations of the relevant parts of a building depicting architectural features with associated detail and features (put-log holes, cracks, peg and mortise holes, nail positions, etc.). Walls adjoining elevations should be depicted in section. The height locations of all plans should be identified.

Details

Separate plans, sections and elevations of representative openings and architectural features, with exploded views to supplement the two-dimensional record where appropriate (e.g. carpentry joints); and representative architectural, decorative and ornamental details, both loose and *in situ* (moulding profiles, inscriptions, setting-out lines, tooling, nail positions, masons' and carpenters' marks, graffiti, etc.).

Analytical records

Plans, sections and elevations depicting boundaries between different types of building material (petrology, brick, tile, wood, metal, glass, etc.); surface finishes (mortar, render, plaster, daub, paint, wallpaper, industrial lining, etc.); building periods, phases of construction and repair; constructional detail (wall alignments and thicknesses, bonding patterns, blockings, put-log holes, beam sockets, chase scars, butt joints, building lifts, gang breaks, fittings, etc.); occupational detail (wear marks, blackened timbers, industrial residues, etc.); and evidence for abandonment or demolition (robbing, salvaging, fire damage, etc.).

Interpretation records

Plans, sections and elevations depicting outline reconstruction of the principal elements and features, for each of the periods identified. Three-dimensional projections may be used to facilitate greater comprehension of the sequence of development.

Intervention records

'As-built' records, showing the extent of conservation or development works, should depict areas of rebuilding, rebedding, repointing, grouting, new fabric insertions, etc.

Measured survey techniques for historic buildings can include (after Dallas 2003a):

Hand-measured

- dimensioned sketch
- hand survey

Instrument-based

- electronic theodolites
- electronic distance measurement
- laser scanning
- total station theodolites

Photographic-based

- pictorial photography
- rectified photography
- stereo photogrammetry
- orthophotography

However, no single survey process is likely to provide a complete record of a building. A combination of techniques often needs to be deployed.

INTEGRATING THE APPROACH

As a part of an historic building conservation or development project, the design of an archaeological recording programme differs significantly from that of a conventional field project, in that the data can form an integral part of the works specification and documentation. Documentation such as scaled plans, elevation drawings and photographs are often the essential basis for detailed works proposals and consent applications. Such

103

records may also be used for issuing instructions to building contractors. Recording programmes should, therefore, be developed not only in advance of works but also in conjunction with all other professional groups involved (particularly the project architect, engineer and principal contractor).

Having agreed an approach, the archaeological response should be:

1. to assist in assessing the extent of any historic fabric interventions (particularly valuable in identifying the causes of specific structural failure or building defects)
2. to conduct (where necessary) a trial evaluation of the fabric's constructional history based on preliminary visual inspection, non-destructive survey, or selective intervention (particularly should health and safety regulations or engineering considerations require)
3. to establish and quantify the degree of proposed intervention during the main works (such as the amount of re-pointing, fabric replacement, stitching, underpinning, etc.)
4. to select the scale and level of recording (comprehensive or selective)
5. to anticipate potential end-user requirements (presentation format, CAD layering conventions, etc.)
6. to select the most appropriate method of basic data capture (hand-measured, instrument-based, photographic-based, or combinations)
7. to approach (where necessary) specialist subcontractors and prepare their works schedules
8. to agree lines of communication, lead-in times and on-site facilities (particularly with the architect and main contractor).

The following is a suggested works programme. The tasks would run consecutively or concurrently, as appropriate:

1. project preparation to organise appropriate data to undertake the proposed works and to establish necessary timetables and contractual obligations
2. documentary research (including the collection of records dealing with past repairs)
3. engineering calculations and recommendation reports
4. execution of survey data capture
5. archaeological recording based on survey data, preliminary analysis based on documentary research and field observation, together with any materials analyses
6. drafting of preliminaries, works schedules, specifications and orders based on record drawings/photographs and taking account of engineering and archaeological considerations
7. execution of the fabric repairs and conservation work according the approved works documentation, together with archaeological monitoring and creation of the 'as-built' record
8. completion of archaeological analysis and interpretation and production of the report.

PROBLEMS AND OPPORTUNITIES

So far in this chapter the importance of record-making has been illustrated and the need for recording to inform building conservation and management strategies has been stressed. Here, some of the problems and opportunities faced by the archaeological profession in this field are addressed.

Background

Over the last twenty years or so, the archaeological profession has passed a number of important milestones with regard to the recording of historic buildings. In particular, the work of Warwick Rodwell was instrumental in laying the modern foundations for the subject, providing a general guide to the archaeological analysis of buildings using churches as examples (Rodwell 1981). From about the mid-1980s, a number of long-term historic fabric surveys were set up by English Heritage (EH) to achieve a greater understanding of the monuments in their care prior to major works. At the initiation of these projects there was no clear specification for work of this type and the archaeological contractors/consultants commissioned by EH had to spend time defining and refining the methodologies employed (see e.g. Wood 1992).

Despite this initial investment and the experience that it generated, it was not until about fifteen years ago that the profession really woke up to both the academic and commercial potential of work in this field. In 1990 it was a difficult job trying to persuade the organising committee of the Institute of Field Archaeologists' (IFA) annual conference that the subject merited more than a half-day session; and this despite the earlier creation of a separate IFA Area of Competence in Recording and Analysis of Buildings. The next year saw the establishment of the IFA Buildings Special Interest Group and the start of a string of successful conferences, day schools and other events to reinforce the message. Publications by the IFA and the Association of Local Government Archaeological Officers followed, anticipating and responding to PPG 15 (Wood 1994; IFA 1996; ALGAO 1997).[4] EH's guidance to grant applicants was revised; the Institute of Historic Building Conservation (IHBC) was launched with a new emphasis on recording and understanding sites as one of its key areas of competence for Conservation Officers; and despite the initial slow take-up, the number of jobs for buildings archaeologists began to steadily increase.

In recent years the number of publications dedicated to the subject has also increased, including a sequence of titles on heritage recording produced by EH (EH 1999b, 2000c, 2003a); general works by Morris (2000), Clark (2001), Dallas (2003b) and Swallow et al. (2004); and conference proceedings edited by Malm (2001) and Pearson and Meeson (2001).

Where does the archaeological profession go next? How many more milestones need to be passed? What are the problems still to be faced and how might these be overcome?

Problems

The first problem is with the words 'archaeology' and 'archaeologist' to describe what is done and who does it. Despite the fact that the Council for British Archaeology has been a statutory consultee for LBC notifications for many years, and that EH until recent reorganisation employed a Chief Archaeologist with overall responsibility for the historic built environment, there still remains a general puzzlement about the involvement of archaeologists with buildings.

A second problem is that, unfortunately, there is still a perception that understanding or recording a building is something that happens – if it happens at all – *after* key decisions have been taken, and usually as a condition of consent. Recording should not be seen as a punishment for bad applications but as a beneficial process that can avoid damage to historic buildings (Clark 1999: xxii). Often overstretched and underresourced, some LPAs have arguably been less rigorous in applying the recording provisions set out in PPG 15. Reports on LPA practice and PPG 15 show that there is no consistency in what LPAs are asking for, and therefore what they are receiving, in terms of records (Oxford Brookes University 1999; Gould 2004).

A third problem is that the early experience of archaeologists in this field was largely gained studying the 'bones' of historic buildings and monuments, rather than their surface

105

finishes, and on the back of major conservation or dismantling and re-erection projects where the scope and level of recording was typically and necessarily of a detailed and comprehensive nature. Small-scale works are much more frequent in planning terms and on the whole require a different approach.

Fourthly, where archaeologists are involved with building conservation there is often a failure of the client team to recognise how and when to involve the archaeologist in the management process, and a failure of the archaeologist to be engaged proactively in decision-making from the outset or to communicate effectively their interpretation. The benefits of a team approach are thus being lost.

Opportunities

Professional links within LPAs

The first opportunity is the prospect of improved links between the planning, conservation, archaeological and architectural professionals at LPA level. The chief benefits that might accrue from such cooperation include greater public awareness of the role of the archaeologist and the importance of recording historic buildings in relation to the planning system (Fig. 8.5).

In the first instance, the responsibility for advising on the need for recording, ensuring the preparation of briefs, the evaluation of project designs and the monitoring of standards often rests with LPA Conservation Officers. The brief and tender stages of recording projects are in many ways the ideal opportunity to bring LPA Conservation and Archaeological Officers together. Sharing responsibility would deliver more confidence and consistency and help to ensure that greater account is taken of regional vernacular traditions in defining the appropriate scope and level of recording. Other benefits of cross-professional cooperation within LPAs include improved procurement arrangements for archaeological contractors/consultants, enhanced record systems and more coherent regional research projects.

The introduction of prequalification procedures by LPAs would, one hopes, ensure that only the most suitably experienced archaeological contractors/consultants are invited to tender for historic building projects. Evaluation of tenders should not be based on cost alone but on organisations' track records of measured survey and analytical recording, studies of building materials and construction history, and general practice philosophy and approach to the project in hand. Ideally, a guide price for the recording works should be provided. Following tender evaluation, LPAs should ensure that information gets fed back to the unsuccessful contractors/consultants to help them understand why they were not selected and so judge how best to improve their services to future clients.

If the quality of LBC applications is enhanced, then the level of documentation held in LPA record systems is also enhanced. Making records is one thing, keeping them is another. This opens the whole debate about what constitutes an appropriate record, where it should be deposited and who has access to it; while the ICT explosion raises the issue of standardisation to which owners, developers and LPAs may aspire.

Finally, more coherent regional research projects for certain types of historic building could be established, fed by, and feeding into, national research frameworks and thematic listing exercises. It also needs to be established whether archaeological research agenda are different from those of other professionals and non-professionals – and if so, why?

Working within multidisciplinary teams

A second opportunity is the prospect of working in close partnerships within multidisciplinary teams on historic building conservation and development projects. The

Recording Historic Buildings in Lancashire
a guide to development in the historic environment

Lancashire County Archaeology Service

Environment Directorate

Lancashire County Council

Figure 8.5. Lancashire County Archaeology Service's information leaflet concisely explains the benefits of recording historic buildings (Lancashire County Council 2000). Although published six years after PPG 15, it was still one of the first county-based guides on the subject produced in the UK. *(Courtesy of Lancashire County Council)*

chief benefits here include pooling knowledge and increasing the responsibilities for archaeologists. Teamwork leads to the establishment of a common language so that professionals coming from different areas can pool their knowledge and help to minimise risk. Working in this way should ensure that the archaeological value and significance of historic buildings are fully appreciated and, where possible, retained or enhanced. It should also lead to a greater understanding of the structural and material performance of the historic fabric, thus avoiding irrevocable damage and allowing for appropriate conservation.

In some instances the archaeologist may play a more extended role in the design of conservation works and in the coordination of related specialists and services (for example, measured survey, dendrochronology, and mortar or paint analysis). The last few years has seen a noticeable shift in the authorship of records, and the ownership of analysis, away from the architect and to the archaeologist. Because of this, some historic buildings projects may benefit from leadership by rotation, with the baton of leadership passing from one professional to another depending on where the project is in the cycle. Because recording occurs early in the cycle, the archaeologist is well placed to assume a leadership role at the outset of a project, before handing over to the architect. This is not a utopian dream (this author has been in such a position), but the concept will inevitably take time to become accepted. Mindsets will gradually change as multidisciplinary working practices become more common. Increased responsibility will also require archaeologists to redouble their efforts to inform the conservation or development process objectively and accurately. In this respect archaeologists must be aware of their legal obligations and the implications of factual or interpretation errors.

Other related benefits include rolling programmes of archaeological recording and the creation of retained archaeologists for certain classes of historic building. Rolling programmes of archaeological recording as part of forward maintenance plans for historic buildings could be introduced. The existing requirements for quadrennial or quinquennial inspections of government estate, National Trust properties, churches and cathedrals could be extended to ease the management of historic buildings in private hands. The creation of 'log books' for historic assets has been raised (BSI 1998; DCMS 2003c). We are obliged to maintain road vehicles, why not buildings? The upkeep of logs could be made a condition of grant aid or encouraged by tax incentives or lower insurance premiums. The idea would also fit well with the government's initiative, which seeks to place the onus on the seller of a private property to provide survey information to the buyer, rather than the other way round (the so-called *Sellers' Packs*).

EH, CADW and Historic Scotland often devolve responsibility for advice and monitoring of their grant-aided works to historic buildings to retained or commissioned architects. Why not also have retained archaeologists to input to schemes at an early stage, particularly for nationally important historic buildings? Cathedrals have a statutory responsibility to appoint archaeologists: perhaps other classes of historic building should receive a similar, dedicated service? At the very least such appointments would give some continuity and formality to advice on matters such as recording, which at the moment is a rather hit-and-miss affair.

Integration of professional bodies

A third opportunity is the prospect of greater integration of the different professional bodies responsible for the management and interpretation of the built environment. The built environment sector, or at least the conservation part of it (including archaeology), is unfortunately too small to support the increasing number of professional institutions and related interest groups. Continued fragmentation is unsustainable. Cooperation, and in the longer term possible merger, is the only logical way forward. The IFA could play a lead role here in helping to advance such proposals, perhaps starting with the Buildings Archaeology Group (BAG) (formerly the Buildings Special Interest Group) sharing resources with similar groups within the IHBC and possibly the Royal Institution of Chartered Surveyors. The BAG sees its role as promoting buildings archaeology and developing links with the wider profession and complimentary professions.

One collaborative project might be the drawing together and publication of a suite of relevant extensive and intensive recording procedures and planning scenarios to illustrate good development control and historic building recording practices.

Training and education

Fourth and finally, all these opportunities could be advanced through enhanced training and education. Although the number of published standards, principles and guidelines continues to increase, nothing replaces the advantages of participation in courses. But at what level and to whom should such courses be aimed? Are existing courses sufficient in number and flexibility to get the message across? The only postgraduate course in the UK dedicated to the archaeology of buildings is at the University of York. Elsewhere, the subject's inclusion in syllabuses of archaeology, architecture, architectural history, building conservation, heritage management, built environment, surveying, planning, engineering, and so on is at best inconsistent, at worst barely visible.

CONCLUSION

Whether undertaken as a result of conservation and development works, or as part of programmes of research, archaeological investigation can broaden understanding and assessment of significance of historic buildings. This knowledge assists the processes of statutory protection for the built heritage and helps to inform strategic policies and record systems for the historic environment as a whole.

Investigation of historic buildings has always formed a significant part of archaeologists' activities. In recent years the role of the archaeologist, and the application of modern archaeological practice, has been extended to inform decision-making in planning, design and conservation. Today, an integrated, multidisciplinary approach can ensure the success of building conservation and development projects in historic contexts. It is only by working in close partnerships with other professionals that the archaeological value and significance of historic buildings can be preserved and appreciated.

NOTES

1. The government has signalled its intention to replace PPG 15, and PPG 16 (*Archaeology and Planning*: DoE 1990a), with a single Planning Policy Statement for the historic environment (PPS 15) (ODPM forthcoming).

2. The government is proposing the phasing out of traditional Structure Plans and Local Plans and their replacement with new style Regional Spatial Strategies and Local Development Frameworks.

3. The whole listing process, including the demarcation between listing and the consent regimes, forms part of a wider review of heritage protection (DCMS 2003c, 2004e; CADW 2003). See also PDP 2003 on streamlining Listed Building Consent. For details regarding the present listing process, see Mynors 1999.

4. Other relevant publications at this time, although not related to PPG 15, included ICOMOS 1990a, RCHME 1991b, Andrews *et al.* 1995 and RCHME 1996.

CHAPTER 9

ECCLESIASTICAL BUILDINGS IN USE

Carl Bianco and Linda Monckton

Great Britain enjoys a rich inheritance of historical ecclesiastical buildings. The Church of England alone supports some 16,400 churches, and with about 13,000 of these listed as being of special architectural or historic interest, the Church has the largest estate of Listed Buildings in England. Furthermore, 40 per cent of these are listed at Grade I (EH 2002a: 6), representing over 30 per cent of the nation's Grade 1 buildings (*Conservation Bulletin* issue 34, July 1998). The Church of Scotland and the Church in Wales also own many Listed Buildings, as do the Nonconformist churches and the Roman Catholic Church. Increasingly there is recognition of Jewish synagogues and related structures, as well as older Muslim and Hindu places of worship, which might be listed as many are former chapels, halls or cinemas for example. Together, these represent a unique and highly significant part of Britain's heritage.

However, while these sites are indeed immeasurably important from an architectural, archaeological, historical and artistic point of view, they are not museums. They are the centre of living, growing communities, their form shaped by the needs of those who have worshipped in them over centuries. As with most historic sites, a great deal of their value (both academic and aesthetic) lies in the evidence they display of change. Whether the result of major rebuilding, repair or internal re-ordering, any alteration to the fabric and setting of a church can reveal much about its community's response to shifting climates of religious, social and political feeling. At the same time, however, the very change that has made these buildings what they are also has the potential, if uncontrolled, to destroy forever their historic character.

The standing fabric of a church, its contents and its surroundings (both above and below ground) constitute an archaeological entity. Any work in or around a church therefore has the potential to destroy valuable evidence for the evolution of that site. The provision of new heating or drainage systems, the digging of modern foundation trenches for an extension, the relaying of floors or the disturbance of monuments or ground levels within a churchyard can all have major archaeological implications. Equally harmful are works to the standing fabric of a church. The piercing of historic masonry to form a new entrance, the stripping of unwanted plaster, the re-pointing of stonework or the alteration or removal of internal fittings can all be highly damaging from an archaeological viewpoint if undertaken without appropriate advice (for a detailed discussion of the archaeological study of churches, and the threats to which they are vulnerable, see Morris 1989; Parsons 1989; Rodwell 1989; and for cathedrals in particular, Tatton-Brown 1989; and Tatton-Brown and Munby 1996).

The archaeological management of these buildings and their surroundings must therefore balance the interest of conservation with the needs of an evolving, dynamic faith. It cannot seek to prohibit change, but must ensure that all work is controlled and that, where archaeological evidence is to be unavoidably destroyed, appropriate provision is made for its recording. Of course, this problem of potentially conflicting interests is not in itself unique to church archaeology. What is unique, however, is the special legal status afforded to ecclesiastical buildings in use, which places them outside the secular system of Listed Building control.

The significance to the historic environment and to society generally of other places of worship, in particular those of non-Christian denominations, is being increasingly acknowledged within the conservation movement. Only a relatively small number of buildings in this category are currently listed. This chapter, however, will look only at those religious organisations and denominations that are exempt from Listed Building Consent and that, therefore, have in hand their own systems of internal control. This ecclesiastical exemption will be discussed in general terms before exploring its practical application primarily through reference to the Church of England's internal system of control.

ECCLESIASTICAL EXEMPTION

In the period leading up to the Ancient Monuments Consolidation and Amendment Act 1913, the Archbishop of Canterbury, Randall Davidson, had requested that the Church of England be exempt from its provisions in order to safeguard its freedom of worship. In return, he gave an undertaking that the Church would review and enhance its own existing system of building control, the faculty jurisdiction (of medieval origin). Ecclesiastical exemption was thus granted on the understanding that the Church of England would provide a system of protection for its historic buildings comparable to that exercised by the state, and since that time the Church has developed and expanded its internal administration to meet this requirement. Curiously, however, cathedrals and non-Anglican churches – while they made no such promise of good conduct – managed to shelter under the umbrella of the exemption for more than seventy years despite the fact that they operated no equivalent internal controls until the 1990s (see below).

While the original exemption was in response to the issue of scheduling, when the principle of statutory protection for buildings and inhabited structures was introduced (initially in the 1932 and 1947 Planning Acts and taking something of its current form in the 1968 Town and Country Planning Act), ecclesiastical buildings could be listed, but the exemption from the secular legislation was thereby extended to Listed Building Consent. Section 60 of the subsequent Planning (Listed Buildings and Conservation Areas) Act 1990 states that any 'ecclesiastical building which is for the time being used for ecclesiastical purposes' is exempt from Listed Building control except where the Secretary of State provides by Order. Pursuant to this Act is the Ecclesiastical Exemption (Listed Buildings and Conservation Areas) Order 1994 which granted exemption from Listed Building Consent and Conservation Area consent only for those denominations which had in place, or were introducing, appropriate internal forms of control (that is churches and cathedrals of the Church of England; buildings of the Church in Wales; Roman Catholic churches; those buildings owned or held in trust by the Methodist Church, the Baptist Union and the United Reformed Church). Peculiars and other special cases were also granted exemption on a temporary basis and are discussed further below. The term 'ecclesiastical purposes' is not defined, although it excludes any building used by a minister of religion primarily as a residence. Cases from the courts have, however, demonstrated that the term 'ecclesiastical' does not solely mean Anglican. Current government policy is that the retention of the exemption is dependent on periodic reviews assessing the effectiveness of the control systems in place. The criteria against which such reviews take place are set out in *Planning Policy Guidance* (PPG) *15* (para. 8.4), which provides the government's code of practice for exempt denominations.

There is no such exemption from the Town and Country Planning Act 1990, and planning permission is still required for any development, defined as 'the carrying out of building, engineering mining or other operations in, on, over or under land, or the making of any material change in the use of any building or other land' (Section 55 (1) 3). Thus, for example, the extension of a church building would require applications under both secular planning law and the relevant system of ecclesiastical control. Maintenance, internal works, and works that will not materially affect the external appearance of a building are excluded from this definition. There is similarly no exemption from Scheduled Monument Consent, although the Ancient Monuments and Archaeological Areas Act 1979 prohibits the scheduling of 'an ecclesiastical building in use for ecclesiastical purposes' (Section 61 (8)). However, other items associated with the church may be scheduled and are not exempt, and therefore work to any Scheduled Monument within the consecrated area of a church (for an example an Anglo-Saxon cross or a lych gate) would still require Scheduled Monument Consent, as would works to scheduled sites within churchyards.

The exemption has, not surprisingly, had its share of opponents from the outset. These consider that the interests of conservation would be better served by removing churches from internal control and making them subject to the same secular legislation as other historic buildings. In January 1984 this concern prompted the Department of the Environment (DoE, now the DCMS – The Department of Culture Media and Sport) to issue a consultation paper on the subject. Subsequent discussions with representatives of the Church of England and of the Churches' Main Committee (a body representing all main Christian denominations) resulted in a decision by the government that the exemption should be generally retained, subject to certain amendments. This decision was announced by Lord Skelmersdale in the debate on the Housing and Planning Bill in the House of Lords (see Hansard for 13 October 1986; and also DoE 1987). As a result the legislation was amended to give power to the Secretary of State to restrict the exemption by Order. The two major points arising from the Skelmersdale statement were that the exemption would not cover total demolition of a church (except, in the case of the Church of England, as part of redundancy scheme under the Pastoral Measure 1983, see below); and that further discussions should take place on how far the exemption should extend to objects or structures within the curtilage of a church. This latter point was resolved by the 1994 Order which stated that the exemption applies to structures within the curtilage of the principal ecclesiastical building except where that structure is separately listed in its own right.

The Church of England had, by the time of the Skelmersdale statement, conducted its own review through a commission established under the Bishop of Chichester in response to the introduction of government funding for church repairs. The final report of the Faculty Jurisdiction Commission (FJC 1984) made a number of recommendations for improving the Church of England's system of control, and was influential in persuading the government of the validity of the exemption. These recommendations finally achieved statutory authority in the Care of Cathedrals Measure 1990 and the Care of Churches and Ecclesiastical Jurisdiction Measure 1991 (for those unfamiliar with the organisational structure of the Church of England see Welsby 1985; and more recently Hill 2001 for a good introduction).

After the introduction of the 1994 Order the government carried out a review of the internal systems for control for the exempt denominations in 1997 known as the Newman Review (Newman 1997). This review aimed to assess whether or not the systems in place met the requirements of the Order and thereby enabled a continuation of the exemption. The key requirements of the exemption include the provision for an independent body to take decisions on changes affecting the character of Listed Buildings; this body taking into account conservation issues and consulting with English Heritage (EH), the local planning authority and the national amenity societies. Public display of applications and the provision of effective enforcement and appeal procedures, comparable in principle to the secular system, were also required. The government issued a response to the recommendations in the Newman Review in January 1999 (DCMS 1999). These documents resulted in various specific recommendations being made to improve or amend the current systems. These recommendations, the responses to them by the exempt denominations and the various systems of control in place will now be discussed.

THE FACULTY JURISDICTION

The principles of faculty jurisdiction and its operation are currently set out in the Care of Churches and Ecclesiastical Jurisdiction Measure 1991 (hereafter referred to as the Care of Churches Measure 1991). This amended and superseded the Ecclesiastical Jurisdiction Measure 1963, which embodied reforms in the court system, and the Faculty Jurisdiction Measure 1964. Rules following the introduction of the 1991 Measure were initially issued in 1992 (FJR 1992) although these have been superseded by the Faculty Jurisdiction Rules 2000 (FJR 2000), of which more below. Measures and their associated rules are passed by General Synod (the governing body of the Church of England), but are also ratified by parliament, and thus have the full force of English law. Under this system of control, any parish within the Church of England must apply for a faculty (licence) if it intends to make any change, internal or external, within its consecrated area. This includes everything in or on the land as well as the fabric, ornaments and furniture of the church. Faculties are granted within the consistory court by the chancellor of the diocese (a lawyer) although the authority to grant faculties is given to archdeacons in uncontentious or unopposed cases. Archdeacons also have the power to issue licences for temporary reordering.

All those carrying out functions of care and conservation under the Care of Churches Measure 1991 should have due regard for the role of the church as a local centre of worship and mission, with the exception of the chancellor whose role is instead a judicial one (Hill 2001: 171 2). Proposals must be formally advertised for a period of not less than twenty-eight days, and all interested parties (which includes the local authority, EH and the national amenity societies) are at liberty to make representations regarding those proposals. As the faculty system applies to all parish churches it actually provides protection to all churches whether listed or not.

Before making an application for a faculty the parish must obtain advice from the Diocesan Advisory Committee (DAC), a body including people with knowledge of architecture, archaeology, art and history and experience of the care of historic buildings and their contents including nominees from EH, the national amenity societies and the local planning authority as well as members of the clergy (including archdeacons). Legally established under the Faculty Jurisdiction Measure 1938 (and with their role then newly defined by the Care of Churches Measure 1991) the DACs had developed informally in the wake of Archbishop Davidson's undertaking to the nation. Through its advisory responsibilities in particular, the DAC can provide valuable assistance to individual parishes in the formulation and execution of proposals (see for example Figs 9.1 and 9.2). Once fully consulted, the DAC issues a certificate that can make one of three recommendations to the chancellor in respect of the proposal for a faculty as follows: recommend, not recommend or no objection.

Many aspects of this system were strengthened by the introduction of the Faculty Jurisdiction (Appeals) Rules 1998 and the Faculty Jurisdiction Rules 2000. Under the

Figure 9.1. All Saints Church, Stock, Essex. This exterior view from the north-east shows an addition to the medieval fabric carried out in a sensitive and successful way. (© *English Heritage*)

earlier Rules (FJR 1992) particularly complex or sensitive cases could be referred to the Council for the Care of Churches (CCC) and other statutory consultees for further advice, whereas under the new rules the chancellor must give notice to EH, the amenity societies and the local planning authority if the works will involve an alteration or extension to a listed church that is likely to affect its character as a building of special architectural or

Figure 9.2. St John's Church, Elmswell, Suffolk. The interior of the galleried west end viewed from the south shows an internal stair and floor added to the inside of a parish church. *(© English Heritage)*

historic interest, or likewise affect the archaeological importance of the church or its archaeological remains existing in the church or its curtilage. Equally, the chancellor must direct consultation with the CCC in relation to proposals that affect articles of particular historic, architectural, archaeological, or artistic interest. The CCC is a national Church advisory body, formed in 1921 and which has a number of functions under the Faculty Jurisdiction Measure 1964, the Care of Churches Measure 1991 and the Pastoral Measure 1983 (see below). In addition to providing a wide range of expert advice, it coordinates the works of the DACs, liaises with national and regional organisations and administers grants for the conservation of church fittings and furnishings (for a history of the CCC see Findlay 1996).

In the majority of cases the chancellor will accept the advice of the DAC (taking into account all comments received from other agencies and individuals), but he is not obliged to do so. Where there is opposition to a proposal, the chancellor may convene a consistory court hearing (usually held at the church in question) at which he or she may call upon witnesses to give evidence; and where the granting of a faculty is contested there are provisions for appeal to higher ecclesiastical courts (for further information and associated case law see Newsom 1988; Suddards and Hargreaves 1996; and Hill 2001). The relative weight of the wishes of the parishioners and the effect on the character of the Listed Building or archaeological remains has, inevitably, been the subject of much debate;

however, the overall approach to the evaluation of evidence has been articulated in a number of consistory court hearings. Such judgements have also tested the importance of assessing proposals in terms of their adverse affect on the character of the building (for further information see Mynors 1989 section 13.5.5). Such judgements have in turn helped to refine the system and have been influential in the review of the Faculty Jurisdiction Rules 1992. The resultant new 2000 Rules also reflect consideration of points raised in the government's response to the Newman Review. Subsequently, in order to ensure clearly defined needs and to demonstrate an understanding of the impact of a proposal on the special character of a building or churchyard, it is now a principle that where a proposal includes significant changes to a listed church then a *Statement of Significance* and *Statement of Needs* should be produced by the parish and that in the same instances consultation at an early stage should take place with EH, the national amenity societies and the local planning authority. One of the recommendations that came out of the Newman Review was that the dioceses should appoint professionally trained conservation officers to assist DAC Secretaries. Conservation expertise already exists within the DACs and the CCC, although a general agreement to consider additional diocesan support where required and where affordable was made during the government's post-Newman consultation with the Church of England. While the new rules took these concerns into account and provided a strengthening of procedures and a greater emphasis on understanding significance, it is interesting to note that at the time of writing there exist only three areas where new posts have been created: one as a specific follow-up to this recommendation is in the Exeter diocese, where a conservation officer post attached to the DAC to help with conservation issues is jointly funded by the diocese and EH. Two further posts, of development officers rather than strictly speaking conservation officers, exist in the diocese of Manchester, where a pilot project is jointly funded by the diocese and EH, and in the diocese of London, for which the church provides full funding. However, the CCC has taken a lead in promoting and developing conservation expertise within the existing diocesan structure, most notably through the creation of bespoke training courses run for DAC Secretaries in association with West Dean College, Chichester.

REDUNDANCY

When a parish church within the Church of England is deemed to be surplus to requirements (either for pastoral reasons or because the cost of repair is considered to be too great) it can be declared redundant under the Pastoral Measure 1983. This provides the legal framework for the disposal of such buildings and ensures that conservation issues are given a hearing. The issue of derelict and disused churches arrived on the agenda of the CCC in its earliest days. A series of high-profile cases eventually led in 1958 to a commission led by Lord Bridges which discovered that 370 churches were effectively redundant in 1960 when the report was published. At this stage churches could be demolished under the faculty jurisdiction process, but as a result of the report a new measure, the Pastoral Measure 1968, was developed, which set up diocesan redundant churches committees, a central advisory body (the Advisory Board for Redundant Churches) and the Redundant Churches Fund to take into care buildings worthy of preservation in the interests of the Church and the nation.

This was superseded by the 1983 Measure, which makes a provision that before putting forward a proposal for the redundancy of a church, the Diocesan Pastoral Committee must ascertain the views of the local planning authority, and obtain from the CCC a report on the historic and architectural qualities of the church, its contents and its churchyard, and of other churches in the area. After possible amendment the proposal is then sent to the

Church Commissioners, who will consult the Advisory Board for Redundant Churches (ABRC) before sending the draft pastoral scheme to all interested parties. Any comments received will then be considered by the commissioners when finalising the scheme for final approval by Her Majesty in Council.

The pastoral scheme itself is primarily concerned with the future of the parish as a whole, while the fate of the building is normally handled through a redundancy scheme made under Section 48 of the Pastoral Measure, which requires that notices be served on the diocesan Board of Finance, the ABRC and the local planning authority. The proposals are also advertised in the local press and any interested party is eligible to comment.

One of three courses may be advocated at this stage: that the building be demolished; that an alternative use be found; or that the building be vested in a guardianship body, most commonly the Churches Conservation Trust (CCT) (before 1994 the CCT was known as the Redundant Churches Fund). This last course (and the most desirable from an archaeological viewpoint) is taken if the Church Commissioners accept the ABRC advice that the church 'is of such historic and archaeological interest or architectural quality that it ought to be preserved in the interests of the nation and the Church of England' (Section 47). The CCT, funded jointly by the DCMS and the Church Commissioners, currently cares for over 330 former parish churches (at least 310 of which are listed Grade I or II*) and aims to maintain a church broadly as it was at the time of its redundancy. Changes in the funding agreement for the CCT mean that at the last review (in 2001) the figures remained at their 1989 levels with 70 per cent of the funds being provided by DCMS (a shift from 40 per cent originally), although the decision-making process remains with the Church Commissioners (CCT 2002).

If the ABRC considers that a church is of insufficient interest to warrant guardianship, the Church Commissioners may recommend that an alternative use for the building be found or, more rarely, that it be demolished. There then follows a 'waiting period' that, because of the often protracted process of seeking a new use, can afford plenty of opportunity for the abandoned church to fall into ruin through neglect or vandalism, ultimately increasing the likelihood of its eventual demolition, as at Holy Trinity, Birkenhead. However, even if a new use is found, as is generally considered desirable, the result can often be highly damaging archaeologically. It can be a particular challenge to ensure that conversions (for example to office, residential or community use) are appropriately sensitive to the internal space of the building and to its historic fittings, and many fine churches – even if not fine enough to be placed in guardianship – have been ruined in this way (for examples of conversions, good and bad, see Powell and de la Hey 1987; for the problems of redundancy in general see also Binney and Burman 1977a, 1977b; Rodwell and Rodwell 1977). Of course, once a church has formally been declared redundant the exemption from Listed Building control ceases to apply – it being no longer a building in ecclesiastical use – and planning permission will always be required for any change of use or material alteration.

However, if total or partial demolition is ultimately recommended under a redundancy scheme, the exemption still applies. In return, the Church Commissioners have agreed to notify the Secretary of State in all cases where the proposed demolition of a listed church (or an unlisted church in a Conservation Area) is opposed by EH, the ABRC, the local planning authority or the national amenity societies. The Secretary of State is then empowered to convene a non-statutory public enquiry, and may recommend either that the building be vested in the CCT or that further efforts be made to find an alternative use. The first such non-statutory enquiry was held over the future of Holy Trinity, Rugby, in 1980 and, despite the recommendation of the Secretary of State that it should be preserved, the commissioners finally secured its demolition in 1983. However, the commissioners have since undertaken to accept recommendations for transfer to the CCT (see DoE 1987).

Since 1969 about fifty churches a year have been made redundant (22 per cent demolished, 57 per cent have alternative uses and 21 per cent are preserved, mainly by the CCT; EH 2002a: 25). In the past five years the number of redundancies has fallen to an average of nineteen per year; however, the number of Pastoral Measure reports by the CCC has increased considerably and it is currently unclear whether this means that there is a real risk of a significant increase in redundancies or whether this reflects a different approach to assessing potential redundancies within particular areas. A major review of the process of redundancy under the Pastoral Measure began in March 2001, and the resulting report was debated by the General Synod in February 2004 (GS 1528, 2004). The resultant legislation (the Draft Diocese Pastoral and Mission Measure) had its first reading by the General Synod in July 2006. A number of significant changes in this legislation affect the structure that processes applications for redundancy. In particular the ABRC will be disbanded and its functions taken on by the Council for the Care of Churches, with the aim that one body will be able to provide a holistic approach to the use and possible redundancy of a church, rather than considering the latter in isolation. This will necessitate a new constitution for the CCC, which will in the process of change be renamed the Church Buildings Council. This would still need to demonstrate an acceptable level of independence and would report direct to the Church Commissioners. This approach might enable groups of churches to be considered within dioceses or parishes together with comparative judgements being made about how a number of churches could be managed. It is anticipated that the new legislation will come into force in 2008. Another aspect of the report, however, is taking a separate path through the legislation; this involves approval of a change in the law which would enable part of a church to be leased out for non-worship related functions providing that worship remains the primary use of the church. This could reduce the number of applications for redundancy by introducing a level of flexibility currently absent. The resultant legislation, the Pastoral (Amendment) Measure, was granted Royal Assent in July 2006, with an imminent start date.

ARCHAEOLOGY IN THE DIOCESES

The Dibdin Commission of 1913–14, conducting the first review of the faculty jurisdiction as promised by Archbishop Davidson, stated clearly that both the Chancellor and the DAC had a duty to have regard to matters architectural, archaeological, historic and artistic. In 1986 the CCC and the then Cathedrals Advisory Commission established a working party to review the Church's response to archaeology in the light of these clear obligations. Its report, *Archaeology and the Church of England* (CCC 1988), made a number of recommendations regarding archaeological management at parish, diocesan and national levels, but many of these were, in the end, not implemented.

However, with the approval of the Care of Churches Measure 1991, archaeology at least received the formal recognition promised by the 1913 Commission. Under its provisions, DACs are required to have within their membership at least one person 'with a knowledge of archaeology', and are to advise on all matters relating to 'the architecture, archaeology, art and history of places of worship'. They must also:

> Review and assess the degree of risk to materials, or of loss to archaeological or historic remains or records, arising from any proposals relating to the conservation, repair or alteration of places of worship, churchyards and burial grounds and the contents of such places (Schedules 1 and 2).

When the Council for British Archaeology (CBA) established its Churches Committee in 1972, one of its earliest initiatives was to compile a list of those archaeologists who would be suitable to serve as consultants to DACs. In conjunction with the then Council for Places of Worship (now the CCC) the CBA urged each diocese to appoint one of these nominees as a full member of its DAC, or at least recognise him or her as an independent consultant. Consequently, by the advent of the 1991 Measure, most DACs were provided with some form of archaeological support. The effectiveness of the system is to a large extent, however, dependent on the attitude of the individual DAC and the ability of the archaeologist involved.

Of course, archaeology in the dioceses can be most effectively managed through the proper consultation at an early stage, as stressed in *Planning Policy Guidance Note 16: Archaeology and Planning* (DoE 1990a). In the same way that a local planning authority is required to ensure that archaeological considerations are taken fully into account (and that appropriate mitigation strategies are incorporated into all developments) so the chancellor, on the advice of the DAC, can attach archaeological conditions to the granting of a faculty.

However, the financial implications of national policy are rather less easy to translate into the ecclesiastical sphere. PPG 16 places a clear obligation upon the developer to bear the cost of archaeological work arising from a project, but ever since its introduction it has been argued that churches (and indeed other charities), while they may assume the role of developer in a technical sense, should receive special consideration, as they are non-profit-making. On the other hand, it might be argued that it is equally unreasonable to release churches from all financial obligations and thereby to encourage a situation in which it becomes expected that some external agency will foot the entire bill for consequential archaeological work. Indeed in the CCC's 1988 report it was stated that the 'the primary responsibility for the archaeological care of a parish church rests with the PCC [Parochial Church Council], under the guidance of the faculty jurisdiction' (CCC 1988: Section 5.1). Attempting to ensure that parishes understand the importance and relevance of this responsibility is a long-term educative process, and resistance to it is most often based in concerns about financial implications. Despite the CCC's report in 1988, it soon became clear that its various recommendations could not be realistically implemented and that it did not address the range of issues. A new working party was formed to address this and it was established with the following agenda:

- to discover the current level of resourcing for archaeological issues in each diocese and the status of the archaeological advisor
- to consider how the Church of England could best fulfil its obligations to archaeology, and how to improve the evaluation on archaeological concerns by the DACs and the CCC
- to produce a programme of education through publications, seminars etc.
- to encourage mutual understanding between archaeologists and parishes.

The subsequent report, *Church Archaeology: Its Care and Management* (CCC 1999), stated that the system in place was adequate but that its execution was patchy and the resources made available for archaeology were wholly inadequate. The reason for this seemed to be based on what the report identified as 'a lack of knowledge of and sympathy with archaeology at all levels of the Church's system of building control from the CCC to the parishes' and the subsequent lack of central guidelines and local policies. This was a sad indictment on the Church's response to the increasing profile of archaeology within law and guidance within both secular and ecclesiastical spheres. Having said this, the education and resourcing of the largely voluntary staff that support the parishes and advise the DACs over as many as 16,000 parishes is no easy matter and by no means lends itself to a quick fix. The fact that the Church was prepared to carry out such a comprehensive and soul-searching review of its own modus operandi demonstrated the real commitment at a central level to addressing the archaeological issues. This commitment was further demonstrated in 1999 by the implementation of one of the key recommendations of the report, that of the employment by the CCC of a full-time professional archaeology officer. The post, which is involved with both faculty jurisdiction and the CCCs role in the Pastoral Measure procedures, has enabled archaeology to be given a profile previously absent from the central structure. In particular it enabled the commencement of national and regional seminars intended to bring together those working within the local authority and DAC spheres. Since 1999, therefore, there has been an increase in the number of dioceses producing archaeological policy documents, although some dioceses have yet to complete this exercise. Further professional unity has been provided by the formation in 2000 of the Association of Diocesan and Cathedral Archaeologists, also based on a recommendation by the working party report, which exists to provide a forum for debate as well as promote professional standards within Church archaeology. The definition of the role of the advisor has therefore been developed and addressed, although it is noteworthy that still most Diocesan Archaeological Advisors either give their time voluntarily or the services are provided by archaeological professionals within a local authority.

The process of education of course is not restricted to those actually carrying out the archaeological works, and who are often responsive to the demands placed upon them. The report articulated the issue of the ultimate responsibility of the parish. Lingering resentment over the requirement to spend money on archaeology existed (and exists), and much of this stemmed from the general lack of understanding about the purpose and benefits of archaeology. It short, there existed a lack of ownership by the parishes. This represents a problem that requires long-term education and a change in culture, which has been developing ever since the introduction of the 1991 Measure and PPG 16 and its sister document PPG 15 on *Planning and the Historic Environment* issued in 1995. All the responsibility, however, should not fall at the doors of the parish, and the issue of consistent advice at a diocesan level continually needs to be addressed in order to ensure that parishes are getting the right assistance and guidance.

One practical way forward identified by the report for parishes was the creation of a *Statement of Significance* that highlighted the important and interesting features of the church, churchyard and fittings. The references to the need for such a document in the Faculty Jurisdiction Rules 2000 (see above) show how the legislative procedures have been able to respond positively to this report and other reviews (such as the Newman Review).

Although the provision for archaeological support at a diocesan and a central level has increased over the past ten years (and further scope exists for improvement), the problem of funding archaeological work has not receded. The 1993 version of this paper identified the need for a national policy for the realistic funding of Church archaeology. The requirement for archaeological work has continued to grow since then, and, despite having been identified as a priority eleven years ago, this plea remains the same today. This is of particular relevance in relation to projects for repair and maintenance. Where a parish is carrying out a development it can be reasonably argued that project costs and therefore fundraising goals should include full provision for archaeological works. Early evaluation can of course enable a mitigation of potential costs as well as a mitigation of the impact on the archaeological resource. EH (state) aid for churches was introduced in August 1977 for the financial year 1977–8: this was superseded by the 'joint scheme for churches' launched by EH and the Heritage Lottery Fund in 1996. However, these funds are specifically for repair and not for archaeology, and until 1996 eligibility was restricted to Grade I and Grade II* churches (the HLF now makes particular provision for Grade II churches). Although recording can be included as part of a repair programme and evaluation and survey as part of a stage 1 grant, there is no provision for grant-aid for archaeological recording where the repair itself is not eligible.

Archaeological involvement in the process of general fabric maintenance would inevitably assist in identifying risks to buildings of particular architectural and archaeological character, and the logical place for this is within the system of regular quinquennial inspections that have to be carried out by a qualified architect or building surveyor under the Inspection of Churches Measure 1955. Such an involvement is already a requirement for cathedrals (see below). The introduction in the new rules (FJR 2000) of the *Statement of Significance* for parish churches should additionally assist in enabling the parish to identify the likely impact of a particular proposal.

CATHEDRALS

Church of England cathedral churches lie wholly outside the scope of the faculty system, and until 1991 had no equivalent accountability whatsoever. A Cathedrals Advisory Commission was established under the Cathedrals Measure 1963, which existed to offer expert advice to cathedral chapters, but it had no statutory authority; in practice each cathedral could do as it pleased. The obvious potential for abuse prompted the Faculty Jurisdiction Commission to recommend in its 1984 report that works to cathedral churches should be brought under statutory control. The result was the Care of Cathedrals Measure 1990 (CCM) and the associated Rules (Statutory Instrument No. 2335 1990), which came into force on 1 March 1991, and then the corresponding enforcement legislation (Care of Cathedrals (Supplementary Provisions) Measure 1994).

Under this 1990 Measure the administrative body of a cathedral must obtain external approval for any works that would:

> materially affect the architectural, archaeological, artistic or historic character of the cathedral church or any building within the precinct of the cathedral church which is for the time being used for ecclesiastical purposes, the immediate setting of the cathedral church, or any archaeological remains within the precinct of the cathedral church (Section 2).

Approval must also be sought for the sale, loan or permanent disposal of any object of architectural, archaeological, artistic or historic interest, and for the permanent addition of any object. Applications for approval must be made to either the Cathedrals Fabric Commission for England (CFCE), or the cathedral's own Fabric Advisory Committee (FAC), depending on the exact nature of the proposed works, and there is a right of appeal against their decisions.

The CFCE is a national body established under the CCM in 1990, and superseded the earlier Cathedrals Advisory Commission. Its function is to ensure the highest possible standards of care and conservation, while having due regard to the fact that the cathedral is the seat of the bishop and a centre for Christian worship and mission. Its members are chosen after consultation with a wide range of specialist national bodies representing the interests of both conservation and worship and mission; the CFCE maintains close links with these organisations in both its judicial and advisory roles.

The CFCE determines all applications for proposals that would involve the permanent alteration or demolition of the fabric (Fig. 9.3), the disturbance or destruction of

Figure 9.3. Conservation work taking place at Ely Cathedral. All cathedral proposals for conservation and restoration require approval under the CCM in order to ensure appropriate recording, craftsmanship, and choice and quality of materials. *(© English Heritage)*

archaeological remains within the cathedral precinct, and the sale or loan of objects designated as being of outstanding interest. It also has the authority to call in for its own determination any proposal deemed to give rise to special considerations. When an application is made to the CFCE, notices must be placed on public display for not less than twenty-eight days and also sent to the local planning authority, to the national amenity societies, and to EH. All interested parties have a right to make representations, and any comments received must be taken into account by the CFCE when determining the case.

Each cathedral has its own FAC, half of its members being nominated by the administrative body and half by the CFCE. The FAC's primary role is to advise the administrative body upon all proposed works, and it has power to determine all those applications that do not require referral to the Commission. Notices of all such applications are placed on public display for not less than twenty-one days and sent to the CFCE and (in certain instances) the local planning authority for comment.

Listed Building Consent is still required for all buildings not in use for 'ecclesiastical purposes', and Scheduled Monument Consent must also be obtained where necessary. This means that where a cathedral precinct is scheduled, a system of dual control exists and permission is required under both secular and ecclesiastical authorities. This excludes the cathedral church itself, which cannot be scheduled (see above). The CFCE must be notified of all applications for Listed Building Consent and Scheduled Monument Consent made by the administrative body. The provisions of the Town and Country Planning Act 1990 also apply to all developments, and in cases where planning permission is required, cathedral bodies are encouraged to seek approval from the CFCE first. This is desirable from a practical viewpoint; since applications under the measure can often be processed more quickly than secular planning applications, and it also enables the local planning authority to ascertain the views of the CFCE before reaching its decision. The Measure inevitably includes a right of appeal, and the Enforcement Measure provides for the diocesan bishop to be called in using his visitorial powers to carry out enforcement proceedings in the event of an infringement of the CCM.

Since the Cathedrals Measure 1963, the administrative body of every cathedral has been required to appoint a cathedral architect. Under the 1990 Measure archaeology received similar recognition, and the appointment of an archaeological consultant became a statutory requirement. A number of archaeologists already served cathedrals in a less official capacity before this date. The 1990 Measure also provides for the architect's quinquennial inspection of the fabric to be undertaken in consultation with the archaeological consultant, and both are obliged to attend all FAC meetings. At the time the statutory post of the Cathedral Archaeological Consultant was one of the most significant developments in the legislative standing of archaeology in the Church of England, and certainly gives the cathedral consultant an authority denied to his or her diocesan counterpart. In 1995, and arising out of a series of annual symposia organised by the CFCE, the Association of Cathedral Archaeologists was formed. In 2000 this was re-formed to become the Association of Diocesan and Cathedral Archaeologists, in line with recommendations from the Church of England Working Party on Archaeology.

The 1990 Measure as a whole provides a far more secure framework for the control of archaeological projects than exists in the dioceses, not least because all proposals involving the disturbance or destruction of archaeological remains require approval at a national level by the CFCE. The commission is therefore able to implement the principles of government codes of practice to a consistent standard. It will insist on a full evaluation of the site and the formulation of an impact assessment and mitigation strategy before considering any scheme, and then may attach such conditions as it deems appropriate. Early consultation is encouraged and standards of project management are required to conform to current national guidelines.

In the early days of the implementation of the CCM there was, inevitably, a mixed response from cathedral chapters, many of whom resented the loss of previous autonomy. Just over ten years on the system is now clearly established and only minor points were raised by Newman in his 1997 Review. However, neither the enforcement procedures nor the appeal process have yet been fully tested in practice. Although this may raise concerns that the system has not been fully tested, the Commission has consistently worked with cathedral chapters and with those bodies that have a statutory right of comment on applications in an attempt to gain an appropriate balance between the requirements for worship and mission and those of care and conservation.

Despite this, a process of continual education is required. Some frustration among chapters is still evident (perhaps inevitably in such a young system), although rather than specifically relating to below-ground archaeology or fabric recording this may manifest itself instead in issues concerning conservation. In this context this rather overarching term refers to the general conflict between the presumption in favour of preservation and the pressures for a changing environment for worship and mission. It is often, in fact, fittings, furnishings and decorative schemes in cathedrals that are under threat, and mitigation by recording may not always be acceptable. The challenge is convincing chapters of the need to include an understanding of the significance of these items (both in their own right and as witnesses to the building's history and its Christian tradition) at an early stage of thinking about proposals for change: this understanding should inform the decision-making process rather than be attached to a proposal as an afterthought.

The mechanism and the working of the cathedrals system as a whole have undergone a recent further evaluation by the planned review of the measure, which began in 1999. This has led to the Care of Cathedrals (Amendment) Measure, which had its final reading in General Synod in February 2003. Having received the required parliamentary ratification and Royal Assent, the new Measure came into force on 1 April 2006. The review process for the 1990 Measure established that no matters of principle needed to be addressed within the current system, but that details to enforce or reinforce good practice based on ten years of the CCM being in operation were required. These have included an explicit requirement to take account of a presumption in favour of preservation and have strengthened the position of archaeology. For example, in relation to the archaeological provisions of the CCM, the archaeological consultant will have a more prominent role in the formulation of the quinquennial inspection report and will be required to produce a report on the archaeology of the cathedral church and its precinct; this might, for example, identify vulnerable aspects of the archaeological resource, establish the current level of understanding concerning any remains and set out strategic objectives for the future. In addition, annual reports to the cathedral chapter and copies to the CFCE will assess to what extent any policies or objectives have been met. As well as raising further the profile of the consultant as a key professional advisor to the cathedral chapter, these provisions should also promote strategic approaches and aid planning in addition to the continuing need to respond to particular pressures or projects.

The measure and its implementation have therefore provided significant advantages for the management of the archaeological resource at cathedrals. One of the advantages for cathedrals themselves was the introduction in 1991 of grant-aid from EH. In 1977, when the issue of grant-aid for churches was discussed between government and the Church of England, it was considered that the needs of the parish churches were greatest, and cathedrals were excluded partly on the grounds that they had better fundraising capabilities and partly because no system equivalent to Listed Building Consent was in place. However, this situation was reviewed in April 1991 and after a Government White Paper (*This Common Inheritance*) it was announced that £11.5 million would be made available to Anglican and Roman Catholic cathedrals over three years. The terms of the funding scheme was based on a survey of the condition of cathedrals carried out by EH in 1991, which identified that £185 million of work was needed to support cathedrals over a ten-year period, with £117 million being related to urgent fabric repairs. Although the scheme still exists, EH has carried out a review of how much of that projected work has actually been carried out (it maintains 85 per cent of the work identified in 1991 is completed) and has concluded, after analysis of a further condition survey, that a projected £57 million is required over the next five years. Subsequently the level of grant, although still available, is now reduced, and the State of the Historic Environment Report 2002 concludes that the scheme has achieved its objectives of slowing deterioration and assisting the management of the historic environment. Based on EH's recent condition survey, therefore, the future of the cathedral grants scheme is uncertain (and there is currently a commitment to provide grant aid until 2008, albeit on a reduced basis). The grants can include archaeological recording as part of the first stage of a conservation or repair that requires significant intervention into the fabric. In the event that EH ends its cathedral grant scheme, it will remain to be seen whether the programmes of maintenance and conservation, and the associated archaeological recording, can continue. The impact of the possible loss of the scheme would be not only one of the loss of available money at a particular level, but also would undermine the sense of confidence that has developed as a result of the reassurance of the partnership between the cathedrals and the state. This confidence has enabled and promoted planning for the future, and in combination with the regulatory system of the CCM has promoted the importance of good record-keeping and appropriate levels of archaeological recording.

PECULIARS

While the cathedrals were provided with an internal system of control in 1991 to enable the retention of ecclesiastical exemption under the 1994 Order, the so-called 'Peculiars' were granted the exemption on a temporary basis pending a review. Peculiars include naval, college and school chapels, chapels belonging to a public or charitable institution or owned by a religious community, and buildings within a peculiar of the Church of England (this includes Royal Peculiars which come under the direct control of Her Majesty via her Lord Chancellor). Surprisingly, these remained outside the statutory frameworks of the secular and ecclesiastical systems until the introduction of the Care of Places of Worship Measure 1999, which established the option for these buildings (with the exception of the Royal Peculiars) to be placed on a list held by the CCC, and thereby elect to come within the faculty jurisdiction; for those not on the list the ecclesiastical exemption ceases and they fall within the secular system.

The two major churches that fall into the category of Royal Peculiars are Westminster Abbey and St George's Chapel, Windsor; both of these opted to retain the exemption and, after extended discussions in the late 1990s between them and the DCMS, they set up their own formal planning committees (which at the Abbey already existed on an informal and advisory basis only) in an attempt to meet the requirements for continued exemption and in anticipation of the revision of the 1994 Order. Therefore, while the committees have been made statutory, unlike the cathedral system they are set up under their own statutes rather than by a separate structure. Despite this move to comply with the system of accountability and openness, inherent in the CCM for example, the overall systems of accountability and operation of the Royal Peculiars was also falling under scrutiny (and the public gaze). A comprehensive review of the situation was clearly required, and although the initiation of the review was a long time coming, a commission under the chairmanship of Professor Averil Cameron was established (Cameron 2001). This review was much broader in its terms of reference than just fabric issues, but in relation to these the report concluded that the current and recently adopted systems did not appropriately meet the criteria set out in PPG 15. The current systems were considered to lack the required level of independence from their institutions thereby not meeting the need for external evaluation and accountability that is inherent in the terms of the 1994 Order. Subsequently, the recommendation was that these two nationally important buildings should be subject to the same system as cathedrals, with which they can be most easily compared, and therefore be included within the terms of the Care of Cathedrals Measure. Resistance to this recommendation from the peculiars themselves (reminiscent of that shown by cathedrals in the late 1980s and early 1990s) has been demonstrated during the consultation period.

One might have expected the response to the report and the decision of the Lord Chancellor's Department (now the Department of Constitutional Affairs – DCA) to consider carefully whether the current situation is both politically sustainable and in the best interests of the buildings as major contributors to our national consciousness and heritage. However, a press release from the DCA in February 2004, which is the only public response to the Cameron Review so far, agreed to the recommendation for an independent assessor to consider disputes, but failed to acknowledge or comment upon the issues relating to the care of the fabric of the buildings in questions. This rather weak response might be considered disappointing by those who saw the possibility of Westminster Abbey or St George's Windsor coming under the umbrella of the CCM as a way to ensure standards across a range of architecturally comparable buildings. In the absence of any further formal comment on the Cameron Report, the question of whether the current arrangements are sufficiently independent and accountable, arguably, still remains.

NON-ANGLICAN CHURCHES

It will by now be apparent that, at least in so far as it related to the Church of England, the term 'ecclesiastical exemption' is something of a misnomer, for the Church is no way exempt from legal control of its historic buildings. Rather it has been given leave to administer its own system of control and this in turn has been ratified by parliament. Indeed, it could be argued that the Church of England controls for parish churches and cathedrals are actually superior to those exercised under the secular system in a number of respects. Firstly, Listed Building control is concerned specifically with matters of architectural and historic interest, while the Church's system also makes provision for safeguarding the archaeological and artistic character of a building. In addition, while Listed Building Consent is concerned only with demolition, alteration and extension, and internally only with fixtures, ecclesiastical control also covers repair and extends its protection to moveable contents.

As already mentioned, the 'ecclesiastical exemption' initially referred to all buildings in ecclesiastical use and therefore many denominations reaped the benefits of exemption without ever having established suitable alternative systems (never having made the promise of good conduct given by the Church of England). The preparation of the 1994 Order enabled major religious organisations to evaluate whether to be considered for exemption, and those that opted in were required to respond by putting in place their own systems of internal control. The government then was able to decide which denominations would be covered by the Order. As with the Church of England, these systems have to meet the criteria in the government's Code of Practice encapsulated in PPG 16 (DoE 1990a, para. 8.4), which sets out the need for the following: an independent decision-making body, public accountability and representation from public bodies, appeal procedures, maintenance of records and a quinquennial inspection system for the buildings. The Roman Catholic and the main Nonconformist churches chose exemption, while those buildings belonging to other faiths, such as synagogues and mosques, which had previous enjoyed exemption without providing any control, came under the secular system (for a brief summary see DNH 1994; also Fig. 9.4). The other exempt denominations (the Church in Wales, the Roman Catholic Church, the Baptist Union, the Methodist Church and the United Reformed Church), were therefore also reviewed by Newman in 1997. The systems pertaining to these denominations are briefly set out below.

The same basic principles apply to the Church in Wales as the Church of England, since the faculty system survived the Disestablishment of the Church in 1919. In 1991 the Governing Body of the Church in Wales established a Commission on Faculties to review both the faculty jurisdiction itself and the overall framework for the care of churches (Church in Wales 1992). As a result of this, and taking into account the then new measures of the Church of England, the faculty system continued on a diocesan basis and a central commission was established to deal with matters relating to cathedrals. Newman

Figure 9.4. The interior of Brighton and Hove Hebrew Congregation Synagogue. Non-Anglican places of worship are now increasingly being considered within listing and designation, and in the future may be allowed the same 'privilege' of ecclesiastical exemption. *(© English Heritage)*

concluded that the results of this review had the potential to be effective, and the government went on to make a series of recommendations to bring the system more in line with accepted procedures for consultation within other systems. Since then the system has undergone a further internal reorganisation, and now both the cathedrals and the parish churches are handled under the faculty jurisdiction system at a diocesan level with DACs and chancellors. A central body (akin to the CCC) exists to advise on cathedral projects and other applications for parish churches that have a significant effect on the character of the building or are considered controversial.

In the early 1990s the Roman Catholics provided no central administrative structure for monitoring works to its buildings and individual dioceses were almost wholly autonomous, with arrangements being made predominantly at the discretion of the bishop. A central committee was established after 1994 and, as currently constituted, is a subcommittee of the Art and Patrimony Division of the Bishops Conference. This works in a similar way to the CCC and coordinates the Historic Church Committees of the dioceses, which, after due application and public notification, can determine applications for approval of proposals. A Code of Practice was produced in 1995, and Newman considered that with some amendments, which were subsequently accepted by the subcommittee, the system would be effective.

The Methodist Church already had a central Church Property Division in place that handled applications for works over a certain financial limit and therefore the creation of a single Listed Buildings Advisory Committee within this Division, in order to comply with the 1994 Order, was not complex. This committee acts as advisory to the Property Secretary of the Methodist Conference and, unlike the Roman Catholic system, is supported by a conservation officer, who was employed pre-Newman.

While the existing administrative structure of the Methodist Church lent itself to the need for a centralised system of planning control for Listed Buildings, the same was not true for the Baptist Union, which is a more dispersed and disaggregated union of small units. Although a central Listed Buildings Advisory Committee was established, Newman concluded that this was not providing the required level of protection and ordered an emergency review of the system within twelve months of his report. A statistical review of the administrative procedures was subsequently carried out, which identified a lack of applications but an overall improvement. In 1999, among other things, the government urged for the speedy production of guidance notes on good practice, which have been put in hand subsequently and for the appointment of a conservation officer. The latter has not been implemented.

The system adopted by the United Reformed Church is centralised only to the extent that the general secretary coordinates the work of the provincial surveyors; the decision-making bodies are based in each of the twelve provinces, although like all regionalised committees the workload that falls on each is variable.

In January 1999 the government stated that there would be a further review of the exempt denominations within the current parliament, and with this in mind issued a consultation document for a revised version of the 1994 Order. Subsequently this was put on hold as the specifics of the exemption were pushed slightly further down the agenda by the consideration of more general issues facing the historic environment into which church buildings inevitably fit. The result was the production of the following documents: in December 2000, *The Power of Place* (led by EH and in partnership with the heritage sector; EH 2000a); and in December 2001, *A Force for Our Future* (by the DCMS and the Department for Transport, Local Governments and the Regions – DTLGR; DCMS and DTLGR 2001). These set out to understand how the public considered issues relating to the historic environment generally and then to identify a policy agenda that responds appropriately to those findings. Although there is not space here to discuss these in detail, two particular outcomes have been the decision to raise the profile, within EH, of places of worship generally and the implementation of a comprehensive review of the system of designation for sites and monuments.

Although it was anticipated that the review of the denominations would have been within the context of the designation review, the latter occurred in advance and a separate paper on the ecclesiastical question was produced, the public consultation on which ended in May 2004 (DCMS 2004f). This paper proposed that the exemption should continue to operate, but under 'management agreements' to be made with EH. It further suggested that EH should have the power to validate and monitor the effectiveness of the exemption systems of control. The responses to the DCMS review were varied and it could be considered that this review has provided neither the level of comprehensive analysis nor the independent scrutiny evident in the Newman Review. It is not clear at present how this will be taken forward, or indeed what the precise role of EH should be.

The principle of encouraging management agreements does, however, relate closely to the overall approach being adopted as part of the Heritage Protection Review which is currently being administered by EH. Currently, for example, a number of pilot projects for church buildings are taking place in order to assess how any proposed new designation system could apply to churchyards and buildings, and in particular how the issue of including burial grounds and the ground under churches, currently exempt from scheduling, would be handled. These pilots will also be used to consider how management agreements between local authorities, the dioceses and EH might work. Proposed reform of the designation system, of which these ecclesiastical pilots are part, will lead directly to a white paper, which, at the time of writing, is scheduled for late 2006. However, it is not yet clear how the proposed role of EH will either take account of the current holistic approach already being implemented under the Care of Cathedrals Measure, for example, nor how it will relate within a statutory context to the decision-making role of the ecclesiastical bodies currently operating.

Perhaps one of the most interesting proposals in the consultation document is the suggestion that the exemption could be extended, as an option, to denominations and faith groups that were not entitled to the exemption after the 1994 Order. It will be interesting to see how, if adopted, this more socially inclusive policy might be implemented and operated.

CONCLUSIONS

Although the system for Church of England parish churches has long been established, the last fifteen years have seen the successful implementation of the Care of Cathedrals Measure 1990 and the much needed introduction of a comparable system of accountability for non-Anglican denominations. And while the precise fate of the Royal Peculiars remains unclear, the tide has been moving in the direction of an accountable system. Although the exemption is rightly under constant observation and regular review it is by no means clear that a simple withdrawal of that exemption and a transfer to the secular system as it stands would provide the level of protection that is now expected for churches, their fittings, furnishings and churchyards. The importance of the stock of church buildings to the historic environment as a whole has been most recently recognised in the first State of the Historic Environment Report (EH 2002a). The Church of England has now also produced a public statement on its built heritage (Church of England 2004). This document seeks to demonstrate the community value of churches, seeks out partnerships, and clarifies the role of the various church bodies which plan for their continuing and developing role in training, education, and support for those directly responsible for building maintenance and care. This document is to be commended as it indicates a willingness of the Church of England to have ownership over some of the pertinent issues and because it is the first united response from the many central parts of the Church of England on church buildings. However, while clearly of political benefit, it may not be perceived universally as cutting to the heart of the matter concerning both funding issues and the sustainable future of church buildings, with their inherent architectural and archaeological value. The pressure remains on all those involved in archaeology and conservation to maintain high standards, to educate and to address the perennial problem of funding.

It is true to say that the role of archaeology in the planning process has come a long way since the spate of conservation and archaeology related laws and guidance notes that emerged in the early 1990s. The process of both internal and external review of the procedures and practices within the system of ecclesiastical exemption has enabled and promoted continuous adaptation and revision. The CCC and the CFCE continue to address the problems that face church archaeology in particular, and a major review and investigation into the legal, ethical and archaeological issues surrounding the treatment of human remains is currently under way.

Many of the issues concerning education and appreciation of the importance of the archaeological resource are, of course, not unique to the church environment. With this in mind it is interesting that the spate of television programmes in recent years focusing on archaeology and history have clearly both responded to and significantly increased popular demand, and this is likely to have an overall benefit in raising the profile of archaeology and explaining its value in a very general way. This, however, is a far cry from the realities of the poverty-stricken parish, dependent on voluntary labour and not eligible for grant-aid that faces urgent repair work. Archaeology is often not as glamorous nor as easy as the media portrays.

Furthermore, while this chapter has concentrated on those buildings and places covered by the ecclesiastical systems of control, there are a large number of sites that were once ecclesiastical and yet now fall under secular control. The most common example of this, other than a redundant church, is a closed churchyard which may or may not be linked to an extant church building. Excavations of burial grounds now divorced from their historical connection with a parish or cathedral building pose yet more problems. The publicity in early 2003 concerning the excavation of a large burial ground for the construction of the new Eurostar station at St Pancras highlighted the dangers of a major developer placing unrealistic timescales on excavations, and demonstrated how as a result there would have been a significant loss of artefacts and human remains. One lesson in this case, apparently still sadly needing to be learnt, is of course the critical importance of a comprehensive appraisal and evaluation and the subsequent need for realistic provision to be made for excavation and recording. The remonstrations against the proposal to clear the site without proper archaeological mitigation in this case were largely led by the Council for the Care of Churches with EH. While the significance of this site to church, urban and social archaeology may be easy to identify, there still exist comparable problems on less publicised projects. The scope of the Church's interest and investment in archaeology therefore stretches far beyond the strict application of its own legal jurisdiction and into the wider world of the archaeology and the history of places of worship.

CHAPTER 10

LOCAL AUTHORITY OPPORTUNITIES

David Baker and Ken Smith with Ian Shepherd
(Scottish dimension)

The uncertainties affecting archaeological opportunities available to local authorities twelve years ago (Baker and Shepherd 1993) have not diminished. In 2005, while Scotland and Wales have sets of unitary councils, England has a motley collection of unitaries, counties and districts, the product of an incomplete review in the mid-1990s: all three countries now have National Parks, some of which are planning authorities. There is a question mark over the role of English county councils, as hosts to many of the local authority historic environment services, because of government policies for regional government.and new planning legislation, though the rejection of regionalisation by the North-East (November 2004) may have reduced the threat.

Yet circumstances are changing and may bring new opportunities. The current system of heritage designations and consent procedures for works affecting historic assets is being reviewed by government; proposals being developed by English Heritage (EH) for England could simplify matters and make them more widely understandable if government priorities allow sufficient parliamentary time for the required primary legislation. One outcome of the concurrent review of Sites and Monuments Records (SMRs) is formal government support for their existence as a statutory requirement of local authorities. A conflation of PPGs 15 and 16 into a single new PPS for the historic environment, in draft at the time of writing, will greet a sector striving to become an integrated community, with an Historic Environment Forum seeking to present a united response to the political agenda being developed by the All-Party Parliamentary Archaeology Group (APPAG) (Chapter 4).

Local government attitudes are also being reorientated: 'authority' is less the watchword than 'customer'; services should be responsive to the needs of users and communities rather than be provided to a grateful public. The shift of emphasis towards users has been driven by government policies for improving community and individual access to culture in all its forms, at last recognising the role of the historic environment in social, economic and environmental policy. There is now less talk of a finite and non-renewable cultural resource that can be seen as an obstacle to economic regeneration, and more emphasis on conservation as the intelligent management of change to places that are cherished because they are familiar, in the interests of society and economy, today and tomorrow. However, delivery continues to be frustrated by the lack of adequate resources.

This review considers local authority opportunities through the archaeological processes of historical conservation, which is essentially a knowledge-based activity, acquiring, analysing and communicating with a range of present and future users. It concentrates primarily upon the historic landscape and archaeological sites rather than historic buildings, which, like maritime archaeology, are covered elsewhere. It was completed in 2004, amid a flurry of relevant initiatives from government and in the sector.

THE PURPOSES AND PROCESSES OF HISTORICAL CONSERVATION

The process model presented twelve years ago (Baker and Shepherd 1993) still holds good. It envisaged historical conservation as a continuous, multi-staged activity, involving a variety of organisations, and serving a range of social interests, through a continuous broad cycle of conservation processes containing within it a narrow cycle of management. At the outset, classes of survival are defined as having historic interest. The population of survivals is identified through survey, whose information product is stored in record systems with dual functions as archives and management tools. The management cycle draws upon understanding of historical interest, also generating new information to be fed back into the records system; by adding to knowledge of class, place or period and about the condition of the surviving resource, it increases potential understanding for future management.

The end of the model (where too often resources tend to run out) listed the diverse set of reasons for doing it all, including research as an activity to find out more about the human past, education to give the rising generations historical awareness and appreciation, satisfaction of the curiosity of local people and tourists, and management of the environment through land-use planning and other processes. Together, these outputs contribute to the human cultures that own those remains, and to general interest and support that can be expressed through the political process. In turn, they feed back to the general awareness of heritage and its value, which is the basis of conservation work.

That model shows how much of this task can be achieved, directly or by facilitation, through the broad spread of services provided by local authorities. A local authority perspective reinforces the ubiquity of the historic environment in time and space: each region, county, district, parish and National Park has a historic landscape with settlement patterns, settlements, sites, buildings and artefacts.

ORGANISATIONAL REQUIREMENTS

In 1995, the then Department of National Heritage (DNH) gave advice to local authorities, then in the throes of reorganisation, about the kind of historical conservation services they should provide. The advice was notable for its comprehensive nature and the failure to follow it up properly. Twelve years ago we wrote that successful conservation depends upon a combination of information and expertise. This was elaborated in EH's *Heritage under Pressure* (Baker and Chitty 2002) which identified two sets of categories of resources needed for a successful service. One, incorporating four principal elements, comprises expert *personnel*, non-core-staff *budgets* for grant aid, proactive casework and project work, *information* resources and *partnerships* with other environmental and development agencies. The other, dominated by four contextual ones, comprises clarity of legislation, *policy* and guidance, an *organisation* that is supportive structurally and culturally, and a *political climate* that is informed and supportive and a local *community* of informed stakeholders. Their presence or absence can be tested by recently introduced 'continuous performance assessment' under the new 'best value' regimes; three performance indicators for historic environment services have been included in the consultation set formalised by the Audit Commission for 2005.

The main effect of PPG 16 (DoE 1990a) on local authority archaeological services has been felt through the 'purchaser'/'provider' model of service structures, mistranslated frequently as 'curator' and 'contractor', with the latter 'out-sourced' despite the inability of knowledge-based activities to cope with largely unregulated market forces. The proliferation of independent field units and consultancies has tended to put local authorities into the role of service purchaser and project monitor rather than implementer. The necessary division between so-called curatorial and contracting functions has hardened into a chasm across which the need for bridges is increasingly recognised. An exception to these arrangements is in Wales, where the four trusts serve the unitary councils of Wales and combine regulatory and research/recording functions, separated by Chinese walls.

The world of archaeology may have fragmented, but a broader approach to historical conservation has developed, attempting to unite the below- and above-ground, historic urban settlements and rural landscapes. Methodologically, a difficult transition has started, towards recognising that a 'small-a' archaeological approach – analysing and understanding physical evidence before making decisions about conservation or explaining it – should be common to all aspects of the historic environment; it has to make headway against fears that it is a bid by 'buried' interests to take over 'built' ones. The idea has now taken root, both in principle and in practice in some authorities, although its delivery is still frustrated by inherited divisions of legislation, organisational frameworks and training-based professional culture. Implementation of the government's response to the review of heritage designations and SMRs should remove at least some of these blockages.

Meanwhile, it continues to be the case that many archaeological services are provided from county level, and most of those for the historic built environment from district level; the new unitary councils that now exist have not all automatically created combined services. However, the combination of the outcomes of the above-mentioned reviews and implementation of the Planning and Compulsory Purchase Act (2004) is likely to see a radical transformation of historic environment services as a response to the need to develop Local Development Frameworks based on Regional Spatial Strategies, to be delivered principally through district and unitary authorities.

DEFINITION

Twelve years ago we wrote that local authorities have a largely passive role in defining what elements of the environment have historic value, and can get caught between contradictory tendencies: on the one hand, industrial archaeology can be hated for its association with the dereliction and redundancies of deindustrialisation; on the other, an almost universal awareness of 'heritage' too easily leads to an unfocused confusion of history and fiction. Time here is showing itself to be a great healer, with the new generations showing a positive interest in the industrial legacy, and people in some localities expressing regret that so much was cleared away. The confusion of 'heritage' and history is gaining some perspective, not by emphasising a hard distinction so much as by promoting the ubiquity of the historic environment. The established built environment concept of the 'cherished local scene' has been broadened into a more comprehensive sense of place, made up of a range of specific items designated as of varying formal value, and sitting within wider frameworks of landscape or townscape characterisation. This connects with the positive inclusion of people in the celebration and enjoyment of their local cultural heritage, and the cherishing of local landmarks and scenes, the elements that combine to provide an area's 'local distinctiveness'.

The opportunities for local authorities are considerable: the risk is that in a context of limited resources it is seen as a choice or a departmental competition between environment versus culture, or conservation versus enjoyment, rather than no conservation without explanation. Ideally, the 'enjoyment' capability promotes conservation attitudes and explains conservation needs as part of its educational remit, while the 'conservation' side has time to explain its advice in terms of a wider community interest and participate in broader schemes of environmental definition and explanation. The greatest potential scope for the latter probably lies in the descriptive and analytical process that ought to be followed in making Conservation Area Appraisals, either as part of new designations or as an explanation and justification of existing ones. Such projects would properly be led by built environment aspects, but equally should include all others, including the archaeology of settlement planning, landscape context, significant former sites and historic buildings. These can enable individuals, members of local amenity and archaeological or historical societies, or classes from local schools, to learn for themselves that some things are historic, thus gaining personal ownership of discovery.

IDENTIFICATION SURVEY

The scope of survey work and the opportunities it provides local authorities have broadened over the last twelve years, partly because of national initiatives led by EH, and partly because of the growing recognition of how characterisation can help in seeking to identify 'heritage assets'. An approach to identification survey that is more structured and focused has been developed through three schemes in particular, as partnerships between EH and local authorities.

Urban archaeological assessment

The Urban Archaeological Assessment programme – and the resultant Urban Archaeological Databases (UADs) – handle the detailed and complex evidence in the historic centres of major towns and cities with the aid of Geographical Information Systems (GIS). Survey and data collection create a database usable interactively for casework, which in turn brings in more information. Technical drawbacks have been the relatively early cut-off date that makes integration with historic buildings difficult and insufficient spatial integration with the local SMRs; the time and resources needed to complete a project through to the final stage of archaeological strategy has also been a problem with several potential UADs not even started.

Extensive urban survey programme

This programme offers a more structured approach to surveying the towns and larger villages for which a UAD is not appropriate. Not only does it aim to stock the SMR adequately, but it also generates a series of map-based summaries and reconstructions that have a wider application for telling local people about it all and feeding into Conservation Area Appraisals.

Historic landscape characterisation

Over the last decade, a significant development in understanding landcape change has been the EH-led Historic Landscape Characterisation initiative (Chapter 17). This work began in Cornwall and is now either completed or under way across almost 60 per cent of England. It has led to a significant increase in understanding how landscape has developed over time, then used for development control and rural land management. It has also made a significant contribution to the development of landscape character assessment, a holistic approach that takes account of the historic component. Landscape character assessment is an essential tool for identifying landscape management needs and solutions; it has been actively promoted and initially grant-aided by the Countryside Agency for a number of years (Swanwick and Land Use Consultants 2002).

DATA STORAGE

Accessible information is the basic intelligence about landscape, habitation, fabric and deposit, without which significance cannot be ascertained, decay slowed, change wisely promoted, character and appearance enhanced, or significance and understanding communicated. It is also the medium by which inherited knowledge is transmitted to future generations, in parallel with, or as a substitute for, the physical survivals themselves. It supports continuing research and brings the past and its material remains to a wide range of interests. In the last five years, there has been much stronger emphasis placed on what is now called 'informed conservation', having sufficient information to make good conservation decisions, which in turn relies upon having information systems (Clark 2001).

Full coverage of England and Wales by SMRs was achieved by the late 1980s. Numbers of local record systems have increased by over 50 per cent in the last ten years because of local government reorganisation and the development of Urban Archaeological Databases for major historic cities and towns; 88 were counted in 1998, and 110 in 2002. An SMR has been defined as 'a definitive permanent general record of the local historic environment in its national context, publicly and professionally maintained, whose data are accessible and retrievable for a wide range of purposes' (Baker 1999a: 3, 1999b: 3).

Increasingly, SMRs are including historic buildings and historic landcape characterisation data, developing into Historic Environment Records (HERs), while others have become part of wider environmental databases. A majority now have GIS linked to their databases.

During the last ten years, SMRs have gained in status. Their role in the planning process, established by the General Development Order of 1988 and repeated in PPG 16 (DoE 1990a), has been confirmed in 2004 with a commitment by government to achieving both statutory status and the resources required to achieve the first stage of the benchmark process (see below) (DCMS 2004e). Recognition as the potentially definitive local detailed record, in a long-awaited agreement made with the former Royal Commission on the Historical Monuments of England in 1996, allowed the National Monuments Record to develop a new facilitating and coordinating role, confirmed in a recent review (EH 2004). This has included data standards, a data audit scheme for individual SMRs, the 'event-monument-archive' model of data organisation, and thesauri of terms.

The situation in Wales has always been rather different, with SMRs attached to the four regional Archaeological Trusts, and substantially funded by the Welsh Royal Commission. The opportunity provided by a relatively small area and relatively uniform arrangements is allowing the development of an Extended National Database (END), to include records from the four trusts, CADW's scheduled monument database, the Royal Commission's National Monuments Record, and the National Museums and Galleries of Wales. At the time of writing more direct and detailed access to the four SMRs is being considered through a single internet entry point.

As part of the drive to bring SMRs up to a consistent standard, those of Wales, England and Scotland were assessed in the later 1990s (Baker 1997, 1999a, 1999b), showing a situation improving on that reported here in 1993, and subsequently taken further still. The English and Scottish assessments introduced the idea of a general standard to which it was reasonable to expect a fully stocked, properly organised and adequately resourced SMR to aspire. The English assessment showed that the average for the seventy-five SMRs it covered was 50 per cent of the standard, with sixty-seven of them in a well-defined range between 35 and 64 per cent. The SMR Content and Computing Survey of 2002 produced some directly comparable material: use of a computerised database had increased from 81 to 93 per cent, not least because of the availability of new software: the number of SMRs using GIS rose from twenty-five to eighty-two (Newman 2002).

A report for EH on *Historic Environment Records – Benchmarks for Good Practice* (Chitty 2002) laid out a two-stage process by which SMRs might attain a standard and status attributed to that title. A further project has investigated the costs of bringing SMRs to the first stage, that of a fully effective SMR in the traditional archaeological sense, providing an indicative figure of £8.2 million (Baker *et al.* 2004).

The continuing fall-out from local government review perpetuates its wild-card status, exacerbated now by the developing regional agenda. SMRs were set up on a county basis, but spend most of their time providing information to district planning officers. Few districts have viable SMRs, apart from the growing number of UADs. Many district and unitary authorities are too small to support a viable record but the Planning and Compulsory Purchase Act (2004) locates the local planning process firmly at that level of local government, at the expense of the counties. The move towards a single designation list and statutory status for SMRs will undoubtedly require any amount of fancy footwork to ensure that, at worst, the current level of historic environment service provision is maintained and, at best, that an integrated and comprehensive system of historic environment service is provided across a region and beyond. As part of this process, SMRs and UADs will need to move towards integration, combining the strengths of both types of system, as has been successfully done with Newcastle and the Tyne and Wear Joint Service.

PLANNING

It is through the land-use planning system that the greatest opportunities arise for the beneficial management of the cultural resource, given its primary concern with the balance between the economic benefits of development and the conservation of the physical environment. The key documents for archaeology currently remain the Ancient Monuments and Archaeological Areas Act 1979 (AMAA Act 1979), PPG 16 (DoE 1990a) and PPG15 (DoE and DNH 1994). Further formal consultation on PPS 15, a new Planning Policy Statement and Guidance for the historic environment, combining the two PPGs, is to be delayed, perhaps until 2007, pending the overall outcomes of the review of heritage designations.

That review is likely to have a significant impact on management of the historic environment through the planning process, not least through the creation of a single register of historic sites and buildings in England. It will also see significant changes to the process of designation, which is likely to become the responsibility of EH rather than DCMS, and of consents – all of which will become the responsibility of local authorities. It proposes significant enhancement of the nature and extent of community and individual engagement with the overall process of designation and management of the historic environment.

Plans

The Planning and Compensation Act 1991 clarified the importance of development plans by stating a clear presumption in favour of granting permission for proposals that conform to their policies. Thus plans at all levels should between them have set a framework capable of ensuring that most aspects of the historic environment are at least taken into account when considering site-specific issues.

The existing framework of regional planning guidance, structure, local, waste, minerals and unitary development plans, developed over several decades, is about to change significantly with the implementation of the Planning and Compulsory Purchase Act 2004. Government wishes to move speedily to Regional Spatial Strategies prepared by regional planning bodies and Local Development Frameworks containing development plan documents prepared by a range of non-county authorities – district councils, unitary authorities, Broads Authority, National Park authorities: the latter will include minerals and waste development plan documents prepared by county councils.

Local Development Framework

In delivering the spatial strategy, the Local Development Framework will focus not only on location and land use but also include economic, social and environmental matters – the 'triptych of sustainability'. All local authorities must submit a Local Development Scheme to the Secretary of State within prescribed timescales, setting out their portfolio of local development documents. It will comprise three types of document. First, a core strategy will provide the planning framework for the area and all development plan documents, including generic development control policies, site-specific allocations and policies, Area Action plans for key areas of change or conservation, and criteria-based policies to ensure that development meets the requirements of the core strategy and is in conformity with it. This set of documents will be separately illustrated by regularly revised proposals maps. Second, supplementary planning documents will provide policy guidance on a wide range of issues, both thematic and site-specific, supplementing the policies and proposals in the development plan documents; examples are design guides, area development briefs or issue-based documents. Third, a statement of community involvement will set out the standards by which the plan-making authority intends to involve the community in preparing, altering and continuously reviewing all the local development documents. It will not be a development plan document per se, but will be subject to examination.

Strategic Environmental Assessment

Also important in this context is Strategic Environmental Assessment (SEA). The European SEA Directive (2001/42/EC) requires a formal environmental assessment of certain plans and programmes that includes land use and planning. Implemented from 21 July 2004, its objective is 'to provide for a high level of protection of the environment and to contribute to the integration of environmental considerations into the preparation and adoption of plans and programmes with a view to promoting sustainable development'. It is mandatory for plans and programmes prepared for agriculture, forestry, fisheries, energy, industry, transport, waste management, water management, telecommunications, tourism, town and country planning or land use and also for those which because of their likely effect on sites require an assessment under the Habitats Directive.

It is a requirement that the environmental report includes an assessment of the likely significant effects on, *inter alia*, 'cultural heritage including architectural and archaeological heritage' (Annex 1 of the Directive). The responsibility for providing (though not necessarily doing) the assessment lies with the authority that produces the plans and the environmental report should be made available at the same time as any draft plan or programme and be an integral part of the consultation process. There is a requirement for public consultation as part of the SEA process, as well as with the designated authorities with environmental responsibilities. For England, this currently (2005) means the Countryside Agency, EH, English Nature and the Environment Agency.

When a plan or programme is adopted, there is a duty to inform, among others, the environmental authorities and the public, making available the plan as adopted with a statement summarising how environmental considerations have been taken into consideration. It must also explain how the Environmental Report (and the opinions expressed in it) has been taken into account and why particular options have been chosen when there is a range to chose from. Monitoring measures must also be identified and implementation has to be monitored.

These changes in the development plan system leave county councils with responsibility only for minerals and waste development plans. In seeing how the system might work, and assessing its strengths and weaknesses, several issues need to be taken into account, including those arising from government decisions in June 2004 on the results of the consultations on the review of designations and on SMRs. At present, most HERs are lodged with county councils, and most conservation officers with district, unitary and National Park authorities. There will need to be a significant re-examination of the relationship between councils regarding the provision of historic environment data from HERs for the purpose of development control and other local authority services. Among other things, this will need to ensure that appropriate economies of scale are achieved in order that cost-effective advice and other provision can be delivered.

As part of the designations review, responsibility for consents within the proposed single Register of Historic Sites and Buildings of England will rest with local authorities, presumably local planning authorities, that is, district, unitary and National Park authorities. Resources for local historical conservation services generally were reduced by 8 per cent in real terms between 1997 and 2002 (Baker and Chitty 2002). The number of planning applications warranting an archaeological intervention has increased slightly but only to about 5 per cent of the overall total, while historic environment issues have begun to infiltrate areas such as education, information and outreach with a small but growing engagement in community and inclusion issues. Conservation officer provision has been characterised as suffering from isolated, overworked officers, often at a junior level and with too few resources to provide effective levels of integrated and sustainable management.

There are issues about adequate resourcing, recognised in the designations review response from government which proposed piloting sub-regional teams as a way of providing integrated information, advice and action for the historic environment. These proposals will need significant further work in order successfully to provide a system that is fit for purpose, delivering cost-effective information and advice at an appropriate level that meets community needs and expectations.

Development control

Development control ought to provide opportunities for positive conservation as well as what is perceived as the negative defence of site, building or area. Too often the latter obtains because the developer has either not secured the relevant information early enough, or is hoping to bulldoze the opposition. The process known as 'Informed Conservation' (Clark 2001) works on the basis that understanding the value of what might be at risk can facilitate acceptable compromises or otherwise unlooked-for gains.

Not only should applicants be fully aware of any potential archaeological constraints before they formally submit their proposals, but there should also be good communication between planning officers and specialist conservation and/or archaeological officers drawing upon their own information systems. The identity of significant items recorded on the information system must be registered on the overall planning constraints maps maintained either as hard copy or, increasingly, as a GIS layer within the planning department. This enables a potential impact to trigger a specialist consultation that allows the extent of any problem to be fully explored.

Defining what ought to be registered as a constraint is a difficult exercise requiring judgement and a measure of realism, bearing in mind the intensity and variety of survivals in most areas of England. Listed Buildings and Scheduled Monuments have always been obvious and should remain so as entries on the new register, but other categories are more problematical. Important unlisted buildings might be identified through a local list or by their location in a Conservation Area. Important unscheduled sites might have already been identified through the scoring processes undertaken by local government archaeological officers participating in EH's Monument Protection Programme (MPP): however, if a realistic threshold is not adopted, too much land may appear to be constrained, with a corresponding loss of credibility. To justify landscapes as constraints requires that they are distinctively identifiable or have been designed in some way. Some of the challenges, themselves an opportunity for local authorities, are how to apply what has been learnt about historic landscapes over the last decade to operations either subject to planning control or controllable only through management agreements.

In order to assess the impact of any planning application it is essential to have sufficient information about what is proposed. It might affect a place where there may be a site, a building that might have as yet unidentified qualities, or a landscape whose spatial and temporal components have not yet been identified. Getting the rather obvious requirement for information generally accepted as a principle and in practice for all kinds of heritage assets has had to combat a strong political tide which effectively rates the time taken to process an application above the quality of decision. Some local authorities have espoused 'informed conservation' wholeheartedly, not least because resolution of contentious issues at the pre-application stage can facilitate smooth problem-free processing of the application subsequently submitted. This is particularly so with the increased delegation of the decision-making process to officers, rather than to planning committees. A statutory requirement that all local authorities maintain or have access to an Historic Environment Record can only improve information flows in development control.

An accepted flexible, staged approach to the investigation of land threatened by development is now well established. Classically, it involves an appraisal to see if there is a potential problem, a desk-top assessment of all existing readily available information, and, if needed, a programme of field evaluation. The latter can involve a combination of documentary research, aerial photography, fieldwalking, earthwork survey, geophysical prospecting and test pits or trial trenches. The overall result is intended to underpin proposals for mitigation of impact that can range from amendments to increase preservation *in situ*, through securing provision for recording in advance of destruction, to outright refusal of consent. Mitigation in the form of pre-destruction recording is achieved by the use of a now familiar 'negative' planning condition requiring implementation by the applicant of a scheme of work approved by the local planning authority in advance of the commencement of development.

The initial appraisal is conducted by the curatorial archaeologist within the local authority, while the assessments, evaluations and other field work are usually undertaken by archaeological contractors, to briefs usually (but not always) provided by the curatorial archaeologist. These are sometimes drawn up directly by the contractors or through archaeological consultants retained by the developer. Both the Institute of Field Archaeologists (IFA) and the Association of Local Government Archaeological Officers (ALGAO) have issued guidance. All work, whether by curator, contractor or consultant is expected to be undertaken by individuals working to the standards and codes of conduct for the profession produced by the IFA. The IFA has a Register of Archaeological Organisations (RAO) scheme of accreditation, which is often erroneously perceived as being for contracting organisations only. The IFA is currently reviewing its standards in order to close an increasingly divisive gap within the profession between contractors and curators, to focus upon the common task of sustainably managing the historic environment.

The process of appraisal, assessment and evaluation has opened up tremendous opportunities but has also conferred new and heavy responsibilities that are a key indicator of archaeology's political arrival. These include an awareness of the interests of others, together with a sense of the values that help to integrate rather than divide archaeology and society. All Britain may be a palimpsest of archaeological survivals, but this does not justify automatic and possibly expensive fieldwork evaluation of all proposals without valid predictive archaeological information. Similarly, archaeological recommendations for mitigation must be economical with both the historic resource and developers' resources, especially when the latter's profit is social rather than financial, and otherwise acceptable proposals are economically marginal. Ingenuity and sensitivity on such matters are required to wean unreconstructed local planning authorities away from refusing to ask for evaluation prior to consent, and only imposing it as a condition to allow post-determination recording, the latter leaving little scope for mitigation by preservation *in situ* except on a voluntary basis.

The workloads involved with dealing with this aspect of conservation of the historic environment continue to be heavy, as has been confirmed by a series of surveys of planning statistics by ALGAO. These demonstrate only a slight increase in the number of planning applications requiring archaeological intervention, but an increase in the degree of detail or sophistication involved.

Not all the local authority archaeologist's casework comes through the planning system. Utility companies delivering gas and water carry out works that can have an archaeological impact, yet usually do not need planning permission. While codes of conduct exist to regulate their activities and adherence to them has improved, it remains patchy nationwide and is often reliant on individual perceptions of an organisation's responsibilities rather than a corporate approach. The Forestry Commission has also built up a significant track record of consultation about grant-aided schemes for planting; conservation of the historic environment within woodlands is an objective of, for example, the England Forest Plan. There remains an issue of resourcing much of the archaeological work that is considered appropriate within woodlands or proposed areas of woodland, without a dedicated budget to meet such costs. At the same time, the consultation process takes no cognisance of historic landscape character in the design of woodlands through these applications.

Road schemes ultimately require planning permission, but only at the stage when the route is finally fixed. While this can involve a heavy archaeological input to the development stages it has in the past not always guaranteed appropriate resource allocation (particularly time) to carry out essential archaeological works once the scheme has been approved. Gaining appropriate archaeological input to initiatives such as Design, Fund, Build and Operate (DFBO) schemes has also proved contentious. Recent initiatives for large schemes, such as that for Stonehenge, involve the concept of early contractor involvement. This has led to the consideration of archaeological issues from the outset, potentially leading to appropriate archaeological evaluation and resource provision.

MANAGEMENT FOR SUSTAINABILITY

There is a whole suite of work beyond development control, beginning with preventative measures incorporated in development plans, such as the ability to identify in Minerals Plans areas of sensitivity to be evaluated before any application to extract can be considered. Local authorities are also empowered under the AMAA Act 1979 to give grants to assist with the cost of the preservation, maintenance or management of any ancient monuments in their areas, and with the costs of archaeological investigations (Chapter 5).

There are other facilitating possibilities for the local authority archaeologist. There is tremendous scope for local authorities with active countryside interests in working with landowners and the farming community to promote historical conservation in the range of agricultural initiatives that have been sweeping across the countryside, many sprouting from the European Commission (see Chapter 22). The Agriculture Act 1986 led to the creation of the first of the Environmentally Sensitive Areas (ESAs). Although defined as addressing historical issues, the emphasis was firmly on the natural environment and it took many years to establish consideration of historic environment issues. ESAs are constrained within particular areas across England, while the remainder of the country was covered by the Countryside Stewardship Scheme (CSS). This scheme had many positive aspects, including the ability to use its special projects facility to promote appropriate archaeological work on agricultural holdings. Its principal shortcoming was a loss of profits compensation scheme, by which farmers who had destroyed or damaged archaeological features on their land could receive remuneration if they agreed to adopt a beneficial management in future, while farmers who had always managed their land beneficially could not be rewarded for continuing that practice because no profits were forgone.

These two schemes have been replaced by a new Environmental Stewardship Scheme. This is based on the shift within the Common Agricultural Policy away from production support to environmental conservation and one of the four principal objectives of the scheme is conservation of the historic environment. This is a welcome recognition by the Department of Environment Food and Rural Affairs (DEFRA) of the overall role it plays in the positive management of the rural historic environment. Environmental Stewardship comprises two tiers, the Entry Level Stewardship (ELS) and the Higher Level Stewardship (HLS). Entry to ELS is non-competitive and all applicants are guaranteed entry to a level that is essentially one step up from Good Farming Practice. Entry into HLS, which replaces ESAs and CSS, is competitive and entry is not guaranteed and requires previous entry into ELS. Options for the conservation of historic environment features occur at both levels and cross-compliance plays an additional conservation role. HLS requires the development of a Farm Environmental Plan that identifies features of importance on a holding, including historic environment features. Provision of historic environment data from HERs to the environmental map element of ELS has not proved easy to accomplish, not least because of the need to provide DEFRA with selected data in a particular format, for which many HERs, developed to service the planning process, are not currently geared. Reliance has had to be placed on a selection of data from EH's National Monuments Record (NMR), which is also providing digital data for all scheduled monuments in England.

EH has also made available funds to local authoritities, on a tapering basis, for the provision of Historic Environment Countryside Advisor posts. These posts have enabled a number of local authorities to maximise the historic environment conservation potential within CSS agreements in particular and they will play a vital role in the application and development of Environmental Stewardship. However, the future of these posts at the end of the tapering funding is uncertain. Meanwhile, DEFRA has been increasingly active in establishing its role in the sustainable management of the historic environment. At the time of writing, it is creating up to eleven archaeological posts within its Rural Development Service, to facilitate the establishment of Environmental Stewardship and ensure its impact on the historic environment is a positive one.

The basis for all such countryside work is information about sites and landscapes, which provide both a context and a predictive framework for as yet undiscovered sites and features of significance. The ultimate objective must be the preparation of a management plan for every Scheduled Monument and locally important site, backed up by management agreements for scheduled sites, grants for repair of erosion on earthworks and ruins, and grants for the provision of interpretative facilities. Initiatives like Environmental Stewardship, though organised at national level, give local authorities mechanisms to make significant progress in consciousness-raising and management, building upon the important contribution over the last decade from the EH-led historic landscape characterisation initiative in understanding landcape change.

Positive management of archaeological sites can also be dovetailed neatly into other major local authority programmes. Hampshire has become a major partner in the care, investigation and interpretation of Danebury hillfort in one of its country parks. Some local authorities with extensive rural as well as urban estates have undertaken a systematic survey to identify archaeological sites, assess their importance and condition, and to make recommendations about their management, protection and public presentation.

The AMAA Act 1979 permits local authorities to take scheduled sites into their guardianship. In some areas, such as Norfolk, the establishment of an independent trust has enabled a number of sites to be taken into positive ownership and management. Such trusts have been able to take advantage of grants from a variety of local, regional, national and even European sources, to acquire and establish beneficial long-term management regimes. The ever-changing nature of funding regimes can mean however that such arrangements are not a sustainable long-term solution in themselves. It is also essential that councils retain the expertise for continuing management, given the poor reputation of some in looking after their historic assets.

Increasingly, local authorities are being discouraged from such direct intervention, and positively encouraged to divest themselves of such assets, instead adopting the role of enabler or facilitator, identifying and supporting others in attempts to secure a sustainable future for sites, monuments, buildings and landscapes. Partly this arises because so many grant schemes now require significant if not complete community or other stakeholder engagement and leadership. Unfortunately, such leadership is often the product of the enthusiasm of a small number of individuals which, when it wanes or moves on, results in the demise of the project. On other occasions, communities are quite happy to engage in the process of identifying what they want to enhance their locality but are reluctant to engage in grant applications and project management. They require someone else to enable them to realise their dreams, often for lack of time rather than lack of interest or expertise. Long-term underpinning support from local authority engagement with community projects is increasingly being lost, to the detriment of good initiatives.

Some local authorities, particularly those adjacent to, or overlapping with, National Parks, may have the opportunity to become involved in more extensive management regimes for designated land such as Areas of Outstanding Natural Beauty and Environmentally Sensitive Areas (Chapter 22). The uplands of Dartmoor, Exmoor and the Peak District, coinciding with some of the richest areas of prehistoric and medieval settlement, remain relatively undamaged by the impact of repetitive lowland cultivation. This does not mean however that there are no impediments to their sustainable management. Public access has to be managed, sometimes extensively, to prevent people's natural and laudable enthusiasm for the outdoors from destroying the very features they wish to enjoy. Sometimes this management requires rerouting or even temporary closure of popular routes, to relieve the pressure on monuments and landscapes. Programmes of work have to be instigated, to repair damage caused by thousands of feet, litter and fire hearths, mountain and trail bikes and use of 4×4 off-road vehicles.

Current concerns revolve around the implementation of the Countryside and Rights of Way Act (2000), popularly known as the CRoW Act. This has identified extensive areas of landscape, classed as mountain, moor, heath or down, which are to be made accessible to people. Landowners are concerned about the impact of access on their estates; others are concerned about the impact on the historic and natural environments and on the landscape in general. Considerable work was done in the Peak District, for example, in 2003–05, to identify the archaeological component of the new areas of access (some 90 square miles, doubling that already available under access management agreements between landowners and the National Park Authority). This was then assessed for its vulnerability and mitigation proposals were developed to ensure that it survived the potential rigours of access. Much of this work consisted of identifying likely desire lines, focal erosion locations in open countryside and at places such as access points. Consideration was also given to the location and potential impact of access paraphernalia such as stiles, gates and parking places, where none previously existed but where provision was deemed necessary for public safety reasons or to lessen the overall impact of access on the environment. As ever, the decision-making process was based on the provision of appropriate historic environment information.

The currency of these rural issues should not overshadow urban archaeological opportunities. Research aspects are covered elsewhere in this volume (Chapter 2), and urban survey work has already been discussed. A topic that has come to the fore in the last twelve years is the role of archaeology in urban regeneration. Local authority archaeologists are potentially in a pivotal position to argue that the historical significance of an urban area under redevelopment is certainly a social, and should be an economic, plus. Renewed communities need roots, and archaeological understanding of buried evidence and evolved townscapes can help look back through the distress of degeneration (and the need for regeneration) and contribute positively to the way forward.

OUTPUT AND FEEDBACK

Local authorities can make a fundamental contribution to many users of the historic environment. How far 'can' has become 'do' is another matter, though there has been some positive progress over the last decade. PPG 16 is now recognised as a weak instrument for ensuring that the knowledge-gain from development-related fieldwork, the reason for doing it in the first place, feeds back effectively into research and the communities where the work was done. Explaining what has been found is not prominent in the culture of environmental planning and rare in that of developers labouring under environmental constraints (Baker and Morris 2001). 'Grey literature' technical reports accumulate in SMRs, but poor connections between academic research and development-related investigations often leave them buried there.

Too many SMRs have difficulty in finding time to bring their material to wider public notice outside servicing the planning function. Nationally, a growing political emphasis upon public access to, and social inclusion in, cultural activities has seen government resources for cultural access channelled to libraries, archives and museums, rather than to environmental databases. Yet the slow take-up for SMR outreach project grants from the Heritage Lottery Fund showed that, for too many, such work was not possible without an adequate level of basic structural development; otherwise it would be a dangerous diversion of resources away from their primary planning role. When the provision of HERs becomes statutory, many more local authorities will be able to realise the potential of their databases to meet a growing demand for information outside the planning process.

Already several SMRs have explored the possibilities and are providing a welcome combination of access and outreach using internet facilities. The development of information technology and the scope for 'interoperability' is opening up further opportunities. Every local archaeological service can now have its own web-page on the website of its parent authority, where the scope of the SMR can be explained, even if direct access to index material is not possible. Information linkages are being developed with museums and archives services. The work of the Archaeology Data Service at York University is increasing access to SMR material, by acting as a portal through which it is possible to search across the records on several SMRs (see Chapter 19). One outcome of the recent review of the NMR is the commitment by EH to progress the development of an historic environment portal for access to NMR and locally based records. It is now possible to contemplate virtual regional (and wider) record systems, the sum of local records that nonetheless maintain their local responsibility.

Education as such is outside the scope of this chapter, but there are huge waves of interest in archaeology that local authority services can help satisfy. The greatest scope probably lies in preparation of teaching materials to meet curriculum needs, in conjunction with museums and archive services. In turn this requires good working relationships within local authorities between educational, environmental and cultural services.

THE SCOTTISH DIMENSION

Local authority involvement in archaeology in Scotland has certainly strengthened over the last twelve years, albeit from the comparatively low base, compared with England, noted previously. The 'gross inequalities of provision' between the local authority archaeological services in Scotland and England remain fundamental, although the Scottish position, in terms of geographical coverage if not of actual posts on the ground, has improved. Three key events can be identified since the first edition: the promulgation, in 1994, of the *National Planning Policy Guidelines 5* on *Archaeology and Planning* (SOEnD 1994a), the wholesale reorganisation of local government in 1996 and the publication of the Baker Report on Scottish SMR provision in 1999. In addition, two important audits, both critical of the current system of provision for historic environment management and conservation, were conducted (Raemaekers and Boyack 1999; Swanson 2001).

The effect of NPPG 5 has been to entrench the practice of developer-funding of archaeological work covered by the planning system. The definition of an SMR in the accompanying *Planning Advice Note 42* as a service of archaeological information and advice (including the professional staff) has provided a convenient model to use in campaigning for the completion of the coverage of SMRs (SOEnD 1994b). It has also resulted in the conscious decision to stick with this term meantime rather than risk confusion by adopting the term HER seen in the south. A later NPPG (18), *Planning and the Historic Environment* (1999), deals primarily with Listed Buildings, designed landscapes and so on.

The reorganisation of local government in 1996 was more far-reaching than in England, creating thirty-two unitary authorities out of the previous two-tier system of regional and district councils. Its impact was initially largely negative, seriously damaging the effectiveness of several well-established regional SMRs and requiring a variety of local arrangements for joint or agency arrangements with neighbouring councils. At the time of writing, all but one of the thirty-two unitary authorities now have access to the services of a professionally curated SMR, although the issues of low staffing numbers remain. Several of these SMRs are provided by separate trusts, supported by the councils.

The survey, by David Baker, in 1998 (Baker 1999b) of the provision of SMRs in Scotland, which had been commissioned by the Royal Commission on the Ancient and Historical Monuments of Scotland, in conjunction with ARIA (Association of Regional and Island Archaeologists) gave for the first time a baseline assessment of SMR provision, as well as charting a way forward. Its principal conclusion, that no Scottish SMR had yet emerged from the initial developmental phase of information gathering and so needed additional resources, above normal day-to-day requirements, was salutory. A simplified scoring system (Baker 1999b: 1) showed that, as a group, the eighteen SMRs surveyed achieved an average of only 47 per cent, with thirteen in the range 39–58 per cent, only two over 65 per cent and four below 40 per cent. Baker's reference to the 'poverty' of staffing provision, reflected in a score of only 46 per cent for management context, is still justified.

The prescription of a Sites and Monuments Record Forum to bring together all levels of responsibility for SMR provision in Scotland with the aim of concentrating on the required improvement in the standards of the records that had been identified in the survey has not been as successful as hoped. However, efforts by individual SMRs to apply UK-wide standards such as evidenced by thesauri (see above) will continue to increase once the decision to merge ARIA with ALGAO in 2006 takes effect.

The overall Scottish context of these events, in terms of the model of the historic conservation process and the definition of the SMR as a definitive permanent record described at the beginning of this chapter, holds good, as does, in general, the split between curators and contractors (see Swanson 2001 for detailed discussion). In many ways, the structure now pertaining may be more stable than that described above for England. However, there is no question that the continuing failure to secure adequate resources for the development of local services, through a combination of scant local means and the inability of central bodies to find the appropriate mechanism for assistance, will continue to vitiate the development of the sector. By way of illustration, the RCAHMS, when facing structural change in a bill before the Scottish Parliament in late 2002, indicated that it was seeking to remove the role of overseeing SMRs, currently in its Royal Warrant, in favour of developing relations with individual SMRs.

The wish to see a statutory basis for SMRs continues: successive reports of the AMBS (Ancient Monuments Board for Scotland), up to its demise in April 2003, called for this, and it has been lobbied for by ARIA and other national bodies such as the Council for Scottish Archaeology. A forthcoming planning bill in the Scottish Parliament provides another opportunity.

The national context does differ markedly from that described above. There is no MPP, no plans to emulate *Power of Place* (EH 2000a), and a much more limited use of consultants as the third arm of the curator/contractor combination. The NMRS (National Monuments Record for Scotland) is rather more developed that the NMR. Its role as the national archive for excavation and evaluation material from the whole country is generally accepted, but currently there is some perceived competition – or confusion – of record roles between CANMORE (the online system) and local SMRs. A statement of cooperation between ARIA and the RCAHMS was ratified in 2004, while an HLF-funded scheme, *Accessing Scotland's Past*, intending to make the NMRS entries more comprehensible, and with two local authority partners, may provide a model for future cooperation (www.accessingscotlandspast.org.uk). The impact of the first National Parks in Scotland (Loch Lomond and Trossachs and Cairngorms) on the treatment of cultural heritage within their boundaries has yet to be assessed.

Local usage of the planning system bears comparison with arrangements in the south: suspensive clauses to ensure a programme of archaeological work, supported by policies (increasingly telegraphic) in structure and local plans, briefs and specifications. These last show less emphasis on geophysics than was formerly the case and now generally prescribe a sample of 5 per cent or more. There is now a greater emphasis on preservation by record. Similar pressures to keep an authority's place in development control league tables can also be seen. Use of formal constraint maps varies greatly according to the policy and practice of each authority; increasing access to a corporate GIS containing the full SMR is leading to less reliance on them. Monitoring of work specified is important, and challenging given the size of the areas involved (see Barclay 1992a: 106–7, fig. 38). The curator/contractor split is acknowledged in the vast majority of mainland authorities, but it is accepted that the particular circumstances of remote island authorities may require at times a less rigorous division of labour.

Non-planning related work is often as, if not more, important, given the dominant land uses in different areas. The accommodation with forestry reached in 1988 (Shepherd 1992) continues to an extent under the new Scottish Forestry Grants Scheme. By no means all SMRs participate in the consultation scheme, owing to the lack of opportunity to recover costs from the forestry industry (an issue currently under renewed discussion). By contrast, charging is allowed for the most recent Scottish agri-environment scheme, the Rural Stewardship Scheme, which requires applicants to check with their SMRs whether any archaeological feature is involved. This is now a powerful tool for informing landowners of the existence of sites of which they may well have been ignorant, particularly those identified through aerial survey, and suggesting, where appropriate, suitable management. Significant issues of personnel resources must be addressed if the scheme is to continue in its present form. This perennial theme, of constrained resourcing limiting many authorities to core planning tasks, is highlighted in the planning audit referred to above (Raemaekers and Boyack 1999).

By way of a final example, the role of archaeology in some local tourism strategies has waxed and waned, but considerable work on interpretation has been done, from trails, leaflets and websites to full-blown prehistory parks and other visitor centres in those areas that are able to accord this work sufficient priority. Issues of widening public access to information are also driving some authorities to place at least parts of their SMRs online (e.g. www.aberdeenshire.gov.uk/archaeology) and to participate in the map-enabled query system, PASTMAP (www.pastmap.co.uk).

THE FUTURE FOR LOCAL AUTHORITY ARCHAEOLOGY

In 1993 the greatest threat to local authority archaeology seemed to be privatisation or out-sourcing of services, breaking the essential continuity of maintained information systems and local expertise that are fundamental to historical conservation. In 2005 the problem is compounded with the need to ensure services gain or retain sufficient critical mass to perform effectively in circumstances where archaeological considerations are much more widely accepted. On the one hand, there are temptations to achieve that critical mass by pooling resources at a regional or sub-regional level, but, on the other, that would cut the specialists off from the services they advise and the communities they serve.

Twelve years ago it was argued that critical mass could only be achieved at the local level by well-regulated collaboration between the curating and contracting roles. A wide range of expertise is required of the local authority archaeologist, in subjects and periods of time, and in technical matters. An individual with relatively little personal experience of major fieldwork projects will have difficulty in approving a detailed specification of works and monitoring to certify compliance with it. It requires a balancing act so that at financially sensitive points in the conservation cycle they must be, and be seen to be, separate and independent, yet on other matters able to communicate as needed on academic and professional matters.

The number of local authority related field units has dwindled, and competitive tendering makes it difficult for a commercial organisation to provide a public service to a given area. The development of archaeological strategies at local and regional level for both research and conservation has provided a useful focus for all professional interests, whatever their role in the development process. Yet many in-house public services remain demonstrably under-resourced and unable to respond to new opportunities for public service work arising from the growing interest in archaeology of all kinds that has been a hallmark of the last five years.

Nevertheless, the importance of the historic environment, as a critical component in public perceptions of local distinctiveness and a key contributor to sense of place, is increasingly being recognised throughout government at national, regional and local levels. Its contribution to social, economic and environmental development is being acknowledged, in regeneration, education, outreach, inclusion and the overall sustainable management of the environment. Recent developments in agri-environment schemes and status within local authorities bear testimony to this. While there are many issues still to resolve – resources in particular – there remains a confidence that there continues to be an important and increasingly recognised role being played by local authorities in conserving the nation's historic environment.

CHAPTER 11

BRITISH ARCHAEOLOGY IN A WIDER CONTEXT

Henry Cleere

Legislative and administrative structures for the protection of the archaeological heritage are now in place in virtually every country in the world. Their diversity and efficacy reflect their political and historical contexts. In Sweden, for example, where the world's first monuments protection law was promulgated by Royal Proclamation in 1666, the concept of archaeological remains as part of the cultural heritage of the nation is deeply entrenched in the national consciousness and is given material substance through strong legislation and a comprehensive antiquities service. Many of the recently created nation states in the Pacific region, by contrast, have little or no monuments protection legislation and rudimentary antiquities services. The former communist countries of the now defunct Eastern Bloc are still in the process of readjusting their systems to the realities of an economy in which priorities are set by market forces.

It would be impossible within the compass of this chapter to provide a comprehensive overview of all the systems operating in the first decade of the twenty-first century. Instead, it is proposed to describe broad categories, with examples from individual states, in the fields of legislation and organisation, concluding with a section on international and interregional legislative instruments and institutions.

LEGISLATION

A comparative study of world antiquities legislation reveals gradations of scope, ranging from the assertion of state ownership of all types of antiquity, whether portable or monumental, to the application of protective measures for only selected categories. A number of surveys of antiquities legislation have been published, both regional (e.g. Hingst and Lipowschek 1975; CoE 1979) and international (e.g. Burnham 1974; UNESCO 1985 onwards) but unfortunately these are soon out of date, since these laws are subject to a process of continual revision and amendment, springing from political changes and new approaches to heritage protection. The most recent compilation was the series of *Reports on Cultural Heritage Policies in Europe*, produced for the Cultural Heritage Committee of the Council of Europe (CoE 1996); individual summaries for twenth-seven of the member states were published, but these have not been updated since that time. Of more value, perhaps, are the relatively few comparative analytical studies that have been published, such as that by Tesch (1984) and above all the monumental work of O'Keefe and Prott, which is still in progress (1984; also Prott and O'Keefe 1989).

The most comprehensive form of legislative protection for the archaeological heritage is unquestionably that in countries with an authoritarian, communist form of government. Put quite simply, these laws assert a state title to all archaeological materials, both portable and monumental, without exception, and prescribe severe penalties for destroying, damaging, or stealing them, along with regulation of any works that may have an impact on them. This was the case in the countries of the Eastern Bloc (e.g. Herrmann

1981; Jaworski 1981; Princ 1984) but in all of them this strong legislation has been replaced by more selective (and in most cases less comprehensive) protection comparable with that in Western Europe. The transition is vividly illustrated in a series of papers published in *Antiquity* shortly after the fall of the Berlin Wall (Bökönyi 1993; Dolukhanov 1993; Gringmuth-Dallmer 1993; Miraj and Zeqo 1993; Neustupný 1993; Schild 1993; Velkov 1993). One of the most serious consequences for the heritage in these countries has been the application of the principle of restitution. With the abolition of state ownership of all property, the former owners of archaeological sites and monuments have been entitled to resume their property rights, which led to some serious losses of heritage, more particularly in the period between the end of communist rule and the enactment of new protection legislation.

Only in the People's Republic of China (Zhuang 1989), North Korea, and Vietnam has strong legislation survived into the twenty-first century, and there are indications that, even in these countries, legislative protection will become progressively weaker as economic development becomes paramount in government policies. This is dramatically illustrated by the flooding of important areas of immense archaeological and historical importance as a result of the construction of the Three Gorges Dam on the Yangtse River in China. An awareness of the gravity of the present situation lies behind the *Principles for the Conservation of Heritage Sites in China* (Agnew and Demas 2002), prepared with the assistance of the Getty Conservation Institute.

Comprehensive legislative protection of this kind is, however, not confined to communist states. The Scandinavian tradition, stemming from the Swedish Royal Proclamation of 1666, is equally emphatic in maintaining a public interest in all aspects of antiquity. The Norwegian Cultural Heritage Act 1979 extends protection to any example from an exhaustive list of monument categories from the earliest times to AD 1537 (Section 4) and to all portable antiquities over the same period for which no owner can be identified (Section 12). The situation in Sweden and Denmark (Kristiansen 1984) is comparable with that in Norway; in Germany a similar form of protection applies in Schleswig-Holstein, because of its historical links with Denmark (Reichstein 1984: 40). In the Scandinavian countries this protection extends to undiscovered antiquities: they are automatically protected from the moment of their discovery, and there is a presumption in law that they are protected before the moment of discovery. A number of other countries have similar legislative protection, but there are few where it is effectively implemented. Greece is one such example; of those in the Third World, Mexico is another (Lorenzo 1984).

A more restricted form of legislative protection is that which applies not to all movable and immovable heritage properties in specified categories but only to those that are identified by means of registers of protected monuments and objects. This is the system in operation in, for example, Italy (d'Agostino 1984) and Japan (Tanaka 1984). In Italy landowners are obliged to notify the competent authorities of discoveries of archaeological material, but it is necessary for the authorities in turn to inform the owner of the state interest in the discovery for full legislative protection to be extended to it; this principle is known as the *vincolo*, and applies equally to works of art and antiquities. The Japanese system, based on the 1975 revision of the Law for the Protection of Cultural Properties 1950, is broadly similar to that in Italy. A similar protection system applies in Europe in Austria, the Republic of Ireland, Spain (García Fernández 1989), and Switzerland, although in the case of the last two, direct responsibility for implementation is delegated to *Comunidades Autónomas* and *Cantons*, respectively.

In many countries, there is little, if any, protection extended to portable antiquities, and only those monuments on statutory lists are protected. This is, of course, the situation in Great Britain (but not Northern Ireland, see Appendix to Part Two) if the archaic nonsense of Treasure Trove, even in its amended form, is disregarded (Palmer 1981; Sparrow 1982; but see Chapter 6). Among European countries such a system applies in most of the German *Länder* (Hingst 1964; Brönner 1982; Reichstein 1984), France, The Netherlands and Portugal. Belgium is an interesting case: until recently, the legislative protection of the heritage was minimal, but constitutional changes have resulted in the creation of three separate legislative codes, for the Flemish- and French-speaking regions and for multilingual Brussels, respectively, broadly on the Italian model.

Finally, there is the situation where there is legislative protection for both monumental and portable antiquities, but where this applies only to a portion of the land surface of the country. This is the case in the USA (King *et al.* 1977; McGimsey and Davis 1984; Carnett 1991), where federal legislation, such as the Antiquities Act 1906, the Archaeological and Historic Preservation Act 1974, and the Archaeological Resources Protection Act 1979, applies only to federally owned or Indian lands and to projects funded by federal agencies. The National Historic Preservation Act 1966 (as amended) creates procedures for approved state programmes, and this initiative has resulted in legislation with varying degrees of effectiveness being enacted by the fifty States of the Union. Federal and Indian lands represent only some 40 per cent of the land surface of the USA, and the protection afforded to antiquities on them is becoming stronger every year with the increasingly successful enforcement of the Archaeological Resources Protection Act 1979 (Smith and Ehrenhard 1991). Sadly, however, the rate of erosion of antiquities on the remaining 60 per cent shows no signs of slackening.

One factor common to the great majority of national legislations is the requirement of authorisation to excavate. In some legislations (e.g. Great Britain and the USA) this applies only to excavations on protected (listed) monuments, but in others, such as France, any archaeological excavation, whether on a protected monument or not, requires official authorisation, a point that is picked up in the 1992 European Convention (see below).

Any study of comparative antiquities legislation highlights one basic fact: there is an inverse relationship between the effectiveness of the legislation and the length and complexity of the laws themselves. One extreme is that represented by Scandinavian legal texts. The Norwegian Cultural Heritage Act 1979 encompasses protection of ancient monuments, historic buildings, and portable antiquities in a mere twenty-nine clauses, supported by regulations set out in six clauses. The Danish Conservation of Nature Act, which covers the entire field of cultural and natural conservation, devotes no more than six clauses out of a total of seventy-one to archaeological monument protection. At the other end of the scale is the UK Ancient Monuments and Archaeological Areas Act 1979, with its sixty-five clauses and five schedules (to which must be added the lengthy provisions of town and country planning legislation in respect of historic buildings). In Spain the admirable Spanish Historic Heritage Law 1985 runs to sixty-six clauses plus three lengthy annexes, but to this have to be added seventeen statutes in the *Comunidades Autónomas*. The total assemblage of national and provincial laws and regulations covering the protection of Spain's historic heritage fills a volume of more than 1,000 pages (García Fernández 1987), yet British archaeologists visiting Spain will be acutely conscious of the inadequacy of the protection currently available to much of that heritage. The corpus of US federal and state legal instruments is equally gargantuan.

ORGANISATION

The kaleidoscope of antiquities protection laws around the world is mirrored by the organisational structures in place to implement them, though only perhaps in France is there one that is as complex as that in the UK, with its government heritage agencies

(English Heritage, CADW, DoE (NI), and Historic Scotland), Royal Commissions, National Trusts, museums, county archaeologists and units. All these organisations are responsible for the basic heritage management functions of survey and inventory, statutory protection and conservation, rescue archaeology, monument management, and control of portable antiquities. Broadly speaking, they fall into three main categories: centralised national organisations, decentralised national organisations, and federal or quasi-federal organisations.

Typical of the centralised structures is that in Sweden. The Central Board and Museum of Swedish Antiquities (*Riksantikvarieämbetet*), which is based in Stockholm, is responsible for all aspects of implementing the comprehensive Swedish legislation. Much day-to-day work is handled through a network of regional offices, and contracts for rescue excavation and other activities are also placed with local museums and universities. Recently, with the advent of competitive tendering, aspects of market economics have been introduced into the traditional Swedish system and there is a small number of private archaeological contractors.

Norway has a similar system, with the headquarters of the Central Office of Historic Monuments (*Riksantikvaren*) based in Oslo. Here, too, there is some measure of decentralisation, with certain functions delegated to the five major regional museums in Oslo, Stavanger, Bergen, Trondheim, and Tromsø. In addition, *Riksantikvaren* has a number of permanent excavation teams in historic town centres such as Oslo, Tønsberg, and Trondheim. Other centralised systems of this kind exist in the Czech Republic, Hungary, Ireland, Sri Lanka, and a number of countries in Africa and Latin America. In Poland the appropriate elements of the former Institute for the History of Material Culture of the Academy of Sciences and the State Conservation Workshops (PKZ) were brought together in 1991 to create a new State Service for the Protection of Monuments Archaeological Service on the Scandinavian model (Schild 1993), with a strong Department for the Protection of Archaeological Property, created in 2002.

The *Instituto Nacional de Antropologíae Historia* (INAH) is a powerful organisation that covers archaeological sites and other monuments, as well as museums, in Mexico. Its headquarters is in Mexico City, and it has regional offices throughout the country, responsible for the implementation of the draconian national heritage legislation. Recent political changes have threatened its hegemony, but INAH has survived with most of its principal functions intact. In 2002 a Documentation and Research Centre for the Management of World Heritage Archaeological Sites was established at Oaxaca, based on the great archaeological site of Monte Alban (INAH 2002). Its development is worthy of close study by comparable services in other parts of the world.

There is a greater level of decentralisation in other centralised states. In India the Archaeological Survey of India (ASI) has its headquarters in New Delhi and specialised branch offices in various parts of the country, but its work on the ground is the responsibility of its *Circles*, of which there are eleven covering the whole country (Thapar 1984). A number of state governments have archaeological services, but these are largely under-funded and under-resourced: the decision-making body is unquestionably the ASI.

In France responsibility for heritage management is divided between a number of centralised organisations based in Paris – *Monuments Historiques*, *Musées de France*, for example – most of them reporting to different ministries. The nearest approach to a state antiquities service is the *Sous-Direction de l'Archéologie* of the *Direction du Patrimoine*, which comes under the Minister of Culture and Communications. This body is responsible for all rescue excavation in France, working through a number of *Circonscriptions*. Until comparatively recently the *Circonscriptions* were headed for the most part by part-time directors who doubled as university professors and museum directors. Over the past decade, however, the funding of this work has been greatly increased, and this has permitted the appointment of younger *Conservateurs Régionaux de l'Archéologie* to the twenty-five *Circonscriptions* (which include Guadeloupe, French Guiana, and Martinique) and the four national *Centres* devoted to specialised research. They also now have substantial permanent professional staff. Another newer feature of French archaeology has been the increasing number of permanent archaeological posts at *Département* and municipal level.

The fragmentation of French archaeology between bodies such as the *Sous-Direction* and research bodies such as the universities and the *Centre National de la Recherche Scientifique* (CNRS), to say nothing of the museums and the substantial French archaeological effort overseas funded by the Ministry for Foreign Affairs, has been a source of concern to archaeologists there for a number of years. These two factors have resulted in no fewer than five reports being produced over the past thirty years, beginning with that by Jacques Soustelle in 1975, all aimed at improving the structure of French archaeology. However, little has been done to implement their recommendations and as a result confusion and resentment remain.

An increasing amount of French rescue archaeology is now developer-funded and consequently there is a floating population of contract excavators, similar to that in Britain, which has been the source of many problems within the French archaeological community, rising to crisis pitch in 1998 when there was a major strike of archaeologists (Audouze 1998). This led to the promulgation of a new law defining the responsibilities of the French state and confirming the spheres of activity of research and rescue archaeology (Audouze 2001). The new law resulted in the creation of a semi-state agency, the *Institut national de recherches archéologiques preventives* (INRAP), responsible in theory for all activities relating to contract archaeology (Audouze and Demoule 2002), although the position continues to evolve. These periodic crises in French archaeology are regularly reported in the columns of the lively *Nouvelles de l'Archéologie*.

The Archaeology Department of the Portuguese Cultural Heritage Institute (*Instituto Português do Património Cultural* – IPPC) was split off from its parent body in 1997, largely as a result of the campaign to save the Côa Valley rock engravings, to form the *Instituto Português de Arqueologia* (IPA), which has a similar function. However, there is currently a proposal for it to be reabsorbed by IPPC, which is seen by many as a retrograde step (Willems 2002). In Greece and The Netherlands, the *Ephorate* and the *Rijksdienst voor het Oudheidkundig Bodemonderzoek* (ROB) respectively operate through regional offices.

The Italian system takes this type of devolved structure a stage further. Heritage matters are primarily the responsibility of the *Ministerio per i Beni Culturali ed Ambientali* (Ministry of Cultural and Environmental Property), but all field activities are channelled through the regional *Soprintendenze* (d'Agostino 1984), of which there are nearly thirty. The *Soprintendenti* are responsible for all aspects of antiquities protection in their regions, with total administrative and financial autonomy. The field of operations is broad: monitoring of construction and highway projects, rescue and research excavations, field survey, inventory, restoration of monuments, and application of the *vincolo* (see above). Until recently, virtually all archaeological work was carried out either by *Soprintendenze* staff or by universities and museums, but now a considerable amount of work in fields such as rescue excavation, survey, conservation, and restoration is being handled by private organisations on contract.

Austria is constitutionally a federal state, so many functions are delegated to the nine *Länder*. Under the 1929 Constitution, however, the protection of monuments (*Denkmalschutz*) is a matter for federal concern alone and so heritage matters are covered by the 1923 federal law on the protection of monuments (*Bundesdenkmalschutzgesetz*), as amended in 1978. Basic decision-making rests with the Federal Monuments Office (*Bundesdenkmalamt*) based in Vienna. However, a number of the *Länder* have created provincial legislations and established strong provincial archaeological services to which matters of inventory and rescue excavation are delegated by the *Bundesdenkmalamt*, notably Steiermark and Salzburg.

Since the end of the Franco era Spain has increasingly moved in fact, if not in law, towards a federal state, with the delegation of substantial powers to the *Comunidades Autónomas*. The 1985 Law (García Fernández 1989) assigns primary responsibility for implementation to the central government. Archaeology and antiquities are the concern of the Institute for Conservation and Restoration of Cultural Property (*Instituto de Conservación y Restauración de Bienes Culturales*) of the Ministry of Culture. That body is, however, concerned more with overall supervision and policy-making; work on the ground is now largely the concern of the *Comunidades Autónomas*. Here, unfortunately, there is a wide variation in commitment and provision. Much of the individual provincial legislation is directed principally to the monitoring of excavations, to the exclusion of all else, and few have more than a handful of archaeologists in post. However, the situation is steadily improving in Catalonia, Galicia, and elsewhere, not least because of the influence of the heritage in emphasising provincial cultural identity. The study by Querol and Martínez Díaz (1996) offers an often critical overview of the Spanish situation.

Other examples of centralised systems with a substantial measure of decentralisation to provincial administrations are those in Japan (Tanaka 1984) and the People's Republic of China (Zhuang 1989).

The final group of countries covers those that have wholly federal constitutions. The principal example in Europe is Germany, where the Federal Constitution specifically reserves all cultural activities to the *Länder*: there is no federal antiquities legislation nor any federal antiquities service in the *Bundesrepublik*. The spectrum of provision at state level is almost as broad as that across the world, ranging from the excellent structure in Schleswig-Holstein inherited from earlier Danish administration to the minimalist approach in Hesse or the over-complexity of the system in Lower Saxony (Reichstein 1984). While field survey, inventory, excavation, and monument protection all figure in the tasks assigned to *Land* archaeological services, the attention given to them differs greatly.

These comments relate essentially to the eight *Länder* and three independent towns that made up the original Federal German Republic. The former German Democratic Republic, as might be expected, had a very different system before reunification. It was a centralised structure with positive and effective decentralisation to five heritage management centres, which combined and integrated archaeological and historical monument conservation and protection, inventory, excavation, museums and research very efficiently. This theoretically admirable structure (which in fact was at the mercy of economic policies, leading to some dubious decisions) has now been dismantled and adapted to conform with the requirements of the federal constitution.

The USA, too, has a federal constitution which delegates certain activities to states. There is no central federal antiquities service as such, although the National Park Service of the Department of the Interior has a long and distinguished record in this field, and acts as lead agency for all archaeological projects in which federal agencies are involved. One of the most impressive developments in US archaeology over the past three decades has been the way in which federal agencies have acknowledged their responsibilities towards the archaeological heritage and have built up substantial professional archaeological divisions: especially noteworthy are the Department of Defense, the Bureau of Land Management, and the US Department of Agriculture's Forest Service, which employ several hundred full-time professionals between them.

Following the passage of the Archaeological and Historical Protection Act in 1974, which provided for up to 1 per cent of the costs of federal projects to be made available for archaeological mitigation work (survey and excavation), the long-established contracting bodies, largely associated with universities and museums, were unable to cope with the sudden exponential increase in demands for their services. As a result many private archaeological contracting firms were set up. Few US archaeologists would deny that the outcome was a great deal of bad archaeology, inadequately reviewed and largely carried out mechanically to meet the statutory duties imposed upon federal agencies. Reports were produced to conform with statutory requirements in a handful of copies and then buried in agency archives, without being made available to the archaeological community at large. That deplorable situation has considerably improved over the past decade: there is better supervision and monitoring of projects by agency archaeologists and the surviving contract groups work according to infinitely higher standards than their predecessors in the 1970s. Here again, unfortunately, the market economy of the Reagan years has influenced federal procurement regulations so that there is an obligation on agencies to accept lowest tenders irrespective of the quality of research design or resources.

Outside federally owned lands, the level of heritage management varies enormously. The National Historic Preservation Act 1966 established a federal policy of cooperation with state and local governments to protect historic sites and values. Procedures were created for approved state and local government programmes, under the supervision of state historic preservation officers. During the administrations of Reagan and Bush senior, federal funding for this work dwindled, but most state administrations have maintained the programmes from their own resources to lesser or greater degrees.

In Australia, as in Germany, there is no federal antiquities legislation: that is wholly the responsibility of the states. The primary responsibility of the federal Australian Heritage Commission is that of inventory, the compilation of the Register of the National Estate. Each state has its own monuments service responsible for implementing state legislation. Canadian federal legislation covers certain aspects of the protection of historic sites and Indian artefacts, but here again the main thrust is via the provinces, with their own legislations and antiquities services. The Alberta Heritage Act 1973 must be among the most comprehensive anywhere in the world, and it is very effectively implemented by the provincial antiquities service.

One important development in Europe has been the establishment of the Europae Archaeologiae Consilium in 1999 (Willems 1999). This organisation brings together the heads of government archaeological heritage agencies in the countries of Europe. Its objectives are the promotion of the exchange of information and cooperation between these organisations, the establishment of a forum for discussion, acting as an interlocutor for working towards common goals and as a monitoring and advisory body, with special reference to the European Union and the Council of Europe, the promotion and presentation of Europe's archaeological heritage, and the promotion of public enjoyment of that heritage.

It has been possible in this chapter only to highlight certain national structures in order to illustrate the wide range of systems in use across the world. Unfortunately the literature on this subject is relatively slight, with very few detailed accounts of individual systems. Those wishing to learn more about the systems in use in individual countries should consult the invaluable *Directory of Archaeological Heritage Management*, produced by the International Committee on Archaeological Heritage Management (ICAHM) of the International Council on Monuments and Sites (ICOMOS), which lists the addresses of antiquities services in most of the countries of the world (ICOMOS 1990b).

INTERNATIONAL CONVENTIONS AND ORGANISATIONS

At the European level, heritage protection and management is considered to be a component of culture and so falls within the province of the Council of Europe. This organisation is long on ideas and ideals but short on funds. Its main contribution in the field of heritage management has been the promulgation of conventions, of which the revised European Convention on the Protection of the Archaeological Heritage, signed in Malta in January 1992, is the most important.

Following Council of Europe custom, an international group of experts in heritage management and law was responsible for the drafting of this instrument, which was then submitted to council members for comment. The final version lacked some of the sting of earlier drafts, though it is an infinite improvement over the 1954 Convention which it supersedes.

Like all international conventions it begins with a preamble in which the importance of archaeology for the study of the prehistory and history of mankind is underlined. It also emphasises the many threats to the heritage that become apparent as development schemes and natural hazards increase. Perhaps the most important statement in the preamble is that the protection of the archaeological heritage 'should rest not only with the State directly concerned but with all European countries, the aim being to reduce the risk of deterioration and promote conservation by encouraging exchanges of experts and the comparison of experiences'.

The convention defines the archaeological heritage as 'all remains and objects and any other traces of mankind from past epochs' that can illustrate the history of mankind and its relation to the natural environment. Of great importance is the new concept that such remains may be situated both on land and under water, which means that even shipwrecks are now acknowledged as forming part of the heritage.

Among the measures proposed for enhancing protection is the creation of legal instruments, listing protected areas and reserves. Another provision is that anyone who comes across an archaeological object is obliged to report the find. The States Parties must also ensure that only competent persons are permitted to carry out archaeological excavations and non-destructive techniques must be used as far as possible, rather than excavation.

One article deals with ways of integrating archaeology into physical planning procedures. Another addresses the question of who should pay for archaeological excavations resulting from changes in land use. The principle that the 'polluter pays' (that is, whoever causes the destruction of an archaeological site should pay the excavation costs) was put forward in an earlier draft of the convention, but it had to be modified for the final text, since it was too extreme and provocative for certain countries (among them the UK). The convention in the event merely mentions the need for 'suitable measures to ensure that provision is made in major public or private development schemes for covering, from public sector or private sector resources, as appropriate, the total costs of any necessary related archaeological operations'.

All costs for practical field operations and publication are considered to form part of the excavation costs, but not subsequent scientific studies. The convention refers cautiously to 'a publishable scientific summary record before the necessary comprehensive publication of specialised studies'. The obligation to disseminate information to colleagues and to the public at large is also laid upon archaeologists.

Trade in archaeological objects is not illegal or immoral as such, but illicit excavation is a growing activity. The convention lays particular stress on museums and similar institutions under state control not acquiring elements of the archaeological heritage with illicit or questionable backgrounds; other institutions, whose acquisition policies are not under state control, should also be influenced to act in a similar way.

The convention also aims to stimulate mutual technical and scientific cooperation between States Parties in the form of exchange of experiences and experts.

The 1992 Malta Convention marked a significant step forward in archaeological heritage protection and management in Europe. Signature of a convention is only the first step, however: it does not have the force of law in individual countries until it is ratified by them. In the case of the 1954 Convention, for example, it was not until 1975 that it was ratified by the UK government. By December 2005, it had been ratified by thirty-four countries; the UK did so in September 2000, but among those countries that had not ratified it by late 2005 were Austria, Belgium, Greece, Italy, The Netherlands, Russia and Spain.

The Council of Europe has no more than moral force. Financial clout resides with the twenty-five countries of the European Union (EU). Although the Treaty of Rome is broadly drafted enough to bring cultural matters, and especially heritage protection and management, within the purview of the EU, it has been reluctant to involve itself to any great extent with such matters in the past. There is a budget for cultural activities – small by comparison with mainline EU concerns – that has largely been applied to prestige projects such as the restoration of the Athens Acropolis. These funds are now being applied on a more systematic basis, a specific theme being chosen for each year. However, the EU's potential role in heritage matters is much greater in other areas, albeit in a more oblique form. Directives such as those on Environmental Assessment and Environmentally Sensitive Areas (ESAs) provide opportunities for archaeological elements to be introduced, either in Brussels during the drafting procedure or when these are introduced, as they must be, into national legislation: the inclusion of archaeological factors in the definition of ESAs in the UK resulted from concerted action on the part of the natural and historical environmental lobbies. Other areas of EU activity that offer opportunities for better archaeological heritage protection are the regional policies, especially those relating to Least Favoured Areas, which in many cases coincide with areas of high archaeological potential, and those relating to tourism and urban planning.

At the international level, the United Nations Educational, Scientific, and Cultural Organisation (UNESCO) is the UN lead agency for heritage matters. It has been responsible for a series of important recommendations and conventions since its foundation in 1947 (UNESCO 1985). These include:

Convention for the Protection of Cultural Property in the Event of Armed Conflict, 14 May 1954 (the Hague Convention)

Convention on the Means of Prohibiting and Preventing the Illicit Import, Export and Transfer of Ownership of Cultural Property, 14 November 1970

Convention concerning the Protection of the World Cultural and Natural Heritage, 16 November 1972

Convention on the Protection of the Underwater Cultural Heritage, 2 November 2001

Recommendation on International Principles Applicable to Archaeological Excavations, 5 December 1956

Recommendation concerning the Preservation of Cultural Property Endangered by Public or Private Works, 19 November 1968

Recommendation Concerning the International Exchange of Cultural Property, 26 November 1976

Recommendation for the Protection of Movable Cultural Property, 28 November 1978.

Figure 11.1. The basilica at Lepcis Magna, Lybia. Designation as a World Heritage site such as this results from a rigorous system of evaluation. *(Photo: D.J. Breeze)*

The 1954 Hague Convention was demonstrated by the Gulf War and the civil war in Yugoslavia to be something of a dead letter. Its coverage was considerably tightened up in March 2001 by the Second Protocol to the Convention, approved after a tense meeting in The Hague. It did not come into force until 2004, when it had been ratified by twenty countries. The 1956 Recommendations on archaeological excavations are also somewhat outdated, referring to a postwar period when a considerable measure of anarchy reigned in archaeology, especially in the countries of the Third World. Plans have been discussed for a drastic revision of these Recommendations, but action remains to be taken by UNESCO.

It is the 1970 and 1972 Conventions, with their concomitant recommendations, that are most relevant to the present-day situation. The problem of illicit trade in antiquities is one that still needs to be tackled in practical terms. It is no coincidence that the countries in which the main centres of the international trade in art and antiquities are located, such as Germany and The Netherlands, have still failed to ratify the 1970 Convention (it came as a great surprise to those who have been putting pressure on the UK Government to ratify the convention for many years that it finally did so on 1 August 2002). It is to be hoped that the Malta Convention will persuade those countries that have not yet ratified the convention that the time has come to do so. The passage of the Single European Act by the members of the EU, with the consequent abolition of tariff and customs barriers between the member states, has also resulted in intensive study being given to its implications so far as the illicit trade in cultural property is concerned.

The 1972 World Heritage Convention remains somewhat controversial among archaeologists: it is still seen by some as a 'beauty contest' between nations. Nonetheless, since it came into force in 1975, over 600 cultural heritage monuments from more than 130 States Parties have been included on the World Heritage List, to represent, as the preamble to the convention describes it, 'this unique and irreplaceable property, to whatever people it may belong'.

There is a rigorous system of evaluation of nominations made by States Parties for inclusion on the list, involving successive stages of assessment, first by the International Council on Monuments and Sites (ICOMOS) as an independent non-governmental professional and scientific organisation and then by the World Heritage Committee, elected by the States Parties. The primary criterion for inclusion is 'outstanding universal value' in one or more of ten precisely defined categories. However, this must be supported by evidence of adequate conservation measures and management plans being in place. States Parties make regular contributions to the World Heritage Fund, which is used to provide technical assistance for work on World Heritage Monuments, principally in the Third World.

The secretariat for this work is provided by UNESCO, but the convention is autonomous and not subject to decisions of the UNESCO General Assembly. There is, however, another area of UNESCO's work in heritage matters which is its direct responsibility. It has run a number of major international campaigns, largely financed by contributions from member states, over the past fifty years: these include the massive campaign in Nubia in advance of the completion of the Aswan Dam, the restoration of temples at Borobodur (Indonesia) and in the Kathmandu Valley (Nepal), dealing with the problems from rising ground water at Moenjodaro (Pakistan), and the excavations at Carthage (Tunisia).

There is one final international document that should be known to all archaeologists, whether involved in heritage management or not. In 1985 ICOMOS created an International Committee on Archaeological Heritage Management (ICAHM), which identified three major initiatory tasks. It compiled a directory of heritage institutions (ICOMOS 1990b), it held the first international conference on the subject in Sweden in 1988 (ICAHM 1989), and it drafted a Charter for the Protection and Management of the Archaeological Heritage, which was approved by the ICOMOS General Assembly in Lausanne in 1990 (ICAHM 1990). The charter is the seminal doctrinal document for this sphere of professional activity.

Its nine articles cover the whole range of activities and issues with which heritage managers should be concerned. They lay down ethical and professional standards and goals in clearly defined fields: integrated protection policies; legislation and economy; survey; investigation; maintenance and conservation; presentation, information, and reconstruction; professional qualifications; and international cooperation. It is intended that the Lausanne Charter should, like the Venice Charter of 1964, which established standards for the conservation of historic buildings, become the gospel, code of practice, and Hippocratic Oath of all professional archaeologists and heritage managers.

The ICOMOS International Committee for the Conservation of the Underwater Heritage (ICUCH) has produced a Charter on the Protection and Management of Underwater Cultural Heritage, which was approved at the General Assembly in Sofia (Bulgaria) in 1996. This has rapidly been accepted as the standard code of practice and ethics in this field, and it was fundamental in the drafting of the 2001 UNESCO Charter (see Chapter 7).

CHAPTER 12

THE CURATOR'S EGG:
A NEW OVERVIEW

Jane Grenville

INTRODUCTION

This chapter offers a critical commentary on some of the issues raised in this part of the book, and in taking account of changes over the last ten years, considers some longer-term implications for the historic environment sector, both professional and academic. It concentrates, perforce, given its writer's professional experience, on the situation in England, but it is hoped that it will have resonances for the UK as a whole, where equal difficulties pertain in persuading devolved government to move heritage further up the agenda of cultural strategies. As the title of the chapter implies, some, but not all, of this change has been for the better. At the time of writing (the winter of 2004) we appear to stand on the precipice of the most fundamental revision of heritage legislation and policy for half a century, providing a fine opportunity for reflection on policy formation in the past. Two major documents crystallise much of the thinking behind the proposed changes, although, as this chapter will show, they themselves are the result of a decade of radical rethinking; they are *Power of Place* (EH 2000a), and *The Historic Environment: A Force for our Future* (DCMS and DTLGR 2001). The first was a review of policies relating to the historic environment commissioned by the Department of Culture, Media and Sport (DCMS) from the heritage sector, led by English Heritage (EH) but to reflect the thinking of the wider constituency. Its steering group comprised representatives of 'the usual suspects' such as the National Trust, the Heritage Lottery Fund, the Council for the Protection of Rural England and the Council for British Archaeology, but also some members whose inclusion would have seemed less obvious ten years ago: the English Tourism Council, the British Property Federation, the Country Landowners Association, the Black Environment Network and the representatives of other environmental interests such as the Countryside Agency, English Nature and the Commission for Architecture and the Built Environment (a new 'design watchdog' which replaced the Royal Fine Arts Commission in 1999). More than a hundred others, representing both a broader range and a more specialist working knowledge, contributed to the deliberations of five working parties detailed to look at definitions and research, legislation, tourism, access and sustainability. A consultation launched on the internet received more than 600 responses and MORI was commissioned to undertake an opinion poll on the perception of the historic environment among the general public. The resulting document, *Power of Place*, certainly aroused strong reactions, many of disappointment at the time, although with the passage of years it seems to be largely accepted as having had a benign influence in persuading the government to consider the significance of the historic environment in planning for the future. The government's reply, *Force for our Future*, a joint response from DCMS and the (then) Department of Transport, Local Government and the Regions (DCMS and DTLGR 2001), seemed to recognise that significance to a degree, although its emphasis on access (both physical and intellectual) and on education before protection and curation has aroused negative comment. This came not least from the All-Party Parliamentary Archaeology Group (APPAG), which convened in July 2001 and issued its first report, *The Current State of Archaeology in the United Kingdom*, in January 2003, and whose very existence signals a welcome heightening of consciousness in Westminster.

That raising of awareness is reflected in the plethora of proposed changes in the pipeline that makes the writing of an overview chapter so difficult at this particular moment. The current system involves two-track legislation with different agencies handling different aspects of the historic environment: intervention on a Scheduled Ancient Monument requires Scheduled Monument Consent (SMC) and this is determined by the national bodies (EH, Historic Scotland (HS), CADW and DoE (NI)) under the provisions of the Ancient Monuments and Archaeological Areas Act 1979 (AMAA Act: see Chapter 5). Intervention in a Listed Building, whether for purposes of repair or alteration, requires Listed Building Consent (LBC), and demolition of an unlisted building in a Conservation Area requires Conservation Area Consent. Both are granted by local planning authorities under the Planning (Listed Buildings and Conservation Areas) Act 1990. All this is likely to change with the Planning and Compensation Bill which is making its way through the parliamentary process and the overhaul of heritage legislation which is proposed in the next three years; together these measures will introduce the biggest shake up since the 1944 and 1947 Town and Country Planning Acts. Already, the two systems seem to be converging in the areas of policy and advice. It would be fruitless to speculate here on the precise provisions of the new heritage act but it certainly is worth noting that in the vanguard of the revision of heritage legislation come two major reviews under the auspices of the Department of Culture, Media and Sport (DCMS): the designation of heritage assets, whether Scheduled Ancient Monuments, Listed Buildings or Conservation Areas (the Heritage Protection Review); and the functions and status of Sites and Monuments Records (SMRs), or, as they are now becoming known, Historic Environment Records (HERs). A much-trailed revision of *Planning Policy Guidance Note 16: Archaeology and Planning* (PPG 16: DoE 1990a) and *Planning Policy Guidance Note 15: Planning and the Historic Environment* (PPG 15: DoE and DNH 1994) to create a single Planning Policy Statement (PPS) has been halted midflow, after it was realised that the implications of changing the designation system are so great that they would necessitate a further revision of planning advice – twice in two years was not deemed a good use of civil servants' time. In any case, it is certain that the outcome of the Heritage Protection Review will require primary legislation, so the whole process is locked in a circle – whether vicious or virtuous remains to be seen.

No less important, and certainly closely related, are various more focused reviews: reconsiderations of ecclesiastical exemption and of maritime archaeology took place in 2004. A review of agri-environmental schemes is under way and the 1997 Hedgerow Regulations are being revised. Portable antiquities have not escaped attention: the Treasure Act of 1996 has been extended to include deposits of prehistoric base-metal objects, the UK has finally signed up to the 1970 UNESCO Convention on the Illicit Export of Antiquities and a private member's bill makes a new offence of 'dishonestly importing, dealing in or being in possession of any cultural asset illegally excavated or removed from any monument or wreck contrary to local law' (see Chapter 6). The functions and status of the National Monuments Record (NMR) were reviewed in 2004. Indeed, it seems that scarcely any aspect of heritage provision is not up for grabs: at an organisational level, EH itself is halfway through a process of 'modernising'. A major organisational change in England since the first edition of this book has been the merging of the Royal Commission on the Historical Monuments of England into EH in 1999

(Chapter 4) and the regionalisation of the enlarged organisation to nine offices. The series of questions asked in the first edition of this chapter could be thoroughly overhauled to reflect this state of flux, but it seems most fruitful to leave them in place, if slightly reworded, at least for this edition, to act as a benchmark in a rapidly changing situation: these are the headings of the following sections. I have omitted the question posed in the earlier edition: 'How should they be investigated/how are assessments made?' The information such a section might contain is to be found in many other contexts, not least elsewhere in this book.

WHO IDENTIFIES SITES FOR DESIGNATION AND WHO CONTROLS THEIR SUBSEQUENT DESTINY?

Given the current proposals for change, there is much to say here. Designation takes many forms: heritage assets may be statutorily registered as scheduled ancient monuments or as Listed Buildings or as Conservation Areas or on two non-statutory registers (Parks and Gardens; Battlefields), and as World Heritage sites (inscribed by UNESCO under the 1972 World Heritage Convention). The opacity of this system in terms of control has been the principal driver for change: 'the system is now so complex that few people fully understand all parts of it. It is not apparent that monuments, buildings and landscapes need separate regimes' (DCMS 2003c: 9, para. 23). The details of the respective legislation for ancient monuments and Listed Buildings are dealt with elsewhere (Chapters 5 and 9): the briefest of outlines is all that is offered here, to illuminate the commentary that follows.

Historical accident dictates that Scheduled Ancient Monuments and Listed Buildings are designated by the relevant Minister (in England currently the Secretary of State for Culture, Media and Sport, although before 1992 by the Secretary of State for the Environment), on the advice of the relevant national agency (EH, HS, CADW or DoE (NI)). Conservation Areas, by contrast, are designated by local planning authorities. In the British system the identification of heritage assets is relatively inclusive, rather than exclusive. Compare, for instance, England's 371,591 Listed Buildings (EH 2003b: 19) with Japan's figure of 4,352 in 1998 (Kindred 2003a: 36). In addition, 19,446 sites and uninhabited buildings are scheduled as ancient monuments, and this figure expands to 36,117 if individual entries are disaggregated into their separate components (EH 2003b: 17) and there are 9,080 Conservation Areas (EH 2003b: 25). An interesting effect of this is that controls are commensurately weaker. To oversimplify for the purpose of making the point, there are three possibilities: very strict control over a very small number of heritage assets; or looser curation of a larger number; or considerable control over a larger number of monuments as a result of greater critical mass in public awareness (as in Denmark, for example). The UK has opted for the second.

The answer to the question of who, therefore, controls the destiny of sites, remains to a very large extent the owner. Generally speaking, the owner initiates projects and control extends to issues of principle (the granting or refusal of consent) and to the manner in which the process is carried out once consent is granted. It is estimated that around 90 per cent of Listed Building Consent applications are approved (DCMS and DTLGR 2001: 33). Contrasting perceptions of the strength of the controls are to be found in two recent official publications: *Heritage Counts 2003: the State of the Historic Environment* notes, '*only* around 5% of the historic environment is formally protected by an Act of Parliament' (EH 2003b: 16 [italics added]), while the Heritage Protection Review consultation document, *Protecting our Environment: Making the System Work Better*, states that, 'it is widely believed – though the evidence has not been collected – that large numbers of owners simply go ahead with alterations without permission because they do not realise that they need it, because they dread the bureaucracy and delay or because they think they would be stopped from making the change they want' (DCMS 2003c: 15–16, para. 51). So the heritage agency is anxious that too little is protected, while the owners are concerned that the bureaucracy is overpowering. If nothing else, this reflects the tensions that have persisted in the British planning system since its inception over the degree to which the right of private interests to treat private property as they see fit is conceded in the public interest.

Nevertheless, the quantifiable evidence suggests that it is indeed the owner who is the more powerful actor, in whose hands lie the initiative for change or neglect. It is perhaps interesting to note the varying effects of action or neglect on upstanding and subsurface sites: lack of direct human intervention on a subsurface site may be benign, but the effects of natural agents such as rabbits, bracken and water erosion cannot be minimised (see also Chapter 22). In a building, the failure to undertake routine interventionist maintenance is usually a major cause of decay, yet neglect may also prevent the worst excesses of modernisation and loss of original features. Active conservation measures to prevent natural and artificial acceleration of decay are therefore essential for both subsurface sites and buildings. Having said that, once the decision to seek change has been taken, the destiny of the site lies within the control of external agencies (although the wishes of the owner undoubtedly remain a material consideration to be balanced against other matters in the determination of the case). The impact of a single designation system and a single heritage act that wraps up the existing divisions between ancient monuments, Listed Buildings and Conservation Areas will be interesting to observe. The stated aim is to simplify the system and make it more understandable to owners and the public at large. But as Andrew Gilg notes in his entertaining overview of the largely unentertaining, even depressing, history of countryside planning since the Second World War (Gilg 1996), one of the most common outcomes of policy change is the unexpected consequence – of policies blown off course by unforeseen events or by human irrationality in the responses of individuals that undermine structural forces – so the ultimate impact of the proposed streamlining is difficult to predict.

The first comprehensive guide to policy, the Department of the Environment's *Circular 8/87*, was issued in 1987 and concerned the provisions for Listed Buildings and Conservation Areas (DoE 1987). Notwithstanding the fact that it related primarily to historic buildings, one of its most important policies was a harbinger of major changes that have occurred in the 1990s, for it contained, tucked away at paragraph 52, the advice that 'Ancient monuments, and their settings, whether scheduled or not are *of course* a material consideration in the determination of planning applications' (my italics). The appearance of this advice was of the utmost importance. Although it appeared simply to formalise best practice in the most efficient local authorities, it was by no means a matter of course, as implied, to regard archaeology as a material factor in the planning process. Nonetheless, by the mid-1980s most counties held SMRs and the checking of planning applications against this information to look for archaeological significance was beginning to be more common (see Chapter 10). With the formal blessing of the DoE for this practice, the possibilities for the protection of the archaeological resource seemed to be greatly enhanced.

The introduction of *Planning Policy Guidance Note 16* (PPG 16: DoE 1990a; also Welsh Office 1991; for Scottish equivalent see SOEnD 1994a; 1994b) decisively shifted the balance towards the inclusion of archaeology as a material factor in the planning process. PPG 16 advises that 'archaeological remains should be seen as a finite and non-renewable resource . . . Appropriate management is therefore essential to make sure that they survive in good condition' (para. 6). The baseline for this management is clearly set out in paragraph 8: 'Where nationally important archaeological remains, *whether scheduled or not, and their settings*, are affected by proposed development there should be a presumption in favour of their physical preservation' (my italics). The point to note here is that the archaeological resource as a whole is being flagged up and that setting and context, as well as the tightly defined legal lines drawn on maps around scheduled monuments, are being taken into consideration. It might, however, be noted, that the definition of setting seems to be in relation to the monument, that we start from the inside and move outwards, rather than taking the alternative model that monuments subsist in a predefined context. Furthermore, this was the first time that archaeology appeared as a material factor within the planning system in a major document dedicated to that purpose: 'developers and local authorities should take into account archaeological considerations and deal with them from the beginning of the development control process' (para. 18). The relevant personnel are clearly identified: 'All planning authorities should make full use of the expertise of County Archaeological Officers or their equivalents.' There is no obligation to consult EH in the case of non-scheduled monuments although 'local planning authorities may find it helpful' to do so (para. 23). By contrast, as discussed above, they are required to do so in the case of a proposal likely to affect the site of a Scheduled Ancient Monument (para. 23). The second major change heralded by PPG 16 was the introduction of developer funding and with it competitive tendering. Paragraph 25 states that where local planning authorities decide that pre-development excavation is justified, 'it would be entirely reasonable for the planning authority to satisfy itself before granting planning permission, that the developer has made appropriate and satisfactory provision for the excavation and recording of remains' with the caveat that non-profit-making developers such as charities, or individuals, might have recourse to EH for financial assistance. Of course, this latter provision might be more effective were the EH grant-in-aid not to be subject to continual real term cuts. The impact of the introduction of developer funding will be dealt with in more detail below.

In the early 1990s, then, without any legislative changes, there was a significant shift in the perception and treatment of the archaeological resource. While the involvement of central government remained mandatory in the case of SMC, the broadening of the net to include non-scheduled sites brought with it a devolution of powers to the local authorities, which already dealt with Listed Building Consent. County Archaeologists suddenly found themselves with a new role, that of curator and arbiter between developer, planning committee and archaeological contractor, rather than the researcher and excavator of the 1970s and 1980s.

The rebranding of DoE circulars as the more plain-English PPGs necessitated the reconfiguration of *Circular 8/87*, and its replacement document, *Planning Policy Guidance Note 15: Planning and the Historic Environment* (PPG 15), appeared in 1994 after a tough tussle in the drafting stages. One of the principal issues was whether or not the 'presumption in favour' of the retention of a Listed Building (DoE *Circular 8/87*, para. 91: 'the Secretary of State is of the view that the presumption should be in favour of preservation except where a strong case can be made out') should be watered down to the 'starting point' and 'the prime consideration' for the determination of applications for demolition (Draft PPG 15, para. 3.3). In the event, it was retained at paragraph 3.3 of the published PPG: 'there should be a general presumption in favour of the preservation of Listed Buildings' and the basis of the advice remained much as before, although arguably more comprehensibly set out. A major difference between the treatment of buildings and that of below-ground archaeology was that the standards required of archaeological information relating to the two were quite different. PPG 16 positively demanded high-level archaeological information for subsurface sites *before* a planning application could be determined; PPG 15 remained somewhat apologetic. The significance of this disparity is discussed below in the section on excavation and recording.

One significant difference in terms of control and influence within the existing two-track legislation is the consultation system. Applications for Listed Building Consent to demolish or partially demolish are referred by ministerial direction to six national bodies: the Council for British Archaeology (CBA), the Ancient Monuments Society, the Society for the Protection of Ancient Buildings, the Georgian Group, the Victorian Society and the Twentieth Century Society, with the Garden History Society consulted on applications within their interest area (Department of the Environment, Transport and the Regions/Department of Culture, Media and Sport *Circular 14/97*, para. 15). These bodies, known collectively as the amenity societies, use a huge network of well-informed volunteers (both professionals 'moonlighting' and a large band of really knowledgeable amateurs) to visit sites, provide local knowledge and help to frame comments to local planning authorities. There is no parallel mandatory consultation system built in to the process of determining Scheduled Monument Consent, which is handled internally by EH ancient monuments inspectors. PPG 16 suggests at paragraph 23 that County Archaeologists 'may wish to consult locally based museums and archaeological units and societies', but there is no compulsion to do so. Comment from interested parties therefore tends to appear in the form of highly active single issue interest groups, of which prime examples are the Stonehenge Alliance (Fielden 2002; and, in reply, Young 2002), and the Friends of Thornborough Henges (Dormor 2003; Horton 2003) or from the CBA and the IFA in response to formal consultations on broader issues or in editorial comment in their journals, respectively *British Archaeology* and *The Archaeologist*. It is not difficult to see the historical circumstances that give rise to such an anomaly in consultation practices between the Listed Building and the scheduled monument regimes: at the time that LBC became compulsory (Town and Country Planning Act 1968), there was little expertise within local authorities to assess the historical merits of individual buildings, whose selection for listing had been made not by the authority, but by the Inspectorate of Ancient Monuments and Historic Buildings (then a part of the DoE and now reconstituted as EH). Consultation was introduced at the specific request of the planners. By contrast, at the time of the introduction of PPG 16 in November 1990, every county had an archaeological officer, and the SMRs were, to a large extent, locally generated. The soliciting of friendly advice from interested parties might therefore safely be left to the discretion of individual County Archaeologists. Whether or not the sometimes less benign function of statutory consultation might usefully be extended into the realms of PPG 16 is a matter for debate: many outside the national agencies and local government feel that archaeologists working within 'the system' cannot help but be compromised by political (with a small 'p') interests and would welcome an opportunity to influence policy and decision-making from an external position more formally than through the current channels of single-issue pressure groups which have to wait until a public inquiry to be given a formal voice. Those within the national agencies and local government note that idealistic positions cannot be sustained within the tough world of realpolitik and that often the outcome of holding a hardline position will be no development at all, and the further alienation of the development community from archaeology, a potentially dangerous position to arrive at, given current funding arrangements. So formal consultation, intended as a positive step, might have two very different negative consequences: it could blunt the sharpness of external comment or it could result in total sclerosis of the system, in which no compromises would ever be found to be acceptable. It is worth noting that, even after *Power of Place*, the heritage lobby is regarded in Westminster as being notably divided within itself, its disarticulated voice easy to ignore. The same holds true in Edinburgh,

Cardiff and Belfast, where there has been no attempt to devise an equivalent document. The extent of the differences between EH, the National Trust, the Society of Antiquaries, the Council for British Archaeology and the Stonehenge Alliance in the public inquiry into the proposed road scheme at Stonehenge, only reinforces such a perception.

The current designation system, dealing with three types of statutory designation (Scheduled Ancient Monuments, Listed Buildings and Conservation Areas) and two non-statutory registers (Parks and Gardens, and Battlefields), together with World Heritage sites is likely to be radically revised in the near future with the introduction of a single unified list 'to cover any type of historically, archaeologically or architecturally important site . . . It might also cover important historic areas, such as World Heritage sites. Purely local designations – Conservation Areas and locally listed buildings – could be included in a local section of the list. . . A few Conservation Areas considered of special historic importance in a national context could be entered on the main List' (DCMS 2003c: 10, para. 24). It is worth noting, in the light of the comment on Conservation Areas, that this 'main list' will represent a selection rather than a consolidation of all existing designations, and that some will be registered on 'local lists', perhaps implying a demotion in their perceived significance. It is suggested that each item on the new list should be supported by a map showing exactly the area covered by the designation and a statement of significance showing the reasons for listing, what is significant about the asset (DCMS 2003c: 13, para. 41).

These statements of significance would represent a major advance for buildings, which to date have been described in terms of their physical appearance, rather than discussed in terms of their historic, architectural or archaeological significance and the reasons for their designation. Such a process has been in place in scheduling for some time, with the production of generic monument class descriptions in the late 1980s and early 1990s against which individual sites were explicitly compared and ranked against identified criteria in the Monuments Protection Programme (Startin 1993; EH 1996; Nieke 2001). Furthermore, the government 'is minded to require owners, local authorities, amenity societies, parish councils and the public to be informed and consulted when an application is made to place an asset on the List' (DCMS 2003c: 14, para. 45) reflecting a desire for greater openness and public involvement in what has, hitherto, been a somewhat secretive process. The reason for the clandestine nature of the procedure was to avoid pre-emptive demolition where owners, getting wind of a potential listing, demolished or destroyed assets before the listing became legal. The most infamous case of this, the destruction in 1980 of the Firestone Factory, a 1930s Modern Movement building on Western Avenue in London, precipitated the accelerated re-survey of Listed Buildings in the 1980s, but every lister has their tales to tell: my own concerns the loss of two out of three hydraulic accumulator towers in the 1820s docks at Goole in Yorkshire, which disappeared mysteriously between my initial reconnaissance visit and my return to make notes on my recommendations. Under the new system, consultation will almost certainly be required, subject to the essential caveat of the provision of protection during the period of consideration (DCMS 2003c: 14, para. 45), and during that time, a more reasoned decision could be made about whether it was desirable to retain all three towers or whether the one that was randomly retained was a good example or alone sufficed to demonstrate the historical significance of what was, at the time of its construction, a radical new technological advance.

The implications of a unified list for a new consent regime have not been fully worked out but, interestingly, a 'suite of consents' seems to be envisaged. This would build upon a development in both ancient monuments and Listed Buildings administration: that of the management agreement, whereby certain agreed interventions are given 'blanket consent' for the period of the agreement (usually ten years). Provision for voluntary management agreements was made made under Section 17 of the Ancient Monuments and Archaeological Areas Act of 1979, and EH produced its *Developing Guidelines for the Management of Listed Buildings* in 1995 (EH 1995b). It has been noted that management agreements have been of some value for the care of ancient monuments but that their coverage of individual monuments only has been a hindrance to their wider effectiveness: 'agricultural management can be achieved if sufficiently large areas are tackled but it is very difficult to achieve on a small scale' (Fairclough 1999a: 33), raising once more the issues of context and setting that are yet to be resolved. Their efficacy in the curation of Listed Buildings has been tested only on twentieth-century listings so far, and even then only eighteen examples are recorded, partly, it would seem, because of anxieties over their non-statutory status: 'without statutory backing no agreement can replace the degree of certainty and clarity that potentially gives the building owner and/or manager the confidence to proceed, unfettered by the normal Listed Building Consent process, or, in failing to obtain it, obviating the risk of enforcement or prosecution' (Kindred 2003b: 14). It seems likely that the introduction of management agreements to the suite of consents proposed in the Heritage Protection Review will address this problem. The anxiety is that it is driven by a government deregulatory agenda and that the certainties of control of each different proposal for a designated site or building will be lost, thus opening the door to incremental loss of significance through cumulative small changes, a problem warned against in PPG 15: 'minor works of indifferent quality, which may seem individually of little importance, can cumulatively be very destructive of a building's special interest' (para. 3.13).

Behind the proposal for a single list lies a decade or more of thinking about the nature and significance of the material remains of the past. Vocabulary is often a good indicator of change: rather than subdivide our surroundings into discrete 'monuments' (with all the intellectual baggage that concepts of monumentality carry (Carver 1996)), archaeological sites, standing buildings and Conservation Areas, we have become accustomed to referring to the whole as the 'historic environment'. Adopting the terminology of environmentalists in their pursuit of sustainability, we have come to understand our historic environment as 'heritage assets' or 'environmental capital', and to work in partnership with other interests, not only in the ecology sector but also in local communities to 'manage change' (a phrase one hears constantly bandied about, as an antidote to the 'pickled in aspic' characterisation of the sector by the detractors of conservation). The provision of a unified list will go some way towards combating the disjunct nature of the present system, but yet more radical thinking is afoot. Strong arguments were being made within EH and beyond in the mid-1990s for Historic Landscape Characterisation (EH 1997a; Fairclough 1999a). This is a broader assessment of whole rural or urban landscapes within the framework of the Countryside Character Map which was produced by the Countryside Agency in collaboration with English Nature and EH and subdivided the country into 159 areas defined as 'biogeographic zones which reflect the geological foundation, the natural systems and processes and wildlife in different parts of England, *and provide a framework for setting objectives for nature conservation*' (UK Biodiversity Steering Group 1995: 100 [my italics]), and EH's *Atlas of Settlement Diversity* (Roberts and Wrathmell 2000). Characterisation is currently under way or completed in more than half of England's counties and does not result in designation or legal protection, and so lies outside the purview of the Heritage Protection Review. It does indeed provide a framework for setting objectives for conservation, but it sends shivers down the backs of those at opposite ends of the spectrum: dichard designators see it as the slippery slope to deregulation while non-sympathetic developers understand it to be an extension of the power of the historic environment lobby to cover absolutely everything. The solution, in the best tradition of British compromise, will probably lie somewhere in between: we are coming to realise that the historic environment is an indivisible whole, and that we can neither ignore parts of it that are not sufficiently significant to designate, nor can we impose blanket protection over the whole of the country. The aim, rather, is to encourage the kind of dialogue that might have led to a more thoughtful approach to the fate of those hydraulic accumulator towers: we might not have saved them all, but we would have made an informed decision.

WHO EVALUATES, INVESTIGATES AND RECORDS?

Archaeological fieldwork in the 1970s and 1980s was largely a matter of excavation and of territoriality (see Chapter 14). Local units were set up to meet the challenge of rescue archaeology. Some were funded by local authorities, others supported by museums or university departments. Yet others formed as independent charitable trusts. Each confined its activities to its home town (e.g. York or Winchester), county (e.g. West Yorkshire), or region (e.g. Wessex). Some university units effectively became regional or county units (Birmingham covering the West Midlands, for instance, or the Institute of Archaeology Field Unit, which concentrated operations in Sussex). The only true roving unit was the Historic Buildings and Monuments Commission's Central Excavation Unit, which acted in the capacity of a national flying squad. The territorial norm, however, was sanctioned in the framing of the AMAA Act 1979, for when areas of archaeological importance were to be designated, a local unit was to be named as the investigating body, setting the brief and carrying it out.

The advent of large-scale developer funding at the end of the 1980s followed the principle of 'polluter pays' that was being widely adopted at the time in environmental conservation, and which suited a Conservative government dedicated to the reduction of government involvement in public projects. It was formalised in the advice of PPG 16, leading to the almost universal adoption of competitive tendering systems in the early 1990s. This is, perhaps, hardly surprising, given that it would not occur to a property developer to use a particular firm of architects or engineers simply because they happened to operate locally. Nevertheless, for a discipline like archaeology, which has always regarded itself as fundamentally research-led, the change proved to be somewhat traumatic. The debate continues over the relative importance of the need for firmly based local knowledge upon which to build an effective research programme versus an assumed gain in technical/financial efficiency. John Walker first raised the issue in 1996 in *British Archaeology* (Walker 1996). More recently the report of the All-Party Parliamentary Archaeology Group (APPAG) recommends that 'urgent consideration should be given to replacing the present system of competitive tendering in developer-funded archaeological investigations by a local franchise system' (APPAG 2003: 21, para. 72), a suggestion brusquely dismissed by Martin Carver in his first *Antiquity* editorial as a very dead horse (Carver 2003: 7) and by David Jennings, director of Oxford Archaeology, as 'dead in the water' (as quoted in *The Archaeologist*, Anon 2003: 8).

The impact of PPG 16 has been surveyed by the Archaeological Investigations Project (AIP), commissioned by EH from the School of Conservation Sciences at Bournemouth University (Darvill and Russell 2002). Some 89 per cent of archaeological investigations (variously defined from assessment to evaluation to excavation) are now triggered by the planning system and carried out by professional archaeological contractors. The upbeat conclusion of the report is that archaeological investigations have increased sevenfold and field evaluations by a factor of two and a half. Watching briefs have increased more than twentyfold, excavations undertaken as a condition of consent numbered about 200 in 1999, and the report suggests that worst fears about the loss of area excavation and the knowledge derived from it have not been realised. Nevertheless, there remains considerable disquiet within the archaeological community about the degree to which research questions are able to be formulated and answered under this regime; a consistent anxiety, again articulated most recently by APPAG (2003: 35, para. 169) concerns the proliferation of 'grey literature', technical site and finds reports which are never made generally available and which add little, therefore, to the sum of archaeological research.

Turning to policy for historic buildings, the effects of PPG 15 are less well documented. The recording of buildings is being carried out in both planning and non-planning contexts but, as signalled above, the requirements of PPG 15 for recording are set out in a more disparate way than those in PPG 16 and hence are easier for applicants, and indeed, local authority curators, to ignore. Nevertheless, they are there. The requirements for pre-determination investigation to provide information germane to the decision-making process are given at paragraphs 2.11 and 3.24. The former states that local planning authorities 'should expect developers to assess the likely impact of their proposals on the special interest of the site or structure in question, and to provide such written information or drawings as may be required to understand [its] significance . . . before an application is determined', and 3.24 that they should consider where 'to require exploratory opening up, with Listed Building Consent as necessary, before considering consent for the main works'. Post-determination conditions are also provided for: local authorities should consider 'in all cases of alteration or demolition whether it would be appropriate to make it a condition of consent that applicants arrange suitable programmes of recording of features that would be destroyed in the course of works for which consent is being sought' (para. 3.23) and 'if there is any likelihood that hidden features will be revealed, the local planning authority should attach an appropriate condition to the Listed Building Consent to ensure their proper retention or recording' (para. 3.24). The importance of using these provisions was quickly made known to both archaeologists and the historic buildings conservation sector (Rosier 1996; 1997; Wood et al. 1994; Wood 1995) and the publication of Informed Conservation by EH (Clark 2001) provides much useful information on the techniques of investigation for buildings. Nevertheless, building recording has not become as commonplace as one might have hoped, given the number of LBC applications each year (SHER figures show these as fairly steady between c. 31,000 and 32,500 between 2001 and 2003 (EH 2003b: 25)). The 200 or so building recording projects logged by the AIP in 1999, compared to numbers in single figures at the beginning of the decade, show that this is an area of work that is being developed (Darvill and Russell 2002: 52), although more recently early results from the Yorkshire Archaeological Research Framework suggest that these figures were optimistic (Steve Roskams pers. comm.). Whatever the precise quantification, there is little doubt that this is an area of archaeological endeavour that is progressing less quickly than envisaged in the first edition of this chapter.

It would, however, be misleading to suggest that all archaeological investigation is carried out under contract and funded by developers. The AIP reported that about 3,156 (11 per cent of all investigations between 1990 and 1999) were not triggered by the planning process (Darvill and Russell 2002: 45–9). Contracting units, universities, the Scottish and Welsh Royal Commissions, EH's own survey teams (some inherited from the Royal Commission on Historical Monuments for England at merger in 1999) and amateur societies are still able to undertake research excavations and surveys where funding is available (see below). The APPAG, however, notes the tendency among universities to situate their research outside the UK on the grounds of costs and the impact of international projects on ranking within the Research Assessment Exercise (to which I return at the end of this chapter) and the report argues that this results in a lack of cohesion within the discipline (APPAG 2003: 30, paras 132–4 and 138).

As to who undertakes this work, the answer is about 275 archaeological contractors, both commercial and local authority or university-based. The top twenty contractors carried out 48 per cent of the recorded field evaluations and their dominance in the market is illustrated in the AIP's findings on other types of investigation. The degree to which the profession has embraced commercialism may be judged by the contents of the advertising section of the *IFA Yearbook*, with its glossy notices for companies offering general and specialist services that would have been unthinkable even fifteen years ago (although the much lamented Mark Gregson spotted what was coming as early as 1981, and had some great ideas about how to short-circuit a potential disaster (Gregson 1982)). The archaeology of buildings is apparently growing in importance: increasing numbers of archaeological contractors are including building recording services in their portfolios. The IFA supports an active Buildings Special Interest Group to promote professional standards in this area, but interestingly, only the University of York offers a specialist training course at postgraduate level. The AIP report notes the continuing contribution of what it describes as 'the independent sector' – museums, university departments, amateur societies and interested individuals – and defines their activities outside the planning process as 'research'. It would be interesting to undertake a more detailed survey to establish how far the planning of projects reflects this perceived difference between research and contract work. Darvill and Russell (2002: 42) suggest that 'the supposed division between "research" investigations and "contract" investigations is far less sharp than is often portrayed', but it is unclear whether this refers to aims and objectives or to purely methodological matters.

HOW IS THE MONEY CONTROLLED?

Other chapters in this volume cover the problems of funding, and they should be referred to for a broader discussion (e.g. Chapters 4 and 13). Nevertheless, it is important to allude to them here, for there are implications for the relationship of curation to research to be discussed in the final section.

Developer funding seems, at the moment, to be the accepted form of financing the bulk of archaeological rescue work, with £68.3 million from that source alone in 2000 (Aitchison 2002). As a result, the archaeological field profession has become locked into broader economic cycles more tightly than hitherto. As in the building trade, cyclical boom and bust has severe implications for the retention of a skilled workforce already compromised by persistently low salaries and poor professional progression (Aitchison 1999; Aitchison and Edwards 2003), which may be the result of competitive tendering, or may, as David Jennings suggests, find their roots in structural problems extending over the last thirty years (as quoted in *The Archaeologist*; Anon 2003: 8). Whatever the cause, the insecurity of such a workforce must surely carry implications for the quality of research.

Finance for non-planning-led work may emanate from EH in the form of the Archaeology Commissions budgets, or 'Rescue budget', but this has been dramatically reduced in the past decade from a peak of *c.* £7 million in 1994 to *c.* £4 million in 1999 (Darvill and Russell 2002: 37) and is now holding something like a steady state, with a budget of £4.64 million in 2003–4 (*ex inf.* EH). Current reorganisation within EH will involve the movement of some funds previously ring-fenced for excavation and survey into a new budget for building recording and conservation research. This is a development regarded as retrogressive by some (not because buildings and their conservation are seen as unworthy of support, but because this should not be at the expense of an already cash-strapped section of the budget). In recent years EH has administered the substantial funding (£3.8 million in 2003–4 and c. £3 million in 2004–5) released by the Aggregates Levy Sustainability Fund (ALSF) introduced in the 2000 budget to derive enviromental benefits from the aggregates industry. Additionally, there are university research funds (although these are comparatively meagre and hard fought over), the learned societies and local or county-based amateur societies. Such funding tends on the whole to be fairly small-scale. The AIP reports a significant, if anecdotal, problem of 'initiative fatigue', whereby the bidding process for project funding from these sources is seen to be so time-consuming (and hence money-consuming also) that its outweighs the benefits of the occasional 'win' (Darvill and Russell 2002: 54).

Contrast these relatively tiny sums with the £366 million committed in 2002–3 to heritage projects by the Heritage Lottery Fund, and the sums in excess of £2 billion that it has dispensed to c. 12,000 projects since it was set up in 1995 (HLF 2003). The problem, as APPAG has pointed out, is that the terms of reference of the HLF, with its emphasis on education and access, conservation and regeneration, make it difficult to release funding for archaeological research per se, and in particular its rules prevent the support of training excavations (APPAG 2003: paras 37, 22, 44). HLF funding has occasionally been won for large-scale investigation – the project to reveal and display the considerable archaeological heritage of Portmahomack in Easter Ross is a notable, but all too rare, example.

Funding by the research councils might be regarded as another source of central support for the profession. On the whole, however, grant aid from the Arts and Humanities Research Board (AHRB) (now reconstituted as a fully fledged Research Council) and the Natural Environment Research Council (NERC) tends to support individual projects at doctoral or postdoctoral level. Applications to the AHRB for archaeological projects are considered by a panel that also deals with history and Classics, and does not ring-fence sums to the different disciplines: the perception is that often archaeology loses out in a tough competition. NERC projects tend to find favour where the emphasis is on the science rather than the archaeology, which serves simply as a convenient means of testing or illustrating some novel scientific application. While one might argue that it is the responsibility of the profession to ensure that such work has relevance for the wider research agenda, it is clear that the disjunctions noted in the earlier recension of this chapter between academic and professional archaeology are, if anything, rather wider than they were. The reasons for and implications of this unhappy state of affairs will be considered in the final section.

THE RELATIONSHIP OF CURATION TO RESEARCH

The implications of the foregoing summary for the relationship of curation to research are formidable. Various trends have been identified:

- changing definitions of the historic environment
- conflicting visions for its future
- changing modes of curation from 'policing the monuments' to 'managing change in the historic environment'
- the harmonisation of above- and below-ground archaeology in designation and policy
- the widening of the fault line than runs between professional and academic archaeology.

All these have an impact on the relationship of research and curation as the following amplifications will demonstrate.

Changing definitions of the historic environment

The influence of both the modern and the postmodern intellectual movements in academia (for archaeology see Johnson 2000, for planning see Gilg 1996 and for conservation of the built environment see Earl 2003) has resulted in the extension of the boundaries of their fields of study to embrace broader (and particularly more recent) timespans and more extensive categories of material (that is, not simply the high-status, aesthetically accomplished structures and artefacts, but also low-status material culture and evidence for quotidian economic and social activity). What is 'valuable' is not therefore restricted to the ancient, the rare and the beautiful, but to the representative, the informative and the mundane. In addition, as noted above in the discussion of designation reforms, lessons have been learnt from the ecological lobby about the limited value of tightly drawn physical boundaries around areas for protection – birds and animals, after all, cannot be corralled within Sites of Special Scientific Interest. The response has been to broaden the approach through the methodology of characterisation of whole areas (Cooke 1999; Fairclough 1999a; Chapter 17).

The envelope of inclusion within the definition of 'historic environment' has stretched almost infinitely. The trend of the last ten years has been away from the identification of single sites and single buildings or of clearly defined Conservation Areas, towards a more holistic approach to the significance of the historic environment. To an extent this simply continues an existing historical trajectory: all developments in the history of designation since its inception in 1882 have tended towards greater inclusiveness, with the range expanded from unoccupied scheduled monuments to Listed Buildings to Conservation Areas, to parks and gardens and battlefields (see Hunter 1996 for an interesting set of essays on these nineteenth and twentieth century developments). Yet, the definition offered in *Power of Place* was broadbrush indeed: 'The historic environment is what generations of people have made of the places in which they lived. It is all about us . . . Most of our towns and cities, and all of our countryside, are made up of layer upon layer of human activity. Each generation has made its mark' (EH 2000a: 4; para. 02). Nor does the DCMS demur from this hyper-holistic approach: 'The past is all around us. We live our lives, whether consciously or not, against a rich backdrop formed by historic buildings, landscapes and other physical survivals of our past. But the historic environment is more than just a matter of material remains. It is central to how we see ourselves and to our identity as individuals, communities and as a nation. It is a physical record of how *our country* is, how it came to be, its successes and failures. It is a collective memory, containing *an infinity* of stories, some ancient, some recent: stories written in stone, wood, brick, glass, steel; stories inscribed in the field patterns, hedgerows, designed landscapes and other features of the countryside' (DCMS and DTLGR 2001: 7, para. 1 [my italics]). The persistence of earlier intellectual baggage in the form of an insistence on national identity as the cornerstone of heritage as well as the impact of the postmodernist agenda of plurality is very easy to deconstruct from the DCMS statement and perhaps less so from the *Power of Place* definition, framed as it was by a committee dominated by academics acutely sensitive to the potential for semantic analysis from their fellows. Those same academics might care to take note of what happened to their words when given a makeover by policy boffins.

This broad definition may suit an academic bent of mind, but it raises uncomfortable questions about operational utility. As definitions become endlessly flexible, advocates of a 'real world' approach to heritage conservation are orchestrating a backlash. In recent discussions regarding the Heritage Protection Review, the possibilities of *reducing* the number of items on the list have been raised (DCMS 2003c: 12, Qu. 4.2 'Should some of the items at Grade II move onto [*sic*] local lists?') and in a DCMS-sponsored seminar on the consultation paper, I have heard the warmly expressed opinion that 'the dross' at the 'lower end' of the Grade II category should be de-listed gain considerable assent around the table. The various controversies over the listing of twentieth-century buildings, particularly those that result from experiments in social housing held by many to have been largely unsuccessful (Buckingham 2000), also demonstrate a disjunction between academic/professional and public opinion. This is acknowledged by the heritage profession: 'ministers have had the courage to take possibly unpopular decisions where they felt that the architectural evidence for the importance of these buildings has been convincingly established' (Smith 2000: 16).

Current problems over capacity may also be exacerbated by ever-expanding definitions of value. DCMS may be comfortable with the broad definition it espouses above, but neither it nor the Office of the Deputy Prime Minister, currently responsible for planning matters, seem willing to accept the financial implications. Anxieties about the fragility of the existing planning framework and the pressure under which historic environment professionals operate are expressed in a report on *Local Authority Conservation Provision*. This highlights the tensions in the curation of the above-ground resource: an average of 1.7 Conservation Officers per local planning authority spend over half their time dealing with development control casework and suffer from the lowly status of their sector within planning departments as a whole (Grover 2003). County Archaeological Officers experience similar institutional difficulties, in part associated with the government priorities noted above, in that they find themselves operating outside the planning department entirely, sometimes in libraries and museums sections, and sometimes in leisure departments, and almost always with workloads that exceed capacity.

Conflicting visions for the future

Taking an expanded resource base as read, then, and given the difficulties and opportunities it provides, what are the stated aims of the various agencies and pressure groups for the historic environment? The *Power of Place* consultation suggests that the need for change is widely accepted: 'although people value the historic environment, this does not represent resistance to change' (EH 2000a: 4: para. 05). Rather, the objective should be to promote good decision-making in planning. The headings of the subsections of the document (and the order in which they appear) give a strong indication of the curatorial imperatives and priorities that the *Power of Place* team culled from their extensive consultation:

- 'conservation-led renewal: unlocking the value'
- 'reinvestment: the benefits of old and new'
- 'prevention not cure: common sense makes economic sense'
- 'people and place: reflecting wider values' (this section being principally concerned with child education, lifelong education, tourism and access issues)
- 'managing change and enhancing character'
- 'the first precondition: knowledge'
- 'the second precondition: leadership'.

Notice how economic development and the integration of historic environment issues into the planning cycle dominate the beginning of the document, how education, social inclusion and tourism are privileged above research (notwithstanding its characterisation as 'the first precondition') and how the functions of 'authority' are considered last.

The DCMS and DTLGR (2001) reply, *The Historic Environment: Force for our Future*, takes the same elements and orders them differently:

- providing leadership
- realising educational potential
- including and involving people
- protecting and sustaining
- optimising economic potential.

It is interesting that economic development seems to take such a low place in this agenda, but we should remember that the document was chiefly the product of DCMS, with some input from DTLGR but none from the Department of Trade and Industry. Even the regulatory aspect of the system takes a back seat. Instead, the two central planks of the Culture, Media and Sport agenda, education and access, along with a 'leadership' role that envisages facilitation rather than coercion, dominate. It is here that the criticism has come.

The APPAG has taken up the cudgels against such current policy development with vigour: 'The past is a fragile and non-renewable resource and must be properly *protected and preserved*. The Government's priorities are expressed in terms of broadening access to and developing the educational potential of the cultural sector. These aims, while worthy in themselves, force Government-funded bodies with responsibilities for archaeology to divert attention away from what should be *their core aims, to identify, protect and sustain* the historic environment, towards other goals. National agencies and national and regional museums find that their activities are increasingly skewed to those initiatives for which the Government is sometimes willing to provide funding, but which do not necessarily correspond to the wider priorities. Without the preservation of this fundamental resource, there will be nothing left to provide access to or to educate people about' (APPAG 2003: 6 [my italics]).

Clearly there is a difference of opinion here about precisely what are the fundamental aims of historic environment management. Is it above all an exercise in protection? If so, protection of what, from what and for whom and with what social and economic consequences? Are audiences more important than resources or do resources cease to exist as meaningful entities without their audiences, as some recent academic thinking might suggest? And does this kind of thinking play into the hands of a pragmatic civil service, ever alert to the possibilities of subverting one political process in favour of another, in this case the protection of the historic environment in favour of regeneration, access and education agendas? Certainly the heritage profession needs to continue its research into the events of the past and their material remains, but perhaps it also needs to lose yet more innocence and turn a more sophisticated eye to the theoretical issues of heritage management, of which more below.

Changing modes of curation

In its current modernisation programme, EH (2002f) identifies three audiences:

- future generations, who should have an opportunity of enjoying England's historic environment in a condition at least as good as that which we currently enjoy
- the people of today who live in or visit England and whom [*sic*] we want to enjoy, appreciate and learn from their historic surroundings
- those people who want to make changes to the historic environment; individual owners or corporate bodies that engage with EH because they are involved with changes to the historic environment.

This is, perhaps, another way of identifying its statutory core duties (to secure the preservation of ancient monuments and historic buildings and to promote the preservation and enhancement of the character and appearance of Conservation Areas in England and to promote the public's enjoyment of and advance their knowledge of those assets and their preservation (National Heritage Act 1983 Section 33)), but the very formulation in this way reflects a sea change in approaches to public duty that affects not only central government but also local authorities. In a management briefing note of June 2002 the Chief Executive, Simon Thurley, is very explicit about this: 'What is the modernising programme about? Recognising that we are a *service organisation*' and 'I want to give us a much clearer *client focus*' (original emphasis). In external documents the same message is sent out. The *User's Guide*, which is undated but was distributed in 2002, has this to say: 'We use this role [adviser to local planning authorities] to achieve positive improvements to historic buildings, and to ensure that new buildings are of a high quality. Each year we provide advice on around 18,000 planning and Listed Building Consent applications. Many still see us as a reactive regulator, but we are working hard to combat that image. We work proactively and in partnership to ensure that change recognises potential' (EH n.d. c: 41).

This change in attitude from regulator to enabler owes much to political pressure, as the Conservative administration of 1979–97 pursued its avowed goal of rolling back state intervention and its successor, the New Labour government of 1997 onwards shows little sign of wishing to take an alternative view, at least in the realm of planning. Archaeologists have fought shy of hard hitting political analysis of their situation in print, if not in the pub, and I argue that now, more than ever, the academic discipline needs to abandon its precious approach to its subject matter as being 'the past and nothing but the past' and to admit that unless we understand, and through understanding take some control over, the conditions under which that knowledge is generated, we shall be unable to resolve the current furious debate over whether the academic discipline and its

Figure 12.1. The introduction of a single Planning Policy Statement will effectively minimise the recording disparities between above- and below-ground recording. The illustration shows surveying being undertaken at Whiteleaf Hill, Buckinghamshire. *(©: Oxford Archaeological Unit. Photo Ros Smith)*

173

contracting/policy making colleagues are there to protect, to preserve, to research, to manage change or to educate (whom and about what?). Until we have clarified the theoretical and political issues that underpin this debate, we shall continue to appear at Stonehenge enquiries into the next century divided and divisive. We can no longer afford to fight battles across the boardroom of EH and the planning committees of the local authorities in the absence of a fundamental analysis of the role of the past in the present. At first sight, the current government policy, as articulated by EH in its modernisation programme, chimes well with recent thinking in academic sociology, in which the role of the intellectual is seen as changing from that of a legislator to that of a facilitator (Baumann 1987, and for a specifically archaeological spin, see Smith 1994, 2004; Smith *et al.* 2003). Gilg (1996: 8) suggests that ideologically left or left-of-centre parties are instinctively interveners and it is the right wing that favours non-intervention – archaeologists need to ask themselves how they might, or indeed whether they want to, reconcile the new role of facilitator with a perceived wish for continued intervention in the form of strict controls over designation and development of the archaeological resource. More research remains to be undertaken regarding the potential and political implications of new ways of managing both the historic environment and its audiences, for we are as yet uncertain about the consequences, or even the pragmatic methods, of this kind of approach.

The harmonisation of above- and below-ground archaeology in designation and policy

The introduction of a single Planning Policy Statement (PPS) to cover planning for the historic environment, whether buildings or subsurface sites, and the current proposals for a single designation system suggest that two-track legislation is on its way out and that a harmonised system will be in operation within the next few years. How this will work out in practice is difficult to predict, for the devil, as always, will be in the detail. The proposal to include a statement of significance in each list entry is a response to the puzzlement of many house owners, when faced with a bald list description that simply describes the appearance of their home, and the needs of many developers who have little help in adjudging the relative archaeological importance of the site they wish to develop until after they have commissioned an initial appraisal. The statement of significance, borrowed from Conservation Plan terminology, is intended to provide a justification for the inclusion of the site, structure or landscape element on the list and to identify the cultural assets of the place that it is desirable to retain in making plans for its future use. The DCMS consultation document *Protecting our Historic Environment* has suggested that they could go as far as 'indicating the works for which consent would be needed' (DCMS 2003c: 13) but, arguably, this is to confuse two stages in the operation – the first being the identification and formal assessment of significance and the second being the application of explicit tests to adjudge whether *specific* proposals would have detrimental impact upon that significance. At present, the view of EH is that the two parts of the process should remain very clearly separated so as not to lose the opportunity at the stage of determination of consent to investigate the precise nature of the proposals. They might be broadly acceptable but problematic in certain details, or conversely, they may represent an acceptable practical solution to the introduction of a change that might, in general terms, seem incompatible with the retention of the significance of the place.

For the archaeological community with its interest in the research potential of archaeology above ground (see, for example, Wood *et al.* 1994), the disparity between the recording requirements imposed upon the developers of subsurface sites as opposed to above-ground archaeology has long been a matter of concern. The reissue of planning policy advice in a single PPS, rather than two PPGs, will almost certainly signal the beginning of the end of this long-running saga. It is likely that policies for the thorough pre-application investigation of significance and the impact of proposed changes will be harmonised and clearer guidance given on post-determination conditions for recording. Of course, the necessity to produce statements of significance for each item on the list will involve a good deal of additional research of the type that has been called for over the years, and the mechanism for achieving this remains unknown at the time of writing: will there be yet another grand 'Listed Buildings re-survey/MPP' project, designed to bring all the listings up to date in as short a time as possible, or will statements of significance be required for existing designations as and when applications for consent are made in their respect? And if the latter, whose financial responsibility will that be – the developer's or the state's?

The fault line between professional and academic archaeology

In the first edition of this book, I closed with the comment that 'academia and the field profession cannot afford to operate in mutual isolation: such a course would without doubt lead to the terminal stagnation of the discipline' (Grenville 1993: 133). Twelve years on from writing this comment, the situation seems little improved. The profession continues to complain that the universities do not turn out adequately *trained* archaeologists: 'While most graduates do not intend to use their degree in a professional capacity, there are skills shortages on graduation which have not been adequately addressed by undergraduate courses. These include, for example, fieldwork and the handling of finds, both of which are vital to a full appreciation of the subject' (APPAG 2003: 28–9, para. 123). Such a complaint mirrors those in other sectors and arguably reflects a general dislocation of expectations between employers, who want graduates to step into their first job fully competent and technically trained, and universities, who hope that their graduates will do so, but are more concerned with a wider intellectual training that will add value to their work careers throughout their lives. How far an industry can, and should, set the syllabus for its associated degree courses remains a bugbear in academic areas other than archaeology and planning. Additionally, as the funding of universities is further removed from general taxation and placed at the door of those who benefit from it, in the form of tuition fees, how far will archaeology, with its poor pay and conditions after graduation, suffer as an academic discipline? A lack of good students coming through the system and moving into the profession will exacerbate capacity problems that are already causing concern.

Equally worrying has been the tendency of academic archaeology to dig itself deeper into its bunker. The Research Assessment Exercise (RAE), undertaken by the Higher Education Funding Councils, assesses research success of individual departments in each university on a cycle of five to six years. The assessment is made by a panel of peers within each subject, so effectively that panel decides what does and does not constitute 'effective' research. The problem here is that the RAE is the major engine in university development these days. Millions of pounds of additional funding rest on its results and it is, currently, the only means of deriving additional core funding (as opposed to project-specific money) available to universities. Vice-chancellors focus upon it to the point of neurosis, for both the money and the prestige that a high score brings can make or break an institution. Research into the process of research (see e.g. Kuhn 1962) suggests that it is susceptible to fashion in its favoured paradigm. Given that RAE scores are determined by panels of peers, I return to my argument in the previous section: unless or until the academic establishment in archaeology is prepared to accept 'applied' research into the conditions of knowledge generation, the management of the archaeological resource and its reception by a wider public as a legitimate part of archaeological endeavour, then the split between academic and professional archaeology will continue to grow to the intense detriment of both sides.

CONCLUSION

So, how are we doing? Archaeology (in its broadest sense) in the early twenty-first century is arguably more attuned to its audiences, more businesslike in its operations and receives more money (which is different from saying that it is adequately funded in a strategic sense) than it was ten years ago. It continues to dissipate its intellectual talents, through inadequate career structures and poor communication between the field profession, the curatorial arm and the academic community. It produces more data than ever before and is beginning to make some inroads into the business of adequately collating it and telling the stories it reveals to an avid public. It understands, and is beginning to succeed in persuading the public, if not governments, that the historic environment is the fourth dimension of where we live, not a foreign country to be visited.

The extent to which we are still at loggerheads with one another can be observed by attending conferences, reading *The Archaeologist* (the journal of the IFA), *The Digger* (an informal and infrequent 'underground' newspaper produced by the digging fraternity and *Context* (the journal of the Institute of Historic Building Conservation) and by sitting in smoke-filled bars gossiping. Another, quicker way of doing that is to compare two recent comments on the state of affairs. The Archaeological Information Project's conclusion is that 'the archaeological community has a continuing duty to meet its responsibilities towards the raw materials of the discipline (the archaeological resource) and those who have authorised and sanctioned a high-profile place for archaeology in today's society (the general public). In this it has actually done rather well' (Darvill and Russell 2002: 51). We might contrast this with the view of Lord Redesdale, the Chairman of APPAG: 'I really do feel that archaeology *is* in crisis' (Redesdale 2002: 23). Both speak from a position of considerable empirical knowledge of the situation, but one set of data was gathered ostensibly as an objective statistical exercise and the other as a policy-forming exercise: statistics and gut feelings do not seem to match.

LEGISLATION IN NORTHERN IRELAND

Claire Foley

Apart from the Ancient Monuments Protection Act 1882, Ireland has had a quite different history of legislation from Britain. Official care of monuments in Ireland goes back to the disestablishment of the Church of Ireland and the Irish Church Act in 1869. The latter made provision for the future upkeep of certain important ecclesiastical sites: 137 ruined churches and crosses were vested in the Commissioners of Public Works to be maintained as 'national monuments', seventeen of these being in what is now Northern Ireland.

This Irish precedent was quoted in the debates on what eventually became Sir John Lubbock's Ancient Monuments Protection Act in 1882. This legislation applied to Britain and Ireland, and there were eighteen Irish sites in its schedule (three in the north). The Ancient Monuments Protection (Ireland) Act 1892 increased the scope for protection beyond the sites in the 1882 schedule, and under the Irish Lands Acts of 1903 and 1923 the Land Commission was given the power to vest important monuments in the Commissioners of Public Works.

After the partition of Ireland, the twenty-two sites in the six northern counties passed from the Commissioners to the Ministry of Finance for Northern Ireland, and in 1926 the Ancient Monuments Act (Northern Ireland) was passed, giving the state a greatly increased responsibility for the care of monuments. This act provided for State Care through acquisition and guardianship, protection through scheduling and preservation orders, the setting up of an Ancient Monuments Advisory Committee, and the reporting of all archaeological finds to that committee. A supplementary Ancient Monuments Act (Northern Ireland) 1937 introduced a provision from the 1930 Ancient Monuments Act of the Republic of Ireland: the restriction of excavation for archaeological purposes except under licence issued by the 'Ministry' (now the Department of the Environment for Northern Ireland). The Republic's 1930 Act had introduced the reporting of finds, and in these two areas – finds reporting and licensing excavations – Irish legislation, north and south, still differs from the law in Britain.

The next landmark was the Historic Monuments Act (Northern Ireland) 1971. This was a fairly short piece of legislation, in the tradition of the 1926 and 1937 Acts, but it increased the effectiveness of protection through scheduling, provided for the registering of scheduling in the Statutory Charges Register, introduced powers of compulsory acquisition of monuments and provided for the appointment of an advisory Historic Monuments Council.

In 1995, the Historic Monuments and Archaeological Objects (NI) Order was enacted. This was a considerable improvement on the 1971 Act introducing Scheduled Monument Consent to bring Northern Ireland in line with other UK legislation. In addition, it brought restrictions on the use of metal detectors on scheduled sites as well as continuing to require an excavation licence for any archaeological disturbance or for searching generally for archaeological objects anywhere in Northern Ireland including the territorial waters to 12 miles out from shore. The requirement for finds reporting continues. The licensing of excavation and reporting of finds in Northern Ireland comply with the European Convention on the Protection of the Archaeological Heritage (revised) known as the Valletta Convention. DoE (NI) is responsible for administering Treasure Trove in Northern Ireland on behalf of HM Treasury (see also Chapter 6).

The work of protecting archaeological sites and monuments benefits from several other pieces of Northern Ireland legislation. Within DoE (NI), under the Planning (Northern Ireland) Order 1991, Planning Service prepares area plans which, when formally adopted, become the statutory planning framework. A new round of area plan preparation is taking place at this time and the archaeological dimension provided by the Environment and Heritage Service (EHS; see Chapter 4) is regarded as an essential component. EU Agricultural Regulations have been translated into local Northern Ireland legislation for administering the environmentally Sensitive Area Scheme and the Countryside Management Scheme. Agri-environment policy protects all historic monuments registered in the Northern Ireland Sites and Monuments Record as well as other features considered to be historic such as old farm structures, field boundaries and plantations. In addition a *Code of Good Farming Practice* has been developed, which is expected to be observed by farmers in receipt of state aid. The protection of historic buildings came late to Northern Ireland, and was preceded by much vocal lobbying by conservation bodies, especially the Ulster Architectural Heritage Society, founded in 1967. The Planning (Northern Ireland) Order 1972 provided for the listing of buildings of special architectural or historic interest, for grant-aid for conserving Listed Buildings, and for the designation of Conservation Areas. The Historic Buildings Council was appointed in 1973 and the first Conservation Area was designated in 1975. There are now sixty Conservation Areas in Northern Ireland. Grant-aid to listed churches was made possible by the Historic Churches (Northern Ireland) Order 1985. Powers of protection for Listed Buildings were increased in 1990 with the Planning and Building Regulations (Amendment) (Northern Ireland) Order. This provided for urgent repairs to endangered buildings and the serving of repair notices on owners of neglected properties. The historic buildings work is now carried out under the Planning (Northern Ireland) Order 1991, a largely consolidatory measure that embraces the work on churches. The Planning Order also provides for an opportunity to record Listed Buildings when Listed Building Consent (to alter or demolish) has been granted. The Planning (NI) Order 1991 was strengthened in 2003 by the Planning Amendment (NI) Order 2003, which for the first time in Northern Ireland now allows for the 'spot-listing' of *listworthy* buildings considered to be at risk from demolition or alteration.

There are approximately 8,500 listed buildings in Northern Ireland. A second survey of historic buildings in Northern Ireland is currently being conducted at electoral ward level. It is designed, among other things, to give quality assurance to the list, as well as to add to it buildings that have been more recently identified as being listworthy, and to remove those buildings that do not have the '*special architectural or historic interest*' to merit remaining on the list.

CHAPTER 13

ENGLISH HERITAGE FUNDING POLICIES AND THEIR IMPACT ON RESEARCH STRATEGY

Roger M. Thomas

INTRODUCTION AND BACKGROUND

Introduction

Throughout the UK, the postwar decades, and the years from about 1980 in particular, saw both a remarkable level of fieldwork and the transformation of a wide range of organisational structures, policy frameworks and areas of technical and intellectual expertise concerned with the management of the nation's archaeological heritage. Many of these topics are described in more detail elsewhere (including Chapters 1, 4, 14). These developments, taken together, have provided a firm basis for the continuing development of archaeological resource management in the UK: they have to a large extent been made possible by sustained funding and support from the various central government agencies concerned with archaeology.

This chapter considers the archaeological policies of English Heritage (EH), the agency responsible for England, and its predecessor bodies in central government. It will discuss the development of these policies and the ways in which they have been implemented, examine the range of activities towards which funding and support has been directed, briefly review achievements to date (including the realignments of policy after the publication of PPG 16 in 1990: DoE 1990a) and consider the significant changes that have occurred in the policy landscape since 2000. (For a very personal view of developments up to 1999, from someone who was central to many of the initiatives discussed here, see Wainwright 2000.)

It is worth remarking at the outset that many of the policies discussed here have been implemented 'on the ground' by bodies other than EH. The archaeological sections of local authorities, independent archaeological units, universities, the Council for British Archaeology (CBA), the Institute of Field Archaeologists (IFA) and many other organisations have all played major roles in the developments discussed here. These bodies have helped to shape policy both through discussion and debate, and through the experience of applying policies in practice. This contribution is gratefully acknowledged.

English Heritage (statutorily known as the Historic Buildings and Monuments Commission for England: HBMCE) came into being on 1 April 1984 (Chapter 5). The statutory duties of HBMCE as laid down in the National Heritage Act 1983 (NH Act) include the duty ('so far as practicable') to 'secure the preservation of ancient monuments . . . situated in England' and to 'promote the public's enjoyment of, and advance their knowledge of ancient monuments . . . situated in England and their preservation'. 'Ancient monument' in this context has a similar, although not identical, definition to that contained in the Ancient Monuments and Archaeological Areas Act 1979 (AMAA Act; Chapter 5) and is sufficiently broadly defined to encompass most kinds of remains of archaeological interest.

The NH Act confers a range of specific functions on the Commission; it also amended the AMAA Act so as to transfer certain powers contained in that legislation to the Commission, including the power to undertake archaeological investigations and to publish the results. Ancient monuments and archaeological work therefore forms an important component of EH's activities. However, EH has a wide range of other responsibilities so that archaeological concerns are only part of the overall spectrum of its work (detailed in EH's *Annual Reports* from 1985 onwards: see also www.english-heritage.org.uk).

EH is a large organisation, with a staff of about 1,870 and a budget of some £158 million in 2003/04. The larger part of its income is an annual grant (£119.6 million in 2003/04) from central government, with which the organisation, while independent, has close links. In 1992 responsibility for EH, which had lain with the Heritage Division of the Department of the Environment (DoE), was transferred to the newly created Department of National Heritage (DNH). DNH is now called the Department of Culture, Media and Sport (DCMS). As the department of state primarily responsible for heritage matters, DCMS has an interest in broad questions of archaeological policy and funding; it is also responsible for the administration of some aspects of ancient monuments legislation, which it does with professional advice from EH (Chapter 5).

Until the mid-1980s, central government responsibility for archaeology in England lay with the Directorate of Ancient Monuments and Historic Buildings (DAMHB) within DoE. In effect, EH was created by transferring the staff and organisation of this body out of the Civil Service and giving them independent status. Responsibility for ancient monuments and archaeology had earlier lain with the Ministry of Public Buildings and Works, and its predecessors the Ministry of Works and the Office of Works, before the creation of DoE in 1969. The strand of continuity through these departmental changes was the Inspectorate of Ancient Monuments. The Inspectorate originated in 1882, and was the engine for the development of many of the funding and other archaeological policies of EH and its predecessors. The Inspectorate does not now exist as a distinct entity within EH, but EH's Inspectors of Ancient Monuments, along with colleagues in EH's Archaeology Division, continue to help in shaping archaeological policy.

An influential role has also been played by the successive panels of external academic advisors (the Ancient Monments Board until 1984, later the Ancient Monuments Advisory Committee and now the English Heritage Advisory Committee), which have helped to guide the work and thinking of officials throughout the period under discussion.

Background: funding policies before 1980

Government financial support for archaeology really began during the Second World War, with resources being provided for the rescue excavation of sites threatened by wartime activities (e.g. Grimes 1960). Support continued through the 1950s and 1960s. During this period, rescue excavations were generally carried out either directly by the Ministry itself or under the auspices of local excavation committees. Ministry excavations were undertaken either by Inspectors or by fee-paid supervisors – sometimes academics or museum staff, sometimes itinerant excavators (Rahtz 1974: 59) – aided by volunteers or paid labourers. Fee-paid supervisors were normally engaged solely for the duration of an excavation; support for subsequent post-excavation work and publication was not always adequate. In a number of places, notably in historic cities and in response to development threats, local initiatives led to the formation of excavation committees: examples include the Roman and Medieval London Excavation Committee (Grimes 1968), the Winchester Research Unit (Biddle 1974) and the Canterbury Excavation Committee. Funding for the activities of such bodies came from the Ministry, from local authorities and from a range of other sources. Again, infrastructure and resources were rarely adequate for the tasks in hand. Elsewhere, archaeological responses to development threats at this period were made, on a more or less ad hoc basis, by museum archaeologists or by local amateurs.

In the late 1960s and early 1970s, there was a considerable upsurge of public and professional concern about the loss of archaeological sites through development of all kinds. The level of government funding began to increase (largely as a result of pressure from the newly formed organisation RESCUE: see Barker 1974). Many more local excavation support organisations and trusts were established, some in particular towns or cities, some in rural areas and some in response to specific threats (notably motorway construction). These bodies derived the bulk of their funding from DoE grants, enabling them to employ professional archaeological officers and to mount excavations. However, not all areas enjoyed such cover. During this period, too, the scale of DoE's direct archaeological programme increased as well, including the major campaigns of excavations by Wainwright on prehistoric monuments in the south and by Stead on Iron Age and Roman sites in Yorkshire (e.g. Wainwright and Longworth 1971; Stead 1991).

The organisational and funding arrangements for archaeology in England before 1973 were embryonic, small-scale (especially early in the period in question) and, by today's standards, ad hoc. However, much important work was done: many sites were excavated which would otherwise have been lost without record. The greatest problems arose in the area of post-excavation and publication work, and it was not until the 1980s and 1990s that many of the excavations carried out at this time were published.

From 1973, DoE planned to establish a network of regional archaeological units that were intended to provide comprehensive archaeological coverage across the country (Chapters 4 and 14). Their organisation was variable: some were independent trusts; others were based on local authorities; and others on museums or, in some cases, universities. Eventually some eighty such organisations were receiving annual DoE grants towards their running costs. The hope that local authorities would assume more responsibility for these costs in due course and the underlying intention of creating a comprehensive archaeological service were not fully realised.

POLICY DEVELOPMENTS 1980–90

The move to project funding

In 1980, DoE announced its intention to end annual grants to organisations and to move to a system in which funds were made available for specific projects of agreed scope, duration and cost. This move from core funding (for establishment costs) to project funding marked a major change in government policies in support of archaeological activity: the move was also, for obvious reasons, widely unpopular. There were two reasons behind it.

The first was that all public expenditure generally requires specific statutory authority. Before 1979, however, there was no explicit statutory basis for central government spending on field archaeology; support was, administratively, more or less ad hoc. The passage of the AMAA 1979 Act changed this; its Section 45 (as amended by the NH Act 1983) provided that EH:

1. may undertake, or assist in, or defray or contribute towards the cost of, an archaeological investigation of any land in England which they consider may contain an ancient monument or anything else of archaeological or historical interest . . .

2. may publish the results of any archaeological investigation undertaken, assisted, or wholly or partly financed by them under this section . . .

This section, which gives the same powers to local authorities, furnished, for the first time, a clear statutory basis previously lacking for government expenditure on archaeology in the United Kingdom. The apparent intent of this section is to provide for the funding of specific projects but not for general subsidies to organisations.

The second reason to adopt project funding was professional and operational. By 1980, approximately 85 per cent of the archaeology budget was taken up with recurrent establishment costs to the aforementioned eighty organisations; a form of stagnation had arisen that was reflected in the ever-increasing backlog of unpublished excavations and the concomitant lack of uncommitted funds assignable to new projects. Project funding would ensure a regular release of funds that would give new ideas, projects and organisations a chance (EH n.d. a).

Behind the legal and policy reasons for this change is a sound academic rationale. It has long been recognised that rescue archaeology must be 'a research activity with an academic basis, the aim of which is to add to the sum of human knowledge' (Wainwright 1978: 11). The move to project funding made it possible for DoE to stipulate that, before a proposed project would be considered for funding, the project director had to provide a written statement (or research design) setting out its aims and justifying its importance in its regional and national academic contexts. This stipulation was designed to improve the quality and direction of the research problems that were to be addressed through archaeological work by ensuring that each project was planned within the framework of a well-designed problem-oriented research strategy. A formal research design has been required for each grant-aided project since 1980.

The context of policy development 1980–90

The project funding system provided a framework within which particular policy objectives could be pursued, to ensure the best use of archaeological resources based on correctly identified strategic priorities. The policies that have been followed, the criteria employed in the allocation of DoE and EH archaeological funding, and the patterns of funding and activity during the 1980s, will be examined shortly. As background, this section considers the range of influences that have affected the development of archaeological policies since 1980.

The archaeological policies of EH and its predecessors did not develop in isolation, but reflect, *inter alia*, wider trends in public policy, the views of advisory bodies and the outcome of consultation and discussion with external archaeological interests. These various influences may be briefly examined.

1. The 1980s saw a continuing emphasis on the need for careful control over, and accountability for, public expenditure and on the need to ensure 'value for money'. Trends in environmental policy, notably the 'polluter pays' principle, have also been of importance. Wider policy trends relating to public expenditure have manifestly had an impact on the development of archaeological funding policies.

2. Before 1984, DAMHB was an arm of central government; its policies had to evolve within the overall framework of government policy as determined by ministers. Contrastingly, policy and strategic direction at EH are its Commissioners' responsibility; archaeological policies are developed within the context of EH's overall remit for the historic environment.

3. Two statutory advisory bodies composed of eminent individuals from the archaeological world successively played an important role in determining and reviewing archaeological policy, including funding policy. Before 1984, the Ancient Monuments Board (AMB) was responsible for advising on the archaeological work of central government. In the 1970s a National Committee on Rescue Archaeology was established as an AMB subcommittee, to advise on the issues arising out of the rescue archaeology programme: for instance, a working party of the committee produced the Frere Report (DoE 1975a) on publication problems (Chapter 19). Area Archaeological Advisory Committees, established in the 1970s, were disbanded in 1979. On the creation of EH, the AMB was replaced by the Ancient Monuments Advisory Committee, a statutory advisory body that provides independent expert advice to the commissioners of EH on ancient monuments and archaeological matters.

4. EH, and DoE previously, has regularly consulted the national archaeological societies and special interest groups about policy matters and individual cases. These groups have also produced statements of academic priorities (e.g. Prehistoric Society 1988) that have helped to inform decisions about resource allocations. Since the inception of project funding, an annual report including expenditure information has been published, enabling the profession to keep in touch with policies and to comment on them.

5. Consultation, both formal and informal, between different sections of the profession is an important mechanism by which policy is developed. EH liaises regularly with CADW and Historic Scotland (HS), with the Royal Commissions and with a range of bodies such as the Council for British Archaeology, the Association of County Archaeological Officers (ACAO), the Standing Conference of Archaeological Unit Managers (SCAUM) and the IFA.

6. Discussions between EH's professional staff and those of archaeological organisations (especially grant recipients and local authority archaeological officers) working on the ground are important for exchanging views on policy and for reviewing the implications and results of particular approaches.

The archaeological funding policies of EH and its predecessors have evolved within a wider policy context and have been developed in consultation with others. The resulting policies therefore reflect a variety of imperatives, views and opinions.

Archaeological policy statements 1980–89

At a time of rapid change in archaeology in the UK, policy has been kept under fairly close review, and has also been implemented reasonably flexibly in response to changing circumstances. A number of clear statements of policy were published during the 1980s, and these have provided the framework within which the patterns of funding for particular activities and projects have developed. These set out the purposes towards which available resources would be directed and the criteria by which decisions about allocations would be made.

In considering this framework, it is important to stress at the outset that, ever since the passing of the first Ancient Monuments Act in 1882, the primary objective of government in this domain has been to secure the preservation of important monuments and archaeological remains. Government involvement in archaeological rescue excavation arose in response to situations where it was not possible to preserve monuments and remains physically, and so the appropriate course of action was to excavate and record that which could not be preserved – the policy of 'preservation by record' is a well-used (and sometimes criticised) phrase. Archaeological excavation has been a last-resort substitute for preservation *in situ*, rather than being a primary objective of policy. This fundamental point is one that it was possible to lose sight of in the rapid expansion of rescue archaeology in the 1970s and 1980s.

A second key point is that government concern has always focused on monuments and remains of national importance. This is the criterion that monuments must meet if they are to be scheduled under the ancient monuments legislation; archaeological projects must also fulfil it if they are to receive funding from EH.

The first such policy statement was the announcement of the change to project funding. At the same time, DoE stated that concurrently its archaeological funding during the 1980s would be based on a strategy encompassing a set of priorities established by the national period and topic societies in conjunction with the AMB. These priorities were:

1. Sites and Monuments Records (SMRs): the compilation of records of identifiable sites was recognised to form an essential database for preservation, management and excavation policies. Increased resources were to be directed towards SMRs in order to facilitate the identification of a representative sample of the features that make up the historic environment.
2. Monument selection procedures: it was proposed that the selection of monuments for scheduling should be within the framework of a sampling policy to ensure the preservation of a representative sample of each class of monument.
3. Environmental evidence: more resources should be directed towards projects with potential for recovering environmental information, particularly in wetlands and waterlogged sites.
4. Landscape archaeology: the investigation of areas of historic landscape should receive increased emphasis.

Stress was again laid on the importance of formulating proper research designs for rescue archaeology projects (EH 1991b: 4–5).

In 1983, the Secretary of State published non-statutory criteria (Chapter 5) governing the selection of monuments of national importance for scheduling. The same criteria, with the accompanying explanatory texts slightly modified, are used to determine whether proposed archaeological projects are of national importance and therefore eligible for funding (for further discussion see Chapter 17). They are as follows:

1. Survival/condition: the survival of archaeological potential is a crucial consideration.
2. Period: it is important to consider the record for the types of monuments that characterise a category or period.
3. Rarity: there are monument categories that are so rare that any destruction must be preceded by a record.
4. Fragility/vulnerability: important archaeological evidence may be destroyed in some cases by a single ploughing episode or similar unsympathetic treatment and must be preceded by a record.
5. Documentation: the significance of a project may be given greater weight by the existence of contemporary records.
6. Group value: the value of the investigation of a single monument may be greatly enhanced by association with a group of related contemporary monuments or with monuments of other periods. Dependent on the nature of the threat, in some cases it

may be preferable to investigate the whole rather than isolated monuments within the group.

7. Potential: on occasion the importance of the remains cannot be precisely specified, but it is possible to document reasons for anticipating a monument's probable existence and so justify the investigation.

In 1986, EH published *Rescue Archaeology Funding: A Policy Statement* (EH 1986). This set out the background to EH's policies, the principles on which funding decisions would be based (including the criteria just described), consultation arrangements and the categories and mechanisms of funding. The document also included the following statement (EH 1986: 7):

4.4 It is important to emphasise that EH allocates the funds at its disposal for recording those archaeological sites which cannot be preserved and whose destruction is taking place beyond the control of agencies with the powers and resources to deal with the problem. The Commission welcomes participation by developers and other bodies in the funding of rescue programmes for its resources are inadequate to carry that burden alone. In particular local planning authorities have a clear role to play in ensuring that the archaeological implications of planning decisions are properly assessed; and, that where destruction of important archaeological sites is unavoidable, due provision for essential archaeological recording is agreed and made before permission for a particular development scheme is given.

This important statement presaged the basic principles of DoE's *Planning Policy Guidance Note 16: Archaeology and Planning* (PPG 16: DoE 1990a) (see below).

EH produced *The Management of Archaeology Projects* in 1989 (EH 1989). This document emphasised the need for sound management of archaeological projects and was felt to be necessary because of the growing complexity, scale and duration of projects (especially urban post-excavation ones) supported by EH. The document, which reflected the broader requirements of control, accountability and value for money in public expenditure, was the forerunner of a much fuller second edition entitled *Management of Archaeological Projects* (EH 1991a). Further important policy statements, published in 1990 and 1991, are considered below.

POLICIES IN PRACTICE 1980–90

The archaeological activities of EH

The foregoing discussion of EH's archaeological policies in the 1980s provides the background for a consideration of the pattern of activities and funding in practice during that decade. Archaeological considerations are central to EH's work in preserving and presenting ancient monuments and historic buildings. The investigation of sites and buildings (whether by survey, excavation, or the archaeological analysis of standing structures), the recording and interpretation of such work, and the publication of the results, has aways accounted for a significant part of EH's budget.

In 1990/91, EH spent some £8.7 million on archaeological activities (Wainwright 1991: 4). The bulk of this sum (£5.5 million) was spent on rescue archaeology grants. This figure included an annual amount of £500,000 transferred to EH by the Department of Transport in respect of archaeological work on new trunk road schemes (the amount actually spent by EH on such work was consistently higher). Nearly £0.7 million was spent on archaeological science (mainly in connection with rescue archaeology projects) through EH's Ancient Monuments Laboratory. Almost £1 million was spent on archaeological recording at EH's own Properties in Care (guardianship monuments), and over £0.4 million on the Monuments Protection Programme (Chapter 17). Further sums were spent on (among other things) publication grants, storage grants, grants for recording monuments and buildings during the course of repair schemes, and work undertaken by the Central Excavation Unit, EH's in-house archaeological unit.

Funding for archaeological projects 1980–90

Grants to external organisations for archaeological work formed the largest part of EH's support for archaeology during the 1980s. The level and pattern of this expenditure had a significant impact on the development of archaeology and the archaeological profession in the country as a whole. The total archaeological grants made by DoE and EH increased fairly steadily over the years. Between 1972 and 1980 the rate of growth was remarkable – from less than £500,000 in 1972–3 to about £3.5 million in 1980–1. By 1989–90 the figure was just over £7 million (see Chapter 14). The rise in available state resources underlay many of the most important developments of the 1970s and 1980s.

The rescue archaeology programme of the 1980s was largely demand-led and, the increase in funding notwithstanding, demand for funds invariably outstripped availability. Selectivity therefore had to be exercised (in accordance with the criteria discussed above). Many projects had to be funded from a variety of sources, with contributions being obtained from developers, local authorities and elsewhere to complement funding from EH. In terms of purposes and objectives, it is possible to divide EH's archaeological grants into four categories in this period:

1. SMRs: support for the establishment or enhancement of comprehensive and retrievable databases.
2. Surveys: grants for extensive strategic surveys (including aerial photographic surveys) to identify and record the archaeological resource in particular areas as an aid to management strategies. Such surveys have generally been carried out in close conjunction with SMRs.
3. Excavations: grants for the excavation and recording of archaeological remains threatened with destruction and not open to preservation *in situ*.
4. Post-excavation: grants for preparing the results of excavations for publication. Unless the results of an excavation are published, there is no general public gain in knowledge or understanding to justify the expenditure of resources on the excavation, and categories (c) and (d) can really be considered together.

The apportionment of funding between the various categories in the period 1982–90 is depicted in Fig. 13.1. The pattern is a striking one. Excavation (X), and post-excavation (PX) work in particular, absorbed by far the largest share of resources and in percentage terms the expenditure on SMRs, surveys (S) and aerial photography (AP) was small (responsibility for the last-mentioned was transferred to RCHME in 1986: Chapter 18). The costs of post-excavation work were particularly heavy and, within this category, urban post-excavation projects accounted for between 35 and 60 per cent of total annual project funding during the 1980s (Fig. 13.2). The importance of careful control of post-excavation projects is obvious. Urban projects of course arise almost entirely from developments under planning control, and the significance of the archaeological planning policies now enshrined in PPG 16 (DoE 1990a) for future funding is clear.

PERCENTAGES

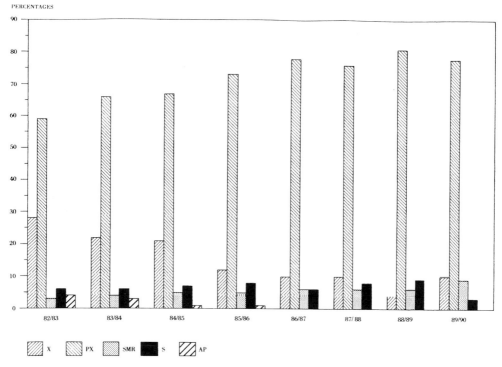

Figure 13.1. Categories of projects funded between 1982 and 1990 as a percentage of costs. *(After English Heritage 1991b: fig. 2)*

PERCENTAGES

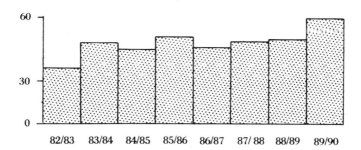

Figure 13.2. Urban post-excavation funding expressed as a percentage of annual project grants. *(After English Heritage 1991b: fig. 6)*

The products of funding

The results of EH's archaeological funding in the 1980s were substantial. The archaeological infrastructure – in terms of staff and the information base – was strengthened, especially through support for SMR and survey projects. A very wide range of important monuments and remains of all periods and types were excavated and recorded in advance of destruction, and analysis and publication of the results has greatly

187

increased our knowledge and understanding of the past and of the character of the archaeological record. These achievements may be briefly reviewed. A fuller account may be found in *Exploring our Past – Strategies for the Archaeology of England* (EH 1991b).

The pursuit of preservation policies through the funding of SMRs (now generally relabelled HERs, Historic Environment Records), in association with ACAO (now ALGAO), has resulted in important developments. These essential databases, on which policies are founded, have been strengthened. SMRs are also important for the prosecution of archaeological planning policies, and have underpinned EH's Monuments Protection Programme. Funding for SMRs has often been linked to agreements on pump-priming funding to assist local authorities in establishing permanent posts, mostly in planning departments, for County Archaeological Officers and SMR Officers. With support from EH, the number of archaeological posts in local authorities rose substantially in the 1980s. All county councils now employ archaeological officers, as do some unitary district and borough councils (notably those in historic urban areas, such as York, Exeter and the London Borough of Southwark).

Preservation policies were also pursued through project funding of survey and aerial reconnaissance. Some surveys were commissioned in response to the need to develop scheduling and management policies for areas of high potential. Into this category fall surveys on claylands (Raunds, Stansted, the Weald), upland areas (such as the Lake District, the Mendip and Quantock Hills, Salisbury Plain, Dartmoor, West Penwith), coastal zones (the Avon Levels, the Essex and Lindsey coasts) and river valleys (the gravels of the Upper Thames, Cambridgeshire and Herefordshire). Other surveys, such as the Stonehenge Environs Project, have had more direct relevance to the rescue programme and have been combined with excavation. Projects in wetland landscapes, such as those in the Fenlands and Somerset Levels, fall into this category.

The execution of surveys, combined where appropriate with excavation, offered an opportunity to begin integrating archaeological considerations into changing countryside policies, reducing the threat to vulnerable areas (Chapter 22). Such initiatives were taken for instance in the Somerset Levels and West Penwith, where the recognition of the archaeological importance of the landscapes has been subsequently confirmed by designation as Environmentally Sensitive Areas (ESAs).

Excavations in advance of development and other threats, and the associated post-excavation work, consistently absorbed the bulk of EH's archaeology budgets in the 1980s. This investment has enhanced our knowledge of the monuments and remains of every period, from the Palaeolithic to the post-medieval, in every region. Projects ranged from fairly modest investigations of individual sites to major, long-term and multidisciplinary landscape projects such as those at Raunds in Northamptonshire and West Heslerton in North Yorkshire. Space does not permit more detailed consideration of the results of the rescue archaeology programme of the 1980s, but published analyses of funding and reviews of results can be found in *Exploring our Past* (EH 1991b), in Wainwright (1984) and in the *Archaeology Review*, which was published annually by EH between 1989 and 1999.

PPG 16 AND DEVELOPMENTS IN 1990–2000

PPG 16

From about 1985, a number of county council archaeology services (working in conjunction with EH) began to develop archaeological planning policies that put the onus on applicants for planning permission to assess and accommodate the archaeological implications of their proposals. Uncertainty about the precise extent of the powers of planning authorities in this area led to pressure for DoE to publish a circular on archaeology and planning. The Rose Theatre controversy in the summer of 1989 (Wainwright 1989a) added considerable impetus to this call and, following discussions between EH and DoE and wide consultation by DOE on a draft, PPG 16 was published in November 1990 (DoE 1990a).

PPG 16 emphasises a number of basic principles: the importance government attaches to archaeological remains and their preservation; the need for local planning authorities to take account of archaeology in strategic planning and development control work; the need for the archaeological implications of planning applications to be properly assessed before applications are determined; the need wherever possible to preserve important remains threatened by development; and the expectation, where preservation *in situ* is not possible, that developers should make adequate provision for archaeological excavation and recording. This last policy is usually termed 'developer-funding', and is an application of the 'polluter pays' principle in environmental protection.

In many ways, PPG 16 can be seen as a culmination of policy directions pursued through the 1980s. The implications of PPG 16 (and comparable instruments such as the *Environmental Assessment Regulations* – see Ralston and Thomas 1993) for the funding, organisation and practice of archaeology have been profound. State funding for development-led excavation has been replaced by developer-funding, bringing with it commercialisation of the activity, competitive tendering and the roles of client, contractor, curator and consultant, and a variety of other changes (Darvill and Russell 2002: 4–8).

Archaeological policies in the 1990s

The publication of PPG 16 marked a watershed for EH's archaeological policies, and for the profession as a whole. In 1991 EH issued *Rescue Archaeology Funding: A Policy Statement* (EH 1991d). This replaced EH's 1986 statement, and modified funding policy in the light of PPG 16. The statement said that EH funding may be appropriate where developer-funding is not a possibility (perhaps because of the nature of the threat) and in cases where, despite proper prior assessment, important archaeological remains have unexpectedly come to light after planning permission has been granted and which it would not otherwise be possible to record. In other words, in a development context, EH funding would be the exception, not the norm. In addition, EH would commission projects that would enable it to carry out its statutory duties, and would direct funding to particular problems with this in view.

The years since 1990 have seen a substantial shift in the focus of EH's archaeological spending, accompanied by a significant decline in EH's archaeology budget (but a much greater increase in the level of developer-funding under PPG 16). Reorganisation within EH, including the merger with the RCHME in 1999, has also had an impact on research strategies.

In 1990–1 (the financial year in which PPG 16 was published) the archaeology budget was just over £5.5 million. In 2003/04 it was £4.43 million: a decline of over 43 per cent in real terms. However, it has been estimated that developer spending on archaeological work was £15.6 million in 1990 and £68.3 million in 2002, an increase of some 437 per cent over that period (Aitchison 2000).

Since 1990, EH has concentrated on providing a wider strategic framework for archaeology in England. This has been done in various ways. In 1991, EH published *Management of Archaeological Projects*, widely known as MAP2 (EH 1991a). MAP2 attempts to analyse the processes, both intellectual and managerial, involved in carrying out archaeological projects, and to provide advice and guidance on this subject (Andrews and Thomas 1995). MAP2 is now recognised as an industry standard; this is particularly important in an era of developer-funding and competitive tendering.

A second significant contribution has been the *Exploring Our Past* (EOP) series of documents. The first (EH 1991b) analysed the achievements of the 1980s and set out an agenda for the 1990s in the light of policy changes such as those contained in PPG 16. *Exploring our Past 1998 (EOP98)* was the result of broad consultation with the profession on a 'Draft Research Agenda', and was supported by *Exploring our Past 1998 Implementation Plan.* Both were essentially internal planning documents for EH, but both are publicly available (EH n.d. b).

Within the EOP framework, resources have been directed towards a series of strategic programmes aimed at identifying and evaluating different aspects of the archaeological resource, and at improving the information base for planning and management decisions. Four programmes merit particular mention.

The Historic Landscape Characterisation (HLC) programme is carried out through county council archaeology services and aims to map (using a Geographic Information System (GIS)) the historic character of the present-day rural landscape. The results can be used to inform a wide range of planning and environmental decisions. About half the country has been covered so far (Fairclough *et al.* 1999).

The Urban Archaeological Strategies programme was launched in 1992. It aims to produce detailed Urban Archaeological Databases (UADs), assessments and strategies for thirty-five major historic towns and cities, and Extensive Urban Surveys (EUSs) on a county basis for all smaller towns. The work is funded by EH through local authorities, who use the results for planning and other purposes. About half the programme has been completed so far (Thomas 2001, 2002).

The National Mapping Programme (begun by RCHME in the 1980s, and now being continued with support from EH's archaeology budget) aims to plot and classify all the archaeological evidence from aerial photographs for the entire country. A substantial proportion of England has already been covered (see Chapter 18 part 1).

The Monuments at Risk Survey (MARS) project was commissioned by EH from Bournemouth University in 1994. The aim of MARS was to conduct a general census of the archaeological resource in England, and to assess how the resource had fared in the period 1945 to 1995. The purpose was to provide a basis for the development of strategic policies. The MARS report (Darvill and Fulton 1998) identified widespread losses and attrition, and a number of policy initiatives have since sought to address these problems.

The MARS programme shows that EH has a continuing role in dealing with threatened archaeological remains. PPG 16 covers threats arising within the planning process, but there are many threats that are outside planning control. These include desiccation of wetlands, coastal erosion, many agricultural activities and a variety of other things, such as illicit excavation by metal-detectorists. A range of projects has sought to deal with such threats. Programmes dealing with wetland areas (Coles 2001a) and the coastal zone (Fulford *et al.* 1997) are notable examples.

The advent of PPG 16 has also focused attention on the need to have an adequate academic basis for the archaeological requirements imposed on developers through the planning system (e.g. Thomas 1997). This led EH to launch its Research Frameworks initiative. A survey of the issues was carried out in 1995, and published as *Frameworks for our Past* (EH 1996). This has been followed by a series of regional and other initiatives to produce research frameworks. Published examples include those covering East Anglia (Glazebrook 1997; Brown and Glazebrook 2000) and the Roman period (James and Millett 2001).

The merger of RCHME and EH in 1999 brought lead responsibility for SMRs back into EH. The National Monuments Record is primarily responsible for this key area. EH also acts as adviser to the Heritage Lottery Fund on bids for online public access to SMRs. Statutory status for SMRs is also under consideration at present (DCMS 2004e; Chapter 10).

The problem of how best to disseminate the results of fieldwork continues to attract attention. The volume of developer-funded work now taking place and the multiplicity of archaeological contractors involved make keeping track of what is happening difficult (Thomas 1991). To this end, EH has supported the Archaeological Investigations Project (AIP) which has published annual gazetteers of all fieldwork in England (Darvill and Russell 2002: 4-6). EH has also supported a Council for British Archaeology survey of the needs of users of archaeological publications (Jones *et al.* 2001).

A further problem concerns the synthesis of the proliferating results of developer-funded and other fieldwork. Much of this work is individually small-scale and needs to be interpreted in a wider context. Some progress is being made in this area (at the time of writing, for instance, Professor Richard Bradley is undertaking a major new synthesis of British prehistory, based largely on the results of developer-funded fieldwork: Bradley 2002b), but much remains to be done. The issue is a pressing one: without wider synthesis, the value of much fieldwork will never be properly realised.

EH also supports the development of what one might call 'professional infrastructure'. Methodological studies, training courses of various kinds, surveys of employment in the profession, studentships and administrative help for ALGAO have all received EH financial support. The *Profiling the Profession* report (Aitchison 1999) is an example: this report on archaeological employment and salaries was undertaken by the IFA with funding from EH.

2000 AND BEYOND

The new millennium saw further new directions, with significant changes in philosophy, legislation, policy and practice either in place or in prospect.

The *Power of Place* report, produced by EH at the request of government on behalf of the whole heritage sector, advocated taking a wide and socially inclusive view of the historic environment (EH 2000a). The report was criticised by some for paying insufficient attention to archaeology. The government response, *The Historic Environment: A Force for Our Future* (DCMS and DTLGR 2001) broadly endorses *Power of Place* and emphasises the potential social, economic and educational benefits of the historic environment. The contribution that the historic environment can make to regeneration is now a key focus of EH's work (EH 2002c).

Within a *Power of Place* perspective, there is little in the physical environment that is not potentially of archaeological interest. It is now difficult to see where, in traditional terms, the boundaries of archaeology lie, if indeed it has any boundaries at all. In effect, archaeology is now emerging as a way of looking at the environment (that is, as evidence for the past), rather than being defined by reference to particular types of subject matter (things which are buried, ancient, or both). This very wide perspective poses new challenges for policy makers and funding bodies such as EH.

In any event, archaeology is now taking its place as a key component of this trend to treat the historic environment as an integrated whole and to value it for its contribution to all parts of society. The 2003 *State of the Historic Environment Report* (SHER) illustrates this trend well (EH 2003b).

At the time of writing there is, though, considerable uncertainty ahead. The planning system is undergoing wholesale change following the Planning and Compulsory Purchase

Figure 13.3. *Power of Place* – a key document in English Heritage's vision of the future.

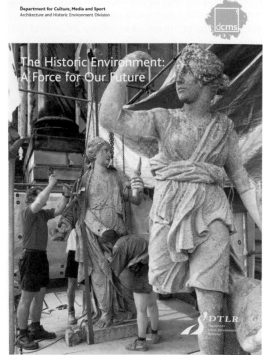

Figure 13.4. *A Force for Our Future* – the government's response to management of the historic environment.

Act 2004. A fundamental review of heritage protection legislation is in progress, and proposes replacing the various statutory regimes (listing, scheduling and so forth) with a single designation (DCMS 2004e: ch. 12). A review of PPGs 15 and 16 has also been signalled.

Some legislative change has already occurred. The National Heritage Act 2002 gives EH the legal power (which it formerly lacked) to work below the low-water mark, out to the 12-mile limit: in other words, to undertake maritime archaeology. Responsibility for this subject has now been transferred from DCMS to EH. This removes a long-standing anomaly; the challenge for EH now is to develop a uniform approach to archaeological resource management across terrestrial and maritime environments (EH 2002d).

At the level of practice, there is an increasing emphasis on working more closely with a range of non-archaeological partners. A good example is EH's work with DEFRA on agricultural damage to archaeological remains (Lambrick 2002). Here, archaeological understanding and EH's policy remit are being brought to bear on this long-standing and difficult issue.

SUMMARY AND CONCLUSIONS

In the 1970s, DoE was by far the largest funder of archaeology, and the pressing need at that time was to establish structures and to respond reactively to immediate threats to the archaeological heritage. The 1980s in particular saw the emergence and consolidation of a coherent organisational and policy structure, much of it local-authority based, for the management of the archaeological resource. Project funding from DoE and EH was important in making this possible.

The 1990s saw the burden of the costs of archaeological work occasioned by development lifted from EH by PPG 16, enabling resources to be redirected to other activities. Strategic programmes of survey and assessment, projects to deal with threats outside planning control, and the development of professional infrastructure were particular foci of activity. Archaeological resource management is now a diverse and often decentralised activity, and there is an important place for a central agency that can provide strategic overview, direction and support.

The years since 2000 have seen a wide range of policy developments in the heritage sector as a whole (against the background of a government that has a modernising agenda). These developments have located archaeology as one component of a broader concern with the historic environment in its entirety, and the focus is very much on finding ways in which the historic environment can benefit society at large.

Much of the apparatus of archaeological resource management in England is under review, in one form or another, at present. It is difficult to predict the outcome of all the changes which are in the air at the time of writing (early 2005). However, the real challenge for EH, and for the profession as a whole, will increasingly be to ensure that real benefits for society are drawn from the very substantial amount of money (much of it coming from private sector developers) which is now being spent on archaeology in England annually. Public benefit has always been the justification for central government involvement in, and expenditure on, archaeology. This will continue to be the case, and it is entirely right that this should be so.

CHAPTER 14

PROFESSIONAL PRACTICES IN ARCHAEOLOGY

Andrew J. Lawson

INTRODUCTION

Professional archaeological practices have become the major employers of archaeologists in Britain. By necessity they have the staff skills and resources to provide both innovative and routine solutions to potential demands on the historic environment. Between them they undertake a large proportion of the country's archaeological research, whether in or out of the field, frequently giving practical application to techniques developed in research institutions. Today, many professional practices are retained by clients who are not themselves directly concerned with the study of the past but who appreciate the ability of the practice to meet the client's needs while also satisfying broader academic, public and professional requirements.

Although the provision of professional archaeological services is now well established, it is a development of a maturing profession with a relatively short history. Until the 1970s most archaeological research was undertaken through academic institutions, museums or local societies, or through government departments such as the predecessors of English Heritage (EH) in England. However, in the 1970s new organisations employing full-time professional archaeologists (or 'units') were established, their work frequently sponsored by central government or local authorities. In the late 1980s this funding arrangement changed so that developers and land owners were expected to make their own arrangements for any archaeological work necessitated by their schemes: an innovation at the time, archaeologists were to be directly employed by the private sector rather than be grant-aided by government.

This change, brought about by government policy, had a very profound effect on the practice of archaeology in Britain. It caused archaeologists to reconfigure working practices, particularly in the light of experience in the USA where privately sponsored archaeology was the norm. Today, the roles played by different archaeologists in a professional forum are better known, and an understanding of who is responsible to whom for what has emerged. With professional ethics defined and different roles respected, a greater emphasis on team-working to find the best result has emerged.

Britain is among other leading nations that recognise the need for more stringent environmental protection, and within such a movement there is a widening appreciation of the relationship between different aspects of the cultural heritage. The study and appropriate management of these different aspects requires specialised knowledge and skills. As a consequence, if a practice concerned with the historic environment were to offer a full range of expertise today, it would inevitably be a large organisation. Currently, the larger professional practices employ more than a hundred staff, some twice that number, with the ability to study every period of the past, from the Palaeolithic to the twentieth century, on land, beneath the water, or from the air, whether of local or landscape scale, ruinous or surviving. Such skills may even be deployed abroad where local expertise cannot be found.

Before exploring these working arrangements more fully, it is instructive to review in more detail the way in which the modern profession developed out of the need to rescue archaeological information before it was lost, especially through the postwar rebuilding of the country. This chapter specifically relates to England (different arrangements occur in other parts of the United Kingdom, see for example Carter 2002 (for Scotland) or Briggs 2003 and Hughes 2004 (for Wales)).

THE INITIAL ESTABLISHMENT OF PROFESSIONAL TEAMS

The rise of 'rescue archaeology' has been conveniently chronicled in a small volume edited by Philip Rahtz (1974). By the early 1970s specific threats to archaeological sites resulting from postwar redevelopment had led to various localised responses, so that, for example, in 1972 the York Archaeological Trust for Excavation and Research was constituted, drawing heavily on experience gained during the previous decade in Winchester and other historic cities. From October of that year it employed a unit of eleven people (Addyman 1974: 162). Similarly, the establishment of the British motorway network led to the formation of committees intent on rescuing archaeological information in advance of (or more often during) the destruction of rural sites (Fowler 1974: 114–29). Threats to the survival of archaeological sites were perceived throughout the nation, and local initiatives spawned an increasing number of professional teams, referred to as 'units'. The situation in Kent (here expressed in rather heroic terms) was typical:

> By the end of 1971 it had become clear that, with the ever-increasing threat in Dover and on so many other sites in Kent, the situation had changed out of all recognition . . . For years several of the leading individuals had grossly neglected their business affairs and full-time jobs, but now even this was not enough. The never-ending work of rescue demanded a greater sacrifice, and so four of the team forsook their own professions to become full-time rescue archaeologists, hoping to survive on a small subsistence level wage. (Philp 1974: 77)

The profession of field archaeology progressed enormously in the latter part of the twentieth century in the realisation that archaeology would otherwise neither attract nor retain the best staff on part-time or subsistence level wages (below).

Elsewhere, for example in Norfolk, individual archaeologists each investigating a different site within a common geographical area came together to pool resources and expertise so as to make professional cover more efficient. The structure for an archaeological unit designed to cover the breadth of archaeology with different period specialists was defined in Norfolk in 1972. Staff were recruited to fill gaps in expertise and the unit was formally launched in April 1973. Here it was realised by an enlightened county council that the newly formed unit provided a valuable service to the community and would help to fulfil the authority's policies. Consequently, the council was prepared initially to underwrite certain salary costs, and eventually to absorb the unit totally within its Museums Service. Although Suffolk and Essex did likewise, not all English counties could offer such support for a team dedicated to their area. Where gaps in district or county provision necessitated the establishment of a unit, regional bodies were established, such as CRAAGS (the Committee for Rescue Archaeology in Avon, Gloucestershire and Somerset) and the Wessex Archaeological Committee. In each, a centralised organisation was preferred to a number of dispersed individual archaeologists.

The concept behind local archaeological units was that they should become centres of local excellence as experience grew. It was suggested that in time accrued knowledge would lead to a more efficient selection of priorities, especially in post-excavation studies.

By the mid-1970s, although national coverage by local units was neither uniform nor comprehensive, their proliferation was coming to an end. Yet, there was a need to provide cover in the areas poorly served. The solution from the Inspectorate of Ancient Monuments (IAM, the predecessor of EH) was to establish the Central Excavation Unit (CEU). It was to fill the gaps, to excavate on nationally important sites and to ensure that where the Department of the Environment was obliged to excavate (as a result of notice served under the contemporary Ancient Monuments Acts) provision had been made. The unit was to be based at Fort Cumberland near Portsmouth, from where projects throughout the country would be mounted. It laid the foundations of EH's Central Archaeological Service which, with a revised role, is still based in the fort.

The origin and growth of professional archaeological organisations has been closely linked to funding arrangements. The initial establishment of a network of units and a steady expansion in the work they undertook was only possible because of an increase in central government funds. In the 1970s block grants were made to units to underpin their costs. The work of each unit was focused on agreed projects, whether survey, excavation or post-excavation, selected on the advice of regional advisory committees (below). However, a modification of legislation (in the form of the Ancient Monuments and Archaeological Areas Act 1979) meant that government funds could only be used for specific pieces of work and not to pay directly for the maintenance of institutions. Consequently, from 1981 project funding became the norm: it required much closer attention to the management of units and passed the problem of seeking sufficient paying work to sustain staff from the funder to the employer. Exceptionally, as in the case of CRAAGS, units that could no longer propose projects attractive to the Inspectorate of Ancient Monuments went into liquidation.

In the early 1980s government funds were acknowledged as the major source of revenue for rescue archaeology either through the IAM, employment initiatives such as the Manpower Services Commission, or local authorities. However, government policy, in line with the increasing influence of the European Community, tended towards holding developers responsible for the effects of their respective schemes. In short, if private companies were to profit from the development of land, the tax-paying public should not have to bear the expense of any necessary archaeological work. Instead, this should be paid for by the developer. In 1983 the duties of the IAM were transferred to a new body, the Historic Buildings and Monuments Commission for England (HBMC, popularly known as English Heritage). Immediately it was clear that government funds were no longer to be the only source of revenue:

> The role of the HBMC is that of joint funder of individual projects . . . participating in discussions with other sponsors where this can be helpful (EH n.d. a: 1).

It was not long before an even strong indication of the change of funding policy was given:

> The Commission welcomes participation by developers . . . in the funding of rescue programmes (EH 1986: 7).

Because most developments are controlled through the planning system administered by local authorities, the 'participation by developers' was seen to be best negotiated during the planning process and, hence, the part that could be played by local authorities was highlighted. In 1990, the government issued guidance on archaeology (below) and EH confirmed its view that:

It would be entirely reasonable for the planning authority to satisfy itself before granting permission that the developer has made appropriate and satisfactory provision for the excavation and recording of the remains (EH 1991d).

Although it is open for a developer to seek funds from any source to ensure 'satisfactory provision', in practice it means that the onus is on the developer to fund the work. The results of this policy is that financial provision for rescue archaeology necessitated by development is now commensurate with the size of the threat, and that the ability of archaeologists to respond is not unacceptably restricted by limited government funds. Although holding developers responsible for the archaeological work necessitated by their proposals may be politically correct, archaeological practices had to learn to respond to the same economic fluctuations as other professions. The pace of development, which is strongly linked to the economy of the country, largely dictates the scale of professional archaeological work and hence the number of archaeologists employed. It is estimated that the total number of people employed in archaeology in November 2003 was 6,800, including 1,100 non-archaeologists working in a support role. The largest proportion of those employed in archaeology (41 per cent) work in the commercial sector, compared with 22 per cent in local government, 16 per cent in universities, 15 per cent in central government and 6 per cent in other categories (Aitchison and Edwards 2003: xi).

It should be stressed that although the growth of professional practices can be linked to development-led opportunities, this was seldom their sole function. Released from the burden of specific development-led threats, EH could sponsor more strategic projects, which concentrated on subjects not easily addressed through individual site investigation – for example, coastal erosion (Fulford *et al.* 1997), or Lower Palaeolithic sites (Wymer 1999). Similarly, many archaeological practices do not restrict their portfolio to rescue archaeology alone but also engage in proactive conservation, management or methodological initiatives, as well as outreach. Nonetheless, although there are many different forms of threat to the historic environment (Darvill and Fulton 1998), funds for tackling them are relatively scarce in comparison with those linked to development. Hence, it is not surprising that professional archaeologists are predominantly engaged in development-related work.

'UNITS' IN THE LATE TWENTIETH CENTURY

For more than twenty years the term 'archaeological unit' was used to describe a team of professional archaeologists working together to identify the need for archaeological intervention, to undertake rescue recording and subsequently to report on the results. Because no cohesive strategy to establish an even network of professional teams throughout the country was ever achieved, coverage by units was extremely variable. Originally, many worked within defined geographical areas, and sought sponsorship from a variety of sources. Local solutions differed, so that the management committees or employed units were affiliated to local authorities (e.g. Norfolk County Council, Winchester District, Poole Borough), universities (e.g. University of Birmingham, University of London Institute of Archaeology), or were independent bodies (e.g. Trust for Wessex Archaeology Ltd). Some units, such as the Oxford Archaeological Unit, were able to attract resources from several sources in return for various services: in that example, the county council, city council and district authorities.

Soon many of the managing committees wished to be independent and properly constituted to take full advantage of tax concessions and to protect their members. Their ambitions were broadly to undertake archaeological research and to educate the public, in all its guises, in archaeology. Bearing in mind that they were funded by public funds, it

Figure 14.1. *Time Team* has been the most successful of a number of popular archaeological programmes that have introduced millions of viewers to archaeological techniques. Participation requires particular professionalism and communication skill. Here Tony Robinson (left) assisted by Prof. Mick Aston (in characteristic striped jumper) and Phil Harding (in characteristic hat), help during a public event as part of British Archaeology Day. (*© Wessex Archaeology; Photo: Elaine Wakefield*)

was appropriate that some became charitable trusts. However, once employers, they became liable for the full range of governance and employment responsibilities. Consequently, many committees became limited companies. This refers to the limited liability that the members of a company have in the event of an inability to pay its debts.

Their work may have included some or all of a range of tasks including the maintenance of Sites and Monuments Records (SMRs), the monitoring of planning applications, advising on appropriate archaeological action, fundraising, excavation, publication, public education (Fig. 14.1), conservation, storage and so forth.

Placing the responsibility for funding archaeology with developers has, however, led to significant changes in professional arrangements necessitating a careful definition of the roles played during the negotiation for planning consent (below). The Local Government Act 1988 wished to see a clear separation between those who required work to be done (the enabler) and those who were paid to undertake the work (the service provider) lest restrictive practices might prevent those paying for the work from obtaining the best value. It was also argued that a developer should also be at liberty to choose whom to employ to do any work required, provided it reached the appropriate standard. The result was that some units were chosen by developers to work outside the geographical territory in which they had traditionally worked: for example, in 1987, the extensive excavations at Reading Business Park (then) in Berkshire were awarded to Oxford Archaeological Unit (Moore and Jennings 1992: 2), although earlier work had been undertaken by Wessex Archaeology, in whose traditional area the site lay.

Such changes inevitably caused considerable concern among many archaeologists, who warned of the possible erosion of the quality of work and of threats to the viability of various organisations. Some objected to the principle of free-ranging professional teams on the basis that local knowledge and experience is essential in the interpretation of discoveries. Conversely, many saw the employment opportunities for entrepreneurial individuals or for new units presented by these more commercial practices. The early 1990s witnessed the establishment of small private companies, partnerships or self-employed individuals trading in a commercial way in competition with the older units.

The desire for a separation of roles and for choice of service provider, together with increasing pressure on local government spending and reorganisation, caused many local authorities to reconsider their support for the archaeological units that they had previously sponsored. While by 2004 some units remained within local authorities (for example, in Cambridgeshire, Essex and Surrey), others had been externalised. Whatever their context, all practices are now expected to sell their services in a commercial way. National coverage remains variable, in part reflecting the pace of development in different areas: for example, in the last decade parts of Yorkshire and London have provided work for more than forty competing practices, whereas Cornwall or Hereford has seen less than a dozen (Darvill and Russell 2002: 61). Inevitably, and in common with any other business, archaeologists frequently work close to home where costs (such as travel and accommodation) can be minimised. However, it is not uncommon to find the same archaeological practice operating flexibly anywhere in Britain (or beyond), this pattern of work being governed both by the aims of the practice and the preference of the client in an open market economy.

By 2000, the term 'unit' had all but disappeared from the trading title of archaeological practices, although the term remains readily understood by most archaeologists. Today, it is not obvious purely from its name what is the basis and remit of an organisation. For example, the title Wessex Archaeology is a convenient abbreviation for the Trust for Wessex Archaeology Ltd, a registered charity and a limited company registered in England. However it may be perceived, the inclusion of 'Wessex' in the title does not mean that the company restricts its business to an historic area, any more than the Halifax Building Society restricts itself to the city in which it originated. Whereas some practices, especially small or sole traders, make clear that they are 'consultants', others include 'archaeology', 'services' or 'solutions' in their titles. The *IFA Yearbook and Directory* is therefore a valuable source of basic information for anyone wishing to know the size of an archaeological practice, the services it offers and the geographical area in which it operates.

THE CONTEXT OF PRIVATELY FUNDED ARCHAEOLOGY

During the later stages of the twentieth century, archaeology benefited from a general increase in environmental awareness and international pressures for developers to be held responsible for the effects of their schemes. Thus, the European Community Directive *The Assessment of the Effects of Certain Public and Private Projects on the Environment* (85/337/EEC), which came into effect in Britain in July 1988, required a formal environmental assessment of major developments before they could proceed. The published procedures (HMSO 1989) defined which types of development required these assessments, but also made clear that the 'Cultural Heritage' (defined as the architectural and archaeological heritage) was one of the matters that had to be addressed. (The requirements are currently sought under Statutory Instrument 1999 No. 293.) The general principle that developers had to give adequate information on the effects of their schemes and on the arrangements made to deal with these effects (mitigation) was also soon to be reflected more widely in government policy. These measures resulted in the need for a professional archaeological input in a wide variety of different situations, including road schemes, pipelines, airports, ports, waste disposal sites and so forth.

In November 1990, the (then) Department of the Environment published a policy for the preservation and recording of archaeological remains in England. This was arguably the most important government statement since the first Ancient Monuments Act a century earlier. The *Planning Policy Guidance Note 16: Archaeology and Planning* (PPG 16) gave specific advice on the handling of archaeological remains on sites which were to be developed (DoE 1990a). It quickly and radically altered the practice of archaeology in Britain.

Fundamentally, the policy:

- placed decisions about the future of archaeological sites threatened by development in the hands of local planning authorities
- ensured that archaeological responses were an integral part of decision-making, not an afterthought
- made developers responsible for commissioning any necessary archaeological work
- meant that professional archaeologists would normally undertake work directly for developers rather than through government grant aid
- made the funding of archaeology commensurate with the scale of development not constrained by a sum allowed by the Treasury.

As philosophy about the relationship between archaeological remains and other more visible traces of the past developed, a second policy, *Planning Policy Guidance Note 15: Planning and the Historic Environment* (PPG 15), was published in September 1994 (DoE and DNH 1994). This publication offered guidance on the wider historic environment and drew attention to the need to consider important buildings, Conservation Areas, inscribed World Heritage sites, Registered Parks and Gardens, Battlefields and so forth, alongside the often buried archaeological remains. The guidance recognised that evidence from the past was not the preserve of excavation sites alone. Despite its much wider application, response to PPG 15 has not been as marked as that to PPG 16. Nonetheless, professional practices have often had to expand their expertise to cover its requirements (Figs 14.2 and 14.3).

The construction of the national network of trunk roads and motorways is not subject to planning law but to its own statutory framework. Similarly, new railways (such as the Channel Tunnel Rail Link) have been built under their own legal framework. At the present time, solutions to transport problems are considered by regional government offices, which must consider all potential forms of transport, not just the use of private cars. Hence, these studies are referred to as 'multi-modal studies'. Guidance on the way in which effects on the cultural heritage are assessed have been published (DETR 1998a, 1998b, 2000). However, a useful website (www.webtag.org.uk) provides the most up-to-date guidance on the objective 'to protect the heritage of historic resources'. If a specific road solution has been identified, it is formally assessed in defined stages with increasing levels of detail being provided at each stage. The scope of work for each stage and the need for formal Environmental Assessment are set out in the Highways Agency's *Design Manual for Roads and Bridges* (*DMRB*) and subsequent amendments (Highways Agency 1992). Although not specifically within the normal planning process, *DMRB* adopts the same principles for the protection of the historic environment as PPGs 15 and 16. As recommended in PPG 16, the purpose of staged assessment is to provide sufficient information for decisions to be made about the proposals so that they can progress from

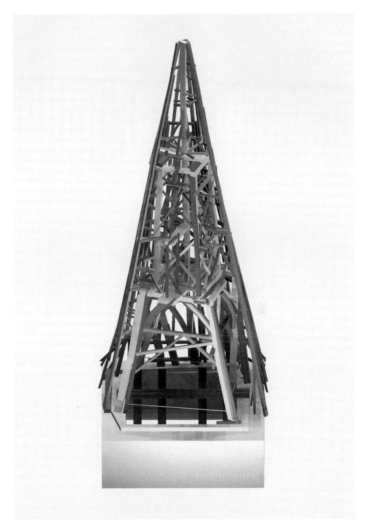

Figure 14.2. 3-D digital model of the internal wooden structure of the medieval spire of St Brannock's Church, Braunton, Devon. Modern recording techniques can help in the analysis and management of historic buildings. In this model each individual timber is located in three dimensions but the images of specific cant posts have been removed to facilitate the view of the inner structure. (© *Wessex Archaeology*)

one stage of design to another, and ultimately to construction. The impact of new roads on archaeological sites became apparent once the motorway network was established (above), and the mitigation of such impacts remains a major area of professional archaeological work (Fig. 14.4). Although many impacts are avoided during the design stages of a road scheme, some are unavoidable and may necessitate the archaeological investigation of some sites. The scale of the work can be gauged from the fact that between 1995 and 1998, the Highways Agency spent more than £4 million on archaeological projects relating to sixteen different road schemes. At the same time they indicated that work was being done on sixteen further schemes in 1998–9 alone (Highways Agency 1999).

Both PPG 15 and PPG 16 are concerned with archaeological sites on land. However, a growing awareness of the wealth and vulnerability of historic coastal and maritime sites (JNAPC 1989; Fulford *et al.* 1997) led to codes of conduct for those who work on the

Figure 14.3. Recording the interior of the medieval wooden spire of St Brannock's Church, Braunton, Devon. Professional practice is not restricted to open-air excavation. PPG 15 has prompted the closer involvement of archaeologists in the management of historic buildings (see Chapter 8), while health and safety policies require attention to personal safety. (© *Wessex Archaeology; Photo: Elaine Wakefield*)

seabed and an enhancement of EH's responsibilities for remains at sea. The National Heritage Act 2002 gave EH the remit to consider the protection of archaeological sites from the low-water mark to the 12-mile limit around England. Although practice in this environment is still developing, essentially all dimensions of the historic environment are now covered by similar principles.

The policy guidance notes identify the need for a staged approach to the input of archaeological information into the decision-making process. It points out that initial assessment of the historical or archaeological importance of a development site can be undertaken using existing records, published accounts or archives. If undertaken by experienced staff, such desk-based assessment can be completed relatively quickly and inexpensively. Should such an assessment identify the potential for archaeological remains within the site, the relevant planning authority may require further information from the developer before a decision can be made. Such information is frequently

Figure 14.4. Excavations by Wessex Archaeology at Springhead, Kent in advance of the Channel Tunnel Rail Link. Large-scale investigations in advance of major infrastructure schemes provide a wealth of information about rural sites of all periods. (© *Wessex Archaeology; Photograph Courtesy of Union Railways (North): Photo: Elaine Wakefield*)

acquired through a field evaluation, which may involve non-intrusive survey (such as geophysical surveying), small-scale excavation or both. The proportion of the site investigated would be dictated by the potential importance and complexity of the buried remains but might vary between 2 and 5 per cent (but see below). The results of the evaluation should be sufficient to determine whether the remains should be preserved or recorded before destruction, or are of such little importance that they can be lost. Where it is considered that archaeological remains do not merit preservation but merit recording, the process of recording through excavation is seen to lessen or mitigate the destructive effect of development. In each case, the requirement for a developer to bear the expense of mitigation recording must be reasonable and justified.

During this process, it is normal for the planning authority to be advised by its own archaeologist (usually a member of the Association of Local Government Archaeological Officers (ALGAO)) while the developer takes independent advice from an archaeological practice or consultant. With a common professional background, the archaeological representatives of both parties should be able to reach agreement on the appropriate response in each instance, although it is not unknown for one party to challenge the proposals of the other.

Archaeological sites and monuments considered to be of national importance may be scheduled and protected by law (under the Ancient Monuments and Archaeological Areas Act 1979). It is an offence to undertake any work to such a monument without Scheduled Monument Consent from the Secretary of State. Where a development might affect a

Scheduled Monument, it is necessary to discuss the work to the monument with EH and so the network of professional liaison broadens. Although the purpose of scheduling is to protect certain monuments, it does not always mean that development cannot happen at a Scheduled Monument. However, the need to balance the requirements of preservation with those of the development necessitates a good understanding of both needs. The resolution of potentially conflicting requirements in such circumstances is typical ground for debate among professional archaeologists, and hence specialist knowledge and experience are essential. Similar discussions may also be necessary over different components of a historic landscape where protection is sought: for example, Listed Buildings, Conservation Areas, Registered Parks and Gardens, battlefields and even hedgerows (see also Chapter 17).

As a result of the implementation of the PPGs the onus is placed on developers to provide information and to propose mitigation measures, preferably with professional archaeological help. The effectiveness of the policies has been reviewed periodically (EH 1992c, 1995c) and the most recent study conducted by Bournemouth University has concluded that work undertaken in this way 'now accounts for nearly 90 per cent of all archaeological fieldwork in England' (Darvill and Russell 2002: 3). The study indicates that in the nine years after the introduction of the PPGs:

- the number of desk based assessments conducted rose sevenfold
- the number of field evaluations rose two and a half times
- the number of mitigation exercises rose twelve and a half times.

Bournemouth University's review of PPG 16 indicates the *annual* number of individual pieces of archaeological work being undertaken under these familiar headings (bearing in mind that not all are necessarily recorded) to be approximately 700 desk based assessments, 1,250 field evaluations, 230 excavations and 2,100 watching briefs. These considerable numbers of projects indicate that there is significant pressure on the nation's finite archaeological remains, and that such pressure generates a huge amount of archaeological research. Some of the necessary research, such as desk-based assessment, synthesises existing information, while other research, such as field evaluation or excavation may provide completely new information. Because the work is normally focused on a particular site and its immediate surroundings, it is likely that the focus of the work is novel and the results of each project make a valuable contribution to the general advancement of knowledge of the past. No precise figure is available for the total financial value of such work, but available estimates show a very significant increase in recent years – from £36 million in 1996 to £42 million in 1999 (Darvill and Russell 2002: 62), and to £75 million in 2002 (APPAG 2003: para. 28). By comparison, the sums available from the Inspectorate of Ancient Monuments in 1973–4 were less then £1 million and in 1983–4 less than £5 million (EH n.d. a, 1991c).

These different forms of work (desk-based, survey, conservation or mitigation) and their documentation form the bulk of the work of many practices. The scope is not necessarily restricted to excavation but to the wider needs of the cultural heritage and, hence, embraces landscapes and townscapes as much as individual sites or buildings, albeit that the trend is towards urban locations (Fig. 14.5).

The requirement for such work shows no signs of diminishing and the indicators from those normally undertaking the work is that demand continues to grow. Few local planning authorities keep a precise record of the number of planning applications that actually require some form of archaeological response, but the proportion is 2 per cent in Cornwall and 1.6 per cent in London (Darvill and Russell 2002: 57). As the number of

Figure 14.5. Excavations by Wessex Archaeology at Addington Street, London. The redevelopment of historic towns and cities continues to provide the opportunity for the recovery of important archaeological evidence, sometimes even where the site has been developed previously. The balance of professional work falls in urban areas. (© *Wessex Archaeology; Photo: Elaine Wakefield*)

planning applications made in England is approximately half a million each year, if only 1 per cent of these required archaeological work, then 5,000 archaeological projects would be created each year.

Currently, this workload is undertaken by more than 400 archaeological practices, albeit that nearly half the overall number of projects are undertaken by a 'top twenty' headed by MoLAS (the Museum of London Archaeological Service) and Wessex Archaeology (Darvill and Russell 2002: 62). The majority of practices are relatively small, with more than 70 per cent of the overall total employing fewer than ten people, and only ten organisations employing more than fifty people each (Aitchison and Edwards 2003: 15). Anyone who needs the services of a professional archaeological practice, therefore, has a considerable choice. As mentioned above, for those who have little knowledge of the range of services available, details and advertisements can be found in the yearbook of the Institute of Field Archaeologists (IFA) (below). A list of practices working within a particular geographic area is also sometimes made available by local planning authorities.

STANDARDS IN PROFESSIONAL ARCHAEOLOGICAL WORK

Since the establishment of professional archaeological teams in the 1970s, there has been an admirable desire among those involved to ensure a universally high standard of work. Standards have been published so as to ensure appropriate:

- ethics (establishing the way in which archaeologists should conduct their professional affairs)
- practice (defining different scopes of work)
- management (formalising management procedures)

so there would be a common understanding of what is required. Allied to these are documents (research frameworks) that suggest academic objectives for archaeological work, so that the increase in knowledge is maximised with each opportunity.

Established in 1975, the Standing Committee for Archaeological Unit Managers (SCAUM) was constituted to enable constructive debate between employers. Initially it distributed advice on a variety of topics (such as wages, agreements with mineral operators and so forth) in an attempt to mould corporate good practice. The most significant of these advice notes, however, relates to the requirements of health and safety legislation. Bearing in mind that building sites are known to be particularly hazardous and that archaeologists frequently work in such situations, the revised SCAUM Manual (1997) is an important introduction to the complexities of the requirements to which all professional archaeologists must submit, whether in the field, laboratory or office.

Recently, SCAUM has revived interest in its original concerns with the role of its members as employers. In 1999 it adopted principles for the employment of archaeologists (SCAUM 1999) and, building on these, in 2004 introduced a *Manual of Best Practice in Archaeological Employment* (SCAUM 2004). Drafted by a personnel consultant, the manual offers guidance for all sizes of organisation 'including universities, local authorities, charitable trusts, partnerships' on the range of issues that confront all employers. It covers such matters as legislation, contracts, terms and conditions, recruitment, interviews, induction, appraisal, development, training, absenteeism, discipline, grievance, redundancy and so forth. Most employers will be familiar with these matters and will act in exemplary fashion. Nonetheless, as with SCAUM's Health and Safety Manual (above), the Employment Manual is a most useful guide for employers and employees alike and may be used as a basic standard for any responsible organisation.

Since 1982 it has been mainly the IFA that has taken on the role of developing professional standards – indeed, their strap-line is 'setting standards in archaeology'. Membership of the IFA is open to all archaeological practitioners, not just those in professional practices. However, all those who subscribe must adhere to its defined codes of ethical practice, its disciplinary procedures and its published standards (IFA 1999). By regulating archaeological behaviour in this fashion, and by validating the credentials of its members, the IFA offers a measure of reassurance to those who commission archaeological work that standards of professional practice are upheld. This is in effect a measure of self-policing by the profession, independent of other political motives.

Although membership of the IFA is only open to individuals, most major archaeological projects are commissioned from archaeological organisations or practices.

Hence in 1995 a scheme of registration for organisations which subscribed to the same ethics and standards as individual members was introduced by the IFA. In this registration scheme, a named 'responsible post holder', usually the most senior archaeologist in the organisation, is held to account for the conduct of the whole body. The scheme thus extends the desired standard throughout the work of the organisation, irrespective of whether or not any particular employee is a member of the IFA. Those who commission archaeological work from registered organisations have the reassurance that it subscribes to the published codes of practice and is regularly monitored by archaeological peers. Although by 2004 there were an estimated 400 archaeological practices in Britain, perhaps surprisingly only forty-six of these were registered (IFA 2004).

Historically, one of the main issues with which IFA was concerned was the issue of the transfer of responsibility of funding archaeological work from government to the private sector (above). Members were aware that in the USA privately sponsored archaeology was common practice and that those who undertook the work did so under legally binding agreements or contracts. Almost immediately after its inauguration, the IFA established a Contract Archaeology Committee, which soon began to analyse the way in which archaeology was handled. The committee identified a variety of different roles for those involved in the negotiation of archaeological projects. The labelling of these roles into:

- curator – those responsible for the conservation and management of the historic environment
- client – those who commissioned work (whether an individual, developer, landowner, government body)
- contractor – those who undertook the work
- consultant – those who offered advice

was instructive (and reflected a degree of analysis that underlined the processual archaeological philosophy of the time). Nonetheless, its initial effect was to provoke a degree of suspicion and polarisation within the profession. Today, these roles are better understood and negotiation over appropriate archaeological work adopts a mature approach: while the identification of the roles remains valid, frequently there is no necessity to insist that different roles are played out by different people. Those commissioning work frequently accept that a single organisation can offer sound advice, safeguard a variety of interests and undertake work in a wholly professional manner without the need for complex arrangements involving many different people, especially where the financial value of the work does not justify them.

As noted above, PPG 16 suggests that different levels of information are required as potential developments are discussed with the archaeologists of local planning authorities (curators). As this required information is likely to be commissioned by the developer (the client) from archaeological practices (contractors), there needs to be a common understanding of terminology and practice. Consequently, definitions of the meanings of basic terms to cover a basic scope of works (the brief) or more detailed definition (specification) have been published. Similarly, different forms of work of increasing complexity were defined and basic standards established for each (ACAO 1993; IFA 1999). Thus, terms such as Desk-based Assessment or Field Evaluation now have common meanings that can be related to the process of understanding the importance of archaeological remains sought in PPG 16.

Standardisation of terminology has also been accompanied by a standardisation of the approach to the gathering of information. Published IFA standards (above) suggest the scope for different stages of work, but sampling strategies tend to adopt a common approach, especially for field evaluation. The effectiveness of these has been reviewed from time to time. The first review published by EH (EH 1995d) contained a useful statistical study by Professor Shennan (1989: 39–40) which demonstrated the proportion of a site which would serve as an adequate sample for the detection of an archaeological structure of a given size. This proportion was relatively large (and hence would be costly to achieve). Once this factor is added to the problem that the size of features that might be contained within a site is not usually known, sampling strategies consequently adopted a more pragmatic approach. A more recent review of assessment strategies, undertaken at the behest of Kent County Council (the 'Planarch Report': Hey and Lacey 2001), selected twelve projects where extensive field evaluation had been followed by large-scale excavation, to test the effectiveness of the field evaluation in predicting the content of the site. Inevitably, the review found that results were variable and concluded, among many other things, that the size of gaps between sampling trenches was the most important element of the sampling exercise. This confirmed the expectation that excavation sampling strategies cannot use a uniform approach and that each must be designed according to the particular circumstances on each site, especially the anticipated date of archaeological remains within it. Alternative approaches have also been advocated (Orton 2000), but clearly the skill necessary to design and execute a sampling strategy to achieve the best result in any set of circumstances is essential in professional practice.

The transfer of the funding of development-led archaeology to the private sector introduced archaeologists to the normal working practices of the commercial world within which the criteria used for the selection of an archaeological contractor were not necessarily the same as those used previously. Then, as now, it became important for archaeological practices to be able to demonstrate persuasively that they could:

- offer the necessary expertise
- marshal appropriate resources
- offer good value
- complete the tasks within time and budget
- work effectively with the client
- enhance both the client's and their own good name.

Credentials, the evidence of previous achievements and trustworthiness, demonstrable cost-effectiveness and the ability to 'sell' proposals are as important as academic reputation. Whereas the practice must retain its reputation in the eyes of its peers, it must also do so in the eyes of its potential future clients. Academic peers may judge a practice from the quality of its interpretation and reporting, but additional qualities will be valued by those who commission the practice.

Because commercial competition between archaeological practices was an emotive and contentious subject (RESCUE/SCAUM 1991), IFA considered the ethics of selection procedures. In 1990 it formally adopted a *Code of Approved Practice for the Regulation of Contractual Arrangements in Field Archaeology*, which has subsequently been amended (IFA 1999). This specifically provides guidance on professional behaviour where more than one individual or organisation is competing for the same piece of work. While competitive tendering remains current, some continue to advocate a franchise arrangement (APPAG 2003: para. 72). In effect, the latter exists where an archaeological practice has a preferred contractor status or has won a framework agreement with a client, having been selected so as to provide the particular range of archaeological services to meet the client's needs. Such needs will undoubtedly vary between clients, but may be influenced by such factors as:

- location (for example, the required work is centred on London or the south-west of England)
- specialism (for example, the work may be maritime or ecclesiastical)
- scale (it does not require more than one person, or it normally requires a large team)

and so forth. The time and cost of conducting a realistic selection competition can be great and in many situations could be disproportionate to the value of the work to be done. Consequently, simplified selection based on personal recommendation, or simply availability, is commonplace.

Each archaeological organisation will set its own objectives and may guard its own independence, but many will also enjoy collaborating with others. It is common practice for large-scale development projects to be run as joint ventures in which different companies share the overall burden of the project by pooling expertise and resources according to the demands of the work. The same is true of archaeological projects. Despite understandable initial concerns about working in a competitive way, professional practices now form joint ventures while also maintaining their separate trading activities. Framework Archaeology, for example, is not a separate company but a successful joint venture established by Wessex Archaeology and Oxford Archaeology to provide archaeological services to BAA plc (the former British Airports Authority). The scale of the work, which has included major excavations at Heathrow, Stanstead and Gatwick, was perceived to be too great for a single archaeological organisation and consequently the two companies joined forces. Working closely with BAA's own consultants, the joint venture has put into practice novel approaches to fieldwork and publication, which undoubtedly have potential for wider use (Andrews *et al.* 2000). The collaboration in this joint venture has demonstrated the potential for challenging established views and for advancing new ideas in a mature fashion.

In 1991 EH (EH 1991a) published a booklet entitled *Management of Archaeological Projects*. This guidance (or as the Chief Archaeologist's Preface suggested, 'formal procedures') was promulgated 'with the aim of ultimately establishing a consensus on good professional and management standards and practice in all areas of archaeological work'. It identifies a series of phases common to many fieldwork projects and puts forward a specification for the documentation of various important criteria for each stage, such as the objectives, tasks, review procedures, products, resources and timetables, which should be understood by all those involved. The booklet, usually referred to as MAP2 (the first edition, MAP, having been replaced rapidly by the second edition) remains the basic reference work on the subject. It is a model of the type of published standard introduced to foster better performance of a rapidly expanding profession. Nonetheless, as it is a guideline it should not be applied inflexibly so that the description of material remains (the record) is separated from interpretation, the creation of a site narrative, or the fashioning of historical knowledge (see also Chapter 19).

The focus of any project on its research objectives is a crucial element. As has been demonstrated, 'clear research objectives facilitate management and can lead to significant cost savings' (Andrews *et al.* 2000: 526), as well as ensuring a 'harmony between curatorial and academic objectives' (EH 1996: 2). The research objectives of any project seek to maximise the advancement of historical knowledge from the opportunities presented by the project, concentrating effort (and hence potentially cost) on the most rewarding elements. They are set with reference to perceived needs in areas where understanding of the past is weakest. Different researchers have different interests and hence their strategies are expressed from different perspectives. They may make reference, for example, to a particular geographic area (such as a city or county), conventional period (prehistoric or medieval), or diachronic theme (ceramics or forts). Such strategies are not normally prescriptive and only offer a framework because the context within which they are set is dynamic, individual site circumstances will each be unique, and inevitably the strength of opinion and degree of consensus will vary.

Nonetheless, publication of research strategies or frameworks is important to make known the necessary direction for effort. Such strategies have been in existence since at least the 1920s; they prioritised the work of units (e.g. Scole Committee 1973; Ellison 1981), and directed EH funding in the 1990s (EH 1991b). A valuable index of research frameworks was compiled by Adrian Olivier (EH 1996: Appendix 8). Revision of such strategies is normally based on an assessment of previous achievement and is frequently accompanied by an extension of range so as to achieve a better geographical or topical balance. Engagement with this process forms an important cross-sectoral activity within archaeology, and professional practices can make a valuable contribution to it. The research framework for East Anglia (Glazebrook 1997; Brown and Glazebrook 2000) provides a model of the approach advocated by EH (Thomas 1994). It builds on a much earlier example (Scole Committee 1973) and results from broad consultation, fine collaboration and the input of many archaeologists working within a single geographical region.

THE ROLE OF THE CONTRACTOR

Under the structured system outlined above, the scope for archaeological work is frequently prescribed by the curator. Because the curator must safeguard the resource he or she must set out precisely what must be done to satisfy this concern. The work required may be set down in outline as a brief; for example, 'the site should be excavated using an appropriate sampling strategy'. However, the brief must then be expanded through a specification to be precise about the requirements. In PPG 16 (para. 30), the specification is referred to as 'a written scheme of investigation'. The specification has to be a very carefully thought-out strategy, its requirements being 'fair, reasonable and practicable' and directly related to the particular circumstances. The importance of the specification must be stressed because it dictates what will happen to a site and may prescribe the final opportunity for recording irreplaceable evidence. It may be very time-consuming even for an experienced fieldworker to produce a well-thought-out specification, and frequently help from others is sought. Furthermore, it is always wise to identify the need to vary the work in the light of unforeseeable discoveries because by its nature archaeology is not totally predictable.

Contractors are invited to consider doing the work defined in the specification. The IFA by-laws dictate that only those with the requisite qualifications, expertise and experience should take up the offer. Consequently, the contractor has to demonstrate that he or she has the qualities to meet the criteria and can undertake the work cost-effectively at the appropriate time. The decision of which contractor to use will be the client's. The decision may be guided by advice on a variety of aspects, such as the suitability of the contractor, previous employment or price. The price for the work is usually submitted as a tender and where prices are sought from several units the process is referred to as 'competitive tendering'. Once a tender is accepted the agreement reached between client and contractor is usually confirmed in a binding contract, the form of which can vary from a simple exchange of letters to long, complicated documents that cover every circumstance (Darvill and Atkins 1991). Once a contract has been won the contractor will use its best endeavours to discharge its obligations in a way that reflects well on itself and its client. The work to be done will have been defined in the specification and any variation from it, possibly necessitated by discoveries on site, will have to be negotiated with the client and the curator. Variations in work may lead to a variation in cost and time, and consequently agreements may also have to be modified. The contractor will have to comply with all appropriate legislation governing employment, taxation, working conditions and so on. For example, it is a statutory requirement for contractors employing more than five people to implement a health and safety policy. The demands of safety and the avoidance of risks are high but are essential for the protection of employees and the public.

ORGANISATIONAL MANAGEMENT

Guidelines on the way in which individual projects should be managed have been set out by EH (MAP2, above). However, the way in which a professional practice organises itself to manage its workload successfully is its own concern. Obviously, it will wish to ensure that it is so structured that individual tasks can be undertaken and controlled effectively within the context of appropriate governance required by company or charity law. Procedures must be understood by all staff, so the communication of working practice is essential.

Wessex Archaeology is one of the largest historic environment practices in England and employs nearly 200 people engaged on a comparable number of projects each year. It is a charitable company and therefore has an organisational structure that reflects this status in line with its published Memorandum and Articles. In this instance, the structure is straightforward and does not involve separate trading companies or subsidiaries, which are sometimes preferred by other organisations. The composition of the trust comprises a group of members who appoint a Board of Directors and Trustees to supervise the work of the organisation. The Board meets regularly but places the responsibility of day-to-day functions in the hands of a Chief Executive, who is in turn supported by a team of senior executives, each with a particular remit (such as finance, operations or resources). Whereas the principal executives and all other staff are employed, neither the members nor the directors receive any remuneration for their work by virtue of the organisation's charitable status. Different spheres of activity (for example, relating to maritime, conservation, or transport infrastructure projects) demand particular knowledge and experience, and consequently the workload of the company is divided between appropriately skilled divisional heads working within an operational management team. The responsibility for running projects is delegated to a series of project managers, each of whom controls several projects simultaneously. Other specialist managers (environmental, graphics etc) have responsibilities for aspects of work common to many projects. Whereas these specialist managers control the standard of work in their sphere and advise project managers on the best approach to individual projects, it is the latter who have overall responsibility for the projects. Projects will vary in scale and duration and may involve different numbers of staff according to the particular circumstances of the project. Consequently, a large overall staff is necessary to complete the workload of the practice, and the staff must be deployed skillfully to ensure operational and financial efficiency.

Naturally, different management systems are used by different companies according to the nature of their business. The activities of such companies may be purely archaeological or may form part of a broader concern in which archaeology is a common component. Thus, archaeologists may be part of a planning consultancy (for example, CgMs), civil engineers (Gifford and Partners) and so forth. Unlike the example of Wessex Archaeology (above), these are not registered charities and are not subject to the same legal constraints.

When they were first established, grant-receiving archaeological bodies did not make a financial surplus and registered charities cannot distribute a surplus to their members or directors. However, the availability of funds over and above immediate costs is what enables any organisation, commercial or charitable, to weather temporary lulls in their markets, to build essential working capital, to research and develop new ideas, to improve working practice and standards and to allow for capital investment. Profits can also offer a return on investment, and hence shareholders will expect a return to justify their investment. (As noted above, directors of charitable companies cannot be remunerated.) Many commercial companies also operate salary schemes in which good personal performance is rewarded with a share of the profits. Now that archaeologists work in a commercial milieu they have managed to embrace the concept of profit and the abovementioned benefits it provides. Nonetheless, as the relative cost of archaeological work is currently cheap, and there are legitimate calls for increased expenditure in basic employment (below), the scope for investment through the generation of operational surplus is frequently limited.

SHORTCOMINGS OF THE SYSTEM

In July 2001 the All-Party Parliamentary Group (APPAG) was set up under the chairmanship of Lord Redesdale 'to act as a focus for Parliamentary interest in all matters relating to archaeology in the United Kingdom'. This formidable body of parliamentarians, enthusiastically applauded in many quarters, took evidence from a wide range of organisations and individuals. In January 2003 it published its first report, *The Current State of Archaeology in the United Kingdom* (APPAG 2003). Far from being content with the current arrangements, APPAG aimed 'to reflect the concerns of all those with an interest in archaeology' and identified a total of forty-eight recommendations to improve matters.

One of the key recommendations was that 'there is an urgent need to improve pay and conditions'(APPAG 2003: 7, No. 3). At the beginning of the 1970s full-time employees hoped 'to survive on a small subsistence-level wage' made available by occasional grants from public funds but, despite an undoubted improvement in job security, remuneration remains poor. Salaries offered for archaeological employment can be gauged from job advertisements at any time, but the situation has been analysed more systematically. Both in 1999 and 2003 specific studies were conducted so as to make available 'labour market information on the archaeology sector'. *Profiling the Profession: A Survey of Archaeological Jobs and Job Profiles in the UK* (Aitchison 1999) showed that the average salary of all archaeological workers in 1998 was £17,562. More than 95 per cent of all employed archaeologists earned salaries in the narrow range between £10,000 and £30,000, so it was not just the newcomers but also the senior staff who experienced low pay. *Archaeology Labour Market Intelligence: Profiling the Profession 2002/3* (Aitchison and Edwards 2003) showed that improvement had been slow in the intervening five years. Although the average annual salary had increased by 12 per cent to £19,161, nationally average salaries in other professions had increased by 28 per cent – effectively the salaries of archaeologists were slipping further behind the national average. The survey demonstrated regional variation with the slowest growth in London, where the cost of living is arguably the highest. Unlike many other professions, salaries were relatively low in the commercial sector, whereas archaeologists in government or academic employment were relatively better off. Bearing in mind that 90 per cent of archaeologists are graduates, their salaries do not compare favourably with other professions.

By way of comparison, *The Business Life Salary Survey 2004* (British Airways 2004) considered the average earnings of more than 120 occupations. It did not include archaeologists, but, if it had, entry-level archaeologists (paid on average £12,140 in 2003) would have been near the bottom of the survey list, earning less than a shelf-filler, car park attendant or road-sweeper. The average archaeological salary would have been well below the 2004 national average of £25,170 and below a sheet-metal worker, bus driver, and most of the other occupations cited. This situation has arisen from a number of factors including:

- low starting point – the subsistence level wage
- relationship to local authority scales – stemming from the 1970s hope that units would be based in authorities
- rapid change to a competitive market.

There is no doubt that employment conditions, benefits and working environments have improved immeasurably in the last thirty years, but there remain many substantial challenges to the profession: finding the means to improve remuneration, creating a better structure, better training and career development (Chitty 1999: 28). Rapid expansion of the profession has threatened a skills shortage as growth in expertise cannot keep pace with increased demand. Substantial improvement in all these areas will not be achieved by one organisation alone (as it will price itself out of the market), so there needs to be a wholesale approach. This is the traditional area of activity for employee associations and trades unions, and the adoption of Prospect (a trade union) by the larger employers heralds a new era of negotiation in this area. However, as long as some archaeologists offer their services in a competitive market in return for a subsistence wage and thus force competitors to adopt similarly low fees, there will be limited scope for improvement. Other disciplines that also employ graduates and which are related to the development-led world, such as architecture or engineering, have established better rewards for their employees and better represent the aspirations of young professionals. There could hardly be a stronger endorsement for change than that of a large group of parliamentarians (APPAG 2003).

Another area of concern for APPAG was what happens at the end of the site investigation process. In the planning system, emphasis has been placed on the location and characterisation of remains, and the mitigation of effects, without a comparable focus on the completion of the process. It might be argued that the public, in whose name the recording is undertaken, derives the greatest benefit once archaeologists have applied their expertise in creating an accessible account. Yet, the accessibility of site archives (records and finds), the appropriate publication of structured reports and the lack of syntheses are among the aspects of modern archaeology criticised by APPAG (2003: paras 157, 167).

Professional practices are normally required to deposit their site and research archives in a publicly accessible depository. However, many repositories do not have the capacity to accept such archives, or the resources to service their collections (Swain et al. 1998; Resource 2001), leaving those who wish to deposit archives in the rightful place with a dilemma – do they throw away the archives they have been asked to create or absorb the increasing cost of storage?

Reports produced as part of professional practice tend to be either structured in such a way as to meet the needs of the planning system, or in the traditional, detailed style of excavation reports. Neither is very appealing to the average member of the public even if they have a keen interest in archaeology. Modern technology provides the means for making data and analyses available through electronic media, thus saving the cost of publication and speeding up dissemination without reducing scholarship, and hence there is little need for expensively printed monographs (Jones et al. 2001).

However, requirements placed on a developer, such as suitable arrangements for archaeology, must relate only to the development site. Under such an arrangement there is little scope for syntheses or broader studies that modify previously held views. It has been suggested (Sophie Jackson quoted in Pickering 2002: 65) that 'PPG 16 encouraged a reactive site by site approach to archaeology . . . rather than considering the importance of the site within the wider archaeological landscape over the longer term'. Similarly (Rob Whytehead quoted in Pickering 2002: 66), 'there was a need for synthetic works aimed at the popular audience'. These views reflect a sense of frustration among many observers who identify a critical public need but do not find the means to meet that need: maximising the advancement of knowledge and creating the greatest public benefit have yet to be realised.

As professional archaeology is part of a dynamic world subject to a plethora of political, economic and academic factors, it cannot remain static. Equally, as regular appraisal is a tenet of good management, it is not surprising that a survey such as that undertaken by APPAG has identified areas requiring attention. Despite perceived weaknesses, professional archaeology has established itself rapidly and become an indispensable element of environmental conservation. As an appreciation of the value to society of the historic environment increases, so will the need for professional practices strengthen. Professional practices have developed rapidly and will continue to be essential to the application of archaeology in modern society.

CHAPTER 15

THE ARCHAEOLOGIST AS CONSULTANT

Simon Collcutt

INTRODUCTION

Any expert may give advice when asked: a reactive role. Consultants offer advisory services as a part or the whole of their function: a proactive role highly dependent upon situation and vested interest. Hunter and Ralston (1993a: 37) put it accurately, if brutally, when they spoke of 'the emergence of archaeological consultants, the latest group to be spawned by the demands of the commercial world'.

In the first (1993) edition of this chapter, I wrote that there were no significant overview texts on British archaeological consultancy: indeed, there were surprisingly few books on consultancy in any sphere. There were some interesting reports from the USA, but the context was so very different that the American experience could not usefully be discussed (cf. *BAN* Editorial 1988; Burrow and Hunter 1990). Lack of reference in mainland European literature was giving the false impression that archaeological consultancy was not practised at all outside these islands. Consultants did not, as a rule, talk openly about their activities; they published only on procedural aspects and, until 1992, they had had no specific professional forum or association. There thus appeared to be no way of estimating how many archaeological consultants were practising in 1993, in one capacity or another, in Britain. Above all, there was the question (unanswerable at that time) of how much the then visibility of consultants was a fad, a transient reflection of factors outside archaeology, and how much a real phenomenon, representing significant shifts in professional philosophy and structure.

Ten years on, very little has changed save (apparent) numbers. At the start of the period, some information became available concerning the 1991 situation (Bell *et al.* 1993). The Institute of Field Archaeologists (IFA) had sent a basic structure questionnaire to twenty-five organisations or individuals considered to be consultancies, receiving answers from fourteen, 70 per cent of whom had been practising for less than five years. By 2002, Carter and Robertson had noted 123 independent consultant and specialist organisations, employing 150 individuals (thus, showing the preponderance of sole traders); they also noted thirty-one commercial mixed-practice consultancies (see below for definition) apparently with a further 175 archaeologists, although it is unclear whether these were all or even mostly employed in a consultancy role themselves. In their recent survey, Aitchison and Edwards (2003) have noted that commercial organisations 'providing historic environment advice and information services' are either 'independent consultants or specialists' or 'other commercial organisations'. They have estimated that *c.* 170 organisations provide such services, employing 7 per cent of the current archaeological workforce (thus, *c.* 400 persons), although it is again unclear as to how many of these individuals fulfil primary consultancy roles. A common search engine in September 2003, restricted to UK websites, returned 415 entries for archaeological consultants, and 11,542 entries for [+ archaeolog* + consultant*] – downright scary! Nevertheless, there are no new texts on British archaeological consultancy. Consultants still do not communicate. The Association of Professional Archaeological Consultants is defunct – one might even say it was still-born – because of lack of sufficient interest from practitioners. At least we have a medium-term answer to that question: archaeological consultancy is indeed a real phenomenon, for good or ill.

This chapter cannot be revised into formal textbook style, each section constructed around received wisdom. The continuing concerns of and about consultants are described, drawing upon the experience of the author, a practising consultant. After another ten years, the result is still a collection of observations and assertions, with many more questions than answers.

DEFINITIONS

An archaeological consultant provides expert archaeological advice. Terminology is still very broad and imprecise. The definitions given below are as self-explanatory as possible, and will be used consistently in the present chapter; used elsewhere, these terms will not automatically communicate the desired meaning. Each category has been included on a de facto basis, as, in every case, practitioners have used the terms consultant or consultancy to refer to some aspect of their work in the published literature.

A freelance consultant offers consultancy services as an unattached individual. A part-time consultant offers services that are (presumably) merely incidental to other employment. An institutional consultant offers services from within an archaeological organisation with wider objectives than consultancy; for instance, many, if not all, archaeological units/trusts now supply consultancy services. A mixed-practice consultant is an archaeologist operating from within a broader-based consultancy firm: examples include practices specialising in tourism, town and country planning, environmental monitoring or engineering. An archaeological practice consultant operates from within a specifically archaeological (or cultural heritage) consultancy firm. The commercial status of archaeological consultancy practices is varied, but private limited companies and formal partnerships began to appear in the 1980s. In 1991, nearly 60 per cent of (the few) respondents to the IFA questionnaire (Bell et al. 1993) were self-employed and, at a guess, this large proportion has probably diminished only slightly today (cf. Carter and Robertson 2002).

Consultants are expected to have a broad grasp of all archaeological issues but a consultant specialist concentrates on particular areas of expertise, often involving artefact, period or environmental studies (it seems likely that a large proportion of British archaeologists, especially sole traders, calling themselves 'consultants' currently fall into this category). The phrase consultant technical specialist may be useful, referring to firms with archaeological personnel that provide scientific support. Non-archaeologists who supply advisory services directly to archaeology may be called ancillary consultants: there are a growing number of aerial photographers, geophysicists and remote-sensing specialists in this category (Chapter18), as well as solicitors and barristers who specialise in Listed-Building and other archaeology-related legislation. It is noteworthy that, in the IFA review of 1991 (Bell et al. 1993), respondent consultants noted 'survey', 'research' and 'excavation' services more, or at least as, commonly as 'cultural resource management'. In the similarly small response sample (only twenty-five) in the most recent survey (Aitchison and Edwards 2003), individual consultants employed in 'field investigation and research services' were almost twice as numerous as those employed in 'historic environment advice and information services', although the organisations for which these same individuals worked categorised their firms' roles in the reverse proportions.

Individuals in all these categories provide advice to external organisations. However, some consultants hold posts in-house. A public tied consultant operates within and provides advice more or less exclusively to a public organisation. A commercial tied consultant operates from within and provides advice exclusively to a single developer firm; so far such positions are very rare. Some consultants may be partially tied through an exclusivity contract with a particular developer. This entails both a pre-emptive right (to exclude other archaeological advisers) and an obligation (to provide advice to that developer) and would usually also involve an agreement to avoid contracts with other parties when there might be competition or conflict with the interests of that developer. Tied situations have also been described as 'embedded' or 'agency' positions (Barnes 2003), although the latter term (given the difference between the commercial/financial and political meanings) may not be appropriate in most tied cases. An advisor is usually a relatively senior, experienced archaeologist who provides occasional advice to a public organisation (the term will be written thus here, leaving the more common spelling adviser to denote an unspecified role); remuneration for such a role may range from zero to full fees.

A consultee is a person or organisation with the non-commercial right (statutory, delegated or otherwise) to be consulted in a given situation; consultees will often have vested interests different from those of consultors. Planning authorities and other governmental agencies are usually the formal consultor, but other individuals (developers and their agents) would do well to contact consultees directly – even if it is unfortunately a growing trend for consultees to act evasively, or even adversarially, from the outset towards commercial interests. The most obvious examples of consultees include central government organisations (including quangos and departmental sections) or archaeological organisations appointed by local authorities that have no internal archaeological sections. The advice of consultees is usually free (that is, costs are borne by the consultee organisation) but there are situations in which costs may be recovered. For instance, a consultant may be given temporary powers (subject only to the High Court or equivalent) to act (under statute) for the purposes of arbitration and is entitled to include his or her fees as part of the taxation. Alternatively, he or she may be appointed with a set honorarium as a professional witness (e.g. by a coroner) or as an assessor (to assist the planning inspectorate). Included in the category of consultees are those persons normally called curators (e.g. local, county or regional archaeologists, governmental agencies with specific curatorial responsibilities, or managing archaeologists appointed by a landowner) whose advice, when based upon policy, statute and property law, has the power of a directive subject only to public inquiry, ministerial veto or the courts.

The reader is encouraged to search such publications as *British Archaeology* (and other CBA documents, cf. www.britarch.ac.uk) or *The Archaeologist* (and other IFA documents, cf. www.archaeologists.net) for examples of practitioners in the categories defined above. This is a valuable exercise that will demonstrate the levels of expertise involved, the increasing rate of personnel transfer from other roles to consultancy and the growing willingness to use the label consultancy to cover existing activities. However, it should not be assumed that individuals can be permanently labelled using the above classification: many persons have multiple roles, with the proper classification being dependent on the situation in a particular application. There has also been a shift in stress from the individual (a person with a known history) to the organisation or firm, a more anonymous unit.

THE HISTORICAL CONTEXT

Archaeological consultancy is the result of a number of trends, more or less directly related to factors inherent in the development of the discipline itself. The story is too convoluted to attempt a linear history here; many of these matters are dealt with from different perspectives elsewhere in this volume (Chapters 1, 4, 14 and 16).

Since the Second World War there has been a steady decline in the vigour of many learned societies, a result both of intrinsic factors (including competition from home-based interests such as television) and growing friction between amateurs and professionals. With the boom in university posts in archaeology in the 1960s and earlier 1970s, the demand for advice could be satisfied, but in the 1980s academic priorities changed. This source of expertise is no longer generally available at the consultancy level, and few academics now have an understanding of how public archaeology is practised – so much so that the present author feels justified, at least in the shorthand of this chapter, to exclude mainstream university activity from the term public archaeology.

A parallel boom-and-retrenchment development occurred in public archaeology. The good years saw an increase in the influence of the Royal Commissions and the establishment of a system of Sites and Monuments Records (SMRs), local, county and regional archaeologists and fieldwork units. The raised profile of archaeology eventually brought new legislation and planning policy. Advice was readily available from consultees but, probably by default rather than design, with an increasingly authoritarian tenor, unqualified from any other quarter. Then the public money began to dry up. Units lost much local and central government funding, many struggled to become financially independent and some went to the wall. Over the past fifteen to twenty years, curators have had to cope with often erratic resourcing and steadily increasing workload. The lead role of central government bodies has been redefined, and loss of confidence has occurred, especially in England, where it is particularly difficult for outsiders to perceive the current state of play (or even the location of the playing field) in the tug of war between central government and English Heritage (EH).

Another consequence of the raised profile of public archaeology in the 1970s was the crystallisation of the concept of professionalism, the most obvious result being the establishment and increasing influence of the IFA. Such a movement has three aspects: the search for standards; the formulation of career structures, and the exclusion of non-professionals (not of amateurs or academics per se, but of persons unable or unwilling to meet emerging standards) – which, no matter how regrettable under certain circumstances, are inseparable.

It is the author's experience that, on the whole, private developers have reacted as reasonably as could be expected to changing planning requirements. It is unfortunate that many public development agencies have so often dragged their feet, a situation that has not greatly improved between the two editions of this book. However, even less enlightened firms could not fail to have noticed the fact that the price of public acceptability is increased developer funding. Developers, needing assurances over cost-effectiveness and avoidance of delays, regularly express distrust of the motives of archaeologists (*all* archaeologists) and concerns over their managerial abilities. The commercial consultant is made aware, on an almost daily basis, of the full extent of this distrust. Despite early enquiries by developers concerning the viability of commercial tied consultants (the normal response to a need for expertise in larger development firms), very few such posts yet exist, probably another reflection of distrust which, in general, seems mutual.

The fortunes of public archaeology are not simply a function of the gross economy. As archaeological standards have risen and it has been admitted that field archaeologists and their families might be allowed to live in something more substantial than tents, public archaeology has certainly become vastly more expensive, making this the major preoccupation of all concerned. However, the economic link may sometimes be less direct and predictable. The Green issue, from which archaeology has benefited so much (even a little improperly at times), is a case in point. Born during the good times and quickly sending an offshoot to integrate with the postwar town and country planning initiative, the environmental movement seemed to gain strength during the 1980s slump. One bizarre effect of this environmental linkage, perhaps together with growing familiarity, has been that many planning consultants now feel themselves competent to write the cultural heritage section of an Environmental Statement (sometimes without – or even despite – a background report from a heritage professional). The ministerial shift in emphasis from the DoE to the Department of Culture, Media and Sport (DCMS) is weakening the links between archaeology and natural environment again, although the current availability of rural management grants gives archaeologists an incentive to resist total divorce. Each of the trends noted in this section has a particular but different momentum, producing a constantly shifting situation as positive and negative feedback drifts into and out of play.

By the mid-1980s there was conflict between, on the one hand, raised professional standards, career expectations and university output of graduates and, on the other, shrinking employment prospects in many areas of archaeology. The more or less arbitrary nature of salary freezes, resource shrinkage and actual cuts in posts meant that there was little correspondence between the quality of personnel and the fact of dissatisfaction or redundancy. These problems caused a toughening in the call for further standards and increasing resentment of amateurs and academics who might threaten job prospects in other sectors: competition between surviving organisations became acute (cf. Baker 1987). Indeed, it may be suggested that the proper evolution of the IFA towards a chartered institute representing the profession as a whole has been seriously damaged as the gulf between members and non-members has widened. Over the last ten years, the public archaeology profession has grown overall (although permanent, as opposed to project-funded, posts do not seem to be much more common), but the relevant problem now probably lies in low salary ceilings and advancement bottlenecks for the large majority of practitioners.

The frustration of the undervalued and the unemployed can have only one of two possible results, in archaeology as in any other sphere. The disillusioned have left the profession. Those who refused to abandon their self-esteem and the belief in the worth of their expert knowledge gained through long vocational training, started to offer their services directly in the marketplace, where, in the face of rising costs, demand for advice was growing.

The massive growth in all types of consultancy in British industry and commerce since 1980 is no accident, but a consequence of our current society. Space to discuss this broad topic is lacking here, although the key factors may be listed: the shifting economics of in-house versus external expertise, economics based upon increasingly short-term criteria; employers' increasing inability or unwillingness to shoulder the rising cost and complexity of training; the dangers to employees of participating in the training of potential younger or cheaper replacements; the expertise famine in the early boom years; the later expertise glut following rationalisation, merger or bankruptcy; the inability of the now commercialised education sector to keep track of changing skills requirements in the outside world; the replacement of employer loyalty by the ethos of sustainable profit, causing decreasing job security; the replacement of employee loyalty by the ethos of personal development, causing decreased employee reliability; the decreasing willingness to allow downward delegation of decision-making; the appalling social strain caused by the geographical mobility (job-hopping) now required to attain advancement; the philosophy that job satisfaction can be more closely equated with financial success; the value placed by our society upon assertiveness; and the total uncoupling between salaries and the hours white-collar staff are expected to work – in brief, the perceived personal risk now involved in putting all one's eggs in one basket with a single primary- or secondary-sector employer. After a little thought, reasonable archaeologists will admit that many of these factors are not so different from those operative in their own profession.

The archaeologist contemplating unattached consultancy is usually faced with the following realities: little or no capital; expertise, possibly in some aspects of public archaeology (although rarely in the fine details of cultural heritage management), but no experience in accountancy and cashflow management, employment and contract law, marketing, or the workings of the businesses of prospective clients and co-consultants; immediate infrastructure needs (office space, computing, communications, transport, insurance); no commercial reputation; and absolutely no safety net. Anyone who thinks that taking this course is an easy way to fortune is a fool. Given very hard work over several years and good luck, a degree of security may be achieved, although affluence is likely to remain beyond reach.

Career prospects in archaeological consultancy are already changing because those who have survived from the earliest ad hoc stages have perforce taught themselves and clients to anticipate high professional standards, in both archaeology and commerce. Any fledgling consultant who cannot contrive to spring more or less fully armed into action now has a poor life expectancy. The establishment of new consultancies has not stopped, but it has already slowed (save for the case of the sole trader consultant specialist); personnel will be drawn into existing practices at trainee and probationer level. When a qualified consultant is ready to move on, he or she will find that there are increasing opportunities in mixed and tied situations as an alternative to unattached practice. The move to consultancy must not be seen as an irrevocable step. There are already a few examples of individuals transferring back from consultancy practices to units, universities or museums; although reasons for transfer so far have perhaps most commonly been negative, the broadening of experience accumulated as the profession increasingly finds it natural for individuals to move between roles can only benefit the subject.

THE ROLE OF THE CONSULTANT

Consultancy represents a spectrum that may be subdivided according to two criteria, vested interest and intrinsic powers. On the one hand, there are consultants whose responsibilities (apart from allegiance to professional ethics, general to all archaeologists and currently best articulated in various IFA codes) are to a specific organisation with a set of defined objectives. From these objectives flow more or less explicit powers that require that the opinions expressed be given weight, not necessarily in proportion to the purely archaeological merit of the argument. On the other hand, there are consultants whose responsibilities are commercial: to the financial well-being of their own organisations and to the fulfilment of particular contracts. Such consultants have no intrinsic powers beyond those conferred by reputation, competence and force of argument. In reality, most consultants (or, more properly, individual consultancy situations) fall somewhere between these two extremes, although there is indeed a degree of polarisation.

It will be useful to discuss the concepts of independence, impartiality and objectivity here. An independent organisation is one that is self-contained (*pace* Selkirk 1988), while an impartial one has no vested interest in the outcome of a particular issue. EH, a state-dependent organisation, is not impartial when advising on the importance of an unexpected find if there may be compensation or project-funding implications for the public purse, just as independent consultants are not impartial when advising on a project costing that their own firm proposes to implement. Again, the degree of impartiality has nothing to do with actual performance: a consultant in any position may decide to let vested interest govern decisions entirely or may try to keep such interest at a distance and reach a decision more nearly based upon the facts, an approximation to an objective decision. Financial interests are not the only issue; for instance, if one seeks advice from an expert in a particular field, there is a trade-off between increased depth of understanding and increased myopia on judgement of comparative importance.

The crux of the matter is that all archaeologists have vested interests of various kinds that cannot be ignored. The relevance of interests is conditional on the situation in each case; the wise sponsor should recognise these interests while the wise consultant (considering long-term benefit) should make sure that relevant interests are fully declared, a point of particular importance for independent consultants where there is less immediate peer oversight. There should be no a priori problem with Chinese walls (the internal separation of functions, such as that between development control and contracting arms in local authority archaeology sections) as long as they are explicit (*pace* Pugh-Smith 2000); such arrangements can often have compensatory advantages with respect to continuity and efficiency. In fact, the use of consultants can help with problems (real or perceived) of vested interest in other sectors of the profession. For instance, some large development interests (including governmental agencies) have toyed with the idea of disqualifying the archaeological contractors who carried out the evaluation at a given site from tendering for the resulting mitigation works. However, such disqualification may have undesirable archaeological effects and the use of monitoring consultants should be a sufficient safeguard for developers (Collcutt 1995b).

As long as archaeology has a reasonably high profile there will be conflicts of interests, irrespective of the particular economic or political climate. Shifting combinations of advisers are useful, even indispensable, for all parties in order to help balance the interests sufficiently for those parties to feel able to reach a consensus in each case (cf. Redman 1990; Griffiths 1991). That many advisers will style themselves consultants is merely an honest statement that someone must pay to keep their services operative. Rational archaeological decisions cannot stem from monopoly nor the free market but only from a guaranteed mixed economy – a suggestion that goes beyond fashionable metaphor to pragmatism (cf. Addyman in CAWP 1988). It is a stereotypic complaint from lay persons that one cannot get two or more archaeologists to agree on any substantive matter. In fact, the lay persons (and commonly the archaeologists too) are missing the point: it is the vested interests of the different archaeologists that cause most clashes, and a careful and honest analysis of any specific discussion will usually identify these interests, together with a core of professional archaeological agreement and, most importantly, topics where the professionals feel they do not (yet) have enough information to offer more than cautionary advice.

Since the nature of consultancy is so situation-dependent, it would be futile to try to describe representative cases, although archaeological consultants are not involved only with the planning system (for instance, there are practitioners who deal with taxation, insurance and even forensic science; cf. the diagram in Fig.15.1 which attempts to give some impression of the range of consultancy activities). However, there are broad categories where the responsibilities are materially different, and not necessarily as a function of the type of consultancy organisation involved. The most obvious category is that of adviser, involving first-data retrieval and interpretation, followed by project design and logistics; the role may develop into that of supervisor, with implementation of

BACKGROUND KNOWLEDGE

National, Regional & Local Planning Policy • Regimes of Four UK Nations, IoM & Channel Islands • Heritage Statute • Governmental Agencies (ODPMS, DCMS, Commissions) • Professional Archaeological Standards (e.g. IFA, EH MAP2, World Heritage Convention, UNESCO Guidelines, Paris/Granada/Valletta Conventions) • Heritage Consultees, National & Regional Archaeological Bodies • Utilities Companies, Agencies & Government Departments as Developers & Land-Users • Crown & Ecclesiastical Issues • National Parks • Archaeological Firms & Capabilities

SPECIAL DESIGNATIONS

Scheduled Ancient Monuments • Areas of Archaeological Interest • Listed Buildings • Conservation Areas • Historic Battlefields • Historic Parks & Gardens • Historic Landscapes • Historic Wrecks • Historic Hedgerows • World Heritage Sites • Local Heritage Designations • Natural Environment Sites (SSSIs, NRs, ESAs, etc.)

INITIAL ADVICE

Scoping Report • Standards • Contract Terms

DOCUMENTARY ASSESSMENT

Regional & National Sites & Monuments Records • Published Archaeological Literature • Museum Collections & Archives • Physical Context (geology, hydrology, morphology, pedology, etc.) • Unpublished Archives • Historic Maps & Texts • Aerial Photographs • Multi-Spectral & Satellite Images • Microtopographic & Geophysical Mapping • Building Plans & Elevations • Industrial Archaeological Issues • Local Perception • Individual Informants • Site Walkover • Development Proposals

FINDINGS

Data & Technique Validation • Statistical Analysis • Building, Monument, Site & Area Appraisal • Condition/Survival, Stability & Vulnerability Analysis • Historic Landscape Analysis • Heritage & Urban Regeneration • Sensitivity Survey • Setting Issues • Development Impact (awareness of industrial, extractive & constructional processes) • Indirect Impacts (e.g. ground-water drawdown, seismic survey vibration, quarry blasting) • Archaeological Impact Statement • Environmental Assessment (Domestic, EU & Non-EU)

POSITIVE IMPACT DESIGN

Site Conservation & Repair • Public Relations & Publicity • Public & Educational Presentation • Restoration with Archaeological Themes • Disposal of Portable Antiquities • Popularisation & Authenticity • Tourism

RISK CONTROL

Risk Management Systems • Development Potential & Taxation • Insurance Assessment • Estate Heritage Administration Schemes • Management Agreements & Grants

MITIGATION

Planning Negotiation • Design Mitigation of Cultural Impact • Statement of Intent Drafting • Planning Applications • SM & LB Consent Applications • Legal Agreement Drafting • Conditioned Scheme Drafting • Resourcing Analysis

Above and opposite: **Figure 15.1.** The range of archaeological consultancy activities.

SELF-REGULATION
Quality Control • Continuing Professional Development • Maintenance of Relevant Competence & Qualification • Avoidance of Conflict of Interest

TRAINING
University Teaching • Planning Inspectorate Training • Submissions to Professional Fora • Theory Publication

ARCHAEOLOGICAL CONSULTANCY

POLICY FORMULATION
LPA Policy Documents (Plans & specific research issues, e.g. wetlands) • Regulatory Impact Assessments (Statutory Plans) • DCMS Consultations & Focus Groups • New Concepts (e.g. Sustainability) • National & Regional Research Agendas • Industry Initiatives & Liaison

DISPUTES & TRIBUNALS
Negotiation & Agreed Matter Preparation • Adversarial Procedures & Rebuttal/Recalculation of Official Assessments (e.g. assessments of monument importance) • Public Inquiries (Planning Appeals & Hearings, Appeals Against Non-Determination, Call-In Inquiries, SMC & LBC Inquiries, Hearings Prior to Scheduling, Written Representations) • Local Subject Plan Examinations in Public • Litigation Briefing, Pleadings & Evidence • Professional Negligence Claim Assessment • Arbitration, Mediation & Conciliation • Land Boundary Disputes • Land Tribunal & Heritage Import of Legal Covenants • Court Expert Witness • Public Inquiry Assessor

PUBLIC ASSESSMENT
Monument Assessments (e.g. for LPAs, EH/CADW/HS, etc.) • Statements of Significance (forthcoming for Heritage Lists)

MANAGEMENT
Briefs • Project Specification & Cost Estimation • Tender Competition Management • Contracts • Commissioning of Evaluation & Mitigation Fieldwork • Logistics • Fieldwork Coordination & Monitoring • Health & Safety • Site Security & Unlawful Interference • Human Remains • Treasure • Multiple Contractor Coordination & Interest Conflict Management • Post-Excavation Management • Report Validation • Resolution of Contractor Disputes • Owner/Tenant/Developer Liaison • Unexpected Archaeological Discovery

SPECIALIST FIELDWORK
Terrain Evaluation • Standing Building & Earthwork Appraisal • Critical Path Fieldwork • Technical Fieldwork (e.g. Preservation Potential Assessment) • Technique Innovation & Testing • Forensic Science

NIMBY & COMMERCIAL INTERFERENCE
Counter Claims & Adversarial Evidence

management or monitoring strategies. When the agreement of others besides the sponsor or client must be sought, the consultant becomes a negotiator. The consultant always has the task of mediator, and should ensure that he or she has both the data and the understanding to improve communication between the different parties involved. If agreement cannot be achieved, the consultant must become an advocate, not of the sponsor or client but of his or her professional opinion as a consultant. The adversarial situation thus precipitated is a basic and necessary mechanism of the British planning and legal systems, designed to break deadlock. However uncomfortable the role may become at times, it would be professional cowardice to refuse to participate (cf. Dalwood 1987; Chippindale 1991). In rarer cases, the consultant may be an arbitrator, with powers to judge between opposing advocates – an even more uncomfortable position owing to the responsibilities involved.

Leaving aside tasks related to individual projects, the consultant has an ambassadorial role, striving to earn the developer's respect for archaeology and archaeologists. This is a difficult job when so many archaeologists seem to have a constitutional disrespect for the objectives of developers. The consultant may also be a fundraiser, showing clients how to instigate projects of public benefit (and what rewards might be expected in publicity terms). However, the consultant who abuses the position by failing to define the exact boundary between statutory responsibilities and benefaction is no better than the consultant who neglects to bring material facts to the attention of curators. There is also the role of populariser: in education, the media, display and tourism. This is perhaps the least formalised but most responsibility-laden task of all, since it will be the main (in some cases, only) point of contact with the public in general – the role of ultimate if often unwitting, even unwilling, sponsors of archaeology.

What sort of person will make the best consultant? Many people (including a few practitioners) have an image of consultants as pushy, arrogant and confrontational individuals. It is true that the effective consultant needs a robust line in argument, an ability to project the voice and a very thick skin in order to survive the daily onslaught, often simultaneously from different quarters. However, it is surely the qualities of perseverance and self-assurance, continually justified by thorough preparation, that are most valuable. Few women (other than in the sphere of consultant specialist) have so far chosen to become consultants, especially in the commercial sector, probably because the aggressive image is unattractive – but all the more reason why their greater involvement would be welcome.

THE STATE OF PLAY

Opposition to archaeological consultancy is articulated most strongly by other archaeologists. Calls for restrictive practices are endemic in the literature, with talk of 'approved organisations' or 'regulation and procurement' (cf. CASG 1988; IFA 1988; Gater 1990; BADLG 1991); even no doubt well-meaning parliamentarians talk up the idea of late (APPAG 2003). At least the practice of local authority select lists of approved contractors has now generally achieved a fairer standard (ever since the Ombudsman took a hand). Tender competitions that categorically require that the proposed project be directed by an IFA member are increasingly common. The English case of statutory Areas of Archaeological Importance is a salutary example of the limitations of the closed shop: on balance, the legally designated monopolies have produced satisfactory services on a day-to-day basis (Jagger and Scrase 1997; cf. *BAN* Editorial 1989 for a note on some problems) but consultants have often had to be used to help cut through conflicts of interest with respect to general policy (cf. Arup 1991). Even when appointed to given tasks, archaeologists do not have an exclusive position: they must resign themselves to monitoring, either by quantity surveyors (cf. Lawrence 1989) who have no archaeological priorities whatsoever, or by archaeological consultants trained to understand the priorities of both the archaeologist and the client or sponsor – perhaps a case of better the devil you know?

Developers rarely perceive archaeological consultants as independent: the consultant is usually treated either as employee or Trojan Horse. Developers themselves tend not to express their opinion of archaeologists in print (but cf. Edwards 1989): in the early days of PPG 16, it was left to the pastiche that was the 'Developer Column' in the *Field Archaeologist* (see especially 'Fitzpatrick' 1991, 1992) to warn of the very real preconceptions, biases and legitimate worries of developers. More recently, a barrister closer to home has had his trenchant say (Pugh-Smith 2000), with points of particular relevance to all archaeological advisers.

Consultants themselves are becoming justifiably annoyed at the tawdry image imposed upon them, as can be seen for example in the call to use the phrase 'consulting archaeologist' (Strickland 1992b). The move by so many County Archaeologists and senior unit and museum staff to consultancy both underlines the quality of personnel now to be found in this specialisation and begs the question what intolerable resource and intellectual constraints have prompted what is still a very risky career shift.

There has been some encouragement for consultants from several quarters in recent years, but, superficial antagonisms aside, attitudes have not always been unequivocal. In the section 'Who is it for?' of an early pamphlet (IFA n.d.) designed to encourage archaeologists to join the IFA, thirteen different types of archaeologists were listed, with no mention of consultants: it took a new addition (October 1992) to rectify this omission. The first IFA *Directory of Members* (IFA 1989) contained a list of those members available for consultancy, a well-meaning but useless step, since there was no clear indication of vested interest. Nowadays, most archaeological firms offer consultancy services, although there has not been the debate about Chinese walls (consultancy versus contracting) that has occurred in planning authorities (consultees versus contracting). Government guidance (e.g. PPG 15 and 16 in England) suggests that developers might wish to make use of consultants for advice during the planning process. However, government commissions to consultants send a different signal. Why was a report on best practice for mineral operators with respect to archaeology included in a commission to a non-archaeological environmental consultancy (Roy Waller Associates Ltd 1991) and why were reports on the performance of PPG 16 commissioned from non-archaeological planning consultancies (Pagoda Projects: EH 1992c; Roger Tym and Partners and Pagoda Associates: EH 1995c)? Individual antipathy is one thing, but organisational reluctance or paralysis is another and cannot be shrugged off simply as a perceptual problem.

Moving to more specific problems, it has been suggested that consultancy practices cream off the more profitable aspects of contracts, leaving major fieldwork and the even more financially risky post-fieldwork projects to units (as implied in *BAN* 1990). The real situation is not that simple. Firstly, it is common practice for consultants in non-archaeological disciplines to gather information, from the field if necessary, upon which to base their advice; it is permissible for archaeological consultants to do the same, to carry out certain forms of field evaluation if adequately qualified (conversely, it appears that archaeologists offering 'evaluation services' now commonly refer to themselves as 'consultants'). Secondly, most units now provide consultancy services. Thirdly, from a commercial viewpoint, field evaluation is seen by many units as a troublesome, scrappy process, but necessary in order to win commissions for more substantial excavations; indeed, they may hold a very significant competitive advantage over less diversified firms by loss-leading in both desk-based assessment and field evaluation. Evaluation is arguably the most important yet underrated aspect of modern public archaeology (cf. Darvill and Gerrard 1992), and requires a special set of skills (in both desktop and fieldwork modes) from totally committed teams, however constituted. It would be damaging, and quite unnecessary, to let an artificial demarcation dispute develop here: all types of organisation must recognise that a reliable operating surplus can only stem from solutions that are both academically sound and cost-effective for sponsors or clients.

It is obvious that archaeologists in tied and mixed practices must come to terms with a strong set of vested interests in their parent organisations, although it would be unfair to assume that these persons necessarily lack objectivity. However, the problem, if problem it is allowed to become, is in fact much wider. Most larger projects involve a consultancy team, usually with either a planning consultant or barrister as lead; the pressures upon an archaeologist to conform are likely to be even greater in this situation than in a mixed practice. Archaeologists must clearly be prepared to work conscientiously in the team environment. However, it is imperative that the concept of planning and management balance be maintained (cf. Davies 1991) and that there be no invisible trawl of issues, no setting aside of minor constraints until they have been openly weighed against all other material considerations. It should not be forgotten that the team context also provides the invaluable opportunity for archaeologists to inform their team colleagues (and vice versa) in a confidential setting where all parties can safely expose and examine their motives.

Allied to the above problem is the issue of data suppression (Heaton 1988; Hinton 1992). When the consultant has presented a report to the client, the contract is fulfilled. The client is not entitled to edit the report and pass it on as the consultant's work, but the client may legally decide not to pass on the report at all or to edit it to remove all reference to the consultant. The latter practices are much more common than the reader might think, and it is important to realise that few non-archaeological consultants see any ethical dilemma in such actions. The IFA *Code of Conduct* (IFA 2000a) is generally applicable to this problem, but is currently not specific enough. It is a legal fact that a consultant's advice is given in confidence and must remain confidential if the client so wishes. However, during a project the archaeological consultant may gather field data. It is advisable that a clear statement be included in all contractual arrangements that any 'primary archaeological data', together with 'proximal interpretation' (the basic commentary that renders bare facts useful), must be released to the relevant SMR before a planning or management decision is taken regarding the land in question (cf. Collcutt 1991). The concept may be widened to 'primary archaeological documents' (those not yet recorded in the SMR but clearly containing data relevant to a decision); a list of such documents, with no comment, may be sent to the SMR if the consultant's report has not been made available.

Contracts present another problem for consultants. There are a number of complex model contracts and contract guidelines in circulation (cf. Darvill and Atkins 1991; see also Chapter 16). However, clients for consultancy will not use these forms and any attempt to force the issue may lose the consultant the contract. The consultant will normally discuss the project with the client (possibly after receiving documentation) and will then send a free-style letter of proposal, including any specific conditions relevant to the particular case (consultants should include general statements upon contract conditions, such as adherence to professional codes or standards, in their publicity brochures, which are a legal part of all contractual agreements); the client will then reply with a free-style letter of commission. When a client has earned a degree of trust, the consultant may even be expected or willing to act upon verbal instructions. Formal contracts may of course be necessary when imposed by clients, as is often the case on private infrastructure and government projects. Nevertheless, the nature of most consultancy tasks, commonly involving intermittent or emergency input over long periods in response to changing situations, is not amenable to prior formal contractual definition. Since it is the consultant who takes the commercial risk (and all consultants should learn their contract law thoroughly), the profession must allow consultants to use their judgement on the conditions of contract in any particular case and not try to impose pro forma documents. The only situation in which more rigorous definition (usually in the form of a detailed specification) is systematically needed (to safeguard the archaeological resource rather than the consultant) is when the consultant proposes to carry out significant fieldwork.

The matter of contract is different from that of brief. A brief is a statement of objectives, stripped of administrative and financial provisions (Chapter 16). Whatever method is used to establish the brief, the consultant should make sure that both he or she and the client understand and agree on its meaning. This is not usually a problem, except in the case of competitive tendering (CT). There was much early discussion of the latter topic in archaeology (e.g. Hobley in CAWP 1988; Richard Hughes reported in Marvell 1990; Watson 1990; Heaton 1991; Swain 1991). The IFA *Code of Approved Practice for the Regulation of Contractual Arrangements in Field Archaeology* (IFA 2000b) is a laudable attempt to mitigate the worst possible effects of CT (cf. also Lawson 1989; EH 1990, 1991a) – an attempt which is working no better now than it was ten years ago. Both public and private sectors are resisting proper tender practices every inch of the way, and archaeological tenderers are letting it happen. The main problem is that many developers (or their lead planning consultants) seem to think that they can both write the brief and judge the tenders themselves. If the IFA really wants to make design rather than cost the competition criterion, more forceful action must be taken to ensure that members maintain solidarity and refuse to tender to briefs that have no input from a qualified archaeologist, either curator or consultant. Similarly, it is good practice for a brief to state the name(s) of the competition judge(s), the period during which requests for further details may be made (and answers circulated equally to all tenderers), the tender deadline and the judgement date. These provisions are not mandatory, but many people (archaeologists and developers) do not seem to realise that any demonstrable instance of unfair tender practice is potentially cause for civil action. This is not an attempt to drum up business for consultants: consultants running a tender competition are automatically disqualified from competing themselves, other than under the most exceptional and explicit circumstances (including prior warning to other prospective tenderers). The use of tendering is definitely on the increase, and now includes even minor projects. Many conscientious firms of consultants and fieldwork teams put very considerable effort into tenders; if the ground rules are not equitable, this effort (and the money it entails) is wasted. CT briefs must contain a statement of the full objectives of a project (including contingencies), together with a thorough set of rubrics indicating the different types of information the tenderer should submit. If no fee has been paid, the specification submitted by a tendering firm is that firm's copyright; all archaeologists should be very wary of any specification that has obviously been prepared by someone with archaeological expertise but which has no acknowledgement of the author. Even if a specification mentions its professional author, the exact wording may give away the fact that, before inept editing by a third party, the document was once a tender.

The question of legal liabilities arises in any consultancy context. Consultants are extremely exposed when advising on archaeological matters affecting the viability of multimillion-pound projects. All contractors will carry substantial public liability insurance, sometimes with special clauses to cover fieldwork. Such insurance is affordable since it has a relatively low premium-to-cover ratio. Advice is quite another matter, requiring full professional indemnity (similar to that held by solicitors; cf. Collcutt 1995a) at much more significant premiums.

Consultants cannot ignore the questions of standards and quality assurance (Chapter 16). Many IFA documents may fail to appreciate the gamut of constraints upon commercial practitioners; the IFA should bring a wider range of expertise to bear upon the matter of standards. A formal standard must be viable in contexts rarely under the total control of archaeologists, and must, by very definition, contain mechanisms for at least qualitative measurement of performance. As for quality assurance (QA), the British Standard is a daunting prospect, especially when one realises that eligibility for the kitemark will be relatively costly. There are, however, several consultancy practices that already have a QA scheme in place (cf. Strickland 1992a). The important point is that the British Standard and the relevant supporting documentation contain a clear statement of what is involved in quality assurance, under the two main rubrics of 'Procedures' (explicit instructions to staff on how to go about a task and how to document progress) and 'Audit' (checking and improving performance at various project stages or before subsequent projects). Any archaeologist can set up a rudimentary QA scheme that can be refined and expanded (incorporating detailed professional standards as they appear) over a period of years, indeed, logically, for ever. It is not difficult to devise formal written procedures to cover many aspects of consultancy work, together with simple internal audit mechanisms. Compact questionnaires may be issued with reports, so that both clients and curators can contribute external audit statistics. The IFA's Registered Archaeological Organisation (RAO) Scheme is meant to be a customised QA approach; it is most regrettable that the IFA decided against allowing actual incorporated entities (that is, legal persons) or other Board-governed organisations to join this scheme in their own right, preferring to place the onus upon individual archaeological employees.

Consultants operate in the marketplace and must be allowed to set their fees as they see fit. Commercially acceptable fee rates rose steadily in real terms during the 1980s, so that, at the time of writing of the first edition of this chapter, archaeological consultants could attract remuneration (from which all overheads had to be financed) comparable to the lowest rate for, say, generalist solicitors (but still significantly below those for most other types of professional consultant). Larger developers or projects could pay such rates, but small developers and most members of the general public could not and still cannot. Similarly, some local planning authorities do not consider archaeologists to be in the same category as other planning consultants and will usually balk at the cost of archaeological support at public enquiries (Saville 1990). Consultants must decide under what circumstances they are available to advise upon the public heritage. The interim solution already adopted by some firms is a *pro bono* allocation from operating surplus, with all non-profit-making applicants eligible, but choice of projects to receive partial or full subsidy being made by the consultancy management on criteria of pure archaeological merit. The matter has been made more difficult by the fact that, in the intervening years, real fee values have slowly declined (thus slipping even further with respect to the 'old' professions) and an experienced archaeological consultant must now expect remuneration not significantly different from that of colleagues of the similar level of qualifications, experience and seniority in other public archaeology posts. One of the 'comments' in the employment survey by Aitchison and Edwards (2003: 116, 5th comment) rings true in this context, noting that archaeological consultants in mixed-practice firms tend not to be as well paid as their colleagues responsible for other issues.

There continue to be problems inherent in consultancy training. Indeed, there is still considerable worry over the whole question of suitability of the available tertiary education in all areas of public archaeology. Consultants should give more lectures and seminars aimed primarily at training rather than publicity. Personnel exchange and on-the-job training schemes may be difficult to organise because of commercial issues and confidentiality; nevertheless, at least larger firms should be able to find some occasions when such training might be possible. In-post continuous or upgrade training will be easier within firms, through shadow and post-mortem systems, but should also include as much exposure as possible to relevant colloquia and other Continuing Professional Development events. Every individual should be encouraged to maintain a project-by-project appendix to their curriculum vitae, noting precisely the nature of their input. This will be useful to a current employer, in order to check for and rectify any imbalance in experience, and also invaluable (supported by references or certification) if the individual changes employment or needs to demonstrate competence for a particular contract.

Finally, one may ask whether consultants can contribute more directly and visibly to the evolution of the profession. The most obvious example of such contribution is the very large body of essentially academic compendia produced by consultant specialists, whose range has probably been broadened because of their consultancy role. The next visible group comprises the specialist lawyers who have provided the excellent textbooks on heritage law (e.g. Suddards and Hargreaves 1996; Pugh-Smith and Samuels 1996b; Mynors 1999) necessary to train and inform the profession. However, it is interesting to note that these lawyers usually stick to 'explicit law', that is, those situations clearly governed by statute and case law. In reality, the great majority of day-to-day problems in public archaeology are not (obviously) covered by this 'explicit law'. When a lawyer alone tries to go beyond the obvious, he or she will often come unstuck (e.g. the terrible conundrums set by Cookson 2000), probably because of insufficient familiarity with detailed archaeological procedures and objectives. When a specialist lawyer and a consultant archaeologist collaborate, greater insight may be achieved (e.g. Pugh-Smith and Samuels 1993); just the few pages on 'practical concerns and consequences' in Pugh-Smith and Samuels (1996b: 114–23) are worth their weight in gold, as is a further article by the same team (Pugh-Smith and Samuels 1996a). Eventually, the archaeological consultant is driven to try to fill these difficult, interdisciplinary voids in practice (the risk of coming unstuck being less important to the profession as a whole, since lawyers will probably get the last say anyway). Examples from the present author's work (often tedious in the extreme, because of the need to examine the topic carefully from every possible angle) include resource specification and the legal requirement for precision in a planning condition (Collcutt 1997); the setting of heritage features (Collcutt 1999); additional planning conditions upon the approval of reserved matters (Collcutt 2001); and the proper provision of evaluation information (Petchey and Collcutt 2002). None of these archaeologically crucial topics is covered adequately in the 'explicit law' textbooks, simply because there is no such law. And, of course, we are just about to receive 'rationalised' guidance on heritage matters (a Planning Policy Statement), together with – probably – thoroughly revised legislation (cf. DCMS 2003c). More work for consultants, I dare say.

CHAPTER 16

WORKING PRACTICES IN FIELD ARCHAEOLOGY

Timothy Darvill

INTRODUCTION

One of the most pervasive changes in archaeological resource management during the second half of the twentieth century was the way in which field archaeology of all kinds was carried out in terms of the working practices applied, namely the professionally accepted, normal arrangements and frameworks for the performance of archaeological tasks. The causes of these changes are numerous and complicated, but some are relevant to an understanding of the present situation. Principal among these is the proliferation of legislative measures that bear on archaeological work, and the tighter definition of roles and areas of responsibility for individuals and organisations. A defining moment in the establishment of the working practices that now obtain was in 1977 when it was announced that central government support for archaeology would henceforth be based on 'project funding' and 'problem-orientated fieldwork' (DoE 1977; Wainwright 1978, 2000: 919). Until that time, block grants were allocated to archaeological units and other organisations engaged in rescue archaeology for them to spend as they thought appropriate. Since the late 1970s most archaeological fieldwork has been carried out as a series of relatively discrete jobs or projects, the need for which is determined by its anticipated contribution to an understanding of the past. Such understandings may be in terms of knowing about particular deposits or areas in order to assist in managing or preserving them, or it may be related to broader questions about what people did, when, and where in antiquity.

Over the last twenty-five years or so the business of doing archaeology has become a complicated affair (Darvill 2004; Tainter 2004), and inevitably this short account is a highly selective outline of a wide topic. It is divided into four main sections. The first deals in a general way with project management, and some of the schemes that have been applied to archaeological situations. In the second section attention is directed towards more operational matters connected with the development and running of projects, including relationships of various sorts within the profession and between archaeologists and other parties. The third section briefly reviews the general regulation of archaeological work through legislation and related instruments, while the final section looks in more detail at archaeological contracts and some of the key issues covered by such documents. Specifically excluded here is any consideration of employment arrangements; the important matter of health and safety is only given cursory treatment.

Many of the matters discussed here are subject to almost constant modification in the light of government intervention, shared experiences and collective debate. This reflects the relative youthfulness and buoyancy of the profession, as well as the result of working within the much wider professional *mélange* represented in local authorities and the development industry. Change is not always welcomed by all, and can sometimes be hard to accommodate quickly within local working environments while maintaining professional dignity, the authority of advice already given, and indeed the *raison d'être* for a particular existing organisational structure or arrangement. For this reason, both the stimulus for, and the implementation of, changes in working practices in archaeology are generally incremental rather than radical in nature, and localised rather than widespread in their effects. However, regardless of whether the organisation is concerned with contracting, curating the resource, consultancy, presentation and display, academic research, or a combination of these, tried and tested working practices are essential. The scale of archaeological work now taking place can be guaged from a comprehensive study of archaeological activity in England between 1990 and 1999 (Darvill and Russell 2002). This showed that during the 1990s the number of archaeological projects involving the direct investigation of archaeological remains undertaken each year increased threefold to reach about 4,500 separate events per annum by the turn of the millennium (Darvill and Russell 2002: 52). About 89 per cent of those investigations were prompted through the planning system and the control of development in protected places.

PROJECT MANAGEMENT

Projects come in many shapes and sizes, but all are journeys into the unknown, fraught with risk, whose exact course can never accurately be predicted and whose final outcome is never completely guaranteed. Project management is a well-established discipline within the field of management studies, and aims to minimise risks, order and direct resources, and relate objectives to attainable goals so that work is finished on time, within budget and to an acceptable standard.

Four main sorts of project are generally recognised, each with its distinctive type of management system (Lock 1988):

- manufacturing projects (making cars, books, tins of baked beans etc.)
- construction projects (building houses, bridges, offices, factories etc.)
- management projects (relocating a company or organisation etc.)
- research projects (creating some new knowledge or understanding of a topic etc.).

The execution of archaeological fieldwork projects is most closely allied to the kind of management systems associated with construction projects, which typically involves a closely ordered incremental series steps or work-packages, each of which, for those carrying them out, might seem like mini-projects in their own right. In fact, archaeological organisations become involved in all four kinds of project at different times during their existence. The most difficult to manage, and the least well documented in available literature, are research projects. This is mainly because it is sometimes hard to visualise the content and form of the final product.

All kinds of projects can be planned and executed in a simple staged approach, which in very broad terms can be represented as a lifecycle of five steps:

1. Recognition of the task or job needing to be done
2. Planning an approach, including background research, experimentation and testing
3. Decision to go ahead with the main project
4. Programme of work forming the main project
5. Completion, conclusion, and review.

Depending on the complexity of the project, these essential steps can be expanded and subdivided almost infinitely, although keeping tabs on what is going on will usually require the attention of a trained project manager. Complexity in such cases can be roughly measured in terms of the number of work-packages and task-sets, the number of individuals and organisations who will perform those tasks, and the degree of coordination required between task-sets. English Heritage (EH) has published useful guidance on archaeological project management in a volume entitled *The Management of Archaeological Projects*, colloquially known as MAP2 (EH 1991a). Here the general staged approach noted above is translated into more explicitly archaeological thinking as a four-stage structure involving proposal, decision, data-collection, and review stages arranged as a cycle (Fig. 16.1). The dynamic element is provided by the fact that each rotation of the cycle begins with a proposal and ends with a review that in turn defines the proposal for the next rotation. Each turn of the cycle should have clearly defined objectives and be appropriately resourced in terms of staff, equipment, time and costs, but by breaking large projects down in this way such things can be relatively easily controlled.

The majority of archaeological fieldwork carried out in recent decades follows more or less closely this cyclical process, which in its most general form involves site selection, assessment and investigation. This has become known as the 'management

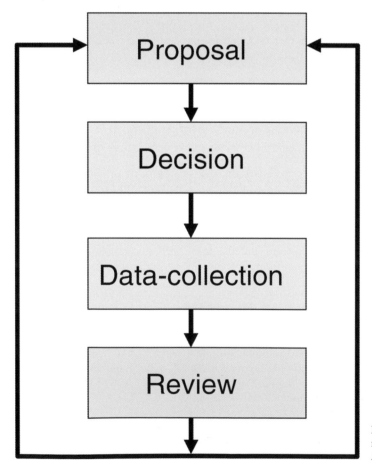

Figure 16.1. Four-step management model. *(After EH 1991a: fig. 2)*

cycle' (Darvill and Gerrard 1992, 1994: 171; and see also Willems 1997: fig. 1). Similar approaches can be detected in development-prompted work within the planning system as well as in non-planning related situations, although the emphasis given to particular stages and the expected outputs from them vary according to the circumstances of individual programmes. Fig. 16.2 shows an idealised model, recognising work-packages of the sort touched upon in other chapters and in some cases discussed further in later sections. Each element of this overall scheme contains within it the four-stage structure represented, but, simultaneously, the whole endeavour can be visualised within an overarching four-stage cycle. Increasingly critical in this overall structure is the decision stage. Within planning-related work this refers mainly to the determination of a planning application or Scheduled Monument Consent application with the result that operations in the first half of the process are often refered to as pre-determination works while those coming after the decision stage are referred to as post-determination works. In projects that are not related to the planning system or development process, the decision stage often relates to the granting of permissions, licences and funds to carry out the work.

For excavation and fieldwork projects, most of which would be post-determination works, EH has expanded the basic four-stage model to emphasise the relationships between the separate stages of the cycle as actually carried out, the broader phases representing the unfolding of the project as a whole and the outputs/products expected from each phase (Fig. 16.3). This model has been tried and tested many times and provides a useful template for thinking through the development of a potential project and for creating the documentation that allows its evaluation and monitoring (EH 1991a; Andrews and Thomas 1995).

All projects need to be executed by a qualified, competent and motivated team, but the key figure is the project manager (see also Chapter 14). He or she leads the team and takes overall responsibility for the success of the project. The project manager is concerned with optimising and coordinating resources of all kinds to achieve the defined goals. The project manager's authority can vary from executive responsibility in a line management sense through to coordinator by persuasion.

Project management increasingly involves the use of sophisticated techniques for analysing a proposed project, computing possible routes that increase the likelihood of success, and modelling resource requirements as the project unfolds. Such management tools include critical-path analysis, network analysis, and cascade diagrams of various sorts (especially Gantt charts).

PROJECT DEVELOPMENT

The idea for a project does not simply appear from nowhere. Usually, there is some kind of a question or problem to be solved, and this may be developed through a 'problem-orientated' approach or a 'curiosity-orientated' approach. In the former, questions are prompted through some fairly formal process: the need to obtain an understanding of archaeological deposits within a development site; the need to excavate, record and understand the archaeology of a particular piece of land; the need to investigate some clearly defined aspect of the archaeological record, and so on. In the latter the potential for a project is recognised through a more fluid relationship with the archaeological material itself, new questions being recognised through serendipitous encounters with previously unseen deposits, new discoveries, or the recognition of unexplained patterns and relationships. The whole process can be greatly assisted by the creation of a 'research framework' for an area, site, period or topic.

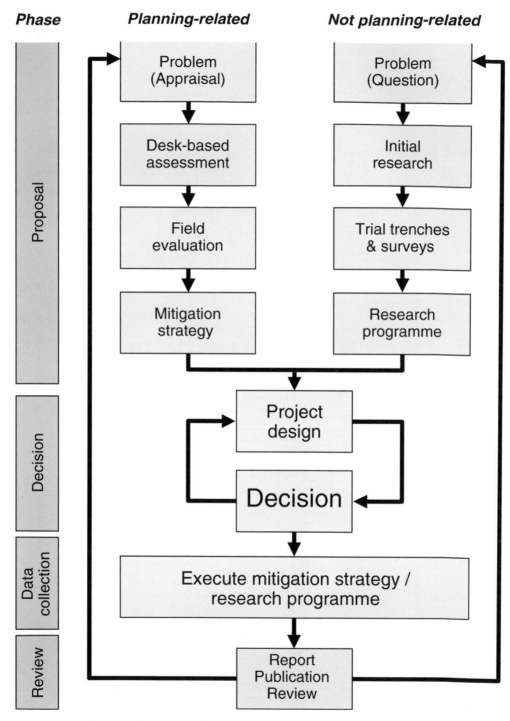

Figure 16.2. Idealised model of archaeological endeavour as a series of stages within two separate but broadly parallel cycles. *(After Darvill and Russell 2002: ill. 1)*

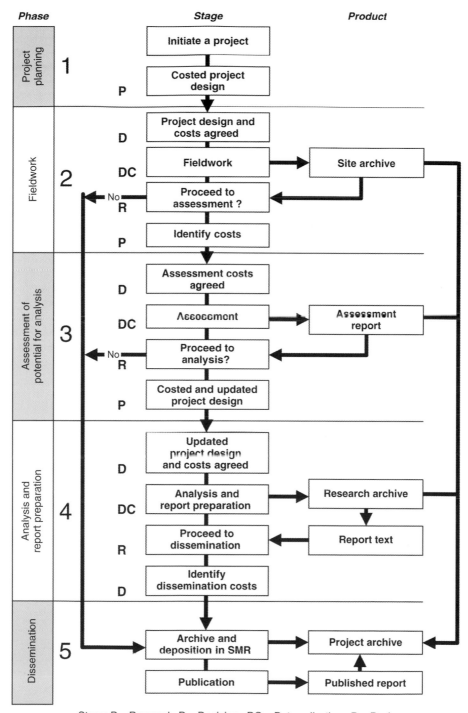

Figure 16.3. Phased scheme for archaeological fieldwork. *(After EH 1991a: fig. 1)*

Research frameworks

In an archaeological context, a research framework is essentially a tool for promoting and facilitating a wide range of problem-orientated and curiosity-drived research in such a way as to make the best of any and every opportunity to extend knowledge and understandings of the archaeology of an area (EH 1996; Thomas 1997; Olivier 2002). A research framework typically comprises three main components:

- *Resource Assessment*: a statement of the current state of knowledge and a description of the archaeological resource. Effectively, a critical review of existing achievements linked to a series of maps and listings of key investigations and publications.
- *Research Agenda*: a list of perceived gaps in current knowledge, work which could usefully be done, linked to explicit potential for the resource to answer the questions posed. Essentially, a statement of the main identifiable issues and priorities for systematic incremental investigation over the next decade or so.
- *Research Strategy*: a statement setting out priorities, methods and a selection of initiatives that can be pursued to address the agenda. Essentially, proposals for progressing all kinds of archaeological research by matching needs to anticipated operations and providing a structure to link recognised objectives with unanticipated opportunities in the future.

These components fit together in a tightly structured way (Fig. 16.4) so that the resource assessment relates to what has happened (i.e. past research). Defining the research issues or setting the agenda is very much a contemporary exercise (i.e. present research), while taking these issues forward involves the formulation of new programmes and initiatives (i.e., future research).

Building on the well-established tradition of developing policy documents of various kinds in British archaeology (CBA 1948; Thomas 1983), the new generation of research frameworks are providing extensive coverage through regional studies (e.g. East Anglia, Glazebrook 1997; Brown and Glazebrook 2000), site-based and sub-regional studies (e.g. Greater Thames Estuary, Williams and Brown 2001; Avebury, AAHRG 2001;

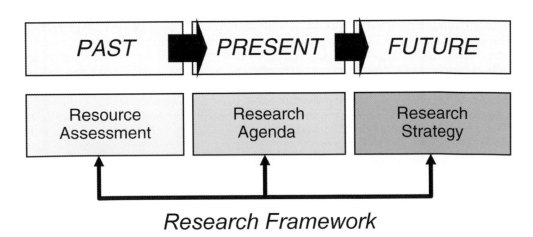

Figure 16.4. Research frameworks. *(After EH 1996: fig. 1)*

Stonehenge, Darvill 2005), and period-based studies (e.g. the British Iron Age, Haselgrove *et al.* 2001). Many more are in preparation. The impact of these documents, which should be regularly updated, is potentially very considerable, not least in commercial archaeology where the basis for both pre-determination and post-determination works is usually set out as a brief, specification, mitigation strategy, or project design.

Briefs and specifications

The terms brief and specification, often prefaced by 'project', are sometimes used interchangeably, although each has an accepted meaning acquired by usage within archaeological project management. Each kind of document should only be employed for its intended purpose; thus it is important to know and recognise the differences.

- a brief is an outline for an archaeological project (IFA 1990: 6), usually little more than the definition of objectives, the rationale or justification for their pursuit, an indication of the methods that might be used, and the operational parameters on the execution of the work. A specimen brief has been published (Chadwick 1991).
- a specification is usually taken to mean a detailed statement of the necessary works associated with the undertaking of a particular project (IFA 1990: 6). It might form the basis for soliciting competitive tenders.

Both the brief and the specification are normally prepared by, or agreed with, the relevant archaeological curator before implementation.

Mitigation strategy

A mitigation strategy is a programme of works developed in order to conserve, protect, record, and/or investigate archaeological structures and deposits that are threatened by wholesale or partial destruction through some kind of development programme. Such proposals may, for example, include the use of particular foundation designs to minimise the impact of construction on buried deposits, or the use of open space to allow the *in situ* preservation of significant remains. Equally, a mitigation strategy may comprise rescue excavations and site recording operations in advance of destruction. The selection of options is based on weighing up the nature and significance of the archaeological remains in relation to the expected impact and overall importance of the proposed development. For large schemes it is likely that multi-option mitigation strategies will be proposed in which different zones within the site will be treated in different ways – some might be fully excavated, some deposits preserved *in situ*, and some areas simply monitored during groundworks. A mitigation strategy is usually prepared as the final review stage prior to the determination of a planning application or Scheduled Monument Consent application, in certain cases incorporated within an Environmental Impact Statement (DoE 1989a). Most are modified during the debate and consultation inherent to the decision stage, with the result that each strand within the strategy is likely to be elaborated as a project design in the project planning that represents the first part of the post-determination work.

Project design

A project design is the document that represents the outcome of a project planning stage (Black and Jolly 2003). In some cases this might be at the very beginning of a project, before a decision is made about whether a piece of work goes ahead (see Fig. 16.3). In other cases one or more project designs may be prepared as a result of a decision stage in the planning process and here it will represent a critical preparation for post-determination works. Either way, a project design comprises a number of key elements (EH 1991a: 27–9; and see HS 1996b):

- Background
  - description of the area/site/problem to be examined
  - review of previous work and its implications
  - the reasons for and circumstances of the proposed new project
  - Statement of the anticipated outputs and where archaeological materials and archives will be deposited

- Aims and objectives
  - the overarching aim of the work
  - specific research questions to be addressed, linked to objectives set in relevant research frameworks
  - publications, presentations, and other expected outputs

- Methods statement
  - techniques and approaches to be used
  - data sources
  - sampling strategies
  - links between the methods and the defined objectives

- Resources and programming
  - staffing and equipment
  - timetable
  - budget.

Creating a project design involves a considerable amount of research, including sometimes a pilot scheme to test methodology and develop appropriate costing and timetable models. Throughout, a significant aspect of the work involves estimating costs and creating a workable programme.

Estimating

Costing archaeological projects in terms of the resources required to achieve set objectives is far from easy. It needs a considerable input of time, consultation with all members of a project team, and the use of results from the tracking of similar projects previously undertaken. There is no common method for costing archaeological work, nor are there generally available price guides for regularly executed operations.

There are also different ways of specifying the price of a task or service detailed in a project specification. The most straightforward way of specifying costs is as a fixed price. Here the contactor undertakes to execute an agreed project for a specified sum, this being set down in a contract (see below). Where the full extent of the work is uncertain at the time a contract is made, the contract may provide that the price be ascertained by measuring the work actually done against items in a bill of quantities or a schedule of rates.

Adjustments to a fixed-price contract may be permitted if there is: (1) a fluctuation clause in the contract entitling the contractor to be reimbursed for any increase in labour or materials costs, or giving the client the benefit of any decrease therein; (2) a clause requiring adjustment to the fixed price where there is any variation; and (3) a general clause whereby contractors may claim an increase in the actual work such as may be caused by late instructions from the client.

Where no price is fixed, the contractor is entitled to claim a reasonable amount from a client. Determining what is reasonable must depend on circumstances but may include payment for the skill, supervision, experience, and services of the contractor as well as materials and labour supplied. It should be noted, however, that market prices used to calculate a price set down in a contract are taken to be those at the time the contract is signed, unless the contract itself says otherwise.

Another method of calculating price is the costs-plus principle. Here the contract contains detailed provision for the calculation of costs with an agreed additional percentage of costs to cover overheads (including a profit margin if that is appropriate). The contract may provide for the contractor to be paid an additional sum in the event of the completion of work before a stipulated date.

Competitive tendering

Competitive tendering (CT) for archaeological projects developed during the later 1980s; its introduction caused considerable debate at the time (Swain 1991). The system, which provides for a number of contractors to submit quotations for undertaking a piece of work defined by a brief, specification, or project design is basically straightforward and perfectly legal so long as tendering is undertaken in an even-handed way. Policy statements have been issued by a number of government agencies (EH 1991b: 27–8; HS 1996a).

The Institute of Field Archaeologists' *Code of Approved Practice for the Regulation of Contractual Arrangements in Field Archaeology* (IFA 1990 with later revisions) includes the following clauses relating to CT:

> 12. An archaeologist involved in commissioning or undertaking works will satisfy himself or herself that the scope of any agreed brief or specification is adequate for the declared purpose, conforms with accepted academic standards and does not needlessly place the resource at risk.
> 13. An archaeologist involved in seeking tenders must endeavour to ensure that all potential contractors consider the same brief, are provided with the same information regarding the criteria for selection, form of tender and deadline, and are clearly notified of the selections procedures and who will select tenders. An archaeologist must treat each such tender as a confidential document unless otherwise specified and the contents of the tender must not be divulged to other tenderers prior to the selection of a contractor.
> 14. An archaeologist shall not select a contractor or recommend a contractor for selection on the basis of price alone. Having satisfied himself or herself that competitors are adequately qualified and are available to undertake the work, an archaeologist will select or recommend for selection from competing tenders those which: meet the brief; are least damaging to the resource; are the most comprehensive; and are the most cost effective.

Of these, clause 13 is probably the most onerous. It requires careful documentation of the tendering process lest procedures are later called into question. Clause 14 has proved slightly more problematic in practice than its drafters expected because one interpretation of its wording essentially allows competition by design: devising an acceptable specification becomes part of the competition itself. This is less than ideal since it encourages specifications that involve the minimum work possible rather than an appropriate and realistic response to the problem in hand. Moreover, contractors find it hard to justify the commitment of resources to the preparation of detailed specifications in a competitive situation when, probabilistically, the chances of success are stacked against them. Currently, the trend seems to be towards greater attention to the preparation of a single project specification (usually by a curator or consultant), this document being used as the basis for all tenders. To judge from practice in other professions, however, even this is unlikely to prevent submissions of non-conforming tenders.

Territoriality

Closely linked to the issue of CT has been that of territoriality (see also Chapters 4 and 14), particularly the notion that where an archaeological unit has been practising for a considerable time, accumulating a database and providing a community service, then it is the most appropriate body to undertake archaeological contracts in its own neighbourhood. The idea that any archaeological organisation should enjoy exclusive rights over a defined area was never really sustainable in the economic and political climate of the UK in the late 1980s (see Lambrick 1991: 23–4), although variation on the idea including some kind of franchise scheme continue to surface from time to time (Walker 1996; APPAG 2003: 20–1). Detailed studies of archaeological activity in England over the ten-year period from 1990 to 1999 show that in practice most archaeological contractors work mainly within a defined market area centred on their headquarters, in effect a home territory (Darvill and Russell 2002: 59–65; and see Fig. 16.5).

Obligations to other parties and the declaration of interests

Archaeological organisations typically work either for a number of clients or carry out a range of roles. Whichever, overlaps of interest are likely to occur and it is important that these are declared before conflicts arise. The IFA's *Code of Approved Practice for the Regulation of Contractual Arrangements in Field Archaeology* includes the following clauses to deal with these matters:

> 22. An archaeologist whose professional responsibilities combine recommendations about preservation and recording with its execution must clearly indicate the combination of these interests to all relevant parties in order that any potential conflicts of interest can be clearly identified. So as to avoid unfair accusations of commercial advantage, an archaeologist should not normally hold such joint responsibilities. If, at any time, during the life of a project, circumstances change so that an archaeologist holds joint responsibilities, this must be notified to all interested parties without delay.
> 23. An archaeologist will declare to other parties within a contractual arrangement any other relevant business interests, and will execute the contract faithfully, conscientiously, fairly and without inducements to show favour.
> 24. An archaeologist should exercise caution in undertaking, for different organisations, a series of contracts relating to a single site or monument where conflicts of interest may arise.

Clause 22 applies, for example, in the case of integrated archaeological organisations that both provide planning advice to local authorities (curatorial role) and offer an archaeological contracting service. Many developers are distrustful of such arrangements even when there is an apparent organisational distinction between the two sections. The trend is towards the complete separation of curatorial from contractual responsibilities; this already applies in many parts of the country.

Competency and qualification

Importance is attached to being qualified and competent for the kinds of archaeological work expected of individuals and organisations, as poorly executed work by unqualified and incompetent practitioners would bring the whole profession into disrepute. The IFA's

Figure 16.5. The distribution of the headquarters of the top twenty archaeological contracting units involved in undertaking the greatest number of investigations recorded by the Archaeological Investigations Project (AIP) in the period from 1990 to 1999. The circle drawn around each unit's headquarters is scaled to reflect the Mean Intervention Distance (MID) for all investigations. *(After Darvill and Russell 2002: ill. 42)*

Code of Approved Practice for the Regulation of Contractual Arrangements in Field Archaeology includes the following relevant, and fairly stringent, clauses:

> 10. An archaeologist may advertise his or her services but must ensure that the services offered are consistent with the *Code of Conduct* and that claims of competence match the task in hand.
>
> 11. An archaeologist shall not offer, recommend the offer of, or accept a contract of work unless he or she is satisfied that the work can be satisfactorily discharged. The archaeologist undertaking the work should have the requisite qualifications, expertise and experience and be able to meet the projected timescale.

Attaining appropriate levels of competence and experience is not simply about qualifying and then practising but rather about gaining proper experience and then maintaining skills through continuing professional development (CPD). The various classes of corporate membership of the IFA (in ascending order: practitioner, associate, member) recognise accumulating experience through time-service. An increasing number of curators insist that project managers and staff superintending archaeological works are members of the IFA at an appropriate level (identifiable by the distinctions: PIFA, AIFA and MIFA).

Some professional bodies require that qualifications are maintained through the annual accumulation of CPD credits for courses and training programmes attended. In archaeology at present, attending training programmes is voluntary, although it is likely that it will become compulsory within the foreseeable future.

Best practice, standards and quality assurance

Closely related to the matter of qualifications and competency are the questions of quality and compliance. The IFA has published a series of documents setting out best practice and acceptable standards for key kinds of archaeological activity:

1. Desk-based assessment (Published October 1994. Revised September 1999)
2. Field evaluations (Published October 1994. Revised September 1999)
3. Archaeological excavation (Published September 1995. Revised September 1999)
4. Archaeological watching brief (Published October 1994. Revised September 1999)
5. Archaeological investigation and recording of standing buildings or structures (Published September 1996. Revised September 1999).

These documents are intended to state the main principles for different types of project, and deal with outcomes rather than technical details on the achievement of those outcomes. The aim is to make good practice the norm, and to promote best practice wherever possible.

Internally operated quality assurance checks frequently form an element of project tracking procedures used by archaeological organisations. Indeed, Total Quality Management (TQM) is now an ambition for some archaeological organisations; it is expected that before long successful ones will be awarded a 'kitemark' for quality assurance under BS 5750 recently introduced by the British Standards Institution. The principal advantage of such quality assurance systems is that procedures can be audited through a formal review system.

Compliance is about the match between what is required in the documents setting out what needs to be done (usually a specification, project design, or licence) and what is actually done in the field and produced as the output. At present this is a task undertaken by curatorial archaeologists, especially national and local government officers who visit fieldwork programmes to monitor work as it is being carried out.

Subcontracting

One way of increasing the scope of work that an archaeological organisation can discharge is through subcontracting elements of projects. This generally works well, although there are important contractual implications (Darvill and Atkins 1991: 2).

Any archaeological organisation may secure assistance with the performance of part of a project through subcontracting, except where there is an express prohibition in a contract of some kind. It should be borne in mind that an archaeological organisation will be liable for defects in a subcontractor's work as if it had performed the work itself. There should be a clause in the subcontract indemnifying the archaeological organisation for any loss arising as a result of the subcontracted work. If the subcontractor breaches the main contract the archaeological organisation can recover from the subcontractor losses suffered as a result. It may be expedient to include a clause in the subcontract whereby the subcontractor agrees to be bound by the main contract, but this will not necessarily incorporate all the terms of the main contract. Terms must be expressly incorporated to apply to the subcontract.

Professional indemnity

Much archaeological work is based on professional judgement and inevitably there will be occasions, rare it is to be hoped, when such judgements are found to be deficient. For this reason all archaeological organisations (including individuals in private practice) should be covered by professional indemnity insurance. Premiums are usually linked to annual turnover, degree of risk, and the nature of the work.

REGULATING WORKING PRACTICES

Everything that professional archaeologists undertake occurs within overlapping frameworks of regulatory measures of greater or lesser stringency. Some frameworks relate to the definition and scope of operations, others to the acceptability and quality of performance. Four main regulatory mechanisms are explored hereafter.

Legislation

Field archaeology is not a regulated profession (cf. medicine, law), but archaeological resources and their treatment are determined by provisions scattered through a substantial raft of primary legislation, supporting instruments and associated guidance notes. The general impact of these on working practices may be gauged from the descriptions of the legislation in Chapters 5 and 10. A few specific provisions can, however, be highlighted here, especially those contained in the Ancient Monuments and Archaeological Areas Act 1979 (AMAA Act 1979).

Permissions are required under statute to carry out some kinds of archaeological work. The most notable of these is Scheduled Monument Consent: the definition of 'works' extends to archaeological investigations and many kinds of management operation (AMAA Act 1979: Section 3). The use of geophysical equipment within 'protected places' (Scheduled Monuments, Guardianship Monuments, Areas of Archaeological Importance (AAIs)) also requires prior written consent (AMAA Act 1979: Section 42).

Licences are also normally required under Section 25 of the Burial Act 1857 for the removal of the remains of any body from any place of burial; full details and variations in Scotland have been summarised by Garrett-Frost (1992).

Licences for other kinds of archaeological excavation are required in Northern Ireland (see Chapter 4; also Appendix to Part Two) and the Isle of Man, but not currently in England, Wales or Scotland. The European Convention of the Protection of the Archaeological Heritage, signed in Malta in January 1992 and ratified by the UK Government in March 2001, includes provisions for the authorisation and supervision of archaeological activities (CoE 1992: Art. 3). How this clause might be implemented in the UK, if at all, is a matter of considerable debate (Selkirk 2001; APPAG 2003: 16).

Within AAIs, some aspects of working practice are defined by legislation (AMAA Act 1979: Part II), among them timetables for responding to operations notices and the scope of works that can be carried out by an investigating authority (see Chapter 5).

Although very rarely used, powers of entry to private property may be authorised by the Secretary of State for the purposes of inspecting Scheduled Monuments and recording matters of archaeological or historical interest (AMAA Act 1979: Sections 6, 26). Provision also exists for the temporary custody of finds and objects of interest recovered during visits under such powers for the purposes of investigation, analysis, restoration or preservation (AMAA Act 1979: Section 54).

Discretionary expenditure on the acquisition and preservation of ancient monuments (AMAA Act 1979: Section 24) and on archaeological investigations (AMAA Act 1979: Section 45) is provided through the legislation. In England, a policy relating to the disbursement of such 'rescue' funding has been issued and subsequently reinforced by a full strategy document (EH 1986, 1991b). Three special areas for funding are established: projects where all possibilities of saving a site or for obtaining funds elsewhere have been exhausted; commissioned projects that enable EH to carry out its statutory duties, including funding research work with such duties in view; and projects where it is not practicable for the developer to make full provision for the kind of archaeological works required (EH 1991b: 33–4).

Other areas of legislation have a bearing on working practices in archaeology, most notably that dealing with health and safety at work. The Health and Safety at Work Act 1974 provided for a comprehensive and integrated legal framework for dealing with the health and safety of virtually all people at work, while also providing for the protection of members of the public where they may be affected by work activities; it also set up a Commission and Executive responsible to ministers for administering the legislation. A manual on these topics from an archaeological perspective has been published (Allen and Holt 1986) and a useful guide to safe working during field survey is also available from the Council for British Archaeology (Olivier 1989).

Codes of practice, agreements, and ethics

There are three main codes, drawn up to assist in the definition and regulation of work within particular industries, in routine use in Britain.

The code promulgated by the British Archaeologists and Developers Liaison Group (BADLG 1991), and supported by a wide range of archaeological organisations, sets out to define areas of responsibility and acceptable means and procedures for the integration of archaeological recording and investigation in the development process.

The second code, published by the Confederation of British Industry (CBI 1991), considers similar issues with respect to minerals operations. Finally, mention may be made of the *Code of Practice on Conservation, Access and Recreation* for the water industry, published by a number of government departments (DoE 1989b). The man-made environment receives special attention in this code.

On a wider front, international agreements are increasingly important, as for example the Vermillion Accord on the treatment of human remains adopted by the World Archaeological Congress in 1989 at its inter-congress meeting in South Dakota, USA. The six items in the accord specify respect for the mortal remains of the dead; respect for the wishes of the of the dead where known or reasonably inferred; respect for the wishes of local communities, relatives or guardians; respect for the scientific value of human remains; the need for negotiated agreements on the disposition of human remains; and the recognition of concerns held by various ethnic groups.

Professional ethics is an area of professional practice that is being increasingly discussed and debated, much of the most stimulating contributions emenating from North America (Green 1984; Lynott and Wylie 2002; Vitelli 1996) and northern Europe (Karlsson 2004). Key issues include stewardship, accountability to archaeologists and other interest groups, affected peoples, reburial of human remains, looting and repatriation, commercialisation, public education and outreach, intellectual property and the public availability of archaeological records.

Professional regulation

The need for a professional institute for archaeologists had long been recognised, although it was not until 1982 that the Institute of Field Archaeologists (IFA) finally came into being (Addyman 1989; Darvill 1999). Its objectives, set out in its Memorandum of Association (IFA 1987: 1) are:

> to advance the practice of field archaeology and allied disciplines, to define and maintain proper professional standards and ethics in training and education in field archaeology, in the execution and supervision of work, and in the conservation of the archaeological heritage; to disseminate information about field archaeologists and their areas of interest.

Field archaeology is broadly defined by the IFA. Its membership, which now exceeds 1,400 individuals, includes practitioners working in units, local authorities, government departments, government-sponsored organisations, museums, universities, and those in private practice. A survey of employment in 1998 showed that roughly one-third of the 4,000 or so people working in archaeology were employed as contractors, about one-third as curators at national and local level, and about one-third in other parts of the sector (Aitchison 1999; Fig. 16.6).

On joining the IFA members agree to abide by the Code of Conduct and all other by-laws. There is a disciplinary procedure open to members and non-members alike to investigate allegations of misconduct by members; if allegations are upheld then sanctions can be brought against the member concerned. At the core of the Code of Conduct (IFA 1999; first issued 1988) are five principles:

1. The archaeologist shall adhere to the highest standards of ethical and responsible behaviour in the conduct of archaeological affairs
2. The archaeologist has a responsibility for the conservation of the archaeological heritage
3. The archaeologist shall conduct his or her work in such a way that reliable information about the past may be acquired, and shall ensure that the results are properly recorded
4. The archaeologist has a responsibility for making available the results of archaeological work with reasonable dispatch
5. The archaeologist shall recognise the aspirations of employees, colleagues and helpers with regard to all matters relating to employment, including career development, health and safety, terms and conditions of employment and equality of opportunity.

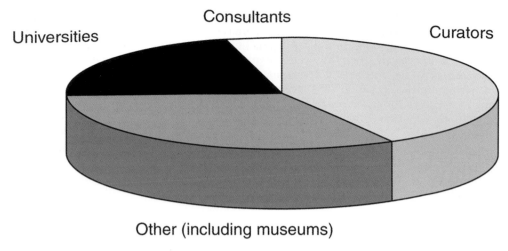

Consultants

Universities

Curators

Other (including museums)

Figure 16.6. Pie-chart showing the distribution of people employed in archaeological work in 1998 according to their principal roles. *(Data from Aitchison 1999: table 6)*

Each principle is developed as a set of rules. Collectively they serve as a foundation for the development of other by-laws relating to specific areas of working practice, for example on contractual arrangements (IFA 1990). On a broader scale, the European Association of Archaeologists, established in 1992, has a professional code of practice and guidance for those working in the field of contract archaeology (EAA 1997, 1998).

Peer review

Much archaeological work is subject to peer review, although not always visible as such. Applications for grants and for membership of learned societies and the IFA are based on peer validation of documentation and peer approval of proposals. The same applies to briefs and specifications relating to fieldwork programmes. Most manuscripts are refereed before acceptance for publication. As an academically based discipline, printed reviews of published works are commonplace.

Peer review serves to regulate archaeological work by promoting innovative and forward-looking projects, endorsing good work practices, and supporting what are collectively regarded as worthwhile endeavours. Looking into the future it will be interesting to see whether archaeologists in Britain are sufficiently confident to allow more penetrating peer review of their work, perhaps along the lines already practised in the USA (Burrow and Hunter 1990: 196).

CONTRACTS AND CONTRACTUAL RELATIONSHIPS

Within the broad mechanisms for the regulation of working practices outlined in the previous section, much of the detail in terms of what should be done, how it should be done, and how the various contributors relate to one another and to the project is governed by some kind of contract. The tighter definition of roles among archaeologists, more closely defined responsibilities, and the fuller integration of archaeological work with that of other professions over recent decades mean that the question of relationships between parties, whether they are all archaeologists or not, has become more critical in recent times (Francis 1998; Heaton 2002; see also Chapter 15). The main players in such networks of relationships are the four 'Cs': curators, contractors, consultants and clients. They may all be involved in the development and negotiation of contracts at various times, and may well be party to some contracts, but the majority of contracts establish relationships between clients and contractors.

Contracts have been widely used in archaeology for more than twenty years (Darvill and Atkins 1991). Many specimen examples and pro formas have been developed, the most recent and wide-ranging as a result of discussions between the Institution of Civil Engineers, the IFA and a range of other professional bodies (ICE 2004). A written contract may range from an informal letter through to a tightly structured document compiled by a solicitor. In all cases a contract must contain:

1. The names of the parties, or a sufficient description of them
2. A description of the subject matter
3. All material terms
4. Details of any consideration.

A standard form contract is a pro forma document regularly used in particular situations to which it specifically relates, although it may be necessary to vary some clauses according to the requirements of a particular application. Such contracts are likely to be useful for routine, well-defined tasks such as watching briefs, evaluations and the recording of standing buildings. Many archaeological contracts undertaken today are of the 'design and execute' type. In these, the contractor devises a programme of work (described in a specification), agrees it with the employer and appropriate archaeological curators, and then carries it out.

The three basic elements of any contract are the agreement, the contractual intention, and the consideration. The *agreement* involves the unqualified acceptance by one party of an offer made by another party, this acceptance being brought to the attention of the party making the offer. A tender may be invited from potential suppliers of goods and/or services. In such cases each tender submitted is an offer: the organisation that invited the tenders can accept any tender to bring into existence a binding contract. For this reason it is important to include with any tender the terms and conditions under which it can be fulfilled. A *contractual intention* must exist to create a legally binding contract. If there is no intention then despite the existence of an apparent agreement supported by a consideration there will not be an enforceable contract. The *consideration* is a benefit that one party must confer on the other in return for the benefit received. Whether the consideration is a promise, goods, or services, it is usually of considerable value although the benefits conferred need not be of the same value (e.g. cost), or the same kind (e.g. financial as against intellectual), as the benefits received. Where an archaeological organisation has been granted charitable status the nature of any consideration has to be examined very closely.

It is also important, irrespective of whether the consideration is deemed a donation or a payment for services, that it is clearly stated that costs or sums payable are inclusive or exclusive of Value Added Tax (VAT), even if VAT is not being charged, in order to reduce the possibility of a VAT liability arising subsequently.

Contracts are not just records of agreements. Their construction should be regarded as a useful exercise in thinking through the circumstances of a project, how it will be executed, and the various effects that it might have on other people. Their negotiation provides an agenda for discussions between the main parties and the chance to express views on particular points. Their implementation may be used as a management tool to keep the project on course.

Most important, however, is that contracts should not simply be documents familiar to project managers and negotiators. In order that a contract for services can be fully executed it is vital that each level of management is aware of those elements of the contract that are relevant to their responsibilities. Many archaeological organisations use contracts to regulate work undertaken for developers and other non-archaeological organisations. Contracts are also used for subcontracted work between archaeological organisations and specialists of various sorts. Specimen model contracts for archaeological services have been published (BADLG 1989; Darvill and Atkins 1991). A review of the main components of the contract and an outline checklist of points to consider follows (and see CBA 1982; Darvill and Atkins 1991).

Definition of site or area for investigation

Any archaeological contract must specify precisely where the land to be investigated lies. A scaled plan of the site and its environs is often helpful. Where possible the plan should include delineation of the area(s) to be excavated; information on access; land ownership; adjacent holdings and surrounding structures; proposed locations of spoil heaps and on-site accommodation for the archaeological organisation; and known live services. It is often necessary, having regard to the design of the proposed development or subsequent land use, to specify a maximum depth of archaeological investigation, related to a datum point. A procedure for reviewing this restriction may also be agreed.

Purpose and scope of contracted work or services

Obligations imposed on developers by clauses in a development agreement, conditions of planning consent, or conditions attached to a Scheduled Monument Consent may be the reason for engaging an archaeological contractor. In such cases it is often helpful to make this clear in preliminary sections of a contract, not least so that it can be used to demonstrate intent by a developer to statutory bodies and/or local authorities. The works to be undertaken should be listed in a schedule. The importance of a well-considered specification that includes a provisional programme cannot be underestimated; extracts from such a document may usefully be included in the schedule. In adapting the project specification to the requirements of a contract, however, there must always be adequate account taken of the need to retain some flexibility for the post-excavation and publication programme as well as the site-works proper.

Licence period and work programme

It is important to state when work will start, either as a date or as a time determined by the completion of some other task, and how long the work will take. A summary programme will frequently be included in the project specification that forms part of the schedule. In order to control work schedules, it is usually helpful to specify the notice period that a developer is required to give before works commence. Arrangements for changes in the duration of the work programme, premature termination or postponement must be made. Arrangements for checking standing buildings before or during demolition must be specified. This provision allows observations that may help with subsequent interpretation of excavated features; detailed recording of standing buildings or remains of historic interest would be contained in the specification. Arrangements for any continuing observation of the development by the contractor after the conclusion of the agreed archaeological programme must be specified, including statutory safety provisions and indemnity for consequent delays.

The following points might be considered when establishing the length of a contract:

1. Date of commencement on site
2. Dates of phased sectional entries/completions
3. Dates of final completion on site
4. Date of interim report to client
5. Date of final report
6. Extensions to contract period (reasons/agreements required/consequential costs).

Consents and access

Responsibilities for obtaining any licences or consents required need to be specified. Who undertakes such duties as organising disconnection of live services should be specified. Arrangements for access need to be defined, including the following:

1. Kinds of access point(s) (vehicular, pedestrian) and kinds of access required (e.g. for lorries, caravans)
2. Wayleave restriction(s) on site
3. Wayleave restriction(s) over adjacent properties (who pays?)
4. Sites for infrastructure works (offices/soil heaps/finds processing/stores/parking)
5. Invited visitors/sponsor's representatives
6. Access by the general public
7. Access for contractors (shared use of space/access points?)
8. Licences.

Ownership and disposal of finds and records

The ownership of finds and responsibilities for the costs of conservation of such finds, where appropriate, should be established before excavation commences (see also Chapter 6). Special permission may be required for the archaeological contractor to take temporary custody of finds and structural remains for the purposes of study and reporting. Arrangements for the final disposal of finds, any structural remains recovered, and the records relating to the archaeological work should be agreed.

Financial arrangements

It is important to establish who is paying for the work, how much they are paying, how they are to pay it, and whether the amounts payable include VAT or not. All sources of finance for a given project forming the subject of a contract should be declared. The following points may be considered when looking at the financial structure:

1. Price: fixed price/contract price plus market fluctuations/costs-plus/contingency sums (percentage or flat rate)
2. Payments: in advance (part or whole)/interim payments (frequency?/dates due?)/ basis of claim (costs or programmed payment)/minimum amount of interim claim/ final account due
3. Retentions: interim claims/on completion of reports
4. Interest: on overdue payments/cost of project finance (cashflow)
5. Penalties: late completion/non-performance/delays to the archaeological programme
6. Extras: publication costs/storage grants/special conservation work/displays/ receptions and publicity
7. Compensation: tenant's rights/grazing/loss of crops/damage to land drains, fences, access, etc.
8. Reinstatement: compaction/surfaces/imported aggregate, etc.

Developer's assistance

It is often cost-effective for developers to offer assistance in kind, especially things that an archaeological contractor would probably have to subcontract anyway. Lighting, fencing/hoarding, shoring, sheet piling, spoil removal and effluent disposal (ground water, chemical toilet waste, rubbish etc.), the provision of facilities (e.g. shelters, offices, toilets) and plant (e.g. mechanical excavators, pumps, dumper-trucks) might be considered. Agreed forms of assistance should be specified.

Site condition before and after licence period

Agreement should be reached on the site's condition when taken over by the archaeological contractor (e.g. cleared of buildings, levelled, topsoil removed) and on its return to the owner and/or developer at the conclusion of work (e.g. wholly/partially backfilled, degree of compaction, topsoil correctly replaced, resurfaced). It is good practice to photograph the site before and after archaeological work.

Arrangements for inspection and monitoring

The developer or his representative must have the right to inspect the site and the archaeological activities at any time. Where works are carried out in fulfilment of a planning consent or Scheduled Monument Consent some monitoring of the progress and standard of the archaeological work will often be required. This is almost always in the interest of both parties: in many cases such monitoring would be undertaken by the county archaeological officer or an EH/CADW/Historic Scotland (HS) inspector. In some cases, all parties concerned may agree to engage an independent archaeological consultant to monitor the work at the expense of one or more of the parties (this work would be the subject of a separate contract). Exact arrangements for such monitoring should be set out in the specification, but the contract must always state arrangements for access to the site by the person undertaking the monitoring.

Security

Agreement should be reached on responsibility for and the nature of site security, given that sites may be in joint occupation. The following aspects might be taken into account:

1. Boundary features, e.g. fences, hedges
2. Stock fences
3. Hoardings
4. Gates and entrances (locks, bolts, availability of keys, etc.)
5. Lighting
6. Temporary trench protection
7. Public viewing areas and platforms
8. Offices, stores and displays
9. Mobile equipment and vehicles
10. Shoring.

Size of team, safety and work practices

In some cases the number of people (including visitors) permitted on site may be limited. General safety considerations will be an implied term in most archaeological contracts, although reference may be made to areas of responsibility. Special consideration may be given to matters such as:

1. Keeping paths and roads clean
2. Noise pollution (night operation of machinery)
3. Support for surrounding buildings
4. Reductions in ground-water levels
5. Silts and sludge entering drains
6. Special shoring.

Insurance and liabilities

Most projects will require various types of insurance (e.g. public liability, employer's liability, plant hire, special conditions/equipment). Limits and areas of liability may usefully be specified in the contract.

Assignment, subletting and subcontracting

The extent to which these aspects need to be controlled varies greatly by project. These matters should be dealt with in the contract. Subcontracting will often feature in major projects and might include fencing, earthmoving, dewatering, geophysical and academic inputs among other things.

Change of site ownership

On occasions, during the execution of an archaeological project the freehold, leasehold or other interest in the site has changed, thereby necessitating renewed negotiations at inopportune times, at considerable extra cost, and with potentially serious consequences. It is better if the terms of contract can be tied to the site.

Termination or suspension of construction work

If the archaeological organisation has the power to stop construction work that is putting in peril archaeological remains it is important to specify exactly who can issue a stop command; and the consequent procedures. This section of a contract would normally conform with and be cross-referenced to, for example, a development agreement.

Termination or suspension of archaeological work

The possibility that one or other party to a contract may wish to terminate or suspend work must be considered along with the financial and timetabling implications. The most likely causes of such an eventuality include:

1. Little of archaeological importance being found
2. Major change in development plans and/or changing threat to the site
3. Land-use restrictions.

Publication and publicity

The need for publications of various sorts, films, information packs, reports for the client, and data to update the Sites and Monuments Record should be reflected in the contract and specifically in the project design. Publicity is a special problem with much archaeological work and requires careful control so that neither party to the contract has cause for complaint. Special care is needed in the case of work funded from charitable donations.

Arbitration and settlement of disputes

Provision should be made for any dispute that arises to be settled by a third party.

Monitoring and tracking

Four principal kinds of monitoring can be identified in archaeology today:

1. Curator monitoring
2. Client monitoring (including monitoring by a consultant acting as agent)
3. Project tracking (i.e. internal monitoring)
4. Third-party monitoring.

The last is rare; such monitoring mainly relates to cases of dispute or disagreement. Project tracking is something that organisations should undertake as part of their internal project management system. Both curator and client monitoring usually involve regular liaison with contractors and periodic inspections of ongoing work.

All monitoring has three facets: observation, recording, and reporting. The three elements most likely to be the subject of attention are: performance, time and cost. Assessment of performance includes its quality and is measured with reference to the expectations included in the project design. Time is a measure of progress and can be gauged with reference to milestones identified at the project planning stage. Cost can be calculated in real terms but is more likely to be measured as the proportion of the budget actually used.

Reports from monitoring and tracking exercises give insights into project progress. Decisions can be made about any changes necessary to keep the project on target.

Confidentiality

As archaeological work is brought further forward in the development process so the question of confidentiality becomes more important. Archaeological assessments and field evaluations may be carried out before land is purchased or options exercised. In such circumstances archaeological information has financial implications as well as academic value. Information is power: even when the outline of a scheme is publicly known there may be tactical reasons for making technical information available in a predetermined order and under controlled circumstances, as for example in a consolidated report containing information on all technical studies undertaken. Sometimes the archaeologist may be caught between the client's need to work or negotiate with the archaeological information generated by initial investigations kept in-house, and the wider professional obligations to make results available. Given that archaeologists have been notoriously bad about making publicly available the results of their work the idea that everything should be disclosed immediately seems rather hypocritical. Equally though, improvements on past performance must be sought and item 27 of the IFA's *Code of Approved Practice for the Regulation of Contractual Arrangements in Field Archaeology* suggests six months as a reasonable period after which access to primary records should be allowed. Thought may be given to exactly which elements of a project are confidential: that a given kind of archaeological operation has taken place at a particular locality is unlikely to be privileged information, although exact details of the findings may be sensitive. Throughout, a pragmatic line agreeable to all parties concerned is needed.

CHAPTER 17

FROM ASSESSMENT TO CHARACTERISATION: CURRENT APPROACHES TO UNDERSTANDING THE HISTORIC ENVIRONMENT

Graham Fairclough

INTRODUCTION

The archaeological profession has changed enormously since the first edition of this book in 1993. In particular, there have been immense changes to how archaeological resource management (ARM) is carried out in the UK, and how it fits in with other types of environmental and heritage management. In 1993, PPG 16 was relatively new and its impact was only just beginning to be fully felt. The thinking-through of the implications for ARM of sustainable development had hardly started, and in some quarters even the idea that ARM needed to be more closely integrated to building conservation, let alone to nature conservation and landscape appreciation, was still novel. The issue of how to make ARM more socially inclusive had been anticipated to some extent by 1993, but its importance has grown in a much more far-reaching way than was foreseen. Social relevance and inclusion, and community participation, are now much more commonly found among the stated goals of ARM, which influences how decisions are taken about which parts of the material remains of the past are significant and why.

Moreover, as the terminology used above shows, our vocabulary and concepts have also changed since that used in the first edition. The archaeological resource is now usually referred to as the 'historic environment' in recognition of the much wider breadth (chronological, thematic and formal) that it is now understood to have. An archaeological site is now more likely to mean a whole landscape or a complete city. It could just as easily be a 1980s missile silo as a Bronze Age barrow. It may not even be wholly material – we might also now include anthropological, phenomenological or experiential aspects – Sites and Monuments Records (SMRs) have become Historic Environment Records (HERs) in name as well as hope. The development of ARM within the discipline can also be measured by comparing the size and character of this book's bibliography with that of the first edition. Papers and books on ARM theory were then rare, whereas now they are numerous. The bibliographic field is still growing, in maturity and theoretical consciousness as well as in numbers.

Archaeological resource managers now worry about local values and local distinctiveness as well as national importance. They are concerned with overall character and perception as well as with the materiality of objects and sites. Context, both geographical and thematic, is much more to the forefront, and in particular the context of the observer, the person who is making an assessment, is increasingly recognised. It is rarely now enough simply to say that an archaeological site, for example, is important because of its own intrinsic attributes as a repository of knowledge about the past: its other attributes, social benefits and affordances need to be considered as well.

Although some of these changes were predicted in the first edition of this book (e.g. Parker Pearson 1993), this new edition nevertheless describes a different world. Perhaps of no first edition chapter is this truer than of Chapter 17, 'The Assessment of Field Remains' (Startin 1993), where Startin described the beginnings of the Monuments Protection Programme (MPP) and the new rigorous methods necessary for the MPP to proceed. More than ten years later, the MPP can be judged on its achievements and seen clearly not just as a scheduling programme (which it never was solely), nor even just as the national (English) management-led review of the archaeological resource that it was designed to be. It was one of the harbingers of a more ambitious and theoretically informed approach to ARM, and a main contributor to the unified approach to the protection and management of the historic environment that was wished for by some contributors to the first edition (notably Breeze 1993) and which has been gaining acceptance over the past few years. Such an approach now appears to many as a serious prospect for the future in the context of government intentions set out in 2003–4 in the consultation paper *Protecting our Historic Environment: Making the System Work Better* and the decision document, *Looking Forward to the Past: The Future for Heritage Protection* (DCMS 2003c, 2004g).

Startin's chapter was at the time absolutely up to date, indeed innovative and ahead of its time. Since then, in the most recent years alone, we have seen the Historic Environment (Heritage) Review that produced *Power of Place*, and the government's response to it in *The Historic Environment: A Force for our Future* (EH 2000a; DCMS and DTLRG 2001), with a similar document in Wales (WAG 2003). Most recently, in England, there has been an important and far-reaching government consultation, already mentioned, on a new unified approach to designation (DCMS 2004g). By 2004, around the time that this second edition was being finalised, a quite different account was thus developing of how we approach the question of importance. This present chapter therefore takes a different direction to that of the first edition. Startin's chapter described a search for rigorous and repeatable, transparent and transferable ways to evaluate or assess the field monuments of England in order to select the most important, that is 'assessment'. The equivalent search today is for comprehensive and inclusive ways to improve holistic understanding of the whole of the historic environment, that is 'characterisation' (EH web page 2003c; Fairclough 2003a, 2003b, 2003c; Darlington 2003; Clark *et al.* 2004).

This new chapter was written shortly after the incorporation of the MPP into a new unified designation department in English Heritage (EH). This organisational change, mirrored by the creation of a small group to promote characterisation, was intended as one of the steps towards a new heritage designation system. The new system was intended to be founded not only on many aspects of MPP theory and practice but also on broader shifts in thinking on issues such as local distinctiveness, sustainability and integrated conservation (EH *et al.* 1996; EH 1997a, 1997b; HS 2002; Clark 1999; Countryside Commission *et al.* 1997; Countryside Agency *et al.* 2001). This chapter will try to summarise some of these changes.

Like Startin's chapter, this new edition is a view from England. Different practices and customs naturally exist in the other countries of the UK, but basic ideas, philosophy and objectives are largely similar across the whole of the UK. The evident acceleration in the divergence of practice between the constituent parts of the UK is another area of change since 1993, especially since the establishment of EH and its siblings in Scotland, Wales and Northern Ireland. This also reflects the establishment of the Scottish Parliament and the Welsh Assembly and the quite different governance arrangements in Man and (especially) Northern Ireland. Yet, despite this, ARM in the UK's countries still mainly shares common legislation and practice, and these countries are still more closely aligned to each other than to other European countries. 'National' in this chapter is nevertheless used (subject to context) to mean English, or Welsh, rather than UK, practice.

One example concerns the practice of historic landscape characterisation (HLC) developed in England (Clark *et al.* 2004), for example (see below). After its first implementation in Cornwall (Herring 1998), HLC was adopted in modified form in Scotland as Historic Land Use Assessment (Dyson-Bruce *et al.* 1999; Dixon and Hingley 2002; Macinnes 2002). In Northern Ireland it is being considered as a way of adding historic depth to an existing, largely non-historic, landscape character assessment, and is perhaps soon to be carried out in the Isle of Man. In Wales, it has influenced some of the characterisation methods used as part of the register-based characterisation programme in Wales (see web pages of the Welsh Trusts, or CADW 2003), but otherwise different approaches are utilised (CADW *et al.* 1998, 2001, 2003).

THE ASSESSMENT OF FIELD REMAINS

'The Assessment of Field Remains' (Chapter 17, first edition) was partly a reflection of widespread concerns coming to a head early in the 1980s about the scope, comprehensiveness and defensibility of the English part of the Schedule of Ancient Monuments. Consensus had grown that the schedule was too small in relation to, and more importantly that it was unrepresentative of, the national resource. *England's Archaeological Resource* put statistical flesh on this perception (EH 1984) and it was accepted that more rigorous, transparent and consistent value-judgements than hitherto were required to define the nationally important part of the archaeological resource that was eligible for inclusion on the schedule. Startin's chapter therefore described the institutional and historical context for these, notably the establishment in 1986 of the MPP. It was written at the end of the first phase of the MPP at a point when the MPP's theory and its basic evaluation method had been defined, but while its full application for actual scheduling was still in its early stages. Ten years on, in 2004, scheduling was no longer carried out as part of this dedicated programme, but operated in tandem with the listing of historic buildings and the registration of parks and gardens as part of EH's integrated 'Designation Team' established in 2002 as a transitional step towards the fully integrated 'list' envisaged by the Heritage Protection Review (DCMS 2003c).

Between 1990 and 2002 the monument evaluation method that was described in 'The Assessment of Field Remains' was used in England to drive forward an intensive twelve-year programme of new scheduling and revision of the pre-existing schedule. The very unevenly documented 1986 Schedule of *c.* 12,500 monuments had grown up largely ad hoc since 1882, when the first Ancient Monuments Act listed 68 monuments in a schedule attached to the Act (26 in England, 21 in Scotland, 18 in Ireland and 3 in Wales; see Chapter 5). This original schedule had been expanded by 2002 into a modern schedule of nearly 20,000 entries (Scheduled Monuments) that contained over 32,000 defined and separately recorded archaeological sites, or archaeological items. Nearly three-quarters of these 20,000 entries are modern well-documented schedulings using the full MPP standards of map and text documentation (Nieke 1997).

Only about half of the 14,000 or so schedulings documented by the MPP, however, were based on the assessment techniques described in the first edition of this book (and in Darvill *et al.* 1987). Those techniques were designed for the comparative assessment of relatively straightforward archaeological sites, termed 'single monuments', such as long barrows, stone circles, hill-forts, moats or monastic sites. For such types of monument, relatively good data existed in county SMRs, which, when marshalled within a framework of newly written 'Monument Class Descriptions', was sufficient for the operation of the assessment method. Between 1990 and 1992, over 230 monument classes were evaluated nationally using these techniques and lists were produced of those sites which, after field inspection, were deemed likely to be eligible for scheduling as monuments of national importance. Scottish and Welsh scheduling programmes during the 1990s were, as a matter of national policy, not founded principally on a dedicated scheduling unit, but kept scheduling as only one activity of a multifaceted inspectorate. They also drew material more directly from traditional types of area-based or thematic archaeological survey. We do not have a clear assessment of the similarities and differences between the schedule in these three countries (or indeed in Northern Ireland or the Isle of Man) but it would make a useful subject for innumerable Ph.D. theses.

In England, as Startin's original chapter anticipated, different methods of evaluation were soon needed for the many areas of the archaeological resource where existing SMR information was inadequate or non-existent. At the same time, perspectives of what the archaeological resource comprised continued to expand. People's view of the scale and character of the resource, and of the best way to look after it, changed after 1990 in the light of PPG 16 (DoE 1990a) and, later, of the MARS project (Darvill and Fulton 1998). New ideas also emerged about the aim and purpose of heritage management and its wider social context, of sustainability (Countryside Commission *et al.* 1993; EH *et al.* 1996; EH 1997a). In time, many aspects of the assessment or evaluation technique described by Startin were amalgamated with the wider ideas of characterisation that were emerging during the 1990s, and which can be said to be now a dominant strand of new thinking in heritage management. While this chapter therefore begins with Startin's original paper, it also sets out to describe and examine the development of different ideas about value and significance, sensitivity and character, and indeed some of the fundamental purposes of heritage management, that have arisen between 1993 and 2003.

THE 1993 STARTING POINT

Perhaps the biggest change since 1993 is that there is now a wider perspective on value, and a more focused appreciation and justification of it. The principal starting point of Startin's chapter was the concept of archaeological national importance predominantly defined (because of the context of scheduling) by relatively narrow issues of traditional archaeological, or evidential and informational, importance. Because of the effect of the inherited 1983 non-statutory criteria for scheduling (DoE 1983, 1990a Annex), most emphasis in the early MPP procedures was on the potential of field remains for information gain using archaeological techniques.

The question 'why are archaeological remains important' was answered thus: 'principal(ly) . . . for the information they contain about the past'. Startin of course fully recognised that other values – 'wider public interest' – sit among these, but in 1993 their more detailed examination still lay in the future.

The original chapter, reflecting its historic context, focused on the attempt to decide management and protection priorities by establishing relative importance. This process always, sometimes correctly, carried an intention to include some monuments and exclude others. It was all about judgement (professional judgement, structured within a framework of criteria and classification-led systems) with the implication that the judgement to be exercised was that of archaeologists. All these issues remain important, and Startin's 1993 chapter should still be required reading for archaeological curators and students. Its discussion, however, is now part of a wider concept of information, understanding and awareness-raising that is designed to help a wider range of people, from other professions to the local community, to align archaeological values and character with other values and benefits. In currently emerging theory, they are accompanied by methods of prioritisation based not just on relative importance but on aspects such as sensitivity, vulnerability and the capacity to absorb change. This is furthermore a part of a general expansion of ARM ambitions, so that more than previously ARM seeks to manage change everywhere rather than merely passively to protect selected highlights.

In part this arises from a recognition that the most important places (e.g. the White Tower, Stonehenge) are not always those that need the most care, and that sometimes lesser sites might be higher management priorities, and that different communities or parts of society will have different views of priority. There is also a debate about local distinctiveness, reflecting that monuments of supposed local importance may be more important in their own context, for example to community perception or to sense of place, than nationally important monuments in that area. At the end of the argument, national importance is an issue of thematic comparison, related to communities of *interest*, whereas local importance is an issue of spatial context and relevance, related to communities of *place*.

WHY ARE ARCHAEOLOGICAL REMAINS IMPORTANT?

It is just as necessary now as it was in 1993 to be clear about what we mean by 'important'. Archaeologists, as mentioned above, have mainly taken this to mean academic value, or evidential value, but other values, such as education, recreation, symbolism or amenity, have always been recognised, though perhaps not explicitly enough. The principal change in thinking during the 1990s, perhaps, was just this point – that the other values existing alongside academic values have been promoted from the second rank and put on a more equal footing for archaeologists and other heritage managers. The most recent and publicly accessible statements of this multiplicity of value are in *Power of Place* and *The Historic Environment: A Force for our Future*, in the consultation preceding *Power of Place* (HER 2000), in their Welsh and Scottish equivalents (WAG 2003; HS 2002 respectively), and (perhaps the most concise yet detailed and influential) in *Sustaining the Historic Environment* (EH 1997a).

There are some dangers in this for archaeology. Notably there is a risk that the scientific and historical roots of the archaeological discipline may be undermined by too focused an application on managing change in the present day. As is sometimes said of PPG 16-driven excavation, the practice of archaeology might lose its roots as a method to find out what happened in the past and merely act as a way of clearing sites of encumbrances. These various aims need not be mutually exclusive, however. In practice, distinctive archaeologists' perspectives on all of them are developing, for instance on time-depth in townscape, on the use of the past to create personal, regional and national identity, or on the central contribution of change to landscape character and to the historic environment that we have inherited. A modern consensus is forming that archaeology not only studies the past but also explains the present and helps to shape the future – that it is a socially embedded practical discipline as well as an academic pursuit (e.g. Bloemers 2002) – 'applied archaeology'.

There also arose during the 1990s a much greater awareness of the need for integrated working across the whole historic environment sector, and between it and other environmental sectors, and gradually too a recognition of this by other sectors (Macinnes and Wickham Jones 1992; Berry and Brown 1995; Grenville 1999; Palang and Fry 2003; Cooke 1999). All these ideas travelled on the sustainable development bandwagon. Now integration is being taken even further, so that environmental concerns are routinely accepted as being hand-in-hand with social and economic concerns, as the tripod of sustainable development, even if practice (and implementation) too often trails behind the theory and the aspiration (EU 2000; CoE 2000; DoE 1994; Fairclough and Rippon 2002).

THE MONUMENTS PROTECTION PROGRAMME

The first phase of the MPP operated very successfully, applying the techniques and procedures that were described in the first edition of this chapter (also Darvill *et al.* 1987) to well-defined and discrete components of the archaeological resource. The resource had been subdivided into monument classes, for each of which a Monument Class Description was produced to frame class discrimination and monument assessment. In this sequential system, the Monument Class Description (MCDs) was the key to subsequent SMR-based evaluation. They were drawn from a synthesis of current knowledge and are therefore always provisional, subject to change as new data is recorded, and more importantly, as further research and synthesis is undertaken. As well as having being used for the 1989–92 SMR-based MPP evaluations, the MCDs remain a critical framework for taking decisions about scheduling and in many cases they are the only consistent description of monument types. Most of the MCDs are available on the EH web page, and are often used as the starting point for purposes other than scheduling, for example by contractors to inform PPG 16-driven evaluation work.

The SMR-based MPP evaluations had been carried out at county level usually by County Archaeologists and their staff with the assistance of the MPP. A monument discrimination scoring system was devised by the MPP to support professional judgements on the national importance of each monument class, putting them into a consistent context. This was an inclusive approach that was also capable of providing assessments of importance for monuments of more local importance, and which can be extended to new monuments as they are discovered. The evaluations took place as a single desk-based operation, carried out over a relatively short space of time mainly between 1989 and 1992. This gave a national overview as well as a county snapshot. The product was sets of SMR evaluations for most counties, and sometimes for other administrative units such as National Parks or topographic units such as Salisbury Plain. These evaluations contain site-by-site assessments for all classes of monuments for which MCDs had been prepared (by now *c.* 235), and include widely agreed defined thresholds of national importance. They are held in SMRs as working documents.

These scored and ranked evaluated lists of SMR records compiled in the early 1990s have been the basic raw material for at least half of the MPP scheduling action since 1990, and until about 1995, in the MPP's second phase, scheduling was the programme's main activity. The existence of the list has allowed scheduling work by MPP archaeologists to be pre-planned and to maintain a degree of consistency hitherto unachieved since 1882. It allowed scheduling to operate flexibly in relation to geography, theme, risk, threat and priority, while still ensuring that individual scheduling decisions sit in a common framework, guided by the 1983 non-statutory criteria but with a sensible extra layer of professional judgement exercised in the field by MPP archaeologists.

The 1990s, however, saw a great expansion – the word 'explosion' is not a wild exaggeration – away from the original MPP county evaluation lists into wider fields of the resource. Increasingly, thematic evaluation took a larger share of MPP resources. From about 1994–5, the balance between the two stages of MPP work shifted so far that the period 1995–2002 can be defined as a distinct (third) stage of the MPP (EH 1997b), many of whose ideas now form the basis for current approaches to characterisation.

This period of thematic evaluation tackled the more complex and less well-documented parts of the archaeological resource where existing SMR data was inadequate. Poorly recorded or little understood monument classes formed a large part – perhaps 50 per cent or more – of the resource. These were usually classes that until recently were the most under-represented in the schedule precisely because limited knowledge made it difficult to demonstrate national importance and thus to justify designation. Special techniques and programmes of evaluation were needed at a national level, taking account where necessary of regional diversity, and these were developed from about 1993, in the first instance for monuments of industry.

The procedures and methods of this National Evaluation follow a similar approach to the SMR-based evaluations, including classification and characterisation (step 1), data gathering (both broad and detailed, steps 2 and 3 respectively), and assessment and evaluation (step 4). They have been described by Stocker (1995a). The stepped approach was applied not to individual monuments in isolation but nationally to individual industries or activities (e.g. coal mining, water supply) or to broad themes (e.g. medieval settlement), thus ensuring a broad supporting framework for all judgements. In some cases (e.g. twentieth-century military), existing levels of data were so low that data gathering had to precede even initial classification. Between 1993 and 2002 (EH 1998, 2000b), MPP carried out National Evaluation of this sort in several major areas. Three – industrial, twentieth-century military and settlement – will be briefly discussed here to give an idea of MPP's work.

Industrial

It was in the industrial sphere (characterised by large numbers of surviving sites but highly variable databases) that MPP first developed its new National Evaluation technique based on ordered sequences of data-gathering, synthesis and peer-aided judgement (Stocker 1995a). The MPP industrial sub-programme had a wide scope, using a modified version of Raistrick's 1972 classification of materials and process (Cranstone 1995), based on categories such as extractive, inorganic manufacture or power and utilities. For each separate industry within these themes (e.g. lead mining in 'extractive industry') a 'step 1' report was prepared that was functionally analogous to an MCD but very different and more ambitious in format and scope. It set out the main stages of the industry's historical and technological development, established chronology, regional diversity, terminology and defined components and features.

This was the first time that such an overview with the emphasis firmly on the material remains had been produced for most industries. It was produced in consultation with specialist study groups and individual experts at national, regional and local level, and using SMR data and knowledge where available. In a similar way to the MCDs for single monuments, these step 1 reports provide the essential framework for site-specific assessment. In particular, they guided two stages of data collection: the production of a representative shortlist for further study of known sites of each industry (step 2), and initial site assessment and simple low-level surveys of individual sites (step 3), also with iterative consultations with experts and interest groups. The results were also fed back into the SMR system for application on a wide range of heritage management fields because scheduling, although of course a significant use, is by no means the only use for this data.

In order to move from data collection to decision-making, the step 3 results were synthesised and a broad view was taken on importance, significance, technological representivity, rarity, regionality and other aspects. All assessed sites were reviewed, graded and – most importantly – their current uses and likely future management needs

Figure 17.1. Industrial remains provided the first test of EH's national evaluation techniques. The illustration shows a view across the excavated remains of Charles MacIntosh's 1825 mill in Manchester, the world's first commercial rubber factory. Later additions to the site survive to the rear. *(© Oxford Archaeological Unit; Photo: Ian Miller)*

were assessed. The step 4 reports set out this final assessment as a statement of EH policy for protecting and managing the particular industry's remains. Each complex, site or building on the step 3 list is considered in terms of a range of management options, and the most appropriate one is identified. These options include scheduling (or descheduling, usually in favour of listing), listing or regrading, Conservation Areas, management by PPG 16, recording before loss or the need for more research before a sound decision was possible. In this way, scheduling was reserved for those cases where protection and passing on to the future in a largely unchanged state (in an oversimplified word, as a 'monument') was the aim (rather than where protection could be achieved by modification, adaptive reuse or conversion), or where significance could be 'converted' to knowledge (e.g. by recording) before being transferred to the future.

The MPP industrial programme produced over thirty separate step 1 reports (e.g. for tin mining, lead extraction, coal mining, brass production, alum manufacture, electricity generation, water treatment and supply, lime burning, stone quarrying, gas, oil: see bibliography in EH 2000b). All are available in relevant SMRs, with copies being held by the NMR, the Ironbridge Institute for Industrial Archaeology, and the CBA. About one-third of these have so far been taken through to step 4, making management recommendations for about 2,000 sites: of these several hundred have already led to scheduling or listing action. Perhaps the main long-term practical use of step 4 reports, however, goes beyond this initial use. The MPP was always intended to be just as much an SMR-enhancement programme as a designation review. The industrial step reports (and all MPP national evaluation reports) provide a substantial new component for SMRs to use in development control work arising from PPG 16 and in historic environment management work more generally. They will also come to have a growing role in educational and outreach work. In this way, such wide-ranging overviews of the resource move close to being characterisation projects in the sense that will be discussed later: not simply the justification for occasional designations, but practical and accessible information for understanding and managing the whole of the historic environment.

Twentieth-century military

Very similar approaches have been equally successful in the even newer field of mid- and late-twentieth-century war heritage, the archaeological remains of the Second World War and Cold War. A few examples of this part of the archaeological resource have been included in the schedule for many years since at least the 1970s, but perception of its value to the community at large, and public support for its protection, increased rapidly with the various fiftieth and sixtieth anniversaries. For many people, the Second World War was moving from the realm of personal experience or the memory of parents, into the domain of history. It is now seen as requiring physical commemoration, not only by purpose-built war memorials, as formerly, but by retaining some of the physical legacy of the war itself, places that touched the lives of parents and grandparents. At the same time, major changes in national defence policy because of the perceived end of a war that never happened, the Cold War, have led to the sale of large numbers of military installations. This massive disposal of land (which inevitably attracted the obvious analogy to Henry VIII's sale of the

Figure 17.2. Concrete remains of the Second World War in Scapa Flow. These too require archaeological evaluation.

monasteries or Mrs Thatcher's sale of the accumulated assets of post-1945 nationalised industries) led to a search for new uses or for ways to liquidate financial value by redevelopment. Decisions on the best future for individual sites required a sound basis for deciding which sites should be protected and how they, and the others, should be managed.

Evaluating this part of the archaeological resource presented some new practical difficulties for the MPP process (Dobinson *et al.* 1997; EH 1998, EH 2003d). First was the problem of the sheer scale of the resource. Because it was very recent in date, and because it still mainly existed in the relatively conservative framework of MoD land management, there was a high level of survival of Cold War remains. Second World War remains have fared less well, with less than 10 per cent survival in some classes after only fifty-five years. The document-led approach that was adopted by the MPP and later by other parts of the UK, however, allowed survival rates to be seen in context. Contemporary documents survive so well that it is possible to reconstruct complete, original populations, and thus (unusually for ARM which normally operates in ignorance of such matters) to measure survival of the resource against its original extent. A further difficulty was that much of the twentieth-century military resource had never been adequately studied or recorded by archaeologists or historians, and even simple classifications and inventories were lacking. By their character, Cold War monuments are also unusually difficult to classify in terms of the overlap between listing and scheduling regimes, and beyond that, in terms of appropriate sustainable conservation strategies. Finally, especially but not exclusively for early 1940s defensive structures built in a hurry, there is the ephemerality issue – unusual and problematic questions inevitably arise when the long-term management of structures that were built for very short life-spans is considered.

To deal with these problems, MPP in collaboration with the CBA undertook comprehensive assessments of the recent defence heritage. This was aimed at identifying, recording and evaluating at strategic level all monuments relating to the Second World War defence heritage (Dobinson 1998). Reports based on archive sources held at the Public Record Office were completed for ten major categories of twentieth-century military monument, including 1940s anti-invasion defences, Second World War bombing decoy sites, anti-V-bomb sites, the Operation Overlord preparatory sites for the invasion of Europe, radar, civil defences and others categories. Further reports provided annotated handlists of military training bases, R&D and experimental sites and POW camps. The archive-based reports are substantial documents based on the analysis of comprehensive defence records, containing a high level of historical and technical detail and precise geographical data, and they have been circulated to all SMRs and the NMR (Dobinson 1996–2000). The series has since been expanded to cover Wales, Scotland and Northern Ireland (Redfern 1998). A series of books using the research is also being published and is attracting the anticipated wide audience (Dobinson 2000, 2001, forthcoming).

These document-based reports follow the industrial archaeology Step 1 reports in reviewing knowledge of each class of monument, including information on typology, chronological framework and – for most classes – location. Rapid follow-up work using the most recent aerial photography established maximum levels of survival for several categories (anti-aircraft artillery, bombing decoys, coast artillery and radar), thus enabling targeted field survey (Anderton and Schofield 1999; Schofield 2001, 2002). Given that very little survives for most of these classes, the monuments that merit some protection are generally self-selecting. There is sometimes greater difficulty, for example with the large numbers of pillboxes that survive. For these 1939–40 anti-invasion defences, however, the CBA's Defence of Britain Project database provided both classification and inventory of the seventy types of anti-invasion defence structures built during the Second World War. The MPP adopted an area-based approach that prioritises the management of the best surviving clusters, notably at defended nodes or focal points. For the Cold War, the MPP used research by the former RCHME that defined thirty-five monument classes from the V-bomber bases and missile sites to defence research sites, regional seats of government and food stores (Cocroft and Thomas 2003).

With these topics, ARM comes almost fully up to date, into areas well within living memory – and areas that are still highly contested. Startin's 1993 chapter used the example of then recently excavated Nazi bunkers in Berlin, brought to public notice and controversy as a consequence of the collapse of the Iron Curtain, to raise the new issues of perception and the difficulties of recent heritage. This was just a slight foretaste of the current position (e.g. Schofield and Anderton 2000; Uzzell 1998). When this chapter's first draft was written, for example, monument types that have just been evaluated by the MPP – Cold War USAF and RAF bases in England – were back on the TV screen as B52 bombers took off from them to bomb Baghdad. Living Heritage?

Settlement

Much of the MPP's work aimed to give a wider holistic context to specific aspects of the heritage, and this is particularly true of rural settlement and fields. The settlement and field patterns of England have long been recognised as a rich palimpsest produced principally by cultural rather than natural factors over a period of several thousand years. We need to understand this patterning before conservation can be sensitive to the crucial, but sometimes subtle, regional and local distinctions (Stocker 1995b). Central to this work was a project carried out by the University of Durham to map the diversity of settlement in England, and thus to provide the wider context for period-specific evaluation projects. This project defined the main characteristics of settlement and mapped their distribution, based on the distinction between nucleated and dispersed settlement. The result – the *English Heritage Atlas of Rural Settlement* (Roberts and Wrathmell 2000) – shows a patterned spectrum of settlement types across the country, from areas at one extreme where almost all settlements are nucleated to those where almost all are dispersed, with a full range of combinations in between. In general terms, this has allowed the country to be seen as three broad provinces (a central province characterised by villages and open fields, and two provinces to the south and east and to the north and west with entirely different patterns of mainly dispersed settlement and anciently enclosed fields) that are historically long-standing, being traceable to at least the late Saxon period and providing a solid basis for more wide-ranging study of landscape and settlement history (Roberts and Wrathmell 2002).These provinces each contain great variety, and can be subdivided into twenty-five 'sub-provinces' and 180 'local regions'.

The Settlement Atlas provided a new framework for MPP-type evaluation and for landscape understanding and management. The division of the country into the Roberts and Wrathmell settlement zones allowed the MPP to select nearly 2,000 medieval and later settlement sites as candidates for scheduling. The ability to compare like-with-like on a regional scale led to more easily defensible selections.

In addition, the atlas defined regional diversity (as did the industrial work and the Historic Landscape Characterisation projects, see below) not in opposition to national importance (the dichotomy of local or national), but as an aspect of it. This view acknowledges that something can be nationally important, perhaps irrespective of its inherent qualities, simply because it contributed to the nationally important matter of preserving local or regional distinctiveness. It is a task of national importance to maintain local and regional distinctiveness, therefore sites of local or regional significance can be nationally important precisely for that reason. Further work in each local region could help in understanding the development of the distinctive settlement patterns which have evolved, for example, in understanding the distinctions between different field patterns in the Central Midlands and in East Anglia (e.g. Hall 2001; Anderton and Went 2002; Martin and Satchell forthcoming). The particular use of the atlas to inform scheduling decisions, though valuable, should not obscure the wider significance of this, as other, MPP projects. Many other aspects of ARM and indeed archaeological research can be based on the work.

WHY DO WE SCHEDULE – WHEN DO WE NEED TO SCHEDULE (OR LIST)?

Assessment (i.e. demonstrating national importance) was a key issue of the MPP's early work, and is central to scheduling and all other designations, but it is only half the ARM story. The MPP system came to recognise two stages in the designation decision-making process – a first stage of determining national importance (or not), and a second stage of deciding whether scheduling is the most effective (or even an appropriate) way to ensure that this importance survives. This involves asking and answering the question, not 'is this monument important enough to schedule?', but 'is the SMC regime [that scheduling would necessarily impose], necessary and appropriate?'

A contrasting view is that scheduling should be simply a certificate of importance or an award of merit, to be applied as automatically and comprehensively as possible to all nationally important monuments and areas. Indeed, before 1981 that had more or less been the aim, even if resources forbade achieving it. Before 1981 (when the Ancient Monuments and Archaeological Areas Act 1979 came into force), the law gave scheduling no real teeth, in the sense that it introduced no protective regulation other than an obligation to give three months' notice of works to a Scheduled Ancient Monument, which could (but might not) trigger the introduction of a stronger restriction called an 'Interim Preservation Notice' (IPN), itself needing to be confirmed as a full 'Preservation Order' (PO). IPNs and POs were rarely issued, not least because they involved two complex and bureaucratic administrative processes, and required rapid action, and a strength of will, that were not always present in the civil service administration in the 1950s, 1960s and 1970s. But the important point here is that this system of confirmation by PO was in effect the second test as defined above, separate to the decision to schedule – that is, scheduling in itself did not automatically 'protect' a monument.

The 1979 Act changed this radically. At the time, the response of most archaeologists was simply to welcome SMC as a stronger, modern consent system, one that actually offered the capacity to protect Scheduled Monuments (SMs, not SAMs – the 1979 Act also dropped the word 'ancient' from Section 1). In truth, however (although not widely recognised until PPG 16 and the work of MPP after about 1990), the new SMC procedure changed the character of scheduling itself, not just of the control procedures. The obligation to obtain SMC pushed together into a single stage all the previous decision stages, that is, both scheduling and a decision on how strong a restriction would be imposed. Scheduling became an inevitable trigger for the need to obtain SMC when work was proposed, no matter how minor that work's impact would be. The second test became combined with the first.

This confusion of scheduling with its control regime (SMC), conflating a statement that something has a certain level of importance with a decision about the best way to manage that importance, was in some ways helpful, however. It clarified the purpose of scheduling, and allowed the MPP from the early 1990s to begin to make a distinction between designation and management by introducing a formal second stage to the decision-making process of scheduling (e.g. the step 4 of the industrial evaluation process described above). This second stage was based on the appropriateness of SMC as a management tool and on the question of whether SMC is the best form of protection for every nationally important monument, in the light of aspirations for its future management. When appropriate, the MPP advised the Secretary of State to use discretion over when to schedule nationally important sites and when not to do so. The listing of buildings had never exercised this sort of discretion, but for scheduling the existence of discretion based on appropriateness was tested by the Rose Theatre case, and upheld by the High Court. This idea of a double test of whether a site should be scheduled sat at the heart of the government's 2003 proposal for a unified designation in England that would separate the decision to list from the decision of what level of control, if any, to impose (DCMS 2003c).

The MPP's criteria for this second test of appropriateness were not fully explicit or transparent, because the most important aspects of the test are flexibility and professional judgement. They can best be explained by offering examples with reference to alternatives to SMC protection regimes.

SMC and the planning process

PPG 16 introduced into the planning process a higher level of control over most known, knowable (through pre-determined field evaluation) or predicted archaeological deposits and sites that were threatened by development (in the legal sense of this as defined by the Town and Country Planning Acts). In practice, of course, these controls have largely leant towards recording not preservation, although PPG 16 clearly set physical preservation as the first preferred option. For any site, therefore, PPG 16 rendered SMC control either less necessary (for example where the response to threat was usually to excavate the site anyway, which the planning system could as easily deliver) or actually undesirable (because for some sites it led to fragmented and uncoordinated decision-making). Few would argue that the City of London, from the top of the newest tower to the bottom of the deepest well, is an archaeological complex of national, indeed international, archaeological importance.

The aim of ARM in a city like London, however, is less often to preserve buried deposits than to minimise damage and ensure appropriate archaeological retrieval of information as a way of using the resource, to liquidate its environmental capital, so to speak. These aims can be achieved with the planning system better than through SMC, and achieved more holistically, more comprehensively and in careful integration with other conservation and planning interests that have a social, environmental and economic basis. Therefore the MPP rarely scheduled within the City of London, or in other still-living historic cores. Where the MPP did propose scheduling in urban areas, it was because the management aim was the retention of a monument in largely unchanged form, and in cities this usually involved obvious monuments such as town walls, monasteries or ruined churches, in which case the higher hurdle of the SMC system was thought to be appropriate. EH policy on managing the urban archaeological resource was based on this approach, leading to the Extensive Urban Survey (EUS) and Urban Archaeological Database programmes to create the ordered and accessible knowledge base necessary for informed planning decisions (EH 1992b, 2000b: 9–10).

SMC and LBC

The Listed Building legislation, for all its imperfections and sometimes opaque selectivity, brought alternative controls and structure to another part of the archaeological resource. One of the MPP's achievements was to rationalise the boundary between listing and scheduling, which is not (nor should be) defined by building type or date, but rather by the implications of present use and future intended management. The MPP would add ruined buildings or very occasionally sensitive buildings to the schedule, where further change is thought undesirable even if this means that the structure might pass out of entirely mainstream economic or functional use and become only kept for its historic or amenity value. On the other hand, in cases where continued use was seen as the key factor for survival and protection, even if this led to structural change, the MPP would hold back from recommending the scheduling (or would recommend the descheduling) of eligible buildings for which LBC was a preferable management option.

Here, of course, we come up squarely against the concept of change itself, and more particularly of archaeologists' attitudes to change and their attempts to stop, manage or simply study it. This is in some ways at the core of this chapter. Briefly, it could be said that the modern conservation movement began in the 1960s (e.g. at the Euston Arch) at such a low level of resource, infrastructure and political support, as did RESCUE in the 1970s, that only a limited part of the resource could be policed. Determined, and sometimes strident, resistance to any demolition, loss or change was often therefore the only safe and effective response. For archaeological remains, that rhetoric is, one hopes, less necessary now (PPG 16 drove away some of its last vestiges) and managing change rather than simply protection is increasingly accepted as ARM's goal (e.g. Fairclough and Rippon 2002; Clark 2001). This is partly a result of newer ideas of sustainable development, and the perception that the historic environment is a resource (to be used) not an asset (to be kept), which in turn arose from the unsuitability for archaeology of the financial metaphor of 'capital'.

This sea change in attitude goes hand-in-hand with the idea of characterisation (see below), but it is also a reflection of a basic perspective on the past that seems to be shared by archaeologists because of their training and interests. A main theme of archaeological research is, after all, the reason for and consequences of change in the past. Compared to several other conservation-based professions, archaeologists have a different response to the idea of change, perhaps fearing it less but certainly being able to live with its consequences more. A modified building gains extra layers of archaeological meaning even if it loses architectural authenticity or original appearance. A demolished building, even, may provide archaeological deposits for the future; even negatives (absences) can be archaeologically meaningful.

Archaeologists are therefore very familiar with the idea that the material remains of the past have continually changed and been modified, and they therefore recognise more readily that this will continue. At the same time, they also really do see the historic environment as a resource, something to be used if necessary, destroyed by excavation or modified to allow new uses, rather than as merely an asset to be stored. The fact that our principal way of doing this – excavation – means that we must destroy in order to learn, may have something to do with archaeologists' acceptance of change.

SMC and landscape management

The rural landscape is the most complex example of the need for the test of appropriateness when considering whether to schedule something (Fairclough 1999). The English landscape, everywhere at least partly cultural, nowhere totally natural, comprises semi-natural, living historic features as well as monuments, which are just as much a part of the historic environment but require a very different type of stewardship – active management rather than protection. Historic landscape – more properly historic landscape *character* – is ever changing, and is a complex artefact needing understanding and flexible, pragmatic positive management rather than protection. The rationale for not scheduling in towns is that towns and buildings are still alive in the sense that they are in very active use and are constantly being modified in a way that, for example, buried

Figure 17.3. Buildings of all types tend to be in active use with constant modification. This needs to be reflected in the nature of controls applied. Here, a photographic recording undertaken during landscape survey. Compare Fig. 17.4. *(© Oxford Archaeological Unit)*

Figure 17.4. The contribution of archaeological sites to landscape character as a whole needs to be managed differently from that of buildings. Compare Fig. 17.3. The illustration shows Castlerigg Stone circle and its vista towards the central Lakes. *(© Oxford Archaeological Unit; Photo: Jamie Quartermaine)*

267

Figure 17.5. The historic landscape needs to be regarded as not just a collection of archaeological 'sites' but as a human perception created from a rich, complex, ever-changing, mosaic of both built and semi-natural components. Its sustainable management (for example in the spirit of the European Landscape Convention) calls for understanding and the flexible management and planning of change rather than simply from protection. This illustration in the Isle of Man shows the importance of hedgerows and the pattern of land use and land cover in any understanding of the historic landscape.

deposits or earthwork monuments are not. This argument applies powerfully to the whole of the rural landscape, with its rich – and indeed dominant – historic and archaeological dimension representative of change throughout the past and only ever within the context of a continuing, changing environment.

The SMC regime, therefore, with its ethos of close, detailed control, is only fully appropriate to monuments within the landscape, to places or things where we wish to keep their fabric as unchanged as possible. The contribution of archaeological sites to landscape character as a whole needs to be managed differently. So too does the contribution of 'non-sites' such as hedges and their overall pattern (the hedgerow regulations offer another alternative to SMC, although it is doubtful that living hedges could be scheduled) or patterns of land-cover such as heath, wood, moor or water meadow. There is also the question of scale, of how to match ARM objectives to the larger, almost infinite, scale of the whole rural landscape. In England and Scotland the answer to this in the early 1990s was to decide not to extend the scheduling concept to landscape through a proposed Register of Landscape (DoE 1990b), but instead to pursue holistic and comprehensive characterisation and integrated sustainable management linked to the spatial planning system (Smith 1999).

AFTER MPP: 2002 ONWARDS

After fifteen years, we can identify the achievements of the MPP in England as:

- the progress it made in producing a new schedule to remedy the weaknesses identified in England's Archaeological Resource (EH 1984), a very long-term task
- a new, rigorous classification of the archaeological resource – the Monument Class Descriptions and the various types of step 1 and similar thematic characterisations, whose methodology represented a major step forward, in many areas, notably industrial and recent military archaeology, revolutionising our view of the archaeological resource, and making an indispensable foundation for conservation and planning strategies for EH and its partners in local government
- greater clarification of the role of scheduling after PPG 16, a more precise demarcation between scheduling and listing, and a reappraisal of the role of scheduling to ensure that it is not used where other measures would be equally or more appropriate; the presumption that scheduling (and other designations) should take account of management need as well as importance which underlies current government proposals for a unified heritage designation.

The MPP showed that it was practical and effective to draw distinctions between how we manage monuments in different situations. Some classes of monument are important at the moment primarily as a research resource, with potential through careful archaeological exploitation to create a stronger understanding of the heritage (e.g. lithic scatters, crop-mark palimpsests), and for these SMC is really neither desirable nor effective. A second category of monument includes those which need physical protection in the context of managed change but where this can be achieved most effectively by means other than scheduling (e.g. listing, PPG 16, agri-environmental regimes, Sites of Special Scientific Interest). Finally, of course, there is an important group of monuments (those with limited supporting uses, but whose loss would be socially, academically or environmentally damaging) where our requirement is for clear, focused physical preservation with minimal change. These are most closely suited to the particular controls and aspirations of scheduling.

Scheduling, however, is only one aspect of modern archaeological site management and conservation. It must fit within a pluralistic and increasingly sophisticated system which takes in the planning process, listing, Conservation Area work, proactive management, research-led conservation, environment land management schemes and new approaches to the landscape based on the concept of countryside and historic landscape character. The impact of new thinking on sustainability also needed to be taken into account, and it is more and more difficult to take management decisions about archaeological remains without also taking into account ecological, landscape, social or other environmental concerns. All this, therefore, underpinned the emerging new approach to ARM, and in particular to the suite of approaches that is coming to be loosely defined as 'characterisation'.

LANDSCAPE CHARACTERISATION

In the first half of the 1990s, two separate strands of thought – a new definition of what 'landscape' meant in terms of ARM, and an exploration of what the concept of sustainability could bring to ARM – reached similar conclusions. These were, broadly, that ARM should be concerned with:

- managing change throughout the historic environment as well as protecting selected sites one by one
- defining essential 'character' as well as identifying traditional hard archaeological values
- understanding the present (focusing of course on its historic dimension) as well as the past in itself
- identifying and promoting the benefits and uses that the archaeological resource affords, not just its intrinsic values but taking into account if at all possible a view of all communities of place and interest.

The exploration of landscape issues in ARM rapidly established objectives of sustainable holistic management that were unachievable through existing approaches such as scheduling or listing, or even through other conventional assessment, survey or evaluation (Fairclough *et al.* 1999). In the same way, the implications of sustainable development for the practice of ARM (EH 1997a), particularly when viewed in the context of integrated conservation (Berry and Brown 1995) and the development planning system (EH *et al.* 1996), suggested new ways of working and different, more ambitious, objectives.

These new ways, at the time of writing, are often described by the word 'characterisation' (EH web page 2003c). This is a shorthand word, perhaps not immediately transparent, for a set of interlinked objectives and methods that seek to provide generalised and areas-based or thematic information about the historic environment in order to frame decisions by archaeological resource managers, spatial planners and developers. This contrasts with traditional approaches to conservation, which assess the relative importance of individual components, then try to protect those with the highest rankings. Characterisation instead seeks a much wider-ranging, holistic understanding to help a wide range of communities to manage change in the historic environment. The two approaches are complementary and both have flaws as well as advantages. Designation is rigorous and easily defended as being based on hard fact, but it can too easily push ARM and conservation into excluding, reactive, negative and relatively limited mindsets. Characterisation can be accused of being too superficial, broad-brush and subjective, but on the other hand it offers rapid overviews, is wide in scope, inclusive and accessible, and it offers an acceptable trade-off to achieve wider goals. Both approaches are required for sustainable management of the archaeological resource and of the historic environment.

The concept of 'character' is not new to the conservation debate, having been embodied, for example, in the 1967 Conservation Area legislation. But during the 1990s, since the publication of the first edition of this book, it has grown in importance, very largely because of the Countryside Commission's work (Countryside Commission 1998) and the development of the Historic Landscape Characterisation (HLC) programmes (Herring 1998; Fairclough *et al.* 1999; Fairclough 2003a). Using character as a means of debate to influence decision-making represents an attempt to ensure that ARM and its related environmental management practices such as landscape management or nature conservation embraces local distinctiveness as well as national importance. It covers the heritage of place as well as the heritage of sectoral interests. It also reflects the desire to understand and capture the essence of large areas, as well as the more conventional, and now relatively straightforward, understanding of its individual components such as monuments or buildings. The relationship between things, the spaces between them, the patterns they form all constitute character at least as much, or more, as the individual merits of any part of an area. In other words, characterisation takes the lessons learnt from resource management of the historic landscape and applies it more generally as an approach to all aspects of the historic environment above the level of site or building.

Characterisation also looks at the benefits (the so-called 'affordances') of the historic environment rather than at its supposed intrinsic values, and in doing this it draws on a wider range of interest and disciplines (Tomasini 2002). It is integrative, and ideally seeks to see the environment as whole, rather than to break it down into ecology, archaeology or any of the separate disciplines necessary to its study and understanding. It is also more open to non-expert viewpoints such as communities of place as well as of interest and a fuller range of values than just the evidential or academic values that earlier ARM focused on.

Characterisation approaches are also less selective than conventional methods of assessment. They do not by themselves identify one area or thing as having greater value than another. Instead they identify what distinguishes every place (or a part of the historic environment) from others, what makes it distinctive and what gives it its character. It is possible to go on from that position to carry out qualitative evaluation or other forms of prioritisation, but it allows such decisions to be based on a more general understanding of the larger resource and (when deferred to the point of need) in the light of well-defined specific threats or opportunities. Rather than a one-off decision about importance that closes doors and narrows options, characterisation offers the scope for a longer series of targeted decisions about priority, sensitivity to change and management need at the time they are needed.

Characterisation can be used as the starting point to identify parts of the whole resource that merit special treatment (e.g. designation) because of their particular needs, sensitivity or significance. Preliminary characterisation allows such decisions to be taken in a sound context, and does not necessarily imply any devaluation of the remainder of the resource. More usually, however, characterisation provides a level of understanding that can be used to influence development proposals such as the government's Housing Growth Areas in the Thames Gateway (Croft 2004), M11 corridor (Went *et al.* 2003) or Milton Keynes/South Midlands (Green and Kidd 2004) sub-regions as they are being formulated. It can do this for all areas, not just for special areas. Sometimes the objective is to protect and keep part of the historic environment, at other times it is to allow or encourage its modification and re-use, sometimes it is merely to ensure that new development has visible or recognisable roots in the past through design, layout or location. The aim is to influence decisions on development and managing change in a variety of ways, and throughout the historic environment not only in designated places.

At the time of writing, these ideas are most advanced in the area of historic landscape because of the ten-year-old HLC programme organised by EH and local government SMRs. HLC was the first method to try to take a wider view of the historic environment, explicitly as a broad-brush generalised method. It chose to trade-off the depth and detail inherent in the small areas or site level approaches that were traditional to landscape archaeologists in return for the rapid coverage of the whole of (normally) a county council area. EH's urban assessment projects (Urban Archaeological Databases and Extensive Urban Surveys) had achieved something similar, in the field of (largely) buried archaeological remains and urban plan form. HLC sought to be holistic in the sense of spreading its net beyond conventional sites to the pattern of the landscape as a whole. Further, it drew in semi-natural features such as hedgerows and aspects of the landscape such as land use, while maintaining the view that 'landscape' is a concept or a construct, and a matter of perception. It was thus in keeping with the then-emerging (now in force in a growing number of ratifying countries) European Landscape Convention (CoE 2000, 2002).

HLC was also innovative in espousing Geographic Information System (GIS) from the mid-1990s, but most of all for setting itself within the frame of integrated conservation. It always saw itself not as the full answer to all aspects of landscape management, nor as a comprehensive overview of the whole of the archaeological resource, but as one of many contributions (but one hitherto largely missing) towards a holistic view of landscape (Fairclough 1995; Countryside Commission 1996), and as a complement to SMRs. To achieve this, HLC cut across many archaeologists' debates about the definition of landscape and the proper way to approach them. It was very directly created as a resource management tool first, and an academic exercise second. It borrowed significantly from landscape character assessment techniques, not because they were necessarily better but because in that way a common language could be developed to help archaeologists to be heard by landscape ecologists and landscape architects. A major facet of this common language was the scale chosen, particularly the adoption by HLC of an area scale, not a site scale.

Another new aspect of HLC's approach was that it grew out of a search for alternatives to designation. It began to be obvious in the early 1990s, during the EH R&D project that was eventually published as *Yesterday's World, Tomorrow's Landscape* (Fairclough *et al.* 1999), that it was not feasible to extend the scheduling-type approach to protect large areas of the landscape, which also prevent more positive and pragmatic approaches to landscape. Legal and procedural systems designed to cope with discrete monuments (from 1882, and with buildings from 1947) cannot effectively be extended to landscape because the aims of landscape management are rather different from those of monument protection. The sustainable management of the historic environment, both at large scale and in terms of the current broader definition of heritage and the archaeological resource, requires different philosophies (Fairclough 2003c).

In this respect, England and Wales have moved down separate pathways. While English methods embraced comprehensive and holistic landscape characterisation, the Welsh approach was to prioritise the task by establishing a selective Welsh register of outstanding and special areas of the historic landscape. This approach has been successful in Wales, despite the lack of statutory teeth, but its use is largely targeted on development control (CADW *et al.* 2003). Its most important contribution – to the highly effective agri-environmental programme Tir Gofal – has been the result less of the drawing of lines around special areas than of characterisation-type methods carried out by the Welsh Archaeological Trusts within them (see the web page of the trusts, for example). These methods are in some spheres more advanced than the English HLC method, notably in their incorporation of associative and cultural affiliation (Gwyn 2002). The parallel Welsh approach of LANDMAP being carried out by the Countryside Council for Wales, which is a complex environmental database designed for land management, similarly adopts an all-Wales, rather than a selective designatory approach. At the end of the day, the English and Welsh approaches may be different in method, but they converge in their objectives.

Scotland's Historic Land-Use Assessment method was partly based on the HLC method trialled in Cornwall (Herring 1998; Dyson-Bruce *et al.* 1999) and is very similar to England's HLC. The two share many aspects of method, objective and application. In 2003 HLC was carried out for the Irish Midlands by the Discovery Programme as the start of an Irish national programme, while the ideas, if not the precise methods, of HLC are gaining a wider European currency (e.g. Fairclough and Rippon 2002; Clark *et al.* 2003). This is not the place for a detailed discussion of those methods, which can be found elsewhere (e.g. chapters on Hampshire and Lancashire in Fairclough and Rippon 2002; Aldred and Fairclough 2003; Macinnes 2002; Dixon and Hingley 2002; Ede 2002; Fairclough 2002a, 2002b, and 2002c; Dyson-Bruce *et al.* 1999; and Dyson-Bruce 2002);

along with accounts of how HLC is being used in practical applications such as spatial planning, agri-environmental policy, landscape management, research and community involvement (Clark *et al.* 2004).

HLC-type approaches are also now used in urban contexts to characterise townscape, as a broadening of EH's urban programmes (e.g. the Extensive Urban Survey (EUS), and in specific test projects such as Merseyside, or Thames Gateway). Other recent examples include area-based characterisation of the Portsmouth dockyards (Wessex Archaeology 2000) and the Lincoln Archaeological Research Assessment (LARA). LARA has created a complex multilayered GIS providing easy access by period or location to current knowledge and proposed research agendas, as a contribution to the sort of archaeological development control necessary in a historic city (Stocker 2003).

In all of these projects, and in the HLC programme itself, a major challenge that remains un-met is that of releasing characterisation's potential for community involvement. This ought to be achievable in two ways. The HLC product should be able to be a stimulus to more inclusive wider responses by asking communities 'this – i.e. HLC – is our (expert) view, what is yours?', while the HLC process could be used to invite and structure community involvement at earlier stages. There have been experiments in this area (in the New Forest, for example, see NFDC 2000) and in Bowland and Arfon with schools and communities during the EU-funded Culture 2000 project European Pathways to the Cultural Landscape (Clark *et al.* 2003), but these need to be generalised and widened. The first edition of this book in 1993 (e.g. Parker Pearson's chapter 'Visitors Welcome') saw the need for this, and several chapters in the present edition can point to early experiments. If there is a third edition in 2015, it should be able to look back on greater progress in this area, driven by the heightened political profile given to this by *Power of Place* and *A Force for our Future*.

Characterisation projects are usually non-selective and non-prescriptive. They describe character rather than ascribe relative values. Decisions about relative importance, sensitivity to change or desirable limits to modification of the historic environment can all be made at later stages as need arises, in a sound and as far as practical comprehensive context. Limiting characterisation projects (as opposed to their uses) to neutral description (as the Countryside Character map did) is not an abdication from taking hard decisions or making judgements. It is a recognition of two things – that relative value judgements devalue what they exclude as much as they promote what they include, and are most usefully and safely made at the point of need; and that they should be made through as wide a consensus as possible.

Identifying the best areas in isolation of future management needs or uses is likely to be unfocused because it cannot predict future threats or changes against which to measure impact. It rarely takes any real account of sensitivity, vulnerability or capacity to absorb change. It is too black-and-white a perspective for modern spatial planning and other decisions, and it sits badly with sustainability. Too early (once-and-for-all) evaluation or definition of significance in the abstract, unconnected to proposals for change, can in fact be characterised as the real act of denial or abdication. It appears to demonstrate a reluctance to become involved (win or lose) in the difficult detailed process of bargaining and balancing that should sit at the heart of community-based planning. It seems to imply a preference to shelter behind the barricades of designation while change everywhere else in the historic environment is unmodulated and uncontrolled. PPG 16 broke through this attitude for archaeology, and historic characterisation is trying to do the same for all aspects of the historic environment.

Characterisation, however, does not rule out value judgements forever: rather, it pushes them forward in time to the most effective moment, as a form of wide-ranging impact assessment rather than as a certification of significance. It also facilitates decision-making by providing broader contexts and frameworks for decisions, just as the MPP's national evaluations did in the 1990s. Like the designation reform proposals of 2003, it sets significance into the context of proposed or possible change, and turns designation into a sensitive, flexible and pragmatic management tool, not an attribute of the resource. It allows the historic environment to be used as well as protected.

CONCLUSIONS

Characterisation is a tool, a form of applied archaeology, which was foreseen by several contributors to the first edition of this book when they called for archaeologists to move into the position of being part of the social process of change, not merely observers of the past's destruction. This repositioning is sometimes referred to as 'informed conservation', drawing its inspiration from the requirement implicit in PPG 16 that information is the prerequisite for decisions (Bloemers 2002; Clark 2001; Countryside Agency *et al.* 2001; Fairclough 2002b). Conservation Plans (Clark 2001), for example, attempt to draw together disparate perspectives and views in order to reach a consensus on the direction of future change. They are a type of characterisation tailored to a particular use (monument conservation) and scale (complex and large monument).

Underlying the move from assessment to characterisation may be the expansion of social (and economic) processes driving change (in the UK at least) to include (rather than only to confront) the ethos of conservation and sustainable development. The National Trust is said to have more members than the Church of England has church-goers. Conservation itself is therefore now one of the drivers of change almost as powerful a social driver as the marketplace is an economic one. This trend may look like NIMBYism (Not In My Back Yard) but it is underpinned by a broad, generally 'Green', reluctance to accept more major change and a genuine social preference for keeping old things, notably buildings.

To future archaeologists, the late twentieth and early twenty-first centuries in the West may be characterised by their concern for conservation, and their penchant for retaining the remains of the past, as well for development and change. Where they will place its origins is a matter for discussion, but perhaps in the postmodern Western rejection of simple solutions, and in the anxieties about science and progress that grew in the later twentieth century. But however they try to explain it, future archaeologists will be able to recognise a particular period character. This might be defined, for example, by the large number of adaptively re-used or converted barns and mills turned into housing, the retro pastiche design of mass housing, or the creation of 'new nature' in the form of amenity woodland or restored heathland. Whatever form it takes, future archaeologists are likely to be able to see it as a recognisably distinct form of material culture created by a strong awareness of the past beyond memory, by a conscious approach to conservation (and resource management), and by heritage re-use.

Many of the concerns discussed within the characterisation debate rose to prominence in the sphere of landscape, hence the emphasis of the latter parts of this chapter. This was because of landscape's living character and the need to manage and protect landscape processes as part of the management regime, two aspects that highlighted the limits of the traditional designation approach. For landscape, process and change are characteristics, not simply threats to be averted, and the whole landscape cannot be managed as a museum object, but only as a creative, evolving whole. It was therefore more easily evident in the landscape context that designation-based protective approaches can only be expanded so far from its monument-specific origins. It is perhaps also a relevant consideration that the landscape sits within the realm of perception rather than reality: that is, the environment exists as a set of material things, but landscape is an idea, an emotional or intellectual construct based on it. For this reason too it is less susceptible to full material preservation.

As a final point, therefore, it may be worth remarking again that archaeology is very largely the study of change in the environment caused by human beings. This puts archaeologists, when operating as managers of the historic environment, into a rather different position, a different relationship to change and development, and to society, than some of our conservation colleagues (Fairclough 2002c). Our approach may be growing more distant from the Ancient Monuments philosophy of the late nineteenth century, the building conservation movement of the post-1945 years, the RESCUE ethos of the 1960 and 1970s, and even the assessment techniques described by Startin in the first edition of this book. But if so, the move offers to take archaeologists and their discipline towards a wider social relevance and to a deeper engagement with society.

ACKNOWLEDGEMENTS

While I have obviously described the developments of the last ten years from my own viewpoint, equally obviously I owe acknowledgements to a very large number of colleagues and friends with whom I have worked over very many years. Not all of them will agree with everything I have written.

First, in keeping with the English bias of the chapter, I must thank all members of the MPP over the years, and of the current EH Characterisation team. There are too many to list, but I wish to mention Dave Hooley, Jeremy Lake, John Schofield (specifically but not only for his military work on the Second World War and the Cold War, and for permitting me to draw freely on parts of the MPP 2000 written by him), Deborah Porter, David Stocker (specifically but not only for his work on towns, industry and settlements), Margaret Nieke, David Went – and of course Bill Startin for lengthy discussions over many years.

Beyond the small world of the MPP, however, many others have helped me over the years, both within and beyond EH: Lesley Macinnes (Historic Scotland), Carol Somper (Countryside Commission, then Countryside Agency, currently Forum for the Future), Richard Kelly (CCW), David Thompson (GAT), Mike Coupe (EH), Katharine Fletcher (EH), Kate Clark (then EH), the very many friends and colleagues in SMRs who developed HLC over the years (including Peter Herring, John Darlington, George Lambrick, Keith Miler, Lynn Dyson-Bruce, Bob Croft, Stewart Bryant, Oscar Aldred, Jo Clark), Carys Swanwick and colleagues in LUC, and Julie Martin then of ERM, for their collaboration on 'Conservation Issues' and sustainability, and . . . well, so many people that it would be unsustainable to list them all. Many of course have works cited in the bibliographic references and I hope I will be forgiven for not naming everyone. But I must thank as always Liz Page, without whose indefatigable and patient hard work and skill this chapter (like so much that I started) would not have been finished.

CHAPTER 18

DEVELOPMENT OF REMOTE SENSING

Part 1: Aerial survey for archaeology

Robert H. Bewley

INTRODUCTION

Since 1990 there has been a transformation in the use and effectiveness of aerial survey for archaeology, not just in Britain, but throughout Europe and even the Middle East (Bewley and Rączkowksi 2002; British Academy 2001; Kennedy and Bewley 2004). This transformation has been particularly noticeable in England, with changes in the organisation of aerial survey nationally, and the acceleration of the National Mapping Programme from 1999, as a result of merger between the Royal Commission on the Historical Monumens of England (RCHME) and English Heritage (EH) (Bewley 2001). Although resources have temporarily declined (in 2004 and for 2005) the position is still much better than it was a decade ago. In Scotland and Wales there have been similar developments in terms of approaches to mapping and using aerial survey (Musson 1994; Driver 2002a; RCAHMS 1994) but there is still a considerable resourcing and training gap for the next generation of air photo interpreters. Perhaps the most significant change has been a growing awareness of the purpose of all forms of investigation (not just aerial survey) to increase our understanding of the historic environment. It is only through a better understanding of the past that we can improve our management, conservation and care of the historic environment for future generations.

In terms of aerial reconnaissance there have been changes in the way in which the Air Navigation Order (ANO) has been interpreted, which has meant that EH has had to become its own operator of aircraft, to ensure the continuation of its own reconnaissance programmes as well as the work of local flyers; these changes have also affected practitioners in Scotland and Wales, where there are companies with Air Operator's Certificates (AOCs) but these are not easily accessible for archaeologists (especially in Scotland).

In Europe there have been enormous political changes with the ending of the Cold War and the break-up of the Soviet empire, as well as the repeal of laws in Italy, where aerial photography is now legal (for the first time since 1928). There is still much more to be done to open up the skies, by removing unnecessary aviation regulations, so that new reconnaissance projects can begin and new collections can be created. Equally we have to aim to unlock the millions of aerial photographs in closed collections, throughout Europe. The developments over the past ten years have been encouraging for the future development of the subject. The European Union Culture 2000 programme, with NATO and the British Academy, funded a one-year project in 2001, *Conservation through Aerial Archaeology* (see www.english-heritage.org.uk and http.aarg.univie.ac.at). This project helped to increase awareness not only within the archaeological profession but also in the wider sphere, so that those in charge of allocating funds will, in future, consider aerial survey as a realistic and cost-effective approach to improving our understanding of the historic environment, and not just rely on excavation. The success of this one-year project has now been followed by a successful application to the Culture 2000 programme for a three-year project (started in 2004), *European Landscapes: Past, Present and Future*, which will use a variety of survey techniques but will concentrate on aerial survey, to promote a greater understanding of European cultural heritage (www.e-landscapes.com).

THE PURPOSE OF AERIAL SURVEY

Aerial survey's purpose is to improve our understanding of the historic environment through aerial reconnaissance, air photo interpretation and mapping. It can be defined as incorporating a number of activities from taking aerial photographs, interpreting and analysing them, integrating the information with other surveys (e.g. McOmish *et al.* 2000; Driver 2002b), report writing, as well as the storage and retrieval of the photographs and the resulting maps, plans and records.

Aerial survey is only part of archaeological survey: its contribution to complementary techniques is its cost-effectiveness and its comprehensive approach; aerial reconnaissance and air photo interpretation help to improve our understanding of sites and buildings from neolithic enclosures (Oswald *et al.* 2001) to modern urban centres (Cattell *et al.* 2002; Brodie *et al.* 2002; Richardson 1998). It is important to understand that aerial survey is an *interpretative process*. Interpretation begins with selecting the subject for each image taken in the air, and continues with the interpretation of the features on aerial photographs and their translation into archaeological information, both as a map or plan and a written, descriptive record. The creation of archaeological record maps has been going on since the Ordnance Survey (OS) began its work (but especially from 1920 with the creation of the Archaeology Division within the OS). The OS transferred responsibility for this work to the three Royal Commissions (in England, Scotland and Wales) in 1983 and this in turn led to the creation of National Monument Records (NMR). During the 1980s these developed as a combination of map-based information systems and computerised databases. Similarly, the growth of regional or county-based SMRs led to a debate on their purpose and how records and all types of information should be used at both national and local level. It was clear that in England their main purpose was for use in development control and the need for the information they contain to underpin the decision-making for managing the historic environment, recently articulated in the *Power of Place* (EH 2000a) and *Force for our Future* (DCMS and DTLGR 2001) documents. What did emerge was an understanding that the use and accessibility of aerial survey information was patchy and had been compiled by a variety of people with a variety of skills and experience. In conjunction with the national bodies in England, the decision was made (in 1988) to run a pilot programme for mapping and recording landscapes which contained mainly crop-mark sites (Fenner and Dyer 1994) and in 1989 this was expanded to include earthwork sites (Horne and MacLeod 1995); this developed from 1992 into the National Mapping Programme (Bewley 2001), for which see below.

THE DEVELOPMENT OF AERIAL PHOTOGRAPHY

The history of aerial photography has been covered more extensively than space allows here (Crawford 1954; Daniel 1975; Deuel 1969; Hampton 1989; Riley 1987; St Joseph 1951; Whimster 1983; Wilson 1982; 2000).

The earliest aerial photographs were taken from balloons (Deuel 1969: 13). Not surprisingly, one of the first aerial photographs for archaeology was of Stonehenge, taken from a balloon (Capper 1907; Wilson 1982: 11). The development of flying, aircraft and photography during and after the First World War provided the platform from which aerial survey for archaeology could be launched. Without the foresight and understanding of one man, O.G.S. Crawford, the subject would not have taken off so successfully. His early papers (Crawford 1923, 1924) paved the way for the seminal work *Wessex from the Air* (Crawford and Keiller 1928), and his professional papers, *Air Survey and Archaeology* (Crawford 1928) and *Air Photography for Archaeologists* (Crawford 1929), are standard texts.

During the decade leading up to the Second World War, Crawford and a number of colleagues (Major Allen, Sqn Ldr Insall and R.G. Collingwood) developed the technique of aerial photography and combined it with fieldwork. The results were published in the quarterly archaeological journal *Antiquity*, whose founder and editor was Crawford himself. With an expanding empire in the Middle East, some of the most notable contributions from this interwar period were from this region (Maitland 1927; Rees 1929). The Second World War provided the impetus for the development of photography and aviation that would be of immense benefit, and not just for archaeology.

Until 1945 aerial photography in Britain was carried out by a few pioneers, such as Major Allen (Allen 1984), Derrick Riley, Jim Pickering, and Arnold Baker to name but a few. In 1945 what became the Cambridge University Committee for Aerial Photography (CUCAP) (and is now the Unit for Landscape Modelling) began aerial survey in Britain for a variety of purposes, one of which was archaeology (1977). Crop-mark landscapes were recorded in the gravel areas and with the massive rebuilding and new town expansions in the late 1940s and through the 1950s, the gravels, rich in archaeological sites, were also under great threat. This threat was recognised in the 1960 RCHME's publication of *A Matter of Time*, which had a considerable effect on the way in which archaeology in England was carried out, even if it took ten years before the formation of RESCUE (RCHME 1960; Jones 1984; Rahtz 1974). Moreover, aerial photography also allowed for the discovery of new types of site, often as earthworks, and the new discipline of medieval archaeology grew alongside aerial photography (Beresford 1950; Beresford and St Joseph 1977).

After the Second World War the development of aerial photography for archaeology to the present day can be divided into three parts. Each part helped the other to exist; there is not space here to do more than list these major events. Firstly, in 1949 CUCAP was created, a year after the Curatorship in Aerial Photography had been established (St Joseph 1977: 5); some reconnaissance had taken place since 1945 from Cambridge. This unit has been renamed the Unit for Landscape Modelling and is still very active in aerial survey, especially vertical surveys and developing the use of new techniques such as Lidar (Holden *et al.* 2002), and holds a collection of over 400,000 prints.

Secondly, in 1965 the Air Photographs Library within the RCHME was established (Hampton 1989). The RCHME started the Air Photographs Library (now part of EH's National Monument Record in Swindon) 'to implement the Commission's resolution to . . . "use air photography to build up rapidly a record of field monuments throughout England"'(Hampton 1989: 17). Initially this was a collection of the regional and locally based aerial photographers' work, but soon came to include the results of the RCHME's own work (from 1967); this collection now holds approximately 750,000 prints. It also holds the collection of vertical photographs that resulted from the postwar survey by the RAF, which was formerly the Department of the Environment's collection (over a million prints); the RCHME (now EH) was given responsibility for these in 1984 and since then has computerised the original flight traces. The collection also holds verticals from other sources. For any given area of interest the relevant photographs can be listed and made available for consultation (contact the NMR in Swindon).

The Scottish and Welsh Royal Commissions also carry out their own programmes of aerial reconnaissance and have done so since 1976 in Scotland and 1986 in Wales. The results of their work are archived in the National Monuments Records of Scotland (NMRS) and the National Monuments Record of Wales (NMRW). In Scotland there are over 77,600 oblique aerial photographs in the NMRS (see the CANMORE website), and there are over one million vertical photographs available for consultation by prior arrangement.

The RCHME embarked upon its programme of flying in 1967 to support its own terrestrial surveys, including buildings and urban areas (Hampton 1989). Since then the Air Photography Unit (APU), which included the air photo library, has been divided between the NMR (responsible for the archiving, retrieval and access to the photographs) and Aerial Survey (within the Research and Standards part of EH) carrying out over 300 hours of aerial survey per year; the photographs from each survey are accessioned into the NMR. The two locations for aerial reconnaissance, in Swindon and in York, enable aerial surveys over most of England. This objective would not, of course, be possible without the third element in the organisation of aerial photography in Britain.

The locally-based aerial photographers received government funds for the first time in 1976, and this has continued to the present day, in a variety of forms, now funded through EH's Archaeology Commissions Programme (recently renamed the Historic Environment Enabling Programme (HEEP)). Until 1975 all the costs of flying were borne by the flyers themselves, but the dry summers of 1975 and 1976 ushered in a new era. The Council for British Archaeology (CBA) formed an Aerial Archaeology Research Committee that pressed for public funds to be made available for aerial photography. The Department of the Environment, through its Inspectorate for Ancient Monuments (later EH) started funding to the tune of £10,000; this was increased to £20,000 by 1985. In 1986–7 responsibility was transferred from EH to the RCHME for grants to local flyers. These grants were primarily for the flying costs and were seen as joint projects with the local institutions and organisations, which augment them in a number of ways (Griffith 1990; Watson and Musson 1993). The joint nature of the projects is still maintained, but the wider remit allowed by EH means that funds are available for more than just the flying costs.

A similar situation pertains to Wales and Scotland. The Royal Commission on the Ancient and Historical Monuments of Wales (RCAHMW) has its own reconnaissance programme, and has responsibility for coordinating aerial survey in Wales. Grants for aerial reconnaissance are provided to regional flyers based in the Welsh archaeological trusts. RCAHMW also collaborates closely with CADW (Welsh Historic Monuments) in monitoring Scheduled Ancient Monuments (SAMs) from the air. This programme has been under way since the mid 1980s (James 1986; Musson 1994; Driver 2002a) and is largely completed as part of RCAHMW's in-house reconnaissance work. Each year more than 600 SAMs are photographed, with re-visits at three- to four-yearly intervals to monitor site condition and land use. Resultant air photographs are used by ground-based CADW Field Monument Wardens to discuss any issues raised with landowners and occupiers.

In Scotland the Royal Commission on the Ancient and Historical Monuments of Scotland (RCAHMS) also advises and provides practical support to local flyers. As in Wales, the archaeologists are organised on a regional basis and, given the upland nature of the landscapes, have to cover larger areas than in England. RCAHMS has had its own flying programme since 1976, and published a catalogue of aerial photographs annually until 1995. A more detailed version is now available on the internet (www.rcahms.gov.uk), and a new site is being developed for the verticals (www.airphotofinder.com).

TECHNIQUES

There is not space here to cover the techniques of aerial survey for archaeology; the subject has been well covered by Riley (1987: 17–40) and Wilson (1982, 2000). The basic principles of photography and aerial reconnaissance have been very well covered elsewhere (Musson 1994) and air photo interpretation and mapping would require a book for itself, but see Wilson (2000). Riley (1987) describes the mapping techniques available for the air-photo interpreter. These fall into two categories: manual and computerised methods; the aim being to remove the distortion of the oblique view to the plan view. Large-scale detailed plans can be made from aerial photographs using desktop computers as well as more expensive photogrammetric machines; this type of mapping is very important for the management and protection of archaeological sites and landscapes. Decisions as to which site or area is to be mapped or needs protection are dependent on having knowledge of the archaeology of the whole country (see National Mapping Programme below).

For the non-specialist the formation of crop-marks and soilmarks has to be briefly explained. Whenever the subsoil or bedrock has been cut into or altered there is the possibility of crop-marks or soilmarks being formed. A ditch cut into any rock or subsoil will fill up with material of different characteristics to the surrounding bedrock. This difference can manifest itself when the land above the ditch has been ploughed and sown with a crop; the ditch is likely to retain more water and more nutrients than the bedrock through which it has been cut. In dryer years, the crops above the ditch grow taller because their roots can obtain more water and nutrients for stronger growth. As they are growing longer and taller they ripen later than the surrounding crop and are darker for longer. This colour (and height) difference is clearly visible from the air (see Fig. 18.1.1).

With soilmarks the main difference is one of colour: soilmarks are normally seen during the autumn and winter months. When the fields are being ploughed the difference in colour between a ditch that has been filled up with organic matter and the bare soil is clearly visible. A full explanation of the formation of crop-marks and soilmarks, as well as the pitfalls of interpreting these marks, has been well covered by Wilson (1982, 2000) for the interested professional and amateur, and also now for schoolchildren (Corbishley 2004). (See also www.english-heritage.org.uk.)

The basic method for recording these variations in crop growth and soil colour is photography from a stable airborne platform. There are two basic types of aerial photography: *vertical* and *oblique*.

Vertical photographs are used by practitioners in a variety of disciplines, including archaeologists, geographers, soil scientists, planners, engineers and solicitors. Taking vertical photographs is, however, a highly specialised and relatively expensive technique carried out by commercial companies or military institutions utilising expensive cameras and specially adapted aircraft. Usually these photographs are overlapping stereo pairs to allow for proper stereoscopic examination.

Oblique photography, using hand-held cameras, from high-wing aircraft, such as the Cessna 150/152 (two-seater) or the 172 (four-seater) is much more accessible to the archaeologist. Oblique photographs are taken through an open window with either medium-format cameras (using 120, 220 or 70mm films) or 35mm SLR cameras (or both), and are most commonly used in archaeology. Traditionally, photography on black-and-white film (using Ilford FP4 and Agfa's Aviphot (70mm), Kodak Tri-X, TMAX and Technical Pan) has been used, but more colour photography (using slide film and colour-print films) is now being taken. A small amount of false-colour infra-red film is used but the difficulties in handling it outweigh the information gained.

Figure 18.1.1. Crop-mark formation. The height differences in the crop are visible in this diagram, demonstrating the impact of subsoil features; a wall or stonework will reduce the height of the crop whereas a pit or ditch will promote growth. These differences are clearly visible from the air, when the right (dry) conditions prevail. (© *EH*)

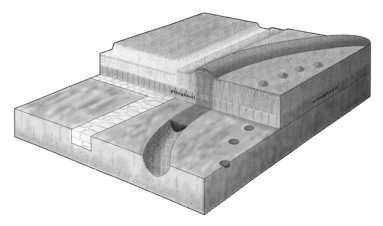

Digital cameras are rapidly becoming standard equipment for all archaeologists and those in the air are no exception. To date no definitive tests and experiments have been carried out but in the pages of *AARGnews* (Driver 2004; Palmer 2004) there have been a number of useful reports. Digital cameras have not, yet, replaced other forms of photography, but it is my prediction that they will become the norm in the next two years. As with any new medium there is an experimentation phase (which we are now in), then the 'acceptance' phase, followed by the 'how did we ever manage without with this kit' phase. Finally there is the 'let's try the old traditional cameras, for fun, phase' (just as the vinyl records are now back in vogue having had fifteen years of CD technology in music). Just as there are some who feel that the digital image has so many advantages over other film types (for example slide film because the main use of slides was for presentations, and so many are moving to the digital presentation) that they feel they can use a digital camera and perhaps one other 'back-up'. Others see the digital camera (as I currently do) as another very useful medium, which is in addition to all other films and cameras types. The benefits are the speed of delivery (the image can be sent electronically, immediately – that is, the same day), and the capabilities of immediate image manipulation. The disadvantages are that the characteristics of the digital camera and lens have to be understood (the focal lengths differ from standard SLR lenses), the quality of the sensors vary, and the long-term storage and archival costs, requirements and needs have yet to be fully worked through. Until the archival needs are taken account of, digital images are at risk, just as improperly stored negatives are. Anyone who wishes to begin a project involving aerial reconnaissance and who feels the need to use a digital camera (which I am sure they would) has to be aware that using *only* a digital camera (and no other form of camera) is a very high risk, given the overall costs and effort required in getting airborne. The discussion about digital cameras has also opened up the question of the use of digital images, taken from negatives or slides, which is now the norm, and some practitioners have all their films processed and scanned onto CD (at the point of processing) so that the images can be used easily for presentations, reports and dissemination, but still have long-term archival quality.

Digital cameras used with lenses designed for standard SLRs and many of the cheaper non-SLR cameras can introduce considerable distortion in images that should be corrected when they are to be used for high-accuracy mapping. Appropriate software is available for this (see http://epaperpress.com/ptlens/index.html).

Figure 18.1.2. Flight traces for all reconnaissance flights in England from 2000 to 2004. EH operates from two airfields (Sherburn-in-Elmet in the north and Oxford in the south). This image and Figs 18.1.3 and 18.1.4 are only made possible by the tracking capability of the GPS systems, which continuously record the flight of the aircraft. *(© EH)*

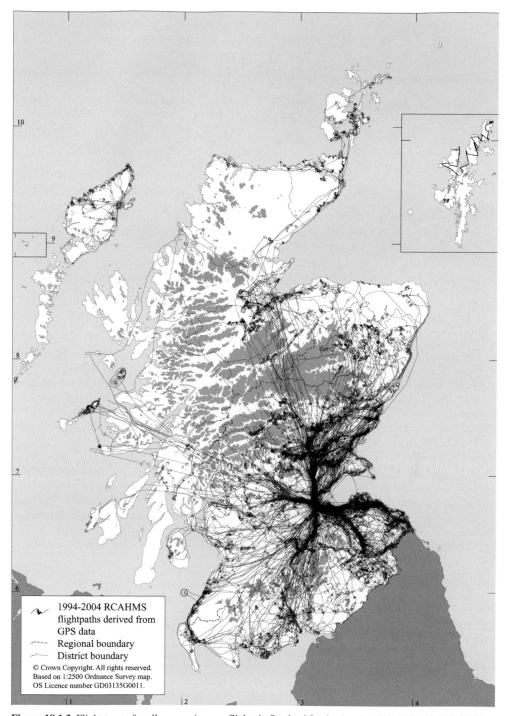

1994-2004 RCAHMS
flightpaths derived from
GPS data
Regional boundary
District boundary

© Crown Copyright. All rights reserved.
Based on 1:2500 Ordnance Survey map.
OS Licence number GD03135G0011.

Figure 18.1.3. Flight traces for all reconnaissance flights in Scotland for the decade 1994–2004. *(© RCAHMS)*

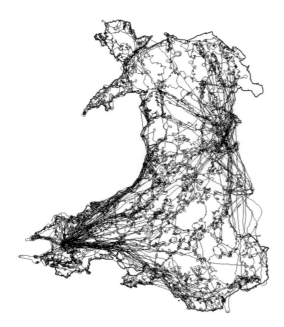

Figure 18.1.4. Flight traces for all reconnaissance flights in Wales from May 2000 to March 2005. *(© RCAHMW)*

The technology and the market are changing so rapidly that, other than general advice, there is no point in setting out which cameras will provide the best results, but as with traditional cameras, certain features remain desirable if not essential. These include shutter speed priority and good quality optics. For digital cameras, high resolution is essential, along with a fast, high capacity storage medium. Auto-focus works well but only if the camera offers a multi-region focus setting. It also the case that the more you pay, may not, necessarily, reflect a better product for aerial photography.

Oblique photography forms part of the annual aerial archaeological surveys throughout the UK, and indeed much of Europe; it has been estimated that over 500 hours of flying is carried out in the UK alone each year. On average this can yield approximately 1,500–2,000 new sites or additional information on known sites, including buildings, each year (Figs 18.1.2–18.1.5). Stereo pairs, using hand-held cameras, can be easily obtained and should be the norm, but taking them requires practice. Their benefit is in the improvement in ability to interpret faint or poorly defined features using a stereoscope.

UNDERTAKING ARCHAEOLOGICAL AERIAL RECONNAISSANCE

Before embarking on any aerial survey there are a number of legal and practical points that have to be observed. The legality of using a particular aircraft and pilot has to be established. The aircraft to be used must have a Certificate of Airworthiness in the Public Transport (Passenger) Category. Every pilot has to have a licence, two categories of which concern us here: a Private Pilot's Licence (PPL) and a Commercial Pilot's Licence (CPL). Currently the majority of pilots who are engaged in aerial photography for archaeology have a CPL; PPL holders can only share the cost of a flight and cannot fly for hire and reward. Fully commercial operations, which charge more for their services, have an Air Operator's Certificate (AOC). The Civil Aviation Authority (CAA) used to issue exemptions from the Air Navigation Order (ANO) to allow pilots to fly 'passengers' for

Figure 18.1.5. Standlake, Oxfordshire. This one image taken in 1990 summarises the range of targets that aerial survey aims to cover. Visible are the buildings of the village, the earthworks of the former manor houses and the crop-mark formations of prehistoric and later sites visible in the arable fields. The threats to our archaeological resource are also highlighted, not just in the arable fields (under threat from the plough) but also the complete destruction of the former landscape by the extraction of sand and gravel; these quarries are now filled with water (top left). *(Crown copyright NMR)*

archaeological aerial photography without an AOC, but this system ended in 2001–2. In 2002 all those engaged in aerial reconnaissance for archaeology in Britain either use operators with an AOC, or their institutions (as in the case of EH) operate aircraft themselves. These changes to the interpretation of the law have meant that archaeologists have had to take full responsibility for each flight; anyone wishing to embark on aerial reconnaissance for archaeology should seek advice from the relevant body (depending on location) on the roles and responsibilities when commissioning a survey. EH has produced a draft Code of Conduct for aerial photography (Grady 2001) and Guidelines for Operating Aircraft (EH 2002e).

Aerial reconnaissance attracts more attention and publicity than other aspects of aerial survey, but is actually the smallest part of aerial survey: it is the work after the photographs have been taken that takes up the most resource. One hour's flight can generate a full day's work in cataloguing and storage of the material; all the photographs are made available via publicly accessible libraries (see below), and in England and Scotland a growing proportion are on the internet (see also the Cambridge University's collection (ULM) website). Following on will be the examination and analysis of the photographs for immediate recording (in EH the photography from any year is assessed rapidly for any new information: see Barber *et al.* 2003) and then the photographs (with others) will be examined as part of the National Mapping Programme (or selective projects).

MAPPING AND INTERPRETATION

English Heritage's National Mapping Programme (NMP)

Since 1992 (after a four-year pilot on crop-mark classification and upland mapping) EH (formerly RCHME) has funded an ambitious programme – the National Mapping Programme (NMP) – to map and record all archaeological sites on the aerial photographs. Originally this was conceived of as a manual approach, using 'sketch plotting' or manual transcription, but the rapid development of computer transformation software and desk-top computers now means this is a totally digital and computerised process. The nominal map scale is 1:10,000 in England, and all the early maps on translucent film overlay (prior to full computerisation) have been scanned.

The overall aim of aerial survey and NMP is to improve our understanding of the historic environment and its change through time. All easily available aerial photographs are examined, interpreted and maps of archaeological features are made using AutoCAD drawing packages and rectification software, for example *Aerial* (now in its fifth version), developed by John Haigh at Bradford University (Haigh 1991) (see also *Airphoto*, developed by Irwin Scollar (Scollar 2002)). A summary of the current progress of NMP can be found on the EH website and in Bewley (2001), but it is important to stress that this is an interpretative exercise, which not only creates an archaeological map but also records sites to a national standard (RCHME/EH 1995). In addition it has a morphological recording module, first developed in 1988 but since revised and refined (see Edis *et al.* 1989): the purpose of morphological recording (i.e. shape and size) is to be able to group or classify sites for which we have no date or function. The assumption in this approach is that sites of a similar size, shape and location *might* have a similar date and/or function. Clearly this will not be the case in some instances, but the approach helps to set up hypotheses that can be tested by further investigation, including sample excavation. Examples of the approach have been published in Stoertz (1997), Bewley (1994), Jones (1998), Winton (1998), and Featherstone and Bewley (2000). As yet unpublished work on the Cornwall NMP project, by Andrew Young, has shown the usefulness of classifying sites in this way in the Camel Estuary. Combining the NMP information with the concurrent Historic Landscape Characterisation project (Fairclough 1999b, 2002b, Fairclough and Rippon 2002) has also revealed an interesting dichotomy of land use in the Camel Estuary, whereby the prehistoric settlements are all on the anciently enclosed land (i.e. the more fertile low-lying areas) and the burials are all on the higher, more recently enclosed land. This distribution pattern has yet to be fully explored (and it may be telling us as much about site visibility (see Carter 1998) as it is about human behaviour). I am grateful to Andrew Young for allowing me to use this example.

NATIONAL MAPPING PROGRAMME

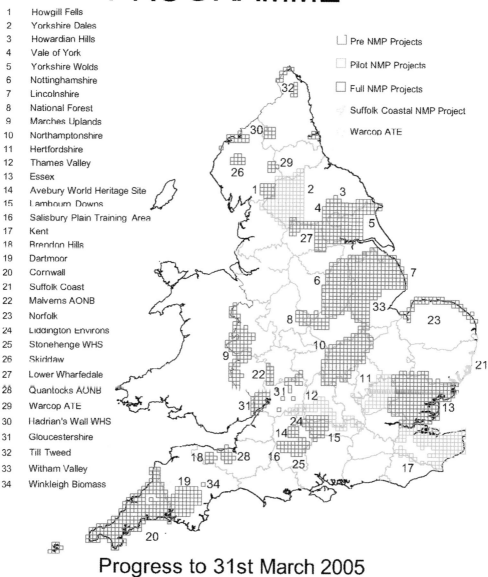

1	Howgill Fells
2	Yorkshire Dales
3	Howardian Hills
4	Vale of York
5	Yorkshire Wolds
6	Nottinghamshire
7	Lincolnshire
8	National Forest
9	Marches Uplands
10	Northamptonshire
11	Hertfordshire
12	Thames Valley
13	Essex
14	Avebury World Heritage Site
15	Lambourn Downs
16	Salisbury Plain Training Area
17	Kent
18	Brendon Hills
19	Dartmoor
20	Cornwall
21	Suffolk Coast
22	Malverns AONB
23	Norfolk
24	Liddington Environs
25	Stonehenge WHS
26	Skiddaw
27	Lower Wharfedale
28	Quantocks AONB
29	Warcop ATE
30	Hadrian's Wall WHS
31	Gloucestershire
32	Till Tweed
33	Witham Valley
34	Winkleigh Biomass

Pre NMP Projects

Pilot NMP Projects

Full NMP Projects

Suffolk Coastal NMP Project

Warcop ATE

Progress to 31st March 2005

Figure 18.1.6. Current progress of the National Mapping Programme in England, showing the number and geographical diversity of the projects completed. *(© EH)*

Each NMP project has its own publication programme as each project area or landscape zone has its own partcular needs. Thus for a small area such as the Lambourn Downs in southern England publication will be in the form of journal articles (Winton 2003), whereas for a large county project, such as Lincolnshire, a monograph has been produced (Bewley 1998), as for Northamptonshire (Deegan forthcoming). For the Vale of York project, which was completed in 2000, the proceedings of a dayschool, based on the results of the NMP project, will be published as an edited volume (Horne and Kershaw forthcoming). Each project produces an internal report, summarising the results and highlighting important discoveries and ways of improving future projects (for example, Boutwood 2002; Crutchley 2000, 2001 and 2002; Deegan 1999 and 2002; Fenner and Dyer 1994; Horne and Macleod 1995, 2001; Small 1999, 2002b).

At the time of writing the NMP Manual (RCHME 1995b) is being revised and updated and will be available from EH in 2005. NMP is a national project (see Fig. 18.1.6) which will produce important national insights, but it also delivers information at a local level for local needs. This may be to answer specific questions of site location in advance of development threats or research problems that assist in improving our understanding of past human settlement and land use. The programme is funded by EH through its Archaeology Commissions programme for external projects (in Cornwall, Essex, Lower Wharfedale, Norfolk, Northamptonshire and Suffolk) and the Aggregates Levy Sustainablity Fund (Till-Tweed project) as well as through core funding for the internal projects (Hadrian's Wall, Vale of York, Gloucestershire NMP, and Quantocks).

In Scotland the approach to mapping and interpretation has been to target specific areas, often in response to a threat or a thematic survey (e.g. a recent survey on cursus monuments, see Gilmour 2002) or in the uplands and those affected by forestry (RCAHMS 1997; Gilmour 2002).

In Wales, a strategy is being developed to integrate air photo mapping and field survey within the Uplands Initiative (www.rcahmw.org.uk/uplands/), where mapping is used to inform field recording, with results then feeding back to update the mapping. Lowland areas are also being targeted for air photo mapping using historical and more recent aerial photography. Air photo mapping and other geographical datasets held by the Royal Commission are being incorporated into a GIS from which will be developed a system enabling easier online public access to the results of archaeological survey and recording work. The datasets form an important part of the national archaeological resource map being developed by RCAHMW.

In England, too, there are specific projects that have used mapping as an integral part, the most recent of which has been the work at Richborough (Small 2002a).

AERIAL PHOTOGRAPHIC LIBRARIES

There are three main sources of aerial photographs for archaeology in Britain. These three hide a multitude of sources and a huge variety of type of library. Fortunately, the National Association of Aerial Photographic Libraries (NAPLIB) has produced a *Directory* of over 360 libraries or sources of aerial photographs. Useful addresses are listed below.

National (specialist) collections of aerial photographs

For England the main sources are EH's National Monuments Record library and the Cambridge University collection (now part of the Unit for Landscape Modelling); a recent computerisation of the card index has meant that searches for the location of photographs can be made via the website (see www.aerial.cam.ac.uk). There are other collections, see *NAPLIB Directory*. There is the Central Register of Air Photography for Wales, at The National Assembly for Wales, Room G-003, Crown Offices, Cathays Park, Cardiff, CF10

3NQ. The NMRW archive at RCAHMW holds its own obliques, and a selection of those taken by the Welsh Archaeological Trusts and Cambridge, along with an extensive collection of verticals and historic RAF obliques. The RCAHMS holds a large collection of oblique aerial photographs taken by its staff, regional flyers and Cambridge University staff. The vertical collection was transferred from the Scottish Office to RCAHMS in 1993, and additions have been made since. (There are national collections of vertical and oblique photographs taken by commercial companies or by the Ordnance Survey for mapping; these are listed in the *NAPLIB Directory*.)

Local or regional collections

Where county councils have been instrumental in commissioning vertical surveys (for census figures for example) collections are often available for archaeological study. There are also the collections that have built up with the grant-aid from the Royal Commissions and are often combined with historic aerial photographs. Norfolk is a good case in point which has a publicly accessible archive, but many other local authorities have accessible collections. Further information about the collections in each county or region can be obtained from the *NAPLIB Directory*.

Private collections

There are a number of private collections throughout the country and by consultation with the appropriate 'curator' or owner of the collection, access may be granted.

FUTURE POTENTIAL

There are three main areas for the future potential and development of the subject. The first is in developing the use and interpretation of remote sensing techniques, used so much in the natural sciences. In particular the use of Lidar (Holden *et al.* 2002; Shell 2002), which uses a laser beam to record the surface of the ground or tree canopy, or buildings, to a high degree of accuracy. Aircraft with this sensor on board also carry other forms of remote sensing, often multispectral imagers (e.g. CASI) recording for example the infrared ranges of light even into the thermal range (Donoghue and Shennan 1988). Archaeologists are beginning to learn the potential of these forms of remote sensing, and there will be many more surveys done over the next decade targeting specific sites and areas (see Bewley *et al.* 2005, on a Lidar survey at Stonehenge). Satellite imagery is often seen as the obvious replacement for the low-tech approach of flying around in light aircraft. However, it is only by combining information from various levels of imagery (satellite to low oblique) that we will improve and develop our techniques: satellite imagery is very useful for monitoring land use changes and detecting larger sites in parts of the world where low-level aerial reconnaissance is not possible (Kennedy 1998). The contribution for archaeology of satellite imagery varies across the globe and with the type of imagery being captured (Donoghue *et al.* 2002) as well as the types of indicator being searched for. A recent example from the Near East, looking at the NDVI (Normalised Difference Vegetation Index), is a novel but useful archaeological adaptation (Mumford and Parcak 2002).

The second is the expansion of the technique and subject into Europe (Kunow 1995). Although there had been much good and pioneering work in France, Germany, Holland and Sweden since 1945, there were large areas of Europe in which aerial survey for archaeology was either illegal (e.g. Spain, Greece and until 2000, Italy) or where the political regime restricted access to maps and photographic information. The ending of the Cold War changed all that, and now there are programmes of reconnaissance in the Czech

Republic, Slovakia, Slovenia and to varying degrees in Poland, Romania, Hungary, Latvia, Lithuania and Estonia (see Bewley and Rączkowksi 2002: Fig. 1). This expansion creates challenges too. Changes are required in the perception of what the study of *archaeology* means; to many it is still synonymous with excavation, but an intellectual debate and engagement with other professional archaeologists is required, and it is only by publishing the results that this debate can begin. Schwarz's recent work (Schwarz 2003) is a very good example of what can be achieved through diligence and careful research over ten years.

Training the next generation of archaeologists in aerial survey is fundamental if we are to reap the benefits of the current expansion across Europe. The Aerial Archaeology Research Group has helped to organise of a number of pioneering European aerial archaeology training courses in recent years (see Bewley *et al.* 1996; http://aarg.univie.ac.at/events/events.html), but these are only a small beginning.

This leads to the third element of the future – unlocking the existing archives of vertical and oblique aerial photographs. Even if there was no more aerial reconnaissance the huge untapped resource of existing archives of aerial photographs would keep many archaeologists busy, interpreting the information on these photographs, for many decades. In Britain there are some three million aerial photographs taken by the RAF over Europe during and after the war, which are accessible but not catalogued; we know there are many other collections still in the basements of official institutions, which need cataloguing. There are similar collections in every country in Europe, so there is a vast resource for archaeological discovery, and these collections are under threat from either neglect (they will deteriorate if not properly archived) or from deliberate disposal. Space in libraries and museums for collections is at a premium and if these boxes of photographs are seen to be of no use and are taking up useful space they will be thrown out.

CONCLUSIONS

Aerial photographs contain information of enormous importance that will improve our understanding of the historic environment, whether it be new information, or for monitoring change or simply illustration. With the increase of threats to archaeology aerial photography is crucial for evaluation work (Palmer and Cox 1993), so that proper mitigation strategies and management plans can be developed. Aerial survey is still an underutilised resource and is often misused. It provides information on early prehistoric sites through to the modern period, including recent and dramatic changes to our industrial and military heritage. One common misconception is that aerial photographic information is synonymous with crop-marks and soilmarks: although crop-marks play an important role in any archaeological study they are only one part of a much wider subject, from prehistoric earthworks to the monuments of the Cold War.

There can be no doubt as to the cost-effective nature of aerial photography and the subsequent mapping and record creation. The nature of the work is such that skilled air-photo interpreters with a good archaeological knowledge are required. The low priority currently given to aerial photography in university research projects and in training courses means that the employing bodies have to train staff. This limits the efficiency with which national programmes can be operated. There are further limitations in the use of aerial photographs: archaeological features recorded by aerial photography represent only one method of survey. As the other section of this chapter will show, there is a whole range of techniques that can also record archaeological sites. Combining the results of the various techniques is an essential component of evaluation and research work (Bowden 1999).

It has been known for many years that sites recorded from aerial photography are in fact a small percentage of what is actually under the surface. The results of this technique should not be used in isolation: follow-up fieldwork and excavation are vital if we are to understand and record the full extent of prehistoric, historic and even modern Britain. However, the largest hurdle to overcome is an intellectual one – to convince those who do not understand the nature of interpretations based on aerial evidence. So often the view is taken by experienced archaeologists, that unless they can excavate, or 'ground-test' a site seen on aerial photograph, that it does not really exist. The success of discovering thousands of new sites, throughout Europe, is tempered by the fact that we have yet to properly fund research based on these discoveries.

ACKNOWLEDGEMENTS

Staff in EH and its National Monuments Record have been very helpful and cooperative, in particular Simon Crutchley, Damian Grady and Pete Horne. Colleagues in Scotland and Wales have supplied information and assisted in my attempts to make this short piece relevant for Great Britain; I am especially grateful to Toby Driver, Jack Stevenson, Marilyn Brown, Dave Cowley and Simon Gilmour. Any errors and omissions are entirely my responsibility.

CONTACT ADDRESSES

Aerial Archaeology Research Group (AARG). This group meets annually to discuss the techniques, discoveries, and all matters concerning aerial photography for archaeology. It has no permanent address, since its officers rotate; for further information see http://aarg.univie.ac.at/

Cambridge University Committee for Aerial Photography (CUCAP) is now the *Unit for Landscape Modelling*, Sir William Hardy Building, Tennis Court Road, Cambridge CB2 1QB. Tel: 01223 764375, Fax: 01223 764381, www.ulm.cam.ac.uk. The collection may be visited by members of the public during normal office hours. Photographs cannot be borrowed but prints can be purchased; orders ordinarily take about a month. Prices depend on print size. Copyright is retained by the University or the Crown.

National Association of Aerial Photographic Libraries (see www.napllb.org.uk).

English Heritage, NMR Enquiry and Research Services, Great Western Village, Kemble Drive, Swindon SN2 2GZ. Tel. 01793 414700, Fax. 01793 414606, nmrinfo@english-heritage.org.uk. This is a branch of the National Monuments Record for England. Photographs can be consulted by prior arrangement. An express service can be provided for urgent requests (costs and details from the above address).

The Royal Commission on the Ancient and Historical Monuments of Wales (RCAHMW), Crown Buildings, Plas Crug, Aberystwyth, Ceredigion, SY23 1NJ. The national body of survey and record for Wales. The National Monuments Record of Wales (NMRW) library and archive can be contacted at the same address. Tel. 01970 621200, Fax. 01970 627701, nmr.wales@rcahmw.org.uk. http://www.rcahmw.org.uk/

The Royal Commission on the Ancient and Historical Monuments of Scotland (RCAHMS), John Sinclair House, 16 Bernard Terrace, Edinburgh EH8 9NX. The national body of survey and record for Scotland. www.rcahms.gov.uk. Photographs are are freely available for public consultation in the NMRS library and copies can be purchased.

CHAPTER 18

DEVELOPMENT OF REMOTE SENSING

Part 2: Practice and method in the application of ground based geophysical techniques in archaeology

Chris Gaffney and John Gater

This section charts the application of geophysical techniques in modern archaeology as practised in Britain. In a recent article (Gaffney *et al.* 2002) the authors discussed the potential of specific techniques and their role in archaeological evaluation. While there is inevitably some overlap between these two works, this part of the chapter considers the wider role of geophysics in archaeological fieldwork. In particular, discussion covers the range of techniques and differing methodologies available to answer a variety of archaeological problems both within research frameworks and the broad context of archaeological resource management. This is not strictly a review of geophysical applications in archaeology; the reader is advised to consult the following references for such information: Aitken 1974; Aspinall 1992; Carr 1982; Clark 1975, 1996; Conyers and Goodman 1997; Gaffney and Gater 2003; Heron and Gaffney 1987; Scollar *et al.* 1990; Tite 1972a, 1972b; Wynn 1986. However, for those readers who are unfamiliar with the background to the involvement of geophysical techniques in archaeology, a summary of the major trends is included.

A BRIEF HISTORY OF GEOPHYSICAL TECHNIQUES IN BRITISH ARCHAEOLOGY

Historically, geophysical techniques have been used to flesh out the excavations of individual sites once features had been identified. For geophysicists, this seemed to be a last resort, an appendage to be used only if time and funding would permit. While this approach had its successes, the input of geophysical data into mature archaeological strategies was rare. Indeed, although the outlets for archaeological publication increased dramatically during the 1960s and 1970s the provision for the dissemination of geophysical results in this period actually decreased, with the virtual demise of the specialist journal *Prospezioni Archeologiche*. Some observers regarded this as a potential new era: the lack of a specialist journal might ensure that results were reported in mainstream archaeological journals. However, this was a false dawn, the reasons for which are not obvious. One may suppose that the initial slow speed and uncertainty of data collection may have had an effect, as would the limited display options available at the time. What is evident, however, is that despite the lack of publications, geophysical techniques have become an accepted part of the British archaeologist's toolkit (Spoerry 1992b).

This acceptance may be described as a product of the inevitable trickle-down of new technology into archaeological applications: during the 1980s dedicated and reliable earth resistance, and more importantly fluxgate gradiometer instruments were marketed in Britain. These instruments included data loggers, thus allowing the automatic recording of digital readings into the rapidly expanding world of computerised data analysis. However, to accept this as a main cause of the acceptance of geophysics would be an oversimplification of the relatively recent establishment of geophysical techniques in British archaeology. The major reason why geophysics has been so successful in the late 1980s, the 1990s and in the early 2000s has less to do with technology, and more to do with the nature of the information required by archaeologists. In short, the ever-increasing pressures on curators to secure the rapid evaluation of large tracts of land has provided the *raison d'être* for geophysical techniques in archaeology. In those instances where traditional archaeological techniques have been found wanting, geophysical applications have become the norm.

The strengths of geophysical techniques as a management tool can be contrasted with traditional archaeological techniques: where information from fieldwalking data can be general, geophysical data are often specific; and where trenching is expensive, geophysical investigation is cheap. The additional information provided by the methodologies used by archaeogeophysicists is greatest in the precise mapping of buried remains. For example, this allows potential land developers to understand their obligation to the study of the area that their work is threatening to destroy. The alternative may be trial excavation resulting in the discovery of a plethora of archaeological features within a trench, a situation in which the archaeologist can merely guess the representative nature of the findings, never mind their extent.

Of course there are disadvantages and it is important that these are acknowledged. For example, it is not possible to date geophysical anomalies except in very general terms, and in several instances archaeological interpretation can also be difficult. Neither of these facts, however, negates the use of the techniques themselves. The latter is more critical in that a thorough knowledge of geology and site conditions is often required to assess the likely success of a technique and hence indicate accurately levels of confidence. Perhaps the most important concept in the evaluation of geophysics is that it should be part of a battery of techniques as a staged approach. Geophysical techniques should not be used uncritically nor should they be the only technique or used as the last resort. Meshed within mature research or evaluation strategies these techniques add significantly to the overall output, but to consider them in isolation is to reduce their impact. Although some restricted studies question their use (e.g. Hey and Lacey 2001), in our opinion they have not taken the holistic approach that is the hallmark of successful multi-staged evaluation strategies.

At the start of the twenty-first century then, in Britain, archaeological geophysics has never been on a stronger footing. Apart from the aforementioned reasons for this renaissance, the effect of the popular series *Time Team* broadcast on Channel 4 television cannot be overlooked. Not only has this made millions of people aware of the potential of the techniques but the programme has alerted potential clients, that is developers, to the advantages of using geophysics in archaeological evaluations (Cave-Penny 1995).

There is again an international journal, *Archaeological Prospection* published by Wiley, dedicated to archaeological geophysics and related disciplines. In addition there is for the first time ever a postgraduate degree course, an M.Sc. in Archaeological Prospection, on offer at the Department of Archaeological Sciences at Bradford University. Once again the subject has entered a new era.

WHICH TECHNIQUES ARE SUITABLE?

At the outset it is necessary to make distinctions between what may be termed evaluation work and investigations that form part of a research project. The list of techniques used in evaluations is limited compared with those used for research purposes. This is primarily because an archaeological evaluation requires that the methods used should be rapid, and the results quick to process and relatively easy to interpret and display. As a consequence, the techniques most often used in evaluations are soil resistance (resistivity), magnetometry (fluxgate gradiometry) and occasionally soil magnetic susceptibility. As the major objective is to map the archaeological potential of an area, and not to estimate depth or stratigraphic relationships, these three techniques are normally ideally suited to the task. However, ground penetrating radar (or GPR/radar for short – see below), which initially had a role specifically to investigate depth phenomena, is now being used more widely in evaluations to also provide plan information.

The principles of all geophysical techniques depend upon the contrast between the physical properties of a feature and those of the surrounding deposits (for a more detailed discussion see Aitken 1974; Tite 1972a). Resistance surveying involves the insertion of electrical currents into the ground and measurement of their resistance in relation to differing buried features. Walls will normally result in high resistance responses and waterlogged ditches will have a low resistance. Magnetic techniques involve the detection of small localised changes in the intensity of the earth's magnetic field associated with buried features. A pottery kiln, for example, will give a very strong magnetic anomaly because of the fired clay/brick structure; a ditch or pit will also produce a measurable anomaly if there is a magnetic contrast between the fill and the strata into which the feature is cut. The contrast is largely dependent upon the magnetic susceptibility of the soil/subsoil and measurement of this phenomenon can form a prospecting technique in its own right. This is because human occupation tends to result in an enhancement of the susceptibility of the soil (Le Borgne 1955; 1960; Tite 1972b). As a result, sites that survive in the topsoil can be detected even if all the features have been destroyed. GPR requires electromagnetic energy pulses to be transmitted through the ground and measures reflected signals that have been produced by interfaces between materials of differing electrical properties. Thus the technique tends to work best where good resistance results can be obtained.

The major advantage of the two common techniques of soil resistance and magnetometry is the simplicity of method, which has been demonstrated in countless surveys. This requires the site to be gridded into typically 20m or 30m blocks with detailed measurements taken within each grid. The sample interval is usually 1m or less and the spacing between traverses 1m. In this way, where conditions are favourable, extremely accurate and detailed maps of buried archaeological features can be obtained. Geophysical techniques can also inform on the less tangible concept of 'activity'.

Activity is used here as a broad category of information that considers man's influence on the environment. This manifests itself as modifications in the physical and/or chemical properties of the topsoil. These may be far-reaching and lie well beyond the traditional definition of a site. Two techniques that are used in this way are soil phosphorus and magnetic susceptibility analysis, although other soil attributes, such as trace element levels, have also been successfully mapped and interpreted as archaeologically significant (see Aston *et al.* 1999; Bintliff *et al.* 1992). In recent years the measurement of topsoil magnetic susceptibility has become the most important of these indicators, although little has been published regarding the validity of field methodologies and sampling strategies at the archaeological level.

To simplify the use of magnetic susceptibility, it is possible to identify three intensities of topsoil sampling: coarse, medium or fine. The coarse sampling interval is more appropriate for identifying potential archaeological areas within a landscape. In such work, sample intervals will be in the order of one measurement every linear 10–50m depending upon the size of the project. This degree of sampling intensity will provide background information with regard to the suitability of an area for more detailed magnetic work as well as indicating the potential of large archaeological sites in the area (see e.g. Clark 1996). Normally any areas of anomalously high susceptibility will be assessed by gradiometer. The second sampling intensity (medium density) requires a sample interval of 10m or less in order to define activity areas (Gaffney *et al.* 1992; Gurney 1992). For producing specific information about activity/features within small sites, a fine sampling interval in the order of every metre will be necessary (see e.g. Allen 1990). However, it is questionable as to whether such a level of work is appropriate to many archaeological problems, especially in topsoil studies where the plough redistributes the soil.

The phenomena measured in area geophysical investigations, such as contrasts of moisture and magnetic minerals, represent bulk changes. Therefore, the methods that are traditionally used give information on what is there rather than how much and at what depth. However, the latter questions are increasingly frequently asked of geophysicists. It must be realised that this is not an attempt to wrestle the spade from the archaeologist's grasp, but another refinement on the information to be assessed before costly excavation. For those people used to geophysical prospecting within the mineral extraction industry an analogy may be useful: the traditional magnetic and resistance tools are used in the location of a scarce resource (archaeology), while the newer questions relate to an estimation of the quantity of that scarce resource that exists and its extraction depth.

Although it is convenient to differentiate the work undertaken in response to the two questions asked by archaeologists, it is an uneasy divide in that resistance and gradiometer data both contain information that can provide rough estimates of depth. Also, by varying the methods, a good approximation of depth can be realised. For example, geological geophysicists have long used expanding resistivity arrays to assess the depths of deposits, while a variation on this also allows vertical pseudo-sections to be constructed (e.g. Edwards 1977). The latter approach has been successfully applied archaeologically because archaeologists are accustomed to viewing data as sections through the earth (e.g. Imai *et al.* 1987; Nishimura and Kamai 1991; Aspinall and Crummett 1997; Neighbour *et al.* 2001). A promising alternative also utilising resistive changes is that of tomography, which is a technique borrowed from medical imagery (e.g. Noel and Walker 1991; Noel and Xu 1991). Both of these are useful appendages in the non-invasive armoury, especially when used in conjunction with an area survey.

Other techniques that have been employed for the collection of vertical section information include seismic methods (e.g. Goulty *et al.* 1990; Ovenden 1994) and GPR (e.g. Stove and Addyman 1989; Conyers and Goodman 1997). Seismic investigation requires an artificially generated seismic wave to be reflected or refracted at interfaces between materials of contrasting reflection coefficients. Unfortunately, claims for the success of the techniques, in particular for GPR, were overstated in early surveys and these provoked considerable attention from specialists within civil engineering and archaeology (e.g. Atkin and Milligan 1992). A review article noted that 'Radar survey techniques currently in use are reminiscent of early days of more conventional geophysical surveys with a noticeable lack of mutual appreciation of the problem of surveyor and archaeologist' (Aspinall 1992: 240). Without wishing to delve too deeply into the problems associated with radar, it is certain that considerable research is required into the resolution of exact depth and individual feature interpretation at the archaeological level. Gross changes can be identified and that is often the limit of the resolution demanded in civil engineering applications. However, for archaeological purposes the level of detail required is much finer and data processing is more prolonged. Often traverses are collected at intervals of 1m or less and the data are sometimes corrected for topographic variation prior to considerable filtering, migration and general enhancement. In an effort to make the radar responses archaeologically comprehensible researchers in this area have developed a technique to extract slices of data from systematic radargrams to form traditional two-dimensional maps. These maps can be equated to time to the response (they are often termed 'timeslices'), which can be linked to an approximate depth. There are many reasons why timeslices are only approximate, but even relative depth is often an important indicator under certain circumstances. What is worth pointing out is that under many circumstances it is inappropriate to use radar, such as the location of features beneath reinforced concrete or clay rich deposits, and that it should not be regarded as the ultimate technique but merely part of the selection available. However, in urban or semi-urban environments it is often true that GPR is the only non-invasive technique that may provide valuable, if limited, archaeological information.

It can be concluded from the above discussion that two avenues are often explored by geophysicists: area survey (mapping of anomalous data after a background has been established) and depth detection of layers and features. It is perhaps useful to summarise the use of geophysical techniques in archaeological geophysics, by thinking of three levels of work (Figs 18.2.1–18.2.3). The first two (Levels I and II) are most widely used in projects associated with planning applications, whereas Level III surveys are more appropriate to archaeological research work and unusual planning problems.

SAMPLING IN AN ARCHAEOLOGICAL CONTEXT

General sampling strategies have been discussed elsewhere (Gaffney *et al.* 2002), and although they are mainly applicable to evaluation work, the criteria for adopting such strategies can apply equally well in research projects that involve, for example, investigating landscapes. Various strategies are outlined here and reference is made to a few case studies. These case studies serve to demonstrate the way sampling strategies can be designed to answer particular archaeological questions.

The scale of some developments can be extremely large, for example, mineral-extraction sites and housing developments; while others are linear in shape, such as pipeline and road schemes. Under such circumstances it is often not possible, nor desirable, to survey the whole of the threatened area, particularly within planning timescales. In deciding upon an appropriate sampling strategy, the nature of the expected archaeology, the ground cover, the topography and the local geology will all affect the way each site is investigated.

A desktop evaluation will usually identify known archaeological sites and these may be targeted for detailed geophysical work. The initial aims of the geophysics may be to define features visible on aerial photographs, investigate the extent of anomalies associated with artefact scatters, evaluate the nature of earthworks, and/or to carry out prospecting in areas adjacent to sensitive and protected sites. Detailed work over predefined areas, with contingency allowances for expansion where necessary, will be appropriate in such instances. It is often required that geophysical techniques will also be used in the investigation of areas of varying archaeological potential within the proposed development. In such instances, a combination of magnetic scanning, magnetic

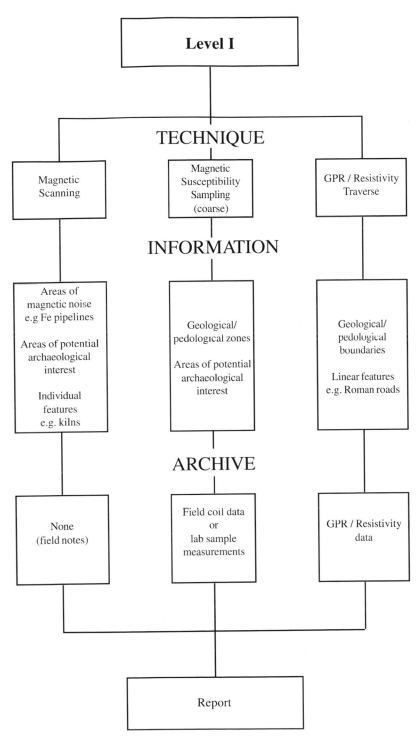

Figure 18.2.1. Some standard strategies considered appropriate to initial prospection work.

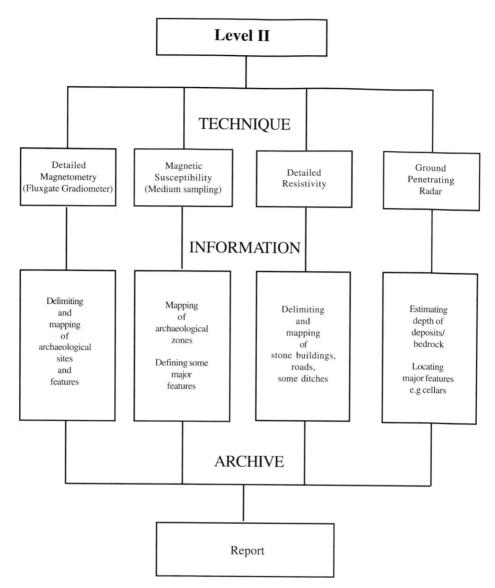

Figure 18.2.2. Common techniques used in archaeological assessment and evaluation.

susceptibility sampling and a modified sampling strategy is usually appropriate. As a general guide it is recommended that the sample blocks for gradiometry should not be less than 40 x 40m, unless other conditions (e.g. easement restrictions) dictate otherwise. This is because a background has to be defined before areas of anomalous readings can be identified. A suitable percentage survey sample usually will be dependent upon the archaeological sensitivity of the area under threat.

The following theoretical (and actual) case studies are examples of the way areas can be evaluated using geophysical techniques.

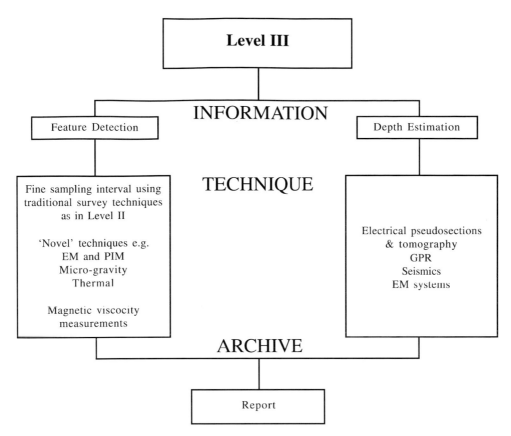

Figure 18.2.3. Some possible techniques used to investigate exact feature location and depth determination.

Projects affecting areas of less than 2ha: Level II and III Surveys

It is debatable as to whether areas affecting less than 2ha should be sampled. Sampling may be appropriate where resistance work is required, but for magnetometry full coverage is desirable. This will provide a far better assessment of a site and diminish the possibility of misinterpretation of the results.

Projects affecting areas greater than 2ha: Level I and II Surveys

In areas where there are no archaeological or topographic determinants, then a modified systematic sampling strategy is appropriate. Survey blocks or transects are positioned within each field based on existing boundaries, unless there is an overriding reason for using the National Grid. Use of the latter can make positioning survey very difficult and does not necessarily facilitate the expansion of the survey samples. By using a grid system based on existing boundaries, blocks can be investigated in a semi-random way or at predefined intervals in order to maximise coverage.

At Shepton Mallet, Somerset, a series of small investigations was carried out for differing developers in different areas on the outskirts of the existing town. While each component survey provided specific information about each field, it was only when

299

viewed in a wider context that the true archaeological importance could be assessed. It became possible to predict confidently the previously unknown limits of the Romano-British settlement based upon geophysical sampling and selected excavation by the Birmingham University Field Archaeology Unit. This information will be of great help in the future planning of the present town, and is an example of how seemingly piecemeal evaluations can contribute to archaeological knowledge.

Linear projects: Level I and II Surveys

Geophysical involvement in linear developments is varied. For example, a pipeline project passing through the archaeologically rich chalk wolds of North Humberside was deemed to warrant a 100 per cent detailed geophysical investigation. By contrast, geophysical work in advance of construction of another major pipeline from Grangemouth to Cheshire was confined to known areas of interest. In a third case, when a pipeline was planned from Humberside to Hertfordshire, a 10 per cent sampling strategy was adopted, in addition to investigating known sensitive areas. In the last case, the exploratory geophysical work identified at least three new major archaeological sites. Most frequently a proposed pipeline or road will be assessed either by a gradiometer in scanning mode or magnetic susceptibility measurements on a 5 or 10m grid. An agreed percentage of the project area will be subject to detailed survey over anomalies located during the scan. Used in this mode of operation, geophysical techniques are a powerful addition to archaeological investigation and complement traditional forms of information gathering such artefact recovery, aerial photography and excavation.

WHAT IS TO BE EXPECTED IN A GEOPHYSICAL REPORT?

At present there are no specific criteria available for those setting geophysical briefs as part of an archaeological evaluation. However, English Heritage (EH) have produced guidelines for geophysical work in field evaluations that should form the basis of routine work as well as containing many important notes on the reporting of evaluations using geophysical techniques (EH 1995e).

While this advice has led to a realisation that specific information must be contained within professional reports, there is still a wide variation in the quality of surveys and reports. Inevitably there must be some variation as to the content of a specialised geophysical report. It is obvious that, for example, the style and display of information will be different when reporting resistance or radar data. However, the reports should still be comprehensible on the same level, namely that any geophysical fieldwork should be followed by a clearly reasoned technical report. There must be sufficient information within the report to allow a specialist reader to understand what instrumentation was used, how the data were collected, what processing has been undertaken and how the results have been displayed. This will allow the specialist to understand the logic behind the interpretation of the data and the limits of confidence that should be placed upon that interpretation.

Specifically the report should contain information on location, topography, geology, soils and the known archaeology of the site. There must be recognition of instances when information on these subjects is not known, as this may affect the certainty of the interpretation.

Data processing and the style of display are the most individual elements of a report. While it is the responsibility of the geophysicist to display the data in a format that illustrates his or her final interpretation it is also true that the effects of each process step

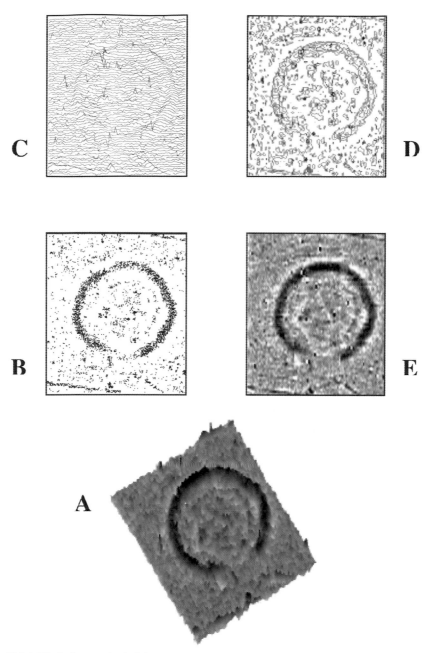

Figure 18.2.4. Displaying geophysical data.

A: 3D Surface Plot
B: DD (0.1 to 3nT)
C: XY Traces / Stacked Profiles (Vertical Scale 10nT / line)
D: Contours (8 levels, 0.1 to 3nT)
E: Grey-scale (White -1 to 3nT Black)

should be documented and displayed. That is, displays of data should be provided after every smoothing or filtering algorithm. This allows an estimation of the quality of the data and a check for any 'artefacts' produced by the processing that may have been mistaken for anomalies produced by archaeological features. In general, as little processing as possible should be undertaken.

It is difficult to apply any rigid rules with regards to the display of geophysical data. The experience of the geophysical operator will decide what is the most appropriate method, depending upon the nature of the results. However, whatever form is chosen – dot density, X–Y traces, grey-scale images, contours, three-dimensional terrain (Fig. 18.2.4) – it is vital that a clear interpretation diagram is included. Additionally, in order for a geophysicist to make an independent assessment of the results, at least one plot of the raw data should be included. An X–Y trace or grey-scale image is often used for this; the former being most effective at showing the full range of magnetic data.

The report should also include a non-technical summary with sufficient information to allow the interested reader to gain an idea of the scope of the work and the general success, or otherwise, of locating archaeological remains. All diagrams should be produced at reasonable scales. By this it is suggested that both the data and separate interpretation diagrams should be reproduced at a scale from which exact measurements can be taken, allowing the efficient positioning of trenches. Summary plots of data and interpretation can be included at a scale allowing an overview of the survey. An appropriate scale for the former might be 1:500 and the latter at the scale at which other information is being summarised (usually 1:1250 or 1:2500). It is not adequate to provide data at only the smaller scale as its quality cannot be assessed at that level. Similarly, it is inappropriate to produce interpretations drawn on top of data diagrams. Interpretative diagrams should be clear, separate diagrams that can be understood by a non-technical client. Those reporting the results should be aware that the interpretation is the bottom line for many of the individuals or groups that commission a survey.

Naturally, it would be useful in all cases for the geophysical report to amalgamate known archaeological information from the proposed development area. However, as geophysical techniques are non-invasive, they are often now used as a primary technique and, accordingly, reports are often required to be submitted before other information can be assimilated. Therefore, those who commission geophysical reports should not be surprised when interpretations are tentative, especially when information such as geological context or expected type of archaeological remains are lacking.

WHAT SHOULD HAPPEN TO THE REPORT AND DATA?

The geophysical report may be a stand-alone piece of work or part of an integrated approach to a proposed development area. As a result, it is expected that the written report will be submitted to the sites and monuments record (SMR) for the region concerned. However, the computerised data must also be maintained for future interrogation, and all competent groups will have some form of data archive that they will attempt to maintain in perpetuity. Although there is no central archiving store for geophysical data in Britain, the Archaeology Data Service (ADS) has produced a document (Schmidt 2002) that endeavours to set best practice in the archiving of geophysical data.

In the majority of surveys excavations are normally undertaken to test the interpretation of the geophysical data and to that end it is remarkable how little feedback there often is after invasive work. While it may be a reasonable guess that no feedback probably means that the interpretation is largely correct, positive criticism is likely to increase the level of confidence that is placed upon future interpretations.

LEGISLATIVE ISSUES

Legislative considerations are often overlooked by clients commissioning geophysical surveys. This fact probably arises because most remote-sensing techniques are by their nature non-invasive. However, although a site will not be physically disturbed by a survey, written permission is still a prerequisite to carrying out work on a Scheduled Ancient Monument. No differentiation is made between surveys carried out as part of a planning evaluation and those that are research oriented. Persons working to strict deadlines, therefore, should be aware that geophysical contractors have to adhere to legal frameworks.

EH will issue a Section 42 Licence on behalf of the Secretary of State for sites in England granting permission to carry out surveys; CADW (Wales), Historic Scotland and the Environment and Heritage Service (Northern Ireland) will act in similar capacities in their respective countries.

ACKNOWLEDGEMENTS

Thanks are due to members of staff at GSB Prospection Ltd who have helped formulate many of the ideas discussed in this chapter.

CHAPTER 19

THE DISSEMINATION OF INFORMATION

Catherine Hills and Julian D. Richards

INTRODUCTION

In the ten years since this chapter was first written there have been major changes in the organisation of archaeological fieldwork in Britain (Chapter 4), in the use of electronic resources, and in the popularity of archaeology, mostly thanks to television. All this has had a significant impact on the dissemination of archaeological information. Julian Richards is co-author of this fully revised chapter, contributing especially to discussion of electronic media.

Different kinds of archaeological information, and a range of audiences, have led to the development of different means of communication. The audience can be divided for convenience into three broad groups: academic archaeologists, field archaeologists and the wider public. In reality of course these groups are not, and should not be, really separate; each has many sub-divisions, and many of us belong to all three.

Academics draw on their own fieldwork, reports on fieldwork by others, archival, laboratory and museum-based research, journals, some now online, other electronic resources, books and personal contacts as sources of information, in order to carry out further research on any aspect of the past and its interpretation, including querying whether such an enterprise is in fact desirable or practicable.

Field archaeologists are mostly employed in the practical world of contract archaeology, where the aim is to complete projects on time and within budget, and to provide a basic report to developers and local authorities. Previous reports, databases and sites and monuments records (SMRs), now renamed historic environment records (HERs), are their main immediate information resources. They are concerned to establish what, if anything, is already known about sites under investigation, and how likely it is that significant archaeological evidence will be affected by proposed developments.

The largest and most important audience is the public, which in reality includes everyone. Archaeologists themselves, whether practical, academic, or both, can only claim detailed knowledge of very small parts of the subject: most of the time they are in the same position as the interested layman. The more general public audience tends to be most interested in discovering what really happened in the past, what it was like to live as a Roman or Saxon, and how archaeologists find out about it, although their interest does not extend to reading detailed excavation reports. They tend to assume that there was a real, knowable past, which archaeologists are uncovering and presenting in as close an approximation to the truth as we are able – which is not a view shared by all academic archaeologists, although it is probably close to the implicit motivation of contract archaeology.

These can appear to be three very different groups, but in fact they have overlapping memberships, and should not be firmly separated: the most theoretical archaeologist does usually do some fieldwork, the most practical digger probably has a degree in archaeology, if not a Ph.D., and still argues about the purpose of digging – and both were once schoolchildren, and remain members of the wider public. Rather than separating this paper into audiences we have therefore divided it according to different types of communication. We find out about any subject through experience and personal contact, and through written text and visual media. The main methods by which we find out about archaeology are listed in the following section.

COMMUNICATION CHANNELS

Experience

Direct personal encounters with archaeological evidence can take various forms. Experience of archaeology by engaging in fieldwork remains one of the best forms of communication: even if it is a small project, with no spectacular finds, working on it will explain better than any number of books and lectures how archaeological evidence is recovered. Talking to other members of the team also provides the commitment to go on and find out more. This is why so many archaeologists began their careers while still at school, as volunteers on local excavations.

Visiting excavations is also good direct experience, but this is less easy than it once was, partly because there are so many excavations, some of very brief duration, but also because developer-funded projects work to tight schedules and are subject to strict health and safety guidelines. They have limited scope for visitors, except on specific open days. Other types of fieldwork do not really lend themselves to visits – rows of fieldwalkers or a team with survey equipment moving over the landscape are not inherently exciting, although their results, when interpreted later, may be. Regional archaeology group meetings often present roundups of recent work, and local societies have regular series of lectures, so it is not difficult to find out what is going on in any given area.

Many groups, such as the Sedgeford Historical and Archaeological Research Project (SHARP) or the Bamburgh Castle Research Project, have often been ahead of their professional counterparts in making effective use of the Internet to keep both the local community and wider audiences informed about their archaeological activities and projects. Project websites can be useful for the recruitment of volunteers, to galvanise support for conservation issues, or simply to provide news. Live webcam broadcasts of excavation trenches are generally less exciting than watching paint dry, once the voyeuristic novelty has worn off. Nonetheless, daily excavation diaries can provide an international audience with an immediate insight into the act of discovery. Through the use of electronic bulletin boards and online discussion lists some projects, notably Catal Höyük, have sought to involve wider audiences in debate and interpretation. Where sites are remote and inaccessible the web can facilitate virtual tours, although there is still no substitute for visiting a site in person.

Archaeological sites, monuments and landscapes can be visited with a pre-existing framework of knowledge, ideally with a guide who knows the place well, or alone with reports and maps, or as part of a group of specialists or students. At many sites there are now information boards – or entire visitor centres – with attractive multimedia displays and up-to-date information which, at the best ones, make the sites accessible to visitors of all levels of knowledge. The centres are often pleasant places to go for an afternoon out, to have tea and take a gentle stroll round the attached monument. Sometimes it can seem as if the visitor centre is substituting for the monument – at Sutton Hoo the exciting objects in the centre eclipse the grassy burial mounds in the nearby field, and at Newgrange, in Ireland, there is a replica of the passage tomb for those unable (or unwilling) to book a trip to see the real thing. Some of the proposed schemes for Stonehenge have a similar emphasis on off-site experience. Perhaps this is not important, as long as the individual visitor is free to choose between a quick look at a replica or a longer trek to the real thing. Scale models and computer graphics certainly play a significant role for many disabled visitors.

Personal contact

Personal contact is still the most effective means of communication in archaeology as in all other aspects of life: we have to find ways of making sense of the ocean of material delivered to our brains daily via eyes, ears, screen or printed page, and our ways of doing that usually go back to something we have been taught, or told, or argued over, with another human being, which might now include virtual contact, via television, e-mail, or the Internet. E-mail discussion lists have introduced new channels for interaction and debate, whether they are focused on a specific television programme, site or topic, or whether they are more generic, such as the *britarch* list, managed by the Council for British Archaeology (CBA). In a limited sense, such open lists do help widen participation and open up knowledge in that anyone from a schoolchild to eminent professor can post questions and responses, and need not admit their offline status. However, in turn these lists often develop into cyber-communities that have their own hierarchies and protocols. E-mail and the Internet may increase the quantity but not necessarily the quality of the information flow.

Education

The first place most people encounter archaeology, or any other subject our society thinks it is worthwhile to teach, is at school. If children start with the idea, however vague, that archaeology is a legitimate subject about which they do know something, they are more likely to take it seriously in the future. It sometimes seems that all that is required of primary school children by the National Curriculum is reading, writing and arithmetic – plus IT – but they do still have time off to do Egypt, Rome, Saxons, Vikings and Aztecs. There are books, some very good, and resource packs, and some imaginative teachers and local archaeologists who manage to communicate enthusiasm for the past to many of their students (see *Internet Archaeology* 12 for discussion and examples). At primary school level dressing up as a Roman soldier or helping to build an Iron Age house works pretty well as an introduction to those periods, although it is true that early prehistory gets little attention. At secondary level the situation is less encouraging, for the whole study of history as well as archaeology. The focus has moved from earlier to more recent periods: even the stalwart Tudors and Stuarts have been eclipsed by Hitler. Although you can still dress up as an evacuee or soldier in a trench there is so much documentary material that inevitably archaeology is not seen as very relevant to these later periods. This creates the problem that archaeology is perceived as kids' stuff, belonging to those periods when society was in its infancy, before reaching the heights of sophistication evidenced by the wars of the twentieth and twenty-first centuries – or alternatively, is taken up as part of a nostalgic romantic reaction against that, a search for an earlier and better way of life.

Lectures still play a major role in university teaching and in communicating to the interested wider public. Some television programmes function in much the same way, with a message delivered by an identifiable presenter. Most professional archaeologists, whether academic or field-based, acquire much new information and ideas directly from colleagues, students or visitors, e-mail or lectures, or by attending conferences, although the latter can serve political and social functions as much as intellectual ones – and many people feel the arguments they have in the pub afterwards are more useful than the formal lectures.

The lecture is not such an easy format for communication as it seems. The ways we absorb information from the written page and through eyes and ears are different. Just reading a paper aloud is often a waste of time: better to photocopy it and hand it round – or put it on the web. But when it works, speaking to an audience communicates more, and better, than reading to them. This depends on the knowledge and personality of the lecturer/presenter: if we feel this is a person we can believe, and if they put over their ideas in a clear and interesting way, we will be receptive to what we are being told. Sometimes the lecturer, or presenter, has such a strong personality that their performance overshadows the content, but that is still (usually) better than someone so boring the audience switches off.

Television

Where television programmes make use of a presenter, producers choose the type of personality they believe will appeal to a wide audience. This currently tends to involve characterful middle-aged men, with occasional experiments with women or good looking younger men. The authority of the older man (Schama, Starkey) seems to outweigh their apparent lack of glamour – which is interestingly counter to wisdom propagated in the media some years ago, that boring old academics could not hold a television audience. Successful archaeology presenters tend to signal their subject by having beards and mud on their boots (Julian Richards, Francis Pryor; see Chapter 20).

Archaeology has had a variable history in TV. In the 1950s the archaeological quiz *Animal, Vegetable, Mineral* achieved great popularity among those who then owned television sets, and its leading participants, Mortimer Wheeler and Glyn Daniel, became successively television personality of the year. The successful formula of a quiz involving eccentric personalities and equally peculiar objects remains to this day at the back of the minds of television executives, although it is not currently on our screens. From the 1960s to the 1980s there were well-informed documentaries, mostly on BBC, including for example programmes with Brian Hope-Taylor on early medieval Britain, the *Chronicle* series, programmes on Sutton Hoo – and many more. It is true that *Chronicle* had its fair share of the popular topics of exotic locations, treasure and bodies with and without flesh, and that in audience ratings terms the most successful programmes were those on Lindow Man (ancient dead body) and the *Mary Rose* (an underwater Pompeii with royal interest). But they also showed that it is possible to go straight from original research, not just excavation results but ideas, to the screen. Thirty years on, the programme on the implications of radiocarbon dating with Magnus Magnusson and Colin Renfrew is still a very good exposition of the subject. When first shown it would have been new to many archaeologists, as well as everyone else.

When the first version of this chapter was produced in the early 1990s it seemed as if this tradition was coming to an end, and that archaeology was fading from TV screens. One new format, the news magazine, was tried with some success, in Channel 4's *Down to Earth*, which was however replaced with what was to become the source of an extraordinary revival in the television fortunes of the subject, *Time Team* (Fig. 19.1). Now, instead of lamenting the disappearance of the subject, it is easier to complain about over-exposure and wonder whether a backlash against a surfeit of archaeological programmes is not about to emerge.

The secret of *Time Team*'s success seems to be that it appeals to a fascination in revealing something hidden under the ground, combined with explaining how that is done, especially through modern technology, and also practical experiments and computer graphics that can build an Iron Age house in a back garden, or turn a fragment into a complete object. The virtual involvement of the audience in the TV excavation, especially in the three-day bank holiday real time events, gives it enormous power. The programme-

Figure 19.1. The *Time Team* under the scrutiny of a young audience in Peterborough.

makers also make effective use of the Internet as a means of providing access to further information and relevant links. As well as strengths, the series has weaknesses (see Hills 2003 for a longer discussion), but it has developed interest in archaeology across a wide spectrum of the public, and encouraged the production of many more, different, television programmes about archaeology. There is now an audience that has learnt history partly through recreation of a day in the life of ordinary people in the past, and in some cases has continued to 'live in the past' as re-enactors at the weekends. Many programmes use this, and deploy actors – whether in masks and fur for the Palaeolithic, rags and pustules for the Plague – or any variety of past armour and weaponry. Some even try to record real life in the past – an Iron Age village or Edwardian house where volunteers have been left alone (except for a TV crew). Most periods and most continents seem to have come at least briefly into view, although maybe Early Man, Rome, and the Vikings have had slightly more than their fair share of attention, together with civilisations apparently destroyed by mysterious catastrophes.

Television is entertainment, but it can also inform, and in many ways is ultimately not different from more academic forms of communication. In both there is always a danger that the packaging, whether on television or in a glossy book – or in a set piece keynote conference speech – will be seen as the end, even if the content is in fact only recycled old material. Presentation is not the same thing as research. Discovering something new, or rethinking a subject from its foundations, is not the same thing as presenting a programme or giving a lecture on the broader context of that discovery. The fine print of detailed data and interpretation remains just that – only accessible by careful reading of detailed texts.

Texts

Written texts of all kinds, addressed to all levels of audience, are still the major form of communication. From bookshops and catalogues, journals and newspapers and even more from the Internet, it might seem that our problem was over-publication, rather than the reverse. Specialists cannot afford either the time or the money to read more than a fraction of what might be relevant, which means some research may be carried out in ignorance of previous comparable work. For all readers finding a critical path through the mass of literature is difficult. The answer for specialists lies through reviews, review articles and bibliographies or abstracts, such as the *British and Irish Archaeological Bibliography* (*BIAB*), now on the web. These are tools, means to an end and not ends in themselves: they are essential guides to the literature, not substitutes for it. Such tools are now much easier to use, thanks to the computer.

For the non-specialist reader there is no simple path; rather, the responsibility of the profession is to produce, as increasingly it does, readable and authoritative introductions, like the Tempus series, for a wider readership. The crucial point about such books is that they should not be simple scissors and paste repackaging of old material but clear summaries of recent research. Readers familiar with new discoveries from television programmes will not be impressed by books that are out of date in relation to factual data; but they will be less able to spot discredited concepts. In Britain we still lack the glossy

Figure 19.2. Written texts of all kinds are still the major form of communication. The illustration shows a selection of research and publication material used in desk based assessment. (© *Oxford Archaeological Unit; Photo: Ros Smith*)

archaeology journals that can be bought in high street newsagents in other European countries, but *Current Archaeology* provides invaluable and accessible summaries of fieldwork results alongside occasionally idiosyncratic commentary on archaeo-politics.

Since the first edition of this book the growth of the Internet has transformed the dissemination of archaeological information and further exacerbated the problems of information overload. Websites may range from a few pages of text describing a specific project to large corporate databases. From its quite anarchic and specialist origins in the academic community, the potential of the Internet has been recognised by commerce and harnessed by government. Lottery funding has enabled large digitisation projects, and government agencies holding archaeological data are encouraged to provide public online access. In Scotland, the National Monuments Record (NMRS) was one of the first national agencies to make its database available online, via its CANMORE interface. Several county and regional records are now following suit, often with the incentive of lottery funding. Other projects, such as the *Defence of Britain* and *Images of England* databases, have relied upon significant amateur involvement. In the Higher and Further Education sector electronic access to information is promoted as solving library under-funding while simultaneously enhancing the learning experience. One of the first electronic-only online journals, *Internet Archaeology*, was produced in our discipline. Traditional journals, such as *Antiquity*, are also enhancing their web presence, and have digitised their back issues. Many of these trends towards electronic access will ultimately make the life of the researcher much easier. Electronic dissemination also provides access to a far richer variety of data types, including searchable databases, unlimited colour images, movies, and virtual reality models. On the down side, finding what you want and, for the non-specialist, assessing the quality of the information provided, have become major issues.

Whether specialists or non-specialists, most people will first try to find relevant Internet resources by using a search engine, such as Google. Although these will generally yield thousands of hits, at least these will be ranked according to relevance to the search term and also frequency of citation, in an attempt to place oft-cited quality resources higher up the list. However, their lists are generated automatically by free-text indexing of web pages and will invariably include both junk and outdated resources. Search engines are also inadequate for searching within non-text resources, including images and databases. Only about one five-hundredth of Internet content is held in text pages. Users searching specifically for archaeological content might alternatively use an information gateway, or list of linked websites, such as that provided by the CBA for the British Isles (http://www.britarch.ac.uk/) or ARCHNET (http://archnet.asu.edu/) in the United States. These benefit from having been compiled by humans and frequently contain short reviews; they still suffer, however, from broken links and are expensive to maintain. In the UK there are several initiatives funded from the university sector, including the Archaeology Data Service, whose remit is to catalogue, preserve and encourage the re-use of digital data (Richards 2003), and HUMBUL (http://www.humbul.ac.uk/), a project that aims to catalogue quality Internet resources useful for humanities teaching and research. These projects are collaborating in research to develop more systematic ways of indexing Internet resources, allowing users to discover what they want more easily. One further aspect of this is the development of a type of web gateway known as a portal, which allows users to search simultaneously across a number of distributed online databases. Thus HEIRPORT (http://ads.ahds.ac.uk/heirport/), a prototype portal for historic environment information resources, allows users to search across a range of databases maintained in different locations, including the collections of the Archaeology Data Service (ADS), the Scottish NMR (CANMORE) and the Portable Antiquities Scheme (PAS). Despite web developers' love of acronyms, this decentralised approach to information delivery is likely to grow, as it is easily extendable across audiences, disciplines and national boundaries (Austin *et al.* 2002).

Creative media

So far we have been talking about types of communication whose purpose is to provide a direct source of information about archaeology. There are also indirect sources of information. Many novelists use archaeological evidence in their recreation of the past in which they have set their story: for example Jean Auel, in *Clan of the Cave Bear*, which evokes life in Neanderthal society, and their encounter with modern humans, as does William Golding's *The Inheritors*. Arthurian Britain has continuing appeal, from Rosemary Sutcliffe to Bernard Cornwell – and many others. One of Lindsay Davies' Roman detective stories is set at Fishbourne, with plausible reconstruction of the building and its dubious inhabitants. None of these necessarily convey much direct information about archaeology, but the authors have usually done their homework, and referenced sources interested readers can follow up. Some novelists have described the process of excavation, and have incorporated it into their work, partly as a means of exploring the complex relationships between past and present, for example Penelope Lively in *Treasures of Time*, or Roger Ackroyd in *First Light*. One of the best evocations of archaeology in fiction is E.H. Carr's *A Month in the Country*, where the lives of an early twentieth-century art historian and an archaeologist are interwoven with the life of the medieval artist whose work – and bones – they are discovering.

Some artists find inspiration in archaeological monuments; others, as Renfrew has argued (Renfrew 2003) explore ways of seeing and interpreting the material world – objects, landscape, bodies – which are different, but parallel, to ways archaeologists see them.

Films, like novels, use archaeological research in the recreation of settings, clothes and weapons, and even events. Some of these are good – the reconstruction of the Roman Forum in the *Fall of the Roman Empire* for example, or, in the same vein, *Gladiator*. Excavation does feature in some films, not usually demonstrating methods one would like to see taken as models for archaeological fieldwork – mostly in Egypt, including assorted *Mummy* horror films, *The English Patient*, and of course *Raiders of the Lost Ark*, with the best known archaeologist in the world, Indiana Jones, and now the computer game inspired, Lara Croft, tomb raider.

These kinds of communication are not a direct message from archaeologists but a reflection of how the subject is perceived by others. In a reflexive process, authors and film-makers take from archaeology what they understand of it, recreate it, and present it to an audience who then come to the subject with preconceptions derived from those fictional versions, which can then feed back into the subject at a professional level. At best, this can be inspirational; but also problematic if it is not ultimately based on a proper understanding of the evidence and its interpretation. Recycling of old material in bright new media perpetuates misconceptions and limits real understanding of new research.

The archaeological report

The foundation of archaeological discussion is the data which has been recovered both from fieldwork and laboratory analysis, and its interpretation within explicit theoretical frameworks. The traditional format in which this is presented is the archaeological report, a printed volume containing an introduction to the site, a summary and discussion of the excavated evidence, conclusions as to its meaning and, at the back, all the evidence – for example, plans, sections and finds catalogues. During the 1960s, publication became the problem it has remained ever since because of the explosion of material, an explosion that resulted from a simultaneous increase in the scale of excavation and in the detail and range of types of information that could be extracted from what was dug up.

In 1975 the Frere Committee (DoE 1975a) tackled the problem of unpublished excavations in an era of rising print costs. This identified four levels of record, of which only Level IV, synthesised descriptions with supporting data and selected finds and specialist reports relevant to synthesis, really needed to be published. What had previously been the bulk of an archaeological report (Level III), full illustration and description of all structural and stratigraphic relationships together with classified finds lists and drawings and specialist analyses, might simply be made available as required: as duplicates, fiche, microfilm or computer printout.

There was disagreement as to the dividing line between Levels III and IV and a suspicion that those with sufficient influence could still publish 'properly' while ordinary mortals would see their work consigned to the wastebasket of fiche, or still worse, archive. Also, the same time and expense were required for post-excavation, even if the results barely saw the light of day, and funding for post-excavation reduced the funds available for excavation.

The Cunliffe Report (Cunliffe 1983) introduced the emphasis on selectivity that has become fundamental: 'the temptation to excavate more than can reasonably be processed . . . should be stringently controlled' (1983: 3). This runs counter to the psychological instincts encouraged by rescue archaeology, especially as it was seen in the 1960s and 1970s (Rahtz 1974) – dig it today because tomorrow it will have been destroyed – which of course partly caused the publication problem. However, in the 1990s *Planning Policy Guidance Note 16* (PPG 16) provided the basis for the requirement for developers to fund the investigation of archaeological remains threatened by construction. This greatly improved the situation vis-à-vis unrecorded destruction of sites; but in so doing greatly exacerbated the problem of publication.

English Heritage (EH) has dealt with this in a policy document which now forms the basis for the organisation of archaeological fieldwork in England funded publicly or by developers, and is implicitly the basis of procedures which have been adopted elsewhere in the UK (EH 1991a). This is *The Management of Archaeological Projects 2*, MAP2, successor to a slim booklet, MAP1, published in 1989. MAP2 was originally compiled in 1991 and is maintained online (http://www.eng-h.gov/guidance/map2). The version consulted and quoted here was last updated in October 1998. MAP2 describes archaeological investigation as a cyclical process of assessment and research, starting with a project design and proceeding through fieldwork, assessment of potential for analysis, redefinition of project design, report preparation, to the final report dissemination. At all stages there is assessment and selection, of whether fieldwork is needed, the scale of work, what should be recorded, how much of the record will remain as archive, how much be further analysed, and what aspects of the results will be more widely disseminated. Decisions are taken by people who have not carried out the excavation, and indeed the report(s) may not be written by the excavator. This is an operation closer to business than research – for good reasons, since most of this work is done within the constraints of the construction industry and planning bureaucracy. The resulting reports follow a fairly logical (and traditional) path from a description of the background to the site investigated, including previous work, history, and geology, to detailed account of the excavation, stratigraphic sequence, specialist reports, discussion and conclusion.

Production of such reports is a bureaucratic and controlled process with little room for individual originality. It is a long way from the old style research project, directed by one person whose vision informed the enterprise from planning to publication. The volume of work carried out requires a system, and this one does ensure some degree of consistency, and it produces a large number of reports each year because production of the report is the end result – the 'preservation by record' of the archaeological heritage. However, the majority of these reports fall within the category of 'grey literature', documents with a very limited circulation. They are widely used in the planning process, and by field archaeologists themselves, but there is a need to find mechanisms for the assimilation and wider dissemination of the information produced by developer-funded excavation, embodied in the grey reports. The list of projects compiled as part of the BIAB for several years went some way to answer this, and they have now become more accessible as a result of putting them on-line as part of the NMR Excavation Index, made available by the ADS. The OASIS project (http://ads.ahds.ac.uk/project/oasis/) has introduced a web-based data collection form for entry of information relating to all archaeological interventions in an effort to maintain an online index, but it will be several years before this is a national system. Nonetheless, such a system has great potential for reducing the duplication inherent in the current system of multiple reporting procedures, and as grey literature reports are gradually made available on the Internet, it will provide easy access to them (Hardman and Richards 2003). However, the results also need to be incorporated into research. The best way forward is to break down the divide between field worker and academic. Results of contract archaeology must be drawn on in research: the distribution of early settlement in eastern England looks very different in the light of recent work – for example, apparently empty land, arable or pasture since at least the later Middle Ages and presumed to have always been farmed or tree-covered, has been found to be full of Iron Age, Roman and Saxon features, as at West Fen Road, Ely (Masser 2001), or Vicars Farm, Cambridge (Lucas and Whittaker 2001). Also, fieldwork should be informed by more than the basic information as to whether anything has been found in the next field. The larger contracting units are well aware of this, and there are a number of national and local initiatives to provide syntheses, but inevitably the pressures of working to a deadline within limited resources mean that it can be difficult to do more than fulfil the basic requirements of the planning brief.

This kind of fieldwork has an implicitly objective theoretical stance: evidence of the past is important, identifiable, and should be recorded for posterity before destruction, in a clear and logical way.

The policy of 'preservation by record' in an archive, with limited circulation reports and selective synthesis, is not without problems. Even where there is a curated archive, as in London, limited use has been made of it (Cunliffe 1990: 671; Merriman and Swain 1999), although this situation may be changing with the promotion of more accessible physical archives, such as the London Archaeological Archive and Research Centre (LAARC), and with the development of online digital archives. The most recent survey to examine the whole question of publication user needs (Jones et al. 2001) recommended the promotion of different publication media and formats to suit different needs and audiences. Whereas previous attempts to publish detailed archaeological data on microfiche had failed with an inadequate and unpopular technology, electronic publication and the dissemination of archival and specialist material in digital format provides a means to overcome the practical limitations of fiche. Despite the dangers of seeing the Internet as a dumping ground for undigested data and of continuing to relegate supporting and specialist reports as secondary material, digital archives offer much potential. Early examples, such as the digital archives for the Royal Opera House and Eynsham Abbey were widely used and individual files, including GIS and CAD, were downloaded hundreds of times (see Richards 2003). Nonetheless, in each case the reports had been prepared for traditional hard copy monographs, and in each case what has been made available online represented the leftovers of the post-excavation process, reflecting the practices of each archaeological contractor.

Where electronic publication can be planned into a project at an earlier stage a more strategic approach can be taken, permitting different levels of access and a seamless transition between publication and archive, as well as different forms of publication. The Fyfield and Overton Down Project was published at a number of levels. A popular book, *The Land of Lettice Sweetapple*, publishes the main results for the general reader (Fowler and Blackwell 1998). The Society of Antiquaries monograph (Fowler 2000) includes the archaeological evidence from the key sites for the academic reader, while in the project digital archive Peter Fowler makes available not only the text of four further monograph-length reports, but also some 100 Fyfield Working Papers, including specialist reports, draft texts, and background documentation. The traditional monograph includes a URL for the archive and basic instructions on how to use it.

Where a site is also published electronically then the full potential of live hypertext links can be explored, allowing the user to move between publication and archive at will. A tentative and preliminary model of some of the possibilities is explored in the layered electronic publication of an Anglian and Anglo-Scandinavian farmstead at Cottam, East Yorkshire, in *Internet Archaeology* (Richards 2001) and the simultaneous release of the archive on the ADS site. At the top level the electronic publication follows the familiar model of a traditional printed report through introduction, methodology, results and discussion. Within the electronic version, however, the reader can follow hypertext links to pull up illustrative material such as plans and photographs, and can also read more detail of the archaeological findings. They can also search an online database of the finds from the excavation, fieldwalking, and metal-detecting. Furthermore, by clicking on further links they can seamlessly move into the archive, reading the specialist reports, the detailed stratigraphic evidence, and are able to download context and finds databases, and raw geophysics surveys and CAD files.

For such approaches to gain ground a new attitude will be required to archives so that they are no longer seen as an afterthought once the report has gone to the editors, and so that academic status is gained as much from a short synthesis and well-ordered archive as from a multivolume hardbound monograph. Many readers will continue to take the easy way out and read only the synthesis, believing it, or not, if they already trust the author (hence the importance, already discussed, of personal contact at all levels of communication). On this basis it is quite legitimate to dismiss all archaeological writing as an exercise in power politics, a form of domination and control (Shanks and Tilley 1987b: 207). If you are an established name in archaeology people will believe your synthesis. If you are not, they will not (unless they are sceptical graduates in which case they will believe only themselves).

The nature of the archaeological record, and how it may be acquired and interpreted, has been the subject of critical theoretical discussion, influenced by anthropology, linguistics and philosophy. This has explored many different views concerning the possibility, or rather impossibility, of knowing the past, and the extent to which any piece of archaeological writing can claim to be an objective view of a real past rather than an exercise in propaganda or personal opinion (e.g. Shanks and Tilley 1987b; Bapty and Yates 1990). The case for multivocality, the need for many different, possibly contradictory accounts, has been argued, especially with relation to the project at Catal Höyük (Hodder 2000). This post-modern approach to the archaeological process has many attractions. It is democratic in allowing all members of the team to contribute, and it shows how contingent all interpretation is on the perspective of the interpreters. It also allows for uncertainty, contradiction and almost by definition requires a continuing dialogue – discussion, reinterpretation, alternative conclusions. Focus on the creation of interpretation is important and necessary: we are too prone to argue as if all sides of any argument were not conditional, as they clearly are, at least in part, on the various intellectual, political and even emotional perspectives of all the proponents.

Some of the Catal Höyük process is not so far from normal fieldwork practice: competent field teams have always discussed what they are doing, and some conclusions are often left unresolved. But for many people, as with novels given alternative endings, not resolving arguments seems both frustrating and perhaps even an avoidance of responsibility. To many, it would seem better to record and report alternative conclusions which do not seem to have the support of most of the evidence – without according those differing views equal status.

It is certainly clear that the multivocal approach could undermine contract archaeology. Why should a developer waste valuable resources on recovering archaeological evidence for which no clear and agreed interpretation can be given? Several archaeologists have addressed this issue (Carver 1996; Andrews *et al.* 2000) and have argued strongly for the reintegration of fieldwork and interpretation. Rather than the neutral retrieval of objective data for future analysis we should work within a framework of historical enquiry intended to provide information about people, not an archive of potsherds. This should not be confined to the rarefied context of well-funded research projects, but should also be central to contract archaeology. Andrews *et al.* argue that this is possible without adding to the cost of projects, while increasing the value of their results – and the satisfaction of those engaged on the work.

CONCLUSION

In summary, archaeology and archaeological results are disseminated to multiple audiences, using various channels of communication. A considerable amount of information and interpretation is communicated, sometimes very effectively. The widespread knowledge of archaeology among the general public is the result of good use of modern media. The results of fieldwork are made available both in traditional format as summary or full reports, online, as limited circulation reports, or in archive. Academic debate continues in all branches of the subject, resulting in a burgeoning academic literature. Yet there are problems that need constant attention. Some are practical problems, where electronic solutions may now be emerging: the volume of information needs to be managed and sorted; excavation results need to be made more widely known; information disseminated to the public needs to be based on proper research, not rehashing of older material. Others are more intractable. The divide between practice and theory, often translated into field archaeologist and academic, is helpful to no one. Academic debate needs data, and fieldwork needs purpose. The easy way might be for the profession to become further divided. This leaves digging to 'preserve by record' uncontroversial evidence which can be packaged up for different audiences, all of whom, specialist or schoolchild, will get simple clear answers to their questions. Meanwhile, the theoretician can disappear into a cloud of unknowing. It is more difficult to take the other path and to try to explain how alternative interpretations can coexist without automatically invalidating each other, to introduce uncertainty and doubt while somehow not denying the possibility of knowing anything. In one direction is a dead subject, whose established details can be elaborated and repackaged, but not changed in essentials, which tells us objective facts about long dead people. In the other is a dynamic attempt to understand human beings in the past and present through their material impact on the world, which involves constant questioning and reappraisal.

CHAPTER 20

VISITORS AND VIEWERS WELCOME?

Mike Parker Pearson and Francis Pryor

INTRODUCTION

Apart from some light editing to allow for the passage of time, much of the second edition of this chapter remains largely unchanged from the original text of 1993. The original chapter is substantially retained as the first part of this text ('Visitors Welcome') – a reference to the ground-breaking English Heritage (EH) publication of the same name (Binks *et al.* 1988) – but a second part is added here ('Viewers Welcome') to take into account the increasing role of the small screen in our archaeological lives. The title has been modified accordingly, with the deliberate addition of a question mark to query the degree of welcome that visitors or television crews actually receive on a significant number of archaeological projects. Experience suggests that this perceived failure to reach out to a wider audience is only sometimes the fault of the archaeological contractor. More often, sadly, it reflects the wish of the client who commissioned the work. Often too, the developer had been advised to maintain a low profile by his or her archaeological consultant in the name of 'commercial sensitivity' or 'client confidentiality'. Whatever one might think of these as excuses (and in certain competitive situations they can have validity) they ultimately have a very negative effect on the wider public's appreciation of the archaeological heritage. Professional archaeologists have an overarching obligation to persuade their clients that good publicity is positive. As Sir Mortimer Wheeler famously noted: 'At the best, excavation is destruction; and destruction unmitigated by all the resources of contemporary knowledge and accumulated experience cannot be too rigorously impugned' (1954: 15). In other words, excavation without publication is merely methodical destruction – and by publication we mean broader dissemination of our results than via the usual 'grey literature' client reports. We should also bear in mind that if enough developers and planners (and behind them the politicians) become convinced that archaeological work is dull, routine and not particularly important (a view heard expressed from time to time) then one day the prevailing climate of planning opinion, in which archaeological remains require sympathetic treatment, might shift – and that would not be in the interests of the resource, research, or the wider community interested in our past.

VISITORS WELCOME

Archaeology is now recognised as a legitimate consideration in planning control. Private organisations are funding large amounts of work. Publicity about archaeological discoveries is copious. And yet for the last three decades there appears to have been a crisis looming over archaeology's survival, either from cuts in public spending or in loss of committed public support. With some exceptions, notably the Heritage Lottery Fund (HLF), professionalisation has forced out the grass-roots participants just when volunteers in nature conservation are growing in numbers. Developers may become less content to pay for archaeology when their expectations of discoveries are not matched by the meagre nature of finds. Despite some spectacular results from 'polluter pays' fieldwork (e.g. the Amesbury Archer, Iron Age chariots in Yorkshire and near Edinburgh, reported in the national press, *British Archaeology, Current Archaeology* and elsewhere), archaeology in Britain continues to run the risk of becoming boring, bureaucratic and inconsequential (see also Biddle 1994).

As well as welcoming visitors, we should be encouraging participants. To carry the public with us requires more than glossy brochures and shop-window consumerism. We require a sea change in professional attitudes to truly involve as many people as possible and to reach the parts we have never reached. But apart from the HLF, where does alternative funding come from? What we would like to do and what we end up doing are often two different things, because of pressures of time and limits of funds. Education, publicity and outreach are some of the first items to be cut from budgets hard-pressed even to ensure that salaries are paid. County archaeologists are often too busy and archaeological education officers are still a rare breed indeed. Perhaps we could be thinking about presentational and educational aspects being included as a matter of routine in the archaeological briefs provided by local authorities in much the same way as they are required in Heritage Lottery funded support (e.g. the Ben Lawers Historic Landscape Project: www.benlawers.org.uk). Against this background archaeologists have always been pretty good at advertising themselves, their institutions, their sponsors and patrons, and their achievements. Very few archaeological organisations have failed to have substantially strengthened their public profile in the last ten years. There are newsheets, newspapers, brochures, teaching packs, site guides, regional tour operators, open days, education officers, resource centres, popular books and multimedia presentations, and now websites in profusion. Some archaeological organisations have specific education and outreach sections (e.g.Wessex Archaeology: www.wessexarch.co.uk); the appointment of Finds Liaison Officers resulting from the implementation of the Treasure Act (see Chapter 6) in its own way also represents a formally funded investment in outreach provision. The use of increasingly sophisticated and expensive means for informing and bringing in visitors has been extensive. Most professional archaeologists no longer need to be apprised of the technical innovations and organisation, as put together so well in *Visitors Welcome* (Binks *et al.* 1988). But perhaps we have concentrated too much on the medium at the expense of the message. The form of presentations may be arresting, intriguing and eye-catching but what about the content?

Everyone has an opinion on what is good for archaeology's public. The differences of opinion can be great. The providers of heritage centres and re-enactments may be vilified for their exploitative and cynical marketing of the past. Those who raise political issues in archaeology may be castigated for their political bias and for rocking the boat. Some organisations have formulated codes of conduct. For example, the 'Campaign for Real Heritage' at Flag Fen is guided by three rules: the past must not be mystified; the past must not be cheapened or trivialised; every interpretation is capable of reinterpretation (Pryor 1989). There continues to be a substantial and continuous flow of literature addressing the philosophical issues that lie behind the presentation of heritage (Lowenthal and Binney 1981; McBryde 1985; Schadla-Hall 1984; Wright 1985; Hewison 1987; Uzzell 1989b, 1989c; Layton 1989a, 1989b; Gathercole and Lowenthal 1990; Stone and MacKenzie 1990; Fowler 1992; Hooper-Greenhill 1991; Skeates 2000; Walsh 1992). Archaeology is, of course, a social phenomenon. Its practice and practitioners are products of the economic and class relationships of contemporary society. Surveys of attitudes towards archaeology (Merriman 1991; Hodder *et al.* 1985; Merriman and Swain 1999) indicate that it still means little to most people from working-class backgrounds. It is part of a plethora of tastes and activities by which dominant cultural groups define themselves as refined, knowledgeable and discerning (see e.g. Bourdieu's 1984 study of class life styles). Nearly all archaeologists

Figure 20.1. Open days continue to provide one of the key public access points to field archaeology, here supported by re-enactment at Durrington Walls, Stonehenge Riverside Project. *(Photo: Megan Price)*

are propagandists for their subject, often with a passion, and few would wish to restrict its appeal to a narrow class niche. So how well have we done in taking archaeology to the people? If only one in four people buy books, then the medium of the written word may be relatively limited in its impact. Exhibitions and displays that use pictorial or three-dimensional representations and spoken words are probably more successful in reaching and appealing to a wider cross-section of the population than text-explained exhibits. Archaeology is regularly reported in the quality papers but almost never – except rather frivolously – in the rest. Bestsellers about the past are either romantic novels or veer towards the mystical, although these are now being complemented by a new genre of archaeological literature based on, and following up, TV programmes such as *Time Team*.

Interestingly, Merriman's 1991 survey indicated that interest in archaeology and the past was not class-restricted among the younger generations. Although archaeology and prehistory receive short shrift in the English National Curriculum, and some national examinations have been axed altogether (only one examination board now offers the subject), there are many teaching resources, support coordinators (education officers in EH, the Councils for British and Scottish Archaeology and local authorities) and enthusiastic teachers who are instilling an interest at an early age (see e.g. Corbishley 1992; Halkon *et al.* 1992; Pearson 2001).

Archaeologists have expanded their passive audience, but their active grass-roots support has declined drastically. The role of the amateur has been marginalised with the necessary professionalisation of the discipline, and opportunities for people to participate in the process are increasingly few and far between, a situation which has been at least partly responsible for the foundation of the Council for Independent Archaeology. As elements of archaeology have joined the consumer culture, the public must increasingly pay for their voyeuristic experiences. Archaeological 'shopping' involves purchases from archaeological dreamsellers of authentic experiences of the past, but sadly misses out on the involvement in discovery and interpretation behind the shop window. You can look, you can even touch, but it is getting harder to join in. Of course, many people are interested yet never want to be involved. Looking through the glass is as close as they want to come. Yet we should surely be encouraging active participation as widely as possible, as at York, for example, where the Archaeology Resource Centre provides the opportunity for 'hands on' activity on a range of processes and crafts for all ages. The comparison with wildlife interests, where many amateurs are acknowledged specialists and experts, is becoming less and less sustainable.

The motives that draw people to archaeology are undoubtedly complex and varied. Escapism, fantasy, curiosity, amusement, and reassurance may be some of the more readily articulated (Lowenthal 1985). In our culture, leisure is positively loaded as a moral value. People may use their leisure time to play, develop their creativity, and improve their psychological well-being (Goodale and Witt 1985). Archaeology may offer some amusement, a sideshow of escapist distractions, but what more does it involve? Social engineering concepts of instruction and moral betterment, expressed in the nineteenth century by Pitt Rivers among others (Bowden 1991: 141–2), are now viewed as patronising, unsophisticated and deeply conservative. But many archaeologists are concerned that mere amusement, 'the happiness of those who cannot think' (Alexander Pope, cited in Goodale and Witt 1985: 3), is not enough.

David Uzzell's (1989b: 10) diagnosis remains valid: 'Despite the use of a profusion of technologies to enhance visitor understanding and enable learning, it would seem from research on the effectiveness of exhibitions that visitors to museums actually do not learn very much.' Similar concerns were once voiced about the popular and successful Jorvik Viking Centre in York (Schadla-Hall 1984), though the reviewer suggested that this was the fault of the presentation rather than the visitor. We may complain that many people simply lack a developed sense of curiosity, but perhaps they are not being sufficiently challenged. Before the changes which overtook the system, a senior Soviet archaeologist, V.I. Masson, made the surprising comment to one of the authors (MPP) that he considered archaeology to be psychology: we must prevent people from becoming Neanderthals living in centrally heated flats! No senior figures in British archaeology had, at that time, expressed such strong sentiments about the purpose of the subject. A few years on, such views are common currency among archaeologists and heritage managers. Interpretation is about encouraging people to think for themselves (Aldridge 1989). It is not instruction but provocation (Tilden 1977: 9).

The primary object of interpretation is to create a sense of discovery and a sense of wonder (Stevens 1989). It is also to provide food for thought; to attempt to shake people out of their 'Neanderthal' docility. In the words of the late French historian Fernand Braudel (1980), we visit the past in order to better understand the present. Through archaeology we visit different times and different cultures, with some aspects similar to our own lives and others very different. In this exploration of sameness/difference we may come to see just how arbitrary and historically rooted are our own 'universal truths'. In the same way that Francis Fukuyama proclaimed 'the end of history' (1992), archaeologists have perhaps unwittingly promulgated the notion that the past is dead, that we are close to the top rung of the ladder of progress. In such ways we reinforce our feelings of superiority to the societies of the past, and teach people to be contemptuous of those primitive peoples from long ago. Through this contempt for the people of the past we are liable to instil contempt for the millions who live in pre- or non-industrial societies (Stone and MacKenzie 1990).

'What's history if you can't bend it a bit?' was the reply to criticisms of deliberate distortion of the past for financial gain during the 1988 Armada celebrations (Hewison

1989). Other forces may also be at play, for example the political correctness of the Trafalgar re-enactment on the 200th aniversary in 2005, which anonymised British and French nationalities into blue or red fleets. The potential misrepresentation of past events for purposes of modern spectacle has been viewed with alarm by archaeologists. The staging of a battle between French and British troops of the Napoleonic period in a Palmerstonian fort has been compared to the hypothetical re-enactment of the Battle of Waterloo in the Tower of London between the Ermine Street Guard and the Sealed Knot (Fowler 1989)! Perhaps a more apt example is the annual gathering of Druids at (or near) Stonehenge. The point still stands, however. But there is a more difficult problem that this opposition between bent history and objective accuracy fails to accommodate. We are all aware of the distortions of prehistory to justify racist and territorial aims under the Nazis (Arnold 1990, 1992). Even without such gross misreadings of the evidence, all reconstructions of the past are in some sense constructs of the present. Our categorisation of past times into eras (Roman, Neolithic, etc.) carries implicit meanings and interpretations that guide our thoughts about what happened, and how, in the past. We may strive to maintain an objective and minimalist stance in interpretation, but such an approach is likely to be misleading as well as boring. Cautious interpretations are likely to invoke a pragmatic utilitarianism in explaining the evidence. Employing our twenty-first-century notions of common sense, we are destined to imprint forever the present onto the past. As a result, we risk learning nothing other than that past cultures were dirtier, technologically less sophisticated versions of ourselves.

This does not mean that anything goes, that we can make up whatever we like regardless of the evidence. Instead, we have to come to terms with realising that the distinction between myth and reality in the past is not as clear-cut as some of us might wish. While we balance a concern for accurate reporting with the need to avoid a dead archaeology of lifeless and meaningless artefacts, we are still constructing creation myths (albeit with a strong component of hard evidence). For example, archaeology in Britain may be used to portray the rise of the nation state, the establishment of democracy, or even the rise of capitalism. Other myths (the insignificance of Britain in world politics until the last 1,000 years; the long history of English individualism, for example) may be ignored or used in other circumstances. All interpretive frameworks are, one way or another, mythic stories that are re-enacted, retold and presented as truth. This relativisation should not make us fearful of how to decide which version of the past is true. Instead, we should relish the possibilities for multiple interpretations and the primacy that this puts on the act of interpretation. The most popular myths about the prehistoric past are fringe beliefs in a golden age of harmony, earth forces and mysticism. The adherents of fringe archaeology are put off by the smug, exclusive, know-it-all condescension of the professionals (Williamson and Bellamy 1983). Through various rhetorical devices (Gero 1989) they cultivate an image of unfairly treated underdog: *they* know the *real* truth but are derided by the blinkered establishment. Such alternative myths are psychological props and legitimations, beyond dispute, to New Age Travellers, among others. Closed minds on both sides are hindrances to tolerance and understanding (see Skeates 2000; Chapter 5). As we develop a more critical archaeology, able to debunk and evaluate competing mythic claims on the past, so we may come to understand better the past in the present rather than simply for its own sake.

The development of the heritage industry in recent years has had a profound impact on archaeology and its presentation to the public. The past and the present are interactive: what happened in history is a question that is answered according to the worries and obsessions of the times we live in. What is happening today is a question that drives us all to examine our history for guidance. The force of the public's interests and enthusiasms moulds the heritage industry's presentations. Archaeologists can feed that force, or struggle against it: in either case, our role as mediator between past and present can be directive but our actions within that role are inherently reflexive. Since the Department of the Environment (DoE) stated that heritage would give a feeling of continuity and a sense of security to face the difficult years ahead (DoE 1975b), there has been an undercurrent of concern for the ways in which heritage differs from history. Within a climate of industrial decline, in which some old-established industries have all but disappeared, some observers viewed the rise of the heritage industry as a bolstering of nationalist sentiment, a thinly disguised presentation of right-wing interests, a sanitisation of some rather dubious past events, and a cloying and nostalgic sentimentality for an 'olde and merrie England' that never existed (Hewison 1987; Ascherson 1987, 1988; Wright 1985). If history is a critical and liberating method of re-evaluating our lives and our society, then heritage is a suffocating embrace of cultural chauvinism (Hewison 1989). When EH once prepared to sell off a number of the nation's monuments, it could be said that the past has been packaged for consumption in every form (see also Chapter 1).

There is no doubt that archaeologists have clung gratefully to the skirts of the heritage boom. The houses and gardens of past aristocracies are, as ever, very much at the heart of this boom, but archaeologists have found ways of using the stimulus and opportunities to good effect. The increasing interest in recording standing buildings and industrial monuments, and in reconstructing historic gardens, has moved the techniques of archaeology into the limelight of more recent history. Archaeology has become not simply the study of the ancient past but also the investigation of material culture right up to the present, including in an exercise that drew on the skills and knowledge of many volunteer recorders – the monuments of the Second World War (e.g. Dobinson et al. 1997; EH 1998). Yet for many practitioners, as well as onlookers, archaeology's contribution may seem little more than the application of a set of techniques, a motiveless yet systematic sifting through the physical rubbish of history. Do we simply provide the evidence and let the purveyors of dreams market the myths and stories that they wish to tell?

If heritage is a distortion of history in terms of accuracy and critical interpretation, it may also purvey a past that is pastiche and collage. According to Hewison (1989), this 'pick 'n' mix' approach weakens our knowledge and understanding of history. There are very obvious implications for archaeology. Most archaeological presentations are site-specific. Equally, our own specialisms are chronologically narrow. Our stories are of fragmented and isolated times and places that rarely relate explicitly to the epic narrative of how the world has changed in the long term. It is possible to use the concept of place to powerful effect; to develop interest in local history and archaeology, as highlighted in EH's *Power of Place* (2000a) and as practised in the growing number of heritage trails (e.g. at Kilmartin, Argyll: www.kilmartin.org). What can be achieved is perhaps less an issue of local pride (pride in another historic market town) than a key to understanding a wider past.

There may be a conflict of interest between 'giving the public what they want' (the consumer is always right in the ideology of the marketplace) and 'instructing the populace in what's good for them' (patronising Victorian-style philanthropism). It can be argued that most people want escapism rather than having to think about the world's problems, and prefer breathtaking spectacle to academic education. For some, the way forward has been a middle ground. The market does not entirely dictate the content, the message, but it does have a considerable impact on the medium. So what are archaeology's messages?

1. *Archaeology is interesting!* You do not have to be an expert to do it. Neither do you have to be white or middle class. There is very little take-up of archaeology by ethnic minorities. Organisations that archaeologists work for may have equal opportunity policies, but there is virtually no attempt to positively encourage minorities. An early project by the Countryside Commission has explored the reasons why members of ethnic

minorities fear the white-dominated countryside. It is a hostile landscape of jealously guarded private property and unfriendly natives. The Countryside Commission once set up a scheme with leaders of Asian communities in northern English towns to take coach parties on days out into the country, so that they might overcome their misgivings and feel confident that the countryside is theirs too. Active involvement of interested amateurs in fieldwork and post-excavation has fallen as professionalism has risen. We must encourage a greater sense of participation if public support is not to be alienated. Archaeological remains are a limited resource and, as such, particularly susceptible to control and exclusion. Self-important power play by professionals is to be avoided wherever possible.

2. *Archaeology is not just about white culture.* While members of ethnic minorities are British citizens, they are often not considered to be English (or Scottish, Welsh or Irish). Such tags have a racial rather than political connotation and have the effect of excluding rather than integrating. We often ignore the multiracial composition of prehistoric and historic Britain (once the subject of a Museum of London exhibition). There were black soldiers in Britain during the Roman period and people of all creeds and colours in the historic period, and it is refreshing to see that a current presentation of the London amphitheatre under the Guildhall Museum is one which also features black soldiers. Equally, considerations of the late medieval and post-medieval periods rarely place Britain in the context of the world system of the time and explain the origins and development of commercial links with different parts of the world. Some valuable work in the eastern USA and in Britain has nonetheless involved local black communities and focused on the identification of black material culture and historical figures rather than on the standard images of enslavement and powerlessness (Paynter 1990; Garrison 1990; Belgrave 1990). Such approaches may need lengthy negotiations with community leaders for their successful development.

3. *Look after the archaeological remains of the past.* In some cases, such as that of the Rose Theatre, the public seemed to be more vigilant and vociferous than the professionals (see Wainwright 1989a). Local opposition to EH's plans for the 'Seahenge' monument in Norfolk provides another example (Skeates 2000: 69) and the Council for Scottish Archaeology's 'Adopt a Monument' scheme offered further reassurance of a wider public involvement and ownership' (www.scottisharchaeology.org.uk/projects/adopt.html). The conservation ethic has increasingly wide support and many people understand and are in sympathy with the basic concepts, as imported from nature conservation. We like to think that this ethic contributes to environmental awareness, yet it can be easily perverted for nationalist and racist ends. For example, the Nazis stressed the value of preservation as a national project to secure the remains of their supposed Germanic ancestors (Arnold 1992).

4. *See how we've been wrecking our environment for millennia, not just the last century.* Upland moors are still viewed by many as natural wildernesses. Archaeology can contribute to the Green issue (Macinnes and Wickham-Jones 1992; see also Chapter 22) and is a good way of providing time depth and social context. Greenpeace already employs such imagery, using the timespans of the earth's existence and of human prehistory, to show how suddenly and relatively recently the scale of global pollution has rocketed.

5. *How do we interpret the past?* Ventures such as the Archaeology Resource Centre in York, Bede's World at Jarrow, or Archaeolink in Aberdeenshire (www.archaeolink.co.uk) help to demystify the archaeologist's task of discovering society and people from bones and stones. The past becomes open, accessible and reinterpretable rather than closed and known. An unidentified iron object in Scunthorpe Museum, labelled 'We don't know what it is either', is not an admission of failure but an invitation to participate. If members of the public are invited to contribute and to learn about the difficulties of interpretation, they will share an involvement rather than remain excluded and passive onlookers.

6. *To be or not to be?* There is a British hypersensitivity about dressing up in costume (Waterson 1989), though dressing up does seem to be successful with children. Perhaps it is problematic, since it contradicts the premise above, presenting the past as if it is known and fully reconstructible. Dressing up in itself demands no mental effort to interpret the past, but it does have the advantage of encouraging ethnographic enquiry. The strangeness and difference of past ways of life can be appreciated if presented well. Effective presentation requires more than dressing up the diggers around the trench or enacting a mock battle. If the point is to be made, it requires a formal theatrical setting and structure.

7. *Have you found any gold?* Everyone loves a good find and it is no surprise that the treasure hunt, the quest for the thing in itself, is still top of the public's agenda. Authentic artefacts are the stuff of the fine-art trade, and relationships with users of metal detectors still have a lot of ground to make up (although the development of the Portable Antiquities Scheme and the employment of Finds Liaison Officers in England and Wales has had a radical impact). The problem of looting and illegal dealing around the world is also likely to get worse rather than better. If popular pressure groups can appear to stop certain sites being destroyed then perhaps more thought should go into mobilising public opinion on dealing in stolen antiquities (but see Chaper 6).

8. *Archaeology, roots and the local community.* There have been relatively successful initiatives in community archaeology, many sponsored by the HLF. Even so, local history, oral tradition and genealogy are considerably more popular. No doubt this is because they can touch the human element more deeply and more immediately. Yet archaeology can be integrated into local studies and is a valuable tool for seeing changes in the physical landscape and built environment now admirably demonstrated in the Scottish PASTMAP facility (www.rcahms.gov.uk). It is instructive to note just how often those most interested in local history are the relatively recent incomers into a community; perhaps the real locals do not need to worship their roots.

9. *The present past.* The archaeological past is faceless, nameless and remote, cut off from the present by a conceptual rift. Many aspects of history before the Industrial Revolution are deemed unimportant for today. Yet we should be using archaeological concepts imaginatively, for the recent past and the present. Several years ago, a TV series on interior decor in the modern house (*Signs of the Times*) was described to one of the authors (MPP) as a great piece of archaeology. Rather than simply using modern contexts to explain archaeological methods (demonstrating stratigraphy through the filling of a dustbin, for example), we should also be doing an 'archaeology of us' based on material culture studies (Rathje 1974; Gould and Schiffer 1981; Shanks and Tilley 1987a). The examination of Torry battery (most recently used immediately after the Second World War to house homeless families) on the coast at Aberdeen offers an example (Cameron 2004: 9).

10. *Early man and early woman – engendering the past.* Stereotypes in the portrayal of men's and women's activities in the past are more likely to be extrapolated from existing roles rather than the archaeological evidence. We should continue to explore multiple interpretations and challenge people to re-evaluate the present; otherwise our models of the past in our own image simply reinforce existing prejudices and universal truths that are, in fact, culturally specific practices. Beware of presenting women in reconstruction drawings as passive background. It is also increasingly important not to forget the children.

11. *Club-wielding cavepersons.* The primitivisation of the past leads to racist attitudes towards non-industrialised nations. Over 20,000 years ago the man buried at the Russian site of Sunghir was wearing a very flashy costume, not a crude hearth rug. Why do prehistoric Britons get portrayed as long-haired, badly dressed hippies/New Agers (or perhaps it is the other way round)? This is completely contrary to the evidence from well-preserved burials of the Danish Bronze Age and from the finds of prehistoric razors,

tweezers and so forth. And why do Romans get presented as clean and tidy ringers for chartered accountants? The Roman period still exercises a powerful hold on the public imagination – perhaps its apparent degree of civilisation, role model for empire, and sameness to our own times need debunking.

12. *Hot interpretation.* This phrase was coined by David Uzzell (1989a) to bring a more powerful, and truthful, impact to interpretation. The past should shock us. One of his examples is the massacre of the Jews at Clifford's Tower in York. He pointed out that today's interpretive displays at the monument have avoided the grisly details of this sordid episode. We tend to glorify past wars and annexations. Perhaps the row over Columbus at the time of the 500th anniversary of the 'discovery' of America represented the beginning of a new attitude.

13. *Skeletons.* It seems that the Home Office has been blissfully unaware of the quantities of human remains exhumed without licences by archaeologists, and their display to a fascinated public, when legally they should be curtained behind screens. Respect for the dead is a big and difficult issue (Layton 1989a; Rahtz 1985: 42–7; Parker Pearson 1999). Providing that the necessary measures are taken to avoid outrage (in Britain, remains from after, say, 1850 or those belonging to particular religious groups), we should be engaging people's curiosity even more, rather than sanctimoniously recommending reburial. Our attitude towards death is already bizarre enough in the way that it is hidden and secret in our culture. It is worse to take away the one opportunity that most people have to see dead bodies in one form or another. The lid is coming off this taboo in Britain, but notions of decency in hiding away the dead still lead to racist judgements of other societies' more up-front attitudes towards death.

14. *Banging the drum.* Armada celebrations, battle re-enactments, and royal pageantry are ceremonial invocations by which the nation state is given substance and legitimated. We like to think that we do not promote a jingoistic and chauvinist notion of nationhood, and undoubtedly other nations have reached greater excesses (Trigger 1984; Gathercole and Lowenthal 1990). However, we frame much of our research and presentation in national terms, without widening the issues to the world society.

This discussion may seem to some to be an exercise in political correctness, rather than in useful and achievable goals for archaeologists committed to their public. Many of these proposals might appear out of reach to the hard-pressed unit manager or fieldworker. Even if we cannot implement such schemes and approaches immediately, perhaps they will provide food for thought. It is not that we should be writing a past where we speak of Neolithic persons as 'vertically challenged', among other forms of politically correct jargon. Rather, we must develop a greater consciousness about our own power as archaeologists and seize the initiative more readily. Otherwise we will just drift along behind the commercial operations, adopting and adapting the cobbled-together ethos and morals of the marketplace.

VIEWERS WELCOME

The award-winning Channel 4 series *Time Team* celebrated the broadcast of its tenth series in 2002. By any standards that was an extraordinary achievement. A decade ago nobody could possibly have predicted that an archaeological series that involved the live or 'as live' (essentially live, but broadcast later) excavation of up to thirteen sites a season was either technically possible or editorially desirable. It is easy to underestimate the sheer technical problems of filming a *Time Team*. To do it properly requires three separate camera crews and directors, state-of-the-art geophysical survey, finds conservation, and of course aerial

Figure 20.2. The excavation of human remains is relatively commonplace in archaeology but is subject to both legal and ethical consideration. The illustration shows a skeleton under excavation. *(© Oxford Archaeological Unit)*

photographic and other background research. The excavation itself must be fully up to current IFA standards, if not a bit better. There may be a sudden need for the services of, say, a dendrochronologist or a specialist in human bone. To make the mix work properly, everyone must be able to communicate, wherever they might find themselves at any particular moment, which may be deep in a cave or overhead in a helicopter. It can be an organisational nightmare or miracle, depending on one's viewpoint. But is it worth all the effort? A cynic might answer 'No', but over three million viewers would firmly disagree.

There is a long-held view that archaeology is far too important to be left to archaeologists alone (Pryor 1989). Not only should it reach a wider audience, it *must* reach one: the current dominant broadcast medium is terrestrial television, so it follows that this ought to be archaeology's natural home – which indeed it is. There is, of course, far more to televised archaeology than *Time Team*, which is used here as a metaphor for a newer style of programming that has moved beyond more traditional approaches, which essentially amounted to a documentary film or series of films. These clearly had roots in literary forms, although occasionally the inspiration may lie in textbooks. If one takes a second look at some of the archaeological programmes of the 1950s and 1960s, it might be rather like attending a university lecture, but with slides that moved. Very little was initially made of television's special potential: the fact that it penetrates deep within the home, right into the heart of the family. There is a huge difference between television and film; the former is essentially private and intimate, the latter is public. This difference should be reflected in the way the message is delivered or the story told. It is more appropriate to lecture or declaim in

Figure 20.3. One of the contributors (FP) talking to Tony Robinson during the recording of a *Time Team* programme.

a film; but on television one must behave rather differently: one can be intimate, but one must also be aware that one is in an unusual, privileged, position within the household. For all one knows, some of the viewers may even be in bed, and it is essential to be honest and not knowingly betray the viewer's trust. It is well to remember that today's viewer holds a remote controller that can switch channels at the slightest detection of self-importance, lack of humour or the merest hint of being patronising. Anything is better than that, even the cheap, televisual wallpaper, which is what reality TV has become.

This is not the place to offer a critique of current archaeological television, for which the reader is referred to Catherine Hills' recent excellent review (Hills 2003). Incidentally, it is encouraging to see that the latest editor of *Antiquity*, Professor Martin Carver, has included television programmes alongside the more usual reviews of books and periodical literature. Who knows, one day a television review may appear in the *Proceedings of the Prehistoric Society*. Some of the intellectual snobbery inherent in the TV=bad versus books=good split within our subject is perhaps beginning to break down, which is to be welcomed. Knee-jerk reactions, of whatever sort, are nearly always a mistake.

Rather than offer a critical overview of current or past television programming, this is a useful opportunity to provide some suggestions for making television programmes that do our subject a service. As professionals we cannot afford to ignore television, and as it shows no signs of going away we would be best advised to treat it with respect. The initial advice is simple: if you want your views on your site or your pet subject to end up on screen, and not on the clichéd cutting-room floor, then be brief and to the point. The more you say, the less will be broadcast. There is a well-used adage for students who were dithering about what to do next on site: 'If in doubt, cut it out'. It pays to spend a few moments thinking about one's response before the question is posed to camera. Some directors hold that this removes spontaneity, although very often they mistake confusion for freshness. Good ideas – even very small ones – have a life of their own: they are not as evanescent as some would have one believe. So it is often as well to think a little first, to visit the territory in one's mind's eye, even if it is not put into actual words (a process which probably *would* remove spontaneity); as Sir Mortimer Wheeler also famously said, 'time spent in reconnaissance is never wasted'.

Excellent advice was given to one of the authors (FP) by the producer of a series being made for BBC Children's Television. He was having trouble doing a short piece to camera and was unable to get it right. The producer appeared and, in a very quiet voice, told him that he was attempting to act a part, to be a character. 'Francis,' he said, 'you're a good actor, but you can only act one role', which of course was himself. In other words, act natural and be yourself. There is no point in pretending to be something you are not. Just because you may be discussing generalities it does not follow that you should put on the mortar board and academic dress of some senior professor. Put another way, it is always better if you can wear your learning lightly.

Some people are naturally highly strung and this can convert to nervousness on camera. There is no easy way to beat television nerves other than to say that such nervousness nearly always feels far worse than it actually appears on the screen. Often slight nervousness can impart a certain edginess or urgency to a contribution – and that can be very appealing. It is also worth remembering that no director is going to retain a contribution where the speaker is plainly very ill at ease. So whatever else happens, you are unlikely to make a fool of yourself in public. For what it's worth, bad attacks of nerves seem to happen less frequently today, possibly because most people are becoming more and more familiar with home video cameras and the like. Also, with the popularity of 'out-take' programmes around Christmas, the process of making a television programme is rapidly becoming demystified.

Today, television programmes are made in a wide-screen format, which is visually attractive but seems to make most contributors look rather broad in the beam. It also can seem to flatten a performance. This has always been a tendency on television, which directors tried to overcome by injecting an additional dose of enthusiasm into their various contributors. Often a seemingly over-the-top performance will actually translate into an enthusiastic, but certainly not over-the-top performance in terms of finished product. In fact it is almost impossible to over-enthuse on television, especially on a topic that genuinely excites one. However, unless you are a very good actor, beware of phoney enthusiasm. The only problem with enthusiasm is that it can sometimes be long-winded – which offends against the golden rule of being succinct. The best solution is a personal compromise that perhaps could be termed disciplined enthusiasm.

Discipline also comes in useful when it comes to consistency in the subsequent retakes of the scene. Incidentally, contrary to what is sometimes heard in many site huts, television retakes are not a symptom of the film-maker's incompetence. Each scene will be shot from several positions, which will be cut together to form the final version. First there will be a 'master take', which will be the one around which the rest will hang. Then there will be separate close-ups of each of the people talking *and* listening and a wide or distant view of the scene, which may sometimes be done without the sound being sychronised to lip movements.

Film-making is a complicated process that involves as much professionalism as, dare one say, archaeology. It is as well to appreciate both its technicalities and its merits; it is the medium through which archaeology can be popularised and through which education can be developed. We would do well to treat the small screen with respect.

CHAPTER 21

MUSEUM ARCHAEOLOGY
Susan Pearce

INTRODUCTION

Museums and their archaeological collections have come into being piecemeal over the past two centuries or so, and both the institutions and the nature of the collections show a corresponding diversity. Institutionally, museums range from the great national bodies, through the major regional museum services, which are in many ways the backbone of archaeological curatorship, to small or specialised museums, such as the one at Fishbourne, which may hold particular material of great interest. The collections these museums hold are themselves part of the intellectual history of modern times, beginning with the seventeenth-century cabinets of curiosities, running through the romantic notions of the later eighteenth- and nineteenth-century barrow diggers, reflecting and encouraging the development of typological accumulations and studies through the nineteenth and twentieth centuries, and witnessing the steady growth of excavation to what would now be recognised as professional standards.

The archaeological museums and their collections need to be understood in terms of their contribution to our understanding of the past, and especially in the light of the developing quality of material culture theory. They need to be understood also as social and intellectual documents in their own right that have contributed, in terms of who collected the material and why, to the creation of ethnic values, gender values and value judgements, and so to the construction of social practice.

An important element in this construction is the body of issues that revolves around present-day problems of acquisition and disposal. The level of excavation activity over the last twenty years or so has meant an enormous accumulation of finds. In London the work of units and societies has generated over 1,000 cubic metres of finds, and the experience is much the same across the country. Although the rate of excavation may be slowing a little, the practice of competitive tendering, which often means that the work is carried out by a non-local unit, has tended to disrupt the good working relationship built up over a number of years between museums and local excavation teams. The proper care of such huge collections would absorb an absurd level of resource, and demands for such resource would be perceived as luxuriously excessive. On the other hand, although collections can be rationalised by various arrangements between museums, the outright disposal or destruction of archaeological material is very difficult because there is no way of knowing what the future knowledge yields of any body of material may be. The best solutions are likely to lie with a cull of some bulk material before museum acquisition, coupled with a mixture of high principle and good professional management within the museum. In this, the Codes of Practice prepared by the Museums Association, and the guidelines (1995) developed by the Society of Museum Archaeologists are very helpful.

Within this broad social and cultural framework, the archaeological museum has three principle areas of responsibility: the management of the archaeological material; the presentation of this material in a wide range of display and interpretative projects; and the practice of research into both the archaeological dimension of the material as this has been traditionally understood, and into its cultural nature as one of the agents that has helped to create our present views about the past. The first two of these responsibilities will be considered in the two main sections that follow, and the third is addressed very briefly in the final section. All three are large areas, which can only be touched on here. The *Standards in the Museum Care of Archaeological Collections* published by the Museums and Galleries Commission (MGC 1992) remains essential reading in the area.

MANAGING COLLECTIONS

The archaeological museum archive

The management of the museum archaeological archive is at the heart of the museum operation, for without collections there would be no broader issues of context and interpretation. The 'archive' was a term brought into prominence by its use in the Frere Report (DoE 1975a), where it meant the whole product of excavation organised in an accessible form, which rendered it capable of critical re-examination. The archive was seen as the prime information source, and the form of final publication correspondingly less significant. The background to the archive concept lay in the enormous increase in excavation that the rescue movement had stimulated, linked with a general refining of recording systems that enabled a much more detailed and precise record of an excavated site to be developed by the early 1970s, and the development in information yield from environmental sampling procedures. With this ran an acute awareness that excavation is essentially a destructive exercise, so that a former site now exists only in its preserved archive. The archive concept can be usefully extended to cover the entirety of archaeological collections.

During the 1990s the notion of the prime importance of the archive was put into a new context with the postmodern realisation that every act in the past is capable of multiple interpretations involving multiple possible histories, for which a single report is, of its nature, an inadequate basis. The same, of course, is also true of any given site archive, which must also carry inherent selectivities; but at least the archive is one step closer to the ancient lived reality than a report can ever be.

The implications of this archive for curatorship are obviously enormous, but the curatorial role is an active, not a passive, one. The curator's relationship with his or her archive is a steady process of interaction in which the existing and incoming collections, the management of museum policies, and the exercise of judgement, are woven together in the explicit actions and decisions that make up every working day.

Collection management policies

The nature of the archive as a whole, both existing and potential, is not simple, but embraces a cross-cutting range of identities, depending upon whether it is seen from a physical, museological, archaeological or historical view. Successful collection management demands recognition of these complexities and an ability to organise and effect strategies that take all this interplay into account. Collection management embraces acquisition and disposal policy, with special emphasis on issues such as collecting-area policies, policies that relate to the type and period of material to be collected, loans, purchases and donations, legal matters such as title and insurance, and collection methods. A collection management policy should relate all these matters to the care needs of the collections in terms of access, documentation, storage and conservation, and each museum will evolve a particular policy that brings the broader issues in line with its specific history and character.

Issues in storage and conservation

The archive embraces not only the archaeological material itself but also a considerable volume of record material. This was originally in written, pictorial, film and printed form, and is now being converted to digital storage. This brings new access possibilities (although it would be a brave – even strange – curator who would actually destroy the old records), and issues of accessibility and security present their own problems and conflicting needs.

Accessibility and security, as in all institutions, can be difficult to combine, and, more particularly, the principle of accessibility means that decisions have to be made about the parts of the collections that are used most, how this should influence the way in which the material is arranged, and how best use can be made of the available space. It would, in the light of this, be relatively easy to devise a use of space that put much-used material in areas equipped as joint store and work rooms, less-used material in the next most accessible stores, possibly linked with the displays and offered as visible storage (Ames 1977), and seldom-used material in more remote stores, perhaps in a separate building if the rest of the collections are held in the museum itself.

There is, however, a major difficulty. For good museological reasons of accession and documentation, there is a strong instinct to keep together the material from a specific excavation or collection and therefore to divide the whole into the three classes on a collections basis; but much research and some display is carried out on a period basis or an artefact-type basis that cuts across collections. Equally, the class-three material is unlikely to comprise complete collections, but rather to involve, for example, the animal bones or undecorated body sherds from excavations whose other material may be frequently consulted. It can, of course, also from an environmental and security point of view, often make good sense to store groups of small finds like coins, Roman brooches or Bronze Age metalwork together, but most curators would hesitate before picking all the worked flints, for example, out of a range of collections and storing these in a single place.

It is very difficult to devise a theoretical system that can take account of these conflicting needs (Watkins 1986), and any such system will prove to be very fragile when it is applied to actual museum situations. In practice, it is usually best to admit that neither hard organisational structures nor ideals of purity are helpful, and to treat the various potential groupings on their own merits, bearing in mind their particular requirements.

There is a large literature on the maintenance of collections in store, which covers this complex subject in detail from all angles. No attempt will be made to summarise it here, and the interested reader should consult Thompson (1978), Leigh (1982) and the *Guidelines for Preparation of Archives for Long-Term Storage* (1990) produced by K. Walker for the United Kingdom Institute for Conservation (UKIC). However, one area of mutual concern to curators and conservators must be mentioned, which surfaced in the 1980s, and is probably incapable of final resolution. In 1983 UKIC issued to its members their *Guidance for Conservation Practice*, which defined the responsibilities of conservators in relation to the care and treatment of objects (see Ashley-Smith 1982; printed in Shell and Robinson 1988: 259–60). It makes clear statements on the need to preserve evidence rather than removing it during the conservation process, and on the desirability of undertaking only treatment that can be reversed. It defines conservation as 'the means by which the true nature of the object is preserved', and uses the term 'true nature' to include evidence about the origin, construction and materials of the piece. It stresses, also, how important it is that both conservators and curators should accept this ethical attitude.

However, in the case of archaeological objects a number of difficulties arise. The object as it emerges from the ground is an encapsulation of its history up to that moment; but the unravelling of that history by the modern investigative techniques of the conservator inevitably involves the destruction of evidence as much as the preservation of a version of the artefact. As Corfield puts it: 'while many general statements have been made about the importance of reversibility in conservation processes, the whole concept has been the subject of scrutiny as it has become more and more apparent that few conservation processes can be considered really reversible' (Corfield 1988: 261).

In a nutshell, the emphasis is now on finding out about a piece, rather than on cleaning it, because the information embedded in the various accretions or products of corrosion may be as diagnostic as the bare object itself. The object that emerges at the end of this process is not, and never again can be, the object that came out of the ground, and therefore a full documentary and photographic record is an essential part of the conservation process (Keene 1980). A most important element in the conservator's responsibility is, therefore, a judgement of the correct balance between, on the one hand, the recovery of evidence and, on the other, the preservation of evidence through minimum intervention and as close an approximation as possible to the ideal of irreversibility.

Investigation in depth requires the closest cooperation between conservator and archaeologist (Cronyn 1980). Detailed work is very time-consuming, and so the choice of objects to be examined in depth is difficult, and must be made on both archaeological and physical grounds, so that the yield in information is as great as possible. The conservators need to know as precisely as possible what questions require answers, and they prefer exact questions put to them about specific objects or groups of objects. Similarly, conservators need information about the context of the find and the structural interpretation the archaeologist puts on it, the approximate date or period of the artefact, and who will undertake its study. The framework for this kind of work is best developed jointly as part of the overall strategy for the excavation site, but it must be very flexible because it is the unexpected that will usually occur.

Documentation

The considerable resources required to store and conserve archaeological archives, and indeed to produce them by excavation or collection in the first place, can only be justified if the archives are genuinely available for use: this cardinal principle means that the material itself, and all related information that pertains to it and is embodied in it, should be accessible, and in turn implies that the information is held on an organised documentation system.

Good documentation also ensures that collection handling and recording is monitored and controlled, and gives clear proof of the ownership of the collection. It helps to establish a sensible acquisitions policy that takes account of existing holdings and monitors the adherence to that policy; it offers satisfactory accounting to interested parties like auditors and insurers; and it provides the information needed by museum staff for exhibition, education, conservation and research, and by outside researchers and the general public.

The problems to be faced in creating a modern and serviceable documentation system are complex, embracing the considerable labour resource involved, the difficulties of system choice (particularly in the modern computer market), and the problems implicit in old collections, frequently poorly recorded, and existing record systems of varying degrees of complexity and incompatibility. To this must be added the difficulties in creating systems that can bring together the needs of excavators and the longer-term requirements of a museum service.

Again, all these issues are being discussed at great length and degree of detail. The reader is advised to consult the specialised journals and groups such as *Computer Applications in Archaeology*, *Archaeological Computing Newsletter* and the Museums Computer Group. In 2000 the Society of Museum Archaeologists and MDA (formerly Museum Documentation Association) issued *Spectrum: Standards in Action: Working with Archaeology* (Longworth and Wood 2000). This is a significant statement, although it reflects the MDA's view that documentation systems can be a way of controlling curatorial processes.

The archive: some conclusions

It is clear that the range of the archaeological archive, as it has come to be understood over the last decade, will require a more informed and more complex documentation system than the traditional approaches could offer. 'The well-tempered archive', to borrow Stewart's phrase (Stewart 1980: 22), would encompass the actual transference of finds and documents to the museum numbering systems, the application of satisfactory documentation and data standards, and the provision of well-organised storage, all expressed in an archival policy. Such a policy would aim to translate into physical premises and working practices all the aspects of collection management that have just been discussed. This must be operated in a climate of genuine cooperation between curators and excavators, and between the curators of different museum services. A few museums, like some of the English county services, are putting an integrated approach to archaeological collections into practice. Such systems, no doubt, represent the ideal rather than the present reality for many museums, but it is the ideal to be aimed at, so that collections are not just held, but truly managed.

MUSEUMS, THE PUBLIC AND THE PAST

Museums and our public

The term 'public' here is used in the simplest and most colourless sense, and means all those people who do not consider themselves to be professional (or quasi-professional) curators or archaeologists. This group, the huge majority of the population, can be divided into three fairly clear sectors. The greater proportion of the adults are those who have no real interest in understanding the past, in the sense that professionals would use that phrase. The smaller section of the adults are those who do take an informed interest in the past. Apart from these, there are the children, whose interests are not yet fixed.

Let us concentrate first on the adults. A number of surveys (Merriman 1991) have made it abundantly clear that, unsurprisingly, the dividing line between the interested adults and the others follows that which separates the better-off and the well-educated from the rest. In this, museums in Britain mirror Bourdieu's perceptive analysis of cultural 'habitus' and 'cultural capital', closely linked to other kinds of economic capital, where possession of the code enables the owner to enjoy what a museum offers, while lack of it means that museum material seems meaningless and rapidly becomes boring (see also Chapter 20). Those who are excluded now question the value of what has no importance for them, and develop an argument that asks why relatively large sums of money should be expended on maintaining institutions for which they see little use, and to whose cultural and intellectual values they do not subscribe. This is the stance of many ley-line enthusiasts, Stonehenge cult-makers and treasure hunters whose alternative archaeology has been described as 'a kind of popular repossession of the past' (Williamson and Bellamy 1983: 57). At the end of the day, these difficulties cannot be met by argument, but only by a prolonged and sympathetic endeavour to teach the cultural code.

Talk of difficulties must be balanced by a further consideration: we have a great deal to build on. Merriman's survey (1991) showed that some 90 per cent of museum visitors and 65 per cent of non-visitors thought that the past was worth knowing about – a large and encouraging proportion. The principal heritage locations like Stonehenge, Jorvik and Bath all attract approaching a million visitors yearly. The popularity of television archaeology, especially *Time Team*, is demonstrated by the consistently huge audiences it attracts. This shows that large numbers of people are interested in the excavation process. Many museums are harnessing this interest, as for example, at the Museum of London, where projects like the opening of a coffin in the gallery bring the element of discovery into the museum (although clearly such enterprises must be carefully handled). Merriman's survey, however, also shows that what the majority of people find most rewarding are objects in their own setting, either out of doors or perhaps in reconstructions, an element of self-discovery, and ideally some kind of link to their own family or neighbourhood. Museums have a particular responsibility towards mediating the past to the public, and it is to the ways in which this is discharged that we must now turn.

Portable antiquities

Most archaeological museums have traditionally offered an enquiry or identification service, through which members of the public could bring in items that they had found. This has always been one of the most important interfaces between archaeology professionals and the wider public, testifying to the genuinely widespread curiosity about the past, and allowing many important details to be recorded. However, the relationship between finders, museums and the wider archaeological world has been transformed by the Treasure Act of 1996, and the Portable Antiquities Scheme (PAS), set up as part of the new thinking in 1997.

Pressure to create the new system came from the treasure hunting groups who felt excluded from archaeological work as it was then perceived, and archaeologists who, undoubtedly correctly, believed that much information of great importance was being lost through the underground activities of metal-detectorists. All this combined with strong dissatisfaction with the ancient law of Treasure Trove to create a rethink. Under the new law, objects, other than coins, at least 300 years old and with a minimum precious metal content of 10 per cent are classed as 'treasure'; so are all associated groups of coins at least 300 years old (where in order to be a 'group' in the case of base metals, the find must number ten or more coins). Objects found in association with 'treasure' also come under the act (see Chapter 6).

Material that counts as 'treasure' must be reported, and there is the official hope that finds of non-treasure will also be reported upon. The finder will receive the full market price, independently assessed, from a museum that wishes to acquire material. In order to make this possible, the PAS set up a network of Finds Liaison Officers to whom finds should be reported.

A number of criticisms can be made of this programme. The network of Finds Liaison Officers began with only eleven people, and although the numbers have improved, the countrywide coverage is patchy. The funding for the network is hand-to-mouth and complex. From a museum angle, a substantial number of the officers are not based in museums, for all the usual reasons of irregular museum distribution. It is also possibly true that the Finds Liaison Officers are only necessary because new moves within the museum world and its funders, over the last fifteen years or so, have undermined the old curatorial network, which was eminently capable of identifying objects brought into it.

There is, however, a very positive side. A very large number – over 50,000 is the number sometimes quoted – of objects have been added to the archaeological record since 1997. New and very positive relationships have been forged with the treasure hunters, and with the broader public, which builds on the efforts of pioneers like David Crowther (1983). New thinking within museums has created resource centres, such as that at the Museum of London, which provide for professional and amateur archaeologists alike. In the long run, the bringing together of people and professionals must be one of the most hopeful and productive enterprises of the late twentieth century (for ongoing information see http://www.finds.org.uk).

Education

Formal education is now seen as life-long as well as school-based. Moves by central government are now making individual schools responsible for deciding how much advantage they take of the education services museums offer, both for school visits to museums and use of specimen loan material (for a good overview of archaeological educational approaches see the Council for British Archaeology website at www.britarch.ac.uk). Originally, there was a fear that, given financial constraints, museum education services would be squeezed out of the school timetable. A balance to these worries was provided by the National Curriculum's emphasis on hands-on experience and the ability to infer general principles from specific evidence: museum archaeology is obviously ideally placed to provide scope for this kind of teaching (Corbishley 1992).

More general tensions were initially seen to underlie the contemporary problems and politics of resource use. Hill (1987: 144) showed that archaeology tended to see education as a commodity, as a way in which archaeologists could communicate what they regarded as the important results of their work to the public, and so justify the public money spent on archaeology in a highly visible and obviously responsible way. Teachers, similarly, saw archaeology as a commodity, making some use of the scope for skills learning and for projects that it offers, but failing to understand the nature of the discipline. Hill also found that the overwhelming majority of teachers have little understanding of modern archaeology, so the result of their use of the discipline is largely misrepresentative, perpetuating dubious stereotypes of what archaeology is and what it can be. The stress placed on teaching the right methods is often at the cost of fact. Several teachers have suggested to the author that it does not matter if the facts are completely wrong, so long as the children learn to use their historical skills correctly. As a result, neither teachers nor archaeologists understood what the other is trying to achieve, and the product is potentially both bad archaeology and bad education.

These differences in intention played their part in how children see the past. An interesting survey undertaken by the Southampton Archaeology in Education team covered 117 children aged 10–12 years from a variety of backgrounds in Southampton, in an effort to understand how children conceive of the past and its people (Emmott 1987). The findings of the survey showed that the children were only just beginning to understand time as an abstract concept, and that they tended to think of history as about kings and queens. Nevertheless, 80 per cent of the replies said that the past was important. The children tended to see past people as less clever than us because they lacked our technology, and they seemed to take a similar view of non-Western cultures. These images of the past 'originate in the content of school curriculum, children's books and television programmes' that generate a 'distorted, ethnocentric and sexist view of the past, which forms a lasting impression and impinges on [children's] images of the present' (Emmott 1987: 139).

In the event many of these fears have melted away. Archaeology is increasingly seen as a way of teaching other key stage skills such as technology, numeracy and art, and as an ideal way of offering transferable skills in an interesting, hands-on mode. Some galleries, for instance the Egyptian gallery at New Walk Museum, Leicester, have been designed with contemporary educational aims in mind. Modern multicultural society has expended the general idea of what human beings are like and has begun to erode stereotyped images and concepts.

Exhibiting archaeology

Education and the exhibiting of archaeology are now often very closely intertwined. Putting archaeology, that is the past in its material aspect, on display is a complex business. Exhibitions in their morphological juxtaposition of plan, selected objects and graphics (in the broadest sense) create their own kinds of knowledge, and may therefore be analysed in such epistemological terms. All human history exhibitions are representational, and so provoke questions about the nature of their relationship to a past reality and to historical change. Archaeological exhibitions are intended to interpret material culture or perhaps to demonstrate how material culture can be interpreted, and therefore face familiar problems surrounding the study of artefacts; and further difficulties revolve around the transmission of all these messages to a viewing public.

Our improving notion of exhibition morphology shows that different exhibition layouts stimulate different kinds of understanding. Displays with strong axial structures, small spaces between display units, and the intention of moving a visitor along a predetermined route, present knowledge as if it were the map of a well-known terrain where all the relationships are well understood, while exhibitions with looser structures and a variety of circulation routes show knowledge as a proposition, stimulating further, or different, propositions. The ground plans of two exhibitions at the British Museum (Figs 21.1 and 21.2) show the kinds of contrasts involved.

All exhibitions are either didactic or intended to evoke feelings, and most hope to be both. The ethical basis of the didactic exhibit is grounded in the belief that knowledge is morally good, partly in an absolute sense and partly because it helps to develop socially responsible citizens who identify constructively with their community and its traditions; it looks back to Victorian ideas about self-betterment, tainted though these are with much political and social hypocrisy. The didactic approach contrasts with the emotive or mood-making exhibition, grounded in the rather different conviction that an experience of the ancient, the exotic and the beautiful is good because it enables us to share in the common scope of human experience, to live more interestingly and to accept more easily the essential precariousness of life.

Museums are now successfully broadening the archaeology exhibition base, by linking displays with a range of object-handling projects. What then, for the visitor constitutes a good experience in an archaeology gallery? What makes an archaeology exhibition successful? There is a broad level of agreement about the ways in which the effectiveness of exhibitions generally can be assessed and the success of exhibitions evaluated (Miles *et al.* 1988; Stansfield 1981), and these involve detailed procedures of observation and feedback linked to very specific recommendations of gallery layout and design. Processes like critical appraisal and market research leading to front-end evaluation and the statement of exhibition objectives, formative evaluation as part of development and

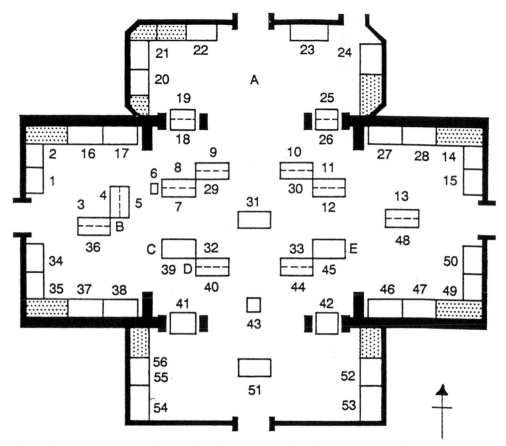

Figure 21.1. Ground plan of the Early Medieval Room at the British Museum as it was in 1991. The sequence of 45 cases includes a series on the migration and post-migration tribes *c*. AD 400–1100 (cases 1–15), a series on the Late Antique and Byzantine World (cases 16–28), a sequence on the Germans, Anglo-Saxons, Celts and Vikings, with a strong British emphasis (cases 29–50) and a separate section on the Sutton Hoo ship burial (cases 51–56). The lattice work plan offers a loose structure and a variety of circulation routes.

production, and summational evaluation undertaken after the exhibition is open, provide a framework through which the operation of the exhibition can be monitored.

In broader terms, which are admittedly difficult to monitor, a successful archaeology display, like a good television programme or book, has to be one that keeps the visitor attracted until the show is finished; if the visitor is carried along with his interest caught, then he will go away with some enlargement of knowledge or sympathy, and that is success.

CONCLUSIONS

The management of museum archaeology, as of all archaeology, ultimately justifies itself in terms of the increase in knowledge and understanding it offers, and the enrichment of our everyday lives it makes possible. Ultimately, all this, in its turn, depends upon

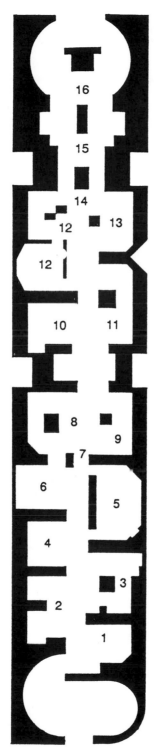

1 Use of Natural Resources
   8000–5000 BC

2 A Way of Life Preserved
   4000–1200 BC

3 Life, Ceremony and Death
   4000–2000 BC

4 Settlement and Defence
   1000 BC–AD 43

5 Landscapes Through Time
   3200 BC–AD 1100

6 A Way of Death
   300–200 BC

7 Master Craftsmen
   100 BC–AD 50

8 Soldiers and the Army
   AD 43–410

9 Pagans and Christians
   50 BC–AD 410

10 Cemeteries and Society
   AD 400–1100

11 Church and Monastery
   AD 650–1650

12 The Medieval Countryside
   AD 600–1650

13 Castles and Norman Lords
   AD 1066–1200

14 Developing Technology
   AD 800–1600

15 The Growth of Medieval Towns
   AD 900–1600

16 Lindow Man

Figure 21.2. Ground plan of the temporary exhibition *Archaeology in Britain* held at the British Museum in 1987. The exhibition has strong axials in a linear structure and expects the visitor to move in a predetermined route. *(From British Museum teaching material 1987)*

337

research work carried out upon the material, work that is designed to enhance our understanding of what material culture from the past can tell us.

Research is often seen as difficult work in museum circles, and this, I believe, is the result of accumulated misunderstandings rather than the outcome of any genuine problems. It is the curator's task to carry out the management of archives, and this, as we have seen, is an active rather than a passive process, which contributes its own positive influence to the research process. The curator must also, it goes without saying, make collections and information available to all comers. It is an equally true but often underestimated fact that the professional management of, for example, the petrological analysis of early lithic material across a collection, contributes directly to our research base. Similarly, understanding of the history and development of collections adds to our understanding of the developing sense of the past and its nature. Intimately intertwined with all this, and to a large extent its product, will be what is sometimes called 'pure' research: that is, the academic study of an aspect of the past. Future research lies in a better understanding of how this can be carried out, and what the outcomes of any piece of work are likely to be. Museums should – as many do – think in terms of the development of research strategies that bring all the different strands together.

This brings us back to our starting point. Museums and their collections are very different, and, like all long-term institutions, embody a variety of strengths and characters. Intelligent development should see this as a power for good, which schemes for regional centres, currently under discussion, could build upon rather than undermine. One hopes that such ideas can be linked up with the new mood in archaeological museums. The past decade or so has seen a profound shift in which the central interest is now the broader public, whose members need to be engaged at every turn. Outreach or education projects are now not enough: public participation is seen as the crucial structuring principle. This creates an integrity of purpose and design across exhibitions, the experience of ancient objects, and research and documentation, blurring distinctions between professional and amateur, 'front of house' and 'backroom' storage, research and participation. Perhaps the new archaeological museums have a message not just for museums or archaeology, but also for wider dialogues about how social interactions can be made vital.

CHAPTER 22

ARCHAEOLOGY AS LAND USE

Lesley Macinnes

INTRODUCTION

Although the recognition of archaeology as a major element in the landscape is not new, its inclusion as a routine aspect of land management is still comparatively recent. The early emphasis of archaeological management was on the conservation of masonry structures, and in particular on monuments in State Care (e.g. Thompson 1981), though there was also recognition of the need for monument protection on a broader front (e.g. Baker 1983). In recent years, however, the management of field monuments and the relationship of this to other land uses has become a focus of serious attention (e.g. Lambrick 1985; Hughes and Rowley 1986; Darvill 1986: 79–85, Darvill 1987; Macinnes and Wickham-Jones 1992; Berry and Brown 1995; Darvill and Fulton 1998: 146–190).

The initial thrust of this aspect of archaeological resource management has been on the protection and management of specific features within the landscape, reflecting current legislation, through which ancient monuments and archaeological sites can be scheduled under the Ancient Monuments and Archaeological Areas Act 1979, and historic buildings listed under the Town and Country Planning Acts (Chapter 5; Suddards 1993; Baker 1993; Dormor 1999). At present, however, there is no specific legislative provision for areas of historic landscape, such as historic parks and gardens, or for the historic fabric of the wider landscape. Despite this, the management of archaeology and the recognition of the historic depth of the modern landscape are now linked to the wider framework of rural land use, a link increasingly recognised within national policy and routine working practices (Grenville 1999; Fairclough and Rippon 2002c; Clark *et al.* 2004: 13–20).

This chapter reviews the relationship between archaeology, historic landscape and land management, and assesses the associated problems and benefits.

ARCHAEOLOGY AND LAND USE

Most land is managed as a mixture of land uses, an increasingly complex combination of agriculture, forestry, natural heritage, recreation and sport. While recognising that these generally take place in combination, for ease and clarity the following section looks at the impact of each of these main uses on archaeology in turn. Subsequent sections consider integrated land management and issues of sustainability.

Farming and agriculture

Agriculture has been a major land use in the British countryside since its introduction in the Neolithic period. Throughout the UK, agricultural practices offer the paradox of being the major factor responsible for the good preservation of archaeological sites in upland areas, and the major agent of destruction in lowland areas, particularly since the Second World War (Darvill and Fulton 1998). There have been numerous studies of crop-mark archaeology, through which the adverse effects of intensive agricultural cultivation on archaeology are well documented (e.g. Hanson and Macinnes 1991; Fulford and Nichols 1992). Many surveys have been undertaken in marginal areas where sites survive well, though relatively few have been explicitly related to the vulnerability of such sites to land improvement.

In upland areas throughout the UK, archaeological sites have survived as visible field monuments in a generally good state of preservation, in heather moorland and unimproved grassland. The degree of survival is often very good, and in many areas extensive areas of relict archaeological landscapes have survived (e.g. Dartmoor (Johnson and Rose 1994) and Perthshire (RCAHMS 1990)). The traditional agricultural management of upland areas, primarily for sheep, deer and game, aims mainly to maintain good quality grassland and moorland, with some tree cover essential for shelter. By and large, these traditional practices have been good for archaeology, though they can be damaging if carried out inappropriately, for instance by erosion caused by overgrazing or uncontrolled muirburn (Berry and Brown 1994; for detailed guidance on the best management of archaeological sites see the websites of the national heritage agencies). At the same time, though, the withdrawal of such management can lead to the development of bracken, scrub and woodland that covers historic landscapes, obscures visible features and damages well-preserved archaeological deposits (e.g. Rees and Mills 1999).

Combining the interests of archaeology and upland farming is not always easy. Grazing archaeological sites is essential to control vegetation, but stocking levels and stock types need to be appropriate: overgrazing can lead to problems of erosion, while undergrazing allows the spread of bracken and other damaging vegetation. Both tree planting and the encouragement of natural regeneration on farmland can damage and obscure archaeological features and historic landscapes, while essential components such as fencing, access tracks and drains can all cause problems if insensitively located from an archaeological point of view. Similarly, the well-preserved archaeological and palaeoenvironmental evidence that survives within peatland is threatened by peat extraction, at domestic as well as commercial scales (Coles 2001a: 23–34).

The continued preservation of archaeological features in the uplands requires the continuation of farming in those areas on a scale comparable to that of the recent past, and the integration of archaeological considerations with other objectives, including those for natural heritage and biodiversity. It is therefore a matter of great concern that the economic pressures of recent years, exacerbated by the foot and mouth outbreak in 2001, are leading to the decline of small farms units, particularly in the uplands: this has severe implications for the continued preservation of the archaeological resource. The reduction or removal of grazing would lead to the establishment of heather and scrub, affecting both buried deposits and the visibility of upstanding features. Yet these archaeological impacts can be minimised, avoided or improved by integrating archaeological needs into strategic land-use planning and farm management plans, and through provisions for positive management of the resource.

In marginal land, archaeological sites often survive as upstanding features in grazed improved grassland, sometimes forming extensive landscapes. Sites or areas of relict landscapes may, however, have been damaged by ploughing in the past. Some may have been drained, enclosed or bisected by fencing; used for quarrying, dumping, storage or feeding stock; affected by vehicle access; or covered in scrub where they have not been actively managed. Gorse, whin and bracken are frequent problems on sites in such locations; while many wetland sites have been affected by agricultural drainage in the recent past, though this is generally no longer supported by grant schemes. Where marginal land is grazed and improved by non-invasive means, archaeological sites will generally benefit, though they will still be subject to localised problems such as stock-related erosion or burrowing animals, while the application of chemicals or liming might affect the composition of buried deposits. Where land is left to revert to an untended or ungrazed state, whether through lack of targeted management, through natural regeneration schemes or as a result of farm abandonment, there will be problems of scrub or tree coverage of archaeological features, and fire-risk from rank grasses and other vegetation.

For archaeological purposes, maintenance of grassland or moorland in good condition is generally the key objective, with avoidance of both overstocking and wholesale stock removal, and with control of burrowing animals (Dunwell and Trout 1999). However, there can be conflict between this aim and the management of land for natural heritage interests, as some of those objectives, such as natural regeneration or the creation of ponds or wetlands, can be detrimental to the archaeological resource. Nevertheless, much of this can be avoided if both objectives are considered within a coherent and integrated conservation management plan (e.g. Thackray *et al*. 1995: 43; Thackray 1999; Clark 1999).

It is in the lowlands that the biggest conflict between farming and archaeology arises, though, ironically, the recognition and visibility of sites that have been reduced to crop-marks in the past largely depends on continued cultivation (e.g. Stoertz 1997; RCAHMS 1994). Arable cultivation damages archaeological features through the reduction, and eventual loss, of earthworks and gradual removal of below-ground deposits; severe damage occurs most quickly where deep ploughing, drainage or subsoiling is carried out. Indeed, recent research suggests that very few sites survive repeated episodes of ploughing intact (Darvill and Fulton 1998: 128–31; DEFRA BD 1701). Nevertheless, ploughing is permissible even on protected sites under the class consent procedures of the Ancient Monuments and Archaeological Areas Act 1979 (Chapter 5).

Even where sites survive as upstanding features in 'islands' within arable fields, they will be at risk from encroachment by the plough, by the growth of trees, scrub or rank vegetation, and by burrowing animals, unless they are actively managed to control these problems. Well-preserved sites have even been deliberately destroyed on occasion because of the inconvenience of having to plough around them. The promotion of natural regeneration within farmland, the expansion of farm woodland and the creation of woodland corridors for wildlife can all similarly have adverse impacts on the archaeological resource.

Nonetheless, even where such farming activities continue, measures can be taken to minimise further damage to archaeological features, by reducing the depth or frequency of ploughing, for example, by avoiding pan-busting or subsoiling, or by leaving a buffer zone around surviving archaeological features. Indeed, such measures help address wider problems such as soil erosion at the same time. Where provision of access is feasible, archaeological sites can also offer an opportunity for farmers to diversify, providing benefits to farmers while at the same time enhancing the conservation, recreational and amenity value of previously intensively farmed land.

Most current agricultural support schemes incorporate the conservation considerations enshrined in Section 17 of the Agriculture Act 1986, and accept archaeological conservation as part of modern land management. Some provision for archaeological management is included within several grant schemes (Grenville 1996). The best models of archaeological needs being integrated into farm-management schemes, however, are the various agri-environmental schemes (detailed information from the Countryside Council for Wales, DEFRA and the Scottish Executive) (all web addresses listed at the end of the chapter). Their main objective is to encourage environmentally friendly and conservation-oriented farming practices, ideally based on integrated management of the whole-farm unit. The schemes have conservation objectives for natural heritage, cultural heritage and landscape. Consequently, they not only allow archaeological management to be related to wider agricultural management, but also enable different conservation objectives to be interrelated. At the level of entry to these schemes, there is a basic requirement to prevent incidental damage to archaeological features and historic landscapes through unsympathetic farming

(a)

(b)

(c)

Opposite, above and following page: **Figure 22.1.** Archaeological sites survive in different forms across the landscape: (a) Roman earthworks in unimproved land; (b) crop-mark enclosure in arable land; (c) medieval earthwork in improved and developed land; (d) some can form extensive relict landscapes. *((a) Crown Copyright: Historic Scotland; (b) and (c) © W.S. Hanson; (d) Crown Copyright: RCAHMS)*

343

(d)

practices: this forms part of the general agricultural and environmental conditions. The schemes additionally offer the option of undertaking active management of archaeological features, such as removal of trees, scrub and burrowing animals, introduction of appropriate grazing regimes and repair of erosion scars. An important element of the schemes is the preparation of whole-farm conservation plans, in which different elements of conservation value are identified and balanced in a single management plan.

Although some conservation objectives are compulsory, however, positive archaeological management is generally optional for the farmer. This means that the full potential of these schemes is seldom met for the archaeological resource. Nevertheless, the provisions allow archaeological management to be undertaken as an integral part of general agricultural management, rather than as a separate activity, and this link helps make the farming community more aware of archaeological features within the farming landscape and their management needs. This is particularly so where archaeological specialists act as farm advisors, helping the archaeological objectives of the schemes to be realised. The current review of the Common Agricultural Policy is likely to lead to the general application of good agricultural and environmental practice in which there will be greater cross-compliance between environmental objectives and farming practice. Heritage objectives are likely to form part of the environmental conditions and should be included in the suite of options for positive management activities, though the details of how these general provisions are implemented will vary across the UK (detailed information from the Countryside Council for Wales, DEFRA and the Scottish Executive).

Forestry

The damaging effects of commercial forestry on archaeology have been well-aired in the literature (Proudfoot 1989; Barclay 1992b; Shepherd 1992). Ground preparation, particularly ploughing, can cause archaeological damage, as can planting and the growth cycle, through root disturbance and masking features. Felling processes can also be destructive, through vehicle damage and the removal and uprooting of trees. Even hand-planted and naturally regenerated scrub or woodland will disturb and obscure archaeological features, though the extent of damage is likely to be reduced in these circumstances. Although most forestry is carried out in upland areas of Britain, where it affects extensive areas of well-preserved archaeological remains, afforestation has also had some impact on the better farmland of the lowlands in recent years, where the rich crop-mark complexes are located. Nevertheless, forestry and woodland can also lead to archaeological benefits: tree coverage has prevented the destruction of archaeological sites by other agencies, such as agricultural ploughing; some sites within woodland are actively managed for conservation, while allowing access to others for recreation is generally beneficial (Yarnell 1993; 1999; Fojut 2002).

It is also important to recognise that woodland has archaeological value of its own, since it has usually been managed or maintained for domestic and industrial activities, and many sites within woodland are directly related to such use (e.g. Smout 2003). Furthermore, the management of woodland can be archaeologically significant in its own right, relating to, for instance, the understanding of such processes as coppicing or woodland pasture. Similarly, areas of ancient, or semi-natural, woodland are both an important element of the historic landscape and a significant store of archaeological information. In this area, the needs of the historic landscape and of archaeological sites within woodland can coincide with those of wider forest management and biodiversity.

The UK Forestry Standard (Forestry Commission 2004) and associated archaeological guidelines form the basis of forestry policy in relation to archaeology, making provision for its consideration in advance of forestry schemes. At a strategic level, the archaeological resource is also addressed within Indicative Forestry Strategies, carried out by local authorities to guide forestry development in their areas, and within more detailed local Forestry Frameworks. Provisions to protect and manage archaeological sites within areas supported by forestry grant schemes are in place throughout the country (further information from the Forestry Commission GB). These cover most forestry in Britain, since relatively little planting now occurs without grant aid, and include both Forestry Enterprise planting schemes and private enterprises. These provisions allow identified archaeological features of importance to be protected, either by their exclusion from a forestry scheme or by adaptations within the scheme. In the former case, archaeological features cease to be a forestry management issue, but in the latter they should ideally become an integral part of forest management. Archaeological features can be incorporated into forest plantations as open spaces for fire breaks or deer lawns, and should be accessible from forest rides for ease of management, though not positioned on the rides themselves as they are then vulnerable to vehicular pressure. In this way, archaeological management can usually be harmonised with other forest management needs. Damage to sites or features already under forest and woodland cover can be ameliorated by removal of trees, with appropriate care, and protection from replanting, activities which Forestry Enterprise now routinely undertake for Scheduled Monuments on their land. Such protection is a basic principle of archaeological management in woodland, together with the avoidance of planted areas close to archaeological features to prevent self-seeding regeneration, and appropriate management to keep features clear of trees, scrub and bracken. These objectives need not conflict with the aims of commercial forestry, as archaeological sites can help provide variety within a woodland habitat and offer a valuable recreational attraction within forests.

In addition to forest plantations, archaeological management is required in relation to the natural regeneration of woodland, which many grant schemes support. Generally, no ploughing is needed for this, though there may be some scarification of the ground surface and limited planting. Nevertheless, archaeological features in these areas require both specific management and the inclusion of more open spaces than management for woodland itself might need.

Although commercial forestry has long been regarded as having transformed the countryside in an unsympathetic way that did not respect the landscape and its component elements, changes in forestry policy and practice have sought to address this problem in recent years (Yarnell 1999). Modern forestry policy supports the concept of multipurpose forestry, which has conservation and recreation objectives as well as economic aims. National forestry schemes now seek to integrate different conservation needs with forest management to enhance the forest environment as a whole and make it a focus for popular interest and recreation (Forestry Commission 2004). Archaeological resource management sits comfortably within this approach, as part of the conservation value and for recreational benefit: indeed archaeological elements are now commonly included within forest trails on Forestry Enterprise land. This situation illustrates how well land uses can be adjusted to integrate competing needs in the landscape. Where forestry is not supported by public grants, however, protection of unscheduled archaeological features can be more difficult to achieve. This can also be more difficult in the context of natural regeneration, particularly where this is consequent upon farm abandonment rather than the result of direct intervention.

Natural processes and natural heritage

The potential impact of major natural processes, such as climate change and coastal erosion, on the natural heritage is well recognised. Similarly, the impacts of human and natural agencies on areas of natural heritage value, such as peatlands and wetlands, is also well understood. Such issues impact equally on the cultural heritage and often demand comparable responses (e.g. Coles and Coles 1996: 104–32; Coles 2001: 171–84; Olivier 2001; Darvill and Fulton 1998: 137–45), yet have been less well documented, with few studies comparable to national or local biodiversity action plans. The consequences for cultural heritage, which cannot be relocated or replaced, can sometimes be catastrophic, and rescue excavation is unrealistic for the extensive nature of the resource as a whole.

There is now quite a body of literature on the integration of archaeological management and natural heritage objectives (e.g. Lambrick 1985; Macinnes and Wickham-Jones 1992; Berry and Brown 1995). Their management needs can be both complementary and conflicting, leading to a close but complicated relationship. Archaeological management can encourage biodiversity on sites, while the management of land for natural heritage value can enhance archaeological management and the setting of monuments. Conflicts arise where, for example, the interests of natural heritage are inimical to good archaeological management and vice versa. In most cases, though, mutually beneficial compromises can be reached.

Archaeological sites can be important areas of natural heritage value (e.g. Berry 1992). Unploughed sites within arable land may, for example, be a key focus of biodiversity in an area, though the vegetation itself might be archaeologically damaging. Similarly, in marginal land 'unimproved' archaeological sites may have particular value for natural heritage, such as hosting old woodland or meadow species. In upland areas there is also often a coincidence of interest; for instance, peatlands and wetlands have both natural and archaeological value (Coles 2001b). Often the natural heritage value is derived from the historic use of a site or area, as with plants introduced for their culinary or medicinal value, for instance; in other cases, biodiversity is an indirect result of particular activities in the past, as with soils enriched by the use of lime mortar in construction which subsequently support lime-dependent species; in other circumstances, archaeological sites simply provide quiet habitats relatively free from modern intrusions (e.g. Macinnes and Ader 1995: 32–4; Hutson 1995: 71–2; Thompson 1995). There is great potential to explore these relationships further in the context of biodiversity strategies and action plans at area and site level, both for research and to inform applied conservation practice.

One of the difficulties in retaining this common value while at the same time avoiding conflict is recognising where management requirements overlap and where they differ. This process is aided by the various formal agreements or concordats that exist between the natural and cultural heritage agencies (see websites for further information). Nevertheless, best results are undoubtedly achieved through regular contact and consultation, which help build mutual understanding and awareness. Designated areas provide the easiest focus for developing such understanding and provide an opportunity to explore the interrelationship between the two interests and to establish complementary management procedures and techniques that can be applied more widely. Such opportunities are often explored most successfully in areas that contain both natural heritage designations and features of archaeological interest, such as National Parks or large estates (Smith 1992; Iles 1992).

Recreation and access

Pressures from access and recreation lead to both threats and opportunities for archaeology. Rights of public access have recently been updated and extended in wide-ranging legislation to allow enhanced access to much of the countryside (Countryside and Rights of Way Act 2000; Land Reform (Scotland) Act 2003). Alongide this, there is an increased economic reliance on tourism, greater personal leisure time, and a widespread diversification of activities within the British landscape, which mean that there is now regular pressure to facilitate access to features of archaeological interest for recreational use. This carries an increased risk of erosion on monuments as a result of higher visitor numbers, as can be clearly seen at some public monuments; and incidental damage, including vandalism. At the same time, however, this also provides more opportunities for interpretation and public education, leading to an enhanced understanding of the past and the features that survive from it. Archaeological features can provide a focus for alternative uses of the landscape that enhance the public's understanding of its development on the one hand and the range, significance and needs of archaeological sites on the other. This potential is widely recognised within areas that promote visitor management, such as National Parks or land owned by the National Trusts, but the archaeological heritage has great value for the wider tourism industry as well. Archaeology and natural heritage have an important complementary value in landscape interpretation, which has been recognised for some time in particular areas, such as Heritage Coasts. There is considerable scope for developing the recreation, and tourism, potential of archaeology and the historic landscape further.

Sporting estates

Sporting estates are an important element of the landscape throughout Britain, though perhaps particularly in Scotland and northern England. In these areas, land is managed

(a)

(b)

Above and opposite: **Figure 22.2.** Archaeological sites are affected by natural processes: (a) decay and encroachment by vegetation; (b) coastal erosion; and by human activity: (c) land use impacts often occur in combination; (d) visitor pressure. *((a—c) Crown Copyright: Historic Scotland; (d) © English Heritage)*

(c)

(d)

primarily for grouse or deer shooting and generally involves a combination of forestry, farming and game management. Archaeological management issues are much as for farming and forestry described above. Generally, high levels of deer stocking help inhibit natural regeneration of woodland, which is beneficial for archaeological conservation, though in some estates deer numbers are reduced specifically to encourage natural regeneration for the benefit of the natural heritage. Muirburn, which is a particular feature of the upland management in sporting estates, is generally beneficial for archaeology so long as it is properly controlled. Indeed, this has itself become a defining characteristic of the modern cultural landscape of upland Britain.

Archaeology and landscape

Although the imprint of human activity is most obvious in the landscape through archaeological and historical remains, attention is increasingly being paid to other historic aspects of the landscape, such as field patterns and vegetation cover. Landscape elements, such as historic parks and gardens or hedgerows, have always been included in agri-environment schemes to some extent (e.g. Jago 1995), but recent techniques that have been developed to map the character of historic land use will facilitate their inclusion more comprehensively. These new techniques of historic landscape characterisation (called *historic landscape characterisation* in England; *historic land-use assessment* in Scotland; *Landmap* in Wales) aim to describe the nature and extent of the historic influence across the landscape (for summaries see Fairclough and Macinnes 2003; Clark *et al.* 2004; Macinnes 2004; Chapter 17).

The techniques behind historic landscape characterisation are essentially simple. They identify broad patterns of land use, including field boundaries, at a landscape scale, usually based on OS 1:25000 maps. The map-based information is supplemented by vertical aerial photographs and other data-sets, such as those for ancient or semi-natural woodland. Historic landscape characterisation also makes use of historic maps, which are increasingly available in digital form. Historic landscape or land use types are identified from this information, based on appropriate parcels of land, reflecting the nature and date of the predominant historic land use within them. Key indicators of historic use include the form of field boundaries, or the size, orientation and use of fields. Information on the period of origin or use, and on past phases of use including, in some cases, relict landscapes, allow change through time to be recognised. The techniques are GIS-based and interactive; they are extremely flexible and capable of great sophistication.

Historic landscape characterisation improves understanding of the time-depth in the landscape; of the impact people have had on land use over time; of the historic origin of the land uses that we can see today; of the degree of continuity and change in the landscape over time; and of the impact of modern change on the historic character of the landscape. The techniques are intended for use alongside historic environment records to inform decisions relating to the protection and management of the archaeological heritage. However, they go beyond individual archaeological features and give a broader context to their management. They help give a fuller appreciation of the historic influence on the modern landscape and its characteristics, such as field patterns and boundaries, and are helping to establish priorities for their management in a land-use context.

Historic landscape characterisation highlights that the landscape has far greater time-depth than is often appreciated, and shows how this has influenced its current character. The techniques can help develop land management strategies that are based upon a better understanding of the historical development of the landscape; and help ensure that the historic dimension of landscape is more fully incorporated into land-use policies and

Figure 22.3. With positive management, archaeological sites can co-exist with most land uses; this prehistoric ritual complex is under light grazing with access for visitors. *(Crown Copyright: Historic Scotland)*

associated grant schemes. They work well with the more established method of describing the natural character of the landscape (Landscape Character Assessment (Swanwick and Land Use Consultants 2002)), providing greater understanding of how much of this character has developed and of its historical significance. Together, these various techniques have the potential to facilitate a better-informed and integrated approach to land use and the management of landscape change, and, ultimately, to help define national and local priorities at a landscape scale. Moreover, site-specific management is increasingly being set within these landscape-wide frameworks.

ARCHAEOLOGY, THE HISTORIC LANDSCAPE AND INTEGRATED LAND MANAGEMENT

Successful protection of archaeological features and historic landscapes requires specific actions to identify, protect, manage and, in some cases, interpret them. Identification, recording and understanding the resource is an essential prerequisite to protecting and managing it, and the maintenance of sites and monuments or historic environment records is fundamental, though also a challenge to resources. In a land-use context, it is particularly important that these records are at a landscape scale and clearly related to land use, and the techniques of historic landscape characterisation mentioned above are helping to ensure this. In addition to general recording, specific audits can be helpful in establishing the condition of the archaeological resource and the potential impact of land uses on it, as the Monuments at Risk Survey demonstrated (Darvill and Fulton 1998).

However, archaeological needs have also to be considered in the context of the competing requirements of different uses of the countryside. The aim is to maximise benefits for archaeology and the historic landscape, while minimising conflicts with other

351

land uses, including natural heritage objectives. This is best achieved in the context of integrated approaches to land management and through the use of conservation planning (Clark 1999). Indeed, this is the real challenge of modern land management, to achieve an integrated strategy that recognises, incorporates and accommodates the various competing values within the landscape.

There are some key frameworks that aim to support such an integrated approach. The various agri-environment and woodland grant schemes already incorporate the protection of the archaeological resource, though sites are not always proactively managed within these schemes. Other frameworks have the potential to incorporate archaeological interests. These include River Basin Management Plans (developed under the Water Framework Directive, which became effective in 2002) which have relevance for archaeological elements within wetland and riverine contexts, and in river catchments (further information from the national environment protection agencies). Similarly, national biodiversity strategies and local biodiversity action plans address habitat or species types, such as moorland or peatlands, which have direct archaeological relevance. However, in most cases the potential of these frameworks to incorporate cultural heritage objectives is not yet realised in practice, and the correlation of interests is seldom recognised or explored. Nevertheless, these could be very important for archaeological resource management in the future. Similarly, the development of strategic planning for rural areas and strategic environmental assessments is likely to have great significance, as these should encourage cross-compliance between relevant agencies and facilitate the inclusion of archaeological objectives in key policies, plans and programmes.

The following examples illustrate how integrated approaches can work for landscape, heritage protection and land-use management, both through regulation and through establishing models of good practice.

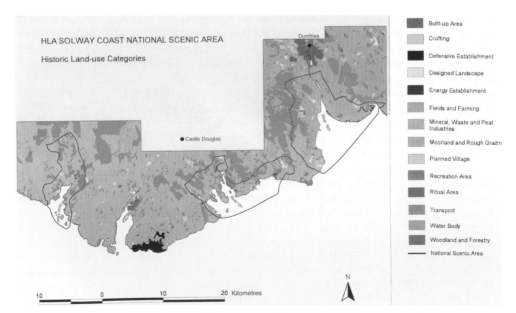

Figure 22.4. This character map shows the historic pattern of the farmed landscape. (*Crown Copyright: Historic Scotland (OS licence number 100017509) and RCAHMS (OS licence number 100020548)*)

Protected areas

There is a complex hierarchy of landscape designations within the UK, with much regional variation. At international level, the World Heritage Convention allows for the protection of both natural and cultural heritage and requires provision to be made for management (Prott 1992). Natural and cultural heritage are treated in separate categories, but the third category of cultural landscape combines them, recognising that they are often closely related (Rössler 2001). World Heritage status will only ever be applied to a few select sites, but does include key archaeological monuments, including Stonehenge, Hadrian's Wall and the Heart of Neolithic Orkney. European Directives and Conventions address natural heritage and cultural heritage issues separately; those for natural heritage are generally stronger and often backed by legislation, whereas those for cultural heritage are more often advisory (e.g. Bell 1997; Marsden 2001). There is scope for including archaeological considerations in the implementation of at least some of these, as recent developments under the Ramsar Convention have demonstrated. The Council of Europe's recent European Landscape Convention actively seeks to promote an integrated approach to the landscape as a whole and improve awareness of landscape issues within spatial and land management planning, addressing both natural and cultural aspects of landscape (Priore 2001; Fairclough 2002c). This was signed by the UK government in early 2006.

At national level, National Parks are found across the country and have both a conservation and a recreational function. These provide a good opportunity for integrated land management, since responsibility for different types of land use is invested in a single management unit (for example, Smith 1992: 127–31). One of the main purposes of National Parks is to preserve and enhance the natural and cultural heritage of the area and promote public enjoyment of them. National Parks can protect archaeological sites and the historic landscape through specific policies, management agreements and through a coordinated approach to land use and land management. Achieving this potential in practice requires understanding of the resource and its needs, which in turn requires specialist databases and advice to inform park plans and policies. In England and Wales, where National Parks have been in place for a long time, most park authorities employ archaeologists directly, but this is not yet the case in Scotland, where National Parks have only recently been established.

Some landscape areas are designated largely for their natural beauty or scenic qualities, such as Areas of Outstanding Natural Beauty and National Scenic Areas. Archaeological objectives may not be included in these explicitly, but archaeological features often contribute significantly to the scenic value and natural beauty of such areas, and can be considered within management objectives. Other designations treat natural and cultural heritage separately: natural heritage is protected through a range of national (e.g. National Nature Reserves and Sites of Special Scientific Interest) and international designations (e.g. Ramsar Convention; Natura 2000 sites) (further information from the natural heritage agencies); cultural heritage is protected through the Ancient Monument and Listed Building legislation (Chapter 5). Historic Gardens, Parks and Designed Landscapes contain both natural and cultural elements and are generally protected through non-Statutory Registers (further information from the national heritage agencies).

Below national level, there is a bewildering array of regional and local landscape and heritage designations, which vary greatly from area to area (specific information from the natural heritage and rural land-use agencies). Although very few such areas are designated primarily for the historic landscape or archaeological resource, these can often be accommodated within management strategies for the protected areas. Indeed, in many cases, regional and local designations provide a good context for integrating the protection and management of the cultural heritage with the natural heritage and broader land management, both formally through management planning and informally through communication and consultation.

Within areas designated for their natural heritage value, there is considerable scope for improving the protection, and in some cases, the management of archaeological sites and their settings. Although archaeology is not a consideration in such designations, in many cases their management need not damage the historic interest within the site. In other cases, however, the management objectives for natural heritage might conflict with the best management of archaeological sites within them, for example, maintaining woodland habitat. Nevertheless, with appropriate consultation, it is often possible to incorporate archaeological management within the framework of designated natural heritage sites, since the former is usually only a small proportion of the latter.

The protection of ancient monuments and archaeological areas under the Ancient Monuments and Archaeological Areas (AMAA) Act 1979 is described elsewhere in this volume. The Act makes provision for the payment of grants for management work on archaeological sites, either as one-off grants for the active management of archaeological or historic features, or as longer-term management agreements. The aim of this management is to maintain archaeological sites or areas in the best possible condition, but natural heritage interests can also be addressed within management actions. Indeed, there is considerable potential to carry out the management of archaeological features in a way that enhances their natural heritage value (Darvill 1987; Wainwright 1989b: 168; Macinnes and Wickham-Jones 1992; Berry and Brown 1995). There are now many good examples of integrating the management of natural heritage with those monuments in care managed directly by the state archaeological bodies (Harding 1995). Although there are no formal designations for the historic landscape, there are inventories or registers of historic parks and gardens, historic landscapes and battlefields, which have improved awareness of the archaeological and historic dimension of the landscape, and facilitated its inclusion in land management strategies (e.g. CADW et al. 1998 and 2001; further information from the national heritage agencies).

Many of these situations allow for integrating archaeological and other environmental objectives. Where this is not achieved, contributory factors can include a lack of awareness that there are other conservation values in a particular area; a lack of understanding of what the management requirements for different values are; and a lack of resources to allow consultation, site meetings and the modified management prescriptions that are necessary for different interests to be combined successfully. Consultations between archaeological and nature heritage bodies have, however, increased markedly in recent years, leading to good examples of integrated policy and practice both nationally and locally.

In addition to designations, the practice of landscape characterisation mentioned above is now becoming more commonplace. This seeks to describe heritage values across the whole of the landscape, not just within protected areas, and to facilitate their inclusion in decision-making concerning development and land-use change. Landscape character assessment highlights both natural and cultural aspects of landscape character, though it focuses particularly on visual character and on most recent historic influences, such as designed landscapes. The techniques of historic landscape characterisation described above bring the human influences into this picture more comprehensively and allow cultural and natural aspects to be more fully integrated. It is likely that the characterisation approach will develop further in the land-use context, and become highly important in setting priorities for protection and management beyond designated areas; it is also helpful, though, in refining priorities within protected areas.

Estate management

Some large estates are owned by public or conservation bodies. Some, such as the National Trust and National Trust for Scotland, have responsibility for both cultural and natural heritage, while others focus primarily on natural heritage (e.g. Wildlife Trusts, Royal Society for the Protection of Birds) or other land uses (e.g. Ministry of Defence and Forestry Commission) (Dwyer and Hodge 1996). Many of these take cultural heritage into consideration in their land management, as, indeed, do some large private estates and public utilities.

The National Trust for England and Wales and The National Trust for Scotland are charitable bodies concerned with the preservation of land and buildings of historic or natural interest. Since the Trusts have large landholdings and have a remit for conservation and interpretation, they have, like National Parks, the potential for a coordinated and integrated approach to land management (Claris 1993). The Trusts do indeed seek to harmonise the wide range of conservation interests within their properties into a holistic approach to landscape management and interpretation. They fully recognise the value of their archaeological resource and employ archaeological teams to research and conserve it, and ensure its integration into overall property management plans (Thackray and Hearn 1985: 51 7; Thackray *et al.* 1995).

The Ministry of Defence (MoD) has made tremendous strides in recent years to include conservation interests within the management of the Defence Estates. This is supported by its regular magazine, *Sanctuary*, which discusses a wide range of conservation subjects related to defence landholdings and MoD activities. This work is guided by Conservation Officers and local conservation groups, on which relevant heritage interests are represented. The MoD also employs archaeologists to advise them on archaeological matters across the UK. The value of this approach for the archaeological resource is emphasised by the Salisbury Plain project, where English Heritage (EH) and the MoD collaborated to produce a management plan for an area of land highly important both archaeologically and for defence purposes (Morgan Evans 1992). The management plan identifies extremely sensitive archaeological areas that will be preserved in all cases (except a national emergency), and areas where sites are sensitively managed within areas used for other land uses or defence activities. One of the MoD's archaeologists is dedicated to the Salisbury Plain training area, showing its commitment to this major archaeological landscape.

There are many other examples of how the management of the archaeological resource can be incorporated into the aims and objectives of other organisations or individuals. For instance, the RSPB, the various Wildlife Trusts and, in Scotland, the John Muir Trust have all supported archaeological work within management of their estates. Similar work has been undertaken within public utility land holdings, and within private estates, where the management of all features falls under the responsibility of a single owner or manager (e.g. Iles 1992).

Overall, then, there is considerable potential for integrated land management where the value of the whole can be enhanced by the judicious management of the component parts. Compromise is involved, but this is acceptable in the vast majority of cases. Integration is easier to achieve where the range of assets has been identified and incorporated in decision-making at the outset. At the same time, however, resources can be a real problem in achieving both the time to prepare integrated management plans, since more time and personnel are involved, and the funds needed to achieve the management objectives, which will tend to be more complex and involve more interest groups. Although the way may be led by designated areas and larger conservation bodies, there are many opportunities to apply the principle more widely, and this is a key area for further development in landscape and archaeological resource management.

THE FUTURE: THE SUSTAINABLE MANAGEMENT OF THE ARCHAEOLOGICAL RESOURCE

The best way to recognise the unity of the landscape in practice is through an integrated form of land management that combines different land objectives (e.g. Miles 1992). This would allow archaeological and cultural heritage considerations to stand alongside natural heritage, agriculture and forestry as a major objective of modern land management and as one of several criteria to be considered in decision-making. The management choices made for any piece of land need to recognise the variety of values within the landscape and seek solutions that balance as many of those interests as possible, even if, on occasion, one is considered to be of paramount importance. Thus, an important historic landscape, for example, might be maintained under a traditional mixed management regime rather than given over to woodland regeneration; or established woodland might be retained on a monument because of particularly important ecological interests.

Currently, sectoral grant schemes, mainly for agriculture and forestry, remain the key mechanism for achieving such integration. These raise common problems for archaeological resource management, including identifying archaeological features and defining the area of archaeological sensitivity. Solutions to these problems differ around the country and depend to a large extent on the quality of the local historic environment database and the availability of archaeological advice. Where archaeological features have been identified, they are generally afforded basic protection within the grant schemes. However, positive management to bring features into best condition is much more problematic, as this is usually an optional element and choices are not always dictated by archaeological priorities or informed by specialist advice.

Nevertheless, integrated approaches to the protection and management of the environment are increasingly the focus of government policy, under the banner of sustainable development (further information from www.sustainable-development.gov.uk). Standard mechanisms for achieving this, such as Environmental Impact Assessment are being improved and developed with new provisions, such as Strategic Environmental Assessment (www.sea-info.net), River Basin Management Plans (see environment agency websites) and Quality of Life Capital (Countryside Agency *et al.* 2001). Land-use policy is increasingly being set within a more holistic framework for rural policy that recognises social and environmental benefit alongside economic benefit.

Cultural heritage is also increasingly embraced within this more holistic approach, and it is becoming recognised that the cultural heritage holds a range of values in modern society beyond its intrinsic or academic worth (Clark 1993; EH 1997a; HS 2002). The archaeological resource is of fundamental importance for what it can tell us about the past, informing environmental history as well as social and technological development. At the same time, it has value for recreation and for tourism; it is an important education resource; it contributes to the sense of place of a community or may be associated with a significant cultural tradition, historical event or local landmark. Such different values all contribute to the overall value of the archaeological resource in relation to other potential uses of the land and allow recognition of the social, environmental and economic benefits of its conservation. This should ultimately lend greater public and policy support to the case for conservation of the archaeological resource.

As not everything can be conserved, however, it is essential within a sustainability scenario to consider ways in which the resource can be used without compromising its value for present and future generations. For the archaeological resource, this concept needs further development to ensure that significant features are not unduly compromised; decisions need to be based on an understanding of the resource, informed by an awareness of the needs of its basic stewardship, and an appreciation of its capacity to absorb change. Established tools, such as conservation planning, and new techniques, such as historic landscape characterisation, carrying capacity studies and Quality of Life Capital, are aiding this decision-making process and will gradually make the conservation of the archaeological resource more sophisticated. As more work of this nature is carried out, models of good practice will become available to guide further work.

Rural land-use policy is in the process of major change. Integrated approaches to the range of land uses are becoming more refined, with social and environmental values beginning to stand alongside economic benefit. A variety of developing frameworks is facilitating this process. If we wish to ensure that the archaeological resource survives in a good state for future generations to study and enjoy, we need to work now towards embedding the management of the archaeological resource within these new frameworks.

ACKNOWLEDGEMENTS

I would like to thank my colleagues D. Breeze, N. Fojut and J. Wordsworth for their help-ful comments on a draft of this text.

APPENDIX: WEB ADDRESSES

National heritage agencies

CADW: www.cadw.wales.gov.uk
English Heritage: www.english-heritage.org.uk
Historic Scotland: www.historic-scotland.gov.uk

Government departments and agencies for environment, rural affairs and forestry

Department for Environment, Food and Rural Affairs: www.defra.gov.uk
Department for Environment, Planning and Countryside: www.countryside.wales.gov.uk
Forestry Commission GB: www.forestry.gov.uk
Scottish Executive: www.scotland.gov.uk

Environmental protection agencies

Environment Agency (England and Wales): www.environment-agency.gov.uk
Scottish Environment Protection Agency: www.sepa.org.uk

Natural heritage agencies

Countryside Agency: www.countryside.gov.uk
Countryside Council for Wales: www.ccw.gov.uk
Scottish Natural Heritage: www.snh.org.uk

National trusts

The National Trust: www.nationaltrust.org.uk
The National Trust for Scotland: www.nts.org.uk

Sustainable development

UK Government Sustainable Development: www.sustainable-development.gov.uk

BIBLIOGRAPHY

AAHRG (Avebury Archaeological and Historical Research Group) 2001 *Archaeological Research Agenda for the Avebury World Heritage Site*. Salisbury: Wessex Archaeology for the AAHRG.

ACAO (Association of County Archaeological Officers) 1993 *Model Briefs and Specifications for Archaeological Assessment and Field Evaluations*. Bedford: ACAO.

ALGAO (Association of Local Government Archaeological Officers) 1997 *Analysis and Recording for the Conservation and Control of Works to Historic Buildings*. Chelmsford: ALGAO.

—— 2001 *Local Records – National Resource, An ALGAO Strategy for Sites and Monuments Records*. London: ALGAO.

AMBS (Ancient Monuments Board for Scotland) 1983 *Ancient Monuments Board for Scotland, Thirtieth Annual Report 1983*. Edinburgh: HMSO.

APPAG (All-Party Parliamentary Archaeology Group) 2003 *The Current State of Archaeology in the United Kingdom*. First Report of the All-Party Parliamentary Archaeology Group, London. Available on www.sal.org.uk.

Adams M. and Brooke C. 1995 'Unmanaging the Past: Truth, Data and the Human Being', *Norwegian Archaeology Review* 28, 93–104.

Addyman P.V. 1974 'York: The Anatomy of a Crisis in Urban Archaeology', in Rahtz 1974, 153–62.

—— 1989 'The Role of the Professional Institution', in Cleere 1989, 302–7.

—— 2001 'Antiquities without Archaeology in the United Kingdom', in Brodie N., Doole J. and Renfrew C. (eds) 2001 *Trade in Illicit Antiquities: The Destruction of the World's Archaeological Heritage*, 141–4. Cambridge: McDonald Institute.

—— and Brodie N. 2002 'Metal Detecting in Britain: Catastrophe or Compromise?', in Brodie and Tubb 2002, 179–84.

Adlercreutz T. 1998 'Property Rights and Protection of the Cultural Heritage in Sweden', *International Journal of Cultural Property* 7/2, 410–33.

Agnew N. and Demas M. (eds) 2002 *Principles for the Conservation of Archaeological Sites in China*. Los Angeles: Getty Conservation Institute.

d'Agostino B. 1984 'Italy', in Cleere 1984, 73–81.

Aitchison K. 1999 *Profiling the Profession: A Survey of Archaeological Jobs in the UK*. York, London and Reading: CBA, EH and IFA.

—— 2000 'The Funding of Professional Archaeological Practice in England', *Cultural Trends* 39, 1–32.

—— 2002 'Footing the Bill', *The Archaeologist* 44, 34.

—— and Edwards R. 2003 *Archaeology Labour Market Intelligence: Profiling the Profession 2002/3*. Bradford and Reading: CHNTO and IFA.

Aitken M.J. 1974 *Physics in Archaeology*. Oxford: Clarendon Press. 2nd edn.

Aldred O. and Fairclough G.J. 2003 *Historic Landscape Characterisation: Taking Stock of the Method – the National HLC Method Review*. London: EH and Somerset County Council.

Aldridge D. 1989 'How the Ship of Interpretation was Blown Off Course in the Tempest: Some Philosophical Thoughts', in Uzzell 1989b, 64–87.

Allen G.W.G. 1984 'Discovery from the Air', *Aerial Archaeology* 10, 1–99.

Allen J.L. and Holt A. St J. 1986 *Health and Safety in Field Archaeology*. London: Standing Conference of Archaeological Unit Managers (with later updates).

Allen M.J. 1990 'Magnetic Susceptibility', in Bell M. (ed) 1990 *Bream Down Excavations 1983–1987*, 197–202. London: HBMC. (EH Archaeol Rep 15.)

Ames M. 1977 'Visible Storage and Public Documentation', *Curator* 20, 65–79.

Anderson J. 1904 'Treasure Trove', *Scottish History Review* 1 (1903–04), 74–80.

Anderton M. and Schofield J. 1999 'Anti-Aircraft Gunsites – Then and Now', *Conservation Bulletin* 36, 11–13.

—— and Went D. 2002 'Turning the Plough: Loss of a Landscape Legacy', *Conservation Bulletin* 42, 52–5.

Andrews D., Blake B., Clowes M. and Wilson K. 1995 *The Survey and Recording of Historic Buildings and Monuments*. Oxford: Association of Archaeological Illustrators and Surveyors. (AAIS Tech Pap 12.)

Andrews G., Barrett J.C. and Lewis J.S.C. 2000 'Interpretation Not Record: The Practice of Archaeology', *Antiquity* 74, 525–30.

—— and Thomas R. 1995 'The Management of Archaeological Projects: Theory and Practice in the UK', in Cooper M.A., Firth A., Carman J. and Wheatley D. (eds) 1995 *Managing Archaeology*, 189–207. London: Routledge.

Anon 1986 *Preservation by Record: The Work of the Central Excavation Unit 1975–85*. London: HBMC.

Anon 1989 'Archaeology and Development: Report of a One-day Conference', *Property Journal, the Journal of the British Property Federation* 14/3, 16–21.

Anon 2003 'Archaeology and Parliament: Responding to the APPAG report', *The Archaeologist*, 50, 7–8.

Apted M.R., Gilyard-Beer R. and Saunders A.D. (eds) 1977 *Ancient Monuments and Their Interpretation. Essays Presented to A. J. Taylor*. London and Chichester: Phillimore.

Archaeological Dialogues 1/1 1994 'Dutch Perspectives on Contemporary Archaeology', Leiden: University of Leiden, Department of Archaeology.

Arnold B. 1990 'The Past as Propaganda in Nazi Germany', *Antiquity* 64, 464–78.

—— 1992 'The Past as Propaganda', *Archaeology* 45/4, 30–7.

Arup (Ove Arup and Partners and the Department of Archaeology, University of York in association with B.Thorpe) 1991 *York Archaeology and Development Study*. Manchester: Ove Arup. (Ove Arup and Dept Archaeol Univ York for York City Council and EH.)

Ascherson N. 1987 'Why "Heritage" is Right-wing', *The Observer*, 8 November 1987, 9.

—— 1988 'Leaving Our Old Curiosity Shop', *The Observer*, 17 January 1988, 7.

Ashley-Smith J. 1982 'The Ethics of Conservation', *The Conservator* 6, 1–5.

Aspinall A. 1992 'New Developments in Geophysical Prospection', *Proceedings of the British Academy* 77, 233–44.

—— and Crummett J.G. 1997 'The Electrical Pseudo-section', *Archaeological Prospection* 4, 37–48.

Aston M.A., Martin M.H. and Jackson A.W. 1998 'The Potential for Heavy Metal Soil Analysis on Low Status Archaeological Sites at Shapwick, Somerset', *Antiquity* 72, 838–47.

Atkin M. and Milligan R. 1992 'Ground-probing Radar in Archaeology – Practicalities and Problems', *Field Archaeologist* 16, 288–91.

Audouze F. 1998 'Une nouvelle crise de l'archéologie en France', *European Archaeologist* 10, 5–7.

—— 2001 'A New Rescue Archaeology Law in France', *European Archaeologist* 15, 4–8.

—— and Demoule J.-P. 2002 'EAA Board Resolution Supporting French Archaeological System', *European Archaeologist* 17, 2–3.

Austin D. 1987 'The Future of Archaeology in British Universities', *Antiquity* 61, 227–38.

Austin T., Pinto F., Richards J. and Ryan N. 2002 'Joined up Writing: An Internet Portal for Research into the Historic Environment', in Burenhult 2002, 243–51.

BADLG (British Archaeologists and Developers Liaison Group) 1989 *Model Agreement between Developer/Client and the Appropriate Archaeological Body*. London: British Property Federation for BADLG (shorter version also available).

—— 1991 *The British Archaeologists and Developers Liaison Group Code of Practice*. London: BADLG (Joint British Property Federation and Standing Committee of Archaeological Unit Managers publication). 3rd edn (first published 1986).

BAN (British Archaeological News) Editorial 1988 'Rescue on the Cheap', *British Archaeological News* 3/2, 13.

BAN Editorial 1989 'The Lessons of York', *British Archaeological News* 4/2, 13.

BAN Editorial 1990 'Archaeology and the Private Sector', *British Archaeological News* 5/4, 42.

BMAPA/EH (British Marine Aggregate Producers Association and English Heritage) 2003 *Marine Aggregate Dredging and the Historic Environment: Guidance Note*. London: British Marine Aggregate Producers Association and EH.

BSI (British Standards Institute) 1998 *Guide to the Principles of the Conservation of Historic Buildings*. London: British Standards Institution. (BS 7913.)

Baker D.B. 1983 *Living With the Past: The Historic Environment*. Bletsoe, Bedfordshire: D. Baker.

—— 1987 'Editorial – Getting the Act Together', *Field Archaeologist* 7, 86–7.

—— 1996 *A Review of the Sites and Monuments Records of the Welsh Archaeological Trusts for the Royal Commission on the Historical Monuments of Wales*. Bedford: Bedfordshire County Council.

—— 1997 *An Assessment of the Welsh Trusts' Sites and Monuments Records*. Aberystwyth: RCAHMW.

—— 1999a. *An Assessment of English Sites and Monuments Records*. London: EH/ALGAO.

—— 1999b. *An Assessment of Scotland's Sites and Monuments Records*. Edinburgh: RCAHMS.

—— and Chitty G.C. 2002 *Heritage under Pressure*. London: EH.

——, Chitty G.C. and Edwards R. 2004 *English SMR Resources Assessment*. EH/ALGAO website.

—— and Morris R. 2001. 'Last Orders?', *Antiquity* 75, 608–11.

—— and Shepherd I.A.G. 1993 'Local Authority Opportunities', in Hunter and Ralston 1993b, 100–14.

Bapty I. and Yates T. (eds) 1990 *Archaeology after Structuralism*. London: Routledge.

Barber M., Grady D. and Winton H. 2003 'From Pit Circles to Propellers: Recent Results from Aerial Survey in Wiltshire', *Wiltshire Archaeological and Natural History Magazine* 96, 48–160.

Barclay G.J. 1992a 'The Scottish Gravels: a Neglected Resource?', in Fulford M. and Nichols E. (eds), *Developing Landscapes of Lowland Britain*, 106–24. London: Society of Antiquaries.

—— 1992b 'Forestry and Archaeology in Scotland', *Scottish Forestry* 46, 27–47.

Barker P. 1974 'The Origins and Development of RESCUE', in Rahtz 1974, 280–5.

—— 1987 'Not Drowning, Just Treading Water', *CBA Annual Report* 37, 70–6.

Barnes I. 2003 'Conference Sessions: Agency Archaeology', *The Archaeologist* 49/12.

Baumann Z. 1987 *Legislators and Interpreters: On Modernity, Post-modernity, and Intellectuals*, Cambridge: Polity Press.

Belgrave R. 1990 'Black People and Museums: The Caribbean Heritage Project in Southampton', in Gathercole and Lowenthal 1990, 63–73.

Bell D., 1997 *The Historic Scotland Guide to International Conservation Charters*. Edinburgh: HS Technical Advice Note 8

Bell M., Drummond-Murray J., Nixon T. and Schaaf L. 1993 'Review of Archaeology in Britain in 1991', *Field Archaeologist* 18, 356–62.

Bender B. (ed.) 1993 *Landscape. Politics and Perspectives*. Providence, RI and Oxford: Berg.

——, Hamilton S. and Tilley C. 1997 'Leskernick: Stone Worlds; Alternative Narratives; Nested Landscapes', *Proceedings of the Prehistoric Society* 63, 147–78.

Beresford M.W. 1950 'Maps and the Medieval Landscape', *Antiquity* 24, 114–18.

—— and St Joseph J.K.S. 1977 *Medieval England. An Aerial Survey*. Cambridge: Cambridge University Press.

Beresford Dew R. 1977 'Rescue Archaeology: Finance 1976–1977', *Rescue News* 13, 4–6.

Berry A.Q. 1992 'Integrating Archaeology and the Countryside: Clwyd County Council's Approach to Archaeological Site Management', in Macinnes and Wickham-Jones 1992, 155–60.

—— and Brown I.W. (eds) 1994 *Erosion on Archaeological Earthworks: Its Prevention, Control and Repair*. Mold: Clwyd County Council.

—— and Brown I.W. (eds) 1995 *Managing Ancient Monuments: An Integrated Approach*. Mold: Assoc County Archaeol Officers and Clwyd County Council.

Bewley R.H. 1994 *Prehistoric and Romano-British Settlement in the Solway Plain, Cumbria*. Oxford: Oxbow Monograph 36.

—— 2001 'Understanding England's Historic Landscapes: An Aerial Perspective', *Landscapes* 2, 74–84.

—— (ed.) 1998 *Lincolnshire's Archaeology from the Air*. Lincoln: Society for Lincolnshire History and Archaeology. (Occas Pap in Lincolnshire History and Archaeology 11.)

——, Braasch O. and Palmer R. 1996 'An Aerial Archaeology Training Week, 15–22 June, held near Siofok, Lake Balaton, Hungary', *Antiquity* 70, 745–50.

——, Crutchley S. and Shell C. 2005. 'New Light on an Ancient Landscape: Lidar Survey in the Stonehenge World Heritage Site', *Antiquity* 79, 636–47.

—— and Rączkowksi W. (eds) 2002 *Aerial Archaeology. Developing Future Practice*. Amsterdam: IOS Press. (Nato Series 1 Life Sciences 337.)

Bianchi R. and Boniface P. (eds) 2002 *The Politics of World Heritage*. Special issue, *International Journal of Heritage Studies* 8/2 (June).

Biddle M. 1974 'The Future of the Urban Past', in Rahtz 1974, 95–112.

—— 1994 *What Future for British Archaeology?* Birmingham: Institute of Field Archaeologists. (Oxbow Lecture 1.)

—— and Hudson D. 1973 *The Future of London's Past*. Worcester: Rescue Publications.

Binford L. 1964 'A Consideration of Archaeological Research Design', *American Antiquity* 29, 425–41.

Binks G., Dyke J. and Dagnell P. 1988 *Visitors Welcome: A Manual on the Presentation and Interpretation of Archaeological Excavations*. London: HMSO.

Binney M. and Burman P. 1977a *Churches and Chapels: Who Cares?* London: British Tourist Authority.

—— and Burman P. (eds) 1977b *Change and Decay: The Future of Our Churches*. London: Macmillan.

Binns G. and Gardiner J. (comp) 1990 *Guide to Undergraduate University Courses in Archaeology, with a Note on Non-University Courses*. London: CBA. 3rd edn.

Bintliff J. 2004 (ed.) *A Companion to Archaeology*. Oxford: Blackwell.

——, Davies B., Gaffney C., Snodgrass A. and Waters A. 1992 'Trace Metal Accumulation in Soils on and around Ancient Settlements in Greece', in Spoerry 1992b, 9–24.

Black S.L. and Jolly K. 2003 *Archaeology by Design*. Walnut Creek and London: AltaMira Press.

Bland R. 1998 'The Treasure Act and the Initiative for the Voluntary Recording of All Archaeological Finds', *Institute of Field Archaeologists Yearbook and Directory of Members 1998*, 36–8.

—— 1999 'The Treasure Act and Portable Antiquities Scheme: A Progress Report', *Art, Antiquity and Law* 4, 191–203.

Bloemers J.H.F. 2002 'Past- and Future-oriented Archaeology: Protecting and Developing the Archaeological-historical Landscape of the Netherlands', in Fairclough and Rippon 2002, 89–96.

Bökönyi S. 1993 'Recent Developments in Hungarian Archaeology', *Antiqutity* 67, 142–5.

Boniface P. 2001 *Dynamic Tourism. Journeying with Change*. Clevedon, UK: Channel View Publications.

—— and Fowler P.J. 1993 *Heritage and Tourism in 'the Global Village'*. London: Routledge.

Bott V. 2003 *Access to Archaeological Archives: A Study for Resource and the Archaeological Archives Forum*. London: Resource.

Boulting N. 1976 'The Law's Delays: Conservationist Legislation in the British Isles', in Fawcett 1976, 9–33.

Bourdieu P. 1984 *Distinction: A Social Critique of the Judgement of Taste*. London: Routledge & Kegan Paul.

Boutwood Y. 2002 *Warcop Army Training Estate. National Mapping Programme Summary Report*. London: EH Internal Report AER/11/2002.

Bowden M. 1991 *Pitt Rivers: The Life and Archaeological Work of Lieutenant-General Augustus Henry Lane Fox Pitt Rivers, DCL, FRS, FSA*. Cambridge: Cambridge University Press.

—— (ed.) 1999 *Unravelling the Landscape. An Inquisitive Approach to Archaeology*. Stroud: Tempus.

Bowler P.J. 1989 *The Invention of Progress. The Victorians and the Past*. Oxford: Blackwell.

Boyne R. and Rattansi A. (eds) 1990 *Postmodernism and Society*. London: Macmillan.

Bradley R. 1983 'Archaeology, Evolution and the Public Good: The Intellectual Development of General Pitt Rivers', *Archaeological Journal* 140, 1–9.

—— 2002a *The Past in Prehistoric Societies*. London: Routledge.

—— 2002b 'Opinion', *The Archaeologist* 46, 24–5.

Braudel F. 1980 *On History*. Chicago: University of Chicago Press.

Breeze D.J. 1993 'Ancient Monuments Legislation', in Hunter and Ralston 1993b, 44–55.

Briggs C.S. 2003 *Towards a Research Agenda for Welsh Archaeology*. Oxford: Brit Archaeol Rep Brit Ser 343.

British Academy 2001 *Aerial Survey for Archaeology. Report of a British Academy Working Party 1999 Compiled by Robert Bewley*. London: British Academy. Available online at: http://www.britac.ac.uk/news/reports/archaeology/asfa.html.

British Airways 2004 'Are you Getting Enough?', *Business Life* (July/Aug. 2004), 38–42.

Brodie D., Croom J. and Davies J.O. 2002 *English Prisons. An Architectural History*. Swindon: EH.

Brodie N. 2002 'Britannia Waives the Rules? The Licensing of Archaeological Material for Export from the UK', in Brodie and Tubb 2002, 185–204.

——, Doole J. and Watson P. 2000 *Stealing History: The Illicit Trade in Cultural Material*. Cambridge: McDonald Institute.

—— and Tubb K.W. (eds) 2002 *Illicit Antiquities: The Theft of Culture and the Extinction of Archaeology*. London: Routledge.

Brönner W. 1982 *Deutsche Denkmalschutzgesetze*. Bonn: Deutsches Nationalkomittee für Denkmalschutz.

Brown N. and Glazebrook J. (eds) 2000 *Research and Archaeology: A Framework for the Eastern Counties*. Vol. 2. *Research Agenda and Strategy*. Norwich: Scole Archaeological Committee for East Anglia. (East Anglian Archaeology Occas Pap 8.)

Buchli V. and Lucas G. (eds) 2001 *Archaeologies of the Contemporary Past*. London: Routledge.

Buckingham S. 2000 'Points (and Slabs) of Interest', *Context* 65, 21–3.

Burenhult G. (ed.) 2002 *Archaeological Informatics: Pushing the Envelope*. Oxford: Brit Archaeol Rep Internat Ser 1016. (Computer Applications and Quantitative Methods in Archaeology, Proceedings of the 29th Conference, Gotland, April 2001.)

Burnham B. 1974 *The Protection of Cultural Property: Handbook of National Legislations*. Paris: International Council of Museums.

Burrow I. 1984 'The History of the Sites and Monuments Records System', in Burrow I. (ed.), *County Archaeological Records: Progress and Potential*, 6–15. Taunton: Association of County Archaeological Officers.

—— and Hunter R. 1990 'Contracting Archaeology? Cultural Resource Management in New Jersey, USA', *Field Archaeologist* 12, 194–200.

Butcher S. and Garwood P. 1994 *Rescue Excavation 1938 to 1972*. London: EH.

CADW (Welsh Historic Monuments) 2003a *Protection of Historical Assets in Wales: A Consultation Paper*. Cardiff: CADW.

—— 2003b *Caring for Historic Landscapes*. Cardiff: CADW.

——, Countryside Council for Wales and ICOMOS UK 1998 *Register of Landscapes of Outstanding Historical Interest in Wales*. Cardiff: CADW.

——, Countryside Council for Wales and ICOMOS UK 2001 *Register of Landscapes of Special Historic Interest in Wales*. Cardiff: CADW.

——, Countryside Council for Wales and the Welsh Archaeological Trusts 2003 *Guide to Good Practice on Using the Register of Landscapes of Historic Interest in Wales in the Planning and Development Processes*. Cardiff: CADW.

CASG (Contract Archaeology Study Group, IFA) 1988 'Report of the Contract Archaeology Study Group', *Field Archaeologist* 8, 115–17.

CAWP (Contract Archaeology Working Party) 1988 *Professional and Public Archaeology – Contract Archaeology Session*. Birmingham: polycopied papers circulated by the IFA Contract Archaeology Working Party at the 1988 Archaeology in Britain Conference.

CBA (Council for British Archaeology) 1948 *A Survey and Policy of Field Research in the Archaeology of Great Britain*. Vol. 1. *Prehistoric and Early Historic Ages to the Seventh Century AD*. London: Council for British Archaeology.

—— 1974 *Archaeology and Government. Report of a Working Party of the CBA and RESCUE*. London: CBA.

—— 1982 *Guidelines for the Preparation of Contracts for Archaeological Excavations*. London: CBA.

—— 1988a (CBA Committee for Nautical Archaeology *et al.*) 1988 'A National Policy for Nautical Archaeology', *British Archaeological News* 3, 31.

—— 1988b (CBA Countryside Committee) 1988 'A Policy for the Countryside', *British Archaeological News*, 3, 57–60.

—— Wales 1988 *Policy and Recommendations for Rescue Archaeology in Wales*. Abermule, Montgomery: CBA Wales.

CBI (Confederation of British Industry) 1991 *Archaeological Investigation – Code of Practice for Minerals Operators*. London: CBI (first published 1982).

CCC (Council for the Care of Churches) 1988 *Archaeology and the Church of England, A Report by the Council for the Care of Churches and the Cathedrals Advisory Commission*. London: Council for the Care of Churches.

—— 1999 *Church Archaeology: Its Care and Management*. London: Council for the Care of Churches.

CCT (Churches Conservation Trust) 2002 *Heart and Identity: The Churches Conservation Trust Review and Report*. London: Churches Conservation Trust.

CMW (The Council of Museums in Wales) 2004 *What's in Store? Towards a Welsh Strategy for the Management of, and Access to, the Archaeological Evidence of our Past*. Cardiff: CMW.

CoE (Council of Europe) 1979 *Monument Protection in Europe*. Deventer: Kluwer.

—— 1992 *European Convention on the Protection of the Archaeological Heritage*. Strasbourg: Council of Europe. (European Treaty Series 143.)

—— 1996 *Report on Cultural Heritage Policies in Europe* (28 documents) Strasbourg: CoE Cultural Heritage Committee.

—— 2000 *European Landscape Convention*. Florence: European Treaty Series, 176. www.coe.int/T/E/cultural-co-operation/Environment/Landscape.

—— 2002 'The European Landscape Convention', *Naturopa* 98 (themed issue). Strasbourg: Council of Europe.

Cameron Averil 2001 *The Royal Peculiars: Report of the Review Group set up by Her Majesty The Queen*. London: Barnard and Westwood.

Cameron Alison 2004 'Torry battery' (Aberdeen Parish), *Discovery and Excavation in Scotland* n.s. 5 (2004), 9.

Capper J.C. 1907 'Photographs of Stonehenge as Seen From a War Balloon', *Archaeologia* 60, 571.

Carey Miller D.L. 2002 'Treasure Trove in Scots Law', in van den Bergh R. (ed.) 2002, *Summa Eloquentia: Essays in Honour of Margaret Hewett*, 75–89. Pretoria: University of South Africa Press.

—— and Sheridan A. 1996 'Treasure Trove in Scots Law', *Art, Antiquity and Law* 1, 393–406.

Carleton J. 1997 'Protecting the National Heritage: The Implications of the British Treasure Act 1996', *International Journal of Cultural Property* 6, 343–52.

Carman J. *et al.* 2000 Five papers on ARM. *International Journal of Heritage Studies* 6, 4.

Carnett C. 1991 *Legal Background of Archaeological Resources Protection*. Washington: US Dept of the Interior, National Park Service, Technical Brief, 11.

Carr C. 1982 *Handbook on Soil Resistivity Surveying*. Evanston, Illinois: Center for American Archaeology Press.

Carter A. 1998 'The Contribution of Aerial Survey: Understanding the Results', in Bewley 1998, 96–104.

Carter S. 2002 'Contract Archaeology in Scotland', *Antiquity* 76, 869–73.

—— and Robertson A. 2002 *Occupational and Functional Mapping of the Archaeological Profession*. Bradford and Reading (Q-West Consultants for CHNTO and IFA).

Carver M.O.H. 1989 'Digging for ideas', *Antiquity* 63, 666–74.

—— 1996 'On Archaeological Value', *Antiquity* 70, 45–56.

—— 2003 Editorial, *Antiquity*, 77, 7.

Cattell J., Ely S. and Jones B. 2002 *The Birmingham Jewellery Quarter: An Architectural Survey of the Manufactories*. London: EH.

Cave-Penny H. 1995 '"Time Team" and the Saxon Cemetery at Winterbourne Gunner', *Field Archaeologist* 23, 6–7.

Chadwick A. 1998 'Archaeology at the Edge of Chaos: Further Towards Reflexive Excavation Methodologies', *Assemblage* 3. http://www.shef.ac.uk/assem/3/3chad.htm

—— 2003 'Reflexive and Reflective? Post-processual, Professional and On-site Recording Methodology – Towards a Radical Field Archaeology', *Archaeological Dialogues* 10/1, 97–117.

Chadwick P. 1991 'Appendix 2: A Model Specification on which to Base a Project Design', in Swain 1991, 55–6.

Childe V.G. 1929 *The Danube in Prehistory*. Oxford: Clarendon Press.

Chippindale C. 1983 *Stonehenge Complete*. London: Thames and Hudson.

—— 1991 'Editorial', *Antiquity* 65, 5–6.

——, Devereux P., Fowler P.J., Jones R. and Sebastian T. 1990 *Who Owns Stonehenge?* London: Batsford.

—— and Gibbins D. (eds) 1990 'Heritage at Sea: Proposals for the Better Protection of British Archaeological Sites Underwater', *Antiquity* 64, 390–400.

Chitty G.C. 1999 *Training in Professional Archaeology: A Preliminary Review*. Carnforth: Hawkshead.

—— 2002 *Historic Environment Records: Benchmarks for Good Practice*. London: EH/ALGAO.

—— and Edwards R. 2004 *Review of Portable Antiquities Scheme 2004*. London: Hawkshead/MLA.

Church in Wales 1992 *Interim Report on the Commission on Faculties*. Penarth: Church in Wales Publications.

Church of England 2004 *Building Faith in our Future: A Statement on Behalf of the Church of England by the Church Heritage Forum*. London: Church House Publishing.

Claris P. 1993 'Archaeology and Nature Conservation in the National Trust', in Swain 1993, 31–2.

Clark A.J. 1975 'Archaeological Prospecting: A Progress Report', *Journal of Archaeological Science* 2, 297–314.

—— 1996 *Seeing Beneath the Soil*. London: Batsford. 2nd edn.

Clark J., Darlington J and Fairclough G.J. 2004 *Using Historic Landscape Characterisation, English Heritage's Review of HLC Applications, 2002–3*. Preston: EH and Lancashire County Council.

Clark J.G.D. 1934 'Archaeology and the State', *Antiquity* 8, 414–28.

Clark K. 1993 'Archaeology and Sustainable Development', in Swain 1993, 87–90.

—— 2001 *Informed Conservation: Understanding Historic Buildings and their Landscapes for Conservation*. London: EH.

—— (ed.) 1999 *Conservation Plans in Action: Proceedings of the Oxford Conference*. London: EH.

——, Darlington J. and Fairclough G.J. 2003 *Pathways to Europe's Landscape*. European Pathways to the Cultural Landscape: EU Culture 2000–03, Heide: EPCL.

Clayton P. 2002 'This Treasured Isle', *Minerva* 13/6, 29.

Cleere H.F. 1991 'Archaeology in the National Parks', *British Archaeological News* 6, 29.

—— (ed.) 1984 *Approaches to the Archaeological Heritage*. Cambridge: Cambridge University Press.

—— (ed.) 1989 *Archaeological Heritage Management in the Modern World*. London: Unwin Hyman. (One World Archaeology 9.)

Clément E. 1995 'The UNESCO Convention on the Means of Prohibiting and Preventing the Illicit Import, Export and Transfer of Ownership of Cultural Property (Paris, 1970)', in Leyten 1995, 45–52.

Cocroft W.D. and Thomas R.J.C. 2003 *Cold War: Building for Nuclear Confrontation*. London: EH.

Coles B. 2001a 'Britain and Ireland', in Coles and Olivier 2001, 23–34.

—— 2001b 'A Past Less Foreign: Wetland Archaeology and its Survival in European Perspective', in Coles and Olivier 2001, 1–6.

—— and Olivier A. (eds) 2001 *The Heritage Management of Wetlands in Europe*. Brussels and Exeter: Europae Archaeologiae Consilium and WARP. (Europae Archaeologiae Consilium Occas Pap 1 and WARP Occas Pap 16.)

Coles J. 2001 'Wetlands, Archaeology and Conservation at AD 2001', in Coles and Olivier 2001, 171–84.

—— and Coles B. 1996 *Enlarging the Past*. Edinburgh: Soc Antiq Scot Monogr Ser 11.

Collcutt S.N. 1991 'Access to Sites and Monuments Records – A User's Pointed View', *Field Archaeologist* 14, 256–7.

—— 1995a 'Professional Indemnity Insurance in Contract Archaeology', *Field Archaeologist* 22, 10–12.

—— 1995b 'Letter to the Editor: Evaluation No Disqualification', *Field Archaeologist* 22, 18.

—— 1997 'Archaeological Works and Development Control: A Case Study in Approval of Funding', *Journal of Planning and Environment Law* (Sept. 1997), 797–814.

—— 1999 'The Setting of Cultural Heritage Features', *Journal of Planning and Environment Law* (June 1999), 498–513.

—— 2001 'Subsequent Conditions: The Conditional Approval of Reserved and Deemed Reserved Matters', *Journal of Planning and Environment Law* (April 2001), 398–403.

Conyers L.B. and Goodman D. 1997 *Ground Penetrating Radar: An Introduction for Archaeologists*. Walnut Creek, California: Altimira Press.

Cooke R.J. 1999 'Nature Conservation: Taking a Wider View', in Grenville 1999, 125–36.

Cookson N. 2000 *Archaeological Heritage Law*. Chichester: Barry Rose Law Publishers Ltd.

Cooper A. and Garrow D. 2000 'Through the Crawlhole: Stories from the Occupants of Çatalhöyük'. (Unpublished TAG paper.)

Corbishley M. 2004 *Aerial Photography*. London: EH.

—— (ed.) 1992 *Archaeology in the National Curriculum*. London: CBA and EH.

Corfield M. 1988 'The Re-shaping of Metal Objects', *Antiquity* 62, 261–5.

Countryside Agency 1999 *Countryside Character*. Cheltenham: Countryside Commission. Vols 4–8. Available at www.countryside.gov.uk/cci

——, EH and English Nature and Environment Agency 2001 *Quality of Life Capital: Managing Environmental, Social and Economic Benefits*. Cheltenham: Countryside Agency.

Countryside Commission 1996 *Views from the Past: Historic Landscape Character in the English Countryside*. Cheltenham: Countryside Commission. (Working Paper CCW4.)

—— 1998 *Countryside Character*. Cheltenham: Countryside Commission. Vols 1–3. Available at www.countryside.gov.uk/cci

——, EH and English Nature 1993 *Conservation Issues in Strategic Plans*. Cheltenham: Countryside Commission. (Working Paper CCP 420.)

——, English Nature and EH 1997 *What Matters and Why: Environmental Capital – A New Approach*. Cheltenham: Countryside Commission.

Cranstone D. 1995 'Step 2 and 3 in the Monuments Protection Programme: A Consultant's View', in Palmer and Neaverson 1995, 115–17.

Crawford O.G.S. 1923 'Air Survey and Archaeology', *Geographical Journal*, May 1923, 324–66.

—— 1924 'The Stonehenge Avenue', *Antiquity* 4, 57–9.

—— 1928 *Air Survey and Archaeology*. Southampton: Ordnance Survey Professional Papers, new ser 7.

—— 1929 *Air Photography for Archaeologists*. Southampton: Ordnance Survey Professional Papers, new ser 12.

—— 1954 'A Century of Air Photography', *Antiquity* 28, 206–10.

Crawford O.G.S. and Keiller A. 1928 *Wessex from the Air*. Oxford: Clarendon Press.

Croft A. 2004 *Thames Gateway Historic Environment Characterisation Project*. Uckfield: Chris Blandford Associates, EH, Kent and Essex County Councils.

Cronyn J. 1980 'The Potential of Conservation', in Keene 1980, 8–9.

Crowther D. 1983 'Swords to Ploughshares: A Nationwide Survey of Archaeologists and Treasure Hunting Clubs', *Archaeological Review from Cambridge* 2/1, 9–20.

Crutchley S. 2000 *Salisbury Plain Training Area. A Report for the National Mapping Programme*. London: EH Internal Report AER/3/2000.

—— 2001 'The Landscape of Salisbury Plain, as Revealed by Aerial Photography', *Landscapes* 2, 46–64.

—— 2002 *Stonehenge World Heritage Site Mapping Project: Management Report*. EH Internal Report AER/14/2002.

Cultural Heritage Consortium 2002 *HEIRNET: Historic Environment Information Resources Network: Users and their Uses of HEIRS*. York: CBA.

Cunliffe B.W. 1983 *The Publication of Archaeological Excavations: Report of a Joint Working Party of the Council for British Archaeology and the Department of the Environment*. London: DoE.

—— 1990 'Publishing in the City', *Antiquity* 64, 667–71.

DCMS (Department for Culture, Media and Sport) 1999 *Portable Antiquities Annual Report 1997–98*. London: DCMS.

—— 2000a *Treasure Annual Report 1997–1998*. London: DCMS.

—— 2000b *Portable Antiquities Annual Report 1998–99*. London: DCMS.

—— 2001a *Treasure Annual Report 1998–1999*. London: DCMS.

—— 2001b *Portable Antiquities Annual Report 1999–2000*. London: DCMS.

—— 2002a *Ministerial Advisory Panel on the Illicit Trade in Cultural Objects, Progress Report (2001)*. London: DCMS.

—— 2002b *Treasure Annual Report 2000*. London: DCMS.

—— 2002c *Portable Antiquities Annual Report 2000–2001*. London: DCMS.

—— 2002d *UK Export Licensing for Cultural Goods: Procedures and Guidance for Exporters of Works of Art and Other Cultural Goods*. London: DCMS.

—— 2002e *Export of Works of Art 2001–2002*. London: DCMS.

—— 2003a *Treasure Annual Report 2001*. London: DCMS.

—— 2003b *The Treasure Act 1996 Code of Practice (Revised)*. London: DCMS.

—— 2003c *Protecting our Historic Environment: Making the System Work Better*. London: DCMS.

—— 2004a *Treasure Annual Report 2002*. London: DCMS.

—— 2004b *The 1970 UNESCO Convention: Guidance for Dealers and Auctioneers in Cultural Property*. London: DCMS.

—— 2004c *Dealing in Tainted Cultural Objects: Guidance on the Dealing in Cultural Objects (Offences) Act 2003*. London: DCMS.

—— 2004d *Protecting Our Marine Historic Environment: Making the System Work Better*. London: DCMS (Consultation Document.)

—— 2004e *Review of Heritage Protection: The Way Forward*. London: DCMS.

—— 2004f *The Future of Ecclesiastical Exemption: A Consultation Paper for England*. London: DCMS.

—— 2004g *Looking Forward to the Past: The Future for Heritage Protection*. London: HMSO.

—— and DTLGR (Department of Transport, Local Government and the Regions) 2001 *The Historic Environment: A Force for our Future*. London: DCMS. www.culture.gov.uk/heritage

—— and Welsh Office 1999 *Follow up to the Review of the Ecclesiastical Exemption (The Newman Report)*. London: DCMS and Welsh Office.

DEFRA (Department for Environment, Food and Rural Affairs) BD 1701 *Review of Agri-environment Schemes; Monitoring and R&D Results*. London: Report to Defra.

DETR (Department of Environment, Transport and the Regions) 1998a *A New Deal for Trunk Roads in England: Understanding the New Approach to Appraisal*. London: DETR.

DETR 1998b *A New Deal for Trunk Roads in England: Guidance on the New Approach to Appraisal*. London: DETR.

—— 2000 *Guidance on the Methodology for Multi-Modal Studies*. London: DETR. 2 vols.

—— and DCMS 1997 *Planning and the Historic Environment: Notification and Directions by the Secretary of State. Circular 14/97*.

DNH (Department of National Heritage) 1994 *The Ecclesiastical Exemption: What it is and How it Works*. London: DNH.

—— 1996 *Portable Antiquities: A Discussion Document*. London: DNH.

—— 1997 *The Treasure Act 1996: Code of Practice (England and Wales)*. London: DNH.

—— and Welsh Office 1996 *Protecting our Past*. London: DNH.

DoE (Department of the Environment) 1975a *Principles of Publication in Rescue Archaeology*. Report by a Working Party of the Ancient Monuments Board for England, Committee for Rescue Archaeology. London: DoE.

—— 1975b *What is Our Heritage? United Kingdom Achievements for European Architectural Heritage Year 1975*. London: HMSO.

—— 1977 *Rescue Archaeology: The Next Phase*. London: DoE.

—— 1978 *The Scientific Treatment of Material from Rescue Excavations. A Report by a Working Party of the Committee for Rescue Archaeology of the Ancient Monuments Board for England*. London: DoE.

—— 1983 *Criteria for the Selection of Ancient Monuments*. London: DoE Press Notice 523.

—— 1987 *Historic Buildings and Conservation Areas: Policy and Procedure*. (DoE *Circular 8/87*.) London: HMSO.

—— 1989a *Environmental Assessment: A Guide to the Procedures*. London: HMSO.

—— 1989b *The Water Act 1989: Code of Practice on Conservation, Access and Recreation*. London: Department of the Environment, Ministry of Agriculture, Fisheries and Food and the Welsh Office.

—— 1990a *Planning Policy Guidance Note 16: Archaeology and Planning*. London: HMSO. (PPG 16.)

—— 1990b *This Common Inheritance*. London. HMSO.

—— 1994 *Sustainable Development: The UK Strategy*. London: Cmd 2426.

—— and DNH (Department of National Heritage) 1994 *Planning Policy Guidance Note 15: Planning and the Historic Environment*. London: DoE and DNH. (PPG 15.)

—— and MAFF (Ministry of Agriculture, Fisheries and Food) 1997 *Statutory Instrument 160, Countryside: The Hedgerow Regulations*. London: HMSO.

—— and Welsh Office 1992 *Planning Policy Guidance Note 20: Coastal Planning*. (PPG 20.) London: HMSO.

—— (NI) 1990 *Finding and Minding 1986–89: A Report on the Archaeological Work of the Department of the Environment for Northern Ireland*. Belfast: DoE (NI).

—— (NI) 1997 *The Treasure Act 1996 Northern Ireland Code of Practice*. Belfast: Environment and Heritage Service, DoE (NI).

—— (NI) 1999 *Planning, Archaeology and Built Heritage*. Belfast: DoE (NI). (PPS 6.)

—— (NI) 2003 *The Treasure Act 1996 Northern Ireland Code of Practice (Revised)*. Belfast: Environment and Heritage Service, DoE (NI).

Dallas R. 2003a 'Measured Surveys of Historic Buildings: User Requirements and Technical Progress', *Journal of Architectural Conservation* 9/2, 58–81.

—— (ed.) 2003b *Measured Survey and Building Recording for Historic Buildings and Structures*. Edinburgh: HS. (Guide for Practitioners 4.)

Daniel G.E. 1975 *A Hundred and Fifty Years of Archaeology*. London: Duckworth.

—— and Chippindale C. (eds) n.d. *The Pastmasters. Eleven Modern Pioneers of Archaeology*. London: Thames and Hudson.

Dalwood H. 1987 'What is Professional Archaeology?', *Field Archaeologist* 7, 104–5.

Darlington J. 2003 'Using a Character-based Approach to Inform and Guide Conservation', *Context* 78 (March 2003), 17–9.

Darvill T. 1986 *The Archaeology of the Uplands: A Rapid Assessment of Archaeological Knowledge and Practice*. London: CBA.

—— 1987 *Ancient Monuments in the Countryside: An Archaeological Management Review*. London: HBMC.

—— 1999 'The IFA: What it Means to be a Member of a Professional Body', in Beavis J. and Hunt A. (eds) *Communicating Archaeology*, 35–48. Oxford: Oxbow Books. (Bournemouth Univ School of Conservation Sciences Occas Pap 4.)

—— 2004 'Public Archaeology: A European Perspective', in Bintliff 2004, 409–34.

—— 2005 *Stonehenge World Heritage Site: An Archaeological Research Framework*. London and Bournemouth: EH and Bournemouth University.

—— and Atkins M. 1991 *Regulating Archaeological Work by Contract*. Birmingham: Inst Field Archaeol Tech Pap 8.

—— and Fulton A. 1998 *MARS. The Monuments at Risk Survey of England, 1995. Main Report*. Bournemouth and London: School of Conservation Sciences, Bournemouth University and EH.

—— and Gerrard C. 1992 'Evaluating Archaeological Sites: The Cotswold Archaeological Trust Approach', in Darvill T. and Holbrook N. (eds) 1992 *Cotswold Archaeological Trust Annual Review* 2 (for 1990), 10–14. Cirencester: Cotswold Archaeological Trust.

—— and Gerrard C. 1994 *Cirencester: Town and Landscape*. Cirencester: Cotswold Archaeological Trust.

—— and Russell B. 2002 *Archaeology after PPG 16: Archaeological Investigations in England 1990–1999*. Bournemouth and London: Bournemouth University in association with English Heritage. (Bournemouth University School of Conservation Sciences Res Rep 10.)

——, Saunders A. and Startin B. 1987 'A Question of National Importance: Approaches to the Evaluation of Ancient Monuments for the Monuments Protection Programme in England', *Antiquity* 61, 393–408.

Davidson J.L. 1986 'The Collection of Antiquarian Information for the Early Ordnance Survey Maps of Scotland', *Proceedings of the Society of Antiquaries of Scotland* 116, 11–16.

—— and Henshall A.S. 1989 *The Chambered Cairns of Orkney*. Edinburgh: Edinburgh University Press.

—— and Henshall A.S. 1991 *The Chambered Cairns of Caithness*. Edinburgh: Edinburgh University Press.

Davies D.R. 1985 'The Management of Guardianship Monuments', *Transactions of the Association for Studies in the Conservation of Historic Buildings* 10, 49–53.

Davies E.J. 1991 'Striking the Balance between Economic Forces and Environmental Constraints', *Journal of Planning and Environment Law Occas Pap* 18, 43–66. London: Sweet and Maxwell.

Deegan A. 1999 *The Nottinghamshire Mapping Project. A Report for the National Mapping Programme*. Swindon: RCHME Internal Report.

—— 2002 *Northamptonshire National Mapping Programme Project. Management Report*. EH and Northamptonshire County Council Internal Document AER/16/2002.

—— and Foard G. forthcoming. *Mapping Ancient Landscapes in Northamptonshire*. EH and Northamptonshire County Council Internal Document.

Deuel L. 1969 *Flights into Yesterday*. New York: St Martin's Press.

Devereux P. 1991 *Earth Memory. The Holistic Earth Mysteries Approach to Decoding Ancient Sacred Sites*. London: Quantum.

Dixon P. and Hingley R. 2002 'Historic Land-use Assessment in Scotland', in Fairclough and Rippon 2002, 85–8.

368

Dobinson C. and Denison S. 1995 *Metal Detecting and Archaeology in England*. London: EH and CBA.

——, Lake J. and Schofield J. 1997 'Monuments of War: Defining England's 20th-century Defence Heritage', *Antiquity* 71, 288–99.

Dobinson C.S. 1996–2000 *Twentieth-century Fortifications in England*. 11 vols and two supplementary papers. York: CBA and EH.

—— 1998 'Twentieth-century Fortifications in England: The MPP Approach', in EH 1998, 2–6.

—— 2000 *Fields of Deception: Britain's Bombing Decoys of the Second World War*. London: Methuen.

—— 2001 *AA Command: Britain's Anti-aircraft Defences*. London: Methuen.

—— 2006. *Building Radar: Forging Britain's Early-Warning Chain, 1935–45*. London: Methuen.

Dolley M. 1977 'Treasure Trove: A Note on Manx Law and Practice', *Antiquity* 51, 137–9.

Dolukhanov P.M. 1993 'Archaeology in the ex-USSR: Post-perestroyka Problems', *Antiquity* 67, 150–6.

Donoghue D., Galiatsatos N., Philip G. and Beck A. 2002 'Satellite Imagery for Archaeological Applications: A Case Study from the Orontes Valley, Syria', in Bewley and Rączkowksi 2002, 211–23.

—— and Shennan I. 1988 'The Application of Multispectral Remote Sensing Techniques to Wetland Archaeology', in Murphy P. and French C. (eds) 1988 *The Exploitation of Wetlands*, vol. 3, 275–85. Oxford: Brit Archaeol Rep 186. 3 vols.

Dormor I. 1999 'Current Planning Policies and Legislation for Historical Rural Landscapes', in Grenville 1999, 43–56.

—— 2003 'Gravel Extraction Threatens "Stonehenge of the North"', *Rescue News* 91, 5.

Dorset Coast Forum 2002 *Old Ship Timbers on Dorset's Beaches*. Dorchester: Dorset Coast Forum.

Drake J.C. and Fahy A.M. 1987 *Guide to Archaeology on Community Programme*. Birmingham: IFA. (Inst Fld Archaeol Occas Pap 2.)

Drewett P.L. 1987 'The Institute of Archaeology and Field Archaeology', *University of London Institute of Archaeology Bulletin* 24, 127–39.

Driver T. 2002a 'Approaches to Aerial Survey and Heritage Management in Wales', in Bewley and Rączkowksi 2002, 247–55.

—— 2002b 'The Applications of Aerial Photography to the Coastal and Intertidal Zone in Wales', in Davidson A. (ed.) 2002 *The Coastal Archaeology of Wales*, 33–42. York: Counc Brit Archaeol Res Rep 131.

—— 2004 'Chairman's Piece', *AARGnews* 29, 6.

Dromgoole S. 1996 'Military Remains on and around the Coast of the United Kingdom: Statutory Mechanisms of Protection', *International Journal of Marine and Coastal Law* 11/1, 23–45.

—— 1999a 'A Note on the Meaning of Wreck', *International Journal of Nautical Archaeology* 28/4, 319–22.

—— 1999b 'United Kingdom', in Dromgoole S. (ed.) *Legal Protection of the Underwater Cultural Heritage: National and International Perspectives*, 181–203. London: Kluwer Law International.

Dunwell A.J. and Trout R.C 1999 *Burrowing Animals and Archaeology*. Edinburgh: HS Technical Advice Note 16.

Dwyer J.C. and Hodge I.D. 1996 *Countryside in Trust: Land Management by Conservation, Recreation and Amenity Organisations*. Chichester: John Wiley.

Dyson-Bruce L. 2002 'Historic Landscape Assessment – the East of England experience', in Burenhult 2002, 35–42.

——, Dixon P., Hingley R. and Stevenson J. 1999 *Historic Landuse Assessment (HLA): Development and Potential of a Technique for Assessing Historic Landscape Patterns, Report of the Pilot Project 1996–98*. Edinburgh: HS and RCAHMS.

EAA (European Association of Archaeologists) 1997 'The EAA Code of Practice', *European Archaeologist* 8, 7–8.

—— 1998 'Principles of Conduct for Archaeologists Involved in Contract Archaeological Work', *European Archaeologist* 10, 2–3.

EH (English Heritage) 1984 *England's Archaeological Resource*. London: EH.

—— 1986 *Rescue Archaeology Funding: A Policy Statement*. London: EH.

—— 1989 *The Management of Archaeology Projects*. London: HBMC.

EH 1990 'Competitive Tendering for Archaeology Projects', *Field Archaeologist* 13, 216.

—— 1991a *The Management of Archaeological Projects*. London: HBMC. 2nd edn.

—— 1991b *Exploring Our Past: Strategies for the Archaeology of England*. London: HBMC.

—— 1991c 'English Heritage Corporate Plan 1991–95', *Conservation Bulletin* 15 (suppl).

—— 1991d 'Rescue Archaeology Funding: A Policy Statement', *Conservation Bulletin* 14, 7–9.

—— 1992a *Managing England's Heritage: Setting Our Priorities for the 1990s*. London: EH.

—— 1992b *Managing the Urban Archaeological Resource*. London: EH.

—— 1992c *An Evaluation of the Impact of PPG 16 on Archaeology and Planning* (prepared by Pagoda Projects). London: HBMC.

—— 1995a *Register of Historic Battlefields*. London: EH.

—— 1995b *Developing Guidelines for the Management of Listed Buildings*. London: EH.

—— 1995c *Review of the Implementation of PPG 16 Archaeology and Planning* (prepared by Roger Tym and Partners and Pagoda Associates). London: HBMC.

—— 1995d *Planning for the Past. A Review of Archaeological Assessment Procedures in England 1982–91*. London: EH. 3 vols.

—— 1995e *Geophysical Survey in Archaeological Field Evaluation*. London: EH. (Research and Professional Services Guideline 1.)

—— 1996 *Frameworks for Our Past: A Review of Research Frameworks, Strategies and Perceptions*. London: EH.

—— 1997a *Sustaining the Historic Environment*. London: EH.

—— 1997b *The Monuments Protection Programme 1986–96 in Retrospect*. London: EH.

—— 1998 *Monuments of War: The Evaluation, Recording and Management of Twentieth-century Military Sites*. London: EH.

—— 1999a *List of Scheduled Monuments*. London: EH. (8 regional volumes.)

—— 1999b *The Presentation of Historic Building Survey in CAD*. London: EH.

—— 2000a *Power of Place: The Future of the Historic Environment*. London: English Heritage. (Historic Environment Review.)

—— 2000b *MPP 2000 A Review of the Monuments Protection Programme, 1986–2000*. London: EH.

—— 2000c *Metric Survey Specifications for English Heritage*. London: EH.

—— 2001 *Buildings at Risk. The Register 2001*. London: EH.

—— 2002a *State of the Historic Environment Report 2002*. London: EH.

—— 2002b *Military Aircraft Crash Sites: Archaeological Guidance on their Significance and Future Management*. London: EH.

—— 2002c *Heritage Dividend 2002. Measuring the Results of Heritage Regeneration 1999–2002*. London: EH.

—— 2002d *Taking to the Water. English Heritage's Initial Policy for the Management of Maritime Archaeology in England*. London: EH.

—— 2002e *Guidelines for Aircraft Operations*. London: EH Internal Report AER/15/2002. (See also EH website.)

—— 2002f *Modernising English Heritage*. London: EH.

—— 2003a *Measured and Drawn: Techniques and Practice for the Metric Survey of Historic Buildings*. London: EH.

—— 2003b *Heritage Counts 2003. The State of England's Historic Environment*. London: EH.

—— 2003c (web page) *Promoting Characterisation*, under 'Conserving Historic Places'. Available at www/english-heritage.org.uk/characterisation

—— 2003d *The Archaeology of Conflict. Conservation Bulletin*. 44 (themed edition).

—— 2004 *Review of the National Monuments Record*. London: EH.

—— n.d. a *An Analysis of Central Government (DAMHB) Support in 1982/3 for the Recording of Archaeological Sites and Landscapes in Advance of their Destruction*. London: HBMC.

EH n.d. b EH website (www.english-heritage.org.uk) Home>Archaeology>Research Agenda (accessed 3 January 2004).

—— n.d. c *English Heritage: A User's Guide*. London: EH.

——, Countryside Commission and English Nature 1996 *Conservation Issues in Local Plans*. London: EH.

—— and RCHME 1996 *England's Coastal Heritage: A Statement on the Management of Coastal Archaeology*. London: EH.

EU (European Union) 2000 *European Spatial Development Perspective*. Potsdam: EU.

Earl J. 2003 *Building Conservation Philosophy*. Shaftesbury: Donhead. 3rd edn.

Ede J. with Darlington J. 2002 *The Lancashire Historic Landscape Characterisation Project Report*. Preston: Lancashire County Council and EH (and on CD). 3rd edn.

Edis J., Macleod D. and Bewley R. 1989 'An Archaeologist's Guide to Classification of Cropmarks and Soilmarks', *Antiquity* 63, 112–26.

Edwards C. 1989 'The Responsible Developer – What Should He Do?', in *Pre-Conference Papers: Archaeological Remains and Development 27th November 1989* (published on a facsimile of the official notepaper of Prudential Portfolio Managers Ltd), 41–6. London: Henry Stewart Conference Studies.

Edwards L.S. 1977 'A Modified Pseudosection for Resistivity and I.P.', *Geophysics* 42, 1020–36.

Egan G. 1998 *The Medieval Household, Daily Living c.1150–c.1450: Medieval Finds from Excavations in London*. London: Stationery Office/Museum of London.

—— and Pritchard F. 1991 *Dress Accessories c.1150–c.1450: Medieval Finds from Excavations in London*. London: HMSO/Museum of London.

Ellison A.B. 1981 *A Policy for Archaeological Investigation in Wessex, 1981–5*. Salisbury: Wessex Archaeological Committee.

Emmott K. 1987 'A Child's Eye View of the Past', *Archaeological Reviews from Cambridge* 6/2, 129–42.

FCO (Foreign and Commonwealth Office) 2001 'UNESCO Convention on Underwater Cultural Heritage: Explanation of Vote'. Unclassified paper.

FJC (Faculty Jurisdiction Commission Report) 1984 *The Continuing Care of Churches and Cathedrals; The Report of the Faculty Jurisdiction Commission*. London: Church Information Office.

FJR (Faculty Jurisdiction Rules) 1992 *Statutory Instrument 1992 No. 2882*. London: HMSO.

—— 2000 *Statutory Instrument 2000 No. 2047*. London: HMSO.

Fairclough G.J. 1995 'The Sum of all its Parts: An Overview of the Politics of Integrated Management in England', in Berry and Brown 1995, 17–28.

—— 1999a 'Protecting the Cultural Landscape – National Designations and Local Character', in Grenville 1999, 27–39.

—— 2002a 'Cultural Landscape, Computers and Characterisation', in Burenhult 2002, 277–94.

—— 2002b 'Cultural Landscape and Spatial Planning: England's Historic Landscape Characterisation Programme', in Green and Bidwell 2002, 123–49.

—— 2002c 'Archaeologists and the European Landscape Convention', in Fairclough and Rippon 2002, 25–37.

—— 2003a 'The Character of the Historic Environment – Heritage Protection and the Sustainable Management of Change', *Von Nutzen und Nachteil der Demkmalpflege für das Leben: 70. Tag für Denkmalpflege*, 103–9. Stuttgart: Theiss. (Jahrestagung der Vereinigung der Landesdenkmalpfleger in der Bundesrepublik Deutschland vom 17–21 Juni 2002 in Wiesbaden: Arbeitsheft 4 des Landesamtes für Denkmalpflege Hessen.)

—— 2003b 'The Long Chain: Archaeology, Historical Landscape Characterization and Time Depth in the Landscape', in Palang and Fry 2003, 295–317.

—— 2003c 'Cultural Landscape, Sustainability and Living with Change?', in Teutonico J.M. and Matero F. (eds) 2003, *Managing Change: Sustainable Approaches to the Conservation of the Built Environment*, 23–46. Los Angeles: The Getty Conservation Institute. (Proc 4th Annual US-ICOMOS Internat Symposium, Philadelphia, PA, April 2001.)

Fairclough G.J. ed. 1999b *Historic Landscape Characterisation: the State of the Art*. London: EH. (Papers presented at an EH Seminar held at the Society of Antiquaries, 11 December 1998.)

——, Lambrick G. and McNab A. 1999 *Yesterday's World, Tomorrow's Landscape. The English Heritage Historic Landscape Project 1992–94*. London: EH.

—— and Macinnes L. 2003 *Understanding Historic Landscape Character. Landscape Character Assessment Guidance for England and Scotland*. N.p.: Countryside Agency and Scottish Natural Heritage Topic Paper No. 5.

—— and Rippon S. (eds) 2002 *Europe's Cultural Landscape: Archaeologists and the Management of Change*. Brussels and London: Europae Archaeologiae Consilium and EH. (Europae Archaeologiae Consilium Occas Pap 2.)

Faulkner N. 2003 *Hidden Treasure: Digging Up Britain's Past*. London: BBC Books.

Fawcett J. (ed.) 1976 *The Future of the Past*. London: Thames and Hudson.

Featherstone M. (ed.) 1990 *Global Culture. Nationalism, Globalization and Modernity*. London: Sage Publications.

Featherstone R. and Bewley R. 2000 'Recent Aerial Reconnaissance in North Oxfordshire', *Oxoniensia* 65, 13–26.

Fenner V.E.P. and Dyer C. 1994 *The Thames Valley Project. A Report for the National Mapping Programme*. Swindon: RCHME Internal Report.

Fernie K. and Gilman P. (eds) 2000 *Informing the Future of the Past: Guidelines for SMRs*. Swindon: EH.

Fielden K. 2002 'So, What *Should* be Done at Stonehenge?' *Rescue News* 88, 4–5.

Findlay D. 1996 *The Protection of our English Churches: The History of the Council for the Care of Churches 1921 – 1996*. London: Council for the Care of Churches.

Firth A. 1995 'Archaeology and Coastal Zone Management', in Berry and Brown 1995, 155–67.

—— 1999 'Making Archaeology: The History of the Protection of Wrecks Act 1973 and the Constitution of an Archaeological Resource', *International Journal of Nautical Archaeology* 28, 10–24.

—— 2002 *Managing Archaeology Underwater: A Theoretical, Historical and Comparative Perspective on Society and its Submerged Past*. Oxford: Brit Archaeol Rep Internat Ser 1055.

'Fitzpatrick L.' (pseudonym) 1991 'Developer Column', *Field Archaeologist* 15, 266.

—— 1992 'Developer Column', *Field Archaeologist* 16, 292.

Fladmark M. (ed.) 1993 *Heritage: Conservation, Interpretation and Enterprise*. London: Donhead Publishing.

—— 1994 *Cultural Tourism*. London: Donhead Publishing.

—— 1995 *Sharing the Earth: Local Identity in a Global Culture*. London: Donhead Publishing.

—— 2000 *Heritage and Museums: Shaping National Identity*. Shaftesbury: Donhead Publishing.

Fletcher-Tomenius P. and Williams M. 1998 'The Protection of Wrecks Act: A Breach of Human Rights?', *International Journal of Marine and Coastal Law* 13/4, 623–42.

—— and Williams M. 1999 'The Draft UNESCO/DOALOS Convention on the Protection of Underwater Cultural Heritage and Conflict with the European Convention on Human Rights', *International Journal of Nautical Archaeology* 28/2, 145–53.

——, O'Keefe P.J. and Williams M.V. 2000 'Salvor in Possession: Friend or Foe to Marine Archaeology', *International Journal of Cultural Property* 9, 263–314.

Fojut N. 2002 'Forestry and Archaeology in Scotland: Ten Years On', *Scottish Forestry* 56/4, 200–9.

Forestry Commission 1991 *Grants and Procedures*. Edinburgh: Forestry Commission.

—— 2004 *The UK Forestry Standard: The Government's Approach to Sustainable Forestry*. Edinburgh: Forestry Commission.

Fowler P.J. 1974 'Motorways and Archaeology', in Rahtz 1974, 113–29.

Fowler P.J. 1976 'US Archaeology through British Eyes', *Antiquity* 50, 230–2.

—— 1987 'What Price the Man-made Heritage?', *Antiquity* 61, 409–23.

—— 1989 'Heritage: A Post-Modernist Perspective', in Uzzell 1989b, 57–63.

—— 1992 *The Past in Contemporary Society. Then, Now*. London: Routledge.

—— 2000 *Landscape Plotted and Pieced: Landscape History and Local Archaeology in Fyfield and Overton, Wiltshire*. London: Society of Antiquaries.

—— 2004 *Landscapes for the World. Conserving a Global Heritage*. Macclesfield: Windgather Press.

—— and Blackwell I. 1998 *The Land of Lettice Sweetapple. An English Countryside Explored*. Stroud: Tempus.

—— and Mills S.A. 2004 'Bede's World, an Early Medieval Landscape: A late 20th Century Creation with 7th Century Fields and Buildings', in Jameson J.H. (ed.) 2004 *The Reconstructed Past. Reconstructions in the Public Interpretation of Archaeology and History*, 103–25. Walnut Creek, CA: Altamira Press.

Francis T. 1998 'Archaeologists: How to Survive Litigation', *The Archaeologist* 32, 19–21.

Frayling C. 1992 *The Face of Tutankhamun*. London: Faber and Faber.

Friell J.G.P. 1991 'Archaeology and the Trunk Roads Programme', *English Heritage Conservation Bulletin* 13, 8.

Fukuyama F. 1992 *The End of History and the Last Man*. Harmondsworth: Penguin.

Fulford M.G., Champion T. and Long A. 1997 *England's Coastal Heritage. A Survey for English Heritage and the RCHME*. London: EH. (English Heritage Archaeol Rep 15.)

—— and Nichols E. (eds) 1992 *Developing Landscapes of Lowland Britain, The Archaeology of the British Gravels: A Review*. London: Soc Antiq Lond Occas Pap 14.

GS (General Synod) 2004 *A Measure for Measure in Mission and Ministry*. London: General Synod Report 1528.

Gaffney C.F. and Gater J. 2003 *Revealing the Buried Past: Geophysics for Archaeologists*. Stroud: Tempus.

——, Gater J.A. and Ovenden S.M. 2002 *The Use of Geophysical Techniques in Archaeological Evaluations*. Reading: Institute of Field Archaeologists. (Inst Field Archaeol Tech Pap 6.)

Gaimster D. 2003 'The Dealing in Cultural Objects (Offences) Bill', *Minerva* 14/6 (November/December 2003), 38–9.

García Fernández J. 1987 *Legislación sobre Patrimonio Histórico*. Madrid: Editorial Tecnos.

—— 1989 'The New Spanish Heritage Legislation', in Cleere 1989, 182–94.

Garrett-Frost S. 1992 *The Law and Burial Archaeology*. Birmingham: IFA. (Inst Fld Archaeol Tech Pap 11.)

Garrison L. 1990 'The Black Historical Past in British Education', in Stone and MacKenzie 1990, 231–44.

Gater J. 1990 'Professional Standards in Archaeological Geophysics', *Field Archaeology* 13, 217.

Gathercole P. and Lowenthal D. (eds) 1990 *The Politics of the Past*. London: Unwin Hyman.

Gero J. 1989 'Producing Prehistory, Controlling the Past: The Case of New England Beehives', in Pinsky V. and Wylie A. (eds) 1989 *Critical Traditions in Contemporary Archaeology: Essays in the Philosophy, History and Socio-politics of Archaeology*. Cambridge: Cambridge University Press, 96–103.

'Gildas' 1988 'Le déclin et la chute de l'archéologie britannique', *Nouvelles archéologiques* 31, 40–2.

Gilg A. 1996 *Countryside Planning: the First Half Century*. London: Routledge.

Gill D. and Chippindale C. 2002 'The Trade in Looted Antiquities and the Return of Cultural Property: A British Parliamentary Inquiry', *International Journal of Cultural Property* 11, 50–64.

Gilmour S. 2002 'Aerial Reconnaissance – NMRS Post-Flight Processes', in *Monuments on Record. Annual Review 2001–2002*, 50–3. Edinburgh: RCAHMS.

Gimbrère S. 1995 'Illicit Traffic in Cultural Property and National and International Law', in Leyten 1995, 53–60.

Glazebrook J. (ed.) 1997 *Research and Archaeology: A Framework for the Eastern Counties*. Vol. 1. *Resource Assessment*. Norwich: Scole Archaeological Committee for East Anglia. (East Anglian Archaeology Occas Pap 3.)

Goddard L. 1998 *Pickering Castle: Information for Teachers*. London: English Heritage Education Service.

Goodale T.L. and Witt P.A. (eds) 1985 *Recreation and Leisure: Issues in an Era of Change*. State College, Pennsylvania: Venture.

Gould R.A. and Schiffer M.B. (eds) 1981 *Modern Material Culture: The Archaeology of Us*. New York: Academic Press.

Gould S. 2004 'Analysing and Recording Historic Buildings', *Context* 84, 23–30.

Goulty N.R., Gibson J.P.C., Moore J.G. and Welfare H. 1990 'Delineation of the Vallum at Vindolanda, Hadrian's Wall, by Shear-wave Seismic Refraction Survey', *Archaeometry* 32, 71–82.

Grady D. 2001 'How Safe Are We in the Air? Draft Code of Conduct for Aerial Reconnaissance', *AARGnews* 22 (March 2001), 30–4.

Graham B., Ashworth G. J. and Tunbridge J. E. 2000 *A Geography of Heritage: Power, Culture and Economy*. London: Arnold.

Green D. and Kidd S. 2004 *Milton Keynes Urban Expansion: Historic Environment Assessment*. Aylesbury: Buckinghamshire County Council, Milton Keynes Unitary Authority and EH (and EH web page 2003).

Green E.L. (ed.) 1984 *Ethics and Values in Archaeology*. New York: The Free Press (Macmillan).

Green L.M. and Bidwell P.T. (eds) 2002 *Heritage of the North Sea Region: Conservation and Interpretation*, 123–49. Shaftesbury: Donhead. (Papers presented at the Historic Environment of the North Sea InterReg IIC Conference, South Shields, 2001.)

Gregson M. 1982 'Corporate Archaeology and the Atelier', in K. Ray (ed.) *Young Archaeologist: Collected Unpublished Papers, Contributions to Archaeological Thinking and Practice from Mark S. Gregson*. Cambridge: privately published.

Grenville J. 1993 'Curation Overview', in Hunter and Ralston 1993b, 125–33.

—— (ed.) 1996 *Archaeological Heritage Management and the English Agricultural Landscape*. York: University of York. (Archaeological Heritage Studies Occas Pap 1.)

—— (ed.) 1999 *Managing the Historic Rural Landscape*. London: Routledge.

——, Harkrader N., Clark J., Hunwicks L. and Rawson D. 2001 *Richmond Castle Conservation Plan*. York: English Heritage. 3 vols.

Griffith F.M. 1990 'Aerial Reconnaissance in Mainland Britain in the Summer of 1989', *Antiquity* 64, 14–33.

Griffiths M. 1991 'Past Perfect? The DoE Planning Policy Guidance on Archaeology and Planning', *Mineral Planning* 46, 9–12.

Griffiths – *see* Mike Griffiths and Associates.

Grimes W.F. 1960 *Excavation on Defence Sites 1939–1945*. London: HMSO.

—— 1968 *The Excavation of Roman and Medieval London*. London: Routledge & Kegan Paul.

Gringmuth-Dallmer E. 1993 'Archaeology in the Former German Democratic Republic', *Antiquity* 67, 135–42.

Grover P. 2003 *Local Authority Conservation Provision in England*. Oxford: School of the Built Environment, Oxford Brookes University. Not published formally: available in full on the English Heritage website at Home > Research and Conservation > Public Policy > Local and Regional Government > Local Authority Conservation Provision or http://www.english-heritage.org.uk/server/show/nav.001002005009006.

Gurney D. 1992 'Phosphate and Magnetic Susceptibility Surveys of the Ploughsoil and Determinations from Features', in Gregory A.K. 1992 *Excavations in Thetford 1980–1982: Fison Way*, 181–7. Dereham: East Anglian Archaeology.

Gwyn D. 2002 'Associative landscape in a Welsh context', in Fairclough and Rippon 2002, 187–92.

HER (Historic Environment Review) 2000 *Viewpoint: Consultation Papers for the Review of Policies Relating to the Historic Environment*. London: EH.

HLF (Heritage Lottery Fund) 2003 *Annual Report and Accounts 2002–3*. London: Stationery Office.

HMSO (Her Majesty's Stationery Office) 1987 *House of Commons. First Report from the Environment Committee, Session 1986–87, Historic Buildings and Ancient Monuments* (Sir Hugh Rossi, Chairman). London: HMSO. 3 vols.

—— 1989 *Environmental Assessment: A Guide to the Procedures*. London: HMSO.

HM Treasury 1952 *Report of the Committee on the Export of Works of Art Etc*. London: HMSO.

HS (Historic Scotland) 1991 *Corporate Plan 1991–94*. Edinburgh: HS.

—— 1994 *Allocation and Disposal of Archaeological Finds*. Edinburgh: HS.

—— 1996a *Contractual and Grant Arrangements in Historic Scotland's Archaeology Programme*. Edinburgh: HS Operational Policy Paper 1.

—— 1996b *Project Design, Implementation and Archiving*. Edinburgh: HS Archaeology Procedure Paper 2.

—— 1997 *The Treatment of Human Remains in Archaeology*. Edinburgh: HS Operational Policy Paper 5.

—— 1998 *Memorandum of Guidance on Listed Buildings and Conservation Areas*. Edinburgh: HS.

—— 1999 *Conserving the Underwater Heritage: Historic Scotland Operational Policy Paper*. Edinburgh. HS Operational Policy Paper 6.

—— 2001 *Acquisition and Disposal of Artefacts*. Edinburgh: HS Operational Policy Paper.

—— 2002 *Passed to the Future: Historic Scotland's Policy for the Sustainable Management of Scotland's Historic Environment*. Edinburgh: HS.

Haigh J.G.B. 1991 'The AERIAL program, Version 4.1', *AARGnews* 3, 31–3.

Halkon P., Corbishley M. and Binns G. (eds) 1992 *The Archaeology Resource Book 1992*. London: CBA and EH.

Hall C.M. and Page S.J. 1999 *The Geography of Tourism and Recreation. Environment, Place and Space*. London: Routledge.

Hall D. 2001 *Turning the Plough – Midland Open Fields: Landscape Character and Proposals for Management*. Northampton: Northamptonshire County Council and EH.

Hamlin A. 1989 'Government Archaeology in Northern Ireland', in Cleere 1989, 171–81.

—— 2000 'Archaeological Heritage Management in Northern Ireland: Challenges and Solutions', in McManamon F.P. and Hatton A. (eds) 2000 *Cultural Resource Management in Contemporary Society*, 66–75. London: Routledge.

—— and Lynn C. (eds) 1988 *Pieces of the Past: Archaeological Excavations by DoE (NI) 1970–1986*. Belfast: HMSO.

Hampton J.N. 1989 'The Air Photography Unit of the Royal Commission on the Historical Monuments of England 1965–85', in Kennedy 1989, 13–28.

Hanson W.S. and Macinnes L. 1991 'The Archaeology of the Scottish Lowlands: Problems and Potential', in Hanson W.S. and Slater E.A. (eds) 1991 *Scottish Archaeology: New Perceptions*, 153–66. Aberdeen: Aberdeen University Press.

Harding P.T. 1995 'Data for Nature Conservation in Statutory and Voluntary Heritage Agencies', in Berry and Brown 1995, 1–15.

Hardman C. and Richards J.D. 2003 'OASIS: Dealing with the Digital Revolution', in Doerr M. and Sarris A. (eds) *CAA2002: The Digital Heritage of Archaeology. Computer Applications and Quantitative Methods in Archaeology 2002*, 325–8. Athens: Archive of Monuments and Publications, Hellenic Ministry of Culture.

Hart M. 1987 'The SERC Experiment in Science-based Archaeology', *Proceeding of the British Academy* 73, 1–22.

Harvey D. 1989 *The Condition of Postmodernity. An Enquiry into the Origins of Cultural Change.* Oxford: Blackwell.

Haselgrove C., Armit I., Champion T., Creighton J., Gwilt A., Hill J.D., Hunter F. and Woodward A. 2001 *Understanding the British Iron Age: An Agenda for Action.* Salisbury: Trust for Wessex Archaeology for the Iron Age Research Seminar and the Prehistoric Society.

Hayes D. and Patton M. 2001 'Proactive Crisis-management Strategies and the Archaeological Heritage', *International Journal of Heritage Studies* 7, 37–58.

Heaton M. 1988 'Contract Archaeology (Review of Proceedings at the 1988 Archaeology in Britain Conference)', *Field Archaeologist* 9, 132.

—— 1991 Letter to the Editor. *Field Archaeologist* 14, 259.

—— 2002 'Model Contracts. Model work?', *The Archaeologist* 43, 16.

Heighway C.M. (ed). 1972 *The Erosion of History: Archaeology and Planning in Towns.* London: CBA.

Henshall A.S. and Ritchie J.N.G. 1995 *The Chambered Cairns of Sutherland.* Edinburgh: Edinburgh University Press.

—— and Ritchie J.N.G. 2001 *The Chambered Cairns of the Central Highlands.* Edinburgh: Edinburgh University Press.

Heritage Lottery Fund 1999 *Unlocking Britain's Past: A Strategic Framework for Support from the Heritage Lottery Fund for Sites and Monuments Records.* London: Heritage Lottery Fund.

Heron C.P. and Gaffney C.F. 1987 'Archaeogeophysics and the Site: Ohm Sweet Ohm?', in Gaffney C.F. and Gaffney V.L. (eds) 1987 *Pragmatic Archaeology: Theory in Crisis?* 71–81. Oxford: Brit Archaeol Rep Brit Ser 167.

Herring P. 1998 *Cornwall's Historic Landscape – Presenting a Method of Historic Landscape Character Assessment.* Truro: Cornwall Archaeological Unit and EH.

Herrmann J. (ed.) 1981 *Gesetze, Verordnungen und Bestimmungen der DDR: Archäologische Denkmale und Umweltgestaltung.* Berlin: Akademie-Verlag.

Hewison R. 1987 *The Heritage Industry: Britain in a Climate of Decline.* London: Methuen.

—— 1989 'Heritage: An Interpretation', in Uzzell 1989b, 15–23.

Hey G. and Lacey M. 2001 *Evaluation of Archaeological Decision Making Processes and Sampling Strategies.* London: EH and IFA.

Highways Agency 1992 *Design Manual for Roads and Bridges.* Vol. 11, *Environmental Assessment.* London: HMSO (and subsequent amendments).

—— 1999 *Roads to the Past: Trunk Roads and Archaeology.* London: Highways Agency.

Hill G.F. 1930 'The Law and Practice of Treasure Trove', *Antiquaries Journal* 10, 228–41.

—— 1936 *Treasure Trove in Law and Practice from the Earliest Time to the Present Day.* Oxford: Clarendon Press.

Hill J. 1987 'Confessions of an Archaeologist Who Dug in School: Or, is Archaeology in Schools a Good or Desirable Thing?', *Archaeological Reviews from Cambridge* 6/2, 143–56.

Hill M. 2001 *Ecclesiastical Law.* Oxford: Oxford University Press.

Hills C. 2003 'What is Television Doing for Us? Reflections on Some Recent British Programmes', *Antiquity* 77, 206–11.

Hingst H. 1964 *Denkmalschutz und Denkmalpflege in Deutschland.* Stuttgart: E. Schweizerbart'sche Verlagsbuchhandlung. (Badische Fundberichte, Sonderheft 7.)

—— and Lipowschek A. (eds) 1975 *Europäische Denkmalschutzgesetze in deutscher Übersetzung.* Neumünster: Karl Wachholtz.

Hinton D.A. 1992 'Confidentiality and PPG 16', *British Archaeological News* 7/6, 74.

Hobbs R. 2001 'Finding our Past: The Portable Antiquities Scheme in England and Wales', in Wise P.J. (ed.) 2001 *Indulgence or Necessity? Research in Museum Archaeology*, 25–31. Colchester: Society of Museum Archaeologists (*The Museum Archaeologist* 26.)

—— 2002 'Finding our Past: the Portable Antiquities Scheme in England and Wales', *Institute of Field Archaeologists Yearbook and Directory 2002*, 33–4.

—— 2003a *Treasure: Finding Our Past*. London: British Museum.

—— 2003b 'In Search of Buried Treasure', *British Museum Magazine* 47 (Winter 2003), 44–51.

Hobbs R. 2003c 'The Trouble with Treasure', *Living History* 9 (December 2003), 67–9.

Hobley B. 1987 'Rescue Archaeology and Planning', *Journal of the Royal Town Planning Institute (The Planner)* 73/5, 25–7.

Hodder I. 1992 *Theory and Practice in Archaeology*. London: Routledge.

—— 1997 'Always Momentary, Fluid and Flexible: Towards a Reflexive Excavation Methodology', *Antiquity* 71, 691–700.

—— 1999 *The Archaeological Process*. Oxford: Blackwell.

—— (ed.) 2000 *Towards Reflexive Method in Archaeology: the Example of Catal Höyük*. Cambridge: McDonald Institute. (British Institute in Ankara Monogr 28.)

——, Parker Pearson M., Peck N. and Stone P. 1985 'Archaeology, Knowledge and Society: Surveys in Britain'. Cambridge: unpublished manuscript.

——, Shanks M. and Alexandri A. (eds) 1997 *Interpreting Archaeology. Finding Meaning in the Past*. London and New York: Routledge.

Hodges A. and Watson S. 2000 'Community-based Heritage Management: A Case Study and Agenda for Research', *International Journal of Heritage Studies* 6, 231–43.

Holden N., Horne P. and Bewley R. 2002 'High-Resolution Digital Airborne Mapping and Archaeology', in Bewley and Rączkowksi 2002, 173–80.

Hooper-Greenhill E. 1991 *Museum and Gallery Education*. Leicester: Leicester University Press.

—— 1992 *Museums and the Shaping of Knowledge*. London: Routledge.

Horne P. and MacLeod D. 1995 *The Yorkshire Dales Mapping Project. A Report for the National Mapping Programme*. Swindon: RCHME Internal Report.

—— and MacLeod D. 2001 'Unravelling a Wharfedale Landscape: A Case Study in Field Enhanced Aerial Survey', *Landscapes* 2, 65–82.

—— and Kershaw A. (eds) forthcoming. 'A Perfect Flat. . . . . Recent Research on the Archaeology of the Vale of York'. EH Monograph.

Horton M. 2003 'Why the "Stonehenge of the North" Should be Saved', *Rescue News* 91, 5.

Howarth, W. 1992 *Widom's Law of Watercourses*. Crayford: Shaw and Sons. 5th edn.

Hughes G. 2004 'The Welsh Archaeological Trusts and the Future of the Historic Environment in Wales', *IFA Yearbook and Directory 2004*, 31–2.

Hughes M. and Rowley L. (eds) 1986 *The Management and Presentation of Field Monuments*. Oxford: University Dept of External Studies.

Hunter J. and Ralston I. 1993a 'The Structure of British Archaeology', in Hunter and Ralston 1993b, 30–43.

—— and Ralston I. (eds) 1993b *Archaeological Resource Management in the UK: An Introduction*. Stroud: Sutton/IFA.

Hunter M. (ed) 1996 *Preserving the Past: The Rise of Heritage in Modern Britain*. Stroud: Sutton.

Hutson A.M. 1995 'Conservation of Bats in the Management of Ancient Monuments', in Berry and Brown 1995, 71–8.

Hvass S. 2001 'Preface by the State Antiquary', *Nationalmuseets Arbejdsmark 2001*, 10–13.

IAM (Inspectorate of Ancient Monuments) 1984 *England's Archaeological Resource: A Rapid Quantification of the National Archaeological Resource and a Comparison with the Schedule of Ancient Monuments*. London: IAM.

ICAHM (International Committee on Archaeological Heritage Management) 1989 *Archaeology and Society: Large Scale Rescue Operations – Their Possibilities and Problems*. (ICAHM Report 1.) Stockholm: ICAHM.

—— 1990 *Charter for the Protection and Management of the Archaeological Heritage*. Paris: ICOMOS.

ICE (Institution of Civil Engineers), 2004 *ICE Conditions of Contract for Archaeological Investigations*. London: Institution of Civil Engineers, Association of Consulting Engineers, Civil Engineering Contractors Association, and IFA. 1st edn.

ICOMOS (International Council on Monuments and Sites) 1990a *Guide to Recording Historic Buildings*. London: Butterworth/ICOMOS.

ICOMOS 1990b *Directory of Archaeological Heritage Management*. Oslo: ICOMOS.

—— 1998 'International Charter on the Protection and Management of Underwater Cultural Heritage', *International Journal of Nautical Archaeology* 27, 183–7.

IFA (Institute of Field Archaeologists) 1987 *The Institute of Field Archaeologists: Memorandum and Articles of Association*. Birmingham: IFA (as amended).

—— 1988 'Report of the Interim Procurement Regulation Steering Committee', in *IFA Annual Report 5*. Birmingham: IFA.

—— 1989 *Directory of Members 1988–1989*. Birmingham: IFA.

—— 1990 *By-Laws of the Institute of Field Archaeologists: Code of Approved Practice for the Regulation of Contractual Arrangements in Field Archaeology*. Birmingham: IFA.

—— 1992 *Directory of Educational Opportunities in Archaeology*. Birmingham: IFA.

—— 1996 *Standard and Guidance for the Archaeological Investigation and Recording of Standing Buildings or Structures*. Reading: IFA (revised 1999).

—— 1999 *By-laws, Standards and Policy Statements of the Institute of Field Archaeologists*. Reading: IFA (occasionally updated).

—— 2000a *Code of Conduct*. Reading: IFA.

—— 2000b *Code of Approved Practice for the Regulation of Contractual Arrangements in Field Archaeology*. Reading: IFA.

—— 2004 *Institute of Field Archaeologists Yearbook and Directory 2004*. Reading: IFA.

—— n.d. Pamphlet on Membership. IFA: Birmingham.

INAH (Instituto Nacional de Antropología e Historia: Mexico) 2002 *Centro de Documentación e Investigación sobre el Manejo de Sitios Arqueológicos del Patrimonio Mundial*. Oaxaca: INAH.

Iles R. 1992 'Integrated Conservation Management on Private Estates', in Macinnes and Wickham-Jones 1992, 134–9.

Imai T., Sakayama T. and Kaiomori T. 1987 'Use of Ground Probing Radar and Resistivity Surveys for Archaeological Investigations', *Geophysics* 52, 137–50.

JNAPC (Joint Nautical Archaeology Policy Committee) 1989 *Heritage at Sea: Proposals for the Better Protection of Archaeological Sites Underwater*. Greenwich: National Maritime Museum.

—— 1998 *Code of Practice for Seabed Developers*. Swindon: RCHME.

—— 2003 *An Interim Report on the Valletta Convention and Heritage Law at Sea*. Wolverhampton: University of Wolverhampton School of Legal Studies.

—— n.d. Joint Nautical Archaeology Policy Committee, British Sub-Aqua Club, Professional Association of Diving Instructors and Sub Aqua Association *Underwater Finds: Guidance for Divers*.

Jacobi R. 2004 'The Late Upper Palaeolithic Lithic Collection from Gough's Cave, Cheddar, Somerset and Human Use of the Cave', *Proceedings of the Prehistoric Society* 70, 1–92.

Jagger M. and Scrase, T. 1997 'In Defence of Areas of Archaeological Importance', *Journal of Planning and Environment Law* (February 1997), 195–8.

Jago M. 1995 'The Countryside Stewartship Scheme: Testing the Way Forward for Integrated Countryside Management', in Berry and Brown 1995, 49–60.

James S. and Millett M. 2001 *Britons and Romans: Advancing an Archaeological Agenda*. York: Counc Brit Archaeol Res Rep 125.

James T.A. 1986 'Discovering and Monitoring Sites by Aerial Survey', in Moore D. and Austin D. (eds) *Welsh Archaeological Heritage. Proceedings of a Conference held by The Cambrian Archaeological Association in 1985*, 137–40. Lampeter: St David's University College.

Jaworski T. 1981 *Legal Foundations of the Protections of Cultural Property in Poland*. Warsaw: Ministry of Culture and Arts.

Jobey G. 1990 'The Society of Antiquaries of Newcastle-upon-Tyne', *Archaeol Aeliana* 5th ser., 18, 197–216.

Johnson M. 2000 *Archaeological Theory*. Oxford: Blackwell.

Johnson N. and Rose P. 1994 *Bodmin Moor: An Archaeological Survey*. Vol. 1, *The Human Landscape to c. 1800*. London: English Heritage/RCHME.

Jones A. 2001 *Archaeological Theory and Scientific Practice*. Cambridge: Cambridge University Press.

Jones D. 1998 'Long Barrows and Neolithic Elongated Enclosures in Lincolnshire: An Analysis of the Air Photographic Evidence', *Proceedings of the Prehistory Society* 64, 83–114.

Jones G.D.B. 1984 *Past Imperfect. The Story of Rescue Archaeology*. London: Heinemann.

Jones S., MacSween A., Jeffrey S., Morris R. and Heyworth M. 2001. *From the Ground Up. The Publication of Archaeological Projects: A User Needs Survey*. York: CBA. Also available at www.britarch.ac.uk/pubs/puns/index.html (accessed 3 January 2004).

Joyce S., Newbury M. and Stone P. (eds) 1987 *Degree, Digging, Dole: Our Future? Papers Presented at YAC '85 Southampton*. Southampton: YAC '85 Organising Committee for Southampton Univ Archaeol Soc.

Karlsson H. (ed.) 2004 *Swedish Archaeologists on Ethics*. Lindome: Bricoleur Press.

Karpodini-Dimitriadi E. (ed.) 1995 *Ethnography of European Traditional Cultures. Their Role and Perspectives in a Multicultural World*. Athens: Institute of Cultural Studies of Europe and the Mediterranean.

Keene S. (ed.) 1980 *Conservation, Archaeology and Museums*. London: Institute of Conservators. (UK Institute for Conservation Occas Pap 1.)

Kennedy D. 1998 'Declassified Satellite Photographs and Archaeology in the Middle East: Case Studies from Turkey', *Antiquity* 72, 553–61.

—— (ed.) 1989 *Into the Sun. Essays in Air Photography in Archaeology in Honour of Derrick Riley*. Sheffield: University Dept of Prehist and Archaeol.

—— and Bewley R. 2004 *Ancient Jordan from the Air*. London: Council for British Research in the Levant.

Kennet W. 1972 *Preservation*. London: Temple Smith.

Keys D. 2003 'It May be Old but is it Art?', *Country Life* (23 October 2003), 68–9.

King T.F., Hickman P.P. and Berg G. 1977 *Anthropology in Historic Preservation; Caring for Culture's Clutter*. New York: Academic Press.

Kindred B. 2003a Review of 'Hozon: Architectural and Urban Conservation in Japan', *Context* 79, 36.

—— 2003b 'Informed Management versus Control', *Context* 79, 13–14.

Kolb D. 1990 *Postmodern Sophistications. Philosophy, Architecture and Tradition*. Chicago and London: University of Chicago Press.

Kristiansen K. 1984 'Denmark', in Cleere 1984, 21–36.

Kuhn T. 1962 *The Structure of Scientific Revolutions*. Chicago: University of Chicago Press.

Kuklick H. 1997 'After Ishmael: The Fieldwork Tradition and Its Future', in Gupta A. and Ferguson J. (eds) *Anthropological Locations. Boundaries and Grounds of a Science*, 47–65. Berkeley and Los Angeles: University of California Press.

Kunow J. (ed.) 1995 *Luftbildarchäologie in Ost- und Mitteleuropa*. Potsdam: Forschungen zur Archäologie im Land Brandendurg 3.

Lamb R.G. 1982 *The Archaeological Sites and Monuments of Scotland, 16: Rousay, Egilsay and Wyre, Orkney Islands Area*. Edinburgh: RCAHMS.

Lambrick G. 1991 'Competitive Tendering and Archaeological Research: The development of a CBA View', in Swain 1991, 21–31.

—— 1992 'The Importance of the Cultural Heritage in a Green World: Towards the Development of Landscape Integrity Assessment', in Macinnes and Wickham-Jones 1992, 105–26.

—— 2001 'From Treasure to Public Good', *British Archaeology* 58, 26.

—— 2002 'Plough Damage: A New Approach to Mitigation', *Conservation Bulletin* 42, 22–3.

—— (ed.) 1985 *Archaeology and Nature Conservation*. Oxford: University Dept of External Studies.

Lancashire County Council 2000 *Recording Historic Buildings in Lancashire: A Guide to Development in the Historic Environment*. Preston: Lancashire County Archaeology Service.

Lang N.A.R. 1992 'Sites and Monuments Records in Great Britain', in Larsen 1992, 171–83.

Larsen C.U. (ed.) 1992 *Sites and Monuments: National Archaeological Records*. Copenhagen: National Museum of Denmark.

Lauwerier R.C.G.M. and Lotte R.M. (eds) 2002 *Archeologiebalans 2002*. Amersfoort: Rijksdienst voor het Oudheidkundig Bodemonderzoek.

Lawrence E. 1989 'The Costs of An Interesting Find', in *Pre-Conference Papers: Archaeological Remains and Development 27th November 1989*, 47–56. London: Henry Stewart Conference Studies.

Lawson A.J. (ed.) 1989 'Draft Approved Practice in Contracting Archaeology and Competitive Tendering', *Field Archaeology* 11, 179.

Layton R. (ed.) 1989a *Conflict in the Archaeology of Living Traditions*. London: Unwin Hyman. (One World Archaeology 8.)

—— (ed.) 1989b *Who Needs the Past? Indigenous Values and Archaeology*. London: Unwin Hyman. (One World Archaeology 5.)

Le Borgne E. 1955 'Susceptibilité magnétique anormale du sol superficiel', *Annales de Géophysique* 11, 399–419.

—— 1960 'Influences du feu sur les propriétés magnétiques du sol et du granit', *Annales de Géophysique* 16, 159–95.

Lee E. (ed.) 1998 *MIDAS – A Manual and Data Standard for Monument Inventories*. Swindon: RCHME (reprinted EH).

Leigh D. 1982 'The Selection, Conservation and Storage of Archaeological Finds', *Museums Journal* 82/2, 115–16.

Levine P. 1986 *The Amateur and the Professional. Antiquarians, Historians and Archaeologists in Victorian England, 1836–1886*. Cambridge: Cambridge University Press.

Lewis G. 1989 *For Instruction and Recreation: A Centenary History of the Museums Association*. London: Quiller Press.

Leyten H. (ed.) 1995 *Illicit Traffic in Cultural Property: Museums against Pillage*. Amsterdam: Royal Tropical Institute.

Lock D. 1988 'Project Management', in Lock D. and Farrow N. (eds) *The Gower Handbook of Management*, 599–630. London: Gower Publishing Co.

Long D.L. 2000 'Cultural Heritage Management in Post-colonial Politics: *Not* the Heritage of the Other', *International Journal of Heritage Studies* 6, 317–22.

Longworth C. and Wood B. 2000 *Standards in Action: Working with Archaeology*. London: Society of Museum Archaeologists/MDA.

Longworth I.W. 1993 'Portable Antiquities', in Hunter and Ralston 1993b, 56–64.

Lorenzo J.L. 1984 'Mexico', in Cleere 1984, 89–100.

Lowenthal D. 1985 *The Past is a Foreign Country*. Cambridge: Cambridge University Press.

—— 1996 *The Heritage Crusade and the Spoils of History*. London: Viking (Penguin).

—— and Binney M. (eds) 1981 *Our Past Before Us. Why Do We Save It?* London: Temple Smith.

Lucas G. 2001a *Critical Approaches to Fieldwork*. London: Routledge.

—— 2001b 'Excavation and the Rhetoric of Destruction', *Norwegian Archaeological Review* 34, 35–46.

—— and Whittaker P. 2001 *Vicar's Farm, Cambridge Post-Excavation Assessment Report*. Cambridge: Cambridge Archaeological Unit Rep 425.

Lynott M.J. and Wylie A. (eds) 2002 *Ethics in American Archaeology*. Washington: Society for American Archaeology. 2nd rev. edn.

MCA (Maritime and Coastguard Agency) n.d. *Wreck Amnesty Final Report: 23rd January–24 April 2001*. Southampton: Maritime and Coastguard Agency.

MGC (Museums and Galleries Commission) 1992 *Standards in the Museum Care of Archaeological Collections*. London: HMSO.

MLA (Museums, Libraries and Archives Council) 2004 *Portable Antiquities Scheme Annual Report 2003/04*. London: MLA.

MoD (Ministry of Defence) 2001a *Report of the Public Consultation on Military Maritime Graves and the Protection of Military Remains Act 1986*. London: MoD.

—— 2001b *Crashed Military Aircraft of Historical Interest: Notes for Guidance of Recovery Groups*. Innsworth, Gloucester: RAF Personnel Management Agency.

MoF (Ministry of Finance, Northern Ireland) 1966 *An Archaeological Survey of County Down*. Belfast: HMSO.

Macinnes L. 2002 'Examples of Current National Approaches – Scotland', in Fairclough and Rippon 2002, 171–4.

—— 2004 'Historic Landscape Characterisation', in Bishop K. and Phillips A. (eds) 2004 *Countryside Planning: New Approaches to Management and Conservation*, 155–69. London: Earthscan.

—— and Ader K. 1995 'Integrated Management Plans: Historic Scotland's Experience', in Berry and Brown 1995, 29–36.

—— and Wickham Jones C.R. (eds) 1992 *All Natural Things: Archaeology and the Green Debate*. Oxford: Oxbow Monograph 21.

MacIvor I. and Fawcett R. 1983 'Planks from the Shipwreck of Time: An Account of Ancient Monumentry, Then and Now', in Magnusson M. (ed.) 1983 *Echoes in Stone*, 9–27. Edinburgh: Scottish Development Department.

MacSween A. 2001 'Historic Battlefields', in Freeman P.W.M. and Pollard A. (eds) 2001 *Fields of Conflict: Progress and Prospect in Battlefield Archaeology*, 291–6. Oxford: Brit Archaeol Rep Internat Ser 958.

Mainman A.J. and Rogers N.S.H. 2000 *Craft, Industry and Everyday Life: Finds from Anglo-Scandinavian York*. York: Council for British Archaeology/York Archaeological Trust.

Maitland Flight Lieutenant 1927 'The Works of Old Men in Arabia', *Antiquity* 1, 197–203.

Malm G. (ed.) 2001 *Archaeology and Buildings*. Oxford: Brit Archaeol Rep Internat Ser 930.

Manley J. 1987 'Archaeology and Planning: A Welsh Perspective', *Journal of Planning and Environment Law* 466–84, 552–63.

Marsden S. 2001 'The Heritage Management of Wetlands: Legislative Designation and Protection: A Viewpoint from England and Wales', in Coles and Olivier 2001, 7–15.

Martin E. and Satchell M. forthcoming. *'Wheare Most Enclosures Be' – Historic Fields in East Anglia*. Norwich: East Anglian Archaeology Reports. (Norfolk County Council and EH.)

Marvell A. 1990 'Evaluating Archaeological Sites – Methods and Techniques: ABC 1990', *Field Archaeology* 13, 230.

Masser P. 2001 *Archaeological Excavations at West Fen and St Johns Roads, Ely, Cambridgeshire – The Trinity and Runciman Lands*. Cambridge: Cambridge. (Archaeological Unit Rep 432.)

Maurice C. and Turnor R. 1992 'The Export Licensing Rules in the United Kingdom and the Waverley Criteria', *International Journal of Cultural Property* 2, 273–95.

McBryde I. (ed.) 1985 *Who Owns the Past?* Oxford: Oxford University Press.

McGimsey C.R. 1972 *Public Archaeology*. New York and London: Seminar Press.

—— and Davies H.A. 1984 'United States of America', in Cleere 1984, 116–24.

McOmish D., Field D. and Brown G. 2000 *The Field Archaeology of Salisbury Plain Training Area*. Swindon: EH.

Mellor D. 1992 'Face to Face with the Facts of Strife', *The Guardian* 2, 4 December 1992.

Mellor J. 1986 'A Community Archaeology Project in Leicestershire', *Rescue News* 40, 3.

—— 1988 'MSC – What Next? The Adult Training Initiative and the Role of Archaeological Bodies', *Rescue News* 45, 3.

Merriman N. 1991 *Beyond the Glass Case: The Past, Heritage and the Public*. Leicester: Leicester University Press.

—— (ed.) 1999 *Making Early Histories in Museums*. Leicester: Leicester University Press.

—— and Swain H. 1999 'Archaeological Archives: Serving the Public Interest?', *European Journal of Archaeology* 2, 249–67.

Mike Griffiths and Associates Ltd 2003 *Environmental Statement: Hungate, York: Technical Appendix D Archaeological Assessment.*

Miles D. 2002 'Portable Antiquities Scheme Extended: Promoting Greater Public Understanding', *Conservation Bulletin* 43, 32–3.

Miles J. 1992 'Environmental Conservation and Archaeology: Is There a Need for Integrated Designations?', in Macinnes and Wickham-Jones 1992, 97–104.

Miles R., Alt M., Gosling D., Lewis B. and Tout A. (eds) 1988 *The Design of Educational Exhibits*. London: Unwin Hyman.

Mills N. 1999 *Medieval Artefacts: Catalogue and Price Guide*. Witham: Greenlight Publishing.

Miraj L. and Zeqo M. 1993 'Conceptual Changes in Albanian Archaeology', *Antiquity* 67, 123–5.

Moore J. and Jennings D. 1992 *Reading Business Park: A Bronze Age Landscape*. Oxford: Oxford Archaeological Unit. (Thames Valley Landscapes: the Kennet Valley, vol. 1.)

Morgan Evans D. 1992 'The Paradox of Salisbury Plain', in Macinnes and Wickham-Jones 1992, 176–80.

Morris E. 2004 'Foreword', in MLA, 3–4.

Morris R. 1989 *Churches in the Landscape*. London: Dent.

—— 1996 'Time Now for Reform of Treasure Trove', *British Archaeology* 11, 11.

Morriss R.K. 2000 *The Archaeology of Buildings*. Stroud: Tempus.

Mumford G. and Parcak S. 2002 'Satellite Image Analysis and Archaeological Fieldwork in El-Markha Plain (South Sinai)', *Antiquity* 76, 953–4.

Murawski P.G. 2003 *Benet's Artefacts of England and the United Kingdom: Current Values*. Cambridge: privately published. 2nd edn.

Murray D.M. 1992 'Towards Harmony: A View of the Scottish National Database', in Larsen 1992, 209–16.

Museums Association 1989 'Museums – a National Resource, a National Responsibility', *Museums Journal* 89/8, 36–7.

Musson C. 1994 *Wales from the Air. Patterns of Past and Present*. Aberystwyth: RCAHMW.

Mynors C. 1989 *Listed Buildings and Conservation Areas*. London: Sweet and Maxwell.

—— 1999 *Listed Buildings, Conservation Areas and Monuments*. London: Sweet and Maxwell. 3rd edn.

Mytum H. and Waugh K. (eds) 1987 *Rescue Archaeology – What's Next?* York: Univ York Dept Archaeol Monogr 6.

NDC (Newbury District Council) 1990 *Newbury Local Plan*. Newbury: Newbury District Council.

NFDC (New Forest District Council) 2000 *New Forest District Landscape Character Assessment: Main Report and Supplementary Annexes*. Lyndhurst: New Forest District Council, Hampshire County Council, the Countryside Agency and EH.

National Board of Antiquities n.d. *Archaeological Heritage Management in Finland*. Helsinski: Helsinki University Press.

Neighbour T., Strachan R. and Hobbs B.A. 2001 'Resistivity Imaging of the Linear Earthworks at the Mull of Galloway, Dumfries and Galloway', *Archaeological Prospection* 8, 157–62.

Newman J. 1997 *A Review of the Ecclesiastical Exemption from Listed Buildings Control, Conducted for the Department for Culture, Media and Sport and the Welsh Office*. London: DCMS.

Newman M. 2001 *The Sites and Monuments Records Data Audit Programme – A Review*. Swindon: EH.

—— 2002 *SMR Content and Computing Survey 2002*. Swindon: EH.

Newsom G.H. 1988 *Faculty Jurisdiction of the Church of England*. London: Sweet and Maxwell.

Nicolle S. 2001 'Treasure Trove (1): Lost, Stolen or Strayed', *The Jersey Law Review* (February 2001), 39–53.

Nieke M.R. 1997 'Ten Years On – the Monuments Protection Programme', *Conservation Bulletin* 31, 10–12.

—— 2001 'Monuments Protection Programme: Knowledge for Managing Change', *Conservation Bulletin* 40, 20–2.

Nishimura Y. and Kamai H. 1991 'A Study on the Application of Geophysical Prospection', in Pernicka and Wagner 1991, 757–63.

Noel M. and Walker R. 1991 'Development of a Resistivity Tomography System for Imaging Archaeological Structures', in Pernicka and Wagner 1991, 767–76.

—— and Xu B. 1991 'Archaeological Investigation by Electrical Resistivity Tomography: A Preliminary Study', *Geophysical Journal International* 107, 95–102.

Normand A. 2003 *Review of Treasure Trove Arrangements in Scotland*. Edinburgh: Scottish Executive.

Neustupný E. 1993 'Czechoslovakia: The Last Three Years', *Antiquity* 67, 129–34.

ODPM (Office of the Deputy Prime Minister) forthcoming. *Planning for the Historic Environment*. London: Office of the Deputy Prime Minister. (PPS 15.)

O'Keefe P.J. 2002 *Shipwrecked Heritage: A Commentary on the UNESCO Convention on Underwater Cultural Heritage*. Leicester: Institute of Art and Law.

—— and Nafziger J.A.R. 1994 'The Draft Convention on the Protection of the Underwater Cultural Heritage', *Ocean Development and International Law* 25, 391–418.

—— and Prott L.V. 1984 *Law and the Cultural Heritage*. Vol. 1. *Discovery and Excavation*. Abingdon: Professional Books.

Olivier A. 1989 *Safety in Archaeological Fieldwork*. London: CBA Practical Handbooks in Archaeology 6.

—— 2001 'A Strategy for the Heritage Management of Wetlands: Statement of Intent', in Coles and Olivier 2001, 185–91.

—— 2002 'Frameworks for Our Past: The Role of the Research Agenda', *The Archaeologist* 46, 34.

Olwig K.R. 2001 '"Time Out of Mind" – "Mind Out of Time": Custom versus Tradition in Environmental Heritage Research and Interpretation', *International Journal of Heritage Studies* 7, 339–54.

Orton C. 2000 *Sampling in Archaeology*. Cambridge: Cambridge University Press.

Oswald A., Dyer C. and Barber M. 2001 *The Creation of Monuments*. Swindon: EH.

Ottaway P. and Rogers N. 2002 *Craft, Industry and Everyday Life: Finds from Medieval York*. York: Council for British Archaeology/York Archaeological Trust.

Ovenden S.M. 1994 'Application of Seismic Refraction to Archaeological Prospecting', *Archaeological Prospection* 1, 53–64.

Owen J. 1995 *Towards an Accessible Archaeological Archive*. London: Society of Museum Archaeologists.

Owen-John H. 1986 *Rescue Archaeology in Wales*. Swansea: University College. (Mainwairing-Hughes Award Ser 3.)

—— 1992 'Who Needs Archaeology?', in Macinnes and Wickham-Jones 1992, 89–96.

Oxford Brookes University 1999 *Local Authority Practice and PPG 15: Information and Effectiveness*. Oxford: Oxford Brookes University, School of Planning, Environmental Design and Conservation Research Group.

Oxley I. 2002 'Scapa Flow and the Protection and Management of Scotland's Historic Military Shipwrecks', *Antiquity* 76, 862–8.

PDP (Paul Drury Partnership) 2003 *Streamlining Listed Building Consent: Lessons from the Use of Management Agreements*. The Paul Drury Partnership with the Environmental Project Consulting Group. London: EH/Office of the Deputy Prime Minister.

Paintin E.M. 2001 *Report on the Operation of the Treasure Act 1996: Review and Recommendations*. London: DCMS.

Palang H. and Fry G. (eds) 2003 *Landscape Interfaces: Cultural Heritage in Changing Landscapes*. Dordrecht: Kluwer Academic Publishers. (Landscape Series 1.)

Palmer M. and Neaverson P. (eds) 1995 *Managing the Industrial Heritage*. Leicester: Leicester Archaeology Monogr 2.

Palmer N.E. 1981 'Treasure Trove and the Protection of Antiquities', *Modern Law Review* 44, 178–87.

Palmer N.E. 1993 'Treasure Trove and Title to Discovered Antiquities', *International Journal of Cultural Property* 2, 275–318.

—— 1996 'Title to Antiquarian Finds: Perpetuating the Impenetrable', *Art, Antiquity and Law* 1, 157–61.

—— and Goyder J. 1992 'Free Movement of Cultural Goods and the European Community', in Pearce S. (ed.) 1992 *Museums and Europe 1992*, 5–23. London: The Athlone Press. (New Research in Museum Studies 3.)

Palmer R. 2004 'Editorial', *AARGnews* 29, 3–4.

—— and Cox C. 1993 *Uses of Aerial Photography in Archaeological Evaluations*. Birmingham: IFA. (IFA Tech Pap 12.)

Parker Pearson M. 1993 'Visitors Welcome', in Hunter and Ralston 1993b, 225–231.

—— 1999 *The Archaeology of Death and Burial*. Stroud: Sutton Publishing.

Parsons D. 1989 *Churches and Chapels: Investigating Places of Worship*. Counc Brit Archaeol Practical Handbook, 8. London: CBA.

Parsons J. 2003 'Finders Keepers, Losers Weepers: Treasure and the Portable Antiquities Recording Scheme', *Glevensis* 36, 43–6.

Paynter R. 1990 'Afro-Americans in the Massachusetts Historical Landscape', in Gathercole and Lowenthal 1990, 49–62.

Pearce S. 1992 *Museum Objects and Collections*. Leicester: Leicester University Press.

Pearson S. and Meeson B. (eds) 2001 *Vernacular Buildings in a Changing World: Understanding, Recording and Conservation*. York: Coun Brit Archaeol Res Rep 126.

Pearson V. 2001 *Teaching the Past: A Practical Guide for Archaeologists*. York: CBA.

Pernicka E. and Wagner G.A. (eds) 1991 *Archaeometry '90* . Basel: Birkhäuser Verlag.

Perrin K. 2002 *Archaeological Archives: Documentation, Access and Deposition. A Way Forward*. London: EH.

Petchey M.R. and Collcutt S.N. 2002 'When to Evaluate? The Provision of Sufficient Archaeological Information in Planning', *Journal of Planning and Environment Law* (May 2002), 528–43.

Petrie W.M.F. 1899 'Sequences in Prehistoric Remains', *Journal of the Anthropological Institute* 29, 295–301.

Philp B. 1974 'Kent, Dover and the CIB Corps', in Rahtz 1974, 73–8.

Pickard R. 2002 'A Comparative Review of Policy for the Protection of the Architectural Heritage of Europe', *International Journal of Heritage Studies* 8, 349–63.

Pickering P. 2002 'Learning from Ten Years of PPG 16', *London Archaeologist* (2002), 64–8.

Pitt Rivers A.H.L.F. 1906 *The Evolution of Culture and Other Essays*. Oxford: Clarendon Press.

Pollard A.M. 1989 'The Funding of Archaeological Science', *Field Archaeologist* 11, 173–5.

—— 1990 *Report of the Co-ordinator for Science-Based Archaeology 1987–1990*. Swindon: Science and Engineering Research Council.

Powell K. and de la Hey C. 1987 *Churches: A Question of Conversion*. London: SAVE Britain's Heritage.

Prehistoric Society 1988 *Saving our Prehistoric Heritage: Landscapes under Threat*. London: Prehistoric Society.

Priore R. 2001 'The Background to the European Landscape Convention', in *The Cultural Landscape: Planning for a Sustainable Partnership between People and Place* 2001, 31–7. London: ICOMOS UK.

Princ M. 1984 'Czechoslovakia', in Cleere 1984, 12–20.

Prott L.V. 1992 'A Common Heritage: The World Heritage Convention', in Macinnes and Wickham-Jones 1992, 65–86.

—— and O'Keefe P.J. 1989 *Law and the Cultural Heritage*. Vol. 3. *Movement*. London: Butterworths.

Proudfoot E.V.W. 1986 'Commentary – the First Forty Years', *Scottish Archaeological Gazette* 12, 2–5.
—— (ed.) 1989 *Our Vanishing Heritage: Forestry and Archaeology*. Edinburgh: Council Scott Archaeol Occas Pap 2.
Pryor F.M.M. 1989 'Look What We've Found' – A Case-study in Public Archaeology', *Antiquity* 63, 51–6.
Pugh-Smith J. 2000 'Archaeologists, Architectural Historians and the Planning Process: Whose Agenda?' *Antiquaries Journal* 80, 15–26.
—— and Samuels J. 1993 'PPG 16: Two Years On', *Journal of Planning and Environment Law* (February 1993), 203–10.
—— and Samuels J. 1996a 'Archaeology and Planning: Recent Trends and Potential Conflicts', *Journal of Planning and Environment Law* (September 1996), 707–24.
—— and Samuels J. 1996b *Archaeology in Law*. London: Sweet and Maxwell.
Querol M.Á. and Martínez Díaz B. 1996 *La gestion del Patrimonio Arqueologico en España*. Madrid: Alianza Editorial.
RCAHMS (Royal Commission on the Ancient and Historical Monuments of Scotland) 1990 *North-East Perth: An Archaeological Landscape*. Edinburgh: HMSO.
—— 1992 *Inventory of Argyll 7*. Edinburgh: HMSO.
—— 1994 *South-East Perth: An Archaeological Landscape*. Edinburgh: HMSO.
—— 1997 *Eastern Dumfriesshire: An Archaeological Landscape*. Edinburgh: HMSO.
RCHME (Royal Commission on the Historical Monuments of England) 1960 *A Matter of Time*. London: RCHME.
—— 1978 *A Survey of Surveys*. London: RCHME.
—— 1991a *The Archaeology of Bokerley Dyke*. London: HMSO.
—— 1991b *Recording Historic Buildings: A Symposium*. London: RCHME.
—— 1992a *Annual Report 1991/92*. London: RCHME.
—— 1992b *Yorkshire Textile Mills: The Buildings of the Yorkshire Textile Industry 1770–1930*. London: HMSO.
—— 1995a *Local Government Act 1992: Guidance from RCHME for New Authorities on the Role of Sites and Monuments Records*. Swindon: RCHME
—— 1995b *Guidelines and Specification Manual for the National Mapping Programme*. London: RCHME Internal Document.
—— 1996 *Recording Historic Buildings: A Descriptive Specification*. London: RCHME, 3rd edn
——, ALGAO and English Heritage 1998 *Unlocking the Past For the New Millennium. A New Statement of Co-operation on Sites and Monuments Records in England between the Royal Commission on the Historical Monuments of England, English Heritage and the Association of Local Government Archaeological Officers*. Swindon: RCHME.
—— and EH 1995 *Thesaurus of Monument Types*. Swindon: RCHME.
—— with English Heritage 1998 *Thesaurus of Monument Types: A Standard for Use in Archaeological and Architectural Recording*. Swindon: RCHME. 2nd edn.
Raemaekers J. and Boyack S. 1999 *Planning and Sustainable Development*. Perth: Scottish Environment Audits, 3.
Rahtz P.A. (ed.) 1974 *Rescue Archaeology*. Harmondsworth: Penguin.
—— 1985 *Invitation to Archaeology*. Oxford: Blackwell.
Ralston I. and Thomas R. (eds) 1993 *Archaeology and Environmental Assessment*. Birmingham: IFA. (Inst Field Archaeol Occas Pap 5.)
Rathje W. 1974 'The Garbage Project: A New Way of Looking at the Problems of Archaeology', *Archaeology* 27, 236–41.
Redesdale R. 2002 'Opinion', *The Archaeologist*, 46, 23.
Redfern N. 1998a *Twentieth Century Fortifications in the United Kingdom*. Vol. 1. *Introduction and Sources*. York: CBA.
—— 1998b *Twentieth Century Fortifications in the United Kingdom*. Vol. 2. *Wales*. York: CBA.

—— 1998c *Twentieth Century Fortifications in the United Kingdom*. Vol. 3. *Scotland*. York: CBA.

—— 1998d *Twentieth Century Fortifications in the United Kingdom*. Vol. 4. *Northern Ireland: Sources*. York: CBA.

Redman M. 1990 'Archaeology and Development', *Journal of Planning and Environment Law* (February 1990), 87–98.

Redmond-Cooper R. and Palmer N.E. (eds) 1999 *Cultural Heritage Statutes*. Leicester: Institute of Art and Law.

Redknap M. (ed.) 1997 *Artefacts from Wrecks: Dated Assemblages from the Late Middle Ages to the Industrial Revolution*. Oxford: Oxbow Monograph 84.

Rees L.W.B. 1929 'The Transjordan Desert', *Antiquity* 3, 389–407.

Rees T. and Mills C. 1999 *Bracken and Archaeology*. Edinburgh: HS Technical Advice Note 17.

Reichstein J. 1984 'Federal Republic of Germany', in Cleere 1984, 37–47.

Renfrew C. 1997 'Stemming the Flood of Looted Antiquities', *British Archaeology* 30 (December 1997), 11.

—— 1998 'Foreword', in Stead 1998, 7–10.

—— 2000 *Loot, Legitimacy and Ownership*. London: Duckworth.

—— 2001 'Amendment Number 2 to the Culture and Recreation Bill', London: Hansard.

—— 2003 *Figuring It Out. The Parallel Views of Artists and Archaeologists*. London: Thames and Hudson.

—— and Bahn P. 1991 *Archaeology. Theories, Methods, and Practice*. London: Thames and Hudson. 2nd edn.

RESCUE/SCAUM (Standing Committee for Archaeological Unit Managers) 1991 *Competitive Tendering in Archaeology. Papers at a One Day Conference in June 1990*. Hertford: RESCUE.

Resource (The Council for Museums, Archives and Libraries) 2001 *Renaissance in the Regions: A Strategic Vision for England's Museums*. London: Council for Museums, Archives and Libraries. Available on www.mla.gov.uk/action/regional/ren_report.asp

—— 2003 *Portable Antiquities Scheme Annual Report 2001/02–2002/03*. London: Resource.

Reynolds P.J. 1979 *Iron-Age Farm. The Butser Experiment*. London: British Museum.

Richards C. 1995 'Knowing about the Past', in I. Hodder *et al.* (eds), *Interpreting Archaeology: Finding Meaning in the Past*, 216–19. London: Routledge.

Richards J.D. 2001 'Anglian and Anglo-Scandinavian Cottam: Linking Digital Publication and Archive', *Internet Archaeology* 10 http://intarch.ac.uk/journal/issue10/richards_index.html

—— 2003 'Digital Preservation and Access', *European Journal of Archaeology* 5, 343–66.

Richardson H. (ed.) 1998 *English Hospitals 1660–1948*. Swindon: RCHME.

Riley D.N. 1987 *Air Photography and Archaeology*. London: Duckworth.

Roberts B.K. and Wrathmell S. 2000 *An Atlas of Rural Settlement in England*. London: EH.

—— and Wrathmell S. 2002 *Region and Place. A Study of English Rural Settlement*. London: EH.

Roberts P. and Trow S. 2002 *Taking to the Water: English Heritage's Initial Policy for the Management of Maritime Archaeology in England*. London: EH.

Rodwell W.J. 1981 *The Archaeology of the English Church*. London: Batsford.

—— 1989 *English Heritage Book of Church Archaeology*. London: Batsford/EH. Rev. edn of Rodwell 1981.

—— and Rodwell K. 1977 *Historic Churches – A Wasting Asset*. London: Counc Brit Archaeol Res Rep 19.

Rosier C. 1996 'PPG 15 and Recording: The Oxfordshire Experience. Part 1', *Context* 52, 20–2.

—— 1997 'PPG 15 and Recording: The Oxfordshire Experience. Part 2', *Context* 53, 20–2 and 35.

Ross M. 1991 *Planning and the Heritage*. London: E. and F.N. Spon.

Rössler M. 2001 'World Heritage Cultural Landscapes in the European Region', in *The Cultural Landscape: Planning for a Sustainable Partnership between People and Place* 2001, 38–45. London: ICOMOS UK.

Roy Waller Associates Ltd 1991 *Environmental Effects of Surface Mineral Workings*. London: HMSO. (Department of the Environment Research Report.)

SCAUM (Standing Committee for Archaeological Unit Managers) 1997 *Health and Safety in Field Archaeology*. London: SCAUM. Rev. edn.

—— 1999 *Archaeology and Employment*. Manchester: SCAUM.

—— 2004 *Employment Practice Manual*. London: SCAUM.

SERC (Science and Engineering Research Council) 1985 *SERC Report: The Funding of Research in Science-based Archaeology in Universities and Polytechnics*. Swindon: SERC.

SOEnD (Scottish Office Environment Department) 1994a *National Planning Policy Guideline 5: Archaeology and Planning*. Edinburgh: SOEnD. (NPPG 5.)

—— 1994b *Planning Advice Note 42: Archaeology and Planning*. Edinburgh: SOEnD. (PAN 42.)

Samuel R. 1994 *Theatres of Memory 1: Past and Present in Contemporary Culture*. London, New York: Verso.

Saunders A. 1983 'A Century of Ancient Monuments Legislation 1882–1982', *Antiquaries Journal* 63, 11–33.

Saville A. 1990 'Public Inquiry Problems – a Note from the Conservation Co-ordinator', *PAST* (Newsletter of the Prehistoric Society) 4, 11–12.

—— 1999 'A Cache of Flint Axeheads and Other Flint Artefacts from Auchenhoan, near Campbeltown, Kintyre, Scotland', *Proceedings of the Prehistoric Society* 65, 83–123.

—— 2000 'Portable Antiquities and Excavated Finds in Scotland', *Institute of Field Archaeologists Yearbook and Directory of Members 2000*, 31–2.

—— 2002 'Treasure Trove in Scotland', *Antiquity* 76, 796–802.

Schadla-Hall R. T. 1984 'Slightly Looted: A Review of the Jorvik Viking Centre', *Museums Journal* 84/2, 62–4.

Schama S. 1995 *Landscape and Memory*. London: Harper Collins.

Schild R. 1993 'Polish Archaeology in Transition', *Antiquity* 67, 146–50.

Schmidt A. 2002 *Geophysical Data in Archaeology: A Guide to Good Practice*. York: Archaeology Data Service.

Schnapp A. 1996 *The Discovery of the Past*. London: British Museum Press.

Schofield J. 2001 'D-Day Sites in England: An Assessment', *Antiquity* 75, 77–83.

—— 2002 'The Role of Aerial Photographs in National Strategic Programmes: Assessing Recent Military Sites in England', in Dewley and Rączkowksi 2002, 269–82.

—— and Anderton M. 2000 'The Queer Archaeology of Green Gate: Interpreting Contested Space at Greenham Common Airbase', *World Archaeology* 32, 236–51.

Schwarz R. 2003 *Pilotstudien. 12 Jahre Luftbildarchäologie in Sachsen-Anhalt*. Halle, Germany.

Scole Committee 1973 *The Problems and Future of East Anglian Archaeology*. Norwich: Scole Committee.

Scollar I. 2002 'Making Things Look Vertical', in Bewley and Rączkowksi 2002, 166–72.

——, Tabbagh A., Hesse A. and Herzog, I. 1990 *Archaeological Geophysics and Remote Sensing*. Cambridge: Cambridge University Press.

Scottish Executive 1999a *Treasure Trove in Scotland. Information on Treasure Trove Procedures: Criteria for Allocation and the Allocation Process*. Edinburgh: Scottish Executive Education Department.

—— 1999b *Treasure Trove in Scotland. Guidelines for Fieldworkers*. Edinburgh: Scottish Executive Education Department.

—— 1999c *National Planning Policy Guideline 18: Planning and the Historic Environment*. Edinburgh: Scottish Executive.

—— 2004 *The Reform of Treasure Trove Arrangements in Scotland*. Edinburgh: Scottish Executive.

Sebire H. 2004 'The Management of the Archaeological Heritage in the Baliwick of Guernsey', in Wise P.J. (ed.) *Past Perfect: Studies in Museum Archaeology*, 59–67. Colchester: Society of Museum Archaeologists (*The Museum Archaeologist* 29).

Selkirk A. 1988 'What's in a Name?', *British Archaeological News* 3/1, 3.

Selkirk A. 1990 'The Current Archaeology Down to Earth Guide to British Archaeology', *Current Archaeology* 11, suppl. i–xxii.

—— 2001 'Government to Outlaw the Amateurs?', *Current Archaeology* 174, 241–43.

Shackley M. 2001 *Managing Sacred Sites: Service Provision and Visitor Experience*. London: Continuum.

Shanks M. and Tilley C. 1987a *Re-constructing Archaeology*. Cambridge: Cambridge University Press.

—— and Tilley C. 1987b *Social Theory and Archaeology*. Cambridge: Polity Press.

Shaw C. and Chase M. (eds) 1989 *The Imagined Past. History and Nostalgia*. Manchester: Manchester University Press.

Shell C. 2002 'Airborne High-Resolution Digital, Visible, Infra-Red and Thermal Sensing for Archaeology', in Bewley and Rączkowksi 2002, 181–95.

—— and Robinson P. 1988 'The Recent Reconstruction of the Bush Barrow Lozenge Plate', *Antiquity* 62, 248–60.

Shennan S. J. (ed.) 1989 *Archaeological Approaches to Cultural Identity*. London: Unwin Hyman.

Shepherd I.A.G. 1986 *Exploring Scotland's Heritage: Grampian*. Edinburgh: HMSO.

—— 1992. 'The Friendly Forester? Archaeology, Forestry and the Green Movement', in Macinnes and Wickham-Jones 1992, 161–8.

—— 1996 *Exploring Scotland's Heritage: Aberdeen and North-East Scotland*. Edinburgh: HMSO.

Sidorsky E. 1996 'The 1995 UNIDROIT Convention on Stolen or Illegally Exported Cultural Objects: the Role of International Arbitration', *International Journal of Cultural Property* 5, 19–72.

Skeates R. 2000 *Debating the Archaeological Heritage*. London: Duckworth.

Small A., Thomas C. and Wilson D.M. 1973 *St Ninian's Isle and its Treasure*. London: Oxford University Press.

Small F. 1999 *The Avebury World Heritage Mapping Project. A Report for the National Mapping Programme*. Swindon: RCHME Internal Report.

—— 2002a *Richborough Environs Project, Kent: Report on the Aerial Photographic Transcription and Analysis*. London: EH Internal Report AER/12/2002.

—— 2002b *The Lambourn Downs. A Report for the National Mapping Programme*. London: EH Internal Report. AER/13/2002.

Smith G.S. and Ehrenhard J.E. 1991 *Protecting the Past*. Boca Raton: CRC Press.

Smith K. 1992 'Protected Landscapes: Integrated Approaches to Conservation Management', in Macinnes and Wickham-Jones, 127–33.

—— 1999 'Sustainable Landscape Management: Peak practice and theory', in Grenville 1999, 111–21.

Smith L. 1986 'The National Trust Archaeological Survey in the East Midlands', *East Midlands Archaeology* 2, 23–6.

—— 1994 'Heritage Management as Post-processual Archaeology?', *Antiquity* 68, 300–9.

—— 2004 *Archaeological Theory and the Politics of Cultural Heritage*. London: Routledge.

——, Morgan A. and van der Meer A. 2003 'Community Driven Research in Cultural Heritage Management: The Waanyi Women's History Project'. *International Journal of Heritage Studies* 9/1, 65–80.

Smith P. 2000 'Post-war Listed Buildings', *Context*, 65, 14–16.

Smout T.C. (ed.) 2003 *People and Woods in Scotland*. Edinburgh: Edinburgh University Press.

Society of Antiquaries of London 1992 *Archaeological Publication, Archives and Collections: Towards a National Policy*. London: Society of Antiquaries.

Sparrow C. 1982 'Treasure Trove: A Lawyer's View', *Antiquity* 56, 199–201.

Spoerry P. 1992a *The Structure and Funding of British Archaeology: The RESCUE Questionnaire 1990–1*. Hertford: Rescue Publications.

—— (ed.) 1992b *Geoprospection in the Archaeological Landscape*. Oxford: Oxbow Books.

St Joseph J.K.S. 1951 'A Survey of Pioneering in Air-photography Past and Future', in Grimes W.F. (ed.) 1951 *Aspects of Archaeology in Britain and Beyond: Essays Presented to O. G. S. Crawford*, 303–15. London: H.W. Edwards.

St Joseph J.K.S. (ed.) 1977 *The Uses of Air Photography*. London: John Baker. 2nd edn.

Stansfield G. 1981 *Effective Interpretative Exhibitions*. Cheltenham: Countryside Commission.

Startin B. 1993 'The Assessment of Fields Remains', in Hunter and Ralston 1993b, 184–96.

Stead I.M. 1991 *Iron Age Cemeteries in East Yorkshire*. London: English Heritage.

—— 1998 *The Salisbury Hoard*. Stroud: Tempus.

Stevens T. 1989 'The Visitor – Who Cares? Interpretation and Consumer Relations', in Uzzell 1989c, 103–7.

Stewart J. 1980 'Integrated Excavation and Museum Recording Systems: Methods, Theories and Problems', *Museum Archaeologist* 5, 11–27.

Strickland T.J. 1992a Letter to the Editor, *Field Archaeologist* 16, 307.

—— 1992b Letter to the Editor, *Field Archaeologist* 17, 338.

Stocker D. 1995a 'Industrial Archaeology and the Monuments Protection Programme in England', in Palmer and Neaverson, 105–13.

—— 1995b 'Who Settled Where, and Why?', *Conservation Bulletin* 26, 17–19.

—— (ed.) 2003 *The City by the Pool. Assessing the Archaeology of the City of Lincoln*. Oxford: Oxbow. (Lincoln Archaeol Stud 10.)

Stoertz C. 1997 *Ancient Landscapes of the Yorkshire Wolds.* Swindon: RCHME.

Stone P.G. and MacKenzie R. (eds) 1990 *The Excluded Past: Archaeology in Education*. London: Unwin Hyman.

—— and Planel P. G. (eds) 1999 *The Constructed Past. Experimental Archaeology, Education and the Public*. London and New York: Routledge.

Stove G.C. and Addyman P.V. 1989 'Ground Probing Impulse Radar: An Experiment in Archaeological Remote Sensing at York', *Antiquity* 63, 337–42.

Stovel H. 1998 *Risk Preparedness: A Management Manual for World Cultural Heritage*. Rome: ICCROM.

Suddards R.W. 1993 'Listed Buildings', in Hunter and Ralston 1993b, 77–88.

—— and Hargreaves J.M. 1996 *Listed Buildings: The Law and Practice of Historic Buildings, Ancient Monuments and Conservation Areas*. London: Sweet and Maxwell. 3rd edn.

Swain H. 1997 'Archaeological Archive Transfer in England, Theory and Practice', in Denford G.T. (ed.) 1997 *Representing Archaeology in Museums*, 122–44. Winchester: Society of Museum Archaeologists. (*Museum Archaeologist* 22.)

—— 1998 *A Survey of Archaeological Archives in England*. London: English Heritage/Museums and Galleries Commission.

—— 2002 'Archives for All: The LAARC Solution', *The Archaeologist* 45, 40–1.

—— 2004 'The Archaeological Archives Forum', *The Archaeologist* 53, 31–2.

—— (ed.) 1991 *Competitive Tendering in Archaeology*. Hertford: Rescue Publications/SCAUM.

—— (ed.) 1993 *Rescuing the Historic Environment: Archaeology, the Green Movement and Conservation Strategies for the British Landscape*. Warwick: RESCUE, The British Archaeological Trust.

——, Rennie A. and Suenson-Taylor K. 1998 *A Survey of Archaeological Archives in England*. London: Museum of London.

Swallow P., Dallas D., Jackson S. and Watt, D. 2004 *Measurement and Recording of Historic Buildings*. Shaftesbury: Donhead. 2nd edn.

Swanson C. 2001 *The Historic Environment*. Perth: Scottish Environment Audits 4.

Swanwick C. and Land Use Consultants 2002 *Landscape Character Assessment: Guidance for England and Scotland*. Wetherby: Countryside Agency and Scottish Natural Heritage.

Tabata R.S. *et al.* (eds) 1992 *Joining Hands for Quality Tourism. Interpretation, Preservation and the Travel Industry*. Honolulu: University of Hawaii. (Procs of the Heritage Interpretation International Third Global Congress, 3–8 November 1991.)

Tainter J. 2004 'Persistent Dilemmas in American Cultural Resource Management', in Bintliffe, 435–53.

Tanaka M. 1984 'Japan', in Cleere 1984, 82–8.

Tarlow S. and West S. (eds) 1999 *The Familiar Past?* London: Routledge.

Tatton-Brown T. 1989 *Great Cathedrals of Britain*. London: BBC Publications.

—— and Munby J. (eds) 1996 *The Archaeology of Cathedrals*. Oxford: Oxford University Institute of Archaeology.

Tesch M. 1984 *Antikengesetze zwischen Denkmalschutz und Forschung: eine vergleichende Untersuchung*. Frankfurt-am-Main: Peter Lang Verlag.

Thackray D.W.R. 1999 'Considering Significance in the Landscape: Developing Priorities through Conservation Planning', in Grenville 1999, 19–26.

—— and Hearn K.A. 1985 'Archaeology and Nature Conservation: The Responsibility of the National Trust', in Lambrick 1985, 51–7.

——, Jarman R. and Burgon J. 1995 'The National Trust's Approach to Integrated Conservation Management', in Berry and Brown 1995, 37–47.

Thapar B.K. 1984 'India', in Cleere 1984, 63–72.

Thomas C. (ed.) 1983 *Research Objectives in British Archaeology*. London: CBA.

Thomas R. 1991 'Drowning in Data? – Publication and Rescue Archaeology in the 1990s', *Antiquity* 65, 822–8.

—— 1994 'Where Next?' Unpublished paper delivered at the IFA Annual Conference, Bradford 1994.

—— 1997 'Research Frameworks: What Are They and Why Do We Need Them?', *The Archaeologist* 29, 10–11.

—— 2001 'Urban Archaeology: Knowledge and Understanding', *Conservation Bulletin* 41, 16–21.

—— 2002 'Market Towns: Highlighting the Assets', *Conservation Bulletin* 42, 68–71.

Thompson G. 1978 *The Museum Environment*. London: Butterworths.

Thompson J. 1995 'The Nature Conservation Importance of Standing Remains', in Berry and Brown 1995, 61–9.

Thompson M.W. 1977 *General Pitt-Rivers: Evolution and Archaeology in the Nineteenth Century*. Bradford-on-Avon: Moonraker Press.

—— 1981 *Ruins: Their Preservation and Display*. London: British Mus Publ.

Tilden F. 1977 *Interpreting Our Heritage*. Chapel Hill: University of North Carolina Press.

Tilley C. 1989 'Excavation as Theatre', *Antiquity* 63, 275–80.

Tindall A. and McDonnell G. 1979 'Universities and Archaeology – a New RESCUE Survey', *Rescue News* 19, 1–3.

Tite M.S. 1972a *Methods of Physical Examination in Archaeology*. London: Seminar Press.

—— 1972b 'The Influence of Geology on the Magnetic Susceptibility of Soils on Archaeological Sites', *Archaeometry* 14, 229–36.

Tomasini, F. 2002 *Heritage and the Making of Place*. Lancaster University: unpublished Ph.D. thesis.

Trigger B. 1984 'Alternative Archaeologies: Nationalist, Colonialist, Imperialist', *Man* n.s. 19, 355–70.

Tubb K.W. (ed.) 1995 *Antiquities Trade or Betrayed: Legal, Ethical and Conservation Issues*. London: Archetype.

—— and Brodie N. 2001 'From Museum to Mantelpiece: The Antiquities Trade in the United Kingdom', in Layton R., Stone P.G. and Thomas J. (eds) 2001 *Destruction and Conservation of Cultural Property*, 102–16. London: Routledge.

UGC (University Grants Committee) 1989 *Report of the Working Party for Archaeology*. London: UGC.

UNESCO 1985 onward *The Protection of Movable Cultural Property*. (1 volume per state; over 40 published to date.) Paris: UNESCO.

UK Biodiversity Steering Group. 1995 *Biodiversity: The UK Steering Group Report*. London, HMSO.

Ucko P.J. 2000 'Enlivening a "Dead" Past', *Conservation and Management of Archaeological Sites* 4, 67–92.

Urban Practitioners 2002 *Heritage Dividend 2002*. London: English Heritage.

Uzzell D.L. 1989a 'The Hot Interpretation of War and Conflict', in Uzzell 1989b, 33–47.

Uzzell D.L. 1998 'The Hot Interpretation of the Cold War', in EH 1998, 18–21.

—— (ed.) 1989b *Heritage Interpretation*. Vol. 1. *The Natural and Built Environment*. London: Belhaven.

—— (ed.) 1989c *Heritage Interpretation*. Vol. 2. *The Visitor Experience*. London: Belhaven.

van der Noort R. and Ellis S. (eds) 2000 *Wetland Heritage of the Hull Valley*. Hull: Humber Wetlands Project, Centre for Wetland Archaeology, University of Hull.

Velkov V. 1993 'Archaeology in Bulgaria', *Antiquity* 67, 125–9.

Vitelli K.D. (ed.) 1996 *Archaeological Ethics*. Walnut Creek and London: AltaMira.

WAG (Welsh Assembly Government) 2003 *Review of the Historic Environment in Wales: A Consultative Document*. Cardiff: HMSO.

Wainwright G.J. 1978 'Theory and Practice in Field Archaeology', in Darvill T.C., Parker Pearson M., Smith R. and Thomas R. (eds) 1978 *New Approaches to Our Past*, 11–27. Southampton: Southampton Univ Archaeol Soc.

—— 1989a 'Saving the Rose', *Antiquity* 63, 430–5.

—— 1989b 'The Management of the English Landscape', in Cleere 1989, 164–70.

—— 1991 *Archaeological Review 1990–1*. London: English Heritage.

—— 1992 *Exploring Our Past*. Southampton University: inaugural lecture.

—— 2000 'Time Please', *Antiquity* 74, 909–43.

—— 2003 'Conflict Resolution in Heritage Management', in de Tejada P.R. and Montoya J.I. (eds) 2003 *Asia-Europe Seminar on Cultural Heritage Training*, 31–5. Madrid: Ministerio de Educación, Cultura y Deporte.

—— and Longworth, I.H. 1971 *Durrington Walls: Excavations 1966–1968*. London: Society of Antiquaries.

Walker J. 1996 'Let Us Have Franchises in Archaeology', *British Archaeology* 20, 11.

Walsh K. 1992 *Representation of the Past: Museums and Heritage in the Post-modern World*. London: Routledge.

Waterson M. 1989 'Opening Doors on the Past', in Uzzell 1989b, 48–56.

Watkins M. 1986 'Order or Chaos', in *Dust to Dust: Field Archaeology and Museums*, 54–9. London: Society of Museum Archaeologists Conference Procs 2.

Watson J. 1990 Letter to the Editor. *Field Archaeologist* 13, 235.

Watson M. and Musson C. 1993 *Shropshire from the Air. Man and the Landscape*. Shrewsbury: Shropshire County Council.

Weaver J. 1992 *Exploring England's Heritage: Cumbria to Northumberland*. London: HMSO.

Welsby P.A. 1985 *How the Church of England Works*. London: Church Information Office Publishing.

Welsh Office 1991 *Planning Policy Guidance Note 16: Archaeology and Planning*. Welsh Office: Cardiff.

—— 1996. *Planning and the Historic Environment: Historic Buildings and Conservation Areas*. Cardiff: Welsh Office. (*Circular 61/96.*)

—— 1998. *Planning and the Historic Environment: Directions by the Secretary of State for Wales*. Cardiff: Welsh Office. (*Circular 1/98.*)

Went D., Dyson-Bruce L. and Vindedal K. 2003 *Historic Environment Issues in the Proposed London–Stansted–Cambridge Growth Area: An Indicative Study of the Harlow–Stansted Area*. London: EH. (www/english-heritage.org.uk)

Wessex Archaeology 2000 *Assessment of the Royal Dockyards at Portsmouth and Devonport*. Salisbury: Wessex Archaeology/EH.

Wheeler R.E.M. 1954 *Archaeology from the Earth*. Harmondsworth: Penguin Books.

Whimster R.P. 1983 'Aerial Reconnaissance from Cambridge: A Retrospective View 1945–80', in

Maxwell G.S. (ed.) 1983 *The Impact of Aerial Reconnaissance on Archaeology*, 92–105. London: Counc Brit Archaeol Res Rep 49.

White R.F. and Iles R. 1991 *Archaeology in National Parks*. Leyburn: National Parks Association.

Willems W.J.H. 1997 'Archaeological Heritage Management in the Netherlands: Past, Present and Future', in Willems W.J.H., Kar H. and Hallewas D.P. (eds) 1997, *Archaeological Heritage Management in the Netherlands*, 3–17. Amersfoort: Rijksdienst voor het Oudheidkundig Bodemonderzoek.

—— 1999 '*Europae Archeologiae Consilium*', *European Archaeologist* 11, 7–8.

—— 2002 'IPA, the Portuguese Institute of Archaeology: Response from the EAA', *European Archaeologist* 17, 1–2.

Williams B. 2002 'The Protection and Management of Archaeological Sites in Strangford Lough', in McErlean T., McConkey R. and Forsythe W. 2002 *Strangford Lough: An Archaeological Survey of the Maritime Cultural Landscape*, 418–22. Belfast: Blackstaff Press.

Williams D. 1997 *Late Saxon Stirrup-Strap Mounts: a Classification and Catalogue*. York: Counc Brit Archaeol Res Rep 111.

Williams J. and Brown N. 2001 *An Archaeological Research Framework for the Greater Thames Estuary*. Maidstone: Essex County Council, Kent County Council, EH and the Thames Estuary Partnership.

Williams M.V. 1995 'Freshwater Archaeology: A Legal Perspective in England and Wales', *International Journal of Nautical Archaeology* 24, 205–10.

Williamson T. and Bellamy L. 1983 'Ley-lines; Sense and Nonsense on the Fringe', *Archaeological Reviews from Cambridge* 2/1, 51–8.

Wilson D.R. 1982 *Air Photo Interpretation for Archaeologists*. London: Batsford.

—— 2000 *Air Photo Interpretation for Archaeologists*. Stroud: Tempus.

Winton H. 1998 'The Cropmark Evidence for Prehistoric and Roman Settlement in West Lincolnshire', in Bewley 1998, 47–68.

—— 2003 'Possible Iron Age Banjo Enclosures on the Lambourn Downs', *Oxoniensia* 68, 15–26.

Wise P.J. 2004 'Current Issues in Portable Antiquities', *Museum Archaeologists News* 38, 2–5.

Wood J. 1992 'Furness Abbey: An Integrated and Multi-disciplinary Approach to the Survey, Recording, Analysis and Interpretation of a Monastic Building', *Medieval Europe 1992*. Vol. 6. *Religion and Belief*. York: Medieval Europe 1992 (Conference), 163–70.

—— 1993 *Buildings Archaeology: Applications in Practice*. Papers Given at the 'Institute of Field Archaeologists Buildings Special Interest Group' Symposium, January 1993: Oxbow Monographs in Archaeology.

—— 1995 'Recording Buildings: Setting the Standard and Delivering the Brief', *Field Archaeologist* 25, 10–12.

—— (ed.) 1994 *Buildings Archaeology: Applications in Practice*. Oxford: Oxbow Books.

Woodward A. and Hughes B. 1998 'A Sense of Time and Space: Sensual Sitescapes at the Iron Age site of Crick, Northamptonshire'. (Unpublished TAG paper.)

Wright P. 1985 *On Living in an Old Country: The National Past in Contemporary Britain*. London: Verso.

Wymer J.J. 1999 *The Lower Palaeolithic Occupation of Britain*. Salisbury: Wessex Archaeology and EH. 2 vols.

Wynn J.C. 1986 'Archaeological Prospection: An Introduction to the Special Issue', *Geophysics* 51, 533–7.

Yarnell T. 1993 'Archaeological Conservation in Woods and Forests', in Swain 1993, 29–30.

—— 1999 'Woods and Forests in the Rural Landscape: Cultural Heritage, Conservation and Management', in Grenville 1999, 101–10.

Young C. 2002 'Stonehenge – An Holistic Approach', *Rescue News* 88, 5.

Zhuang Min 1989 'The Administration of China's Archaeological Heritage', in Cleere 1989, 102–8.

INDEX